ITALIAN BATTLESHIPS

ITALIAN BATTLESHIPS

Conte di Cavour and Duilio Classes 1911–1956

Erminio Bagnasco and Augusto de Toro

Drawings by Roberto Maggi and Maurizio Brescia

Seaforth
PUBLISHING

Frontispiece: *top:* The battleship *Giulio Cesare* at La Spezia in the early 1930s; *bottom:* The battleship *Andrea Doria* and the destroyer *Granatiere* lying disarmed at Taranto in June 1959. (E Bagnasco)

Translated from the Italian by Raphael Riccio

First published in Great Britain in 2021 by
Seaforth Publishing
An imprint of Pen & Sword Books Ltd
47 Church Street, Barnsley
S Yorkshire S70 2AS

www.seaforthpublishing.com
Email info@seaforthpublishing.com

British Library Cataloguing in Publication Data
A CIP data record for this book is available from the British Library

ISBN 978-1-5267-9987-6 (Hardback)

ISBN 978-1-5267-9988-3 (ePub)

ISBN 978-1-5267-9989-0 (Kindle)

Pen & Sword Books Limited incorporates the imprints of Atlas, Archaeology, Aviation, Discovery, Family History, Fiction, History, Maritime, Military, Military Classics, Politics, Select, Transport, True Crime, Air World, Frontline Publishing, Leo Cooper, Remember When, Seaforth Publishing, The Praetorian Press, Wharncliffe Local History, Wharncliffe Transport, Wharncliffe True Crime and White Owl.

Typeset and designed by Stephen Dent
Printed and bound in India by Replika Press Pvt. Ltd

CONTENTS

PREFACE

It is with great pleasure that I present this new and important study, the work of friends (and longtime collaborators) Erminio Bagnasco and Augusto de Toro, relating to the five Italian 'dreadnoughts' of the 'Conte di Cavour' and 'Duilio' classes – designed on the eve of the Great War – four of which also served in the Second World War following extensive reconstruction during the 1930s.

In the introduction that follows, the authors delve deeply into the details of the genesis and development of this work, which describes the technical aspects of these ships and their long careers from the period immediately preceding Italy's entry into the First World War until the years following the Second World War.

This book, originally presented in a two-volume series of monographs in Italian, represents an in-depth and exhaustive study of an uncommon subject, in part because, as the authors correctly point out in their introduction, until now the only complete works on the 'Cavour' and the 'Duilio' classes have been two noteworthy volumes – which are dated and now almost impossible to find – written by Franco Bargoni and Franco Gay in the early 1970s for the old 'Orizzonte mare' series.

The structure of this book has been updated to current editorial standards and, in effect, constitutes a complete work, based on the two original volumes of the series.

The first part of the book, which as originally published in Italian was the first of the two volumes, deals in depth with all of the technical aspects of the two classes, their reconstruction and their operational activity up to Italy's entry into the war on 10 June 1940. The second part addresses the wartime careers between 1940 and 1945, the service of the *Doria* and *Duilio* with the newly constituted Italian Navy until 1956 and the events that relate to the *Cesare*, which was transferred to the Soviet Navy as war reparations.

The first part of the book, which deals in depth with the technical aspects of these ships, is enriched by a great number of large format plans (more than 25) by Roberto Maggi, whom I wish to thank not only for the effort that resulted in such a large number of diagrams, drawings and overall views of the ships but also for the precision and the love of detail that mark all of his works.

Maurizio Brescia
Editor, *STORIA militare*

INTRODUCTION

This book dedicated to the 'Conte di Cavour' and 'Duilio' class battleships is, above all, the result of many requests to complete this analysis of the policy considerations, technical and operational aspects of Italian battleships of the Second World War following our book *The Littorio Class: Italy's Last and Largest Battleships 1937–1948* published in 2011 by this same publisher. In this case as well, the only works that have dealt specifically with the 'Cavour' and 'Duilio' and in a fairly in-depth manner are the two small volumes by Franco Bargoni, Franco Gay and Elio Andò, which date from the 1970s (see Bibliography). As was also the case for the 'Littorio' class, since that time the availability of documentation, including photographs, relating to these battleships has increased considerably and new research has been conducted in various archives, and in all of the records of the Historical Office of the Italian Navy. The result was a volume published in 2020 in Italy by Edizioni 'STORIA militare', which we now present in an English edition. This book follows the general scheme of the earlier book on the Italian '35,000-tonners', with appropriate modifications deriving from the different origins and construction characteristic of the ships, which are of no little importance with respect to their technical and policy profiles.

Their operational life can be considered just as significant. Following their radical modernisation, the two 'Cavours' constituted the only nucleus of 'modern' battleships in the Italian Navy between 1937 and 1940, which, in addition to intensive training activity, carried out numerous missions both military and political in nature; with the two 'Duilio' class, also rebuilt, they took part in the Second World War alongside the three '35,000-tonners', although from 1942 onwards as second-line ships. In the post-war period, when the surviving 'Littorio' class ships were broken up in accordance with the terms of the peace treaty, the two 'Duilios' carried on serving for several years with the Italian Navy, and the *Giulio Cesare* in the Soviet Navy, ceded in accordance with the peace treaty. The *Andrea Doria*, decommissioned in November 1956, was the last battleship to fly the Italian flag shortly before this category of ship vanished forever from the inventories of the principal navies of the world.

The general layout of this book is similar to that employed for the 'Littorio' class and consists of an analysis of Italian naval policy relative to battleships from the early years of the twentieth century, followed by a technical description of the two classes of ships, both in their original as well as rebuilt versions, and completed by an in-depth account of their operational careers. For reasons of space and because of their limited service during the First World War and in the post-war period following both

The battleship *Duilio* at anchor at La Spezia in 1919.

The battleship *Andrea Doria* at Pola in October 1940, at the end of the reconstruction carried out at CRDA of Trieste. (Photo 'Mioni', Trieste)

world wars, we have opted to concentrate our attention on the period between 1940 and 1945, with a few important exceptions, such as the loss and partial recovery of the *Leonardo da Vinci* and the fortunes of the ex-*Giulio Cesare* following its transfer to the Soviet Union. Also, for the first time this book draws extensively on reports and accounts of the results of the training periods of the two 'Cavours' in the years between 1937 and 1940, including statistics of firing exercises up to 1941. These documents provide a more precise idea of their effectiveness, and how they were regarded by the hierarchy of the Italian Navy at the time, than has been previously described.

The numerous drawings that illustrate this book are mainly the work of Roberto Maggi, accompanied by other original drawings that come mainly from the very impressive archives of the Gruppo di Cultura Navale of Bologna, which very courteously made them available to us. The colour plates that reproduce the camouflage schemes and the various liveries adopted by the ships over time are the work of Maurizio Brescia.

The many photographs come in large part from our own collections, and when known the source is indicated in the accompanying caption. Our selection was based on those that were of the best quality, although in some cases we had to use photos that were not perfect in the technical sense as they represented the only images available for a particular time or event.

As a conclusion to this brief introduction, we wish to thank everyone – organisations and individuals – who helped us in our research and in drafting our work, whose names are shown at the end of the volume following the extensive list of principal archival sources consulted and a substantial biography.

E Bagnasco and A de Toro
Milan – Udine, Spring 2020

Chapter 1

THE DREADNOUGHT IN ITALY: FROM CUNIBERTI'S CONCEPT TO THE 'CARACCIOLO' CLASS

An article that appeared in the 1903 edition of *Jane's Fighting Ships* by Naval Engineer Lieutenant Colonel Vittorio Cuniberti proposed as the 'ideal battleship for the Royal Navy' a ship of 17,000 tonnes displacement and refined hull shape, armed with twelve 305mm (12in) guns, with 305mm maximum vertical protection and a speed of fully 24 knots, that is, at least 3 knots faster than that of contemporary battleships (the so-called multi-calibre pre-dreadnoughts) – the Regia Marina [Italian Navy] ignored the idea, even though it derived entirely from Italian design experience. As can be deduced from the article and the attached diagram, shown below, it was a further development of an earlier design for a small 8000-tonne battleship, which was to be named the *Amalfi*, armed with 203mm (8in) guns, and that of the later design of the 'Regina Elena' class battleships, which were still multi-calibre, of more than 12,000 tonnes normal load, which the Italian designer had long promoted during the years that straddled the two centuries. The Italian Navy considered the model proposed by Cuniberti outside of its capabilities and therefore allowed him to divulge it through the young but already prestigious British naval almanac. The idea apparently influenced the mercurial First Lord of the Admiralty, John Fisher, who was receptive to all types of new ideas, especially in the field of large ships, and between 1905 and 1906 Great Britain laid down and completed a battleship inspired by those ideas. The name of this ship, the *Dreadnought*, soon came to define the new type of all-big-gun battleship, which was destined to outclass all those that had preceded it. In truth, other navies, such as the US Navy with the 'Michigan' class, or the German Navy with designs that led to the 'Nassau' class, were independently reaching the same conclusions at much the same time, supported by the naval experience of the 1904–1905 Russo-Japanese war, and it was only speed of construction that made the *Dreadnought* the first single-calibre battleship to enter service. Fisher himself dated the first inspiration to his period in command of the Mediterranean Fleet at the beginning of the century, and even though no definite traces have remained, the Director of Naval Construction of the Royal Navy himself was coming to the same conclusions.

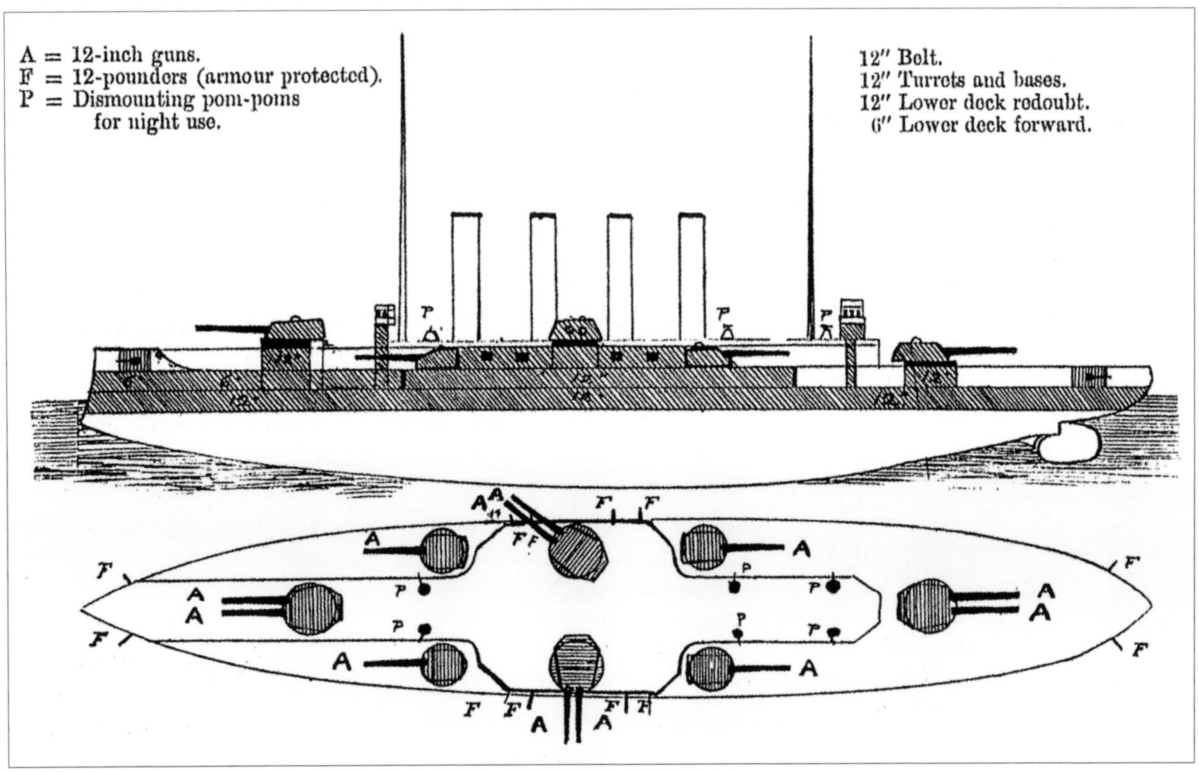

The single-calibre battleship proposed by Cuniberti in the 1903 *Jane's Fighting Ships*.

Some critics consider Cuniberti's idea to be technically impractical because it would have meant, with almost 2000 tonnes less displacement than the *Dreadnought*, building a ship armed with two additional 305mm guns, better protection and with 3 knots more speed – that is to say with an engine output that would have been double that needed to move it at 21 knots. In truth, Cuniberti had set forth a concept and not a design, and thus the technical details were only of relative importance, although with the *Dante Alighieri* those values were actually approached. In any case, what should be noted here is that the Regia Marina, while claiming credit for the idea, did not at the time take advantage of it, stopping at the four 'Regina Elena' class battleships.

These were ships of about 13,000 tonnes displacement under normal load, armed with two 305mm (12in) and twelve 203mm (8in) guns, with a speed of 22 knots and lightly protected. Politically, they were an expression of Italian adherence to the Triple Alliance because of its marked anti-French stance, as it was a type of fast battleship able to challenge the Marine Nationale in the free use of the sea with quick sorties, as the Italian Navy was not able to compete against its overall supremacy. At the time of their design the concept was fairly original and in some senses they were the forerunners of the battlecruiser, so much so that not all experts considered them to be true and proper battleships. Nevertheless, the design advantage was almost completely nullified by the long building time: laid down between 1901 and 1903, they entered service in 1907–1908, by which time the dreadnought type had become generally established.

Although Italy had been part of the Triple Alliance with Germany and Austria-Hungary since 1882, its potential enemy still remained, as an alternative to France, the Hapsburg Empire. Until the early twentieth century the Regia Marina had paid no attention to the Adriatic and to the Austro-Hungarian kaiserlich und königlich (k u k) Kriegsmarine, especially because of its small size, which made it an integral part of the coast defences of the eastern Adriatic. But from 1900 to 1908 its increasing strength began to cause concern. A Navy Staff was set up in 1907 – earlier, from 1882, there was only a staff office within the Navy Ministry that was subordinate, as a directorate general, to the secretary general – and in 1908 the new body submitted a report to the Supreme Commission for the Defence of the State, requesting that a 2:1 ratio be reached, to compensate for the disadvantageous geographic nature of the Adriatic. These aspirations proved to be unachievable, both because of the expansion of naval construction by Vienna as well as delays that afflicted Italian naval construction, so that the estimated ratio was then 1.8:1 in favour of Italy, which in 1911 had fallen to 1.5:1, in 1913 to 1.3:1, and in 1914 to 1.2:1.

The British *Dreadnought* fitting out.

In effect, the lengthening of construction times, which ended up eroding the combat value of the ships still on the ways, was a problem common to a number of navies, including the French, but in Italy it assumed a chronic and extremely accentuated character. Between 1904 and 1906 this and other problems had been the object of a parliamentary inquiry that involved the entire administration and organisation of the navy as well as of the use of finances allocated to it. The outcome was not very flattering because it discovered poor use of the funds provided, less than transparent relations with the industries involved, and the unfavourable cost-to-quality ratio of supplies. One of the criticisms focused on the provision of inferior-quality armour plate by the Terni steel works, motivated by the desire to support the still frail state of the national industry; the navy replied to this criticism by saying that the steel was cheaper than that provided by Krupp and that its strength, even though not as good, was good enough to pass the appropriate tests. It should be said that practices that were not completely regular were also common in other navies. For example, in rival Austria-Hungary, between early 1910 and late 1911, the then head of the navy section of the ministry of war, Admiral Rudolf Montecuccoli, attempted to bypass the parliamentary delays in approving funds for construction of the first two dreadnoughts, the *Viribus Unitis* and the *Tegetthoff*, by resorting, without higher authorisation, to bank credits and advances to the Stabilimento Tecnico Triestino in order to finance the beginning of construction, then shifting the payment burden to the navy treasury. A scandal ensued, which although minimised by Archduke Francis Ferdinand – heir to the throne, the protecting deity of the k u k Kriegsmarine and the chief proponent of its development outside of the Adriatic – led to Montecuccoli's dismissal in 1912, but his actions gave the Austro-Hungarians an advantage over the Italians with respect to dreadnoughts, which they would maintain until 1914.

In Italy, in the years following the parliamentary inquiry, the situation did not improve, at least with respect to the pace of naval construction. Delays afflicted the building of the first dreadnought, the *Dante*, preceded by delays in the supply of armour plate for the last two armoured cruisers, *San Giorgio* and *San Marco*. The battleship was included in the naval programme approved on 17 June 1909 – since 1901 naval construction programmes were financed on a five-year basis – which called for building four single-calibre battleships, three large scouts, twelve destroyers, thirty-four torpedo boats and twelve submarines.

The *Dante* was laid down on 6 June 1909, before any other French or Austro-Hungarian dreadnought. It was a ship of 19,500 tonnes displacement at normal load, armed with twelve 305/46 guns in triple turrets, all on the centreline, and capable of reaching the impressive speed of 23 knots, but at the expense of protection, which was the most modest among the early single-calibre ships. Armstrong of Pozzuoli was chosen to provide the main armament, but it was not delivered until more than a year after the contracted date. As a result, the ship was not turned over to the navy until January 1913, that is to say, after the Austro-Hungarian *Viribus Unitis*, which was laid down at a later date, but before the French *Jean Bart* and *Courbet*, although suffering longer construction times than all of them, as can be seen by the table below. Moreover, the *Viribus Unitis* was the first dreadnought to mount large-calibre triple turrets, all on the centreline and two of which were superfiring.

Ship	Laid down	Launch	Completed	Construction time
Dante Alighieri (Italy)	06.1909	20.08.1910	01.1913	3 years, 7 months
Viribus Unitis (A-H)	07.1910	20.06.1912	10.1912	2 years, 3 months
Jean Bart (France)	11.1910	26.09.1910	6.1913	2 years, 7 months
Courbet (France)	09.1910	23.09.1911	11.1913	3 years, 3 months

The *Dante* design was based on the same principles that had inspired the building of all of the earlier battleships from the 'Italia' class of 1885 onwards, in which protection was sacrificed in favour of armament and speed. This did not leave it free of criticism, as among other faults, it appeared to have only modest transverse stability. Originally, all or some of the dreadnoughts of the 1910 programme were intended to be repeats, but even in the design stage, it was decided to make extensive modifications, so that the following ships ('Conte di Cavour' class), although inspired by the same principles, were to have more balanced characteristics. The three ships – *Conte di Cavour*, *Giulio Cesare* and *Leonardo da Vinci* – were laid down in the summer of 1910. These had greatly increased displacement (more than 23,000 tonnes at normal load), a slightly better armament (thirteen 305/46 guns on the centreline in three triple turrets and two superfiring twin turrets), more extensive protection (although maximum armour thickness varied), and greater stability; but, all things considered, in overall concept they followed the same path as earlier efforts. Compared to the 'Viribus Unitis' and 'Jean Bart' classes, they could be considered generally equal to them or slightly better and rather more balanced in their weight breakdown and stability characteristics.

In 1911 it was decided to include another two dreadnoughts in the naval construction programme, which would constitute the 'Duilio' class. To save time, it was intended to repeat the 'Conte di Cavour' design, of which they were effectively a replica, except for larger-calibre secondary armament: 152mm (6in) instead of 120mm (4.7in). Named the *Duilio* and *Andrea Doria*, they were respectively laid down in February and March 1912. With them the Regia Marina was confident of achieving superiority in dreadnoughts over the Austro-Hungarian Navy by the beginning of 1914.

The Austro-Hungarian dreadnought *Viribus Unitis* launched in 1911. The ship would be lost at Pola in 1918, the first victim of an Italian assault craft.

But these ships suffered the same difficulties that had plagued the naval programmes in the previous decades. Towards the end of 1911 Terni had already built up such serious delays in supplying armour plate for the *Cesare* and the *da Vinci* that it forced the navy to turn to foreign suppliers for orders of many thousands of tonnes, in particular to a consortium formed by the US companies Carnegie Steel and Bethlehem Steel. However, the plate provided by Bethlehem did not meet the contract specification and refusal to take delivery led to new delays. Other problems, costing a year, related to the supply of the 305mm guns for the three 'Cavours', as had already happened with the *Dante*, so that the *Cavour* finally received the 305s that were intended for the *Doria*, in order not to delay her entry into service. The times dragged on for *Duilio* and *Doria* as well, to the point that *Doria* did not enter service until 1916, with the war already under way. The repeated, serious failures in the system led to more parliamentary reaction – not this time a new inquiry, but it did lead to a heated exchange of accusations in March 1913 in the Senate between the Minister of the Navy, Admiral Pasquale Leonardi Cattolica, and his predecessor, Admiral Giovanni Bettolo. It was difficult to ignore the inadequacies of Italian industry, but there was no consensus on the main constraining factors in the execution of the naval programmes: the excessive sub-contracting for each ship, as blamed by Cattolica; poor coordination between technical and administrative departments, as maintained by Bettolo; the over-dependence on supplies from foreign industries, which may have had a vested interest in lengthening delivery times, as maintained by Vice-Admiral Carlo Rocca Rey, at the time the Chief of Staff of the Navy; or even, as pointed out by foreign observers, the approximate and ill-defined budgeting, which did not take into account subsidies and advances by the Navy Ministry to industries. Whatever the underlying reasons, it must be said that the navy hierarchy did not learn from previous experience, formulating programmes that in practice proved to be beyond Italian industrial capabilities. As Rocca Rey recognised at the end of the war in Libya, national industry would not have been able to meet the naval construction demands deemed necessary by the navy, even if parliament had granted the funds to finance them. In conclusion, even though in 1912 the Regia Marina had six dreadnoughts in various phases of building, contrary to expectations it did not achieve numerical parity with its smaller Austrian rival in 1914, and was not able to overtake it until a year later. Nor was the comparison favourable with the Marine Nationale, which was penalised by the same slowness, as can be seen in the following summary.

Number Dreadnoughts/ Country	**Under construction**	**In service 07.1914**	**In service 05.1915**
Italy	6	3	5
France	7	4	4
Austria-Hungary	4	3	3

The Regia Marina saw intense activity during the war in Libya, waged in 1911–1912 against the Ottoman Empire, for the conquest of its north African province, to which was added the occupation of Rhodes and islands of the southern Sporades in the Aegean. With the exception of a few small actions, this did not entail battles with the modest Turkish naval forces, but there were many operations involving landings, security, support for ground troops and shelling of coastal defences. This activity, which was well conducted in an overall sense, highlighted the numerical and qualitative shortage of light units (scouts and destroyers) and the navy's inability to carry out not only escort duties for larger ships, but also long and independent missions on the high seas. This led to a redefinition of construction priorities by the Navy Staff, which now concentrated on light vessels and on battleships, renouncing the middle category (large cruisers), which were deemed to be less essential. Rocca Rey still thought that Italy should have an advantage of two dreadnoughts over the Dual Monarchy, and at least equality with respect to light vessels, in order to remain as the second naval power in the Mediterranean.

With the laying down of the *Duilio* and the *Doria*, the Italian Navy felt confident that it could achieve superiority over the k u k Kriegsmarine by late 1914. But the cumulative delays, the rapid entry into service of the three 'Viribus Unitis' class and, above all, the news that had leaked of Vienna's intention to soon lay down three super-dreadnoughts armed with 356mm (14in) guns, replacing the small coastal armoured ships of the 'Monarch' class, from late 1912 became a nightmare for the Regia Marina staff, fearful that the advantage that it was so laboriously achieving could be soon nullified and overturned by the seven Austro-Hungarian dreadnoughts. In that period, even the modest 'Emanuele Filiberto' and 'Saint Bon' pre-dreadnoughts, more or less contemporaries of the 'Monarch', could have been replaced and, taking into account the ship attrition suffered during the war in Libya, the Italian Navy hierarchy felt that it needed four more dreadnoughts for 1918–1919: two to replace the 'Saint Bon' class and two others to maintain an advantage over the Austro-Hungarian fleet from ten to seven, or ten to eight, if Vienna had decided to also replace an old 'Hapsburg' class battleship along with the three 'Monarch' class.

Funding for the two supplementary battleships would need to be approved by the parliament at the same time as the previous two, given that previous experience had shown the need to prepare the designs and to order the materials for the large ships well in advance. As much as Rocca Rey's fundamental orientation was anti-Austrian, the hypothesis of a conflict with France was always present in his calculations. In fact, the agreements between London, Paris and Saint Petersburg, which in 1907 produced the Triple Entente, the renewed Italo-French tensions over the conquest of Libya, on the one hand, and on the other hand, the renewed Triple Alliance in 1912 and the negotiations in June 1913 for a new naval convention among the three powers, did not preclude such a scenario. Even in that context the strengthening of the battle fleet would have maintained its validity as a deterrent factor.

On 1 April 1913 Vice-Admiral Paolo Thaon di Revel assumed the post of Chief of Staff and with him a new phase opened in the story of the Regia Marina and in naval construction. At the time it marked a closer relationship with the Triple Alliance, culminating in the second naval convention of 14 October 1913 that, compared to the earlier convention, called for joint cooperation, not only by geographic area, with Austria-Hungary and with the few German units present in the Mediterranean, while Rome gave up its role as overall command of the united fleets, which was offered to the commander of the k u k Kriegsmarine, Admiral Anton Haus. Again in 1913, as also in 1914, Italian naval manoeuvres had an anti-French tone and the building programmes supported by Thaon di Revel prioritised destroyers and submarines, this latter type intended for the defence of Italian waters from the Ligurian Sea to the Tyrrhenian Sea and for offensive operations in the western Mediterranean basin. More generally, the ratio that he envisaged to the government in the spring of 1913 was the maintenance of a figure of 60 per cent of the Italian fleet compared to the French and the 4:3 compared to the Austro-Hungarian, a ratio for the latter well below the 2:1 recommended in 1908, but which now appeared acceptable in view of the strengthened ties with the Central Powers.

When outlining future naval programmes up to 1918, by stretching the definition of several classes of French and Austrian pre-dreadnoughts ('Patrie', 'Danton' and 'Radetzky' classes) as single-calibre battleships and by overestimating the financial and building capabilities of the two rival powers, di Revel was able to propose Italian construction of fully nine battleships between 1913 and 1918 in addition to those already in service and building. But what distinguished the plan even more was the supplementary construction by the same date, and beyond current orders, of forty large and three small submarines for defensive and offensive tasks in the central-western Mediterranean, as well as another thirty-four 800–1000-tonne destroyers. It was an unrealistic plan that ignored the critical issues that had previously affected Italian naval industry, as well as the country's financial capabilities. In order to find the required resources, Thaon di Revel was prepared to give up all other categories of ship, including scouts (while simultaneously warning of the need for them), and above all he declared himself against the trend towards gigantic battleships, which at the time was spreading throughout Europe, Italy included.

Thaon di Revel was, moreover, among the few in those years who had realised the power of the submarine, when in other navies – including the German, which was to make the most intense and effective wartime use of the type – there were doubts as to its use and usefulness as an instrument of naval warfare. In these convictions the Italian admiral found the support of the Army Chief of Staff, General Alberto Pollio, who, as a convinced Triple Alliance supporter, saw in the new weapon not only the most ideal tool that a small navy could possess to face a stronger enemy, but especially the best means of defence against presumed French offensives against the coasts or the coastal Italian nerve centres on the Ligurian Sea and the Tyrrhenian, whose vulnerabilities constituted one of the major worries for the Italian Army. In his judgment, by 1920 Italy should aim for a ratio with France with respect to submarines of 3.75:1 and was of the opinion that part of the dreadnought programme should be abandoned in favour of strengthening the underwater arm.

Thaon di Revel did not go that far. He had no doubts about the importance of battleships, but was also persuaded that the high impact of their cost on the overall navy new construction budget should not compromise the monies assigned to destroyers and submarines, which he judged just as indispensable. Also taking into account the economic effects caused by the loss of large ships, of the technical progress of submarines and underwater weapons and of the high vulnerability of major units to this type of offence, in his view, the size of those ships should not exceed 26,000 tons and have a per unit cost less than 80 million lire. However, he was not against large ships, which is shown by his concern over the hiatus between 1915–1916, when the two 'Duilios' were to complete, and 1918, when the 'Caracciolo' class were to begin to enter service. To fill that gap, in November 1914 he suggested to the then Minister of the Navy, Vice-Admiral Leone Viale, that Italy acquire a pair of dreadnoughts from abroad, such as the Argentine *Rivadivia* and *Moreno*, which had just been completed in the United States, and which above all were in line with his technical principles.

The Regia Marina had been considering the construction of super-dreadnoughts since 1910 (that is, since the laying down of the three 'Cavour' class), and in February 1912 the Admirals Committee, the consulting body of the Ministry of the Navy, declared itself for a type of battleship of 27,000–29,000 tons armed with thirteen 356mm (14in) guns in triple and twin turrets on the centreline, twenty 152mm (6in) in casemates and with 48,000 horsepower for a speed of 23–25 knots. This was to be a development of the 'Cavour' and 'Duilio' classes. In the same years similar designs were also maturing in the French and Austro-Hungarian navies with the 'Ersatz Monarch', but all were of traditional concept. However, in February 1913, the navy hierarchy, with the support of the Admirals Committee, decided on

The single-calibre battleship *Rivadavia* under construction in the United States for Argentina in 1912.

ships of 35,000 tons, armed with twelve 381mm (15in) guns in four triple turrets, twenty 152mm in casemates and a speed of 28 knots, equal to or better than that of battlecruisers that had entered service or were under construction in the British, German and Japanese navies; these characteristics marked a qualitative first compared to all of the other navies in the world. The cost per unit was estimated to be 120 million lire. These would be ships of a radically new type, blending the characteristics of the battleship and battlecruiser and therefore forerunners of the large fast battleships of the 1930s that represented the culmination of battleship development. They are usually compared with the British 'Queen Elizabeth' class, but if a comparison must be made, they appear to fall between that class and the battlecruiser *Hood*, which was completed at the end of the war.

When news of the building of the Italian super-dreadnoughts was confirmed, it caused concern in London, as no French battleship under construction or planned could match them, so that several modern battleships of the 'Queen Elizabeth' type would have to be dispatched to the Mediterranean in event of hostilities between the Triple Entente and the Triple Alliance.

The design of the new class of four ships, later designated the 'Caracciolos', was begun in 1911 on the initiative of admirals

Mock-up of a 'Conte di Cavour' class battleship erected in Genoa for the 'Esposizione Coloniale' in 1914.

Leonardi Cattolica and Bettolo, respectively Minister and Chief of Staff of the Navy, and was ultimately entrusted to Major General of Naval Engineers Edgardo Ferrati. But the cost and excessive dimensions compared to the existing dockyard infrastructure quickly led to widespread criticism and in the final design of December 1913 Ferrati reduced the displacement at full load to 31,000 tons with eight 381mm guns in twin turrets and eighteen 152mm, with a reduction in the cost per unit to 100 million lire; speed would remain unchanged at 28 knots. But even these ships did not meet with complete approval within the navy. Before his death in that same year of 1913, Cuniberti opposed the plan, proposing ships of smaller dimensions (25,000 tons and 25 knots speed). Thaon di Revel, basically for the reasons outlined previously, also objected, worried that the huge cost would work to the detriment of light and underwater units; furthermore, in September 1914 he tried, in vain, to reduce the protection and speed characteristics of at least the last ship laid down – the *Francesco Morosini* in Livorno – to save about 20 million lire, to be transferred to financing four 680-ton destroyers and eight 250-ton submarines. Despite the criticisms, the new Minister of the Navy, Vice-Admiral Leone Viale, did not feel it necessary to suspend construction of the four large ships but, in return, assured Thaon di Revel that he would set aside an ample amount from later navy budgets for light and underwater craft.

Except for the *Francesco Caracciolo*, their building proceeded at a snail's pace, provoking in 1914 renewed debate in the senate, and in March 1916 the total suspension of work in favour of the pressing need for smaller ships, once the Austro-Hungarian abandonment of the 'Ersatz Monarch' class had been verified; furthermore, the Triple Entente already enjoyed a great superiority in battleships. For the same reasons, a similar decision was made by Paris with respect to the battleships of the 'Normandie' and 'Lyon' classes.

Ultimately, in May 1915, with Italy's entry into the war alongside the Entente, the Regia Marina could marshal only five battleships (*Dante Alighieri*, three 'Conte di Cavour' class and one 'Duilio'). Even France and Austro-Hungary, at war since August 1914, were able to deploy only first-generation dreadnoughts.

The 'Caracciolo' design

The specifications provided by the Regia Marina for the competition announced in 1911 referred to a battleship with a maximum displacement of 35,000 tons, with a speed of 28 knots, an armament of twelve 381mm guns and twenty of 152mm and adequate protection. Three of the main naval shipyards of the era (Ansaldo, Orlando and Odero) responded to the competition, each with a rough design, and these were complemented by similar studies presented by several naval engineering officers of the Regia Marina, among whom was the then General Edgardo Ferrati. He was in fact given the task of drawing up the preliminary design, which was ready by the end of 1913 and which adopted some of the solutions originally proposed by the shipyards listed above.

This design, which changed many times in order to limit weight and construction costs, called for a fast battleship with the following main characteristics:

Normal displacement: 31,000 tons
Dimensions (metres): 212 overall, 201.6 at perpendiculars x 29.6 max x 9.5
Engines: 20 boilers and four geared turbines on four shafts – maximum power output 105,000 horsepower
Maximum speed: 28 knots
Range: 8000 miles at 10 knots
Protection (mm): armoured belt 300; armoured deck 51; main gun turrets 400 max, main gun barbettes 300
Armament (mm): eight 381/40 (15in) guns in twin turrets; eighteen 152/50 (6in) singles in casemate battery; twenty-four 76mm (3in) in single mounts on deck

The most significant and innovative aspects compared with earlier single-calibre battleships built for the Regia Marina were represented mainly by the main gun armament, with the

'Francesco Caracciolo' class battleship

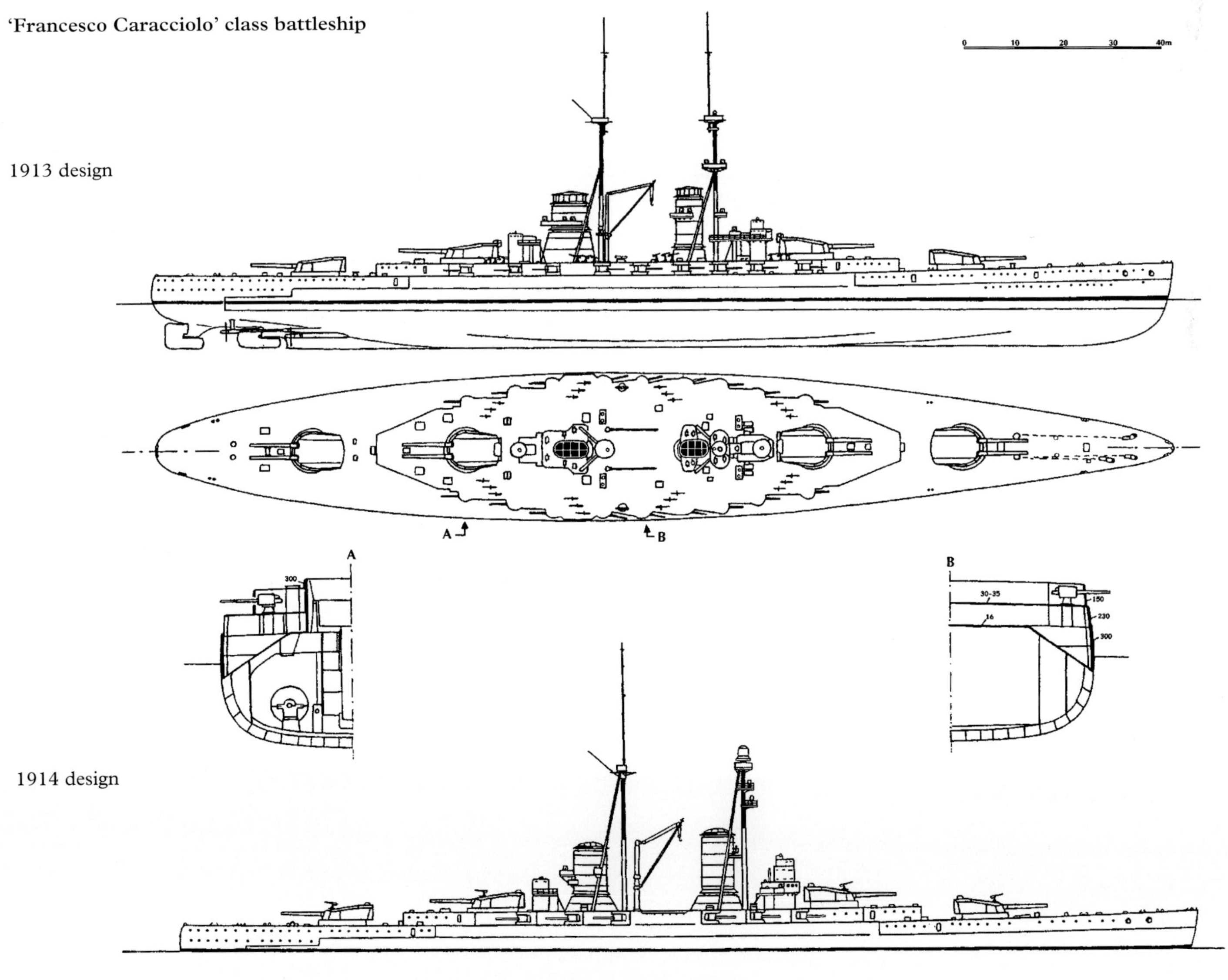

use for the first time in Italy of recent Armstrong and Vickers models of 15in (381mm) guns, and by the configuration of the powerplant. This, in particular, was of decidedly more modern conception than those of the earlier dreadnoughts (*Dante Alighieri* and the 'Conte di Cavour' and 'Duilio' classes), being arrayed on four distinct turbo-reduction groups, mated to the same number of shafts, rather than three turbine groups driving four propellers.

In the new design, each turbine group would be fed by five Yarrow type water-tube boilers, of which three were oil fired and two mixed (oil and coal), working at an operating pressure of 17.5 atmospheres. The two forward turbo-reduction groups drove the two centre propellers, which were the aftermost pair, with the two rear groups connected to the two outboard propellers, further forward. Each group consisted of a high-pressure (HP) turbine and a low-pressure turbine (LP), linked, by a flexible coupling and sprockets, to a helical gear connected to the shaft line. Attached to each group was a cruise turbine, working in series with the HP and LP turbines and working through a sprocket above a gear whose shaft was linked to that of the HP sprocket through a flexible coupling that could be disconnected at fast speed and high power. The astern turbine was incorporated in the LP turbine.

The combined normal full power of the four geared turbines with forced draught was designed to be 70,000 shaft horse-power, increased to 90,000 at extra normal power. By feeding the ten mixed-combustion boilers with oil only, the machinery was to have been able to develop 105,000 shaft horsepower at maximum power. Four 300kw turbo-generators were planned for production of electricity. The Regia Marina's intention was to build a class of four ships – classified in 1914 as 'first-class battleships' – which, according to British press sources at the time, were originally to bear the names *Dandolo*, *Morosini*, and *Goffredo Mameli*, in addition to a somewhat improbable *Giuseppe Mazzini*. In reality the four new battleships would constitute the 'Ammiragli' class or the 'Caracciolo' class, from the name-ship. The *Francesco Caracciolo* was laid down on 16 October 1914 on the ways of the Regio Cantiere di Castellamare di Stabia and was followed in 1915 by *Marcantonio Colonna*, *Cristoforo Colombo* and *Francesco Morosini* laid down respectively on 3 and 14 March at the Cantieri Odero and Cantieri Ansaldo di Genova yards, and on 27 June at the Cantieri Orlando at Livorno.

However, shortly after they were laid down, strong doubts arose regarding the soundness of the design; in particular, horizontal protection (51mm) was held to be totally inade-quate against large-calibre rounds, which at long range hit the decks almost vertically. In addition, the disposition of the powerplant – which grouped about two-thirds of the boilers and two of the geared turbine groups outside of the main longitudinal bulkhead, or too close to the sides of the hull – dangerously exposed the ships to heavy damage in case of torpedo attack. These were serious defects that were difficult to remedy without a radical reworking of the entire design. Nevertheless, in 1916 a new study was prepared that included several modifications to improve horizontal protection, trading weight through a drastic reduction of the secondary armament to twelve 152/45 guns, substitution of the twenty-four 76mm guns by twelve 40/39 rapid-fire guns and other measures. These changes were not deemed to be sufficient to guarantee the safety of the ship in combat, however, and in March of that same year, the Regia Marina staff decided to suspend work on the four 'Caracciolo' class. Cancellation of the relevant contracts followed and the dismantling, in 1918, of the few elements that had been worked on in the Genoa and Livorno yards. For the *Caracciolo*, though, the work that had been suspended in March 1916 resumed after about a year, but only for a few months, to be again interrupted until August 1919, when it resumed in order to complete the hull so that it could be launched to free up the building slip. The *Caracciolo* in fact took to the water on 12 May 1920 and a few days later the large empty hull was towed to La Spezia. It remained there until the following November, when it was moved to Baia, in the Gulf of Naples. There, after several years of lying aban-doned, it was finally sent for breaking when as, as we shall see in Chapter 4, all proposals for alternative uses came to nothing.

Castellammare di Stabia, 12 May 1920: launch of the battleship *Francesco Caracciolo*, which was never completed. (A Fraccaroli collection)

Chapter 2

DESIGN, ORIGINAL CHARACTERISTICS AND BUILDING OF THE 'CONTE DI CAVOUR' AND 'DUILIO' CLASS BATTLESHIPS

The Regia Marina's modern battleships began to take shape on designers' drawing boards in the two-year period after 1906, the year in which Great Britain completed the *Dreadnought*, the first single-calibre battleship whose name, from then on and for many years, marked an entire new category: in fact, all armoured ships that reflected its general characteristic were defined as 'dreadnought', and earlier ships, whose main armament was divided up among two or more calibres, were designated as 'pre-dreadnought'. This division of calibres – as the celebrated battle of Tsushima fought between the Russians and Japanese in 1904 had amply demonstrated – significantly constrained the offensive power of large armoured ships, not allowing them to bring all of their firepower to bear at long ranges. While it is true that in those years the lack of effective fire control equipment limited the accuracy of large-calibre guns at long range, normal combat distances were measured in a few thousand metres, corresponding to the normal run of torpedoes of the day, and this in large measure compensated for the inevitable lack of precision. The years that immediately followed the appearance of single-calibre battleships, however, saw significant improvement in that field and soon new ships were able to use the enormous power of their large-calibre guns more profitably in terms of both range and by the concentration of fire of the greatest possible number of guns.

In this first phase in the new line of development marked by the *Dreadnought* – which also had a modern steam turbine powerplant that gave it a speed in the order of 21 knots, which was notable for the era – all of the major navies quickly adopted

The battleship *Giulio Cesare* ready to be launched on one of the Ansaldo slips at Genoa Sestri.

The battleship *Dante Alighieri*, first of the Italian 'dreadnoughts'. (A Nani drawing)

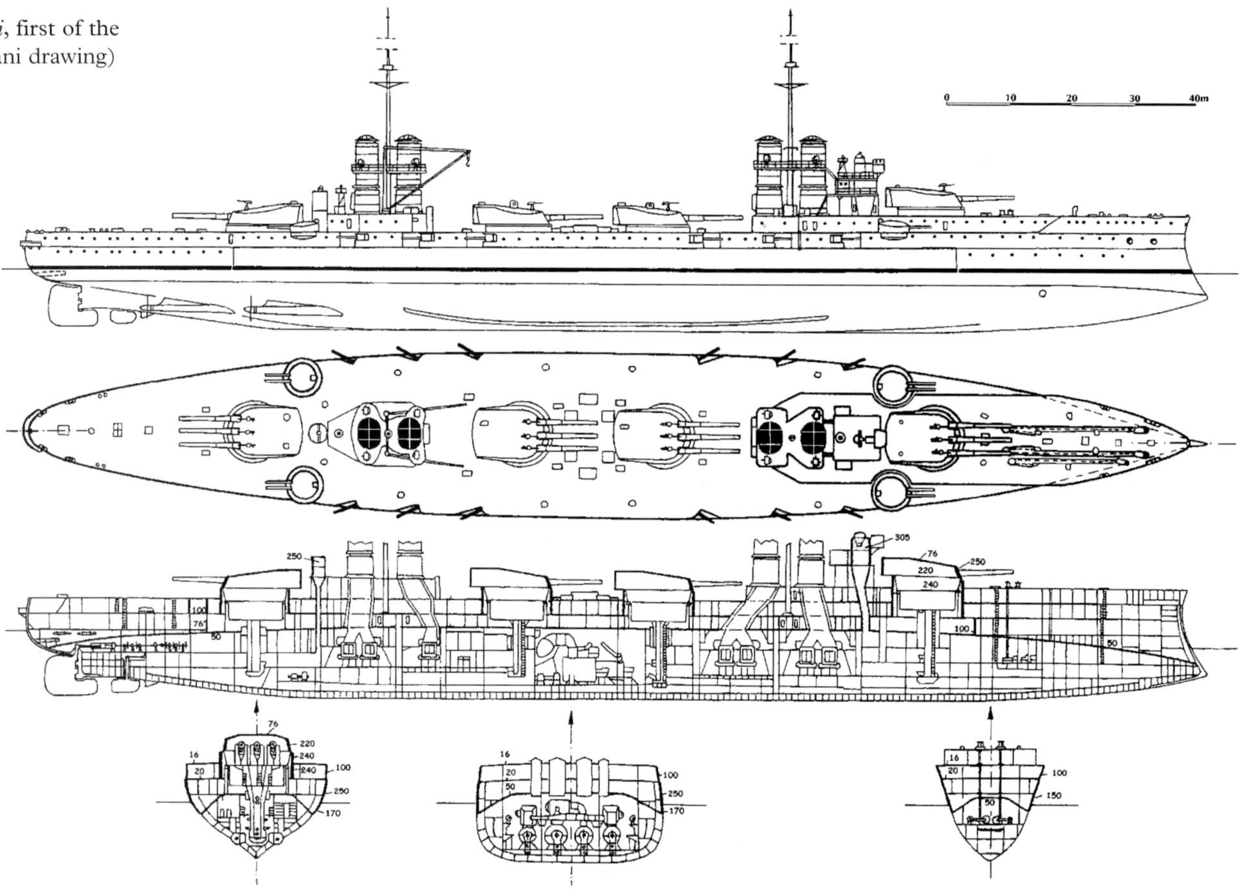

The *Dante* moored at the buoy in Venice in 1919.

this model for their design and building programmes for new battleships.

In Italy, the interesting studies relating to large single-calibre ships conducted since 1903 by the then Naval Engineer Colonel Vittorio Cuniberti never became reality, and the Regia Marina had of necessity gone ahead with construction of the four 'fast battleships' of the 'Regina Elena' class of 13,000 tons normal displacement and 22 knots, designed by Cuniberti himself, but according to the 'classic' formula of dual-calibre main armament (two 305mm [12in] guns and twelve 203mm [8in]) and with reciprocating steam engines. The resulting ships were decent, even though conceptually they were already outdated by the time of their entry into service in 1907–1908.

The *Dante Alighieri*

Contemporaneously, however, studies for the first Italian 'dreadnought' had begun, but for economic reasons, the ship, to be named *Dante Alighieri*, was not laid down at the Regio Cantiere di Castellamare di Stabia until 6 June 1909. The design was completed in 1908 by Naval Engineer General Edoardo Masdea, an authority among the naval engineers of the era and already the designer, among others, of the famous and popular 'Garibaldi' class armoured cruisers. The new ship showed interesting and innovative characteristics, among which was the disposition of the main armament, consisting of twelve Armstrong 305/46 (12in) guns, mounted for the first time in Italy in armoured triple turrets; previously, large-calibre mountings were twin at most. This feature enabled the grouping, with obvious weight and space savings, of all of the large-calibre guns in only four turrets, all disposed along the ship's centreline, making wide arcs of fire possible on both sides. The hull, of high-strength steel, presented significant technical challenges, especially relating to its great length – almost 170 metres compared to about 140 for large ships built up to then. The powerplant was to consist of twenty-three boilers and three groups of steam turbines, but driving four propeller shafts (an arrangement also used in later construction), for a planned total power output of 33,000 horsepower and a speed of 22–23 knots at a normal displacement of 19,500 tons. Protection, whose overall weight was 4020 tons, equal to 18.6 per cent of the displacement, consisted of vertical armour made up of plates whose maximum thickness was 250mm in the central section of the hull, and horizontal armour on three decks with a maximum total thickness of 94mm; in addition, the armoured command space – called the 'blockhouse' – was protected by 280mm plates while those on the frontal portion of the main gun turrets were 250mm thick.

Hull construction of the new ship (overall length of 168.1m and 26.63m breadth) proceeded quickly, so that it could be launched on 20 August, the year after it was laid down. Complete fitting out, however, took another twenty-nine months, and the ship was not delivered to the Regia Marina until 15 January 1913. By contrast, the British *Dreadnought* was completed in only twelve months, a clear illustration of the industrial and economic potential of the United Kingdom compared with that of Italy in the first decade of the twentieth century.

Following its launch, the hull of the *Dante Alighieri* was towed to La Spezia where, under the supervision of the local dockyard, the powerplant was installed (built by Ansaldo in its Genoa-Sampierdarena works) and fitting out was completed. At full power trials, carried out in the Ligurian Sea in June 1912, the *Dante* powerplant developed, at forced draught, 32,189 horsepower for 22.83 knots on 9 June and 35,378 horsepower at 23.825 knots in a later six-hour trial on 16 June; in both trials the average displacement was in the order of 20,140 tonnes, or about 600 tonnes above displacement at normal load.

The three 'Conte di Cavour' class

Before the construction of the *Dante* had begun, on instruction from the Navy Staff, Engineer Masdea revised his entire design in the light of new developments in Great Britain with the 'Bellerophon' class of three ships, the first single-calibre type built after the *Dreadnought*. In addition, as innovative as the new 305/46 triple turret may have been based on the design of the then Naval Engineer Colonel Edgardo Ferrati, it had been observed that the main armament layout of the *Dante Alighieri* allowed only a limited concentration of fire either ahead or astern; in practice, an overall sector of 40 degrees between the bow and the stern could be covered only by the three guns of the two extreme fore and aft turrets, and the entire twelve-gun broadside could only fire over an arc of 80 degrees on each side; *ie*, 40 degrees from beam to bow and 40 degrees from beam to stern. It was therefore necessary to come up with a new layout for the main armament. The solution was found by going from a total of twelve to thirteen 305/46 guns; in fact, with an increase of only one gun and by replacing one of the four triple turrets with two twin turrets – and thus with a relatively modest weight increase – a better and more effective distribution of the volume of fire over a 360-degree arc could be achieved, especially in the forward and after sectors, for an arc of 50 degrees, which increased from three to five guns by arranging a twin turret in

Genoa-Sestri Ponente, 15 October 1911: Launch of the battleship *Giulio Cesare*.

a superfiring position above each of the two outer triple turrets.

At the same time, it was decided to improve protection, not by significantly increasing thicknesses, but rather by extending the armour scheme. In order to retain maximum speed at the same level as that planned for the *Dante* with a powerplant of the same configuration and the same order of power, the increase in weight (from 4020 to 5150 tonnes for the armour alone) required a complete redesign of the hull, which was to be some 10 metres longer and 28m broad instead of 26m. Obviously, the shape of the underwater hull had to be redesigned, improving the value of the coefficient of fineness at the waterline (length/breadth) from 5.91 of the *Dante* to 5.95 of the new design. The coefficient of fineness of the hull (also called the block coefficient, or the ratio between the hull volume and that of a rectangular block of the same length, breadth and depth) marked a clear improvement, going from 0.60 to 0.53; in other words, the shape of the hull was more refined, thus reducing resistance to the ship's forward movement. The designed displacement under normal load conditions initially was to be around 22,000 tonnes against the roughly 19,500 of the *Dante Alighieri*; nonetheless, with a similar available power output, maximum speed was to remain of the same order thanks to the lengthening of the hull and the improvements in the main coefficients of fineness.

The new battleship design, presumably completed in the first half of 1909, convinced the Navy Staff and it soon reached a decision to build three ships of this type, which, based on a royal decree of 2 December 1909, were added to the navy list with the names *Conte di Cavour*, *Giulio Cesare* and *Leonardo da Vinci*. The order for construction of the first ship, the *Cavour*, had however been issued to the Regio Arsenale della Spezia earlier, on 31 July 1908, about a year before the official laying down at Castellamare di Stabia of the *Dante Alighieri*, considered to be the prototype of the new single-calibre battleships. In effect, this first *Conte di Cavour* ordered at La Spezia in 1908 was originally to have been a replica of the *Dante* and only later became the first ship of the three single-calibre battleships of the improved type.

The *Conte di Cavour*, name-ship of the new class, was laid down on building way No 1 of the La Spezia dockyard on 10 August 1910, only a few days after the keel-laying of her sister-ships *Giulio Cesare* and *Leonardo da Vinci* respectively on the building ways of the Cantieri Ansaldo of Genoa-Sestri Ponente and Cantieri Odero & C, also located in the Ligurian capital but at Foce. Before laying down the *Conte di Cavour*, which was almost 177 metres long overall, building way No 1 of the La Spezia yard had to be significantly lengthened. It was situated almost at the northeast limit of the long descent that, despite their demolition in the post-war period, is still called the 'Banchina Scali' (building ways quay) and required the construction of a robust steel extension inland supported by large stonework.

The first of the new battleships to take to the water was the *Conte di Cavour*, launched on 10 August 1911, but which, as we shall see, for various reasons would be the last to be completed. The launch of the *Leonardo da Vinci* followed at Genoa on 14 October 1911 and of the *Giulio Cesare*, also at Genoa, the next day.

Embarking one of the 305/46 main guns aboard the battleship *Giulio Cesare* fitting out in Genoa in 1914.

Preparing the main and secondary armament gun barrels for the 'Conte di Cavour' class ships in the Vickers-Terni works.

Until the launch – a mass consisting of the ship plus a launching cradle, of 8800–9150 tonnes – construction of the three ships had proceeded according to the established schedule that called for machinery trials by 31 December 1912. After that, delays in the delivery of materials (essentially armament and armour plate) that were the responsibility of the Regia Marina began to manifest themselves. This significantly retarded fitting out the ships, so much so that *Cesare* and *da Vinci* were not able to begin trials until 31 August 1913, eight months later than planned, and the *Conte di Cavour* experienced a delay of almost a year and a half.

The contracts for building the 'Cavours' called for the power-plants to be furnished by the same yards that were building the hulls, except that the turbines for the *Leonardo da Vinci* were to be the responsibility of Ansaldo, which was the licensee in Italy for Parsons. The Regia Marina was responsible for providing the armament and armour plate, but their fitting and completion on board were the responsibility of the respective commercial yards and the La Spezia Dockyard. Based on this division of responsibilities, the contracts agreed with the two private shipyards for each ship reckoned a cost of 3,720,000 lire (to which about 1,300,000 lire more would be added for extra-contractual requests to Ansaldo and Odero) which, obviously, did not include the materials provided by the Regia Marina.

With respect to the guns, the Regia Marina ruled that the provision of the large-calibre guns (305/46), including reserve guns, would be divided as follows:

- Vickers-Terni, in its La Spezia works, for guns destined for the *Conte di Cavour*,
- Vickers, in its Elswick works in Great Britain, for those of the *Leonardo da Vinci*,

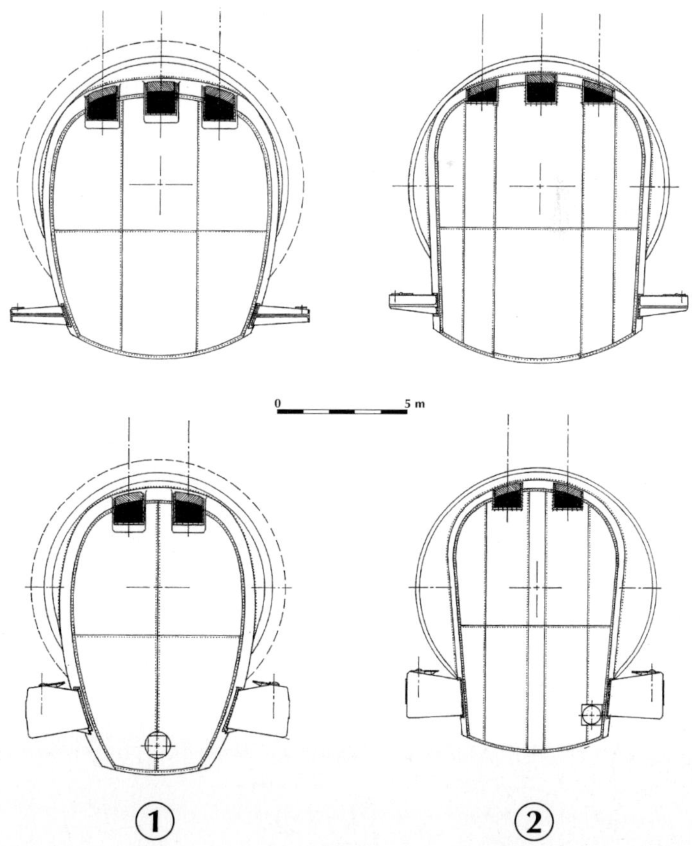

Plan views of the two types (Vickers and Armstrong) of main gun turrets of the 'Conte di Cavour' and 'Duilio' class battleships.

Modernised versions (with rangefinders)
1) Vickers type
2) Armstrong type

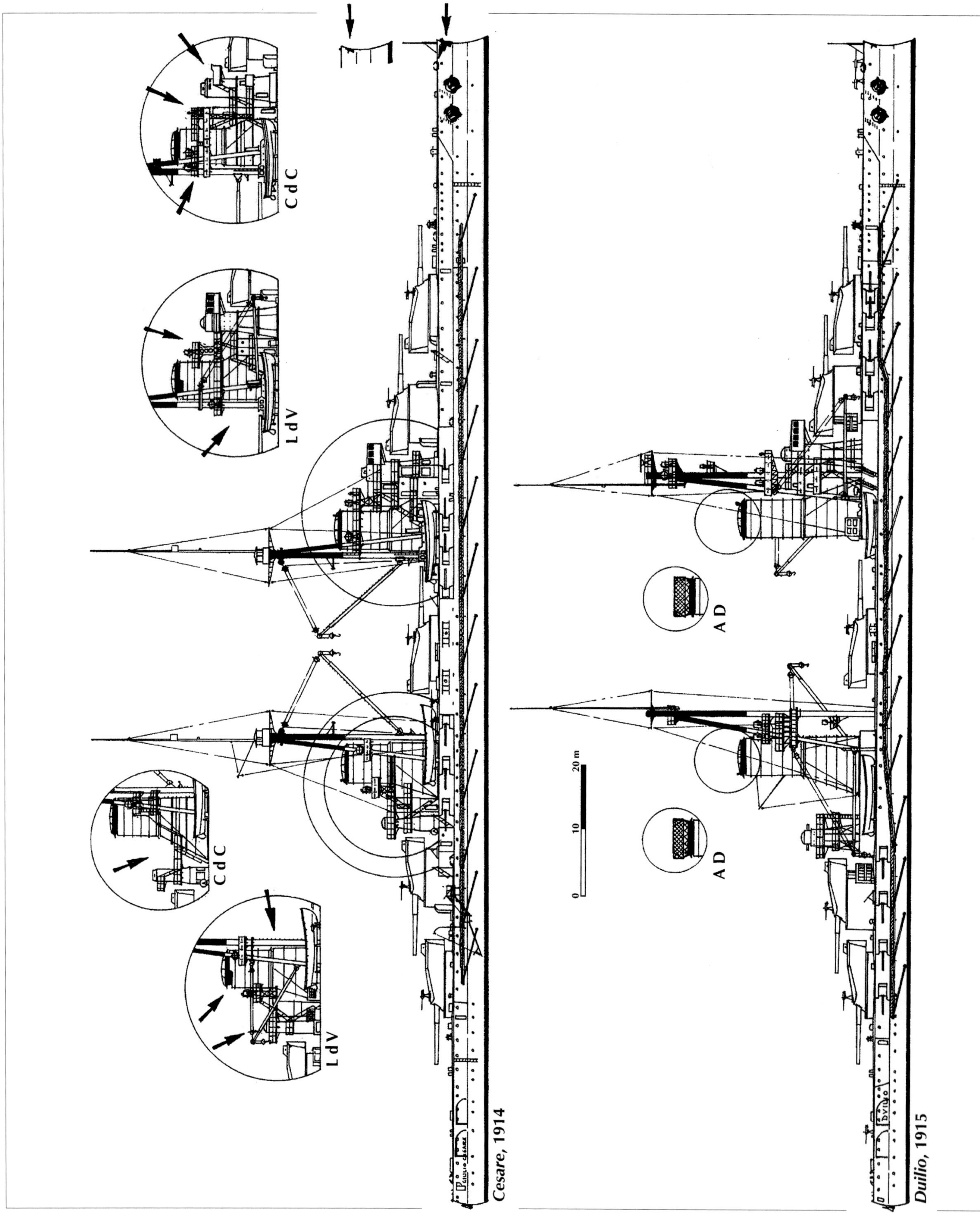

Appearance differences between the three ships of the 'Conte di Cavour' class and the two ships of the 'Duilio' class. (R Maggi drawings)

The battleship *Giulio Cesare* entering Taranto's Mar Piccolo on 21 January 1917 returning from a deployment of the Italian Naval Squadron to Corfu.

The battleship *Conte di Cavour* at Taranto during the Great War. Note at the bow an early form of camouflage – the white false bow wave was intended to make it more difficult for an observer at a distance to estimate the ship's speed accurately.

The battleship *Duilio* fitting out in Genoa, probably in late 1914.

The battleship *Duilio* steaming out for trials in the Gulf of Genoa in January 1915.

The *Andrea Doria* at La Spezia on 1 May 1916. In service only two months, the ship is undergoing training before to moving to Taranto. The anti-bomb grilles over the funnels can be seen clearly.

– Armstrong-Pozzuoli, in its Pozzuoli works, for those destined for the *Giulio Cesare*.

At the same time, it was established that provision of the armour plate would be the responsibility of the Terni company, except for the upper side strakes of the armoured box citadel, which were to be produced by the Carnegie Steel Co of Pittsburgh in the United States. During that period, Terni normally obtained nickel steel from the Glasgow Steel Co in Great Britain and from Bethlehem Steel Co of Bethlehem, Pennsylvania, and from Carnegie Steel, then processed it in its own mills according to the Krupp system.

There were significant delays in the production of the main guns as well as of the armour plate for the 'Cavours'. In particular, the 305mm guns for the *Cesare*, manufactured by Armstrong-Pozzuoli, which relied on assistance from the British mother company and whose delivery was scheduled for June 1912, would not be ready until March 1914; for those slated for the *Leonardo da Vinci* there was more than a year's delay; and, finally, the production of the main guns for the *Cavour*, also scheduled for June 1913, saw such a delay that, in order to make up a few months – in light of significant delays that had already been suffered in fitting out the ship because of other commitments for the dockyard workers – the Regia Marina decided to transfer to that ship the complement of main guns of the same type already completed by Vickers-Terni for the similar battleship *Andrea Doria* (as outlined later).

Upon completion of fitting out, for the 'Cavour' class ships, the weight breakdowns of the main components at light displacement unladen and dry was as follows:

Hull	34.6%
Protection	30.2%
Fitting out and various	12.8%
Powerplant	8.5%
Armament	13.9%
Total	**100%** (20,280 tons)

The results of the speed trials for the ships of the class (examined more closely in Chapter 3) were judged to be satisfactory, even though only the *Cavour* had exceeded the forecast 22 knots, and even then only by a fraction, while the other two only reached 21.5, at an average displacement of 21,700 tonnes, about 1400 tons less than that planned at normal load.

The two 'Duilio' class

When Naval Engineer General Edoardo Masdea died suddenly in 1910, his *Dante Alighieri*, the prototype of the Italian 'dreadnoughts', had not been completed, while the three 'Conte di Cavour' class, whose design the distinguished Neapolitan engineer had worked on most recently, were about to be laid down. In order to meet the target of six modern battleships as called for in the Regia Marina's naval programmes, another two ships were required as quickly as possible, so it was necessary to consider the possibility of repeating the design of the 'Cavour' class, making improvements as needed.

Tasked with overseeing this design was Naval Engineer Giuseppe Valsecchi, who limited himself to only minor modifications to Masdea's last design that would not involve a significant lengthening of the building time. Retaining the overall dimensions, the shape of the hull and the type of powerplant, these modifications would mainly involve the layout and configuration of the superstructure, the arrangement and increase in calibre of the secondary armament and lowering by one deck the midships 305/46 gun turret; the resulting improvement in stability allowed modest changes in protection. In particular, the anti-torpedo armament would change from eighteen 120/50 (4.7in) guns, arranged in a battery on the broadside amidships, to sixteen 152/45 (6in) guns in two separate casemates abreast the fore and aft 305mm turrets. In order to bring the magazines closer together and to gain deck space, the distance between the fore- and aftermost 305mm triples and the superfiring twins was reduced by several metres, leaving the positions of the triple 305mm turret rings unchanged with respect to the bow and stern.

The decision to replace the 120mm guns with 152mm guns stemmed from the continuous increase in the size of seagoing torpedo craft and by the need to counter them at ranges beyond the maximum run of their torpedoes.

As we shall see later, the changes introduced to the protective system led to some improvement, without significant variation in the overall weight of the protection, offset by other modifications.

The new design was completed in about six months and by 2 September 1911 contracts were placed for the two ships, at first defined as the 'improved "Cavour" type'. One ship each went to the Regio Arsenale della Spezia and to the Regio Cantiere di Castellamare di Stabia, where respectively only a few days earlier the *Conte di Cavour* and about a year earlier the *Dante Alighieri* had been launched. In reality, these were the only two free building ways large enough among all of those available in the principal Italian yards.

The two new 'dreadnoughts' were added to the navy list by royal decree dated 6 November 1911 with the names *Duilio* and

The French battleship *Courbet*, launched in 1911, here in the roadstead at Toulon. (M Piovano collection)

'CONTE DI CAVOUR' AND 'DUILIO' CLASS BATTLESHIPS

(official classification at the time of entry in service: 1st class battleships)

'Cavour' class

Conte di Cavour	Builder:	Regio Arsenale della Spezia
	Fitting out:	As above
	Laid down:	10 August 1910
	Launched:	10 August 1911
	Delivered to the Regia Marina:	1 April 1915
	Radically modernised between October 1933 and 1 June 1937 (see Chapter 5 and following)	
Giulio Cesare	Builder:	Ansaldo sa, Genoa
	Fitting out:	As above
	Laid down:	24 June 1910, Cantieri di Genoa-Sestri Ponente
	Launched:	15 October 1911
	Delivered to the Regia Marina:	14 May 1914
	Radically modernised between 1 October 1933 and 1 October 1937 (see Chapter 5 and following)	
Leonardo da Vinci	Builder:	Odero & C, Genoa
	Fitting out:	As above
	Laid down:	18 July 1910, Cantiere di Genoa-Foce
	Launched:	14 October 1911
	Delivered to the Regia Marina:	17 May 1914
	Sunk by internal explosion at Taranto 2 August 1916 Salvaged between 17 September 1919 (raised) and 23 January 1921 (righted) Stricken: 23 March 1923 Broken up at Taranto after 1933	

'Duilio' class

Duilio	Builder:	Regio Cantiere di Castellamare di Stabia
	Fitting out:	Ansaldo sa, Genoa
	Laid down:	24 February 1912
	Launched:	24 April 1913
	Delivered to the Regia Marina:	10 May 1915
	Radically modernised between 1 April 1937 and 15 July 1940 (see Chapter 5 and following)	
Andrea Doria	Builder:	Regio Arsenale della Spezia
	Fitting out:	Odero & C, Genoa
	Laid down:	24 March 1912
	Launched:	30 March 1913
	Delivered to the Regia Marina:	13 March 1916
	Radically modernised between 8 April 1937 and 26 October 1940 (see Chapter 5 and following)	

Andrea Doria. The first was laid down at Castellammare on 24 February 1912 and the second at La Spezia on 24 March that year. It is interesting to note that, as with the famous 1876 battleship, the name *Duilio* was not preceded by the proper prefix *Caio*, as applied to all successive ships of that name.

In order to speed entry into service, the Regia Marina devised a somewhat complex organisation to build these battleships: the hulls would be built by the Arsenale della Spezia (*Doria*) and by Castellammare di Stabia (*Duilio*); fitting out would be entrusted to two private Genoa dockyards, Odero & C (*Doria*) and Ansaldo (*Duilio*); the powerplants would be built by Ansaldo for both ships in its Genoa-Sampierdarena works; and production of the main guns was split between Vickers-Terni of La Spezia (*Doria*) and Armstrong-Pozzuoli (*Duilio*), while armour plate was assigned to Carnegie Steel Co of Pittsburgh in the USA for the *Andrea Doria* and to Acciaierie di Terni for the *Duilio*, plus some elements for the other ship.

Launched respectively on 30 March and 24 April 1913 during solemn ceremonies in the presence of the King, *Doria* and *Duilio* were towed to Genoa to complete their fitting out. Work on the *Duilio* went quickly enough, so that the ship was able to begin sea trials about two months earlier than the 30 June 1915 forecast date. Fitting out the *Andrea Doria* was significantly delayed as its main guns, manufactured by Vickers-Terni, were transferred, as noted earlier, to the *Conte di Cavour*, whose fitting out was way behind schedule, largely because of the late delivery of the guns by the same company.

After having carried out the planned series of sea trials, which did not turn out to be particularly spectacular, *Duilio* was delivered to the Regia Marina on 10 May 1915, just a few days before

'CONTE DI CAVOUR' AND 'DUILIO' CLASS BATTLESHIPS

Principal technical characteristics upon entry in service[1]

		'Cavour' class (*Conte di Cavour, Giulio Cesare* and *Leonardo da Vinci*)	**'Duilio' class** (*Duilio* and *Andrea Doria*)
Displacement (t.):	empty	20,280	20,100
	normal load	23,150	22,970
	full load	25,080	25,200
Dimensions (m):	length overall	176.09	176.09
	length between perpendiculars	168.96	168.96
	breadth overall	29.03	29.03
	draught at full load	9.04	9.05
Power plant:		(*Cavour* and *da Vinci*) Blechynden oil-fired boilers	8 Yarrow oil-fired boilers
		12 Blechynden mixed fuel boilers	12 Yarrow mixed fuel boilers
		(Cesare) 12 B&W oil-fired boilers	
		12 B&W mixed fuel boilers	
		3 groups of Parsons turbines on 4 shafts	As 'Cavours'
	Maximum power output:	31,000 shp	32,000 shp
Speed (knots):		21.5 (maximum at normal load)	As 'Cavours'
Range (miles at knots):		4800/10; ,000/22	As 'Cavours'
		With 1450 tons coal and 850 tons oil	with 1476 tons coal and 845 tons oil
Protection (mm):	Vertical (max at waterline) at centre	250	As 'Cavours'
	at extremes	120, at bow 100, at stern 120	
	tower max	280	As 'Cavours'
	main gun turrets max	280	As 'Cavours'
	secondary batteries max	130	secondary batteries max 150
	horizontal, total, max	85	As 'Cavours'
Armament (mm):		13–305/46 guns (III x 3, II x 2)	As 'Cavours'
		18–120/50 guns (I x 18)	16 152/45 guns (I x 16)
		14–76/50 guns (I x 14)	19 76/50 guns (I x 19)
		3–450mm torpedo tubes	As 'Cavours'
Complement[2]:		894 men (44 officers and 850 NCOs and other ranks)	As 'Cavours'

Notes:
[1] In the absence of significant differences between the ships of the same class the mean values are given.
[2] Excluding staff of flag officers.

Purely by way of example, values shown are for *mean tonnage* (volume of internal spaces), gross (total) and net (subtracting spaces used exclusively for the ships' combat employment) expressed in tonnes of tonnage (1 tonne = 2.3 cubic metres) and valid for all of the ships of the two classes: 13,613 and 7782.5. These values – calculated according to specific national parameters for warships and differing from the classic values for merchant vessels – were used to determine agreements for ports (outside of naval bases), towage and canal transits (Suez, etc).

Italy entered the First World War, while *Andrea Doria* was not completed until 13 March 1916. The full-power speed trials were rather disappointing, as neither ship made more than 21.5 knots, against the 22 that had been planned. In essence, with respect to speed, range and manoeuvrability, the performance of the 'Duilios' almost exactly matched those of the earlier 'Conte di Cavour' class.

In contrast, at the time of entry in service the external appearance of the 'Duilios' differed considerably from that of the earlier class, as can be seen from the plans reproduced on page 22. In particular, the ships of the two classes could be distinguished even at a distance mainly by the shape of their funnels, which were much higher on the 'Duilios'; by the position of the forward tripod (placed abaft the first funnel on the 'Cavours' while it was forward of it on the 'Duilios'); and by the absence on the 'Duilio' of the long midship shelter deck and resulting lower freeboard of the midship triple turret. Another feature that could be seen at a distance, although with some difficulty, was the smaller space between the barbettes of the 305mm turrets of the fore and aft groups of the two 'Duilio' class.

The average unit cost borne by the Regia Marina for building the 'Duilio' class was significantly lower than for the 'Cavours': the mean cost of the 'Duilios' was 84,462,500 lire (of which 37,000,000 was for the guns), against 100,553,800 (36,343,800 for the guns). This was achieved by the reduced use of private industry for the hulls and some economies of scale in fitting out by building ships that were practically the same as the earlier class.

Chapter 3

TECHNICAL DESCRIPTION OF THE 'CONTE DI CAVOUR' AND THE 'DUILIO' CLASSES

For more than twenty years the 'Conte di Cavour' and the similar 'Duilio' classes represented the chief Italian expression of the single-calibre battleship concept. Along with the slightly earlier *Dante Alighieri*, these 'dreadnoughts' constituted the Regia Marina's battle squadron opposing that of Austria-Hungary during the Great War. The conduct of naval operations in the Mediterranean during the course of that conflict did not, however, allow any operational employment other than forming a 'fleet in being' moored at Taranto, except for a brief deployment to Corfù. One of the 'Cavour' class, the *Leonardo da Vinci*, was however lost in port in 1916 due to an internal explosion.

The silhouette of these ships was dominated by two conspicuous funnels that constituted the most prominent element of the superstructure, complemented by the fore and aft command

The new battleship *Duilio* in the port of Genoa shortly after being turned over to the Regia Marina by the Ansaldo shipyard in May 1915.

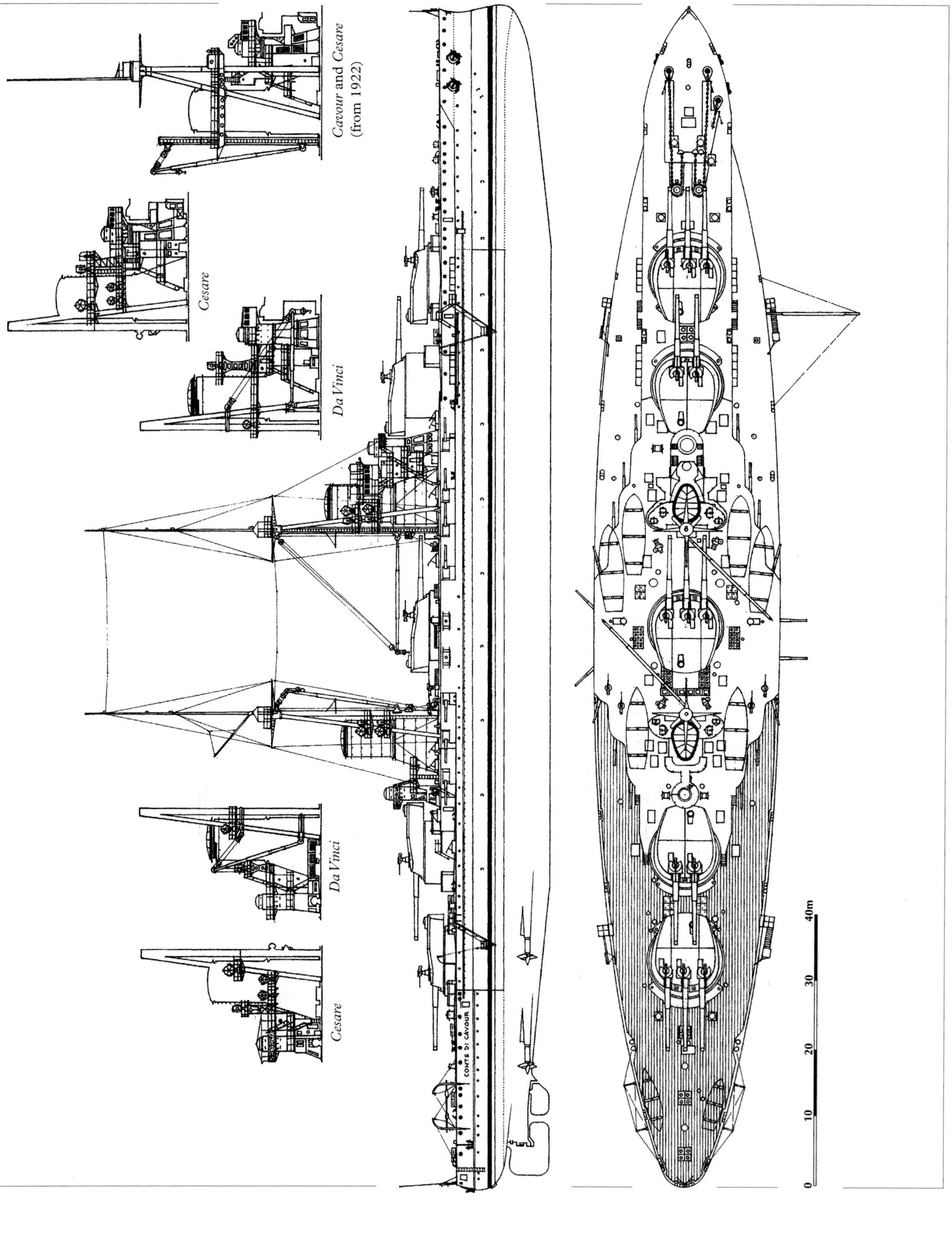

External views of the 'Conte di Cavour class battleships in their original form. (Drawing by R Maggi)

The *Leonardo da Vinci* at Genoa in 1914 about to enter service. (Courtesy M Biorci)

towers, both of rather modest size. Alongside each funnel was a tripod mast of not particularly massive construction, supporting a platform for the spotting tops, which originally were very small, and also spars mainly intended for the long radio antennae. The hull appeared rather low in the water and was dominated by the four main gun turrets fore and aft, while the fifth turret, the central triple turret placed between the funnels, was less prominent. Secondary armament, all in casemates, left the upper decks completely free.

In contrast to all large Italian ships preceding them, the 'Cavours' and 'Duilios' had no ram bow – the last to be fitted with one was actually the *Dante Alighieri* – but their bows featured a slight projection of the fore-foot intended to improve the coefficient of fineness of the keel and reduce resistance.

The original profile of the 'Cavours' underwent a drastic alteration in the early 1920s when, as we shall see, the forward mast arrangement was modified and became more complex, giving the ships a considerably more squat and massive look. The 'Duilios', which were characterised by decidedly higher and less well-proportioned funnels, did not undergo substantial modifications until 1937, when they were subjected to major reconstruction. This followed the same lines as the rebuilding of the two

Detail of the battery layout of several 152/45 (6in) guns on board the *Duilio*.

The battleships *Conte di Cavour*, in the foreground, and *Dante Alighieri* in the anchorage in Taranto during the Great War. Note, in the background, an airship in flight.

remaining 'Cavour' class ships begun in 1933, which radically changed the appearance of all these vessels, giving them lines that were altogether more modern (see Chapter 5 and following).

Hull and superstructure

The hull structure was of high-tensile steel except for those parts subject to possible vibration, where Martin Siemens mild steel was used. The stem post, the stern post, the rudder frame and the propeller shaft brackets were of cast steel. The hull, fitted with a cellular double bottom, was divided into watertight compartments by longitudinal and transverse bulkheads and by various 'platforms' (or decks that did not extend for the entire length of the ship). On the 'Cavours', above the double bottom were more internal plates that constituted a complete triple bottom designed to better protect the ship against underwater threats along with a 22mm thick bulkhead that ran along both sides of the powerplant amidships. On the 'Duilios', instead, the triple bottom was replaced by a more extensive compartmentation in the lower part of the hull.

The battleship *Duilio* fitting out at Genoa in 1914.

There were three continuous decks: the splinter (or protective) deck, the main deck and the upper deck. This became the exposed quarterdeck aft, while forward it was in part covered by the forecastle deck; exterior areas of the upper deck were teak-planked.

In the 'Cavour' class, the forecastle deck, which extended aft for about 62 metres, was followed by the large central shelter deck, which extended from the forward superfiring turret barbette to its after equivalent. The shelter varied in width; amidships, its two bulwarks in fact constituted an extension of the hull sides, while fore and aft the structure was shaped to form the various gun ports of the 120mm secondary armament. The width of the forecastle deck was cut back to allow ahead fire by the eight forward guns of those batteries. Both the forecastle deck and the shelter deck were covered by teak planking.

On the 'Duilio' class the forecastle deck, which was also entirely teak-planked, continued aft of the forward funnel forming the roof of a casemate that housed the gun ports, port and starboard, of the forward 152mm battery; the after battery was positioned on the main deck, one deck lower, with appropriate embrasures that allowed the four aftermost guns to fire directly astern. There was a single superstructure from which arose the second funnel and the small aft control tower.

As can be seen from the plans, applicable to both classes, the hull shape, which had been extensively trialled in a ship testing tank, was particularly advanced. The stern was of the so-called 'cruiser type', with both the main and auxiliary rudders arranged on the ship's centreline, aft of the four propeller shaft fairings.

The hull, below the splinter deck, was subdivided into watertight compartments by eighteen complete transverse bulkheads, by four longitudinal bulkheads delimiting the machinery and magazine spaces, and by various partial bulkheads, transverse as well as longitudinal. Above the splinter deck, the internal spaces were subdivided into watertight compartments by twelve trans-

The battleship *Duilio* at La Spezia in June 1915 shortly after entry into service. (Courtesy Bibl A Mai, Bergamo – Fondo E Occhini)

verse bulkheads that extended as far as the main deck and eleven as far as the forecastle deck, in addition to four longitudinal bulkheads.

Above the weather decks, the superstructure consisted primarily of the two funnels that emerged from extended bases that functioned as 'smoke boxes', in which the exhaust ducts from each group of boilers converged. The 'Duilio' design originally provided for identical funnels to those of the 'Cavours', but while fitting out, their height was increased by about 3 metres in order to keep the smoke as far as possible from the command positions. The remaining superstructure was minimal and consisted of the forward armoured conning tower, with additional bridge platform, and by the similar, but smaller, aft control station.

The mast arrangement consisted of two high tripod structures placed close to the funnels. On the 'Cavour' class, both tripods faced towards amidships with the foremast abaft the first funnel. On the 'Duilio' class, however, the forward tripod was ahead of the fore funnel in the space created by moving the upper 305mm twin turret closer to the lower triple turret. Considerably altering the silhouette of the ships, this modification, was clearly designed to reduce the effect of hot gases from the boilers on the masts themselves, the foretop, and the conning tower from whose upper level the fire of the main guns was directed. The position of the derricks also differed on the ships of the two classes: on the *Cavour* and *Cesare*, the two 20-ton capacity derricks and their associated cable lifts were attached to each tripod's central mast; on the *Leonardo da Vinci* they were separated, with a capacity of 16 tons each and mounted on the two supporting legs (known as 'foxes' in Italian) of the tripods; a similar arrangement to this was then adopted on the two 'Duilios', which had four 20-ton cargo derricks for loading.

In 1922, the fore tripod of the two surviving 'Cavour' class was replaced by a tetrapod – surmounted by the main fire control top – placed immediately ahead of the forward funnel as on the 'Duilios'; the original forward tripod was not removed completely, the lower part of its central leg being retained to act as a support for the derrick. At the same time several minor improvements were made to the command platform arrangements, two fire control positions being installed on the sides of the tetrapod to direct the fire of the secondary guns and a few simplifications were introduced to the structures that surrounded

Detail of the unarmoured wheelhouse of the battleship *Andrea Doria*.

the aft armoured command tower. During those same years, the size of the foretop on the 'Duilio' class was increased for the purpose of main armament fire control.

Protection

The passive defence system on ships of the 'Conte di Cavour' class was of the armoured citadel type with a complete belt at the waterline; total weight was 6124 tonnes disposed as vertical armour and rather fragmented horizontal protection.

The side protection consisted of a belt that extended from bow to stern, from the level where the splinter deck met the hull side, about 1.8 metres below the waterline, up to the main deck. This belt consisted of two strakes of tempered steel armour: the lower strake consisted of a central section 250mm thick, two sections 230mm thick fore and aft that ran as far as the armoured bulkheads of the citadel, and two further sections at the extremes that tapered off to 120mm aft and 100mm forward; the upper strake consisted of a 220mm central section between the two armoured bulkheads and two sections at the extremes tapering down to 80mm. A third strake of armour, between the main and forecastle decks, ran from the stern bulkhead as far as the extreme bow with a thickness at the centre of 130mm that tapered towards the stern to 110mm and towards the bow to 80mm. The central shelter deck where the 120mm guns of the secondary armament were located was protected by 130mm plates. The aft bulkhead consisted of 130mm plates between the splinter deck and the main deck and by 110mm between the main and forecastle decks; the forward section had 130mm plates. The armour plate of the belt and bulkheads were of nickel steel case hardened using the Krupp method; they were fastened with substantial bolts over a backing of wood, while those of the shelter deck rested directly on 14mm thick plating.

Horizontal protection was arranged on four levels and consisted of plates of high resistance special steel of varying thickness. Maximum total thickness, including that of the plating of the various decks, reached 130mm. In particular, the best protected decks were the forecastle and its extension over the central shelter deck (30 + 14mm), the main deck (18 + 13mm) and, obviously, the protective or splinter deck, which was flat in the centre (12 + 12mm thick) and sloped down at the sides (20 + 20mm max) until it met the lower edge of the armoured belt.

To protect the main guns, the revolving turret mechanisms were protected by barbettes up to 220–230mm thick; the gunhouses themselves had 280mm of frontal armour, 240 on the sides and 85 on the roof. The forward armoured conning tower was protected by plates 280mm thick for the cylindrical section and 200mm where it was conical; the communications tube between the tower and the forward control station reached a maximum of 280mm. Protection of the equivalent aft conning tower measured respectively 160, 130 and 100mm thickness.

The arrangements on the 'Duilio' class, while retaining the same armour thicknesses for the vertical and horizontal protection, differed in detail from those of the 'Cavour' class, principally because of the lowering of the midship main gun turret by one deck level and the resulting elimination of the central armoured shelter deck. This significant saving in weight was, however, partly offset by the increase in the thickness of the vertical protection for the secondary battery, which went up from 130 to 150mm, as well as the greater weight of the 152mm guns compared to the 120mm guns.

Overall, by the time they entered service, their protection was considered unsatisfactory: the thickness of their armour was inadequate against modern artillery larger than 300mm at medium ranges, and it was judged of limited effectiveness against plunging fire from large-calibre guns at long ranges. With respect to underwater protection, which was mainly reliant on extensive compartmentation in the lower part of the hull, there was a similarly negative assessment of its effectiveness against mine and torpedo explosions.

As on all of the other large Italian ships of the era, the 'Cavour' and 'Duilio' classes were fitted with steel anti-torpedo nets. These were fitted along the sides, handled by a series of hinged booms. While at sea, these nets were rolled up and lashed to the hull sides; they were in fact utilised only when the ships were in anchorages where surprise attacks by submarines or torpedo boats were deemed possible. Their deployment and re-stowing took considerable time, and the weight of the nets and their associated equipment was also significant. During the war it became clear that battleships rarely anchored in open roadsteads, so in 1916 it was decided to progressively remove them, which was concluded within the year for all of the ships of these two classes.

Given the era, explosions beneath the keel caused by weapons activated by magnetic fuses had not been foreseen nor the effects of heavy and powerful aerial bombs. However, in the final phase of fitting out *Andrea Doria*, completed in the spring of 1916, some defence against attack by the small air-dropped bombs of the period was introduced: the tops of the two funnels were fitted

'Cavour' class central shelter deck.

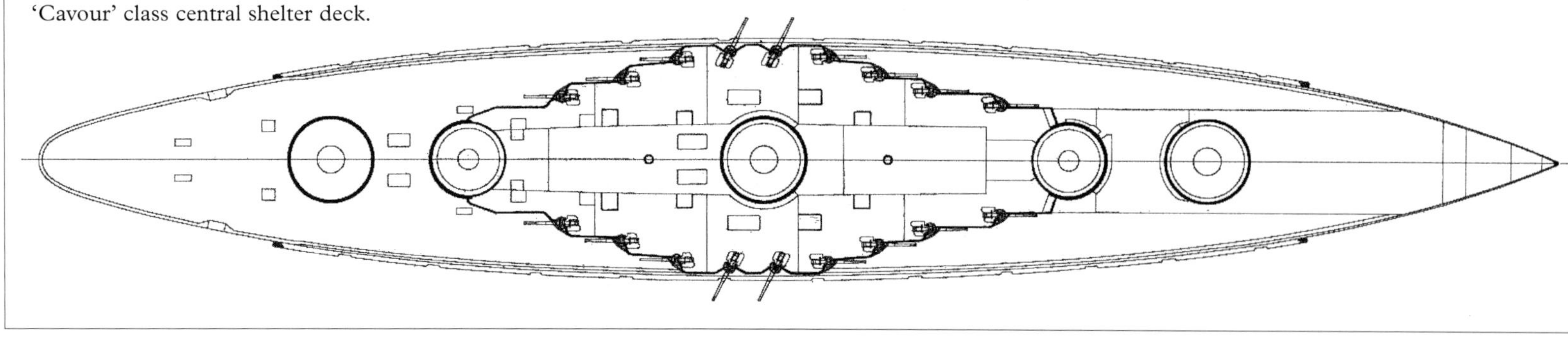

'Duilio' class casemates.

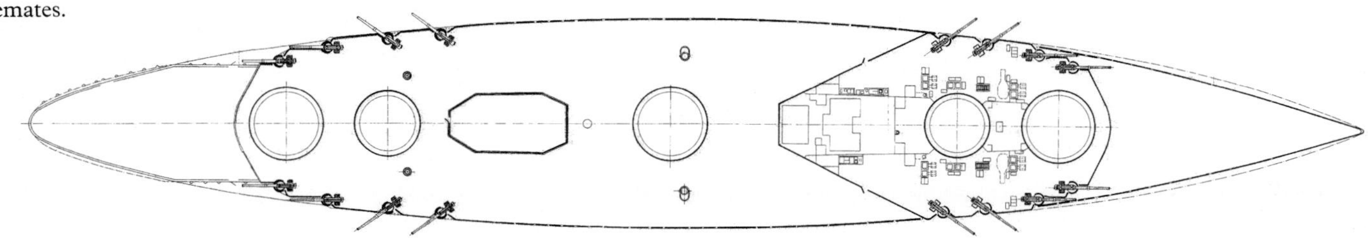

with conspicuous latticework structures covered by metal nets that acted to detonate the bombs before they could penetrate into the boiler uptakes. They proved of limited value and were eliminated during the immediate post-war period.

Powerplant

On the 'Cavour' class, steam-generating equipment consisted of groups of oil fired and mixed combustion (oil + coal) boilers whose composition varied in number and type from ship to ship as appears in the summary tables on pages 96, 97 and 137. All of the boilers were of the water-tube type, functioning at a working pressure of 16 atmospheres, grouped in ten watertight compartments; five forward of the machinery spaces and five aft. The smoke ducts from the fore and after boiler groups each converged at the base of the corresponding funnel. Ventilation of the spaces and the 'forced draught' (achieved by increasing the air pressure in the boiler spaces) was generated by powerful electric fans. For feeding of the mixed combustion boilers there were more than seventy coal bunkers of varying sizes, with a maximum total capacity of 2410 tons, all located under the splinter deck. The maximum oil load (850 tons as designed) was almost totally stowed in thirty compartments of the double and triple bottom, from which it was drawn by electric and steam pumps. The supply of reserve water for the boilers was 330 tons.

The main machinery consisted of three independent Parsons-type steam turbines placed, with their associated auxiliary machinery, in three separate compartments, one on the centreline and two outboard of it. The two outboard groups each drove one shaft, while the centre group drove two, for a total of four shafts. All were fitted with three-bladed bronze propellers, cast in one piece along with the boss, with diameters of 2.3 metres (outboard) and 2.8 metres (centre); the two starboard propellers rotated to the right while the two port side propellers rotated to the left. Each group consisted of a high-pressure turbine (HP) and a low-pressure turbine (LP) for

'CONTE DI CAVOUR' AND 'DUILIO' CLASSES – FULL POWER TRIALS

Ship	*C di Cavour*	*Cesare*	*da Vinci*	*Duilio*	*Doria*
Date	15.1.1915	11.1.1913	2.12.1913	30.1.1915	1.5.1916
Place	Ligurian Sea	Gulf of Genoa	Gulf of Genoa	Gulf of Genoa	On passage[1]
Mean displacement (tons)	21,612	21,700	21,717	22,135	23,620
Mean speed (knots)	21,9	21.56	21.6	21.26	21
Propeller RPM (inboard)	389	394	394	399	–
(outboard)	324	318	319	317	–
Maximum power (shp)	31,278	30,700	32,300	31,700	34,000

[1] From La Spezia to Taranto
(Source: Report of the Director General for Naval Construction to His Excellency the Minister of the Navy, various exercises, see Bibliography)

'Conte di Cavour' and 'Duilio' classes.
General machinery arrangement.

B: boilers;
HP: high-pressure turbines;
LP: low-pressure turbines

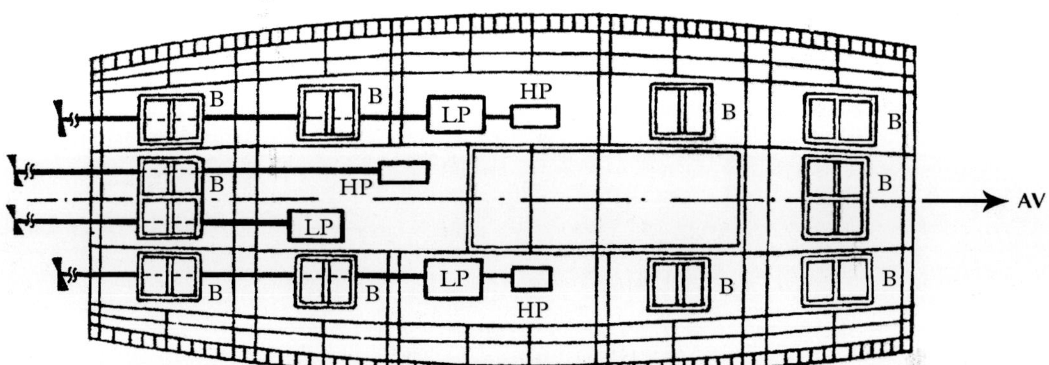

forward speeds. In the outboard groups both the HP and LP turbines were connected directly – that is, without any reduction gearing – to the same single shaft; in the centre group, however, the HP and LP turbines were connected directly each to their own shaft. The outboard groups each had an astern turbine, incorporated into the casing of the LP turbine; the centre group had two astern turbines (that is, one for each shaft), of which the left-hand turbine was independent while the other was incorporated with the LP turbine. The six turbines for forward movement developed a combined total of about 31,000 horsepower; the four astern turbines developed power in the order of 14,000 horsepower.

At normal speed the steam was introduced directly into the three HP turbines; from these, as soon as initial expansion had occurred, it passed to the corresponding LP turbines for further expansion and then was shunted to the respective condensers. Regulation of the number of shaft revolutions ordered was achieved by adjusting the steam delivery valves and was, given the different configuration of the centre group compared to the outboard groups, somewhat laborious. Different speeds were programmed for the two inboard propellers and for the two outboard propellers; at full power, the outboard propellers operated at about 320 revolutions compared with 390 for those inboard. Here we should note that the lack of reduction gearing – an arrangement that became common practice in the years following the design of these ships – meant that neither propellers not turbines were operating at optimum revolutions. There were three main condensers, one for each group of turbines, and four auxiliary. The circulating pumps for the main condensers could draw water from the sea and, in case of emergency, from the bilge.

Electric power for onboard needs was supplied by three electric powerplants, two of which were located in protected areas. Each consisted of two 150 kW generators (turbo-generators) at 110 volts. The general configuration and composition of the powerplant of the 'Duilios', except for the boiler model, were almost identical to those of the 'Conte di Cavour' class.

The results of the full-power trials that preceded their entry into service for both classes were similar and, in general terms, were not particularly spectacular. In fact, mainly because of the weight increases due to modifications made during construction and fitting out, only one of the ships (the *Conte di Cavour*) came close to the designed 22 knots.

Armament, organisation, fire control, ammunition stowage

The armament of these single-calibre battleships consisted of a battery of large-calibre guns, which constituted the main armament, and a battery of medium- and small-calibre guns that represented the secondary armament, also called the anti-torpedo armament, in addition to a small underwater component consisting of three torpedo tubes. As previously mentioned, the medium-calibre armament marked the chief difference between the 'Cavour' and 'Duilio' classes: on the 'Cavours' these consisted of eighteen 120mm guns, while the 'Duilios' had sixteen 152mm guns. There was also a difference in the number of 76mm guns, with fourteen on the 'Cavours' and nineteen on the 'Duilios'.

305/46 systems

The Model 1909 305/46 gun, in four triple turrets manufactured by Armstrong of Pozzuoli, had previously armed the *Dante Alighieri*, the first Italian dreadnought. It was also chosen by the Regia Marina to equip the 'Cavour' and 'Duilio' classes, in triple and twin turrets for a total of thirteen guns per ship. This was a gun designed by Armstrong, characterised by a 'wire-wound'

A salvo from the midship 305/46 turret of the battleship *Leonardo da Vinci*. (A Fraccaroli collection)

Sectional view of a twin 305/46 turret of the type mounted on the battleship *Giulio Cesare*.

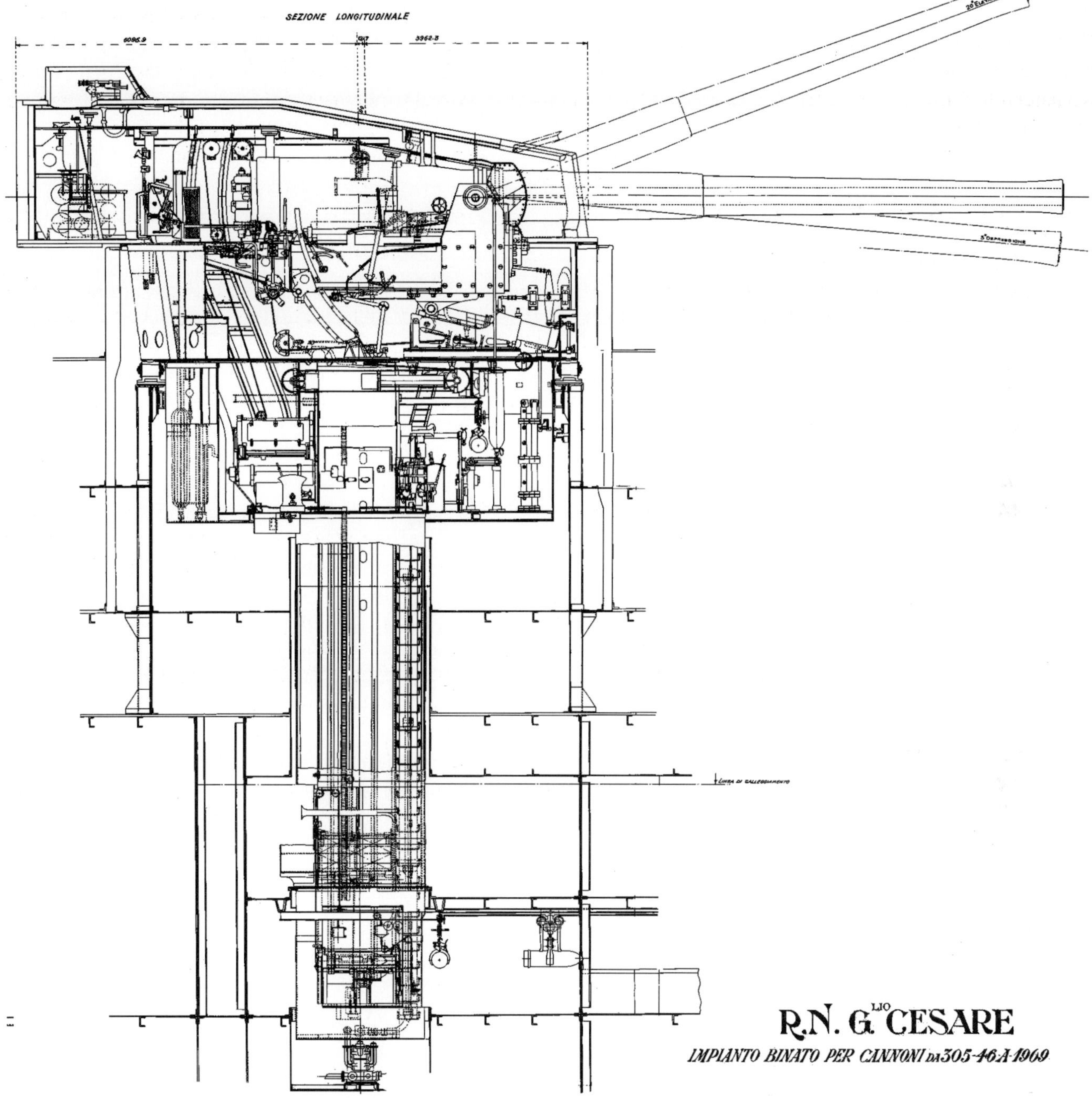

process that consisted of tightly wrapping numerous coils of a ribbon of nickel steel. The gun consisted of a removable core in nickel steel around which was wrapped a first series of rings that were also of nickel steel. Over this, extending from the breech to about half the length of the barrel, was a ring of steel ribbon, while the area towards the muzzle was wrapped in a layer of nickel steel that completed the second layer. This layer was then covered by an outer layer, which comprised the third layer, or 'jacket', in carbon steel. As can be seen in numerous photographs, the guns produced by Armstrong displayed three concentric rings: the 'jacket', an intermediate ring and the liner; guns produced by Vickers showed a total of four rings, as there were two intermediate rings. The liner had seventy-two grooves with a uniform twist, from left to right. The breech had a horizontal sliding screw-type block.

The original characteristics of this widely used and well-proven 12in gun were: weight of the oscillating mass 64,113kg; muzzle velocity of the armour-piercing shell 861m/sec; weight of armour-piercing shell 452kg; weight of fragmentation round 404.6kg; maximum range approximately 21,500 metres, rate of fire one round every thirty seconds. They were mounted in armoured triple and twin turrets on gun carriages on inde-

'CAVOUR' AND 'DUILIO' CLASSES – MAIN GUN TYPE AND ARRANGEMENT

Ship (Builder-fitting out)	**305/46 gun Model**	**No. rings at muzzle**	**Turrets** (see p 19) **Model**	**Elevation**	**Modernising yard 1933–1940** (see Chap 5)	**320/44 gun (ex 305/46) Model**	**No. rings at muzzle**	**Turret**	**Elevation**
Dante Alighieri (RCm-la Spezia)	A 1909	3	A (4 x III)	20°	———	———	———	———	———
Conte di Cavour (Ars Spezia)	V 1909	4	V (3 x III; 2 x II)	20°	CRDA, Trieste	OTO 1934	4	V (2 x III; 2 x II)	27°
Giulio Cesare (Ansaldo, Genoa)	A 1909	3	A (3 x III; 2 x II)	20°	C.del. Tirreno, Genoa	An 1934	3	A (2 x III; (2 x II)	27°
Leonardo da Vinci (Odero, Genoa)	V 1910	4	V (3 x III; 2 x II)	20°	———	———	———	———	
Duilio RCm-Ansaldo, Genoa	A 1909	3	A (3 x III; 2 x II)	20°	C.del. Tirreno, Genoa	An 1936	3	A (2 x III; 2 x II)	30°
Andrea Doria (Ars Spezia-Odero-Genoa)	V 1909	4	V (3 x II; 2 x II)	20°	CRDA, Trieste	OTO 1936	4	V (2 x II; 2 x II)	30°

Abbreviations: Ars Spezia: Arsenale della Spezia; An; Ansaldo, Genoa; A: Armstrong Pozzuoli; OTO: Odero Terni Orlando, La Spezia works, ex-Vickers; CRDA: Cantieri Riuniti dell'adriatico; RCm: Regio Cantiere di Castellammare di Stabia; V: Vickers-Terni, La Spezia works (Elswick for *da Vinci*)

pendent cradles and slides with a maximum elevation of 20 degrees and a depression of -5 degrees. The 305/46 guns of the 'Cavour' and 'Duilio' were produced in part by Armstrong in its Pozzuoli works and in part by Vickers-Terni in its new shops in La Spezia and, for the *Leonardo da Vinci* only, in Vickers' main works in Great Britain.

In all, for these two classes of battleship plus the *Dante Alighieri*, Armstrong-Pozzuoli produced 41 guns including those for reserve and Vickers 42, of which 28 were produced in La Spezia (Mod G) and 14 in Great Britain (Mod T).

Although the performance of these guns and the layouts of the turret systems were broadly similar, the appearance of the armoured gunhouses, triple and twin, built by Armstrong and those built by Vickers were quite different, as can be seen in the drawings and photos. The two sides of the Armstrong turrets were straight and were only slightly narrowed towards the rear, while the Vickers turrets were curved and converged more to the rear. The *Conte di Cavour*, *Leonardo da Vinci* and *Andrea Doria* had Vickers turrets and guns, while the other two ships (*Giulio Cesare* and *Duilio*) were equipped with the Armstrong model (see drawings of the armoured turrets on page 21).

Loading the 305/46, as for all large-calibre guns of the Regia Marina, was of the so-called 'ordinary' type, that is with projectile and separate charge, the charge consisting of a number of cartridge bags containing the propellant, which varied according to the type of charge selected (for example, 1st for combat, with 136kg of cordite; 2nd for coastal fire, etc). In general terms, the turret layout was similar to that of almost all of the comparable systems of the era and consisted of: the so-called 'gun chamber' that held the breech mechanism for the guns; the shell handling room; the carousels and the elevators that aligned the gun axis with the shells and charges coming from the ammunition stowage spaces below. The power to operate these mechanisms, as well as for the rammers to push the projectiles and charges into the guns, was of the hydraulic type with water under pressure furnished by steam pumps. The backup for the electrical main gun turret traverse system was also hydraulic.

Because of its overall characteristics and performance, the 305/46 was considered a good gun, reliable and accurate enough, designed with ample strength margins that, as we shall see, would allow its recalibration to 320mm during the later radical modernisation of the 'Cavour' and 'Duilio' classes (see Chapter 5). The limited original range was essentially dependent on the configuration of the gun mounting, which had a maximum elevation of only 20 degrees, because at the time of the weapon's design, the simple fire control systems did not make for effective employment of naval artillery at ranges greater than 20,000 metres. Nonetheless, during the Great War studies had been undertaken and gunnery range tests carried out to increase elevation to 30 degrees, achieving significant increases in range.

120/50 guns

These 4.7in guns constituted the secondary armament of the three 'Cavour' class and were the 120/50 V Model 1909 on single pedestal mounts, placed in casemates on both sides of the central armoured shelter deck for a total of eighteen guns. Of these, eight were arranged so that they could fire ahead, six fired astern, and four on the broadsides. These 4.7in so-called quick-firing guns were produced by Vickers, in which the propellant charge contained in a brass case was separate from the projectile. Both the loading and the 'ramming' of the projectile into the gun as well as the propellant case were done manually, with a rate of fire of about six round per minute (one every ten seconds). Resupply

The *Conte di Cavour* anchored in Taranto's Mar Grande during the Great War. (USMM)

of ammunition from the magazines to the ready-use lockers on the main deck was by mechanical elevators, while the horizontal movement of projectiles and brass cases to the individual guns was by hand, with the assistance of trays suspended from guide rails on the roof of the casemate.

The main characteristics of this gun, mounted on single carriages with +20 degrees and –5 degrees elevation, were: weight of the oscillating mass 3.7 tons; muzzle velocity 850m/sec; weight of semi-armour-piercing shell and fragmentation shell respectively 22.06 and 23.15kg; maximum range 12,000m; rate of fire about four rounds per minute (one every fifteen seconds).

152/45 guns

These 6in guns constituted the secondary armament of the two 'Duilio' class and were the models 152/45 S 1911 and 1912 in single pedestal mounts, placed in casemates on each side of the forecastle deck and the main deck for a total of sixteen guns subdivided into two groups, fore and aft, of eight guns each. These guns were designed by Schneider and produced by Ansaldo; they were quick-firing and completely manual in operation with ammunition resupply and loading arrangements similar to those of the 120mm guns on the 'Cavour' class.

The main characteristics of these guns, mounted on single carriages with +20 degrees and -5 degrees elevation, were: weight of the oscillating mass 6.4 tons; muzzle velocity 830m/sec; weight of semi-armour-piercing shell and fragmentation shell respectively 48.34 and 44.43kg; maximum range 17,000m; rate of fire 3.5 rounds per minute (one every seventeen seconds or so).

The *Conte di Cavour* in 1918. Note the single 76mm gun positions right forward on the forecastle deck in the anti-torpedo-boat role.

76mm guns

These 3in guns were part of the secondary armament of the 'Cavour' and 'Duilio' classes, in single deck mounts and manually operated and firing fixed ammunition (the round weighed around 10kg) for close-in anti-torpedo [boat] defence.

There were fourteen 76/50 positions (that could be increased to eighteen) for the Vickers 1908 and 1909 and Armstrong 1908 and 1909 types, whose appearance, characteristics and performance were very similar to each other: maximum elevation +20 degrees, maximum depression –5 degees; total weight of the mounting 1.14 tons; muzzle velocity 815m/sec; weight of semi-armour-piercing shell 7kg; maximum range 11,000m; rate of fire fifteen rounds per minute (one round every four seconds).

The guns could be mounted by simply bolting their pedestals down on prepared bases. According to the ships' equipment books, these were thirty in number, of which three were at the extreme forward end of the forecastle deck, twelve on top of the armoured shelter deck, two on deck at the stern and thirteen on the roofs of the main gun turrets.

However, an analysis of the shipyard drawings shows that initially there were to have been twenty-two positions on the

The Regia Marina battle squadron operating in the Ionian Sea in late 1916.

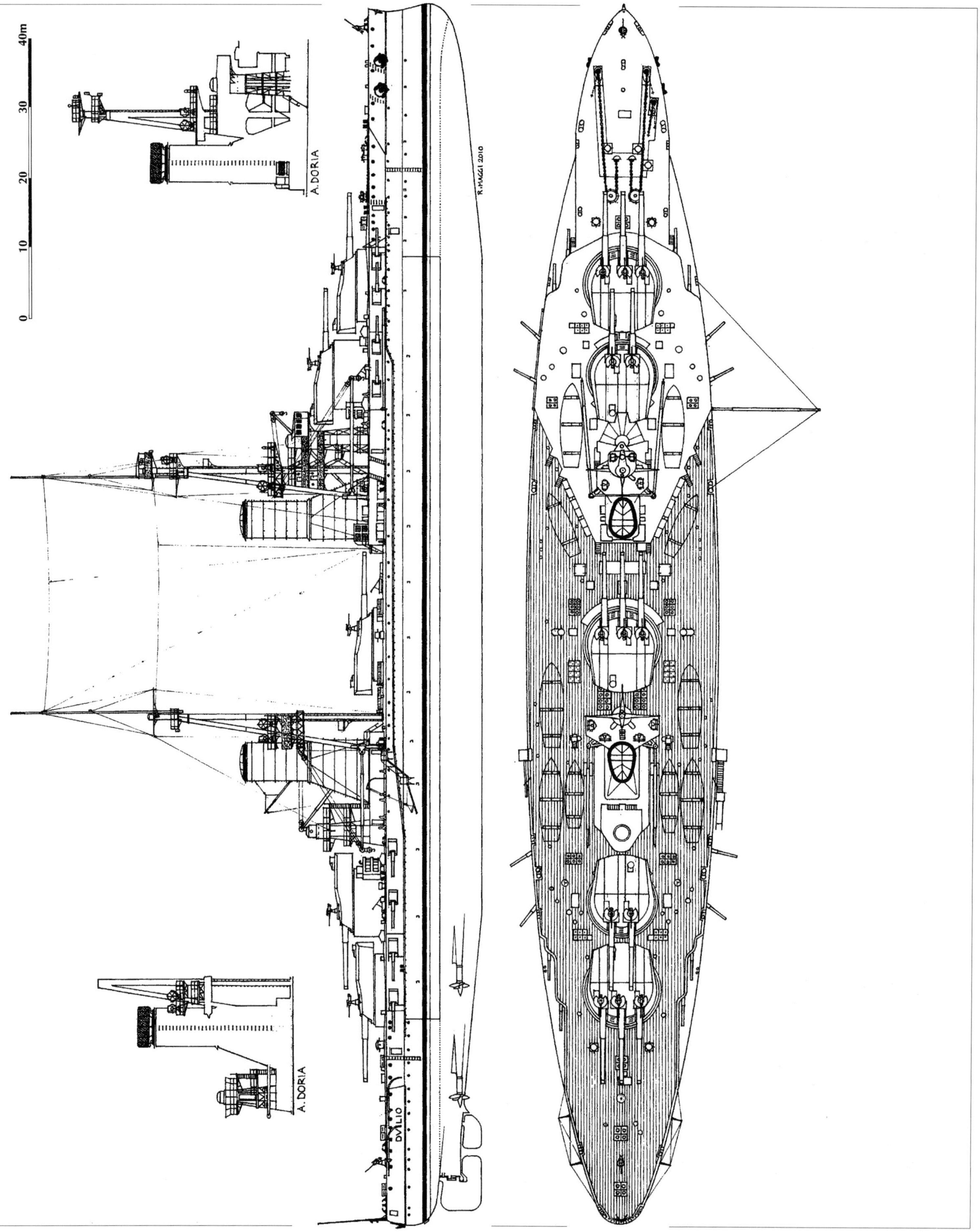

External views of the 'Duilio' class battleships in their original form. (Drawing by R Maggi)

The *Conte di Cavour*, whose forward mast had recently been modified, leaving La Spezia in 1922.

Cavour and *da Vinci* and twenty-three on the *Cesare*. While the main armament was in action, as the 75mm positions had no protection against the blast effects of the main guns, the gun crews had to be 'sheltered' or moved under cover, and thus their guns could not be employed.

On the *Duilio* and the *Doria*, initial plans called for the fitting of single 76/45 Schneider 1912 guns produced by Ansaldo but, as these guns were not yet readily available, it was necessary to fall back on the older 76/50 A 1909 guns also made by Ansaldo. These totalled nineteen guns, which could be fitted in thirty-four positions: three at the forward end of the forecastle deck, eight on the same deck either side of No 2 main gun turret; eight on deck, sided, aft of No 5 turret; two on deck at the extreme stern; and thirteen on the roofs of the main gun turrets. Towards the end of the Great War, six of the 76/50 were replaced by a like number of 76/40 Ansaldo RM 1916 guns adapted for anti-aircraft use, whose characteristics were: elevation from +65 degrees to -5 degrees; total mounting weight 2.9 tons; muzzle velocity 690m/sec; weight of anti-aircraft fragmentation round 6.02kg; maximum horizontal range 10,000m; rate of fire twelve rounds per minute (one round every five seconds). In the immediate post-war period, when they were finally available, the 76/50 on the 'Duilio' class were replaced by a like number of 76/45 S 1912.

In practice, not all of the 76mm guns could be repositioned using the normal onboard hoisting gear (loading derricks, sheer legs, etc), and it was necessary to use dockyard cranes or lifts. On the 'Duilio' class, however, the sixteen positions either side of Nos

The battleship *Duilio* at Pola in the early 1920s.

The *Conte di Cavour* at Genoa on 22 April 1912.

2 and 5 main gun turrets were served by temporary derricks that were able to move the guns through four hatchways that were specially configured to allow the mountings to pass through.

The complement of 76mm guns on the battleships of both classes also included two 76/17 Schneider 1912 guns for the use of landing parties. This was a small howitzer on a wheeled carriage that could be dismantled and which was normally stowed away, as was a 47/40 A 1901 boat gun on a carriage mount.

450mm torpedo tubes

Both the 'Cavour' and 'Duilio' classes were fitted with three torpedo tubes for launching 450mm Type A 95/40 torpedoes. Two were located towards the bow, in the same compartment, with one oriented to the right and one to the left; the third tube was located on the centreline at the extreme stern above the splinter deck. Each tube had three torpedoes, which were launched by compressed air.

Fitting torpedo tubes on board single-calibre battleships may seem anachronistic, as it is unlikely that these ships would operate at ranges where weapons with a run of only a few thousand metres would be useful; nonetheless, it should be remembered that the *Dreadnought*, which inspired the 'Cavour' and 'Duilio' ships, was also fitted with torpedo tubes. However, once it was recognised that they had no practical function, the tubes and their torpedoes were removed from the Italian battleships, probably in the early post-war years.

The underwater equipment of both battleship classes was completed by a pair of paravane otters for protective sweeping, which when stowed were lashed to the sides of the forecastle deck. Forward, to facilitate handling the steel towing cables for the paravanes, a highly visible pair of chains were stretched between a bracket at the fore-foot and the stem-head (see diagram on page 93).

Changes to the armament

In the period between their entry into service, shortly before and during the Great War, and their laying up prior to being modernised in the 1930s, changes to the armament were very minor and essentially involved its smallest element. More important, as we shall see, were changes to the fire control systems of the large- and medium-calibre guns.

The first of a series of small modifications involved the number of 76mm guns of the 'Cavour' class, which was stabilised at thirteen 76/50 guns on the roofs of the main gun turrets, with the addition, as on the 'Duilios', of six 76/40 Ansaldo Mod 1916–1917 anti-aircraft guns positioned three per side on the shelter deck abreast the aft funnel. On the 'Duilio' class for a long period during the 1920s the positions of two of the 76/40 AA guns were fixed, with one on the extreme bow and the other on the aft portion of the roof of No 4 turret.

At the beginning of the same decade, the ships of both classes were fitted with two Vickers 40/39 Model 1915–1917 AA guns positioned one per side on the forecastle deck slightly forward of No 2 main gun turret. These 2pdr guns were automatic weapons weighing a total of 825kg, with a water-cooled recoiling barrel, fed by 50-round magazines with tracers and explosive rounds weighing 1.3kg each, on a cloth belt; the mounting was a platform type, with elevation from +80 degrees to –5 degrees, manually operated; muzzle velocity was 650m/sec and effective range was 4400m. Theoretical rate of fire was 200 rounds per minute, in practice reducing to about 50 because of the somewhat impractical method of replacing the ammunition magazine, which weighed 96.4kg. Produced under licence by Terni, it was at the time subject to frequent jamming, but it was also the only heavy automatic anti-aircraft cannon available in Italy during the early 1920s that used a recoil-dampening type of mount, so did not transmit excessive force to the deck during firing and was subject to only modest vibration.

Organisation of the guns and fire control system

The large number of guns on board, some fifty in total, required a significant number of personnel to man them, so that the size of the two gunnery divisions (3rd and 4th) was much larger than any others, except for the two (7th and 8th) consisting of the numerous stokers and machinery mechanics. Arrangements for centralised fire control were, on the other hand, minimal and of limited effectiveness.

At the time the ships entered service, and for almost the entire duration of the Great War, fire control of the main armament was entrusted to two directors, furnished with small coincidence rangefinders, one being located in the upper portion of the forward armoured control tower and the other, which was smaller, abaft of the aft funnel. The two control tops at the head of the tripod masts were also used to direct the fire of the main guns. There were no mechanical fire control centres, but only simple calculation rules, manually tracked 'prediction tables' and a network of telephones, mechanical indicators and voice pipes for the transmission of data and orders.

It was not until just before the end of the war that the fire control systems, for the main and medium-calibre guns, began to improve with the fitting of more rangefinders and the creation of an embryonic fire control centre located on the main deck near No 2 turret. Essentially, however, it was not until the early post-war era that there was any major improvement. An early, important step was the installation of three 4.7m base 'Triplex' coincidence rangefinders mounted one above the other on a single traversable mounting on the roof of the forward armoured control tower. The first installation of a Triplex system was in late 1917 on the battleship *Dante Alighieri*, the ship designated for carrying out trials, followed in 1918–1919 by installation on the two surviving 'Cavour' class ships and on the two 'Duilios'. Almost contemporaneous with the embarkation of the Triplex, beginning with the 'Duilio' class ships, the equipment on the after control top was progressively improved and 2.74m base rangefinders were fitted on turrets 2, 3 and 4 to be used for independent firing of the individual turrets or of groups of turrets.

From 1919–1920 for the 'Duilios', and later for the 'Cavours', the main armament could be controlled from either of two fire direction centres [SDT – *Stazione di Direzione del Tiro* – Fire Direction Station]: one was located in the fore-top and one in the forward armoured control tower in which were located, respectively, the 1st and 2nd Fire Directors. The fire direction centre in the top was fitted with an APG [*Apparecchiatura di Punteria Generale* – General Aiming Device] of the 'Girardelli' type (through which target designation and turret training angles were determined), and with optical instruments for observation of the fall of shot, indicators for the aiming adjustments to be made, receivers for checking the distance by the rangefinders, an indicator showing the instant of the salvo fall, the electrical warning for 'turrets ready', and a series of telephones and voice tubes. The 2nd DT (Fire Director) centre had all of the same instrumentation except for the APG. The fire control centre, located on the main deck and run by the 3rd DT, had a manual 'prediction table', a Sperry-type course tracker, various chronometer indicators, a simple 'level' to establish the instant of fire when the ship was rolling heavily, repeaters for all of the instruments mentioned, and was linked – by telephone, voice tubes and electromechanical transmitters – with the Triplex, with the aft rangefinder, with the five main gun turrets and the two SDT. In the 'ordinary aiming' mode, the fire control centre, responsible for transmitting the elevations and trajectories to the guns, also

Detail of the conning tower of the battleship *Duilio* moored in Mar Piccolo at Taranto, probably in the early 1930s.

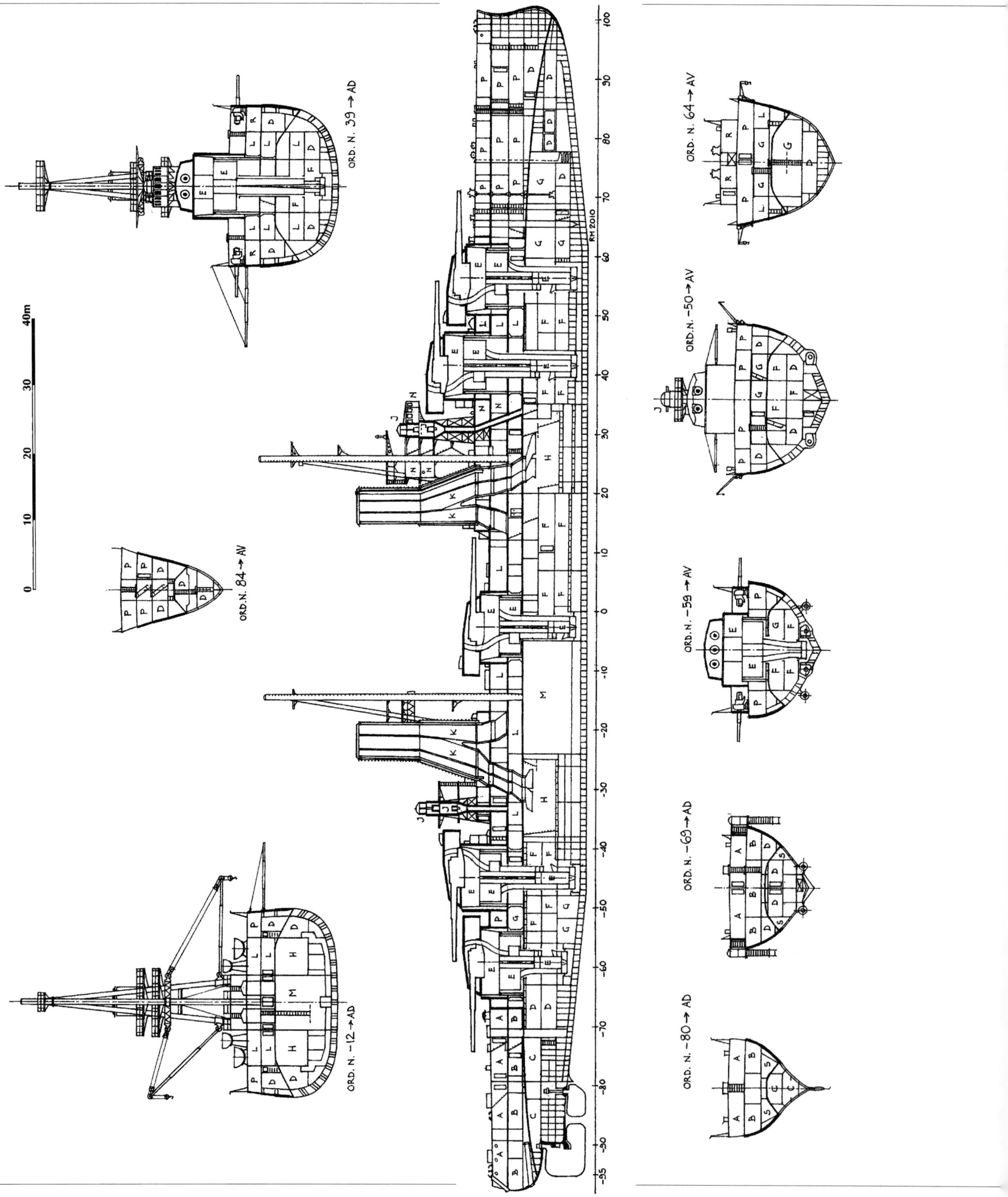

Longitudinal section and transverse sections of the 'Duilio' class battleships. (Drawings by R Maggi)

Forecastle, battery deck and lower deck of the 'Duilio' class in their original form. (Drawings by R Maggi)

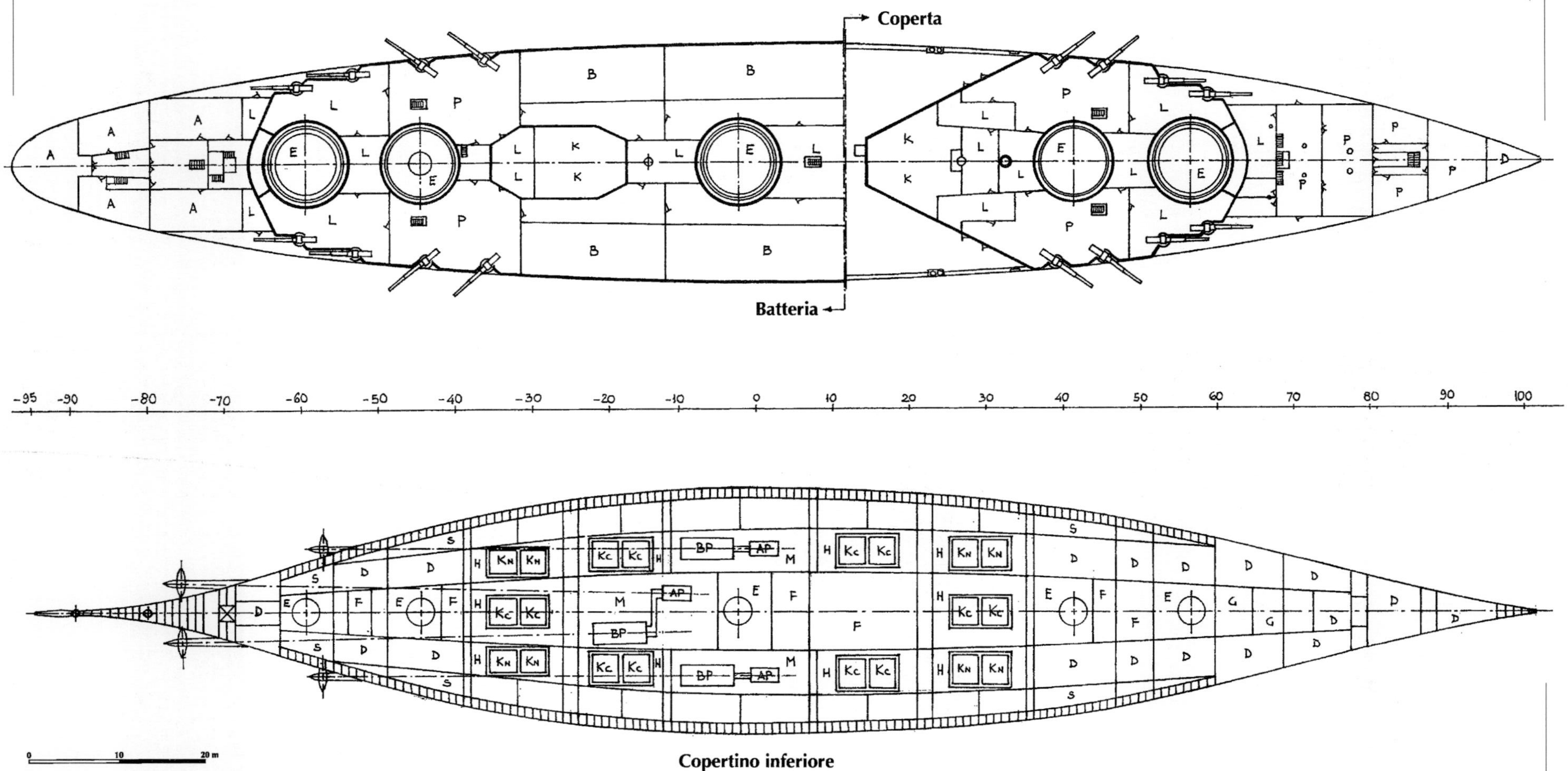

- A Accommodation for admirals and senior officers
- AP High-pressure turbines
- B Officers' quarters
- BP Low-pressure turbines
- C Rudder machinery
- D Storerooms and magazines
- E Main armament turret mountings
- F Ammunition stowage (magazines and shell rooms)
- G Auxiliary machinery
- H Boiler rooms
- J Fire control and direction stations
- K Boiler uptakes
- Kn Oil-fired boilers
- Kc Mixed fuel boilers
- L Various service spaces
- M Engine rooms
- N Command and control spaces
- P Crew quarters
- R NCO quarters
- S Oil and water tanks

determined the instant of fire; alternatively, in the 'general aiming' mode, the order to fire was determined by the 1st, or the 2nd DT.

In the 'independent fire' mode, to be used only when damage or mechanical breakdowns prevented the two other types of aiming described above, it was planned that the main armament would be controlled as follows: 1st group = turrets 1, 2 and 3; 2nd group = turrets 4 and 5. Firing would be directed by officers positioned behind the sighting ports in the two superfiring turrets (2 and 4) furnished with a 2.74m base rangefinder and reduced instrumentation, but sufficient for rapid fire; if necessary, turret 3, also provided with a rangefinder, could fire independently.

During the course of work carried out in 1922 – during which the forward mast arrangement on the 'Cavour' class was modified – for the first time on both ships of this class, fire direction stations for the medium calibres appeared, fitted with 2.74-metre coincidence rangefinders placed in an elevated position on the two sides of the new tetrapod. At the same time the fore-top, designated to act as the main fire direction centre, was significantly enlarged, repeating what had already been done on the 'Duilio' class. On the 'Duilio', there were four fire direction centres for the medium-calibre guns, located on both sides of the lower tops on the fore and after masts. Each of these stations was provided with a general aiming device of the 'Spallazzi' type, with a rangefinder and simplified instrumentation for fire direction for the medium-calibre guns for an entire broadside of the ship or for the forward or aft section of the same battery.

Also in the 1920s, anti-aircraft 'barrage fire' by 76mm guns with anti-aircraft characteristics was directed by a station placed on the navigating bridge that surrounded the aft armoured tower with the aid of a 1.50m base Zeiss rangefinder, employment of an 'abacus' to determine elevation, with orders to the guns transmitted via megaphone.

In the years that followed, except for a progressive, general upgrade of the optical instrumentation for range measurement, there were no substantial changes to the fire control systems of these ships prior to their radical modernisation. It should be remembered that in the early 1930s the Regia Marina's first electromechanical fire control centres were embarked on the 'Duilio' class ships, designed shortly earlier for the new 'Trento' class heavy cruisers.

Ammunition stowage

On both of the battleship classes, there were three main ammunition stowage spaces: one fore, corresponding to the two forward main gun turrets (Nos 1 and 2); one midships below No 3 main gun turret, and one aft, corresponding to the two after 305mm gun turrets. Each space was in turn divided into two levels where, in the upper level, the 305mm firing charges were stowed in the magazine and in the lower level were the projectiles themselves in the shell room; an adjacent space contained the cases and projectiles for the medium-calibre guns. The cased ammunition for the smaller-calibre guns were stowed in separate magazines away from the main ammunition stowage.

On the 'Cavour' class, upon entry in service, total ammunition capacity was 1300 rounds of 305mm (equal to 100 rounds per gun); 3600 of 120mm and 3360 of 76mm. On the 'Duilio' class, the capacity was 1144 rounds of 305mm, 3440 of 152mm and 5265 of 76mm.

All of the magazines were insulated, fitted with 'remote thermometers' to control the temperature from a distance, with protected electric lighting, with sprinkler systems to extinguish

The battleship *Conte di Cavour*, along with other ships of the battle squadron, taken from an airship in the 1920s. (Courtesy G Garello)

Launch of a Macchi M 18 reconnaissance seaplane from the catapult located on the port side of the forecastle of the *Conte di Cavour*.

any small fires and with large seawater pumps, controlled from outside the compartments themselves to quickly flood them if necessary for safety reasons.

Steering and handling equipment, manoeuvring qualities and stability

There were no substantial differences between the two classes of ship with respect to these characteristics.

There were two rudders, of the semi-balanced type, situated on the centreline: a main rudder, located aft on the line of the rear perpendicular, with a surface area of 32 square metres; and an auxiliary rudder, 9 metres forward in line with aft frame 82, with a surface area of 10 square metres. The maximum rudder angle for both was 35 degrees, which could be reached in less than twenty seconds thanks to two 180 horsepower motors, one steam and one electric, able to work in tandem or separately. The rudders, which were divided for safety reasons in case of damage and to increase the ships' manoeuvrability, could be steered separately or in tandem through hydraulic controls located on the navigating bridge, in the fore and aft armoured control stations and in the orders room located under the conning tower. The steering gear could also be operated manually via four large spoked metal wheels, which could be worked by sixteen men. Motors, steering gear and manual backup for the rudders were positioned at the stern under the splinter deck. A mechanical indicator of the 'ball and pyramid' type, situated between the two yards of the aft mast, signalled the rudder movements for the benefit of any other ships that were part of the formation.

The steering qualities of these ships are summarised in the following table, relative to the use of only the main rudder, which indicates the diameter of the turning circle in metres:

Rudder angle	20°	25°	30°	35°
Speed 10 knots	1222	1126	1051	989
Speed 20 knots	1343	1281	1185	1037

The time needed to turn 360 degrees was 8 minutes 20 seconds at 20 knots and 14 minutes 35 seconds at 10 knots at maximum rudder angle.

During stability trials, carried out under normal displacement conditions, the transverse metacentric height (*r-a*) was for all ships between 1.43 metres and 1.66 metres, a clear indication of sufficient stability that reached the maximum righting moment at a 30-degree heel while positive stability was lost between 45 degrees and 48 degrees.

Mooring arrangements and lifesaving equipment

The anchors, all of the Hall type with hinged flukes, were: two bower anchors, which could be hoisted into hawseholes on the sides of the bow; one sheet anchor, also in a hawsehole slightly aft of the bower anchor on the starboard side (each weighing 8 tons); one stream anchor weighing 2.15 tons also in a hawsehole at the extreme stern; and two 800kg kedge anchors, initially secured against the rear bulkhead of the shelter deck and later on the hull quarters below the quarterdeck. The bower anchor chains were 70mm gauge and had a total length of 800 metres, equal to thirty-two 25-metre lengths; the sheet anchor chain, also of the same gauge, was 225 metres long.

The initial complement of boats was eighteen or nineteen of various types, from 14-metre steam pinnaces through 13-metre and 9.5-metre rowing boats to small 5-metre punts. Individual lifebelts were of the canvas and cork type with shoulder straps and safety ribbons and, from the latter period of the Great War, there were a number of Carley float liferafts that were mainly stowed against the bases of the funnels.

Aviation equipment and embarked aircraft

For a brief period in 1918, equipment for raising and towing a 'Draken' type observation balloon was installed, experimentally, on the quarterdeck of the *Andrea Doria*.

The first aircraft appeared on the battleships of both classes in 1925. These were M 18 AR (folding wing) seaplanes, of which one example per ship was mounted on a special framework on the roof of the midships main gun turret. In bad weather, the turret itself was traversed to orient the aircraft into the wind in order to reduce stress on its light construction. The seaplane was lowered on to the sea for take-off and was recovered by the ship's cargo derricks. Produced by Macchi, the M 18 was a three-seat reconnaissance biplane flying boat with wing-mounted floats, weighing 1780kg, with a maximum speed of 187 km/h from a 250 horsepower Isotta-Fraschini 'Asso' engine driving a pusher propeller; range was about 1000 kilometres at a practical ceiling of 5000 metres.

Fitted with radio gear, these aircraft were used for reconnaissance, observation and correction of gunfire when allocated to the 'Cavour' and 'Duilio' classes. There were, however, serious operational limitations because of the need to lower the aircraft onto the water – effectively stopping the ship for several minutes – to allow it to take off, which was only possible when the sea was calm and the wind was moderate. Once its mission had been completed, the aircraft normally diverted to land at a coastal seaplane station, as recovery at sea by the ship would have forced it to heave-to once again and was likewise restricted to landing in the open sea only under favourable weather conditions.

From 1926 the *Conte di Cavour* and then the *Duilio* and *Andrea Doria* were fitted with a long 'Gagnotto' metal catapult working by compressed air and suitable for launching an M 18 AR seaplane. Not traversable and situated on the port side of the forecastle deck, the catapult remained on board until the early 1930s and was the only aircraft equipment worthy of note permanently embarked on these ships.

Colour schemes

From the time of entry into service until the early 1920s these two classes of battleship adopted a uniform paint scheme of the hull and superstructures in 'light ash grey' characteristic of Regia Marina ships of the period. The upper decks, covered in teak planking, retained their natural colour, while the tops of the superstructures and of the main gun turrets received a darker grey colouring compared with the vertical surfaces. A strip of the hull along the waterline, called the boot-topping, was painted black, while underwater the colour of the anti-fouling was usually 'bottle green' but at times replaced by 'brick red'. Colour of interior spaces was 'very light green' except for those that opened to the exterior for which 'dark blue' was adopted in order to avoid reflection.

From the summer of 1915, an early, simple form of camouflage was applied on the *Conte di Cavour* and the *Guilio Cesare* by painting false white 'moustaches' either side of the stem (somewhat showier on the *Cavour* and less prominent on the *Cesare*) to simulate the bow-wave produced at high speeds, with the intention of deceive an observer at a distance as to the actual speed of the ship. The results were probably judged to be modest, as this measure was eliminated after only a short time.

From the early 1920s – except for ships scheduled to operate in warm waters, which retained or adopted an all-over very light grey – Regia Marina ships, including the 'Cavour' and 'Duilio' classes, began to be progressively painted uniformly in 'dark blue-grey', also called 'steel grey'. This paint scheme was retained until 1929–1930 when Italian ships returned to the traditional 'light ash grey' that remained in use until the Second World War was well under way.

Chapter 4

BATTLESHIPS AND ITALIAN NAVAL POLICY BETWEEN THE TWO WORLD WARS

Experiences in the Great War and uncertainty in the post-war period

Given the form that maritime operations took in the Mediterranean and the Adriatic, actions involving Italian dreadnoughts can be counted on the fingers of one hand, and little more need be said about the other major ships either. They had no occasion to do battle against the enemy. On the other hand, on 2 August 1916 the Italian battle squadron suffered the tragic loss of the *Leonardo da Vinci* in Taranto's Mar Piccolo, blamed on Austrian sabotage like the similar action that had led to the sinking of the pre-dreadnought *Benedetto Brin* at the Brindisi anchorage on 27 September 1915. Other authors, however, maintain that in the case of the *da Vinci* it was spontaneous ignition of the main armament propellant charges, as had happened during that period in various navies. There was greater activity involving tactical and firing exercises, conducted almost exclusively in the Gulf of Taranto, which among other things attracted negative comments by British observers about the outdated nature of the training. The Austro-Hungarian dreadnoughts were no more aggressive, taking an active part in very few operations, among which was the fatal June 1918 action that led to the loss of the *Szent Istvàn* at the hands of Luigi Rizzo's *MAS 15* [*Motoscafo Armato Silurante*; roughly equivalent to the British MTB or US PT boats]. The value of the Italian dreadnoughts as a 'fleet in being' was also overstated, as Allied naval strategy was certainly not focussed on the Austro-Hungarian battle fleet: rather, it was driven by the threat of mines and submarines, the lack of profitable targets in the Adriatic, and politically motivated Italian reluctance to cooperate with large Entente naval forces in major operations in the sector. Neither party had any great interest in changing this reality: on the Austro-Hungarian side because it was soon apparent that the submarine was by far the main offensive tool for the war in the Mediterranean, and on the Allied side, because the Austro-Hungarian surface fleet was already neutralised by the simple fact that it was bottled up in the Adriatic.

And yet, if the prospect of a great naval battle soon evaporated – for which until then most of the larger navies been had preparing – such a possibility never entirely disappeared from the concerns of the Regia Marina staff, which, considering the relative strengths of the forces, always feared a sortie by the Austro-Hungarian fleet up to and beyond the Otranto Strait, and made plans for such an eventuality. This preoccupation did not dissipate until June 1918 after the sinking of the *Szent Istvàn* at Premuda, which brought the number of opposing battleships to a more favourable ratio for Italy.

At any rate, wartime experience led all navies to reflect on the role of large battle squadrons and the very principles of naval warfare, centred on the decisive battle and on the exercise of maritime power. There was no decisive battle and the only major encounter between fleets, that of Jutland (or Skagerrak to the Germans), had little immediate effect on the course of the war. Events had, instead, brought the submarine to the forefront, and with it a new type of warfare, which made it possible to contemplate victory at sea simply by impeding its use by the enemy, interrupting its lines of supply. On the other side, it was the weapons of trade defence and anti-submarine warfare that became the main protagonists, first and foremost the smaller ships, while the great surface fleets could not make any real contribution and, in fact, ended up absorbing resources and energy that were needed elsewhere.

Doubts emerged from the technical perspective as well, especially due to the underwater vulnerability of capital ships. It is true that the victims of torpedoes and mines were mainly pre-dreadnoughts and armoured cruisers, while the more modern single-calibre ships survived fairly well – only the *Audacious* and the *Viribus Unitis*, this latter ship in port, were sunk by underwater attack; but it is also true that a new race between protection and subsurface offence threatened an almost unbelievable increase in battleship dimensions. Not least, the appearance of the air arm, although it had not yet had a decisive effect on the conduct of naval operations, foreshadowed extraordinary developments that might revolutionise conventional naval warfare – at the very least, it would require improved horizontal protection for capital ships. For that matter, even the few clashes between large ships had shown the need for greater combat ranges and the resultant increased impact angles of projectiles. In Italy, as elsewhere, by the early 1920s Regia Marina technical organisations had assessed that in order to balance the requisites of high speed, strong armament and effective protection the battleship would have to reach a displacement of at least 50,000 tons (the so-called 'absolute ship').

In those years these and other technical and doctrinal questions were widely debated in military and political spheres in Italy, within the context of the larger problems of public finance, marked by war debts, by the demobilisation of the armed forces, by transition to a peacetime economy and by virulent social conflict. It was this climate of uncertainty and restriction on spending that marked Italian naval policy for many years following the end of the war.

Cancellation of the *Francesco Caracciolo*

The Italian navy had come out of the First World War having made considerable progress in renewing its equipment and in new construction. These efforts had been focused on light, stealthy and auxiliary vessels, both because the conduct of the war favoured their use and also because, with respect to larger ships, the Entente enjoyed a significant superiority over the Austro-Hungarian fleet. For these reasons, in March 1916 construction of the four large battleships of the 'Caracciolo' class was suspended, cancelling the relevant contracts, so that at the end of 1918 the Regia Marina found itself with only its first-generation dreadnoughts: the *Dante*, the two surviving 'Cavour' class and the two 'Duilios', all of modest combat value compared with more recently built British, American and Japanese ships, but equivalent to the contemporary French battleships. The *da Vinci* was also added to the list, as it was soon to be raised in anticipation of its restoration.

The first problem was presented by the *Caracciolo*, the only one of the ships in an advanced stage of construction, on the ways of the government shipyard at Castellammare di Stabia; in addition, part of the 381mm and 152mm armament and of the main machinery for the four ships had already been manufactured. Because of this, work resumed in October 1919, at least to free the building slip, and the large hull was launched on 12 May 1920, amidst uncertain prospects.

The fact was that the 'Caracciolo' class, even though of advanced concept, suffered from the deficiencies listed above, which were only in part attributable to the fact of having been designed before the war. Paying attention to early wartime events at sea, since 1915 Ansaldo had been studying a series of changes to the underwater protection, the most controversial point, even though they understood that it would not be a total solution. In 1916, after the battle of Jutland, the problem of insufficient horizontal protection against projectiles with a high impact angle, or fired at great ranges (plunging fire), also emerged. In this case, the solutions considered would have inevitably increased displacement by several thousand tonnes, reducing the metacentric height and, with it, stability; and by increasing draught, reducing the reserve of power and the already minimal freeboard, impairing their seagoing qualities. To resolve these problems, albeit not completely, it would have been necessary to add bulges, which would have improved underwater protection and stability, but would have also led to a significant loss of speed. It is not

The battleship *Andrea Doria* at the buoy in the splendid bay of Villefranche, on the Cote d'Azur, in 1921. (Courtesy M Biorci)

surprising, therefore, that the then Minister of the Navy, Rear Admiral Giovanni Sechi, was sceptical about completing even one of these ships; finally, parliament refused the 100 million lire funding needed to complete it, accepting the loss of a good part of the 55 million that had already been spent on its construction.

On 25 October 1920 the hull was sold for 6.5 million lire to the Società Generale di Navigazione Italiana of Genoa for completion as a transatlantic liner. However, this scheme collapsed because it would have cost another 75 million to realise and the liner would certainly have turned out to be uneconomic. The next proposal was conversion into a large tanker or, later, into a large cargo ship. The study for the latter was undertaken by the very same Naval Engineer General Edgardo Ferrati who had designed the 'Caracciolo' class, and probably dating to the same period was another idea originating from Ansaldo: transformation into a 'hydroplane transport' and/or an aircraft carrier. Even these ideas were soon abandoned because of the high economic cost; the hull was finally broken up at Baia, near Naples, and the materials salvaged and put to other use.

Abandonment of the *Caracciolo* appears to have been an almost inevitable decision because of the extreme difficulty of applying the essential design modifications to a ship in an advanced stage of construction. Budget restrictions and doubts about the value of such ships in a political climate not favourable to new military expenditures also played a part. Perhaps the contemplated transformation into an aircraft carrier would have been an interesting solution – as later happened in all of the major navies – which would have given the Regia Marina a fast fleet unit with an air capability. Most importantly, this would have provided the technical and operational experience of naval aviation that it lacked during the Second World War, as well as constituting a useful precedent from a political standpoint.

Paradoxically, giving up the opportunity to complete a large and 'modern' battleship was counterbalanced by the raising of the hulk of the *da Vinci* at Taranto, in order to completely restore the ship. The technical aspects are covered in the box on pages 54–57 and the political aspects are discussed later; but it should be said at the outset that the decision turned out to be providential from the standpoint of international relations.

Renewed Italo-French naval rivalry and the 1922 Treaty of Washington

With the end of the war and the dissolution of the Austro-Hungarian Empire, France had become Italy's main rival. In 1918 the French navy had seven dreadnoughts (four 'Jean Bart' class with 305mm guns and three 'Bretagne' class with 340mm guns), all told not much better than the Italian battle fleet and equally inferior to those of the major naval powers. Paris also abandoned the construction of five large (but of obsolete concept) 'Normandie' type battleships, even though they had all been launched, except to transform one into an aircraft carrier (the *Béarn*), as well as the four 'Lyon' class, which were still on the building ways. This renunciation was influenced, even more so than in Italy, by the experience of the recent naval war, aggravated by the fact that at its conclusion France was gravely lacking in modern small surface ships and submarines. Moreover, the discrepancy had become accentuated during the course of the conflict, during which, while Italy had built about 70,000 tons of ships, almost all of which was in those categories, France was able to build barely 28,000 tons, as its industrial base was almost completely committed to army needs. It is not surprising, therefore, that in February 1919 the staff of the Marine Nationale, in fixing priorities for its future programmes, placed torpedo craft at the top, scouts and light cruisers second, and battleships only in third place. This orientation was driven by fears for the safety of traffic between North Africa and metropolitan France along the western Mediterranean routes, which would be perilously exposed to the threat of superior Italian light forces. But overall, even though less balanced than the Italian navy, the French navy could always count on 700,000 tons of ships against 450,000 for the Italians, a superiority that politically always carried a certain weight.

On the other hand, the United States and Japan found themselves in a major naval armaments race with programmes that, if completed, would have in a few years increased the US Navy

Off Corfu, 31 August 1923. Troops of the 14th Artillery Group on board the battleship *Conte di Cavour* which, along with other Italian ships, was engaged in the temporary occupation of the Greek island.

The battleship *Andrea Doria* in May 1926. Note the reconnaissance seaplane on the roof of the midships main gun turret and the uniform dark grey paint scheme, typical of Italian warships of the 1920s.

from 1.5 to 2.5 million tons and the Japanese from 0.7 to 1.6 million tons. In effect, this competition also involved Great Britain, which had begun eliminating 300,000 tons of its 2.3 million tons of naval shipping, but felt obliged at the least to respond with improved warship designs. To put the brakes on a competion that seemed to repeat that of the Anglo-German naval race prior to the Great War and which threatened the finances of the major powers, in late 1921 the United States promoted a conference to reach a reduction and a limitation of naval armaments. The conference, in which the five great powers partici-

Battleships at anchor off Naples on the occasion of the visit of the Spanish royal family on 26 November 1923. *Conte di Cavour* is in the foreground.

The battleship *Duilio* steaming out of Mar Piccolo, Taranto, in 1933.

pated, began in Washington on 12 November 1921 and concluded with the treaty of that name on 6 February 1922, valid until 31 December 1936. It was the basis for the naval policies of all of the signatory powers until the middle of the 1930s so it is useful to summarise its provisions.

On the political plane it fixed a hierarchy among the powers in the ratio of 15, 15, 9, 5, 5, the fruit of assigning to the United States and Britain 525,000 tons of new battleships, 305,000 tons to Japan, and 175,000 to France and Italy and of 135,000, 81,000 and 60,000 tons, respectively, of aircraft carriers, the only other category of shipping for which it was possible to find quantitative agreement. Britain lost its world primacy, now sharing it with the United states but, in turn, the treaty guaranteed the Anglo-Saxon powers an absolute primacy in the world, in each single theatre and category of warship, so much so as to constitute a worldwide *pax*.

In Europe, Britain enjoyed a ratio of 3 to 2 over France and Italy combined, with a safety margin of a third, in case another naval power might arise with a weight equal to the two Latin powers. Italy and France came to the conference with ten battleships each in service: Italy with six modern battleships (the *Dante*, the three 'Conte di Cavour' class and the two 'Duilios') and the four antiquated 'Regina Elena' class for a total of

The battleship *Conte di Cavour* seen from an airship in July 1927.

182,800 tons nominal; France, with the seven modern ships cited above and the three antiquated 'Diderot' class, for a total of 221,700 tons nominal. The *da Vinci* was included in the three 'Cavours', which was allowed because the ship was declared 'under repair', while it was still only a wreck. Thus, if the ship had not been raised and righted, Italy would have been judged to have one fewer 'modern' battleship and 22,500 tons less in total. This would have increased the difference with France and made it more difficult to establish a reasonable relative strength. This was the only – unplanned – advantage of its inspired, but costly operation of partial recovery.

Italy, which had come to the conference with the aim of reaching a ratio of at least 8 to 10 with France, obtained parity and, moreover, at a level that was therefore sustainable financially. From here on in, with this as a strong precedent, parity with the most strongly armed European continental power became the fixed point of Italy's policy of arms reduction in the years to come. The French delegation had tried without much conviction to obtain an overall tonnage of 350,000, equal to ten 35,000-ton battleships, but such a figure would have reopened discussion of the balances agreed between the three oceanic powers and, in the end, they resigned themselves to the 175.000-ton limit and to

Refloating the *Leonardo da Vinci*

The battleship *Leonardo da Vinci*, third ship of the 'Conte di Cavour' class, sank on the evening of 2 August 1916 at its mooring in the Mar Piccolo in Taranto. It was assumed that an act of sabotage (or, alternatively, spontaneous combustion) caused the explosion of the main gun charges stored in the after magazines, the energy of the explosion opening two large holes (each about 10 x 5 metres) in the hull and massively distorting the deck in the area around the aft 305mm triple gun turret. Water immediately flooded the ammunition spaces and, as much of the internal watertight subdivision was destroyed at the same time, it spread to the adjacent compartments until it reached the after boiler spaces through the propeller shafts tunnels, which were open. The ship began to settle rapidly by the stern, initially remaining upright but then began to heel to port. The capsizing of the ship, which rolled about 165 degrees, took place within only about ten minutes following the explosion. The battleship, which had a mean draught of 9.20 metres, corresponding to a displacement in the order of 24,000 tonnes, was moored over a flat seabed about 11.50 metres deep consisting of a layer of mud from around 9 to 15 metres, over a layer of very compacted clay. The rapid spread of water in the interior spaces, made easier by a large number of hatches that could not be closed in time, led to a rapid, progressive loss of both buoyancy and stability. When the extreme stern touched bottom, as muddy and yielding as it was, the reaction that followed contributed to significantly accelerate the loss of stability, thus advancing its capsizing. Due to the rotational effect of the hull, the superstructures and part of the port side towards the stern had dug into the bottom mud. The tallest structures – the funnels and the masts – had largely broken up and collapsed, while the more robust main turrets and the two armoured command towers had been driven into the mud. The situation of the ship resting on the bottom is shown in the drawing on page 56, which is taken from a report made immediately after the sinking. A good part of the hull forward initially remained above water, with the keel rising some 5 metres above the surface; in the months that followed, however, it was discovered that the ship was slowly burying itself and when it finally came to rest in December 1916, only 3.40 metres of the bow was visible.

Raising the wreck presented significant technical difficulties, even though the ship had sunk in sheltered waters and near a dockyard. On 11 August 1916 the Minster of the Navy nominated a special commission 'charged with studying the possibility of raising the ship in serviceable condition, even if only partially so, and inviting technical-economic proposals'. These proposals – signed off by influential engineers who were experts in the field – were not long in coming. These included:

i. suggestions to build a large caisson around the wreck, either of metal or stone which, once emptied of water, would have allowed the necessary repairs to the hull and thus lead to its righting;
ii. righting the ship by digging a deep trench into which to the hull could slide on its side and then to raise it by a cofferdam built around the forecastle deck, etc (from Engineer G Orlando, of the eponymous shipyard);
iii. Naval Engineer General Rota's plan to right the ship using the buoyancy provided by two cargo ships (*Bronte* and *Sterope*) to be sunk alongside the wreck and then raised gradually by pumping compressed air into them with the assistance of two large lighters (*GM 40* ex-battleship *Duilio* and *GM 45* ex-battleship *Ruggero di Lauria*);
iv. and finally the proposal by Naval Engineer General Edgardo Ferrati, which called for raising the overturned hull using compressed air and its righting by selective flooding once it had been refloated.

The commission concluded its work in November 1916, advising adoption of General Ferrati's scheme, but incorporating some specific features from the other plans. Assisted by Naval Engineer Colonel De Vito, Ferrati was commissioned to oversee the work, which he directed almost to its conclusion and, when he died, he was replaced by Naval Engineer General Emanuele Faruffini. Assembling the necessary materials began in late 1916 and preparation for work aboard the *Leonardo da Vinci* itself began in spring of 1917. The first stages progressed quite slowly because of wartime shortages of equipment but consisted of placing a series of decompression and equalising chambers on the ship's hull. By pumping compressed air parity with Italy. The French delegation left the conference disappointed, not so much because of parity with Italy, as the country's perceived demotion with respect to the other powers, which it felt did not reflect its real status as a great power. The French parliament, following very heated discussions, ratified the treaty, but Paris did not want the agreement of capital ship parity with Italy to set a precedent for agreement on smaller warships, a category that it considered to be of greater interest.

With regard to battleships, the treaty fixed the maximum standard displacement for battleships at 35,000 tons and the maximum calibre of the guns at 406mm (16in). Standard displacement was that of a ship completely fitted out and equipped, but without fuel and reserve water for the boilers; it was expressed in English tons (equal to 1016kg). Although it represented an unreal condition of the ship, it allowed an easy comparison of the general characteristics of the ships aside from range, which could be adapted to the needs of different operational theatres in which the ships of the various navies were to operate. In terms of numbers, the treaty indicated by name the battleships existing or under construction that each power could retain (for Italy and France all of those previously mentioned) or convert into aircraft carriers or reduce to auxiliary roles, as well

through these into many interior spaces that had been made completely watertight, a gradual lowering of the water level was achieved. This made it possible to start lightening the wreck by first unloading the remaining ammunition in the forward and midships magazines and later emptying the coal bunkers. These operations were completely successful, so that by November 1917 a slight lifting of the ship's bow was noticeable, which then progressively increased.

Under the direction of Naval Engineer Lieutenant Armando Andri, an officer with significant first-hand experience in underwater work, divers were simultaneously working to seal off all of the external holes and, in particular, the two large open-

The salvaged hull of the *Leonardo da Vinci* in drydock, keel upwards in order to make the initial repairs.

ings in the hull sides, which required complex carpentry. The next problem was safely removing the heavy armoured turrets and main guns, which would be lowered onto the bottom and salvaged later. Raising and lowering the hull slightly by using compressed air, the delicate work of releasing the turrets onto the bottom was completed in early 1918, followed by removing the armoured barbette of No 2 turret and other superstructure, thus lightening the wreck by about 6000 tonnes, leaving a weight of around 18,000 tonnes to be refloated.

During 1918 the underwater work of sealing off all of the exterior hull openings was completed, while in the largest drydock in the shipyard special shoring was prepared to receive and hold the ship in its upturned position. Operations were begun to attach the planned eight large floatation cylinders, placed two on each side of the bow and two per side aft. These cylinders, emptied of the water they contained by means of compressed air, were intended to furnish the buoyancy needed to offset the effect of many internal spaces that were still flooded.

On 4 June 1919, a significant raising of the forward portion of the ship was achieved and in early September the final operations to refloat the ship began by using all of the available pumps, assisted by an underwater electrical connection that had been set up for some time and which was continuously being upgraded.

Taranto, Mar Piccolo, 21 January 1921. Beginning of operations to right the hull of the *Leonardo da Vinci*.

Finally, on 17 September 1919 the *Leonardo da Vinci* was afloat again, overturned but in perfect trim. Quickly towed to the entrance of the drydock, the following day it was delicately

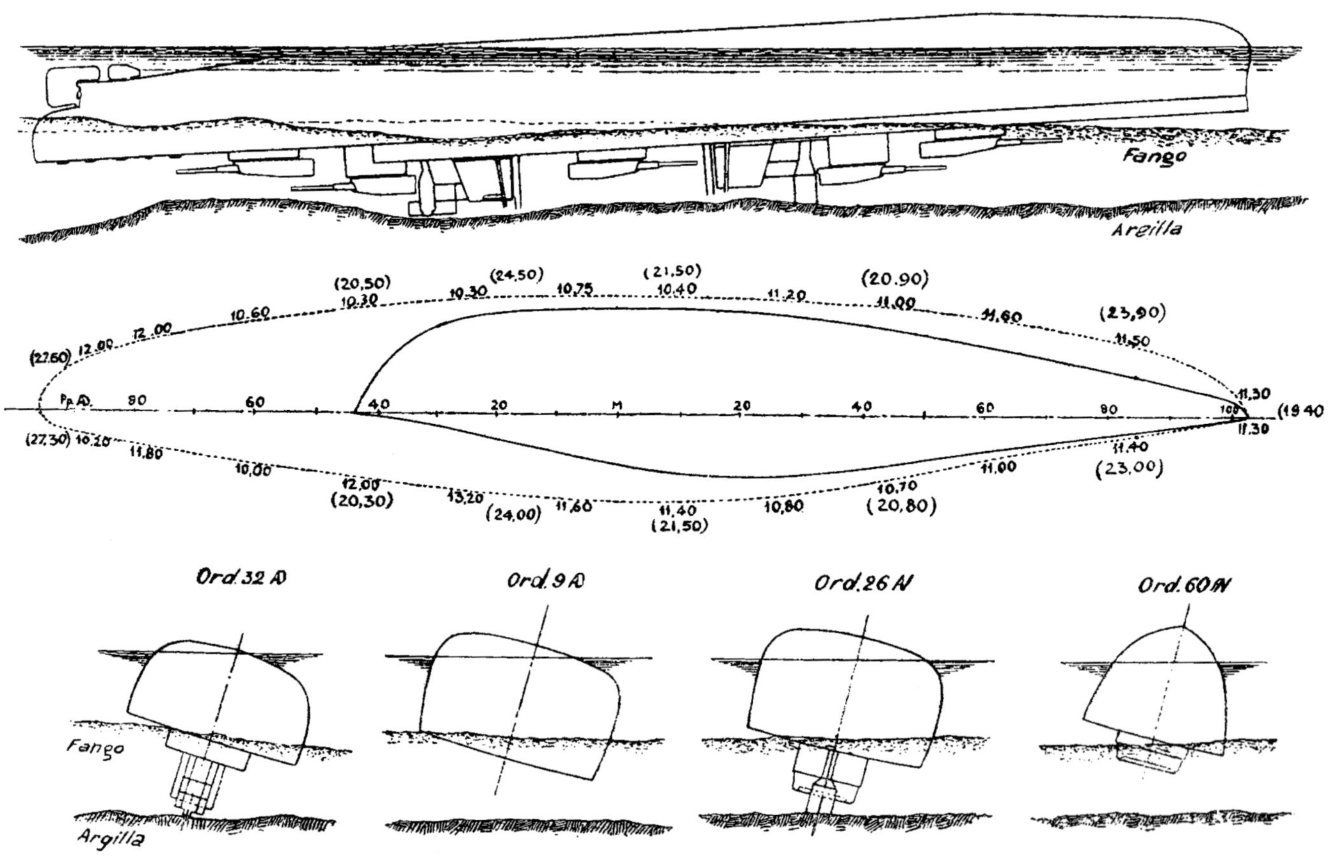

Position of the wreck of the *Leonardo da Vinci* sunk at Taranto.

Hull of the *Leonardo da Vinci* while being completely righted on 26 January 1921.

manoeuvred into the dock, and positioned on the special shoring that had already been prepared. Operations to drain the flooded areas were concluded on 5 October with the ship resting perfectly on the shoring and free of the buoyancy cylinders.

During its time in drydock, which lasted more than a year, the hull was made completely watertight. The after section of the forecastle deck was rebuilt and the hull bottom was stripped of the assorted pipework and catwalks that had been used during the raising operations. The mud, debris and, sadly, the remains of many sailors who had died during the sinking, were removed from all of the interior spaces.

When repainting was completed, the *Leonardo da Vinci* left the drydock on 21 January 1921 and was towed to a large trench more than 20 metres deep that had been excavated by dredgers in the bottom of Mar Piccolo in which the righting was to occur. By pumping water into the double bottom of only the starboard side – using several lighters and with the aid of submarines *N 1* and *N 5* – the ship was made to heel about 45 degrees, corresponding to practically zero stability. Left on its own, the large hull soon after began to increase its heel until, around midday on 24 January, it rotated completely and re-emerged in an upright position, even though it was still heeled some 22 degrees to starboard. The list was soon eliminated by emptying part of the water in the double bottom and the ship was able to be safely towed to a mooring near the drydock that today bears the name of the man who oversaw the difficult recovery of that unlucky battleship. It remained there for several years, while recovery of its main gun turrets was completed by means of a unique underwater structure shaped like a 'doughnut' that was specially built – only for the ship to be sent for breaking up, also at Taranto, as we shall see.

In the annals of naval engineering, the salvage of the *Leonardo da Vinci* represented one of the most difficult and important of those carried out in shallow water on an overturned hull. Executed with perseverance and with considerable, prolonged commitment of human and financial resources, it perhaps deserved a better outcome. Instead, the financial constraints of that period combined with doubts about such a significant investment in a ship that by now was conceptually obsolete, made it impossible to complete the restoration. In the end it was a great effort crowned by success, but quite useless.

Source: Report by General E Faruffini to the College of Naval and Mechanical Engineers, Venice, October 1919 in A Baistrocchi, *Elementi di arte navale*, Livorno, Belforte, 1934 and A Andri, *Recuperi navali in bassi fondali*, Rome, Bizzarri, 1979.

as the replacement plan that would have led in twenty years to the above-mentioned ratios. These ships could also be modernised, but within a 3000-ton limit, an option that would be exercised by various powers, including Italy for the 'Cavours'. The treaty imposed a ban on the construction of new battleships for ten years (the so-called naval holiday), which the replacement plan took into account, except for Italy and France which would be allowed to put 35,000 tons on the ways in 1927 and 1929 in consideration of the low fighting capability of their battleships. The pre-dreadnoughts of the two Latin powers were exceptions, and would be kept on the list until broken up but which could not be replaced. The minimum age at which battleships could be replaced was established as twenty years.

Britain, which had no battleships designed in the light of experience gained at the battle of Jutland, was allowed to build two, the future *Nelson* and *Rodney*, to replace four from among those that could be retained. No quantitative agreement was reached on smaller ships and submarines, but only a qualitative agreement on cruisers, whose standard displacement was not to exceed 10,000 tons with guns no larger than 203mm (8in).

Naval programmes and battleships in the 1920s: the fate of the *Leonardo da Vinci*

The fate of the *Leonardo da Vinci* was sealed during the time frame of the Washington Conference. When the issue came before the senate on 7 February 1921 they voted to restore the ship, against opposition from the Minister of the Navy, Rear Admiral Sechi, who attempted in vain to make the decision on refurbishment subject to the cost involved. On 19 February 1921 Sechi instituted a special commission that was to determine the condition of the ship and propose its best use, confirming whether or not it was advisable to restore it as a battleship and, if so, with what changes to the hull, outfitting and armament. The commission made a favourable assessment, on 9 July presenting its conclusions to the newly installed Minister of the Navy, the Honourable Eugenio Bergamasco – depending on whether the work was done commercially or by a navy shipyard, a complete restoration to its 1915 condition would cost between 31 million and 59 million lire, or between 61 and 73 million lire to incorporate wartime experience. The Minister, who throughout the proceedings relied on the judgments of the navy hierarchy, in mid-August called upon the Comitato progetti navi (Ship Design Committee) for a more precise calculation of costs and a feasibility study. In response, in early September the Navy Chief of Staff, Vice Admiral Giuseppe De Lorenzi, declared recommissioning of the ship to be worthwhile, but that construction of light warships and submarines were a higher priority. With these reservations, on 21 and 22 September, Bergamasco presided over a meeting of the Admirals Committee, the Minister's main consultative body, which expressed itself in favour of restoring the battleship, but had to admit that the sum needed, estimated at 60 million lire, could not be supported by the navy's normal budget; it would require supplemental funding and in that sense the decision was returned to the government.

It was this budget problem that sealed its fate. That same September the Council of Ministers, in fact, refused the supplemental 60 million lire, even if it was spread over three years, nor

Firing the main guns of the *Andrea Doria* in 1920-1921. (A Molinari collection)

would it draw from the ordinary budget, both because of the scope of the restoration work and because ordinary maintenance of the ships of the fleet would suffer. The question again landed in the senate in the form of a motion, which saw the High Chamber – including Thaon di Revel, the more sceptical Sechi and all of the other admirals – invite the government to restore the ship. But the proposition did not make any headway because the necessary funds could not be found. The Admirals Committee took up the question again in a 10 October 1922 meeting, where a number of contrasting opinions emerged and, on 12 March 1923, it finally came to a negative decision. This conclusion took into account the navy's precarious financial situation, deterioration of the hull, and the loss of the battleship *France* (foundered on the Breton coast on 26 August 1922), which Paris declared no intention to replace, even though the Washington Treaty allowed it the option to do so. The *da Vinci* was thus struck from the official list on 22 November 1923 and the hulk sent to Taranto for breaking up.

From the economic point of view the cost of work to raise and right the ship was offset by the value of the material that was salvaged, amounting to more than 18 million lire. It must be said, however, that part of the material could have been salvaged straight from the wreck, without righting the ship.

In the years following the Washington treaty Italy planned its naval construction around annual programmes based on budgetary availability, oriented towards achieving the desired parity with France that, with respect to major ships in 1922, saw it at a disadvantage in tonnage (351,200 tons against 449,200 tons) but with a slight advantage in numbers (142 ships against 135). If only the main types of ships are considered, in France between 1922 and 1929 programmes were authorised for building 130 ships totalling 250,485 tons, with an annual mean of 31,300 tons, against the eighty ships of 163,110 tons authorised in Italy, with an annual mean of 20,400 tons. The French predominance was entirely concentrated on light warships and submarines, demonstrating its intention to outdistance Italy in the categories it valued most; in any case, the mean annual percentage of Italian construction authorised was 65.2 per cent of French programmes, which was a long way from parity.

The February 1929 naval programme and the battleship question

For some time after signing the Treaty of Washington the battleship remained on the margins of Italian naval policy, either directly because of the 'naval holiday' or overshadowed by the emphasis on renewal and strengthening of light craft and submarines. The debate, nevertheless, did not dissipate and took a decisive turn, at least in naval circles, in favour of large ships. This was primarily the result of more careful examination of the Great War at sea, where the battle squadrons exerted an indirect but decisive effect in blockading the Central Powers, while it was no longer certain, mainly for political and legal reasons, that the submarine would be able to repeat its success in the war against seagoing trade. A second consideration was that developments in technology would allow only capital ships to withstand threats from bombs and torpedoes and prevail over lighter warships. Finally, doubts persisted about the real capabilities of the air arm to replace naval power centred on large warships, while an aeronaval integration appeared more likely.

It was not until the late 1920s that the Regia Marina staff examined the building of battleships in preparation for the end of the 'naval holiday' scheduled by the treaty for 1931 and of the concept of defining a multi-year naval construction programme that would guarantee the renewal and growth of the fleet in a structured manner. It should be remembered that the programme had its origins in a September 1927 study by Rear Admiral Romeo Bernotti, at the time recognised as one of the greatest thinkers in the Regia Marina, aimed at giving a solid foundation and direction to Italian naval policy after years of reflection following the Great War.

The Navy Staff formulated its policy a year and a half later, in February 1929. In particular, if fixed the criteria to define a multi-year programme for a systematic renewal of the fleet, including aero-naval cooperation, establishing an auxiliary air arm and the construction of an experimental aircraft carrier. The programme, even though it had not been legislatively sanctioned, influenced Italian naval policy until at least 1934. With respect to battleships, it considered the problem of saving the existing ships as well as that of new construction, after which, in late 1928, the *Dante* had been scrapped, the *Cavour* decommissioned and the *Giulio Cesare* assigned as a training ship.

In favour of saving the old battleships were considerations that were almost exclusively political; these were linked to Italy's position among the major naval powers and the weight that battleship numbers would bring to negotiations in future naval international conferences. Arguing against their retention were many technical and budgetary considerations: the 'Cavour' and 'Duilio' classes were of outdated design, especially because of their high degree of vulnerability to modern air and underwater threats; operationally they were more of a liability than an asset, because of the numerous smaller ships that would be required to escort them; and additionally, their operating costs weighed heavily on the navy budget. In conclusion, for the Navy Staff they represented only an illusion of strength and their gradual decommissioning appeared necessary and advantageous. Only international political considerations argued against hastening the timeline so as not to increase the disparity with France in this category of warship.

A different attitude was expressed towards new capital ships, which the Navy Staff viewed favourably. First and foremost, the programme fixed the minimum number of ships to be built at three, so that at least two could always be operational, and identified two types: one of 23,000 tons with six 381mm (15in) guns, a speed of 28–29 knots and adequate vertical, horizontal and underwater protection; and one type of 35,000 tons with six 406mm (16in) guns, good protection and a speed of 29–30 knots. In the first case, the three ships could be built within the 70,000 tons total limit allowed by the treaty in 1927 and 1929; in the second case the 35,000 tons from 1931 would also have to be used, once the 'naval holiday' ended. The staff tended towards the second option, even though the cost was significantly higher than that of the smaller ships, for the simple reason that it was thought not worth building battleships whose displacement was less than 35,000 tons as long as this maximum limit was in force. The policy, nevertheless, took into account the position of the government, which, without being prejudiced against it, considered a decision on this issue to be premature, mainly for reasons of international politics, as it did not appear fitting that Italy should be the first to begin construction of new battleships. This would, in addition, hamper the renewal and development programme for light craft and submarines, which at that time was considered to have priority, and the Navy Staff decided simply to park the battleship problem and to continue, in the meantime, to look at the two types in question.

The 1930 London Conference and construction of the *Dunkerque* (1931–1932)

The Washington Conference had ended without reaching any agreement on smaller warships and submarines. In 1927 the Geneva conference between the major naval powers failed to find an understanding in those categories; Rome and Paris preferred not to take part because of the impossibility of agreeing on this issue and so as not to aggravate already delicate diplomatic relations. In October 1929 the London government, after having reached a preliminary agreement with Washington, promoted a new conference to regulate the matter from then until 31 December 1936, the date the Treaty of Washington expired. All of the signatory powers of the original treaty attended, even though in the meantime the positions of Italy and France, but also of France and Britain, remained far apart: Rome, which upheld the goal of parity, was determined to achieve it, even at the cost of causing the conference to fail, right down to the lowest level of armament, as long as it was not surpassed by any other continental European power; Paris, formally, did not reject the principle, but put forward quantitative demands that, if agreed to, would have in turn forced Great Britain to renounce the 'two power standard' towards the two most heavily armed continental powers.

The conference began in January 1930 and concluded on 22 April without reaching full agreement, because of the dissension between the two Latin powers. It was agreed to subscribe to a treaty on the points where an agreement had been reached and, as proposed by Italy, not to close but to adjourn the conference,

Aerial photo of the battleship *Andrea Doria* while it was conducting main armament gunnery training in the early 1930s.

The two 'Duilio' class battleships and the two 'Conte di Cavour' class in service at the end of the 1920s anchored in Augusta bay. (E Leproni collection)

in the hope of settling, in a less tense climate and with British mediation, the Franco-Italian dispute on minor warships. The 'holiday' in battleship construction was extended to 31 December 1936 and qualitative limits were established for cruisers, destroyers and submarines as well as rules for replacement. Italy and France subscribed to the treaty, but not to this last part. But even the parts of the treaty that they had signed up for were not ratified by their respective parliaments, so that France and Italy were not legally bound by it, although they remained bound by the Treaty of Washington.

Italo-French negotiations, which resumed with London's mediation in August 1930, fell through in March 1931, just at the time when it seemed that an agreement had been reached. Up to that point the naval rivalry between Rome and Paris had expressed itself only on the issue of light warships, but now a new source of friction arose when France announced the construction of a 23,000-ton standard displacement battleship in response to the first German armoured ship, the *Deutschland*, nominally built within the limitations of the Treaty of Versailles, but with its 280mm (11in) armament, outgunned all of the 'Washington' type cruisers.

In France the development of the navy depended heavily on public opinion and on the humour of the parties, and of parliament by way of funding the budget, and in those circles there was a strong opposition to capital ships. Until 1930 the Marine Nationale had not paid much attention to the subject. Less sensitive than others to the allure of large ships, it had excluded the old 'Jean Bart' and 'Bretagne' classes from radical modernisation and limited itself to changes of no great significance that, even though repeated, did not change their basic characteristics. It was not

The German 'pocket battleship' *Deutschland*, first of a series of three *panzerschiffe* armed with 280mm (11in) guns, whose construction provoked the French to build the *Dunkerque* class.

until 1926–1927 that it began to design 17,500-ton battlecruisers, armed with eight 305mm (12in) guns and with a speed of 35 knots, aimed at challenging the new Italian 'Trento' type cruisers in the western Mediterranean in defence of communications between France and North Africa.

In late 1928, when the general characteristics of the first German armoured ship became known, the French Navy Staff transferred its attention to ships of 23,333 tons that would surpass the German ship in speed (30 knots) and armament (eight 305mm guns), carry armour capable of withstanding the 280mm gun, and possess adequate underwater protection; this would not be achievable in a 17,500-ton battlecruiser. But it was not until the 1930 London Conference that its construction was announced and in October of that year the French government made provisions in draft legislation for its financing. The new battleship was part of the 1931 tranche, whose draft legislation was presented to the parliament with a full ten-month delay and had to wait for the opening session of the new parliament before it could be definitively approved on 31 March 1932. The battleship was laid down on 24 December that year with the name *Dunkerque*, but in the meantime its standard displacement had been raised first to 25,000 tons and then to 26,500 tons in order to be able to carry eight 330mm (13in) guns in quadruple turrets.

It should be made clear that the French Navy Staff did not harbour a preference for battleships of greater displacement. But ultimately, in that era, ships of 26,500 tons were the largest that the Marine Nationale could obtain, and in any case that type was more than capable of dealing with the *Deutschland*, and could be built using existing infrastructure and without interfering too much with the light warship building programmes.

The Italian response to the *Dunkerque*: rebuilding the two 'Conte di Cavour' class (1932–1933)

Faced with the news of the building of the *Dunkerque*, the government in Rome initially decided against following suit, either to await the outcome of the general disarmament conference, which might lead to the reduction of the characteristics of this category of ship, or for budgetary reasons, or because it shared the British idea of reducing the displacement and main gun calibre of capital ships, having even proposed their abolition to the London Conference. It should be made clear that even though the Regia Marina staff could support the proposal to keep down the displacement of the French battleship to 26,000 tons, it was not in favour of renouncing all capital ships, inasmuch as it was convinced that this type of ship was still the most suitable for combat at sea. In this uncertain phase, in order to balance the *Dunkerque*, the Italian Navy developed new studies regarding battleships of various sizes, none of which, however, were of 35,000 tons.

The problem came to a head on 26 November 1932 when the Admirals Committee, presided over by the then Minister of the Navy, Giuseppe Sirianni, was called upon to give an opinion on three new ship designs: one from the Ship Design Committee for a 29,500-ton battleship, about which, however, no details have

Embarking the 330mm (13in) guns in the first of the two forward quadruple turrets of the French battleship *Dunkerque* while fitting out at Brest in 1936.

come to light; two from private shipyards, the result of a competition, of which one was for a 26,000-ton battleship with underwater protection, with 300mm vertical and 130mm horizontal protection, armed with eight 343mm (13.5in) guns and with a speed of 29 knots; and the other for a battleship admittedly similar to the *Deutschland*, but with a displacement of 18,000–20,000 tons, with no underwater protection, but with extensive compartmentation, with six 343mm main guns in two triple turrets and with a speed of 28 knots. To these studies was added a preliminary design for partial reconstruction of the 'Cavour' and 'Duilio' types, after the possibility had been established of providing them with adequate internal underwater protection, while retaining the excellent hull form.

Until then the Regia Marina had not considered modernising these battleships, as it did not seem possible to solve the problem of underwater protection, which was their biggest weakness. However, the study for the new battleships of medium displacement had taken the hull lines of the 'Cavours' as its starting point, and so it became clear to the Ship Design Committee that, given an extensive reconstruction of their hull and powerplant, these ships could well be provided with an effective underwater protection system. This solution had already found favour with the Navy Chief of Staff, Admiral Gino Ducci, and was presented in three meetings to Mussolini who, before deciding, wanted to hear the thoughts of the Admirals Committee.

The preliminary design, drafted by Naval Engineer Colonel Francesco Rotundi, called for a displacement of 23,700 tons, lengthening the ship from 175 to 210 metres, replacing the powerplant with a more modern system with only two shafts for a speed of 29 knots to make space for an internal underwater protection system. Main gun armament could retain the original 305mm calibre, but by eliminating the centre turret, reducing the thirteen to ten guns; alternatively, the calibre of the ten guns could be increased to 320mm (12.6in). In both cases the guns would be re-tubed to increase their performance: in the first case, with the calibre unchanged, thanks to an increased muzzle velocity, and in the second, thanks to an increase in projectile weight and charge size, which would have approached the performance of the 330mm (13in) guns of the *Dunkerque*. In this last case power was estimated to be 1/7 less than that of the French 330mm, offset by the greater number of barrels, ten against eight. By Sirianni's estimate, the combat value of these ships would have been 15–20 per cent lower than that of new ships of equivalent size, such as the *Dunkerque*; according to Rotundi's estimate it would not have been less than 10–15 per cent. The total cost for partial reconstruction of all four ships was estimated to be about 600 million lire to be divided in three annual tranches and corresponding to a cost per ship of between 110 and 125 million lire, including the guns. Sirianni judged this sum to be within foreseeable budget allocations, while leaving sufficient to carry out renewal of lesser warships.

From the beginning Sirianni had directed the meetings of the Admirals Committee towards the 'Rotundi design', so that the other studies were barely taken into consideration, and the favourable final opinion was unanimous – even though the Minister was careful to also submit alternative uses of the same monies for construction of three 10,000-ton heavy cruisers or ships of 12,000 tons armed with 203mm or 305mm guns (ships of so-called free tonnage, but according to the Treaty of Washington categorised as battleships) in order to achieve clear superiority over France in that field. The alternatives were quickly ruled out due to the unanimous desire to have a core of sufficiently modern battleships available as soon as possible, and because the 12,000-ton model would not have represented any real advantage.

Therefore, in late 1932 it was decided to respond to the *Dunkerque* with the reconstruction of all or several of the four 'Cavour/Duilio' classes. The general lines of the modernisation were agreed, except for the calibre of the main gun armament, where there was a difference of opinion between the Chief of Staff and the Minister of the Navy. At the end of February 1933, Ducci observed that at a range of 20,000 metres the penetrating capability of the re-tubed 305mm and 320mm guns was, in fact, almost identical, and that the 320 only had the advantage of a larger propellant charge. As a result, he suggested that, at least for the first two ships to be modernised (the 'Cavours'), it would be better to retain the calibre unchanged, avoiding a prolonged experimental period and thus gaining time in the fitting-out phase. In addition, keeping the 305mm calibre would not require substantial modification of the ammunition, other than for the supply and loading systems of the gun mountings; and, finally, the 305, compared to the 320, could have the tube liner replaced cold. Later, and at a more measured pace, thought could then be given to transform the 'Duilio' guns to 320mm.

Sirianni, although acknowledging the merit of the argument by the Chief of Staff, did not agree, for reasons of morale and, in some respects, from a technical standpoint. Given the agreement on the negligible difference between the two re-tubed guns, renunciation of a larger calibre in ships that were extensively modernised would not have been understood either by navy officers themselves or by public opinion, especially if compared to the *Dunkerque*. Above all, it would not have been sensible to have two classes of ships otherwise similar to each other, but armed with different calibre guns. On 27 February Sirianni submitted the question to the permanent commission for testing military equipment (Mariperman), mainly to determine the compatibility of the times needed for readying the weapons with those of the ships, initially estimated at two years. On 6 March Mariperman specified that, whichever calibre was chosen, the time to produce the weapons would be similar, about twenty-two months, with maybe a savings of two months for the 305, and that readying the gun mountings would need twenty-eight months. In light of this reply and of other technical observations, Sirianni concluded that keeping the 305mm calibre would not speed up the supply of the guns and mountings and that this would have roughly coincided with the time of completing the hulls. He informed Ducci of this on 14 March.

In the spring of 1933, in addition to establishing the calibre of the main guns, there was also a decision on the definitive design, which for the time being involved only the 'Cavours', as the government had preferred to postpone reconstruction of the 'Duilio' class. Originally intended to commence in July 1933, the work actually began the following October in Trieste, at the San Marco shipyard of the Cantieri Riuniti dell'Adriatico (CRDA) for the *Cavour* and at the Cantieri Navali del Tirreno (CNT) of Genoa for the *Cesare*, who had won the contracts. Little more than two years were estimated for the work, but the two ships were completed respectively on 1 June and 1 October 1937, after almost four years. The cost of rebuilding was 161,499,000 lire for the *Cavour* and 160,499,000 lire for the *Cesare*, sums also greater than estimated.

Reconstruction of the two 'Cavour' class represented an interim response to the French decision to build a new medium-displacement battleship – 'watchful waiting' as it was called at the time, both from a political as well as a technical standpoint, which, all things considered, seems understandable. Politically, Mussolini preferred to await developments of the general disarmament conference, from which a drastic reduction in the size of battleships might result, if not their outright abolition, and he was not very inclined to follow France in a competition in this category of ship, other than to safeguard the principle of parity. Technically, a division of relatively modern ships of the battle line seemed to be more than sufficient to balance a 'Dunkerque'; in addition, the rebuilt 'Cavours' could be considered to be qualitatively superior, especially in terms of speed, to the 'Jean Bart' and 'Provence' classes and were also capable of operating with light forces. Given the uncertain future of the capital ship, the Regia Marina hierarchy appeared to be satisfied. After having been opposed for more than a decade to the modernisation of the old battleships, they had found an acceptable design solution, in the medium-displacement category, the minimum they would accept.

The failure of the Italo-French naval negotiations: building the *Strasbourg* and the two 'Littorio' class (1933–1934)

Modernisation of the two 'Cavours' left open the question of naval parity between the two Latin powers. Now Rome had an interest in obtaining offsets (recognition of parity in lesser

The French fast battleship *Dunkerque*, which entered service in April 1937.

warships and other benefits of a more general nature) in exchange for renouncing the construction of battleships larger than the *Dunkerque*; France, on the other hand, wanted to avoid such an eventuality without making too many concessions and to not tie its hands in future conferences. After the March 1931 failure, Anglo-American mediation efforts continued during the general disarmament conference without, however, leading to any results. The admission of Germany to the conference was an additional factor in hardening the French position, which feared that revision of the military clauses of the Treaty of Versailles might occur without adequate guarantees. In October 1933, with Germany's withdrawal from the disarmament conference first, and then from the League of Nations because of the lack of recognition of its 'equality of right', the conference went into a period of stalemate; but on the margins, there appeared unexpected glimmers of hope for settling the Italo-French naval disagreements.

On 16 October 1933 a new phase of negotiations between Rome and Paris got under way to reach agreement on naval programmes up to the end of the Treaty of Washington. These faltered in the spring of 1934 because of the French decision in February to lay down a second ship of the 'Dunkerque' type, the *Strasbourg*, in response to news of a fourth German 'Deutschland' class, but it was driven more by opposition to even implicit recognition of the principle of parity, France assuming that for technical and financial reasons Italy would not even be able to build an equivalent 26,500-ton battleship. Italian reaction materialised with the decision to lay down two '35,000-tonners' armed with 381mm (15in) guns, the *Littorio* and *Vittorio Veneto*, strongly desired by the new Undersecretary of State, Admiral Domenico Cavagnari, who as of 1 June 1934 was also the Navy's Chief of Staff. He had convinced a reluctant Mussolini and also defended his decision in the face of British pressure for Italy to renounce such high tonnage and calibre, fearing that this could have a negative influence on the imminent 1935 naval conference. *Littorio* and *Vittorio Veneto* were laid down on 28 October 1934, respectively, in the Ansaldo yard at Genoa-Sestri Ponente and the CRDA San Marco yard in Trieste. France, in turn, responded by laying down in December 1934 and January 1935 a like number of 35,000-ton battleships, the *Richelieu* and *Jean Bart*.

On the international level it was an event of undoubted importance and marked the zenith of Italo-French naval rivalry, but its importance should not be overstated. Neither the two 'Littorios' nor the two 'Richelieu' class – nor even the rivalry itself – prevented a rapprochement between Italy and France following the failed Nazi coup d'etat in Austria in July 1934, and culminating with the Mussolini-Laval agreements of 7 January 1935 and in the Badoglio-Gamelin military agreements of 19 and 28 June 1935. Anglo-Italian disagreement was marginal; London did not feel that its interests were threatened, but only hindered in its proposals to reduce the limits on battleships in the 1935 conference where the stumbling block was not the existence of the two Italian and two French 35,000-ton ships, but Washington's independent opposition to lowering that threshold.

The two 'Littorios' represented a significant step in Italian naval policy. Following a decade concentrating on lesser warships, the Italian Navy took the road to large battleships that, in truth, it had never shown any real desire to abandon. Between 1930 and 1935, considering only major shipbuilding, France had authorised construction of forty-seven ships for a total of 231,371 tons, among which were four battleships (two of 26,500 and two of 35,000 tons) against seventy-three ships totalling 177,499 tons authorised by Italy, among which were two 35,000-ton battleships but without including rebuilding the two 'Cavours'. The smaller number of ships and greater tonnage on the French side is explained by the additional two new battleships and the greater displacement of individual destroyers. Overall, compared to 1922–1929, Italy was reducing the numerical disparity, while, in tonnage, the Italian annual mean of 29,600 tons now represented only 76.9 per cent of the French mean of 38,500 tons.

The London Conference of 1935–1936 and the end of naval disarmament

The 1930 London naval treaty provided that a year before the expiry of the Treaty of Washington the signatory powers were to meet to reach a new agreement on limiting naval armaments. However, between 1935 and 1936 the international naval situation had been complicated by the Japanese and French renunciation of the Treaty of Washington (29 December 1934 and 2 December 1935), by the Anglo-German naval agreement of 18 June 1935, which had caught Paris off guard and had also irritated Rome, while the Mediterranean crisis and adoption of sanctions by the League of Nations against Italy following the Ethiopian adventure was a further aggravation. On the other hand, tension between Paris and Rome had reduced, now that they were free of the controversy regarding naval parity and on a more general level took a common anti-German position.

The second London Conference opened on 9 December 1935, and Italy attended, despite some uncertainties over tension with Britain. In January Japan walked out of the conference, when its proposals were rejected, among them the 'abolition of offensive ships' (battleships, aircraft carriers and heavy cruisers). The conference ended on 25 March 1936 with a treaty signed only by the United States, Great Britain and France, as Rome preferred not to join because of the worsening Mediterranean crisis. But, for the first time, Rome and Paris had participated in naval negotiations with shared views thanks to an improved political climate and having overcome the naval parity argument. That favoured the abolition of the ratio that had been agreed upon in 1922 in Washington and the consequent hierarchy between the naval powers so each then became free to build the fleet deemed to be most suited to their own needs. During the discussion all of the powers, except the United States, declared themselves in favour of a reduction of the displacement and main gun calibre of battleships. In particular, the Italian and French delegations in unison proposed reduction of the first item to 27,000 tons and of the second to 305mm. In the end, the rigid American stance prevailed and, in fact, a clause was introduced by which the maximum calibre was to be raised to 406mm (16in), if by 1 April 1937 Japan and Italy were not ready to accept the 356mm (14in).

The treaty, therefore, only decided the qualitative clauses, which for battleships maintained the maximum displacement at 35,000 tons but reduced the calibre of the main gun armament from 406 to 356mm. The minimum battleship age (for replacement) was increased from twenty to twenty-six years; lesser age limits were introduced for other categories of ships. The treaty was to remain in effect until 31 December 1942 and called for interim consultations in 1940. Because the value of the treaty depended on the adherence of the other naval powers, the British government tabled a series of bilateral negotiations, the effect of which was that between early 1937 and early 1939 Rome, Berlin, Moscow and minor powers, but not Tokyo, signed on, so that the maximum displacement for battleships rose to 40,000 tons (45,000 for the United States) and the calibre to 406mm, as a result of application of the safeguard clauses. The beginning of the war in September 1939 effectively put an end to all limitations.

Sanctions and new naval construction

The Mediterranean crisis and the application of sanctions against Italy by the League of Nations was not without consequences on Italian naval policy – from a political standpoint, because now Great Britain figured among the ranks of potential enemies and, from the financial standpoint, because restrictions introduced by the Italian government influenced new construction. A meeting of Italian military chiefs was held on 13 August 1935, presided over by the chief of the general staff, to examine the extremely tense situation with Britain. Cavagnari, in contrast to all the other military chiefs, had since January 1935 declared himself in favour of the action in Ethiopia, but made no secret of the absolute inferiority of the Italian fleet compared with the British fleet. Any conflict with Britain would have been very perilous because of the total lack of effective battleships, as the only two in service, the unmodernised *Duilio* and *Andrea Doria*, were of no value. If, instead, the new squadron of modern battleships, formed by the two 'Littorio' class and the two modernised 'Cavours', had been available at that time, the picture would have been different 'even if only from the point of view of risk to the English'. This was a stance that revealed, even before the war, the core of Cavagnari's thinking about the function of battleships: namely, that they would essentially act as a dissuasive element in the face of potential or real enemies.

Detail of the midships section of the battleship HMS *Barham* in a 1937 photo. The British battleships of the 'Queen Elizabeth' class, built on the eve of the Great War, were armed with eight 381mm (15in) guns.

The significance of this thinking came to the fore in October 1935, as soon as Mussolini responded to the imposition of sanctions against Italy with his own very strict directives with respect to imports, even of military supplies. There were to be no orders for machinery, equipment and finished foreign products, and imports of raw materials were to be limited to the minimum necessary, even at the cost of obtaining products of lower quality than ideally required. At least at first, these measures did not have much impact on naval construction, as it was not difficult to give up importing machinery and equipment and, with respect to finished and semi-finished products, they were kept within modest levels. There was greater difficulty regarding raw materials, but for the time being stocks were sufficient to meet almost all of the requirements for the ships under construction, beginning with the 'Littorio' class. Despite the fact that the navy's situation was not yet worrying, in October Cavagnari intervened with General Alfredo Dallolio, commissioner general for wartime production, and with Mussolini, to obtain the most lenient application possible of the limitations that affected him. In his memo to the Duce, he repeated that it was indispensable that Italy, whose development was possible only overseas and which was now hostage to the greatest maritime power, should have a well-balanced naval force, based on large battleships, as they were the only ships that had high offensive and defensive value. Only such a force would be able to ensure respect for Italian rights and aspirations, whatever fluctuation there might be from rivalry to friendship with other powers. Cavagnari's aim was to guarantee the growth and harmonious development of the naval forces with specific regard to battleships and, in the short term, to avoid any slowdown of the construction that was under way.

Reconstruction of the 'Duilios' and studies of 27,000-ton battleships (1935–1937)

Cavagnari's initiatives were not a dead letter. The reconstruction of the two 'Cavour' class ships looked very promising and in mid-

November 1935 the Navy Staff planning office also began to consider reconstruction of the two 'Duilios'. The aim was to harmonise the characteristics with those of the earlier two in order to create a homogeneous division of four ships. Otherwise the two unmodernised 'Duilios', whose combat value was almost zero, would have found it impossible to operate with the 'Cavour' and 'Littorio' classes because of the differences in armament, speed and protection. In February 1936 the Ship Design Committee, in association with CNT and CRDA, began work on transforming the two 'Duilios', using the 'Cavour' scheme as a model, but improving it in light of experience gained in the construction of the two 'Littorios'. The biggest innovations related to anti-torpedo armament (135mm [5.3in] guns instead of 120mm) and anti-aircraft (90mm instead of 100mm) guns, arrangement of fire control systems, which would be similar to those of the 'Littorio', as well as the forward portion of the hull, which would be properly rebuilt rather than just being superimposed on the old structure. The radical modernisation of the two 'Duilios' was, finally, decided upon in early 1937 and the two ships constituted the 1937/1938 programme, which will be addressed later. Work was assigned to the Cantieri Navali del Tirreno for the *Duilio* and to the CRDA San Marco yards for the *Andrea Doria*, in order to capitalise upon the experience that the two yards had acquired with the earlier transformation of the 'Cavour' class. Work on both ships began in April 1937 and ended with the war already in progress, *Duilio* in July and *Doria* in October 1940.

This decision to modernise still gives rise to some questions. It had its origins in Cavagnari's U-turn in favour of strengthening the battle squadron by adding another two ships at a modest cost and by the assessment that almost all of the battleships possessed by the other powers were old types. As these would have formed the bulk of the battle squadrons of the competing powers for many years to come, it was therefore worth Italy modernising its old ships. However, account was not taken of the fact that naval rearmament was being resumed and that the newly built ships would inexorably devalue the rebuilt 'Cavour' and 'Duilio' types, as became evident with the earliest experiences during the war. Furthermore, in a situation of financial stringency in Italy, particularly regarding imports of raw materials, resources devoted to these two battleships must have been at the expense of the much more important 'Littorio' class, competing for steel industry production and slowing down the essential armour plate. Finally, the cost of rebuilding these ships would have been almost the same as that needed to build another 'Littorio'. The cost of rebuilding the *Cesare* was 160,499,000 lire, slightly more than that of the *Cavour*. But rebuilding the *Duilio* cost 302,527,000 lire and 302,969,000 lire for the *Doria*, in total not much less than the 800 million lire for a 'Littorio' of the first group. Even without considering the scrap that could have been gained from their demolition at a time of scarcity, the resources and energy devoted to rebuilding the two battleships, which soon proved to be only second-line, would have been better used in building other ships or in accelerating the completion of the larger battleships, so that in 1942 Italy might have had four 'Littorios' operational. In substance, if the radical modernisation of the two 'Cavours' made some sense because it fell into a period when the fate of disarmament and of battleships were still uncertain, by 1937 when it was decided to rebuild the 'Duilios', the political, military and technical scenarios were radically changed and did not argue in favour of reconstruction. Most of all, if a small group of French and US ships are excluded, all of the other old battleships were, before reconstruction, superior to the corresponding Italian ships because they were much better armed and protected and more suitable to profitable modernisation. But what is most surprising is the lack of any voice of opposition within the Regia Marina, which was certainly not lacking with respect to the contemporary proposal to build new 27,000-ton battleships, and precisely for this reason it is worth mentioning.

In the run up to the London Conference, one of the most popular proposals regarding the future limits for battleships was for a standard displacement of 25,000–27,000 tons and a gun calibre between 305mm and 330mm, that is to say, characteristics equal or close to those of the *Dunkerque*. Great Britain, initially, supported this position, with France and Italy in agreement. In anticipation of this, since September 1935 the ship design committee had been charged with carrying out preliminary feasibility studies, assuming a standard displacement of 26,500 tons and a main gun armament of 305mm or 320mm. The studies, within these limits, offered various design options, and in December 1935 were submitted to the Admirals Committee for consideration, which expressed a rather varied series of judgments and proposals that in early 1936 were again submitted in summary to the attention of the ship design office. The general consensus that emerged from the Admirals Committee outlined a ship of 27,000 tons standard, armed with nine 320mm guns in triple turrets, twelve or sixteen 140mm guns in triple or quadruple turrets, twelve 90mm anti-aircraft guns in single protected mounts and rapid-fire cannon, with protection comparable to that of the 'Littorio' class and a steam plant able to provide a speed of 30 knots and a range of 4000 miles at 20 knots (but capable of being increased for ocean missions).

On 6 February 1936, in reaching its conclusions, the Ship Design Committee pointed out that for ships with these characteristics it would be necessary to increase displacement to 30,000 tons, an escalation also affecting the 'Littorios', whose design at that time (February 1936) already called for 38,500 tons. In order to stay within the 27,000 tons, it would be necessary either to adopt the quadruple turret solution of the *Dunkerque* or to reduce speed to 28 knots, while retaining protection levels similar to those of the 'Littorios'. But, in a climate that favoured large battleships, the committee concluded that it was not appropriate for Italy to build battleships of medium tonnage from choice, but only as a restriction deriving from international treaties; in fact, from the technical standpoint, it would be preferable to continue building more ships of the 'Littorio' type. These studies were not pursued further because the 1936 London Treaty left things essentially unchanged and it would have been pointless to build 27,000-ton battleships when the other powers could build 35,000-ton ships. In short, the two committees confirmed the conclusion already reached in 1934, when considering a ship of the 'Dunkerque' type, that on 27,000 tons it was impossible to achieve the indispensable requirements for a modern battleship. It does not seem that similar considerations were given any weight when deciding to rebuild the 'Duilios'.

From the 'Duilios' to the *Impero*

The Ethiopian war and the Mediterranean crisis, even though far from provoking a general conflict, did leave a profound mark on relations between Rome and London. This was reflected in the war plans of the Regia Marina staff, which from 1936 contemplated a conflict with Great Britain and closer ties to Germany. But the real objective of this planning was to lay the groundwork for a multi-year programme of naval construction that would fix the relative ratios with France, Britain and Germany, the type and size of ships to be built, age and replacement limits, all conforming to the (overestimated) financial and industrial capabilities of the country – or, at the very least, might act as a guide for annual naval programmes. With respect to battleships, all of the studies contemplated a minimum of six (two rebuilt 'Cavours' and one rebuilt 'Duilio' plus three 'Littorios') up to a maximum of eight (four rebuilt battleships and four 'Littorios').

The Italian studies did not get past the embryonic stage, mostly because, except for a minimal programme in 1936, they were far beyond the country's financial means. But they did exercise some influence at least with respect to battleships, in that the 1937/1938 naval programme with the two 'Duilios' was completed by the impressive 1938 supplementary programme, with the construction of another two 'Littorio' types in addition to twelve large scouts (the future 'Capitani Romani' class) and sixteen long-range submarines for a total of 128,000 tons of new ships. The building of the second group of 'Littorio' class ships and of the lesser warships of the supplementary programme was, in fact, decided on 7 January 1938 following consultation between Mussolini, Cavagnari and the Minister of Finance, Paolo Thaon di Revel, grandson of the Grand Admiral of the same name, a year after the decision to rebuild the two 'Duilios'. Building the new '35,000-tonners', which were assigned the names *Impero* and *Roma*, was awarded, as for the earlier ships, respectively to Ansaldo of Genoa-Sestri Ponente and to CRDA of Trieste in its San Marco yard, where they were laid down on 14 May and 18 September 1938. The first was to have been delivered in August 1941, but never entered service, with the second in June 1942, a deadline that was met precisely.

The 1937/1938 naval programme and the supplementary 1938 programme represented the greatest effort to strengthen the fleet made by Italy between the two world wars, the maximum that Italian finance and industry were capable of accomplishing at the time and, possibly, the greatest ever in its history. It might well have been achieved if the war had not imposed other priorities and, in particular, if the fitting out of the *Impero* had been better managed. At any rate, it caused much anxiety within the Marine Nationale staff and its chief, Admiral François Darlan, became concerned that the Italian Navy might equal and overtake the French Navy within a few years and that in the naval conference planned for 1940 France might arrive in a state of relative inferiority. Darlan obtained from the government the 1938 *bis tranche*, an additional budget on top of the 1938 tranche, and consisting of two more 35,000-ton battleships, the *Clemenceau* and the *Gascogne*. All told, the two 1938 French tranches projected the building of two large battleships, two aircraft carriers, two cruisers, seven destroyers, eight torpedo boats and twelve submarines for a total of 156,160 tons. However, this programme met with serious political, technical and logistical difficulties and after the conflict had begun in September 1939, remained entirely uncompleted. Taking into account even the most modest and unimplemented naval programmes of 1939, between 1936 and 1939 France approved fifty-eight ships for 191,342 tons and Italy 157 ships for 277,723 tons, excluding the two 'Duilios' being reconstructed. In summary, the naval programmes between 1922 and 1939 saw the approval of 205 ships of 673,178 tons for France and 286 ships of 599,420 tons for Italy and in 1940, counting only the major ships in service, under construction and programmed, Italy had 280 ships of 700,722 tons compared with 240 ships of 827,972 tons for France; the ratio of tonnage had reached 0.85:1 compared with the 0.63:1 in 1931 and with the 0.64:1 in 1919.

The British battleship *Barham*, in the dark grey of the Home Fleet, steaming in line ahead with other similar ships in the second half of the 1930s. (M. Brescia collection)

The 'Cavours' and the 'Duilios' during and after the Second World War

The experience of the first few months of the war showed the limitations of the rebuilt battleships. Once France had fallen and thus made it impossible to measure themselves against the 'Dunkerque' class or against the antiquated French battleships, they were unable to challenge any of the British battleships in terms of either armament or protection; their only marginal advantage was speed, and this did not apply for the battlecruisers and for the modern 'King George V' class ships. They proved to be barely adequate in terms of speed and manoeuvring characteristics to operate in formation with the 'Littorio' class, to the point that after the early months of the war they were destined to operate only, but not always, when one of the two '35,000-tonners' was not operational, as between late 1941 and early 1942 in the important convoy escort operations to Libya. After this, because of shortages of fuel and of escort vessels, until the end of the war they engaged in no noteworthy actions and were manned at a minimum level. Only the two 'Duilios' were fully manned, in the summer of 1943, in anticipation of possible enemy landings near Taranto, and consideration was given to using them as floating batteries to defend the port. Thus, once the Navy Staff had clearly recognised the limited utility of these ships, it is surprising that after the aerial torpedo attack against Taranto the decision was made to proceed with the costly salvage of the *Cavour* and the later refurbishment work in Trieste. The recovery took place in parallel with the restoration of the much more important *Littorio*, of the *Duilio*, and from April 1941 of the *Vittorio Veneto*, after she had been torpedoed at Gaudo. However, in reality, during 1941 the salvage of the *Cavour* was largely carried out by CRDA personnel and equipment, which had spare capacity beyond what was needed at the time for new construction, including for the *Roma*, so raising the ship was not a great obstacle. Even when the shipyard situation worsened in 1942–1943, restoration of the *Cavour* in Trieste provided a means – agreed between the managers of CRDA and the Regia Marina – to keep specialised dockyard workers in post who otherwise might have been called up or scattered among other yards that were experiencing shortages.

Nevertheless, late in the war these battleships still figured to a certain extent in the plans of the Regia Marina. The navy had never given much thought to what sort of fleet would be wanted after the war, except to preserve the major naval forces as much as possible, extending the principle of the 'fleet in being' to the political arena. As a reflection of how much the battleships mattered to the Navy Staff, even in 1943, it is useful to recall the development programme for the fleet that was put together on 14 June of that year, in which the rebuilt battleships still played a role. This document reaffirmed complete faith in capital ships in the conduct of naval warfare. It argued that wartime limitations on their employment had not been a result of any intrinsic inadequacy in the type of ship, but to external failings such as insufficient numbers and training of air escorts, the number and technical characteristics of the naval escorts, lack of radar, and deficiencies in defences against air attack (but the lack of fuel was not mentioned). The Allies had dealt with those shortcomings and had employed their battleships in all theatres with always decisive results, as recently demonstrated by the invasion of French North Africa. The Navy Staff felt that Italy also would soon be able to overcome the listed weaknesses and the battleship core would have an important part in a long drawn out war and would be a very important factor in peace negotiations. Developing this view, the detailed programme laid out the needs for all of the categories of warship and projected the following availability of battleships:

- 1943: Three 'Littorio' class (*Littorio*, *Veneto* and *Roma*) and three 'Cavour' type (the refitted and modernised *Cavour* after its torpedoing at Taranto and the two 'Duilios'); *Cesare* in reserve;
- 1944 and 1945: four 'Littorios' (as above + *Impero*) and two 'Cavours' (*Cavour* and one 'Duilio'); one 'Duilio' and *Cesare* in reserve;
- Late 1946: four 'Littorios', two 'Cavours', the two 'Dunkerque' class (to be salvaged from Toulon and refurbished); one 'Duilio' and *Cesare* in reserve.

With the fall of Fascism, the loss of the war and with it the country's role as a naval power, the Navy Staff and the post-war Italian government attempted, up until the Paris peace treaty of 10 February 1947 and beyond, to save the two surviving 'Vittorio Veneto' class ships. In a similar vein, at the end of the war, Great Britain and France also completed two large battleships, *Vanguard* and *Jean Bart*, despite the obvious decline of this category of ship. The peace treaty left Italy with only the two useless 'Duilio' class ships, at the same time imposing a prohibition against possessing any other battleships as well as guns with a range of over 30,000 metres. *Roma*, *Impero* and *Cavour* had been lost; the *Cesare*, as we shall see, had to be ceded to the Soviet Union, while *Italia* (formerly the *Littorio*) and *Vittorio Veneto* were scrapped in the early 1950s.

But during those same years the political situation in Italy changed radically, with the ousting from the government of the Socialists and Communists, and later their electoral defeat, and internationally with the lowering of the Iron Curtain in Europe, and the subsequent formation of two ideologically, politically and militarily opposed blocs, one led by the United States and the other by the Soviet Union. On 4 April 1949 Italy aligned itself with the western bloc, joining the Atlantic Pact, a circumstance that also foreshadowed the revision of certain clauses of the peace treaty. Diplomatic activity was crowned in December 1951 with the acceptance by most of the victorious powers of the request by Alcide De Gasperi's government to remove the political and military clauses of the peace treaty, and on 22 December of that year the political clauses were declared outdated and the military clauses obsolete. For the Italian Navy this implied, among other things, the ability to exceed the overall limit of 67,500 tons, to be able to build battleships and to use guns with ranges greater than 30,000 metres.

These last two options, however, were by now outdated and the navy set out on other paths to provide for national defence at sea and to fulfil its recently assumed international obligations. The two 'Duilios', although lacking any combat value, remained in service for some years to come, but only with exclusively training functions or as naval headquarters.

Chapter 5

DESIGN AND RECONSTRUCTION OF THE BATTLESHIPS OF THE 'CONTE DI CAVOUR' AND 'DUILIO' CLASSES

As noted in the preceding chapter, the Admirals Committee meeting of 26 November 1932 was presented with the preliminary design study for the radical modernisation of the 'Conte di Cavour' and 'Duilio' class battleships done by Naval Engineer Colonel Francesco Rotundi, under the auspices of the Ship Design Committee (MARICOMINAV). This project essentially retained the original optimum hull form of those ships, but with a considerable lengthening of the hull and significantly increased the power. It had already been submitted several times to the head of government and thus it can be inferred that the relevant feasibility studies were begun during 1931.

The project involved a partial, but substantial reconstruction of the ships that increased the maximum length from 176 metres to about 210 (later scaled back to 186), with the complete rebuilding of the forward hull, replacement of the entire four-shaft powerplant by new two-shaft machinery, increasing the original 31,000–32,000 horsepower roughly three-fold. The smaller size of the boilers and turbines made it possible to create a suitable underwater protection system without modifying the overall shape of the hull, that is to say without adding external blisters that must inevitably have meant a drastic reduction in speed. It was estimated that a speed of close to 29 knots could be achieved, against the current 21, with a normal displacement of slightly more than 23,700 tonnes. In order to minimise changes to the immersion of the armoured belt, the increase of average hull draught was to be kept as low as possible, at the cost of reducing the effectiveness of the entire vertical protection system.

The key element of the study thus resided in providing the ships with adequate underwater protection without changing either the breadth or the shape of the underwater hull. The solution proposed was the adoption of the system of 'absorbing cylinders', which had been conceived as early as the First World War by then Naval Engineer Lieutenant Colonel Umberto Pugliese. This had already been applied on an experimental basis in the military tankers *Brennero* and *Tarvisio*, built during the 1920s, as well as having featured in noteworthy designs (for example in the study of a 17,500-ton aircraft carrier supervised by Naval Engineer General Filippo Bonfiglietti in 1929) and also proposed for the 35,000-ton standard displacement battleships, for which preliminary design studies were being produced under the supervision of General Pugliese, who was at that time in charge of the General Office of Naval and Mechanical Construction (MARICOST).

Unshipping the 305/46 guns from the *Giulio Cesare* prior to commencing the extensive modernisation work in 1933.

In order to retain the thickness and configuration of the main vertical protection, while considering an increase, however modest, in horizontal protection, in addition to the creation of the new underwater protection system, some weights would need to be reduced if overall displacement were to be kept down. This would come partly from lightening some components like funnels, masts, and so on, but principally from removing the not very effective midships main gun turret and its associated ammunition. Main gun armament would thus be reduced from thirteen to ten guns in two triple and two twin turrets with 305mm guns, or, as was under consideration, re-bored to 320mm. Secondary armament was no longer to be installed in casemates but rather in twin turrets located on each side of the upper deck; the anti-aircraft guns were to be in completely new installations, as there was practically no provision for AA defence in the original configuration of these ships. Overall, the work would entail the dismantling and reconstruction of about 60 per cent of the original structures, leaving only 40 per cent unchanged. It was a significant undertaking, greater proportionally by far than the contemporary modernisations of French, British and even American battleships, entirely justifying the term 'reconstruction' that was frequently used to describe the transformation of the two 'Cavours', and later also of the two 'Duilios'.

In spring of 1933 the decision was made to proceed, for the

The battleship *Conte di Cavour* moored at Trieste in October 1933 before the start of the major modernisation work by the CRDA San Marco yard. Note in the foreground the original seaplane catapult located on the port side of the forecastle.

time being, with the radical modernisation of only the battleships *Conte di Cavour* and *Giulio Cesare*. Having overcome the budget formalities as well as the uncertainties with respect to main gun calibre – as amply covered in Chapter 4 – in early October 1933, with reduced crews formed for the purpose, the two ships left Taranto, where the former had been laid up for some time and the second was being used as a school for gunners. They arrived at Trieste and Genoa respectively, where they were to undergo the planned major work; *Cavour* at the San Marco shipyard, now part of the Cantieri Riuniti dell'Adriatico (CRDA), and the *Cesare* at Cantieri del Tirreno, the two yards that had offered the best prices and guarantees for a successful outcome of the project. The contracts made the yards responsible for every aspect of the fitting-out except for the guns and their associated mountings, which remained the remit of the Regia Marina. That, in turn, would rely on Odero Terni Orlando (OTO, La Spezia works) for the *Cavour* and of Ansaldo of Genoa for the *Cesare*.

Before leaving the base at Taranto, both ships disembarked all ammunition, the 120/50 guns of the secondary armament, all of the 76mm guns and 40/39 rapid-fire guns, the fire control instruments, rangefinders included, as well as all of the gunnery equipment, except for the 305/46 gun mountings themselves. During the transfer to Genoa, the *Giulio Cesare* put into La Spezia, where the midships 305mm turret was taken out, the tops of the other main gun turrets removed and the main gun barrels disembarked. Seven days after arriving in their respective ports, the ships were administratively placed in a 'reserve' category, the *Cavour* moored at the pier of the San Marco yard in Trieste and the *Cesare* alongside the delle Grazie quay in the port of Genoa, facing the local Cantieri del Tirreno workshops.

The original project for modernising the 'Cavour' class

The earliest known document that illustrates the project for the transformation of the two 'Cavours' bears the stamp of MARI-

COMNAV dated September 1933 and presents an elevation and weather-deck plan views, reproduced below. An examination of these drawings, in which the ship has an overall length of 184.6 metres, reveals several features (from the bow):

- There are three anchors, two starboard and one port side, reflecting the original configuration; the forward structure continues well past the hawsepipes and ends with a fine cutwater and a bulbous stem head;
- The forecastle deck runs at full width beyond midships, narrowing into a shelter deck as far as the after superfiring main gun barbette;
- The armoured conning tower is a very simple structure, conical in shape like those on the 'Montecuccoli' class cruisers then under construction, surmounted by a small rangefinder tower with a cylindrical base of rather small dimensions;
- A single funnel rises directly from the forecastle deck, amidships, with a cap inspired by the aforementioned 'Montecuccoli' class and of the more recent '10,000-ton' cruisers;
- The mast consists of a fairly high tripod with two bracing legs facing forward; the cargo derrick is stepped on the main mast itself, so the ship's boats are stowed aft of the tripod;
- Aircraft facilities consist of two catapults that can pivot outboard, positioned either side of the funnel, with trolleys and elevated rails that run aft from the bridge tower, for stowing the four onboard seaplanes which have folding wings;
- The propellers have been reduced from four to two, with associated shafts and brackets, but the rudders, main and auxiliary, placed on the ship's centreline, are the same as the originals;
- The profile of the underwater hull appears unchanged in its general lines, except for the greater length and a more modern shape in the bow area.

The main armament, as planned from the beginning of the modernisation studies, comprises four turrets with ten 320mm guns; secondary armament is subdivided into six 120/50 twin turrets, three per side on the forecastle deck; finally, the anti-aircraft guns consist of four mountings of a new design with four 37mm guns each, also positioned on the forecastle deck, two per side, slightly forward of the tower and between the tripod and the aft superfiring main gun turret.

We will return to a discussion of the main and medium-calibre guns later, but as the quadruple 37mm AA guns never became operational, a few brief items of information are provided here. This was a type of installation being developed in 1933 by the Breda company that was based on pairing two twin Breda 37/54 air-cooled automatic guns of new design on a common traversable platform. In 1933 Breda was producing a water-cooled version of this gun (Mod 32 twin mounts), but in fact the twin air-cooled version (Mod 38) only became operational later. The mounting, which was provided with a small rangefinder with a base of about one metre at the rear of the mount, was power-operated with traverse and elevation motors, and was to be of the enclosed type with 30mm thick plates; overall weight was 18,027kg, including ready-use ammunition (960 rounds, equal

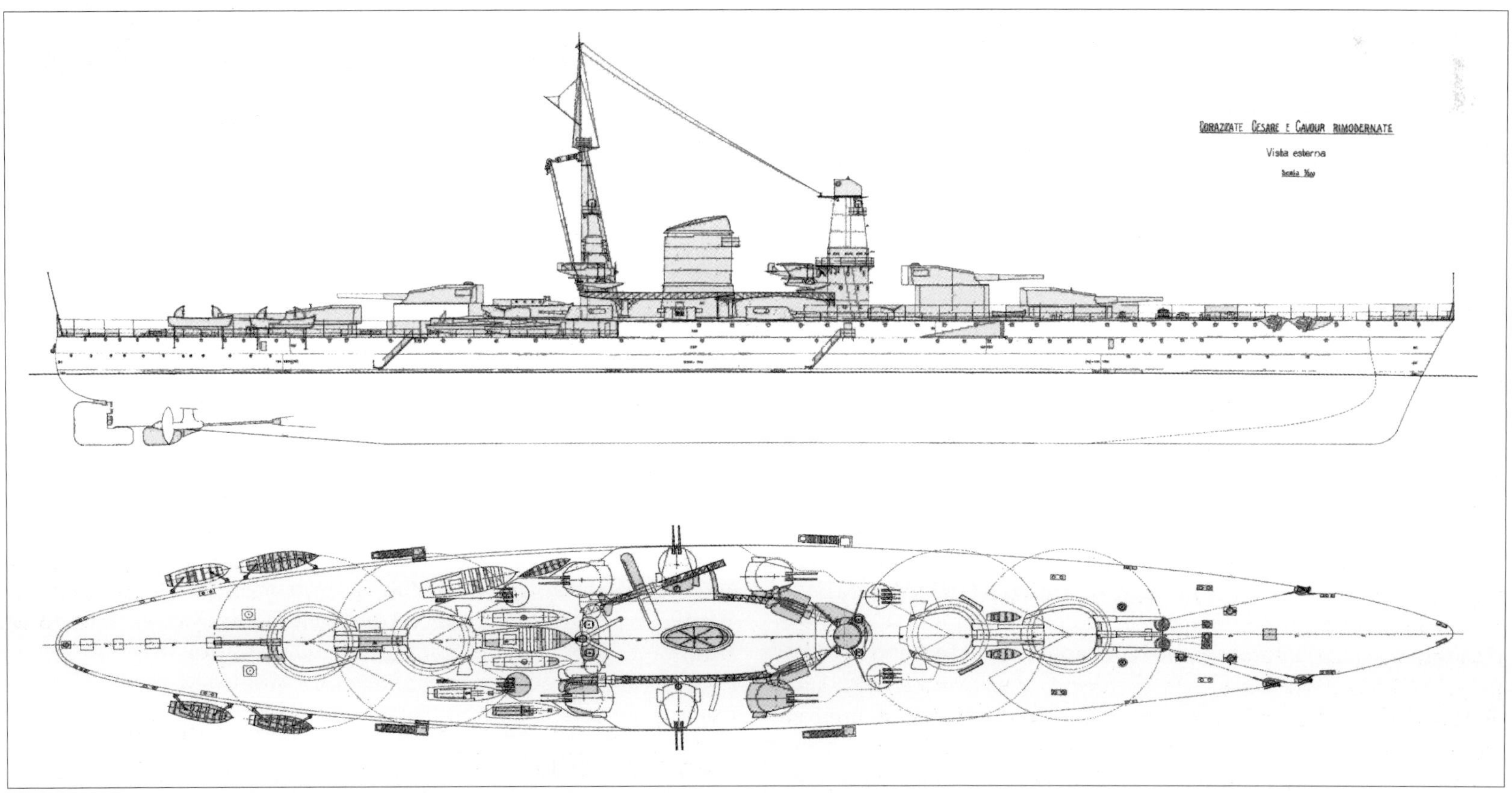

The original design drawn up for radical modernisation of the 'Conte di Cavour' class. Note the single funnel, the simplified conical bridge tower and the presence of two catapults for reconnaissance seaplanes amidships.

The *Conte di Cavour* at Trieste before the major reconstruction began. Moored alongside the battleship are the cruisers *Cadorna* and *Fiume* being fitted out.

to a little less than two minutes of fire). The arrangement involved two twin systems side by side on a single platform, similar to that which would later be employed, for example, in the Bofors 40/56 quadruple mountings widely used during the Second World War by the US Navy; it is probable that the equivalent Italian study was not further pursued because of the excessive vibration while firing deriving from the type of rigid mount that characterised the Breda 37/54, which differed from that of the flexible mount (with recoiling guns) of the analogous Bofors guns that generated lighter forces (of recoil and compression) and modest vibration.

The proposal for a diesel powerplant

It should be recorded that on 19 February 1933, during the preliminary design stage of the battleship modernisation project, Naval Engineer General Curio Bernardis, a renowned designer of submarines with particular experience in the field of internal combustion engines, submitted his proposal to power these ships with a group of large diesel engines in place of the traditional steam plant that had been envisaged. It was a system that was to have been able to develop a total power output in the order of 65,000 horsepower, split into four diesel engines each of 16,500 horsepower at 350 revolutions per minute, powering the same number of shafts. Such a power rating would have allowed these battleships to reach a maximum speed of around 26 knots at a displacement of about 24,000 tonnes. The proposed powerplant was to have been based on development of a 2200 horsepower diesel engine at 400rpm made by Fiat, at the time in the experimental phase but which the designer believed offered the possibility of significant expansion while maintaining sufficient operating reliability and a high output.

Although maximum speed would be a couple of knots less than expected from a traditional steam powerplant of almost 90,000 horsepower, the advantages the diesel machinery could offer, on approximately equal weight, were undeniable: instant readiness, significant flexibility in speed without excessive production of smoke, a drastic reduction in the size of the exhaust ducts (funnels and smoke boxes) and, most important of all, particularly low fuel consumption – for an equal weight of embarked fuel, it meant an increase in range of about double, or rising from 3500 miles at 20 knots to about 7500 miles. On the debit side was the notably higher initial cost, but this would have been offset within a few years by the lower operating costs.

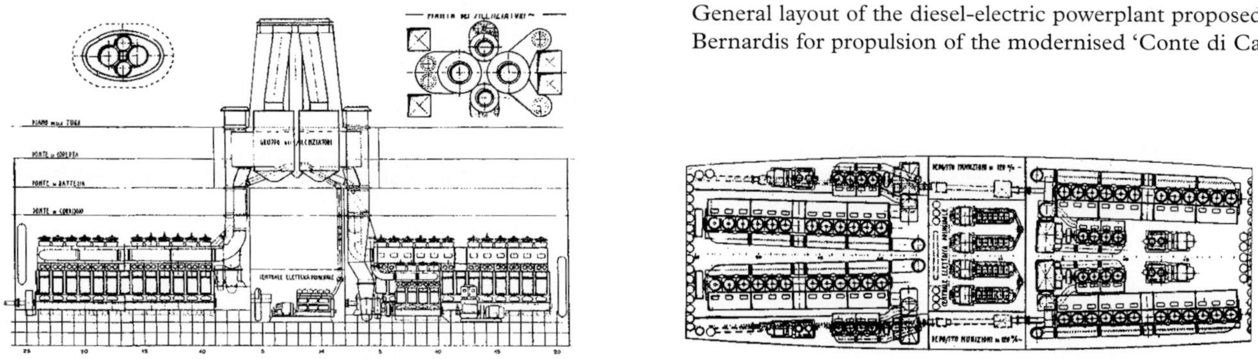

General layout of the diesel-electric powerplant proposed by naval engineer General Bernardis for propulsion of the modernised 'Conte di Cavour' class battleships.

The hull of the *Cavour*, now stripped of all its superstructure, undergoing modernisation work at Trieste.

General Bernardis understood that sacrificing a maximum speed of around 28–29 knots might constitute an insurmountable obstacle to a favourable decision by the Navy Staff on his original proposal, so he also produced a scheme for a more complex powerplant with a total power output of about 80,000 horsepower from a combination of four diesel engines and four diesel-electric motors (see the drawing at the top of this page). Despite the advantages outlined, he knew his proposals would be met with scepticism in an environment not inclined to abandon traditional and proven steam machinery, so as a last resort he suggested adopting diesel propulsion by way of experiment in only one of the four battleships to be modernised.

Trieste, San Marco shipyard. Initial alignment of the original bow structure of the *Conte di Cavour*, in the background, with the new stem, fitted with a bulbous fore-foot, which would soon envelop the old bow. (F Petronio collection)

The *Conte di Cavour* soon after the fitting of the new bow during the modernisation work carried out in Trieste between 1933 and 1937. (Courtesy E Trevisan)

The specific reasons why Bernardis' proposal was rejected have not been found, but it must have weighed heavily against him that the large and powerful Fiat diesel engines that formed the basis of the design did not exist at that stage, even as a prototype. There were many unknowns inherent in this specific industrial sector, so it was logical to suppose that the timescale for their construction and trials could run to many years.

The main modifications carried out during the course of reconstruction work on the *Cavour*

The first stage was removing the main gun turrets and the various elements of the powerplant, including the machinery bedplates, and dismantling of all of the superstructures. In the meantime, the original reconstruction scheme was subjected to a general revision that even included proposals advanced by the participating shipyards, leading to numerous modifications. The arrangement of the superstructure was altered substantially, significantly changing the appearance of the ships: the large central funnel was split into two, rising from a long central shelter deck and connected to a like number of boiler groups; the conning tower, while retaining a conical structure, assumed a more massive and complex shape; the main mast was moved much further aft and the tripod adopted the conventional configuration with the main leg, fitted with a cargo derrick, forward of the two supporting legs; lastly, the anchor hawseholes were reduced to just two, one per side, located at the height of the forecastle deck stringer and positioned about a dozen metres from the stem head. The anti-aircraft armament was conspicuously modified: four twin 100/47 mountings, of the same model as those embarked on the Regia Marina's modern cruisers, replaced one-for-one the quadruple turrets for the new model 37mm guns that had been deleted at the outset; four of the usual twin 35/74 gun mountings – which later, as we shall see, became six – were placed on the forecastle, on the sides of the main gun turrets and on the central shelter deck, while six twin 13.2mm heavy machine guns were placed on tripods on the rear portion of the two superfiring main gun turrets. The planned aircraft arrangements were subjected to significant changes, but, in the event, they were installed only on the *Conte di Cavour* and then only briefly before being replaced by two additional twin 35/74 mountings.

Apart from the modifications to the main armament, which will be addressed later, one of the most challenging aspects of the work was updating the protection system, which at all costs had to be kept within narrow weight limits. As it represented about 30 per cent of the displacement, exceeding the planned weight would have had significant effects on the ship's performance, as it would have increased hull immersion and reduced speed. In addition, it had been decided beforehand that the general structure of the original vertical protection could not be modified, so greater immersion of the ship would have reduced the effectiveness of the entire protective system against shellfire, because the lower edge of the thickest part of the armour belt would be pressed too far below the waterline.

The *Conte di Cavour* at Trieste at the conclusion of the reconstruction.

Mainly for weight considerations, substantial increases in the thickness and/or extension of the original vertical armour had to be rejected, even though it was accepted that the existing scheme was not particularly effective, as previously discussed in Chapter 3. This was, in effect, the crucial weakness of the entire project, but even a partial solution would have involved so much alteration that it would have threatened the cost-effectiveness of the whole project, and made it more difficult to achieve the most important characteristic, namely high speed. This speed, it was believed, would compensate in part for the weakness in protection by manoeuvring, allowing the ship to dictate the combat distance as well as the most favourable tactical position. Nevertheless, a small increase in vertical protection was achieved by adding 50mm thick plates around the upper portion of the main gun turret barbettes spaced 50cm from the existing armour.

Horizontal protection, mainly against the fire of large-calibre guns at great distances (plunging fire) and against aerial bombs, was so inadequate that some improvement was essential. However, even in this case, weight restrictions posed serious restraints, although, in the event, the new underwater protection meant that a significant increase in overall displacement had to be considered. A solution, although partial, was found in creating a protective deck corresponding to the battery or first lower deck. The central part of this deck would consist of 80mm thick plates intended to protect the areas of the powerplant and main ammunition magazines inside the existing 130mm armoured end bulkheads. As can be seen by the transverse section on page 123, part of the original protective deck and its plating (20 + 20mm maximum thicknesses) was removed in order to create more height for the powerplant, while towards the hull side it formed the top of the Pugliese underwater protection system. The thickness of the two higher decks – the forecastle deck and upper deck – were to remain unchanged. In this way, horizontal protection, even though split between three levels, was to have reached a total thickness that varied between 135mm and 116mm over the machinery spaces and magazines; towards the hull sides this variable thickness would be reduced to less than 70mm. It was a rather modest increase, but it was the maximum achievable within the strict weight limits that had been imposed. It was, however, slightly more than that of the French battleships of the 'Courbet' and 'Bretagne' classes, the latter of which were armed with 340mm guns and had just been or were in the course of being modernised in those years. The modernised British battleships of the 'R' class were similar, but not the 'Queen Elizabeth' class, whose maximum horizontal protection was not much more than 160mm, but it was better arranged.

It should be borne in mind that all the above British battleships were armed with 381mm (15in) guns whose performance was well above that of the 320mm (12.6in) Italian guns and that the maximum thickness of their vertical protection was as much as 330mm at the waterline against the Italian 250mm, closer to the 270mm of the French battleships cited above. With respect to speed, the planned 28 knots envisaged for the Italian ships compared very favourably with the 21–22 of the French and 21–24 of the British ships.

Moreover, it should be remembered that modernisation of the 'Cavour' class had been conceived essentially as an anti-French measure, valid when compared to the modernised French battleships, but somewhat problematic in several respects if opposed to the modern *Dunkerque* at 31,000 tons normal displacement with eight 330mm guns, maximum vertical protection of 242mm and horizontal of 140mm and, finally, with a speed of 30 knots.

As previously mentioned, underwater protection of the 'Cavour' was based on the Pugliese type 'absorbing cylinders', arranged longitudinally inside the turn of the bilges for a distance of about 114 metres between the two armoured bulkheads, situated just beyond the extreme main gun turrets and forming the ends of the armoured citadel. This system was designed to protect against torpedoes and mines, as well as bombs or shells, which might explode in direct contact with or close to the sides of the underwater hull bottom abreast the magazines and the entire machinery space.

This system provided for the use of particular structures intended to soak up a great part of the energy developed by an underwater explosion, using calculated hydrodynamic and mechanical effects to reduce the residual pressure on the interior structure and thus limit the resulting damage. On the 'Cavour' class, this system was situated at the hull side, just below the lower

Detail of the extreme stern of the *Conte di Cavour* during the works at Trieste. The main semi-balanced rudder has been temporarily removed, but the auxiliary rudder, slightly forward, has remained in place.

edge of the armoured belt, completely within the existing double bottom structure. It was enclosed within a strong, curved, watertight bulkhead that extended downwards and towards the interior of the hull. In the space between the internal plating of the double bottom and the armoured bulkhead, a steel cylinder of appropriate diameter, called the 'absorber', was inserted, held and interrupted every three or four frames by sheet steel diaphragms placed athwartships. For the system to function effectively, it was essential that both the cylinder and the double bottom be kept empty; the space around the cylinders was always filed with liquids (potable water, fuel, etc), which as they were expended were replaced by seawater as ballast. When subject to an underwater explosion, the pressure wave immediately destroyed the double-bottom cells and pushed into the liquids in the holding tanks; as these liquids could not be compressed, they transmitted the pressure in all directions, acting mainly on the exterior of the cylinder that, being empty and intentionally weak, collapsed, thus absorbing a large part of the kinetic energy of the blast and ensuring the integrity of the curved bulkhead and of any others affected. In other words, a controlled flooding would occur outside the main longitudinal watertight bulkhead. The inevitable listing of the ship on the damaged side would be very rapidly compensated by flooding the cells of the double bottom and of the void spaces of the opposite side by a series of 'automatic balancing channels'.

As confirmed by accurate tests on models, the full effectiveness of the system depended on enough space to set up its constituent parts to the optimum dimensions calculated by the designer, as was the case with the 'Littorio' class battleships. On the 'Cavours', however, size and structural limitations imposed by the existing hulls forced the adoption of many compromises (position and diameter of the absorbing cylinder, width of the void spaces, etc) which undoubtedly reduced the effectiveness of the entire system. Nevertheless, throughout their careers, neither of the 'Cavour' class – nor either of the 'Dorias', which were rebuilt similarly later – suffered any underwater damage that

The after 320/44 battery of the *Giulio Cesare* upon completion of modernisation work and the re-mounting of the guns under the supervision of Ansaldo of Genoa.

directly affected the Pugliese system. Therefore, its effectiveness in the smaller version could not be properly evaluated. In fact, *Cavour* and *Duilio* in 1940 and then the ex-*Cesare* in 1955 were seriously damaged by underwater explosions, the first two by torpedoes with magnetic fuses and the third by a bottom mine, but these all occurred 'under' the hull and thus outside the area of the Pugliese system, conceived mainly – and this should be stressed – for protection on the sides.

Alteration of the main gun armament of the modernised battleships

We have made frequent reference to re-tubing the original 305/46 Mod 1909 guns to 320/44, which was possible because of the wide margin of strength with which the original guns of the 'wire-wound' type had been built at the beginning of the century. This transformation, along with the radical modernisation of the associated mountings, occurred in two phases: the first, with respect to the guns intended for the two 'Cavours', in 1933–1936 and a second in 1937–1940 during the modernisation of the two 'Duilios' that, as will be seen, would be ordered later. Altogether, fifty-two 305mm guns were removed from these four battleships, of which only forty were transformed into 320mm guns and quickly re-employed; the remaining twelve, which were not immediately re-tubed, constituted a reserve of guns for the whole group. The complex procedure of modifying the calibre of the guns began by first removing the original 305mm barrel liners, and the required number of steel coils – which characterised the wire-wound construction of these weapons – before inserting the new 320mm barrel liners. This recalibration to 320/43.77 (later officially rounded up to 44 calibres) was regarded as successful, increasing the perforating projectile weight from 452 to 525kg, but reducing the barrel's longitudinal rigidity – identified by some as the reason for the marked dispersion of fire that later became apparent in these guns.

It should also be recalled that these large-calibre guns were not all of the same model: *Cavour* and *Cesare* mounted, respectively, Vickers-Terni Mod 1909 and Armstrong-Pozzuoli Mod 1909 guns which had similar but not completely identical characteristics. The same can be said for the other pair of battleships, where *Andrea Doria* had the same type guns as *Cavour* and the *Duilio* as *Cesare*. Altering the calibre of the guns and modernising the mountings (by modifying the hydraulic and electrical equipment) did not require changes to the external appearance of the armoured turrets, by OTO of La Spezia for the guns originally produced by Vickers and by Ansaldo for the Armstrong guns. When completed, the 320/44 of the *Cavour* was designated OTO Mod 1934 and the *Cesare*'s Ansaldo Mod 1934, both characterised by elevation being increased from 20 degrees to 27 degrees; the guns of the *Andrea Doria* were given the new designation of OTO Mod 1936 and those of the *Duilio* as Ansaldo Mod 1936, both with a maximum elevation of 30 degrees.

Detail of the muzzle of one of the Armstrong 305/46 Mod 1909 guns of the *Giulio Cesare* re-tubed to 320/44 in 1934.

Completion of work on the 'Conte di Cavour' class

Reconstruction of both 'Cavours' began in October 1933 and was completed respectively in June and October 1937. During this complex process there had been a general, but modest weight increase, accruing from small but widespread modifications carried as the work progressed. This raised some apprehension because it risked greater immersion of the ships, compromising the effectiveness of what was already barely adequate vertical protection, in addition to potentially reducing speed. Nevertheless, during sea trials carried out in 1936, both ships reached and exceeded, if only marginally, the 28 knots specified in the contract; these speeds were later confirmed in February 1938 (see Chapter 7) at higher trial displacements, which were very close to those expected for the ships at full load. Maximum combat speed was therefore set at 26 knots, a sustainable increase of at least 4–5 knots compared with the ships as built and in any case surpassing by a wide margin the operating speed of the modernised dreadnoughts serving at that time with the Marine Nationale and the Royal Navy.

In addition to the excellent output of the new powerplants, the bold architectural solutions that had characterised this reconstruction proved to be, overall, entirely validated. However, it should be observed that defects in the workmanship in parts of the structural modifications did not come to light for some time. For example, there were leaks in the lower part of the hull that often proved very difficult to eliminate completely, especially in the area of the original bow, which the new design had not removed but had instead incorporated in the new structure, creating a number of small 'blind spots' that were almost inaccessible.

From the aesthetic viewpoint, the 'Cavour' class emerged from the reconstruction with a completely new appearance, and rather more modern lines. In addition, the arrangement of the main armament and its associated fire control equipment was much more rational, and underwater protection was certainly more effective, even with all of its dimensional limitations. For horizontal protection, the modest improvements increased effectiveness a little, but not much could be done to improve the vertical protection, which principally depended on the thickness of the belt armour and for reasons of weight this could not be modified.

As early as 1937, however, criticism was levelled against the configuration of the secondary and anti-aircraft armament. In Italy there was no dual-purpose gun available for both defence against modern torpedo boats and directed anti-aircraft use, so the Regia Marina had to resort to two distinct types of gun: respectively the 120/50 OTO Mod 1933, a 4.7in gun previously developed for destroyers, in twin purpose-designed gunhouses with a single cradle (six per ship) with elevation from -2 degrees to + 42 degrees and with a maximum range of 19,000 metres; and the 100/17 (3.9in) OTO Mod 1928 in shielded twin mounts with a single cradle on a flexible mount for anti-aircraft fire (four per ship, the same as those equipping contemporary cruisers) with elevation from -5 degrees to +80 degrees and maximum horizontal range of 15,240 metres. Dividing the secondary armament into two different calibres considerably complicated onboard logistics, but in Italy a single-calibre alternative was not available for the entire duration of the war.

For close-in anti-aircraft defence, Breda Mod 1928 37/54 guns were envisaged, in six twin water-cooled mounts, and the same number of twin Breda 1931 13.2mm heavy machine guns. In the late 1930s, however, this latter automatic weapon was considered to be largely outdated both in calibre and in performance, so that it was gradually replaced by 20mm cannon: on the 'Cavour' class the six original 13.2mm positions were replaced shortly before 1940 by a like number of twin Breda 1935 20/65 guns.

The modernisation design for the 'Conte di Cavour' class included two 'Gagnotto' type catapults, powered by compressed air and traversable outwards, to launch reconnaissance seaplanes. Installed on each side of the central shelter deck, their midships position resulted from insufficient space available at the extreme stern; furthermore, by this time, placing catapults and aircraft on the forecastle deck had fallen from favour in the Regia Marina, largely because they interfered with the ships' seakeeping, after the less than brilliant performance of that type of arrangement on the early 'Condottieri' class and '10,000-ton' cruisers. Following completion of the rebuilding work on the hull, superstructure and powerplant, the *Cavour* had been moved from Trieste to the dockyard at La Spezia, where it was planned to complete the armament and a few fitting-out details. During this phase, a catapult was installed in the early months of 1937, with trials in the

In waters off La Spezia 1937, the test launch of a modern reconnaissance seaplane of the IMAM Ro 43 type from the port side catapult of the *Conte di Cavour*. These experiments revealed that when swung outboard the catapult interfered with the employment of the two twin amidships 120/50 turrets of the secondary armament. As a consequence, all of the aircraft equipment initially envisaged for these battleships was eliminated. (M Piovano collection)

The *Conte di Cavour* with the modernisation work complete, leaving La Spezia for trials in March 1937. Note installation of the port catapult abreast the funnels.

The battleship *Conte di Cavour* while visiting Malta in June 1938.

waters of the Ligurian Sea following in the spring; several launches were made with an IMAM Ro 43 biplane, the most modern of the Regia Aeronautica [Italian royal air force] catapult seaplanes and which at that time equipped all of the modern Italian cruisers. Although the launches were successful, the trials revealed that the excessive size of the two catapults significantly limited the operation of the midships secondary armament 120/50 twin turrets, in addition to subjecting the parked aircraft to excessive blast effects when those guns fired. Considering these factors alongside the need to find space amidships for close-in air defence, it was decided to eliminate the catapults, replacing them with two additional twin mounts for 37/54 rapid-fire gun systems. On the other hand, the large numbers of reconnaissance seaplanes embarked on the catapults of Regia Marina cruisers made it possible to extend their role to cover the battleships as well. After that decision, aircraft arrangements were definitively eliminated from the 'Cavour' class and were not even considered during the later modernisation of the two similar 'Duilio' class battleships.

The modernisation and reconstruction of the 'Duilio' class

As previously mentioned in Chapter 4, the reconstruction of the 'Cavour' class was considered a success, so in order to have a group of four battleships with common characteristics within a relatively short time, in the early months of 1936 work resumed on plans for a similar major modernisation of the other two old dreadnoughts available, *Duilio* and *Andrea Doria*, whose current combat value was practically nil. Bearing in mind the modest

The battleship *Giulio Cesare* at the time of re-entering service following the major modernisation work carried out in Genoa.

technical-economic advantages to be gained from this scheme, as discussed in the previous chapter, the decision to proceed with rebuilding the two 'Duilios' as well was made by the Regia Marina in early 1937. On 15 March the *Duilio* left Taranto to arrive three days later at Genoa, where it was turned over for work to the local Cantieri del Tirreno, which had already seen to the modernisation of the *Cavour*. Soon thereafter the other battleship, the *Andrea Doria*, reached Trieste from La Spezia, where on 8 April it was formally 'taken in charge' by the CRDA San Marco yard.

The radical modernisation of these two ships proceeded along similar lines to the 'Cavour' class, with the above-named shipyards carrying out the modifications to the hulls, powerplants and fittings, but reserving the preparation and fitting of the armament to the Regia Marina, which in turn relied upon cooperation with Odero Terni Orlando (OTO, La Spezia works) and of the Società Ansaldo pa respectively for *Andrea Doria* and *Duilio*.

The scheme for the reconstruction of the 'Duilio' class began with a design substantially the same as the preceding class and sought similar objectives. Therefore, the plans followed the same lines, but incorporated improvements suggested by recent experience with the 'Cavours' and what had been learned from the

Detail of the 'tulip' (or 'live muzzle' as the swell was known in Italy) of a 305/46 Vickers Mod 1909 re-tubed to 320/44 on the battleship *Conte di Cavour*.

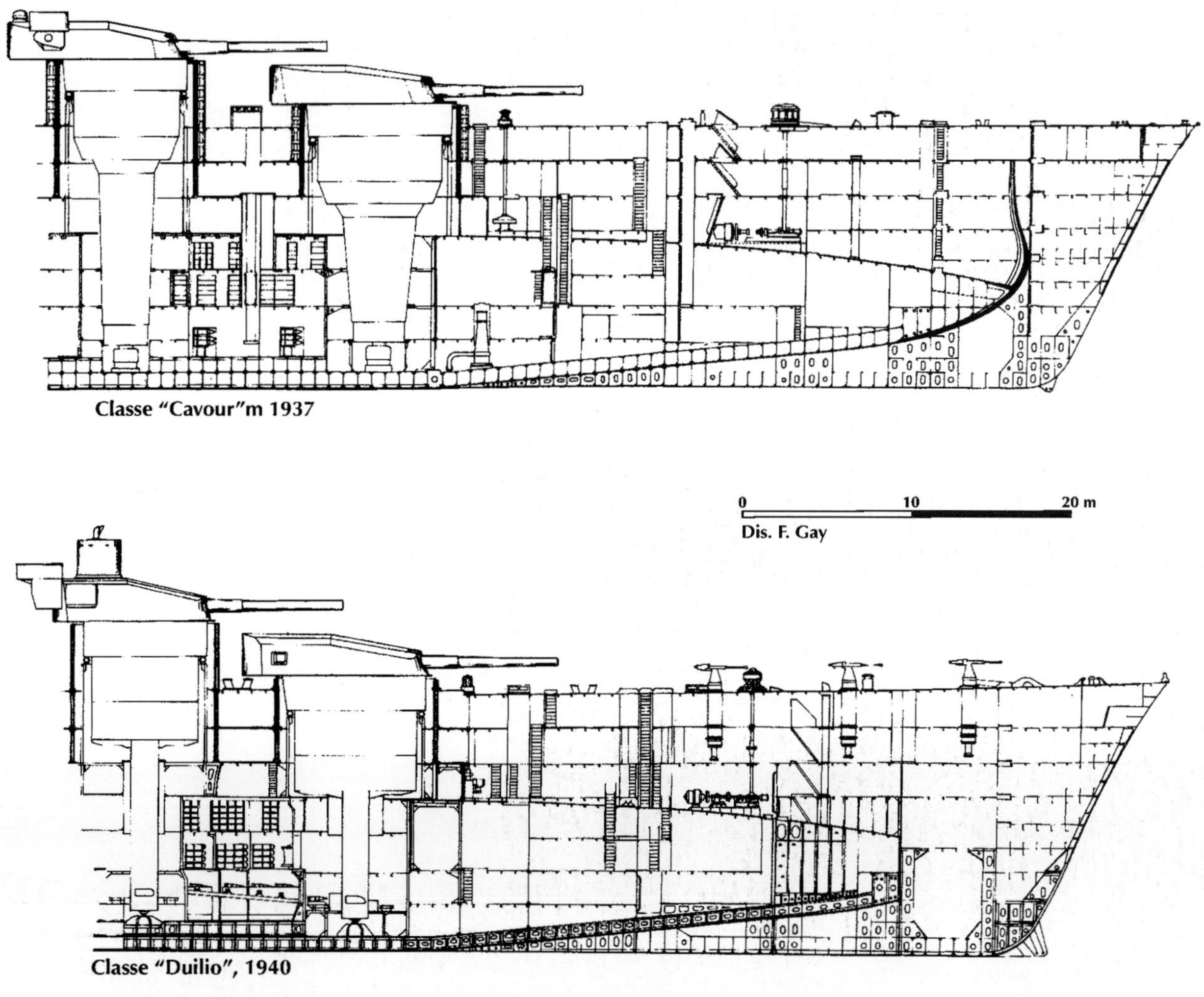

Bow areas of the longitudinal sections of the modernised battleships of the 'Conte di Cavour' (top) and 'Duilio' classes compared. Note that on the first class the new bow structure was superimposed over the original, which remained in place, while on the second the new form replaced the pre-existing structure.

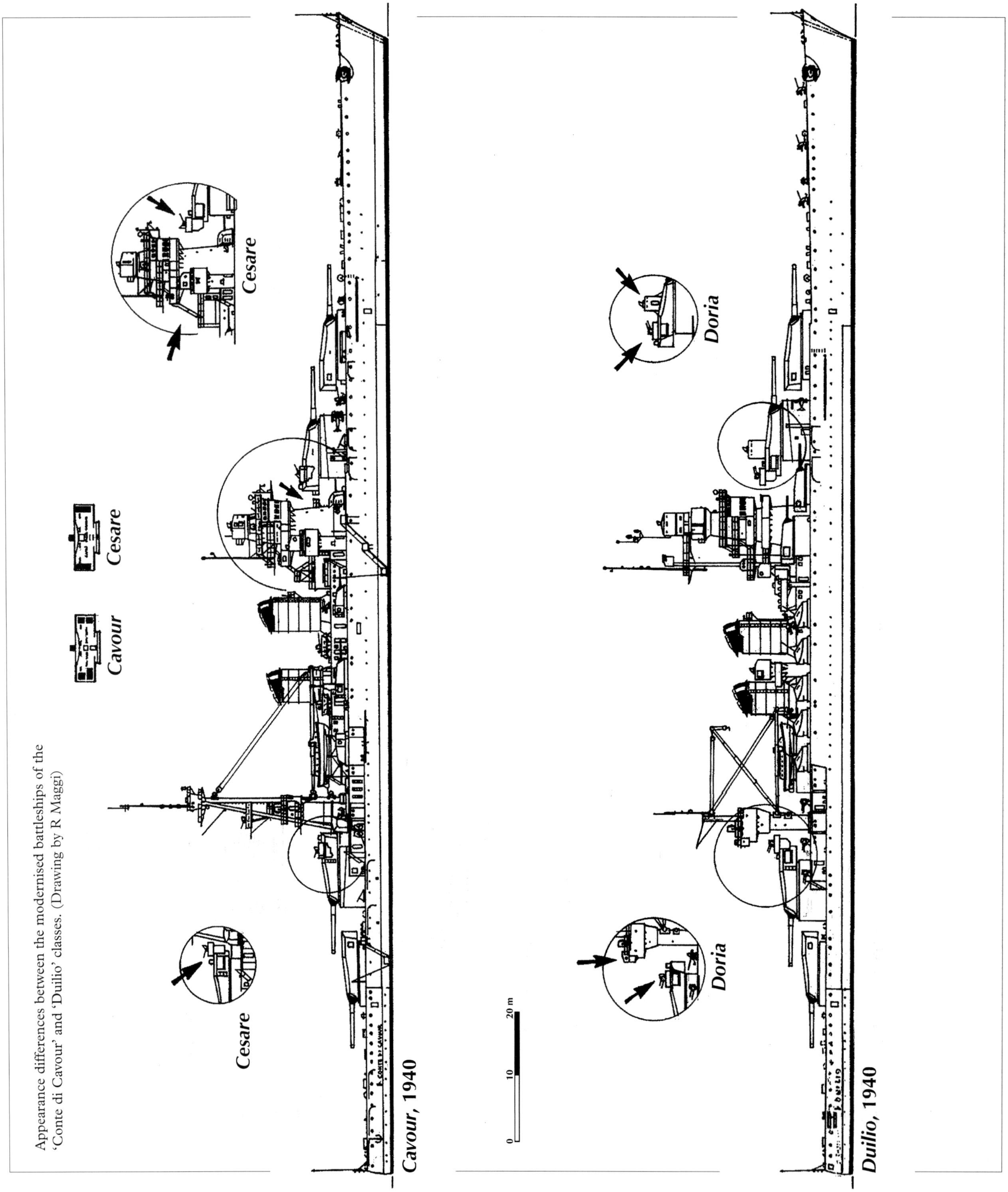

Appearance differences between the modernised battleships of the 'Conte di Cavour' and 'Duilio' classes. (Drawing by R Maggi)

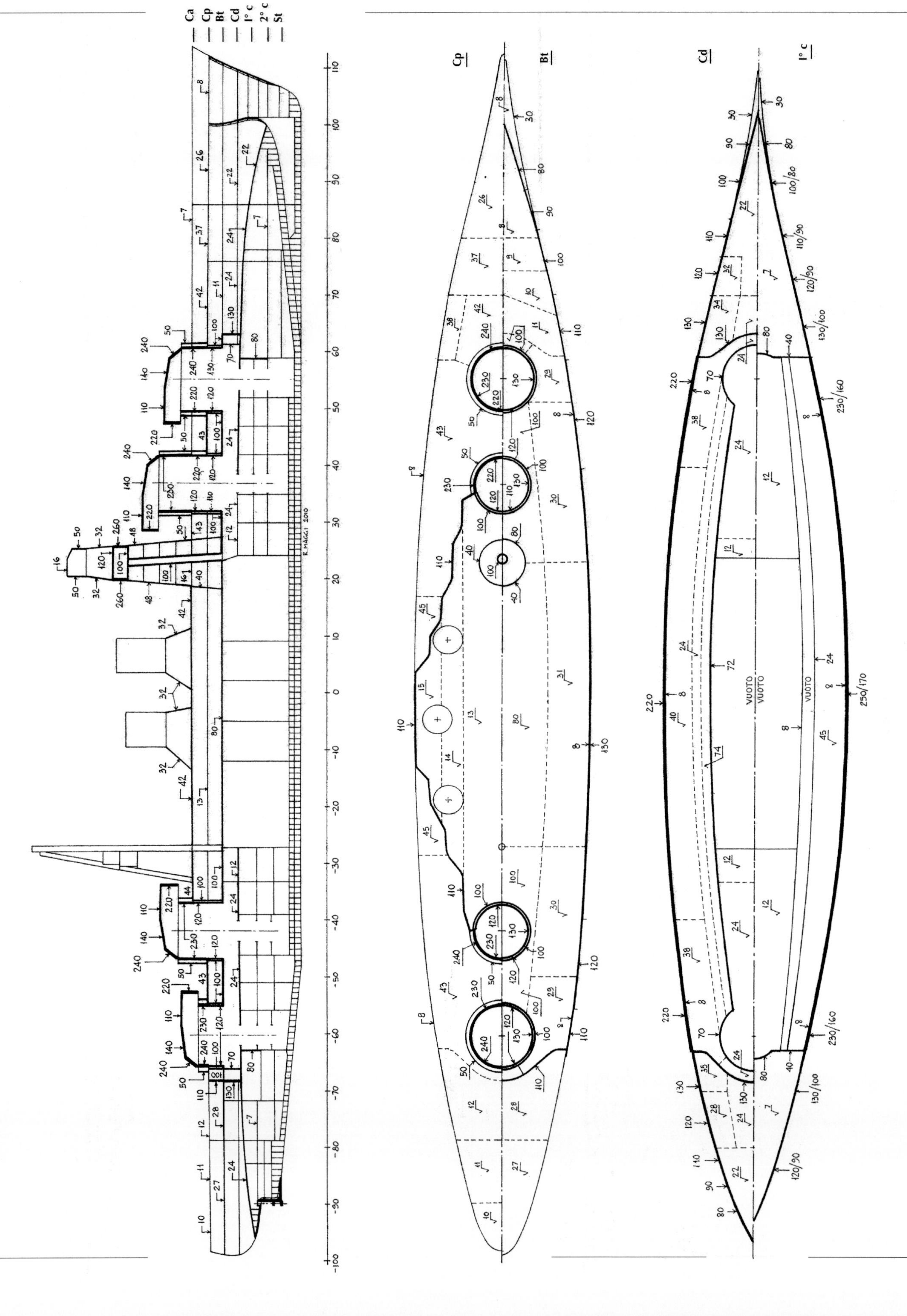

'Conte di Cavour' class modernised. Armour plan.
(Drawing by R Maggi)

Note: measurements in millimetres

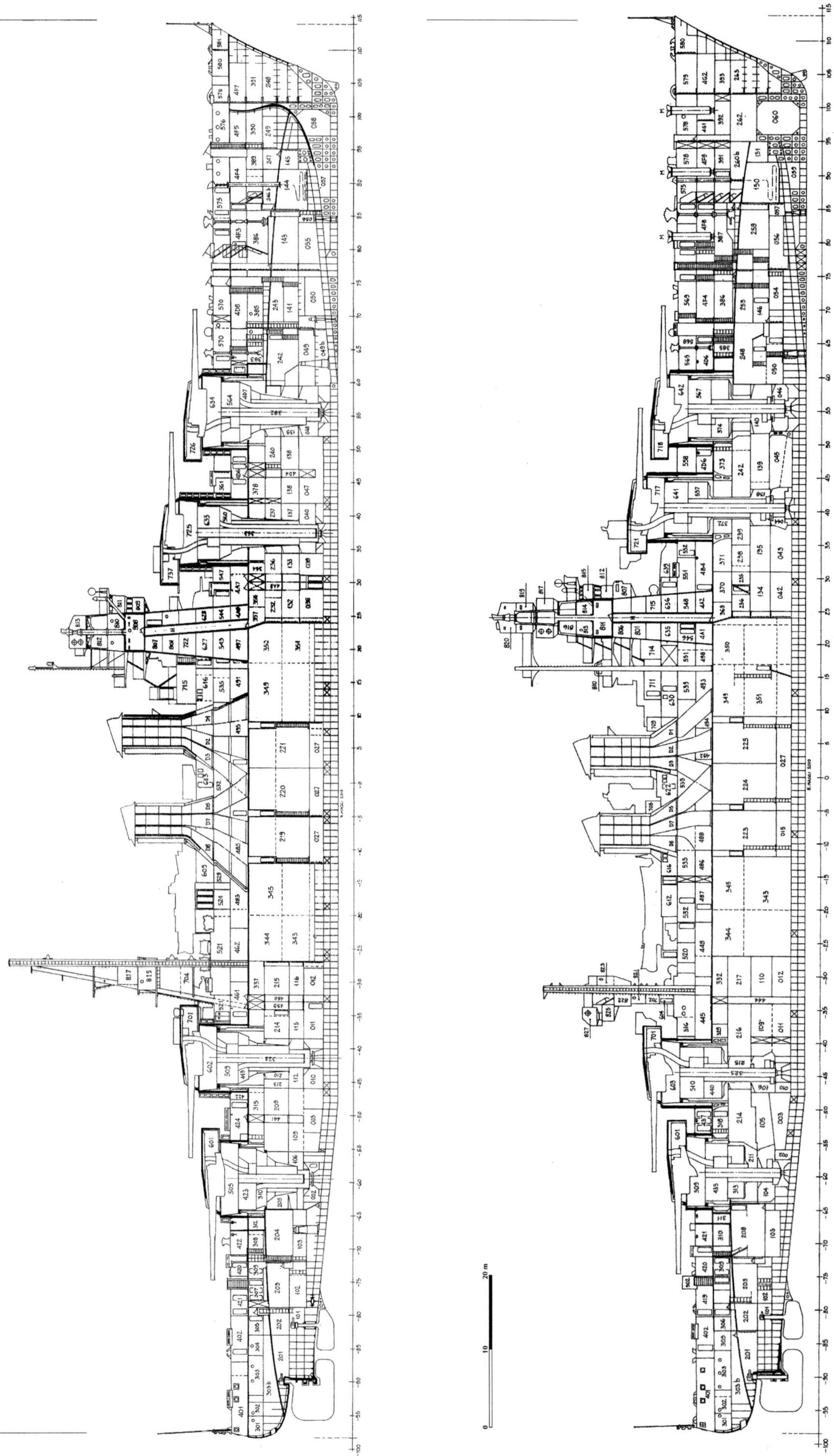

'Conte di Cavour' class (top) and 'Duilio' class modernised. Comparison of longitudinal sections. (Drawing by R Maggi)

For key, see pages 100-103 and 132-134

'Conte di Cavour' class.
Transverse sections
(Drawing by R Maggi)

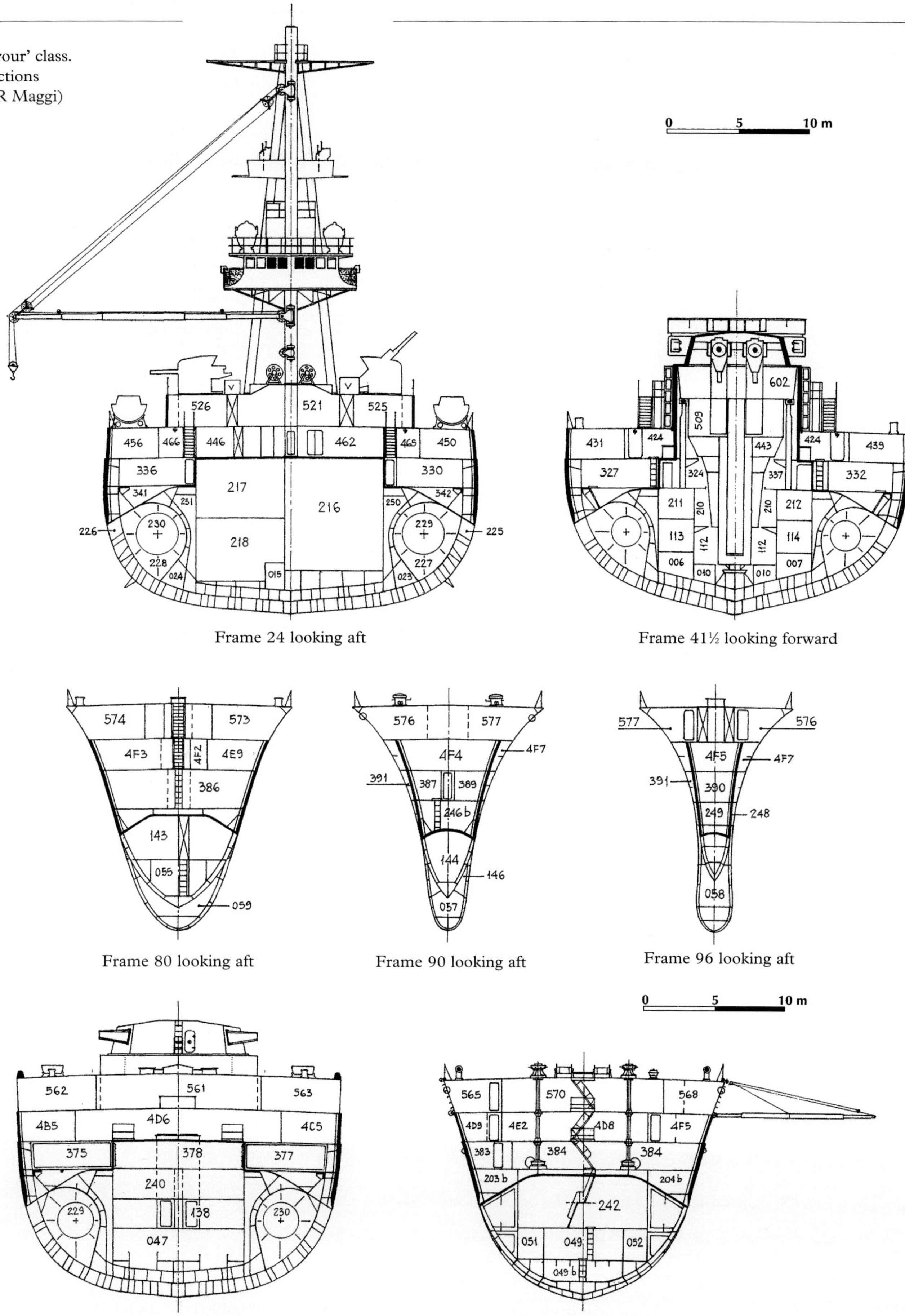

Frame 24 looking aft

Frame 41½ looking forward

Frame 80 looking aft

Frame 90 looking aft

Frame 96 looking aft

Frame 44 looking aft

Frame 64 looking aft

For key, see pages 100-103

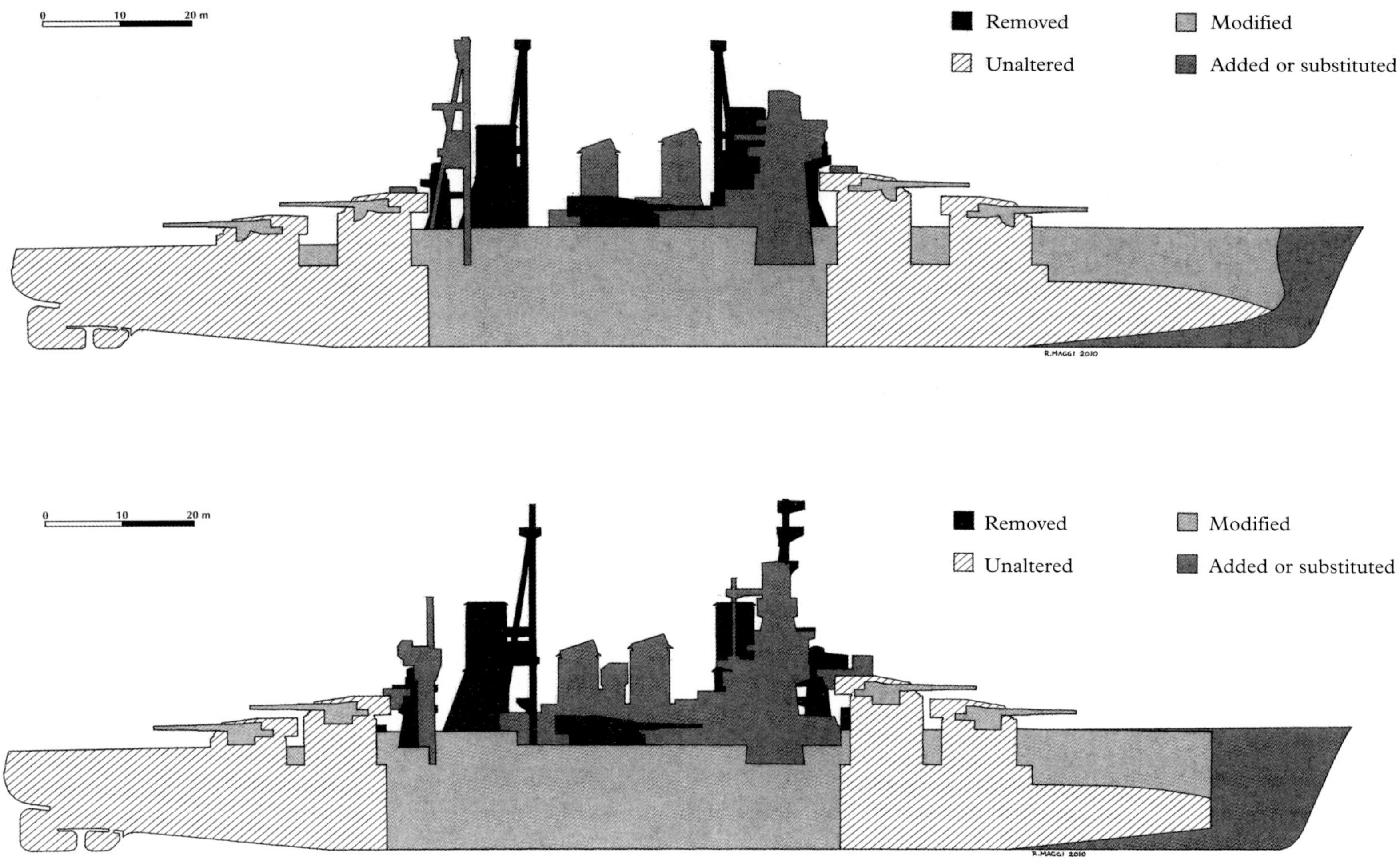

'Conte di Cavour' (top) and 'Duilio' classes. Comparison of the parts that were removed, modified, added and left unaltered during the modernisation work. (Drawing by R Maggi)

work under way on the two new '35,000-ton' battleships, now almost ready to be launched as the *Littorio* and *Vittorio Veneto*.

In particular, with respect to the hull, the greatest differences between the 'Duilios' compared with the 'Cavours' were concentrated in the area of the hull ahead of the forward main gun turrets. Here, instead of superimposing the new bow structure over that of the original, the fore end of the hull in the 'Duilio' class was almost completely dismantled and replaced. This resulted in a significant structural simplification and elimination of most of the problems stemming from water ingress that were mentioned previously when describing the 'Cavour' and which will be addressed again later.

The few changes made to the horizontal protection were the same as those made on the 'Cavour' class. Regarding vertical protection, there was a small difference, but it was largely aesthetic – the layer of additional 50mm armour around the main gun turret barbettes, rather than being positioned at a distance of 50cm from them as in the 'Cavours', was placed directly against the surface in the 'Duilios'. As a result, the 'Cavour' barbettes – which were further apart from each other compared with the 'Duilio' – appeared to be more massive than they were in reality. No substantial changes could be made to the Pugliese underwater protection system, which therefore remained similar. The configuration of the powerplant, designed to develop the same power output, was likewise similar, but on the 'Duilio' class achieved a slightly lower performance.

The major differences between the two classes of modernised battleships were concentrated in the configuration of the superstructures and the composition of the secondary and anti-aircraft armament. In those areas the influence of recent work on the new '35,000-tonners' was so evident that the final appearance of the 'Duilios', although on a smaller scale, was very similar to that of the 'Littorio' class. In particular, compared with the 'Cavour', the bridge tower was taller, with a general layout clearly inspired by the 'Littorios'. As on the latter, the principal mast was immediately aft of the tower, then came the two funnels, which were closer together and moved slightly aft to reduce the effect of smoke interference on the fire control equipment that was mainly located on the bridge tower. Finally, the high tripod mast aft that characterised the 'Cavours' was replaced by a smaller pole mast placed at the top of a special mushroom-shaped structure like that which dominated the after superstructure of the 'Littorios'.

The secondary armament of the 'Duilio' class was completely different from that of the 'Cavours', consisting of twelve modern

One of the twin 320/44 mountings of the *Giulio Cesare* in the Ansaldo artillery works in Genoa.

OTO 1937 135/45 (5.3in) anti-ship guns in four triple turrets, placed in pairs on either side of the bridge tower. These were excellent guns, accurate and with a high rate of fire, with elevation from -7 degrees to +45 degrees, a maximum range of 19,600 metres and capable of anti-aircraft barrage fire as well. However, the main anti-aircraft armament of the 'Duilios' comprised ten Ansaldo and OTO 1938 and 1939 90/50 (3.5in) guns in small stabilised single turrets, the same mounting as those on the 'Littorio' and similarly positioned on the sides of the central shelter deck. The 90/50 was an excellent gun, powerful and with a high rate of fire, but its innovative stabilised mounting (which automatically compensated for the ship's roll and pitch) proved rather delicate and subject to frequent electrical malfunction. For close-in air defence, the 'Duilios' were equipped with a good number of Breda 37/74 (fifteen) and 20/65 (sixteen) guns from the outset.

In terms of rapid-fire cannon, however, a brief note about their effectiveness is in order. All of the automatic weapons embarked on the modernised Italian battleships – and also on other major Regia Marina warships – were gas-operated, developed by Breda in the 1930s and distinguished by good ballistic characteristics as well as a satisfactory rate of fire. However, because only the breech-block recoiled, the guns were installed on rigid twin mounts that, when firing, transmitted significant stresses to the structures on which they were mounted. This generated heavy vibration that had negative effects on the accuracy of prolonged fire and limited the number of weapons that could be embarked because they could only be mounted where there was a support that was structurally very strong. The problem was only solved with the later production of single flexible mounts with partially recoiling barrels – of both the 37/54 (only on the 'Duilio' class and then in limited numbers) as well as the 20/65.

The fire control system on the modernised 'Cavour' class was generally similar to that later installed on the two 'Duilios', except for the inferior standard of the associated equipment, which was somewhat antiquated and whose performance was not as good. Probably to keep down the ever-rising costs of the modernisation, the equipment embarked on the two 'Cavours' was actually poorer than similar equipment of the period such as that already

The *Andrea Doria*, still without armament, while on machinery trials in the Upper Adriatic in February 1939. (F Petronio collection)

available and embarked on, for example, the last of the '10,000-ton' heavy cruisers (the *Bolzano*) and on two 'Garibaldi' class light cruisers. In fitting out the 'Duilios', on the other hand, the equipment employed benefited from experience gained while building the 'Littorios' and turned out to be almost at the same high level as on the 'Littorio' class.

In general terms, all of the equipment for fire control was of Italian design and manufacture: there were rangefinders and aiming equipment of suitable performance, up-to-date electromechanical and calculating stations, but the systems were rather slow in reacting to changes in kinematic situations during surface engagements and, even more so, for anti-aircraft fire. Systems for stabilising the line of sight of aim in heavy seas or movement of the ship platform were not very effective; throughout the war this problem could not be resolved adequately, other than by resorting to archaic firing practices ('at the end of the top of the roll', etc), which, however, slowed the rate of fire significantly. Later, in Chapter 7, some of these issues are addressed in relation to the results of gunnery exercises by the 'Cavour' class battleships on the eve of the conflict where these problems clearly arise – along with others, among which were the marked phenomena of 'dispersion' of the 320mm rounds.

Chapter 6

TECHNICAL DESCRIPTION OF THE MODERNISED 'CONTE DI CAVOUR' CLASS BATTLESHIPS

At the end of this chapter is a summary chronology relating to the two 'Cavour' class ships from the beginning of their modernisation until their breaking-up, as well as the principal technical characteristics at the time of their re-entry into service in 1937. The text that follows furnishes some details that complete and supplement those tables.

The *Conte di Cavour*, not yet completely fitted out, during machinery trials in the Upper Adriatic.

The actual 'reconstruction' proper undergone by these ships involved about 60 per cent of the original structure and equipment, following a design that was without doubt the most extensive modernisation scheme applied to any inter-war battleship. The chief features of this transformation, which involved practically all of the onboard facilities, were indisputably:

- the extensive modifications to the hull previously described, including the installation of an effective underwater protection system and of a pair of anti-roll bilge keels 1.2 metres wide by 54.9 metres long
- the complete replacement of the powerplant, the original four-shaft arrangement becoming two propeller shafts
- and the substantial reconfiguration and reorganisation of the armament.

The battleship *Conte di Cavour* at Trieste after the final completion of the modernisation work.

Above: The battleship *Conte di Cavour* at Taranto in 1938.

Right: Close-up of the after main turrets of the *Giulio Cesare* moored at Genoa in May 1938. Note in the foreground the officers' gangway and associated guard post.

Opposite, top: Detail of the battleship *Giulio Cesare* moored at Genoa in May 1938. (G Alfano collection)

Opposite, bottom: The battleship *Conte di Cavour* at Trieste after the final completion of the modernisation work.

CONTE DI CAVOUR

The battleship *Giulio Cesare* moored in 1939. The crew gangway is abreast the bridge tower.

Close-up of the forward 320mm guns and of the bridge tower of the battleship *Conte di Cavour*. Note the coat of arms that adorns the muzzle tompions.

Replacing the powerplant was undoubtedly one of the more positive aspects of the 'Cavour' modernisation. The power of the new machinery more than doubled output, and actually was almost tripled during speed trials. Steam was produced by two separate groups of four modern subvertical boilers, functioning at a working pressure of 22kg/cm^2, which fed a like number of geared turbines, each consisting of one high-pressure and two low-pressure turbines, with incorporated astern gearing, and associated reduction gearing. Disposed in well-separated spaces, both the condenser units as well as the propulsion units worked independently with a high margin of safety. Starting with the main boilers and the donkey boilers (two) cold, six hours were needed to get under way, but in exceptional circumstances this could be reduced to four.

As discussed in the preceding chapter, the ten re-tubed 320/44 guns of the main armament were divided into four armoured turrets, of which two were triple (weighing 745 tons) and two twin (550 tons); however, the associated fire control installations must now be described. The main SDT [*Stazione di Direzione del Tiro* – Fire Direction Station] included the general aiming equipment [APG, for *Apparecchiatura Punteria Generale*, or General Aiming Device] and two 7.20-metre rangefinders, one stereoscopic and one coincidence, in addition to much other important instrumentation. From this SDT, positioned about 23 metres

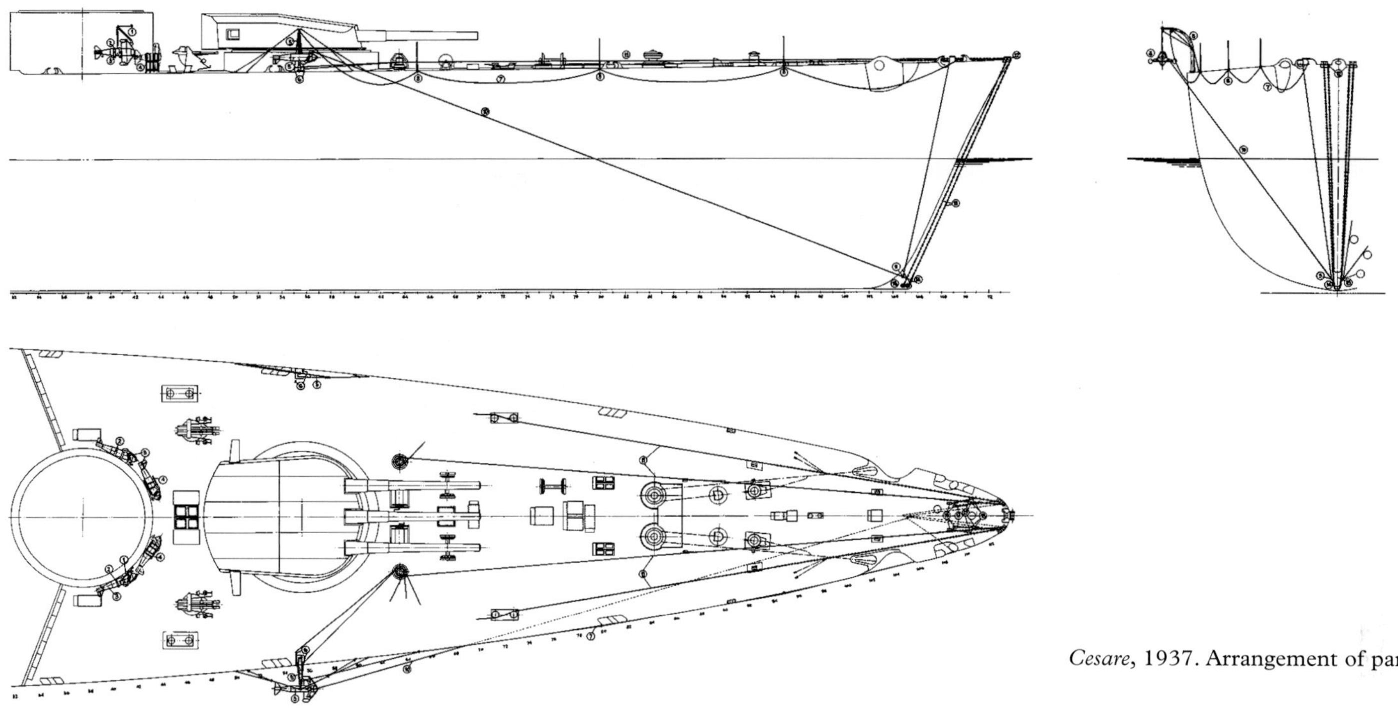

Cesare, 1937. Arrangement of paravanes.

Aerial photo of the *Conte di Cavour* at speed on the eve of the war.

Details of the bridge tower of *Giulio Cesare* in 1940, before the twin 13.2mm machine guns were replaced by those of 20mm.

above the waterline, the 1st DT [*Direttore di Tiro*, or Fire Director] was able to control the entire battery, or of part of it, making use of interconnections with a fire control centre of the OLAP/RM 1 type located in a protected space under the bridge tower on the middle deck. In the event of damage or breakdown of the main system, fire could be directed by the 2nd DT from another position in No 2 main gun turret, at the rear of which was a smaller fire control director of the Galileo RM 2 type and a 9-metre base rangefinder. Alternatively, it was also possible for this SDT to connect with the main fire control centre, and a

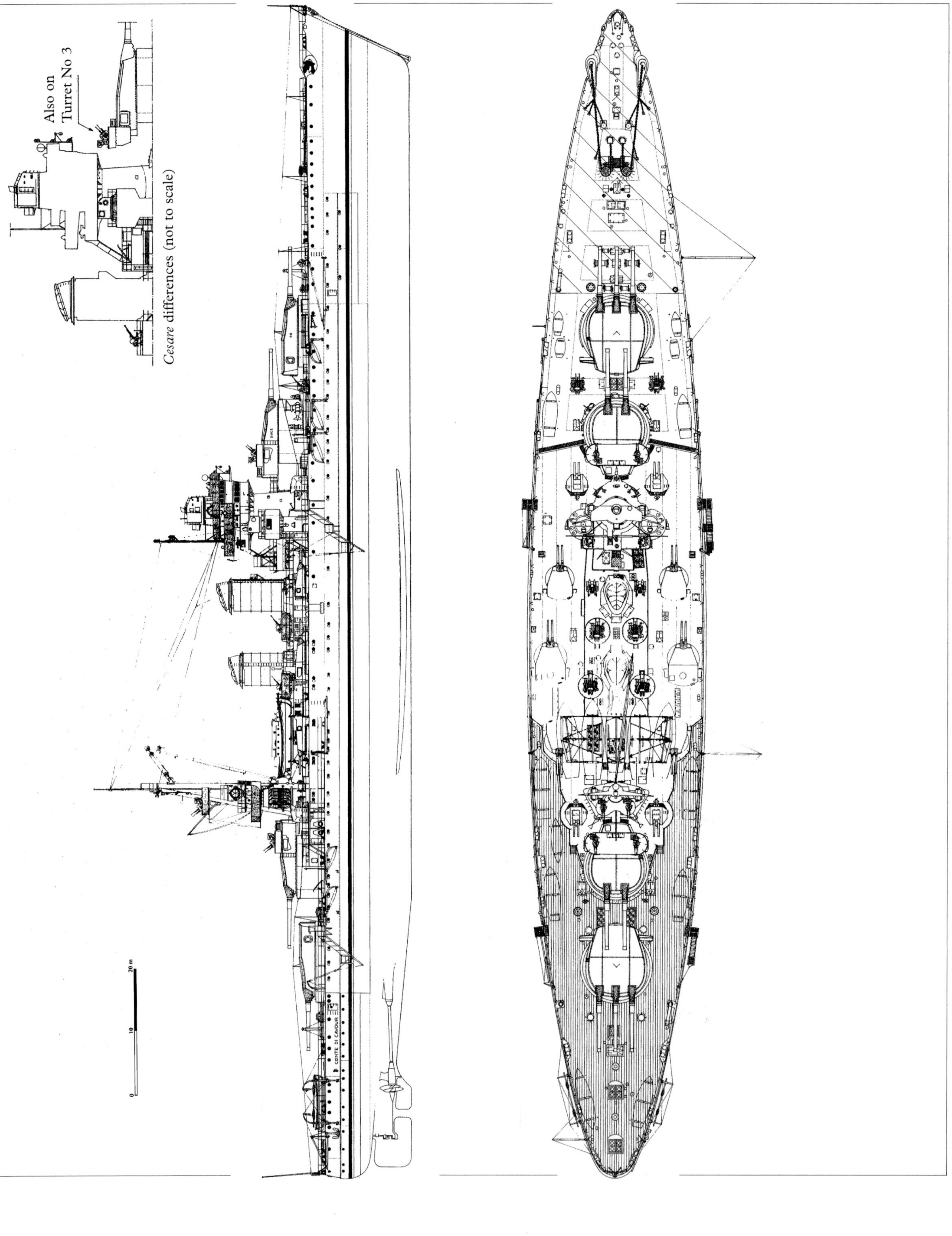

Modernised 'Conte di Cavour' class battleships. External views 1940.
(Drawing by R Maggi)

Conte di Cavour 1940. Fore and aft external views. (Drawing by R Maggi)

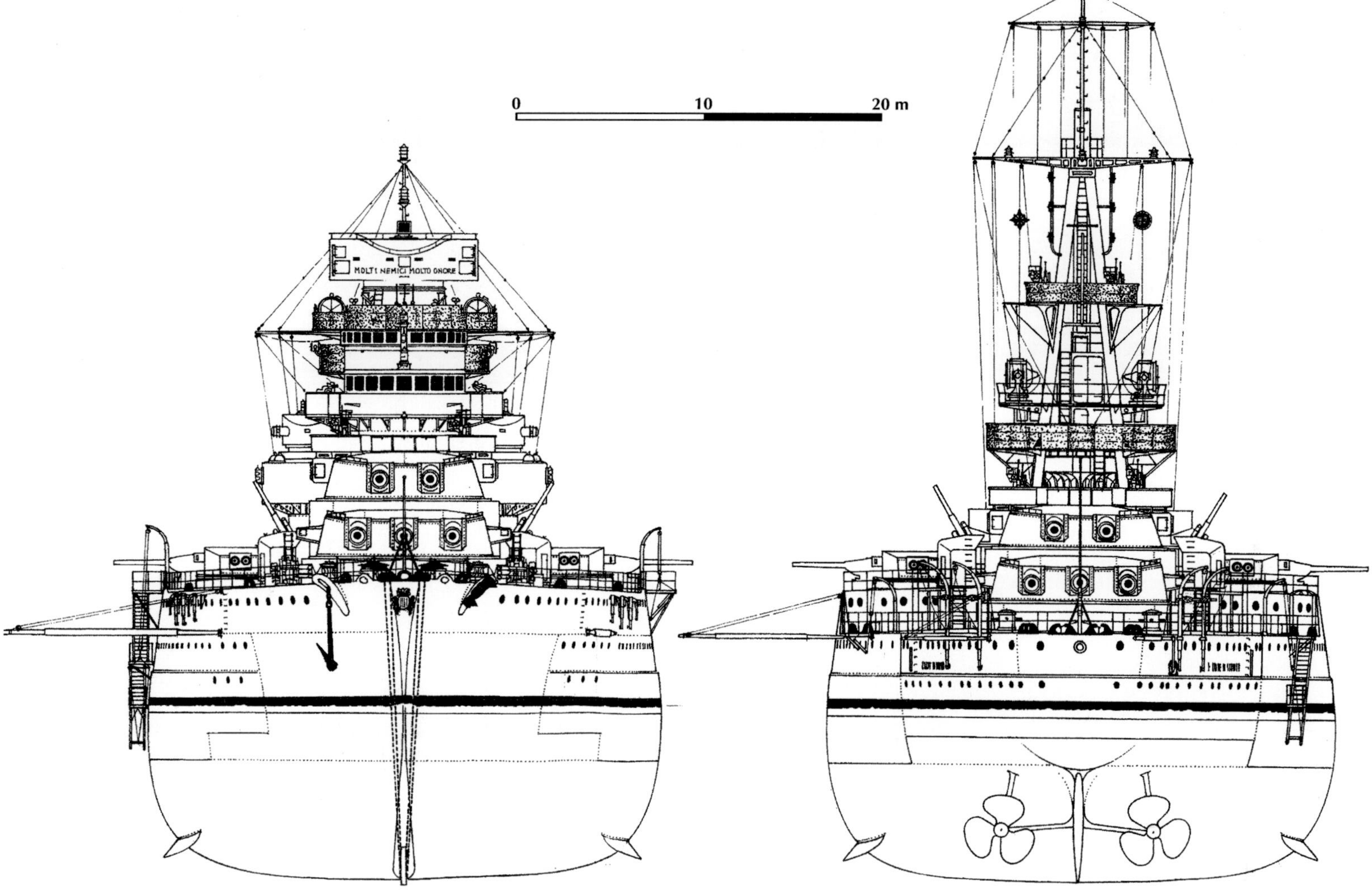

The Breda 1935 20/65 twin mounts that replaced the 13.2mm Breda 1931 guns in the same light AA role on the 'Cavour' class in 1940.

similar system was also present in No 3 main gun turret. The combined use of these SDT allowed various combinations for directing the main guns, including subdivision into firing groups – fore and aft – of the 320mm turrets, which could also operate independently, although with significant limitations.

Anti-ship and anti-aircraft barrage fire by the three starboard and three port 120mm turrets of the secondary armament was directed by two SDT, equipped with a 3-metre base rangefinder and with an APG, placed on the sides of the bridge tower. The associated fire control directors, of the Galileo RM 2 type, were co-located with a 5-metre rangefinder in the rear of the two medium-calibre turrets that, if needed, could also function as secondary SDT.

Two small traversing directors equipped with 1.5-metre stereoscopic rangefinders were located on each side of the wings of the navigating bridge, using calculators to direct daylight anti-aircraft fire by the 100/47 guns and night-time firing by the 120mm guns, supported by illuminating fire by two of the 100mm mountings.

Maximum ammunition issue, per barrel, called for 80 complete rounds for the 320mm guns, 200 for the 120mm, 400 for the 100mm, 1500 for the 37mm and 2400 for the 20mm.

MODERNISED 'CONTE DI CAVOUR' CLASS BATTLESHIPS

Conte di Cavour

Reconstruction/modernisation: Cantieri Riuniti dell'Adriatico (CRDA) c/o 'San Marco' yards of Trieste
Start of work: late October 1933
Completion of work and return to the Regia Marina: 1 June 1937
Sinking by British torpedo-bombers at Taranto: 11 November 1940
Recovery: start of work in December 1940; refloated in July 1941
Transfer under its own power to reach CRDA Trieste; December 1941
Beginning of refit and modernisation: early months of 1942
Continuation of work at a slow pace until suspension in June 1943
9 September 1943: ship abandoned, as incomplete, and capture the following day by the Germans, who later began progressive dismantling.
Sinking: 23–24 February 1945 at Trieste by capsizing following damage by aerial bombing
Stricken: 27 February 1947
Recovery: 29 March 1952, raised in upturned position
Demolition: 1952–1953 in the Bay of Muggia in Trieste without having been righted

Giulio Cesare

Reconstruction/modernisation: Cantieri del Tirreno, Genoa
Start of work: 1 October 1933
Completion of work and return to the Regia Marina: 1 October 1937
Stricken: 15 December 1948; designated as *Z 11* for consignment to the Soviet Union in compliance with the February 1947 peace treaty
Delivery: 6 February 1949 at Valona; renamed *Novorossiysk* in the Soviet Navy
Sinking: 29 October 1955, capsizing in the port of Sebastopol (Crimea) following explosion of an old German bottom mine from the Second World War
Recovery: raised in 1956 in upturned position
Demolition: after 1956 at Sebastopol

Bridge tower and forward main gun turrets of the *Conte di Cavour* in summer 1940.

'CONTE DI CAVOUR' CLASS BATTLESHIPS

Principal technical characteristics upon re-entry in service following reconstruction[1]

		Conte di Cavour	Giulio Cesare
Displacement (t):	standard (st)	26,176	26,140
	at normal load (cn)	27,726	28,455
	at full load (pc)	29,032	29,100
Dimensions (m):			
	Length overall	186.9	
	Length between perpendiculars:	168.9	
	Breadth overall:	28.02	
	Maximum draught at full load:	10.4	

Powerplant:
8 Yarrow type water tube boilers
2 groups of Belluzzo type geared turbines on 2 shafts: 2 three-bladed propellers, diameter 4.8 metres
Maximum designed total output: 75,000 shaft horsepower; during trials more than 90,000 shp

Speed (knots): maximum 27 at normal loading (trials 28, at 238 revolutions per minute)

Range (miles at knots): 6300/12; 4320/20 with 2765 tons oil and 440 tons reserve water for boilers

Protection (mm): maximum vertical at waterline 250; maximum total horizontal 135; main gun turrets 280; main gun barbettes 290; medium calibre turrets 120; maximum conning tower 260; underwater 'absorbing cylinders' Pugliese system

Armament (mm):
10–320/44 guns (in 2 triple turrets and 2 twin)
12–120/50 guns (in 6 twin turrets)
8–100/47 guns (in 4 twin mounts)
12–37/54 rapid-fire guns (in 6 twin mounts)
12–13.2mm heavy machine guns (in 6 twin mounts) [1937–1940]

Later modifications:
12–20/65 rapid-fire guns (in 6 twin mounts) [1940]
16–20/65 rapid-fire guns (in 8 twin mounts) [*Cesare*, 1941–1944]

Complement[2]: 1260 comprising 60 officers and 1200 petty officers and ratings

[1] In the absence of significant differences between the ships of the same class the mean values are given.
[2] Excluding staff of flag officers.

Purely by way of example, values shown are for *mean tonnage* (volume of internal spaces), *gross* (total) and *net* (subtracting spaces used exclusively for the ships' combat employment) expressed in tonnes of tonnage (1 tonne = 2.3 cubic metres) and valid for all of the ships of the two classes: 13,613 and 7782.5. These values – calculated according to specific national parameters for warships and differing from the classic values for merchant vessels – were used to determine agreements for ports (outside of naval bases), towage and canal transits (Suez, etc).

Miscellaneous equipment carried included self-defence gear against moored mines, consisting of four type 'C' paravanes, with several series of cutters along a steel cable that was deployed from a length of chain fitted between the extreme end of the forecastle (stem-head) and the bottom of the stem post (fore-foot). There were also oil-burning fog generating machines of which 4 + 4 were situated in the two funnels and two on the hull sides aft. Capacity of the loading derrick for handling the ship's boats was 20 tonnes.

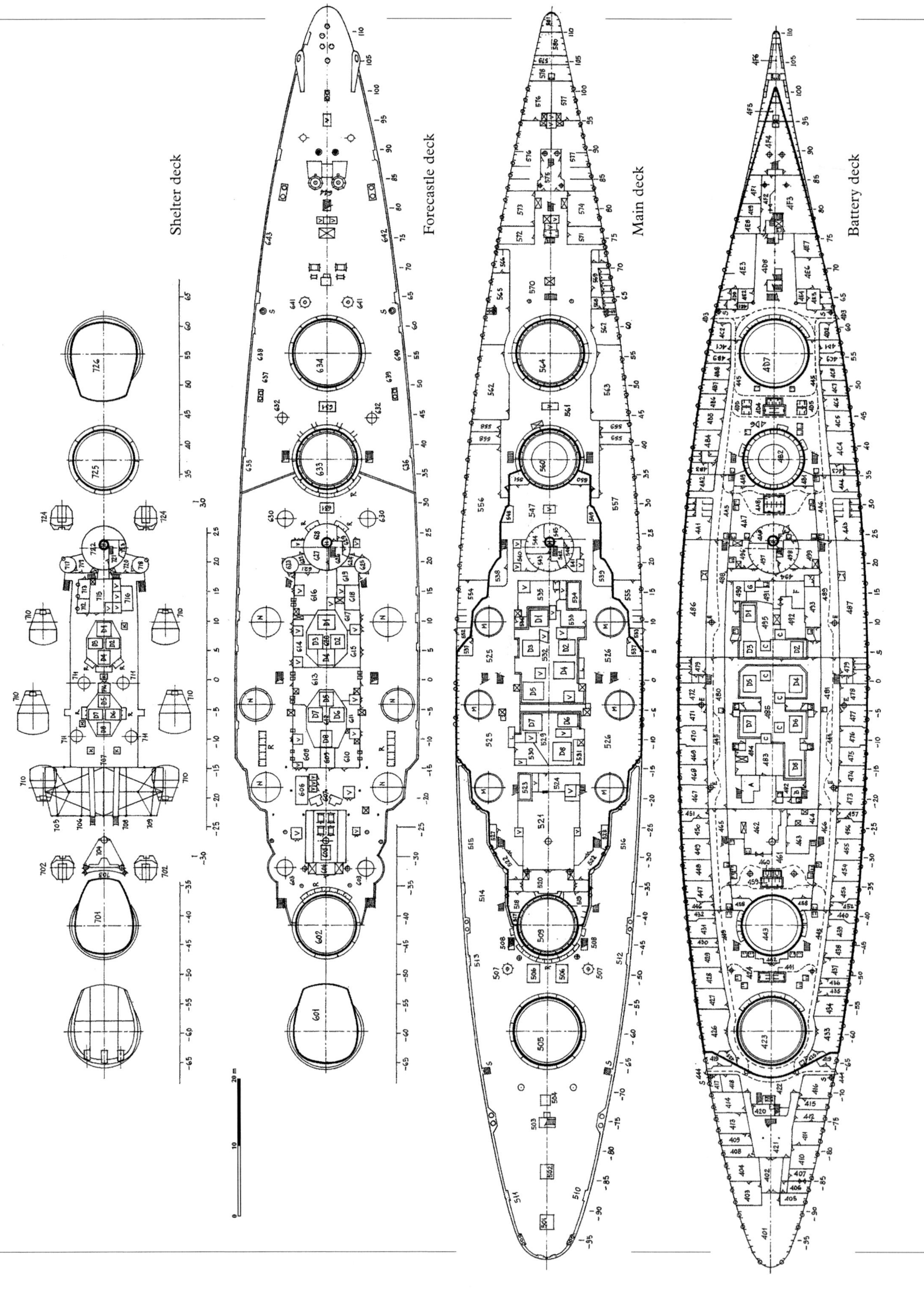

'Conte di Cavour' class. Plans of upper decks (Drawing by R Maggi)

Key overleaf

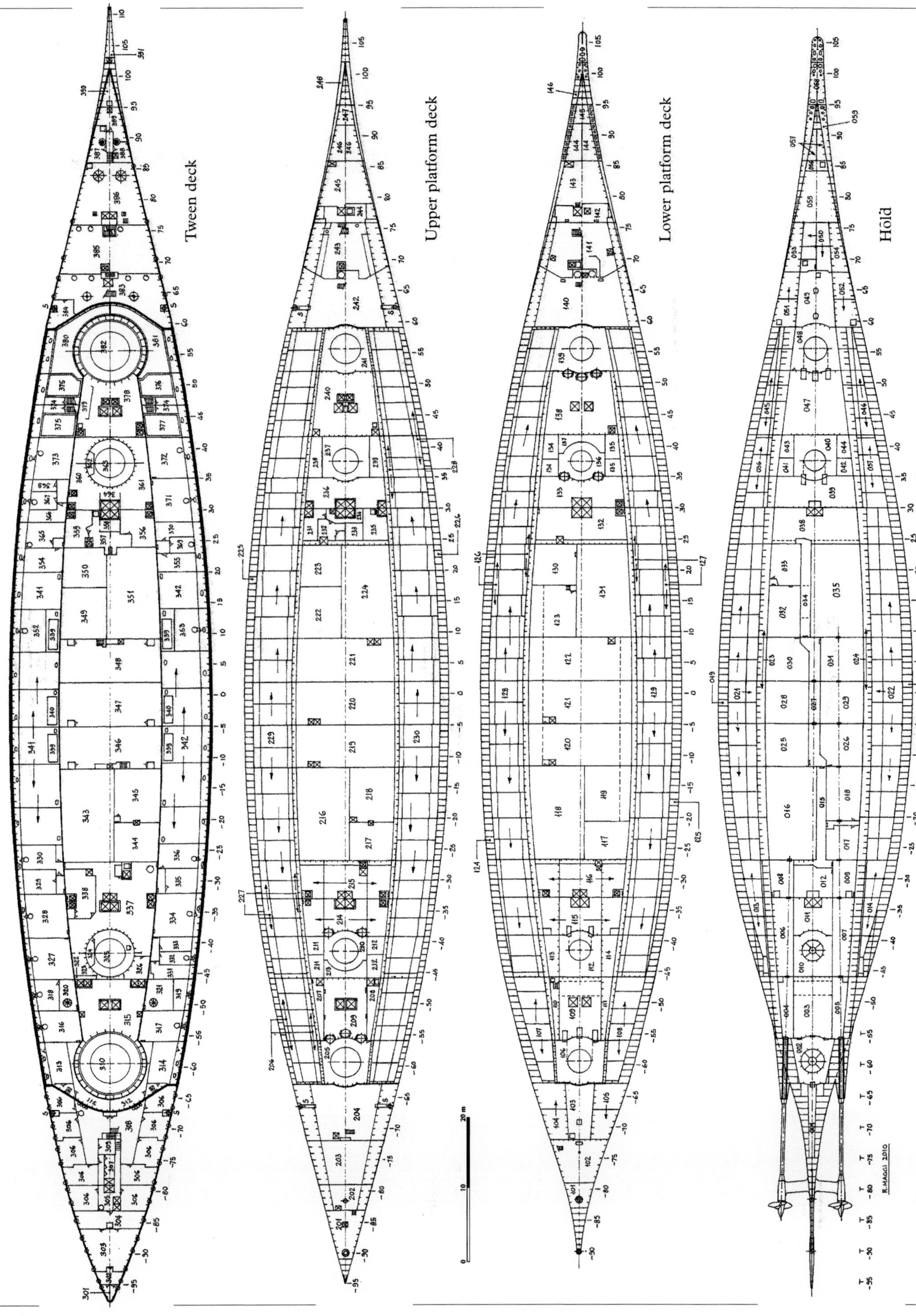

'Conte di Cavour' class. Plans of lower decks (Drawing by R Maggi)

Key overleaf

Key to drawings on pages 84-85 and 98-99.

HOLD
001 Afterpeak
002 No 4 320mm turret bedplate pivot
003 No 4 320mm shell room
004 Aft port shaft tunnel
005 Aft starboard shaft tunnel
006 Middle port shaft tunnel
007 Middle starboard shaft tunnel
008 Fore port shaft tunnel
009 Fore starboard shaft tunnel
010 No 3 320mm turret bedplate pivot
011 No 3 320mm shell room
012 Aft 120 & 100mm shell magazine
013 Aft port oil tanks
014 Aft starboard oil tanks
015 Aft passage
016 Aft engine room (port shaft)
017 Aft auxiliary machinery room
018 No 8 boiler bedplate
019 Port watertight compartments
020 Starboard watertight compartments
021 Middle port oil tanks
022 Middle starboard oil tanks
023 Port cofferdams
024 Starboard cofferdams
025 No 7 boiler bedplate
026 No 6 boiler bedplate
027 Middle passage
028 No 5 boiler bedplate
029 No 4 boiler bedplate
030 No 3 boiler bedplate
031 No 2 boiler bedplate
032 No 1 boiler bedplate
033 Fore auxiliary machinery room
034 Fore passage
035 Fore engine room (starboard shaft)
036 Fore port oil tanks
037 Fore starboard oil tanks
038 Aft No 2 320mm shell room
039 Fore No 2 320mm shell room
040 No 2 320mm shell handling room
041 Fuse magazine
042 Primer magazine
043 Gun powder magazine
044 MG shell magazine
045 Port fresh water compartment
046 Starboard fresh water compartment
047 No 1 320mm shell room
048 No 1 320mm shell handling room
049 Fore pump station
049b Bilge
050 Potable water compartments
051 Port miscellaneous stores
052 Starboard miscellaneous stores
053 Port pantry store
054 Starboard pantry store
055 Boatswain store
056 Log room
057 Chain locker flat
058 Trim control tanks
059 New stem cofferdams

PLATFORM DECK
101 Auxiliary rudder steering gear
102 Boatswain store
103 Aft pump station
104 Aft port miscellaneous stores
105 Aft starboard miscellaneous stores
106 No 4 320mm shell handling room
107 Port boiler feed water tanks
108 Starboard boiler feed water tanks
109 No 4 320mm shell room
110 Port shell handling motors room
111 Starboard shell handling motors room
112 No 3 320mm shell handling room
113 Fuse magazine
114 Primer & detonator magazine
115 No 3 320mm shell room
116 Aft 120 & 100mm shell magazine
117 Aft auxiliary machinery room
118 Aft engine room (port shaft)
119 No 8 boiler room
120 Nos 6 & 7 boiler room
121 Nos 4 & 5 boiler room
122 Nos 2 & 3 boiler room
123 No 1 boiler room
124 Port watertight compartments
125 Starboard watertight compartments
126 Port oil tanks in cylinder cofferdams
127 Starboard oil tanks in cylinder cofferdams
128 Port shock-absorbing cylinders
129 Starboard shock-absorbing cylinders
130 Fore auxiliary machinery room
131 Fore engine room (port shaft)
132 Aft No 2 320mm charge magazine
133 Fore No 2 320mm charge magazine
134 Port ammunition auxiliary magazine
135 Starboard ammunition auxiliary magazine
136 No 2 320mm charge handling room
137 Shell handling auxiliary motors room
138 No 1 320mm charge magazine
139 No 1 320mm charge handling room
140 Fore diesel generator room
141 Lower main pantry
142 Pumps room
143 Wine store
144 Chain locker
145 Sea water cofferdam
146 New stem cofferdams

LOWER DECK
201 Steering gear compartment
202 Main rudder steering gear
203 Steering electric motors
203b Available space
204 Aft diesel generator room
204b Available space
205 No 4 320mm charge handling room
206 Boiler feed water tanks
207 Port charge handling motors room
208 Starboard charge handling motors room
209 No 4 320mm charge magazine
210 No 3 320mm charge handling room
211 Port ammunition auxiliary magazine
212 Starboard ammunition aúxiliary magazine
213 Shell handling auxiliary motors room
214 No 3 320mm charge magazine
215 Aft 120 & 100mm shell magazine
216 Aft engine room (port shaft)
217 Aft turbo-generator room
218 No 8 boiler room
219 Nos 6 & 7 boiler room
220 Nos 4 & 5 boiler room
221 Nos 2 & 3 boiler room
222 No 1 boiler room
223 Fore turbo-generator room
224 Fore engine room (starboard shaft)
225 Port watertight compartments
226 Starboard watertight compartments
227 Starboard oil tanks in cylinder cofferdams
228 Port oil tanks in cylinder cofferdams
229 Port shock-absorbing cylinders
230 Starboard shock-absorbing cylinders
231 Telephone battery room
232 Cypher room
233 Gyrocompass room
234 Passageway lobby
235 Generator room
236 No 2 320mm charge magazine
237 No 2 320mm charge handling room
238 Port ammunition auxiliary magazine
239 Starboard ammunition auxiliary magazine
240 No 1 320mm charge magazine
241 No 1 320mm charge handling room
242 Fore diesel generator room
243 Upper main pantry
244 Pump room
245 Wine store
246 Chain locker
246b Electric rotors store

247 Sea water cofferdam
248 New stem cofferdams
249 Forepeak
250 Port cylinder cofferdams
251 Starboard cylinder cofferdams
S Diesel generator exhaust

MIDDLE DECK
301 Showers
302 Lavatories
303 W&E ensigns & lieutenants j.g. quarters
303b W&E ensigns & lieutenants j.g. baggage store
304 W&E ensigns & lieutenants j.g. wardroom
305 Passageway
306 Non-commissioned officers twin cabins
307 Non-commissioned officers showers
308 Crew space No 1
309 Captain's archive
310 No 4 320mm turret transfer room
311 Port officers' baggage store
312 Starboard officers' baggage store
313 Port towing cables store
314 Starboard towing cables store
315 Crew space No 2
316 First gunner's store
317 Clothing store
318 Gunner's mate store
319 Closet
320 Port warping windlass manoeuvring room
321 Starboard warping windlass manoeuvring room
322 Electric batteries
323 W/T stations store
324 Turret motors room
325 No 3 320mm turret shell hoist
326 Gyrocompass room
327 Signal officer store
328 Aft engineer store
329 Torpedo officer store (available)
330 Second electrical engineer store
331 Officer's wine store
332 Officer's pantry store
333 Admiral's wine and pantry store
334 First electrical engineer store
335 Crew co-op store
336 Coxswains' store
337 No 4 refrigeration machinery compartment
338 W/T receiving station
339 Trim balance oil tanks
340 Trim balance water tanks
341 Port sea water cofferdams
342 Starboard sea water cofferdams
343 Aft engine room (port shaft)
344 Aft turbo-generator room
345 No 8 boiler room
346 Nos 6 & 7 boiler room
347 Nos 4 & 5 boiler room
348 Nos 2 & 3 boiler room
349 No 1 boiler room
350 Fore turbo-generator room
351 Fore engine room (starboard shaft)
352 Port baggage room
353 Starboard baggage room
354 Oakum store
355 W/T equipment store
356 Gunnery fire control room
357 Dispatching control room
358 Passageway
359 Air cooling machinery room
360 No 3 refrigeration machinery compartment
361 No 2 refrigeration machinery compartment
362 Turret motors room
363 No 2 320mm turret shell hoist
364 Evaporators
365 Bed linen store
366 Warrant officers' mess store
367 Crew store room
368 Infirmary store
369 Assistant's store
370 Available store
371 Fore gunners 'store
372 Fore engineers' store
373 Main clothing store
374 Passage to refrigerator rooms
375 Meat refrigerator rooms
376 Vegetables refrigerator rooms
377 Officers' store rooms
378 No 1 refrigeration machinery compartment
379 Ice machines
380 Flour store
381 Biscuit store
382 No 1 320mm turret transfer room
383 Warping windlass manoeuvring room
384 Frequency converters
385 Crew space No 3
386 Capstan manoeuvring room
387 Typography
388 Confinement cell
389 Prison
390 Boatswain's store
391 New stem cofferdams
S Diesel generator exhaust

MAIN DECK
401 Meeting room
402 Admiral's lobby
403 Admiral's stateroom
404 Admiral's cabin
405 Admiral's closet
406 Admiral's secretariat
407 Flag Staff secretariat
408 Admiral's bathroom
409 Captain's bathroom
410 Chief of Staff's stateroom
411 Chief of Staff's cabin
412 Chief of Staff's bathroom
413 Captain's cabin
414 Captain's stateroom
415 Chief of Staff adjutant's bathroom
416 Chief of Staff adjutant's cabin
417 Officers' bathroom
418 Officers' showers
419 Officers' lavatory
420 Flag Staff secretariat
421 Officers' lobby
422 Lobby
423 No 4 320mm turret loading room
424 Crew space v 4
425 Anti-gas safety lobby
426 Officers' library
427 Flag lieutenant's cabin
428 Navigating officer's cabin
429 Staff officer's cabin
430 Staff officer's bathroom
431 Staff officer's cabin
432 Staff officer's bathroom
433 Staff officers' wardroom
434 Chief engineer's cabin
435 Chief engineer's bathroom
436 Executive officer's bathroom
437 Executive officer's cabin
438 Executive officer's stateroom
439 1st gunnery officer's cabin
440 1st gunnery officer's bathroom
441 Ammunition loading hatches to No 4 magazines
442 Admiral's closet
443 No 3 320mm turret transfer room
444 Aft ammunition loading scuttle
445 Ammunition handling rails
446 Staff officer's bathroom
447 Staff officer's cabin
448 Ship's officer's cabin
449 2nd gunnery officer's cabin
450 Staff officer's cabin
451 Staff officer's bathroom
452 1st medical officer's bathroom
453 1st medical officer's cabin
454 Personnel officer's cabin
455 3rd gunnery officer's cabin
456 1st paymaster's cabin
457 1st paymaster's bathroom
458 Flag Staff's secretariats
459 Ammunition loading hatches to No 3 magazine
460 Ammunition loading hatches to medium and small calibre magazines
461 Crew space No 5
462 Shipwright's workshop
463 Gunnery workshop
464 Electrical workshop
465 Port aft officer's passageway

466 Starboard aft officer's passageway
467 W/T officer's cabin
468 Lieutenant's cabin
469 Guest officer's cabin
470 2nd paymaster's cabin
471 Engineer lieutenant commander's cabin
472 Engineer lieutenant commander's cabin
473 Gunnery subordinate officer's cabin
474 Gunnery subordinate officer's cabin
475 Gunnery lieutenant commander's cabin
476 2nd medical officer's cabin
477 Engineer lieutenant commander's cabin
478 Engineer lieutenant commander's cabin
479 Officers' bathrooms & lavatories
480 Port fore officer's aisle
481 Starboard fore officer's aisle
482 Crew showers
483 Crew showers
484 Stewards' showers
485 Nos 5-6-7-8 boiler covers
486 Warrant officers' quarters
487 Warrant officers' quarters
488 Port aft warrant officer's aisle
489 Starboard aft warrant officer's aisle
490 Cloak room
491 Permanganate showers
492 Hot showers
493 Dressing room
494 Passageway
495 Nos 1-2-3-4 boiler covers
496 Electrical service secretariat & archive
497 Powerplant control room
498 Powerplant archive
499 Ship's secretariat
4A0 Powerplant secretariat
4A1 Port warrant officers' showers & lavatories
4A2 Quartermaster's secretariat
4A3 Starboard warrant officers' showers & lavatories
4A4 Daily items distribution secretariat
4A5 Port fore warrant officers' aisle
4A6 Starboard fore warrant officers' aisle
4A7 Crew space No 6
4A8 Ammunition loading hatches to No 2 magazine
4A9 Paymaster's secretariat
4B1 Personnel officer's secretariat
4B2 No 2 320mm turret shell hoist
4B3 Clerks' lavatories & showers
4B4 Warrant officers' twin cabin
4B5 Accountant officers' twin cabin
4B6 1st gunnery WO cabin
4B7 1st adjutant WO cabin
4B8 1st signal WO cabin
4B9 1st W/T WO cabin
4C1 1st engineering assistant WO cabin
4C2 1st infirmary WO cabin
4C3 Civilian guests' lavatories
4C4 Civilian guests' quarters
4C5 Warrant officers' double cabin
4C6 1st electrical service WO cabin
4C7 1st mechanic WO cabin
4C8 1st galley WO cabin
4C9 1st shipwright WO cabin
4D1 1st SQT WO cabin
4D2 1st boatswain WO cabin
4D3 Fore ammunition loading scuttle
4D4 Ammunition loading hatches to No 1 magazine
4D5 Food store access hatches
4D6 Crew space No 7
4D7 No 1 320mm turret transfer room
4D8 Main underdeck access hatch
4D9 Sick-bay lobby & WC
4E1 Laundry store
4E2 Pharmacy
4E3 Crew sick-bay
4E4 Sick-bay linen store
4E5 Disinfection room
4E6 Isolation hospital
4E7 Surgery
4E8 Dental surgery
4E9 Venereal disease prevention treatment room
4F1 Shipwright workshop
4F2 Lobby
4F3 Laundry store
4F4 Crew wash room
4F5 Old boatswain store
4F6 New boatswain store
A Aft engine room air intake
B Aft turbo-generator air intake
C Boiler room air intake
Dx No 'x' boiler funnel uptake
E 120mm mount base
F Fore engine room air intake
G Fore turbo-generator air intake
H Protected communication tube
S Diesel generator exhaust

UPPER DECK
501 Meeting room skylight
502 Admiral's quarters skylight
503 Officers' quarters hatch
504 Staff officers' quarters ventilation skylight
505 No 4 320mm turret loading room
506 Crew spaces ventilation skylight
507 Aft warping windlass
508 Crew spaces hatch
509 No 3 320mm turret transfer room
510 8m oared launch stowage
511 9m whaler stowage
512 8m motor launch stowage
513 8m motor launch stowage
514 7m whaler stowage
515 10m motorboat stowage
516 10m motorboat stowage
517 Closet
518 Wardrobe
519 WC
520 Officers' wardroom lobby
521 Officers' wardroom
522 Lobby
523 Aft engine room cover
524 Officers' galley and pantry
525 Crew space No 8
526 Crew space No 9
527 Engineering department secretariat
528 Gunnery department secretariat
529 Nos 5-6-7-8 funnel uptakes
530 Crew showers
531 Automated telephone switching board
532 Nos 1-2-3-4 funnel uptakes
533 Crew showers
534 Fore engine room cover
535 Crew washplace
536 Storekeeper's closet
537 Crew WC
538 Crew pantry
539 Crew co-op shop
540 Tailor's workshop
541 Load controller's room
542 Bridge platforms staircase
543 Signal room
544 Frequency converters room
545 Gunnery technical secretariat
546 Bridge WC
547 Crew space No 10
548 Mess-tin store
549 Closet
550 WO & POs' barber shop
551 Crew secretariat
552 Port oil loading room
553 Starboard oil loading room
554 Port warrant officers' lavatories
555 Starboard warrant officers' lavatories
556 Port warrant officers' quarters
557 Starboard warrant officers' quarters
558 Port warrant officers' closets
559 Starboard warrant officers' closets
560 No 2 320mm turret shell hoist
561 Crew space No 11
562 Port warrant officers' pantry
563 Starboard warrant officers' pantry
564 No 1 320mm turret loading room
565 Engineer petty officers' quarters
566 Engineer petty officers' lavatories
567 Civilians' quarters
568 Civilians' WC
569 Petty officers' WC
570 Crew space No 12

571 Ironing room
572 Crew barber shop
573 Port crew washplace
574 Starboard crew washplace
575 Crew space lobby
576 Starboard crew WC
577 Port crew WC
578 Boatswain's store room
579 Pump room
580 Gasoline tanks room
581 Paint store
M 120mm mount – Loading room
Dx No 'x' boiler funnel uptake
V Fan
L Food heater
S Diesel generator exhaust
R Ammunition lockers

FORECASTLE
601 No 4 320mm turret – gunhouse
602 No 3 320mm turret – loading room
603 Aft 100mm mount bedplate
604 Fire extinguishers store
605 Officers' wardroom skylight
606 Aft machine room skylight
607 Derrick winches
608 Warrant officers' galley
609 Sick-bay galley
610 Officers' galley
611 Admiral's galley
612 Aft funnel smoke ducts
613 Crew's galley
614 Cafeteria
615 Smelting furnace
616 Bakery
617 Forge
618 Fore machine room skylight
619 Battery charge room
620 Fore funnel smoke ducts
621 Flour store
622 Port bridge pump room
623 Closet
624 Starboard bridge pumps room
625 Machine signal repeater
626 Bridge platforms staircase
627 Captain's day cabin
628 Admiral's day cabin
629 Bridge WC
630 Fore 100mm mounts bedplate
631 Crew spaces skylight
632 37mm machine gun bedplate
633 No 2 320mm turret transfer room
634 No 1 320mm turret loading room
635 7m motorboat stowage
636 7m motorboat stowage
637 3.5m raft stowage
638 4.5m launch stowage
639 3.5m raft stowage
640 4.5m launch stowage
641 Fore warping windlasses
642 7.5m whaler stowage
643 7m dinghy stowage
644 Capstans
Dx No 'x' boiler funnel uptake
V Fan
N 120mm mount barbette
S Diesel generator exhaust
R Ammunition lockers

DECKHOUSE
701 No 2 320mm turret – gunhouse
702 Aft 100mm mounts
703 Platform to access No 2 320mm turret
704 Lifesaver platform
705 12.25m motor pinnace stowage
706 13m motor launch stowage
707 12.25m motor pinnace stowage
708 13m motor launch stowage
709 12.25m motor pinnace stowage
710 120mm mounts
711 37mm machine gun tubs bedplate
712 Seamen's secretariat
713 Flag command secretariat
714 Machine gun spare parts store
715 Miscellaneous store
716 Fore machine room skylight
717 Paint store
718 Foam extinguishers store
719 Port potable water refrigerator room
720 Starboard potable water refrigerator room
721 Bridge platforms staircase
722 Main W/T station room
723 Bridge WC
724 Fore 100mm mounts
725 No 2 320mm turret – loading room
726 No 1 320mm turret – gunhouse
V Fan
Dx No 'x' boiler funnel uptake
R Ammunition lockers
K Galley exhaust

PLATFORMS
801 Chart room
802 Bridge platforms staircase
803 Director bedplate
804 Lookout station
805 3m director
806 Cypher room
807 Communication control room
808 Armoured bridge
809 Navigation bridge
810 Armoured admiral's bridge
811 Admiral's navigation bridge
812 Searchlight storage room
813 7.5m main director
814 Aft signal station
815 Unarmoured W/T receiving station
816 W/T transmitting station
817 Searchlight storage room
818 Machine gun spare parts platform
B Magnetic compass
B1 Detecting compass
B2 Gyrocompass repeater
B3 Standard compass
K Vent
M1 20mm machine gun
P 120mm searchlight
T Searchlight control device
R Ammunition lockers
G Sonar

Chapter 7

CAREERS OF THE 'CONTE DI CAVOUR' CLASS BETWEEN 1937 AND 1940

Once the modernisation work had been completed, *Conte di Cavour* and *Giulio Cesare* were commissioned respectively on 1 June and 12 August 1937, constituting the Battleship Division, soon renamed the 5th Division. They then began to carry out regular training activities. This was regulated by annual exercise programmes fixed by the Navy Staff and split into two or more periods. This continued during the war, especially for battleships and cruisers, but progressively declined for destroyer squadrons because of wartime requirements and the shortage of fuel, as well as their intense employment and the resulting attrition, as these ships were increasingly used for convoy protection.

1937/1938 training year

Artillery and gunnery

The conduct of exercises and main gun firing drill, all carried out with practice rounds, is summarised in the tables below.

Exercises were held in series (each consisting of salvoes of 3 to 5 rounds) with different modes of fire and varied rates.

These were the first exercises executed with the 320/44 guns and the results were not reassuring. Especially worrisome were the high dispersion rates of the series I charge, far above the theoretical dispersion, which already exceeded the maximum limits of 'dispersion' (twice that of the arithmetical median of the impact of the rounds with respect to the centre of the salvo) considered acceptable according to the Regia Marina parameters at the time for a good naval gun (1 per cent of the distance). With respect to the composition of the salvos, median spreads for three rounds were 337 metres, for four rounds 783 metres and for five rounds 658 metres. The causes were variously attributed to aiming errors, imperfect loading of the projectiles, unstable platforms or deformation of the flexible structures due to the effects of firing, abnormal charge combustion, disturbance of the trajectories due to blast effect, and non-optimal behaviour of the projectile along its trajectory.

After further analysis the first and last reasons were discarded, either because the aiming recorders always showed median errors below a thousandth, or because the median difference remained high. In addition, many problems emerged with respect to the mountings and the guns, to which many of the failed rounds (misfires or lost) were imputed, especially on the *Cavour*. In themselves they did not seem very serious, but taken together they revealed an intrinsic weakness of the gun systems, especially those of OTO manufacture. Loading times were also excessive (35 seconds for the *Cavour* and 32 seconds for the *Cesare*, compared to the 28–30 seconds projected) and there were anomalies in the post-recoil return to battery of the various guns, especially on the *Cesare*. All of this led to performing yet more cycles

SUMMARY OF FIRING RESULTS OF THE 320/44 GUNS DURING TRAINING YEAR 1937/1938

Ship	*Cesare*	*Cesare*	*Cavour*	*Cesare*	*Cavour*	*Cesare*	*Cavour*	*Cesare*	*Cavour*	*Cesare*	*Cavour*	*Cavour*
Date of series[1]	02.02	04.08	04.08	...12	02.03	02.03	08.06	15.03	28.06	14.06	11.03	08.06
Charge	I	I	I	III	III	III	III	III	III	III	III	III
Median range (m)	21,720	16,970	18,935	14,400	14,625	16,950	14,425	14,750	14,070	14,440	13,885	14,890
Salvos	7	6	7	11	10	10	10	11	11	12	8	8
Bracketing salvos[2]	3	3	4	5	1	0	4	4	5	6	3	3
Effective salvos	4	2	0	2	1	4	5	4	7	6	1	5
Effective median longitudinal spread(m)[3]	540	774	611	191	309	141	228	294	231	198	265	200
Theoretical median longitudinal spread (m)[4]	353	292	264	170	177	213	184	215	181	189	128	181
Rounds to be fired	30	30	30	50	50	50	60	60	70	70	45	45
Failed rounds	7	2	2	17	19	7	7	6	28	7	4	4

1 Carried out in 1938, except for the III charge series of the *Cesare* in December 1937.
2 Salvos falling within the dispersion limits laid down for gunnery exercises during the training year (1 per cent of distance) even if not straddling.
3 Distance measured on a line parallel to the line of fire between the shortest and longest rounds of the salvo.
4 Longitudinal spread calculated on the basis of firing tables.

AVERAGE FIRING RESULTS OF THE 120/50 GUNS DURING TRAINING YEARS 1937/1938

Date of firing series	14.07.1938	09.02.1938	19.021938	14.06/25.06.1938	25.06.1938
Series executed	4[1]	3	2	2	2
Charge (daytime)	I	III	III	III	III
Average distance (m)	12,793	5997	6880	5925	7375
Salvos	32	29	23	21	20
Bracketing salvos	21	11	7	3	13
Effective salvos[2]	18	8	8	5	9
Effective median longitudinal spread[3]	393	256	200	177	251
Theoretical median longitudinal spread[4]	198	112	112	95	111
Rounds to be fired	192	228	132	120	120
Failed rounds	2	35	4	10	16
Rounds on target	7	/	/	/	/

1 Against the target ship *San Marco*.
2 Salvos falling within the dispersion limits called for by firing exercises for the training year (1 per cent of the distance), even if not bracketing.
3 Distance measured in metres on a line parallel to the line of fire between the shortest and longest rounds of the salvo.
4 Longitudinal spread in metres calculated on the basis of firing tables.

of work to adjust and fine-tune the guns as well as the electric motors and machinery of the Ansaldo mountings, and in greater measure, the OTO equivalents.

With respect to the medium-calibre guns, the exercise results are briefly summarised below, without distinction as to ship.

The results of firing for the series I charge were considered good because of the low number of lost rounds, because the loading times met expectations and because of the good percentage of rounds on target (*San Marco*). It appeared less satisfactory if confined to the eighteen effective salvos, because of their excessive spread due to indiscriminate use of old and new types of 120mm projectiles; salvo spread diminished markedly by using only armour-piercing projectiles, and approached the theoretical limits for both ships. There were also five night-time firings at charge III and one at I with a satisfactory outcome of the illuminating rounds and searchlights, with respect to both range and for the precision of handling.

The Galileo directors, although functioning well, turned out to have several shortcomings.

Both battleships also carried out a series of ten salvos each in daylight with the 100/47 guns at charge I at an initial range of 10,500 metres with such mediocre results because of failure in transmission of the firing data that they were neither reported not taken into consideration.

Hull and powerplant

From 12 November to 16 December 1937, the *Cesare* underwent work in the Taranto naval dockyard that had not been done at the Cantieri del Tirreno (CdT) and which also included elimination of steam leaks from the high-pressure turbines. Also at Taranto, from 16 December 1937 to 28 January 1938 it was the turn of the *Cavour*, where final work was done on the hull as well as fitting-out and work on the powerplant, opening up the HP turbines that were affected by steam leaks. Both of the propeller shafts were discovered to be suffering significant erosion of the white-metal anti-friction bearings of the brackets and stern tube glands. On 16 February, during a transfer from Taranto to Messina, the two ships carried out a full-power speed trial lasting two hours thirty minutes between Punta Alice and Punta Stilo with a force 4 wind on the port bow with the following results:

PRINCIPAL TRIALS FIGURES

	Conte di Cavour	*Giulio Cesare*
Displacement (t)	27,978	28,450
Average speed (knots)	28.04	27.90
Propeller revolutions (rpm)	239.385	241.950
Power at torque meter (shp/shaft)	100,156	110,000 approx
Fuel consumption (tonnes/hour)	38.700	37.500
Fuel consumption (kg/shp/hour)	0.393	0.340

The results achieved proved to be very flattering, except for a small problem with the reduction gearing of the forward power unit on the *Cesare*. There was no steam loss from the HP turbines. The *Cesare* recorded vibration, but not at a worrying level and only in the area of No 3 turret.

1938/1939 training year

Artillery and gunnery

The main guns were not fired in the first period (1 October 1938–15 January 1939), but the 320mm mountings of both ships were the object of remedial work by both of the building firms. Only the *Cesare* carried out a series of eight 120mm daylight salvos and a night-time series of six, from which was noted a certain slowness in loading and the need to replace the calculators with others that functioned more quickly and reliably.

During the second period (16 January–30 September 1939) *Cavour* and *Cesare* conducted a total of fifteen main gun firing series at charges I, II and III with good results in observing the fall of shot. At about two years from entry into service the dispersion of salvos of both ships continued to be worrisome, as is shown in the statistic below of the series I charge. Nor did the

SUMMARY OF I CHARGE SERIES OF THE 320/44 GUNS OF THE *CAVOUR* AND THE *CESARE* DURING TRAINING YEARS 1937/1938 AND 1938/1939

Rounds comprising the salvo	3	3	4	4	5	5
Ship	*Cavour*	*Cesare*	*Cavour*	*Cesare*	*Cavour*	*Cesare*
Salvos	6	4	10	6	6	9
Median distance centre of impact (metres)	21,850	21,320	21,890	20,680	21,040	19,650
Median effective longitudinal spread (metres)[1]	347	567	684	555	843	650
Theoretical effective longitudinal spread (metres)[2]	305	295	370	345	399	413

1 Distance measured on a line parallel to the line of fire between the shortest and longest rounds of the salvo.
2 Longitudinal spread calculated on the basis of firing tables.

functioning of the main gun mountings show any improvement. After fine-tuning the Ansaldo 320mm guns, in addition to old and new problems, they suffered a worsening of irregularities in the rapid run-out return of the guns, while the intrinsic weakness of the OTO mountings was confirmed.

Hull and powerplant

From 26 October to 26 December 1938 the *Cavour* underwent a cycle of major works in drydock at the Taranto naval yard. This work mainly involved the powerplant for final warranty inspections and because of recurring steam leaks in the HP turbines, which were again opened up and reworked with the almost complete elimination of the losses. The fireproof brickwork of the boilers was also extensively repaired and adjustments were made to the gearing of the turbine reduction gears.

Fresh erosion of the white-metal bearings of the propeller shaft brackets was discovered, along with significant corrosion along the shafts themselves, especially inside the stern tubes. Should the problem resurface, the possibility was examined of installing two replacements that had been manufactured as a precautionary measure the previous August. Two remote-controlled smoke generators were also placed aft on the quarterdeck.

From 28 December 1938 until 28 February 1939, it was *Cesare*'s turn in drydock at Taranto. In this case also the most pressing work involved the powerplant – so serious that the HP turbines had to be taken out and sent to the CdT in Genoa for opening up and repairs because of the recurrence of steam leaks. Other relevant work involved the boiler brickwork, replacement of several ventilating systems, attention to the turbine reduction gears because of erosion, as well as repairs to the triple bottom of the hull around No 3 main gun turret. The same phenomena that had plagued the *Cavour* with respect to the propeller shafts and their seals were discovered, but to a lesser extent, and adjustments were accordingly made. Finally, the shelter deck was fitted with a radiotelegraph station and, as on her sister, two remotely controlled smoke generating systems were installed aft on the

The battleship *Conte di Cavour* in 1938.

quarterdeck. From 22 July to 11 August 1939 the *Cesare* continued to undergo a brief cycle of work at Ansaldo in Genoa where, among other things, several improvements were made to the powerplant's feed-water and lubrication circuits.

Both of the battleships suffered leaks of seawater through the armour plate seams, the underlying wood backing and the internal plating of the old hull, especially in the area of the juncture between the new and the original bow. In twenty-five days at the end of 1939, work to seal the bow and the armoured belt area were carried out on the *Cavour* with positive results. The same work on the *Cesare* continued to be postponed, as the problem appeared tolerable, even though it led to flooding of inaccessible spaces (the blind cells) between the old and new bow by 50–60 tons of water, which affected the ship's longitudinal trim, and the maintenance of structures and plates, which could not be reached. No repairs were ever carried out.

The 1939/1940 training year

Artillery and gunnery

During the first period the *Cavour* and *Cesare* each carried out three series at charge III and the fine-tuning of the 320/44 guns continued. The Ansaldo mountings continued to experience anomalies in the post-recoil return of the guns to battery position, although to a reduced degree, but it proved impossible to establish the cause. No trouble was noted in the OTO installations other than minor problems in No 1 turret. It was confirmed that those mountings had several shortcomings since first manufacture that it was hoped to eliminate progressively.

During the second period the two battleships each carried out two series with the main guns at charge II and two series at charge III. Dispersion, especially when firing at charge II, was always considerable, despite the fact that it was possible to exclude errors in the transmission of the aiming data. In compensation, mechanical trouble with the guns and mountings was almost totally eliminated. In the Ansaldo 320/44 guns the rapid return to battery was reduced to such a degree that it no longer caused concern and the mountings could now be said to have reached full working order: during the final series no rounds were lost and there was no trouble with the equipment. With respect to the OTO 320/44 guns, with the latest changes and adjustments the functioning of the systems saw a marked improvement that ensured the absence of any serious problems during firing; the few rounds that were lost in the final series were attributable to human error and any minor issues were immediately resolved during the course of firing.

During the same period two daylight series at charge III were carried out with the 120/50 guns, one of which was a simultaneous collective shoot along with the 320mm and anti-aircraft guns, and two series at charge III at night. The slowness of loading due to the rammers emphasised the need to replace them with a new impulse type that had been adopted for the 135/45 guns of the 'Capitani Romani' class cruisers and of the 'Duilios'. At high elevation the difficulty in extracting the cases also manifested itself, as they had to be removed by hand with a serious delay in the loading rate.

Hull and powerplant

During *Cesare*'s time in the graving dock in Taranto for bottom cleaning and painting (24 November–5 December 1939), corrosion was once again found in the propeller shafts, especially at the stern tubes, and the white metal of the port shaft had to be replaced. On the *Cavour*, which was in drydock in Taranto from 12 December 1939 until 4 January 1940, both of the propeller shafts and the propellers themselves had to be replaced. At the same time maintenance work was done on the hull to deal with corrosion to the plates near the fore-foot and amidships, as well as for small leaks in the armour plate seams and in the rudder riveting. The hull bottom and distorted double-bottom plating was also inspected following a grazing of the seabed on 14 April 1939, verifying they were watertight.

The May 1940 firing exercises

Some of the exercises described above were carried out under ministerial control, or for very specific purposes, differing from those normally established and verified by a special commission. Those conducted in May 1940 are worth noting as they provide a measure of the degree of effectiveness of the 320/44 guns just on the eve of the war.

Functioning of the OTO and Ansaldo 320/44 gun and mounting systems

On the *Cavour* the remedial work that had been carried out made the OTO version much more reliable, but not to the point of guaranteeing a fully trustworthy and prolonged functioning of the guns, as the intrinsic weak points could not be eliminated. At the time of fitting out the *Andrea Doria*, these problem areas, especially in the breech, the secondary elevator and the traverse and locking mechanisms were eliminated in a manner that appeared for the moment to be satisfactory. The Ansaldo mountings could also be said to have been equally free of the biggest problems to the recoil brake and elevation mechanism.

Results of the exercises under ministerial control

During the 6 May 1940 exercises, the rangefinders, fire control centre and aiming systems on the *Cavour* all performed very well. The 320/44 firing sequences were on target with the first salvo and were maintained for the entire series. Mean dispersion was, however, high, even after subtracting five abnormal rounds attributed, variously, to poor preparation of the charges, to the faulty behaviour of the projectiles (exercise rounds) along their trajectory, and to distortion of the barrels. Improper ramming of the projectile was excluded from the list of causes. On the *Cesare* the fire control centre and aiming systems functioned properly, but the rangefinders were short by 1000 metres, despite the fact that for the entire series the five rangefinders used all provided the same data. The series was well directed and executed, but the fire director's work was, as usual, compromised by the wide dispersion of the three-round salvos.

The salvo dispersion problem

In general, for all of the 320/44 and smaller guns mounted on surface vessels the dispersion experienced during the ministerial control exercises in 1940 were on average higher than those noted in 1939. One of the few exceptions was the performance of the 320/44 guns, which in 1940 suffered an average dispersion of 371 metres compared with the 385 metres in 1939. The dispersion problem was a major concern to the Navy Staff, which made it the subject of a specific examination by an ad hoc commission presided over by the Vice Chief of the Navy Staff, Admiral Odoardo Somigli, on 13 May 1940. The main causes were found to be aiming errors, and time-lags in the transmission of gun-aiming data to the fire control clocks according to the system referred to as counterindication. Three corrective actions were proposed as a potential resolution of this difficult issue:

- A return to the older manual system, in which the aimers in the towers 'followed the pointers' transmitted to the towers, aligning a pointer whose movements corresponded to the traverse and elevation of the guns; in this type of aiming, referred to as counterindication, human error was added to electromechanical error.
- Widespread adoption of more efficient aiming devices to achieve better performance and to enable proper training of the aiming personnel by daily, controlled 'cold' [dry fire] drills.
- Reduction of the degree of 'play' in the equipment used for the transmission of fire control data caused over time by use and wear.

It should be noted that, in the significant amount of documentation that the authors consulted from the late 1930s and from the war years, among the various factors called upon to explain the excessive salvo dispersion of Italian guns, there is no mention of variations in projectile and charge weights (for the charges, if anything, dissimilarities in combustion times were noted) attributed to excessive tolerances accepted in the ammunition supply, on which much attention was focused in post-war historiography. The same can be said for other presumed causes, such as excessive muzzle velocity or the 'drooping' of the guns, which were noticed on many occasions, but not with the same emphasis. This does not mean that the problem did not exist, as the Regia Marina hierarchy was aware of it and sought to remedy it, but in an absolute sense, it was not as serious as many would have liked it to be believed, especially if compared with the performance of other big guns such as the 330/50 and 380/45 of the French 'Dunkerque' and 'Richelieu' class battleships. That being said, during the 1939/1940 and 1940/1941 training years the Navy Staff's inspectorate for arms and ammunition arranged to collect statistical data on the performance of 381/50 and 90/50 naval guns drawn from the exercises. A small sample is presented in Appendix 2, where the 320/44 and 381/50 guns from the same companies are compared. It can easily be seen how dispersion and longitudinal spread of the first type were on average higher than those of the second type, but also that an improvement was recorded in the last year.

Naples, morning of 5 May 1938. The battleships *Conte di Cavour*, left, and *Giulio Cesare* moored near the San Vincenzo pier, being inspected by passengers aboard the transatlantic liner *Rex* that had been hired to transport guests to attend Review 'H'.

Career highlights of the 'Conte di Cavour' class up to the outbreak of war

Between commissioning and the earliest months of the war, the *Conte di Cavour* and *Giulio Cesare* were the Regia Marina's only operational battleships and as such were intensively employed, and deeply involved in the politico-military events of the latter part of the 1930s.

The Naples review in honour of Hitler (5 May 1938)

The 5 May 1938 naval review in the Gulf of Naples in honour of the Führer and Chancellor of the Reich, Adolf Hitler, from whose initial the designation 'H' was adopted, was the largest and certainly the most celebrated event of his second visit to Italy between 3 and 9 May 1938, held in return for Mussolini's visit to Germany in September 1937. The Duce intended this to exhibit with great pomp and ceremony Italy's military force and the stage of development it had reached, but without leading to any political consequences, least of all the military alliance that at the time was of most interest to Hitler.

The review was meticulously planned for more than a month, with substantial resources committed, and the 'Cavour' class was involved from 30 March. Unlike earlier reviews, it was characterised by the execution of exercises representing brief tactical and action scenarios, in addition to traditional parade formations, and by the participation of a large number of submarines proceeding on the surface and underwater. The phases were planned to follow one another in varied and uninterrupted forms, showcasing expertise in manoeuvring, such as the spectacular diving and surfacing in unison of a formation of no fewer than eighty-one submarines. In addition, the attendance of many passenger ships ensured the greatest participation by political, military and civilian representatives, by media organisations and by the populace (12,000 invitees, including tourists, in addition to the officials). The overall management of the review, or exercise as it was then called, was the responsibility of the Navy Chief of Staff and Undersecretary of State, Admiral Domenico Cavagnari, on board the *Cavour*. It is not possible to give a full account of so many other personalities, the most important of whom were embarked on the *Cavour*, while the rest were hosted aboard the *Cesare* and other ships; it should be recalled, however, that among the first was Admiral Erich Raeder, commander-in-chief of the Kriegsmarine. The ships involved included almost all of the modern ships in service and other older ships for secondary duties, as summarised in the table below.

There was a total of 2 battleships, 7 heavy cruisers, 11 light cruisers (among the modern ships only the *Raimondo Montecuccoli* was absent), 7 scouts, 18 destroyers, 24 torpedo boats and escorts, 6 old torpedo boats, 85 submarines, 6 support ships, one repair ship, 13 tankers (oil, gasoline and water), 15 tugboats, 1 vedette, 4 motorboats, 6 minesweeping tugs, 72 seaplanes in addition to 20 shipboard aircraft. These ships were joined by 14 passenger ships, among them the *Rex* (Italy's largest and fastest liner), divided into three groups, allowing the many and varied delegations, guests and tourists to follow the review from the sea.

In case of adverse conditions, an alternative programme had been planned, but, thanks to the good weather, on the night before 5 May it was decided to hold the review as planned.

The first movements began in the early hours of 5 May. Mussolini reached the port at 10:00, boarding the *Cavour* first, to

ORGANISATION FOR REVIEW 'H'

I Squadon: 5th, 1st, 8th Division, VII, VIII, IX Destroyer Squadriglias;
II Squadron: 3rd, 7th, 2nd, 4th Division, I Scout Flotilla, X Destroyer Squadriglia;
Torpedo Boat Flotilla (headquarters school): scout *da Recco*, IX, X, XI, XII torpedo boat flotillas;
I Flottiglia MAS, motor torpedo boat *Turr*, 4th, 5th, 8th, 9th, 10th, 11th MAS flotillas;
Submarine group, constituted for the purpose;
Logistic service ships;
Other ships: one antiquated torpedo boat, two school ships, two yachts, one target ship;
Security: two destroyers, VIII and IV torpedo boat flotillas (escorts), five antiquated torpedo boats;
Coastal security (in part by the Guardia di Finanza [Revenue Service]); one vedette, four motorboats, six minesweeping tugs;
Maritime air reconnaissance: 1st 2nd, 3rd, 4th groups

Aerial photo of the battleship *Conte di Cavour* followed by her sister-ship *Giulio Cesare* in the Gulf of Naples on 5 May 1938 for Review 'H'.

The *Conte di Cavour* photographed from a torpedo boat during Review 'H' in the Gulf of Naples on 5 May 1938

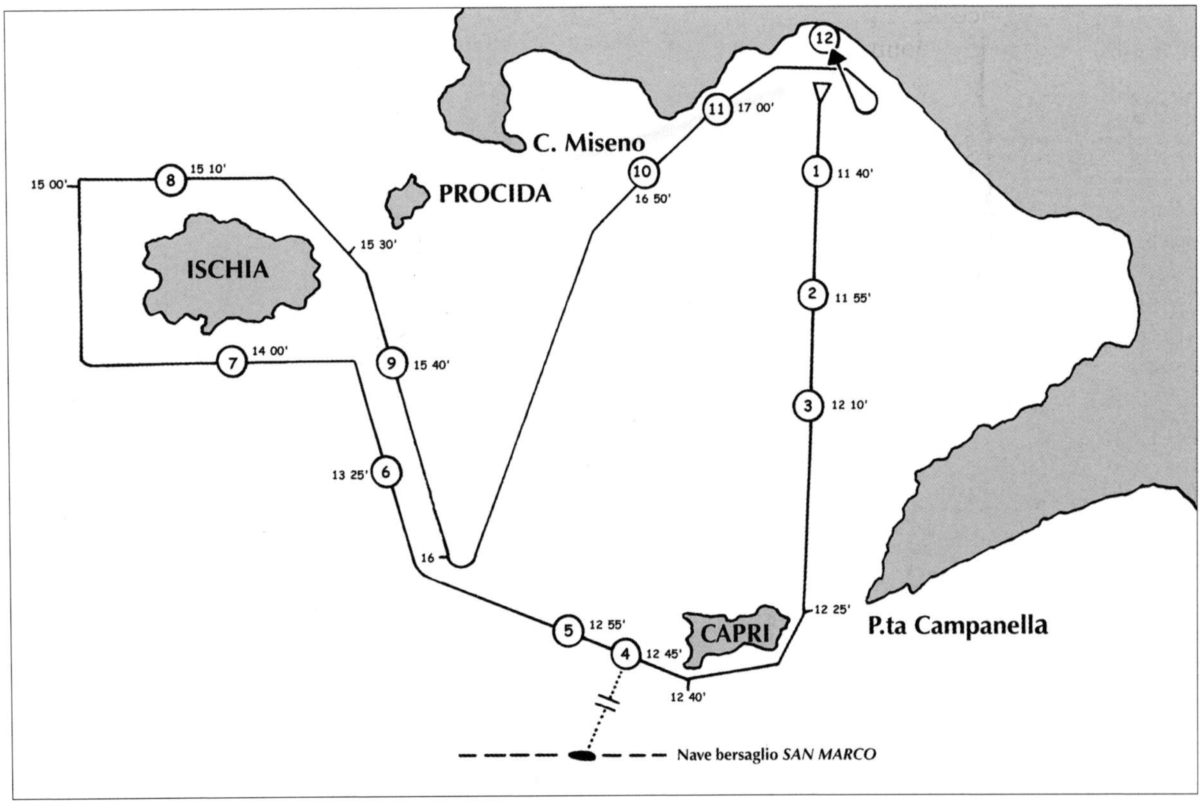

Naples, 5 May 1938. Sequence of Review 'H'. Movements keyed to those of the battleship *Conte di Cavour* aboard which were embarked the King, Hitler and Mussolini.

1 Evolutions of the 1st Squadron.
2 Simulated attack by three submarines.
3 Simulated torpedo boat attack.
4 Firing by heavy cruisers against the target ship *San Marco*.
5 Passing in review by 2nd Squadron.
6 Dive and surfacing in unison by the submarine squadron.
7 Crossing the formation by torpedo boat flotillas.
8 Simulated attacks by a MAS flotilla.
9 Passing in review by the submarine squadron.
10 Fly-past by seaplane squadrons.
11 Review of the two naval squadrons in the roadstead.
12 Return to port.

The battleship *Conte di Cavour* during Review 'H' in the Gulf of Naples, 5 May 1938.

receive the Führer, the King and Prince Umberto who, shortly before, had greeted Hitler at the Napoli-Mergellina railway station and had continued from there in a procession to the port through a huge crowd, much friendlier than had been the case in the preceding days in Rome.

As soon as Hitler and the King had boarded the *Cavour*, between 10:45 and 11:15 the I Squadron emerged from the western mouth of the port, with the 5th Division bringing up the rear. It is not possible to provide here a complete account of the sequence of events of the review (see the very brief summary graphic of the movements of the 5th Division at sea). This evolved in three phases: the first, morning period, culminating in attacks on the *Cavour* by three submerged submarines, in a firing exercise by a section of heavy cruisers and one of scouts against the radio-controlled target ship and by a dive in unison of eighty-one submarines; an afternoon phase, featuring the torpedo boat flotilla crossing the line of file of the two 'Cavours' and the high-speed mass attack by the MAS flotilla against the battleships; an evening phase consisted of light shows in port and in the roadstead.

Of all of the military displays that marked Hitler's visit to Italy, the naval review was certainly the most impressive and spectac-

Torpedo boat *Astore* passing by the stern of the *Conte di Cavour* during Review 'H'.

The battleship *Conte di Cavour* in the Gulf of Naples on 5 May 1938.

Aerial view of the midships of the battleship *Conte di Cavour* in May 1938.

ular. The Führer and his closest entourage were struck by the modernity of the ships and the perfect execution of the manoeuvres, which left a positive impression. Observers from the major navies also made complimentary comments. Major doubts were, however, expressed by the Kriegsmarine, which for quite some time had been following the development of the Italian Navy with an eye towards a possible alliance. Under the circumstances, the most serious German doubts concerned how well the manoeuvres related to actual operational situations. The review did not change its fundamental assessment, which was that although the Regia Marina appeared to be capable of exercising a diversionary effect with respect to the Marine Nationale, it was far from being able to achieve it compared with the Royal Navy. But these judgments did not take into account the propaganda and political aims that the heads of the navy were pushing for: to infuse a naval awareness in the regime and in the country and to nourish a favourable climate with respect to an armed force that consciously aspired to play a major role in military policy and national life.

Visit by the head of government and concentration of the fleet at Genoa (13–31 May 1938)

A visit by Mussolini to Genoa and nearby Ligurian localities had been planned even before Review 'H' had been held. For this occasion, the Duce wanted the entire fleet to take part, in order to demonstrate to the people of Liguria and to the Italians in Piedmont and Lombardy, the two regions that he considered to be the most continental, of the strength that Italy had reached at sea.

Concentrating the fleet in Genoa, by transferring two individual squadrons from Gaeta and from Naples, allowed an exercise during transit that was to be attended by Mussolini himself aboard the *Cavour*. The operational orders provided for participation by a substantial complex of forces, as shown in the table opposite.

Command of the exercise was assumed by Admiral Cavagnari, who hoisted his flag on the *Cavour* on 13 May at Gaeta. During the passage to Genoa, the programme called for night-time torpedo attacks with simulated torpedo launches and fire by major ships against the target ship *San Marco*. Mussolini embarked on the *Cavour* at 16:45 on 13 May and at 17:00 I Squadron left the anchorage at Gaeta, shortly thereafter to join with II Squadron coming from Naples. From 18:00 to 19:00 the two squadrons, with an anti-submarine escort of four Cant Z 501 seaplane sections of the 182nd Flotilla of Marina Napoli and the 85th Seaplane Group of Elmas, carried out complex manoeuvres. The night-time attacks saw the destroyers of I Flotilla engaged with ships completely blacked out. Night-time 120mm firing exercises by *Cavour* and *Cesare* against the *San Marco* followed. Once the exercises were over, the squadrons rejoined each other and sailed on towards Genoa. Off the Portofino promontory, the *Cavour*, followed by the *Cesare* and the VIII Destroyer Squadriglia (a squadriglia was an Italian echelon consisting of four to six minor ships), sailed along the coast as far as Genoa, where they moored at the Sanità quay at 09:15 and shortly afterwards Mussolini disembarked. It was originally planned that *Cavour* and *Cesare* would moor at the Zingari quay, the berth that was closest to the centre of the city, but it was realised that the minimum depth of 9.50 metres would not allow the docking of the two ships, which had a normal draught of 10.40 metres. Even the docking manoeuvre at the Sanità quay, which had a minimum depth of 11 metres, presented some problems.

The visit by the Duce to the Genoa region lasted until the evening of 16 May, when he returned to Rome by train. He gave it a decidedly maritime emphasis, marked not only by his visits to the port installations, to the shipyards and the Ansaldo works, but also, on the afternoon of 14 May, by inspecting the battleship *Littorio*, which was fitting out, and by the keel-laying ceremony of her sister-ship *Impero* at the Ansaldo yards of Genoa Sestri. The fleet laid over in Genoa until the end of the month to cope with the great influx of visitors, which was calculated at 650,000 people, of whom 220,000 had come from the rest of Liguria,

THE FLEET CONCENTRATED IN GENOA, MAY 1938

I Naval Squadron (from Gaeta)
5th Division: battleships *Cavour* (flagship of commander-in-chief I Squadron, Admiral Arturo Riccardi), *Cesare*;
1st Division: heavy cruisers *Fiume, Pola, Zara, Gorizia*;
8th Division: light cruisers *Abruzzi, Garibaldi*;
I Destroyer Flotilla: VII Destroyer Squadriglia: *Freccia, Dardo, Strale, Saetta*; VIII Destroyer Squadriglia: *Lampo, Baleno, Fulmine*, Folgore; IX Destroyer Squadriglia: *Alfieri, Gioberti, Oriani, Carducci.*

II Naval Squadron (from Naples)
3rd Division: heavy cruisers *Trieste* (flagship of Commander-in-Chief II Squadron, Admiral Wladimiro Pini), *Trento, Bolzano*;
7th Division: light cruisers *Eugenio, Aosta, Attendolo*;
2nd Division: light cruisers *Giussano, Bande Nere, Colleoni*;
4th Division: light cruisers *da Barbiano, Diaz, Cadorna*;
I Scout Flotilla: *Usodimare, da Noli, Tarigo, Vivaldi*; X Destroyer Squadriglia: *Maestrale, Grecale, Scirocco, Libeccio.*

I Submarine Group (from la Spezia)
15th Submarine Flotilla: *Fieramosca, Balilla, Sciesa, Millelire, Toti, Calvi, Finzi, Tazzoli*;
13th Submarine Flotilla: *Malachite, Rubino, Topazio, Ambra*;
11th Submarine Flotilla: *Scirè, Neghelli, Gondar, Ascianghi*;
34thSubmarine Flotilla: *Diaspro, Turchese, Medusa, Corallo*;
42nd Submarine Flotilla: *Sirena, Argonauta, Fisalia, Anfitrite, Ondina, Nereide, Naiade, Galatea*;
Submarines: *Foca, Zoea*

II Submarine Group (from Naples)
12th Submarine Flotilla: *Berillo, Onice, Ametista, Zaffiro, Jalea, Jantina, Macallè, Iride*;
14th Submarine Flotilla: *Axum, Alagi, Aradam, Adua*;
21st Submarine Flotilla: *Otaria, Glauco*;
41st Submarine Flotilla: *Ferraris, Galileo, Settimo, Settembrini, Capponi, da Procida, Mameli, Speri*;
Submarines: *Dessiè, Dagabur.*

The battleship *Giulio Cesare* leaving Genoa in May 1938.

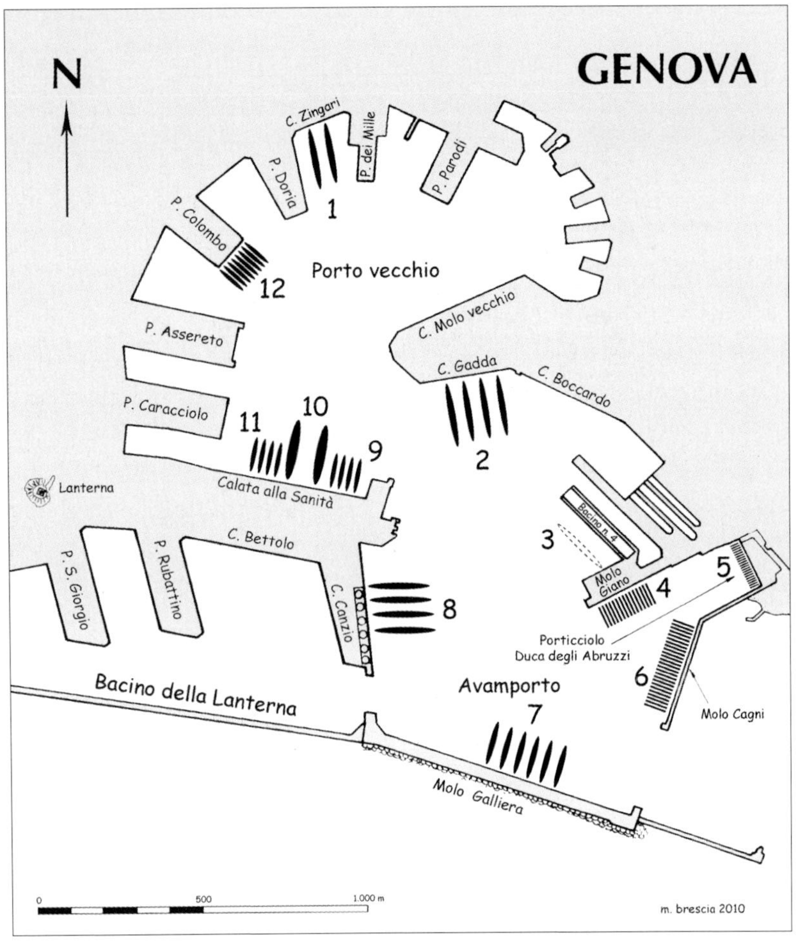

Left: Mooring plan of Regia Marina ships visiting Genoa between 4 and 31 May 1938.

Identification of the ships was made possible by 'cross-referencing' what could be inferred from photos with information reported in the 18, 21 and 22 May 1938 editions of the daily Genoa newspaper *Il Secolo XIX*.

1 Zingari Quay, from the left: *Trieste* and *Trento*
2 Gadda Quay, from the left: *Bolzano, Aosta, Attendolo* and *Eugenio*
3 Possible alternative position of the *Eugenio*, on the seaward side of basin No 4 (at the time known as 'XXVIII October')
4 Giano Quay: 2nd Submarine Group
5 Duca degli Abruzzi Marina: MAS
6 Cagni Quay: 1st Submarine Group
7 Galliera Quay, from the right: *Bande Nere, Colleoni, Di Giussano, Cadorna, Diaz* and *Da Barbiano*
8 Fuelling quay, from top: *Zara, Gorizia, Fiume* and *Pola*
9 Hospital quay: 10th Destroyer Squadriglia – from the right *Maestrale, Grecale, Scirocco* and *Libeccio*
10 From the right: *Cesare* and *Cavour*
11 4th Destroyer Squadriglia – from the right *Usodimare, Da Noli, Vivaldi* and *Tarigo*
12 Colombo Bridge, from top: *Freccia, Dardo, Strale, Saetta* (7th Destroyer Squadriglia); *Baleno, Folgore, Fulmine* and Lampo (8th Destroyer Squadriglia)

(M Brescia, from *Genova, maggio 1938* in 'STORIA militare' No 202, July 2010.)

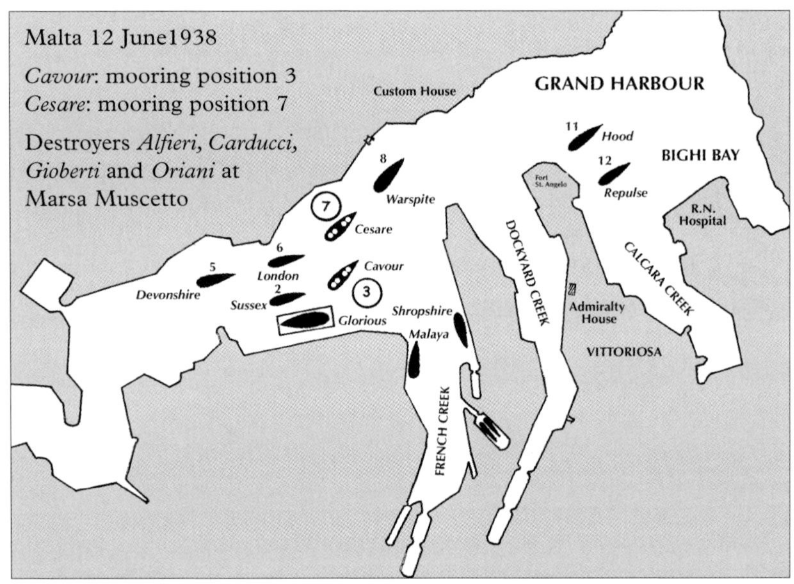

Piedmont and Lombardy. The squadrons left Genoa between the afternoon of 30 May and the morning of 31 May and the 5th Division transferred to La Spezia.

Visit by the 5th Division to Malta (21–24 June 1938)

From 16 to 18 April 1937 the British battleship *Queen Elizabeth*, flagship of Admiral Dudley Pound, commander-in-chief of the Mediterranean Fleet, paid an official visit at La Spezia to the commander-in-chief of the I Squadron, Admiral Arturo Riccardi. The visit, and others that followed, were not immediately exchanged because of new Anglo-Italian tensions in the summer of 1937 during the Spanish Civil War, but in May 1938, right after the conclusion of the Easter Pacts that settled the outstanding questions between Rome and London, including recognition of the Italian empire in East Africa, it seemed that the time had come for a return visit. Between May and June 1938, agreements were reached for a visit by the 5th Division and the IX Destroyer Squadriglia to Malta for 21–24 June 1938.

The battleship *Cavour*, Admiral Ricciardi's flagship, along with *Cesare* and the IX Destroyer Squadriglia (*Alfieri, Gioberti, Oriani* and *Carducci*) weighed anchor from Taranto on 20 June and arrived at Valletta at 08:10 on 21 June. There the ships were guided to assigned moorings: the battleships at the buoys in Grand Harbour, the destroyers at Marsa Muscetto. To receive them almost the whole of the Mediterranean Fleet had assem-

The battleship *Conte di Cavour* manoeuvring in Malta's Grand Harbour in June 1938.

Above: Detail of the bridge tower and part of the forward main gun battery of the battleship *Conte di Cavour* moored at Genoa in May 1938.

Left: The battleship *Giulio Cesare* leaving Taranto's Mar Piccolo in 1938.

Detail of the battleship *Conte di Cavour* manoeuvring in Malta's Grand Harbour in June 1938 (F Bargoni collection)

bled, among which were the battlecruisers *Hood* and *Repulse*, the battleships *Warspite* (Admiral Pound's flagship) and *Malaya* and the aircraft carrier *Glorious*. Despite the recent political tensions, the visit was held in an atmosphere of cordiality, without even the slightest incident. The 5th Division and the IX Flotilla departed from Malta on the morning of 24 June, reaching Taranto the following day.

Visit of the 5th Division to Cattaro (22–24 July 1938) and to Sebenico (25–29 July 1938)

In late May 1938 news reached Rome that a division of very new French light cruisers, returning from a cruise in the waters of the Levant, had visited the Yugoslav ports of Cattaro and Sebenico (modern Kotor and Šibenik). To balance that visit, Cavagnari planned to send the cruisers of the 1st Division to the same ports the following July. Relations between Rome and Belgrade had calmed down since Milan Stojadinovic, a Serb, had become Prime Minister of Yugoslavia and an Italo-Yugoslav pact of friendship and cooperation had been concluded on 25 March 1937. The programme was changed several times, and finally it was decided to send the 5th Division. This would be the second visit by Italian ships in the space of a year, after the training ships *Vespucci* and *Colombo* had visited Cattaro and Ragusa (Dubrovnik) in July 1937. The battleships *Cavour*, Riccardi's flagship, and *Cesare*, escorted by the IX Destroyer Squadriglia left Taranto on 21 July and arrived at the entrance to Cattaro fjord the following morning, where they anchored before Teodo (Tivat), welcomed by Vice-Admiral Marian Polic, commander-in-chief of the Yugoslav fleet, by General Damjanovic, the port commander, and Captain Saskijevic, the naval dockyard commander. The visit was held in an atmosphere of friendliness and with very much appreciated logistic assistance. Paul, the Prince Regent of Yugoslavia, was also to have attended, but was unable to because of mourning for the death of the Queen Mother of Romania. The impression gained by Riccardi was a welcome by the authorities that was sincerely friendly, a respectable degree of effectiveness of the Yugoslav

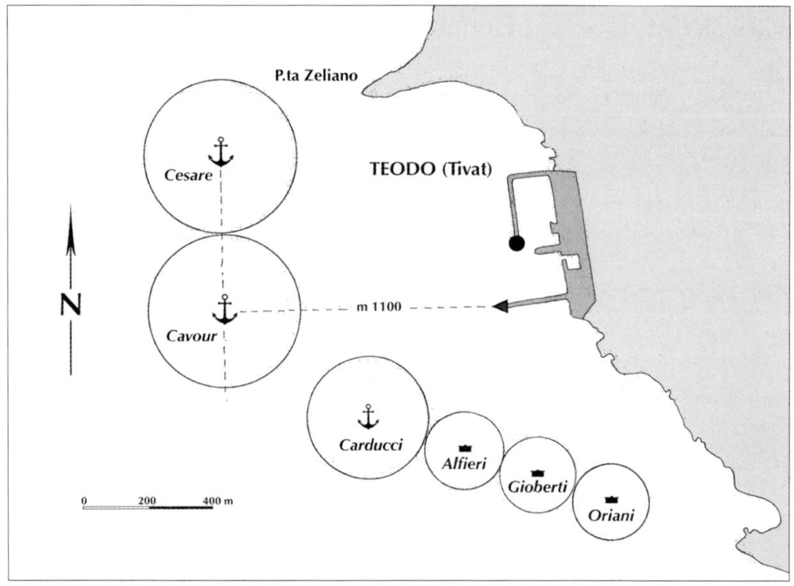

Plan of the anchorage of Italian ships near the Yugoslav naval base of Teodo while visiting Cattaro (modern Kotor) in July 1938.

ships and shore installations and of well-disciplined personnel, but also of an absolute dominance of command by the army over the navy.

On the night of 24 July, the division left Cattaro for Sebenico where, from a political standpoint, the situation was somewhat difficult because of a strong Croatian faction that had been perturbed by the improvement in Italo-Yugoslav relations. For those reasons, in view of the arrival of the Italian ships, the Belgrade government had sent substantial police forces to Sebenico in order to prevent any disorder, and on the Italian side as well several precautions were taken, such as a time limit on shore leave.

The 5th Division and the escorting destroyers reached Sebenico on the morning of 25 July. The choice of anchorages presented some problems for the battleships due to lack of space, given the simultaneous presence of several British destroyers that would have to be moved to make room for the Italian ships. Riccardi preferred, instead, to anchor the battleships in the outer roadstead, in the Sebenico channel, with only the destroyers entering the inner harbour on which the city fronted. Receiving the Italian ships were again Admiral Polic, General Damjanovic and the highest local authorities. The behaviour of the local populace ashore was not hostile and everything went smoothly, except for some negligible incidents between sailors and local men that had little to do with politics. The Regia Marina ships left their anchorages in the early hours of 29 July to return to Italian ports.

Visit of the head of government and of the 5th and 7th divisions to Trieste (18–25 September 1938)

In mid-September 1938, while the Czechoslovakian crisis was on the verge of ending, Mussolini undertook a prolonged visit to the Trieste area, where he arrived at 10:30 on 18 September, sailing from Venice aboard the brand-new destroyer *Camicia Nera* with an honour-guard from the IX Destroyer Squadriglia (*Alfieri, Oriani, Carducci, Gioberti*) and of the VII Destroyer Squadriglia (*Lampo, Fulmine, Folgore* and *Baleno*). For the occasion, on the morning of 19 September the 5th Division – with Admiral Riccardi's flagship *Cavour* and *Cesare*, coming from Taranto with stopovers at Bari, Rimini and Pola – as well as the 7th Division with the light cruisers *Eugenio di Savoia*, flagship of Admiral Odoardo Somigli, and the *Duca d'Aosta* and the torpedo boats *Lira* and *Libra* assembled in the roadstead at Trieste. The head of government took leave of Trieste on the morning of the 20th, then to continue on a tour to Friuli. But for a few days the ships that had accompanied him remained in port and in the roadstead to allow visits by the public, for which trains were organised from Udine, Gorizia, Monfalcone, Pola, Fiume and Postumia. The 5th and 7th divisions left Trieste, respectively, on 24 and 25 September bound for Taranto and Augusta.

Epilogue at sea of the Spanish Civil War. Plans for the escape of the Republican fleet to the Soviet Union (5–7 March 1939)

Even though the two 'Cavours' had entered squadron service in the second half of 1937, battleships were the only ship category that did not participate in the Regia Marina's activities in the Spanish conflict. An exception, at the end of the conflict, was a sortie directed at preventing a possible escape of the Republican fleet to the Soviet Union.

In late February 1939, when the Spanish Republic was close to collapse, there was a military uprising in Madrid, led by Colonel López Segismundo Casado, commander of the Army of the Centre. Its aim was to oust the government of Juan Negrìn, which was supported by the communists and in favour of continuing the war, and to open dialogue with Generalissimo Francisco Franco in an attempt to reach a negotiated peace.

Casado's revolt also had repercussions in Cartagena, a naval base that was already in a state of confusion and in which almost the entire Republican fleet had gathered. In early March there was a revolt conducted by military units sympathetic to Casado and by pro-Franco elements, accompanied by an attempt at a Nationalist landing, both of which failed because of the reaction of forces loyal to Negrìn. But, in the meantime, an ultimatum issued to the fleet by the rebels to leave Cartagena immediately had caused its commander, Admiral Miguel Buiza – not part of the revolt, but favourable to Casado and already inclined to abandon Cartagena in the absence of any peace negotiations – to leave the base shortly after 12:00 on 5 March with all of the operational ships, including the light cruisers *Miguel de Cervantes*, his flagship, *Libertad, Méndez Nùñez* and the destroyers *Lepanto, Almirante Anteguerra, Almirante Valdés, Gravina, Jorge Juan, Almirante Miranda, Escaño* and *Ulloa* and with several hundred civilians on board. The decision was hastened by an air raid by Nationalist aircraft, which that same morning had hit the shipyard area and had seriously damaged the destroyers *Sànchez Barcàiztegui* and *Lazaga* and caused slight damage to the *Gravina*.

SHIPS HUNTING THE SPANISH FLEET

Scouting force:
From La Spezia (5 March): X Destroyer Squadriglia: *Maestrale, Grecale, Scirocco, Libeccio*
From Cagliari (6 March): escort *Procione*; torpedo boat *Spica*
From Tripoli (7 March): School Command Division (Admiral Angelo Iachino) Light cruiser *Bande Nere*; destroyer *da Recco*;
I Torpedo Boat Flotilla: *Airone, Ariel, Aretusa, Alcione*;
VIII Torpedo Boat Flotilla: *Lupo, Lince, Lire, Libra*;
XI Torpedo Boat Flotilla: *Cigno, Climene, Castore, Centauro*;
XII Torpedo Boat Flotilla: *Altair, Aldebaran, Andromeda, Antares*.

Procione and *Spica* were to have reconnoitred the Sardinian Channel; X Destroyer Squadriglia the western approach to the Sicily channel; the School Command Division would patrol the channel to the east and the waters around Malta. The X Torpedo Boat Flotilla was also put on alert in the Aegean (*Vega, Sirio, Perseo, Sagittario*). Naval scouting was integrated with air reconnaissance from the Balearic, Sardinian and Sicilian air force elements in their respective sectors. These forces had the exclusive mission of finding the Republican fleet and maintaining contact without attacking it, while actual interception was reserved for a naval force composed as follows:

Interception force (I Squadron, from Taranto)
1st Division: heavy cruisers *Fiume, Pola, Zara, Gorizia*;
IX Destroyer Squadriglia: *Alfieri, Oriani, Carducci, Gioberti*.
5th Division: battleships *Cavour* (Admiral Arturo Riccardi), *Cesare*;
VII Destroyer Squadriglia: *Freccia, Dardo, Saetta, Strale*.

The sortie by the Republican fleet did not go unobserved by the Nationalist government at Burgos, which asked Rome to prevent its escape to the Soviet Union, from where it would have been very difficult to repatriate it once the war was over. The eventuality had already been considered by the Regia Marina and an aeronaval force was activated to reconnoitre the central-western Mediterranean and to intercept the Republican fleet, composed as shown in the above table.

I Squadron was to have intercepted the Republican fleet and force it to detour to Augusta, without resorting to the use of arms, except in the event of refusal or resistance. On the morning of 7 March, the two divisions took to the sea from Taranto, the 5th only in order to move to Messina. For almost the entire morning of the 6th, no sightings were made, until the Republican fleet was spotted by aircraft from the Balearics off Algiers and was then followed continuously by aircraft for the rest of the day as far as Bizerte, where, finally, it sought refuge. There was, however, no contact at sea. On 7 March, learning of its internment in Bizerte, the end of the emergency was declared and the forces were returned home. It happened that Admiral Buiza, after a night of uncertainty regarding the politico-military situation in Spain, doubtful of the discipline of the crews in case of a return to Cartagena and fearful of destructive air attacks in other less-defended Republican ports, in the early hours of 6 March had decided to sail to Algiers. But the French authorities forced him to sail to Bizerte, where he arrived at night and where the 'Red' fleet was interned. At any rate, the lack of fuel left him no other choice, a circumstance that of itself made it impractical to escape to the Black Sea. Buiza had no inkling of the presence of the Italian forces at sea, nor did he take that into account in his calculations, all of which were focused on Spain's internal situation. The outcome of any encounter therefore remains a matter of speculation. The eleven Republican ships at Bizerte, which were joined on 8 March by the submarine *C 4*, were later consigned to the Spanish government on 2 April 1939, the day following the end of the civil war.

The occupation of Albania (6–9 April 1939)

Italy had exerted a major influence over Albania since the 1920s. From the summer of 1937 the Foreign Minister, Galeazzo Ciano, had been advocating establishing Tirana's complete dependence on Rome, but the issue came to a head in mid-March 1939 following the German occupation of Bohemia and Moravia and the complete dismemberment of Czechoslovakia. That action disconcerted Rome, which had not been forewarned, as it was not the Czechoslovakia created at Versailles that was dissolved, but rather the September 1938 Munich agreement of which Mussolini had been the creator. The desire to balance the German move and to reinforce Italian influence in the Balkans, where there was a fear of new German initiatives, hastened Rome's action.

Differing from Ciano, Mussolini put a priority on following public opinion, so that military preparations were begun days after sending Tirana the draft of a treaty that provided for establishment of an Italian protectorate. King Zog of Albania sought to negotiate and Mussolini, welcoming the opportunity to preserve appearances, on 2 April sent a new outline agreement that nominally preserved Albanian sovereignty; this was accompanied by an ultimatum upon whose expiration, at 12:00 on 6 April, Italy would proceed with military action. As Zog continued to prevaricate, Rome moved militarily.

Meanwhile, in late March the general lines of the operation had been fixed: designated 'Esigenza Oltre Mare Tirana (OMT)' [Overseas Exigency Tirana], it was placed under the aegis of the Minister of War and of the chiefs of staff of the three services under the command of General Alfredo Guzzoni. On April, General Alberto Pariani, Undersecretary of War and Army Chief of Staff, issued the orders. The expeditionary corps was structured with three echelons with a total of 22,000 men; the first echelon was to consist of a landing force and the later echelons were to expand and occupy the zones of penetration into the interior. The Regia Marina was to participate with a large deployment of forces, providing transport even by using requisitioned merchant shipping, providing protection for the expeditionary forces, supporting the landings of the 'San Marco' regiment and its detachments, as well as initial cover for the advance of army columns towards the interior. The Regia Aeronautica was to participate with an air squadron (Squadra Albania) with 384 transport, bomber and fighter aircraft. On the night of 29/30 March the Navy Staff took the first steps to requisition merchant shipping, and on 31 March the commander-in-chief of I Squadron, Admiral Riccardi, issued the general operational orders. The ensemble of naval forces engaged in the four landing areas assigned to the first echelon was as shown in the table below.

On 5 April, the mobilised ships began to arrive in the designated ports. On the morning of the 6th almost all of the assigned

EXIGENCY OMT NAVAL FORCES[1] ENGAGED IN LANDING OPERATIONS ON 7 APRIL 1939

1 Group (from Brindisi to San Giovanni di Medua)
Light cruiser *Bande Nere*; VIII Destroyer Squadriglia section: *Folgore, Fulmine*; XIV Torpedo Boat Squadron section: *Pleiadi, Polluce*; tanker *Pagano*[2]; motor tanker *Garigliano*[2], steamship *Umbria*.

2 Group (from Brindisi, Taranto, to Durazzo)
1st Heavy Cruiser Division: *Fiume* (flagship OMT Command), *Zara, Gorizia, Pola*
IX Destroyer Squadriglia: *Alfieri, Gioberti, Carducci, Oriani*; VIII Torpedo Boat Flotilla: *Lupo, Lince, Libra, Lira*
Destroyer Sella; torpedo boat *Pilo*
Repair ship *Quarnaro*; aircraft support ship *Miraglia*; motor tanker *Tirso*[2]; motorships *Adriatico* and *Barletta*; yachts *Palatino, Toscana, Valsavoia, Aquitania*

3 Group (from Taranto to Valona)
5th Division: battleships *Cavour* (flagship Commander-in-Chief I Squadron), *Cesare*
X Destroyer Squadriglia: *Scirocco, Libeccio, Grecale, Saetta*
XI Torpedo Boat Flotilla: *Cigno, Climene, Centauro, Castore*
Minelayer *Azio*; yachts *Arno* (from Saseno), *Sannio*

4 Group (from Taranto and Brindisi to Santi Quaranta)
8th Division: light cruisers *Abruzzi, Garibaldi*
VIII Destroyer Squadriglia: *Baleno, Lampo, Freccia*
I Torpedo Boat Flotilla: *Airone, Ariel, Aretusa, Alcione*
MAS 512 and 519
Refrigerator ship *Asmara*; motor tankers *Sesia*[2] and *Scrivia*[2]; steamship *Marin Sanudo*; cable layer *Giasone*

Submarines (from Taranto, for ambushes in the Ionian and Lower Adriatic)
Zoea, Guglielmotti, Galilei, Settembrini, Da Procida, Sirena, Nereide, Speri, Galatea, Mameli, Salpa

1 Added to these were various fishing craft and tugs for landing troops and equipment ashore and for associated tasks.
2 Equipped as landing ships.

troops had reached their departure ports, embarkation of men and equipment had begun and the first ship movements had taken place. In the event that negotiations took a positive turn, the operation would be suspended. With respect to the 3rd Group – the only one of concern here – between 4 and 6 April *Cavour*, *Cesare* and the steamship *Sannio* embarked the men, light vehicles and army and militia equipment comprising the Valona (modern Vlorë) column commanded by Colonel Tullio Berardi.

As the ultimatum expired in vain, at 12:46 on 6 April, the OMT became operational and the final embarkation operations were accelerated. At 15:30 the 3rd Group began to move, concluding at 20:00 with the departure from Taranto of the 5th Division escorted by the X Destroyer Squadriglia. On the night of 6/7 April the detachments of IX Torpedo Boat Flotilla followed by those of X Destroyer Squadriglia landed in the port of Valona, which took possession of the port area and major road hubs after weak resistance. During those same hours the bulk of the group arrived in the roadstead and from dawn until afternoon the offloading of men, vehicles and equipment began, with the assistance of the *Azio*, motor trawlers and tugboats.

At 16:30 the *Cavour* joined the action by firing twenty-four rounds from No 5 main gun turret in support of the Bernardi column that was advancing towards the Davoli oilfield area. At 19:00 the 5th Division left Valona for a night-time security patrol, leaving defence of the roadstead to the destroyers; the mission was, however, soon broken off and the battleships returned to Valona around midnight. At 13:00 on 8 April the *Cavour* set sail for Durazzo (modern Durrës) and command at sea in Valona was assumed by the captain of the *Cesare*. On 9 April the 5th Division's mission ended with the return to Taranto of the *Cesare* and of the X Flotilla from Valona and of the *Cavour* from Durazzo, as their presence was no longer needed.

The OMT was concluded on 10 April with the occupation of all of Albania at the cost of twelve dead and eighty-one wounded, mainly from navy landing units, and on 16 April Albania was united with Italy by conferring the crown on Victor Emanuel III. This was the first Italian landing made since the time of the Italo-Turkish war of 1911–1912, with the only other major precedent being the joint manoeuvres in north-western Sicily in August 1937. From a military standpoint it was not a significant test because of the disparity of forces and the weak enemy opposition. However, there were many harsh criticisms of the operation, especially by the head of the general staff, Marshal Pietro Badoglio, who had been left on the margins of the preparations; his comments were directed against the planning as well as the execution, especially from the logistics standpoint. Other criticisms related to the navy's performance, with regard to shortcomings and problems in requisitioning merchant shipping, in distribution of army troops on the ships and in the phasing of landing the men, vehicles and equipment. These latter criticisms do not seem to take sufficient account of the abbreviated execution times, of the fact that the occupation of the landing zones was initially carried out by navy landing detachments – and that, therefore, the first ships of the invasion force were necessarily warships – and that in any case the shallow depths and the rudimentary docking facilities at Durazzo and Valona would only allow landing of the bulk of the first echelon from ships moored in the roadstead.

On the international scene the OMT had no direct backlash, by either London or Belgrade, who had been forewarned and reassured of Italy's non-hostile intentions. But at this point Britain regarded the Easter Pact as a dead letter and considered Italy among the ranks of hostile powers. No documents have been found regarding the Regia Marina's attitude, except for satisfaction voiced by the hierarchy as to how it had carried out the mission it had been assigned. In principle, however, the staff had always been in favour of controlling the eastern shore of the Otranto channel and, on 18 May 1939, the Navy Staff's war plans department commented favourably on the new situation, underscoring the advantages to hermetically sealing the Adriatic with limited forces, of having full access to the anchorage at Valona, of the possibility of neutralising Corfù whenever third parties sought to take it over, and use of Albania for any other military moves in the Balkans.

Cesare and *Cavour* graze the seabed in Taranto's Mar Grande (14 April 1939)

Having returned from Exigency OMT, the 5th Division was to have carried out a firing exercise in the Gulf of Taranto on 14 April. Two days earlier the local naval command notified the headquarters of I Squadron (Admiral Arturo Riccardi on the *Cavour*) that works were in progress for laying net barriers in the channel of the San Vito entrance to Mar Grande on the side of the island of San Paolo and provided a safe route to follow. An examination made by squadron headquarters discovered that the route indicated, although having a depth of more than 12 metres at the entrance, decreased to 10.7 metres near a shoal and close to another of barely 10 metres. Because the battleships had a draught of about 10.5 metres, on 13 April the naval command was requested to modify the route or to dredge the shallows, and orders were given to the ships' captains to be careful to keep a little to the east of that alignment and to proceed at slow speed near the channel, all the more so because entry was scheduled for the night-time hours.

At 09:55 on the 14th the *Cesare* left her moorings in Mar Grande, followed at 10:47 by the *Cavour*. The manoeuvre to steer free of the shallows was carried out as prescribed and the two ships turned into the San Paolo passage between the two buoys marking the entrance at a speed of 6 knots. Even so, while one after the other they were between the two pairs of buoys (inner and outer) over a bottom that on the charts measured 12.4 metres, they both scraped the seabed.

The *Cesare*, which was leading, at 10:26 hit bottom, and hove to for a quick check of potential damage; having discovered that there was none, at 10:40 she continued for the exercises, after having signalled the *Cavour* to wait for another message before proceeding. *Cesare* reported at 11:15 that she had scraped bottom in the middle of the channel between the two pairs of buoys. The *Cavour* received the first message at 10:46 while preparing to get under way, but the second not until 11:27. On the bridge the admiral, due to a sequence of errors, relied on the first message and when the *Cavour* turned into the entrance of the channel, at 11:20, before receiving the second message, she in turn scraped bottom. The captain immediately had the engines stopped and turned to port towards Capo San Vito to clear the channel. When in deeper water, a check of the hull was made with the assistance of a diver. At 13:15, by Riccardi's orders, the mission was cancelled and the *Cavour* re-entered Mar Grande from the San Vito passage, where at 14:50 the ship anchored at the buoy and where an inspection of the hull was resumed. The *Cesare* returned in mid-afternoon though the San Vito passage again, once she had completed the exercises.

The episode had a postscript in the form of an intervention by Admiral Cavagnari, who recognised that the primary cause was of a hydrographic nature, but he criticised organisational short-comings and poor squadron communications as contributing to the unfortunate incident involving *Cesare*, which, several hours later, was found to have some leaks.

The damage sustained did not affect the overall readiness of the two ships (for details see Appendix 4). The repairs would only take a few days, but it would have been necessary to put them, one after the other, into the only drydock in Taranto capable of holding them; because of this, Cavagnari did not hide his disappointment, especially in view of the state of international tension at the time. Therefore, very summary repairs were made with the ships still afloat while more complete repairs were put off until other work requiring drydocking had to be done in the future.

The I Squadron cruise in the western Mediterranean and in the Atlantic (19 June – 9 July 1939)

In early June 1939, with the civil war in Spain barely concluded, the Navy Staff planned a training cruise by I Squadron in the western Mediterranean and eastern Atlantic with stops in Spain and Portugal as well as in Tangiers, a territory subject to a special international regime, of which Italy was a part. Scheduled to take part were the *Cavour*, the 1st and 8th divisions and four submarines.

On 19 June, setting sail from Naples were the *Cavour*, Admiral Riccardi's flagship, with the X Destroyer Squadriglia (*Maestrale, Grecale, Libeccio, Scirocco*), the 1st Division (heavy cruisers *Fiume, Zara, Pola, Gorizia*) with the IX Flotilla (*Alfieri, Carducci, Gioberti and Oriani*) and the 8th Division (*Abruzzi* and *Garibaldi*) with the VII Flotilla (*Freccia, Saetta* and *Strale*). Sailing separately from Naples and from La Spezia were two submarine sections: *Atropo* and *Guglielmotti, Mocenigo* and *Finzi*. The squadron laid over at Palma di Mallorca (21–24 June), Lisbon (27 June–1 July) and Tangiers (2–7 July 1939), then headed back to Italy.

The welcome received at Palma was decidedly warm and cordial. Signs of the war were still evident, such as port obstructions and the torpedo boat *Procione* of the Italian naval mission, while the minelayer *Marte* was present from the Spanish navy. At Lisbon the I Squadron was welcomed by the destroyers *Dao* and *Vouga* and on 29 June they were joined by the submarines *Guglielmotti* and *Atropo*. There were many intense celebrations, but they were marred by the news of the death of Admiral

Italian ships anchored in the roadstead of Palma de Mallorca in the Balearic Islands in June 1939: the battleship *Conte di Cavour* with the light cruisers *Giuseppe Garibaldi* and *Duca degli Abruzzi* further off. Despite the fact that the Spanish Civil War was over, in the foreground the nets protecting the anchorage and the associated buoys can still be seen.

The battleship *Giulio Cesare* at Taranto in late summer 1940. Note the modification to the pole topmast, whose height has been significantly reduced.

Costanzo Ciano, president of the Chamber of Fasces and Corporations, for which on 28 June the Portuguese ships present lowered their flags to half-mast as well. The squadron left Lisbon after being refuelled by the tanker *Bronte*, which had been in place since 25 June.

At Tangiers the visit was marred by poor sea conditions caused by easterly winds up to force 6, which limited traffic to and from shore and thus affected the courtesy visits and spontaneous celebrations. Also present as station ships were the destroyers *Alvise da Mosto* and the French *Forbin*, as well as the Spanish minelayer *Vulcano*. Visits were exchanged with the last two ships, but pleading 'duty', Riccardi restricted the visit with the captain of the *Forbin*, in line with the directive to reduce to a minimum and in strict form any contacts with French military and civil authorities on occasion of visits to foreign ports.

On the eve of 9 July, during the passage back to Italy, *Cavour* experienced the beginning of overheating of the tube band of No 4 boiler, ascribed to the lack of attention by the personnel on duty, with slight damage to several boiler tubes. The damaged tubes were removed with onboard equipment without reducing the efficiency of the boiler. The cruise ended with the squadron's return to Taranto on 9 July and remained the only mission by a 'modern' battleship outside of the Straits and one of the few in the history of the Italian Navy involving battleships.

Chapter 8

TECHNICAL DESCRIPTION OF THE MODERNISED 'DUILIO' CLASS BATTLESHIPS

Chapter 6 has already described the major technical improvements that distinguished the 'Duilio' class modernisation from the 'Cavours'. We will limit ourselves here to providing information regarding changes made to the major equipment, in addition to several organisational changes of major significance made to onboard services.

With respect to the powerplant, the differences between these two classes were minimal and the performance characteristics were similar, except for a slightly lower power output of the 'Duilio' class that translated to one knot less maximum speed, but which did not have a significant impact on the joint operational employment of the ships.

In order to restrain the increase in displacement – as some elements of the modernisation tended to drive up weight beyond what was envisaged – many and varied measures were taken, among which was reducing the weight of ammunition stocks. The official allocation was, in any case, judged to be somewhat excessive, so the 'rounds per barrel' were kept down to 65 complete 320/44 rounds (projectile plus four charges each), 148 rounds of 135/45 and 419 rounds of 90/50.

As previously discussed, the fire control system on the 'Duilio' class was substantially similar to that of the 'Cavours', using analogous equipment but of more modern type. There were, however, substantial differences in some elements. For example, for the main guns, the main SDT, equipped with an APG and located at the top of the bridge tower, did not traverse but was fixed and unarmoured; beneath it, the conspicuous annular turret with two 7.20-metre rangefinders rotated 360 degrees. For the medium-calibre guns, the two SDT with 5-metre rangefinders and associated bases were not positioned at the sides of the bridge tower, but rather one to port and one to starboard in the space between the two funnels. Fire control for the 90/50 guns was provided by two stabilised SDT fitted with 3-metre stereoscopic rangefinders located symmetrically on the two sides abaft the tower. One backup SDT, equipped with a 3-metre rangefinder, was located on the 'mushroom' at the base of the aft mast along with two

The battleship *Andrea Doria*, with the basic reconstruction work completed, during one of its first sorties in the open sea for trials in the waters off Trieste.

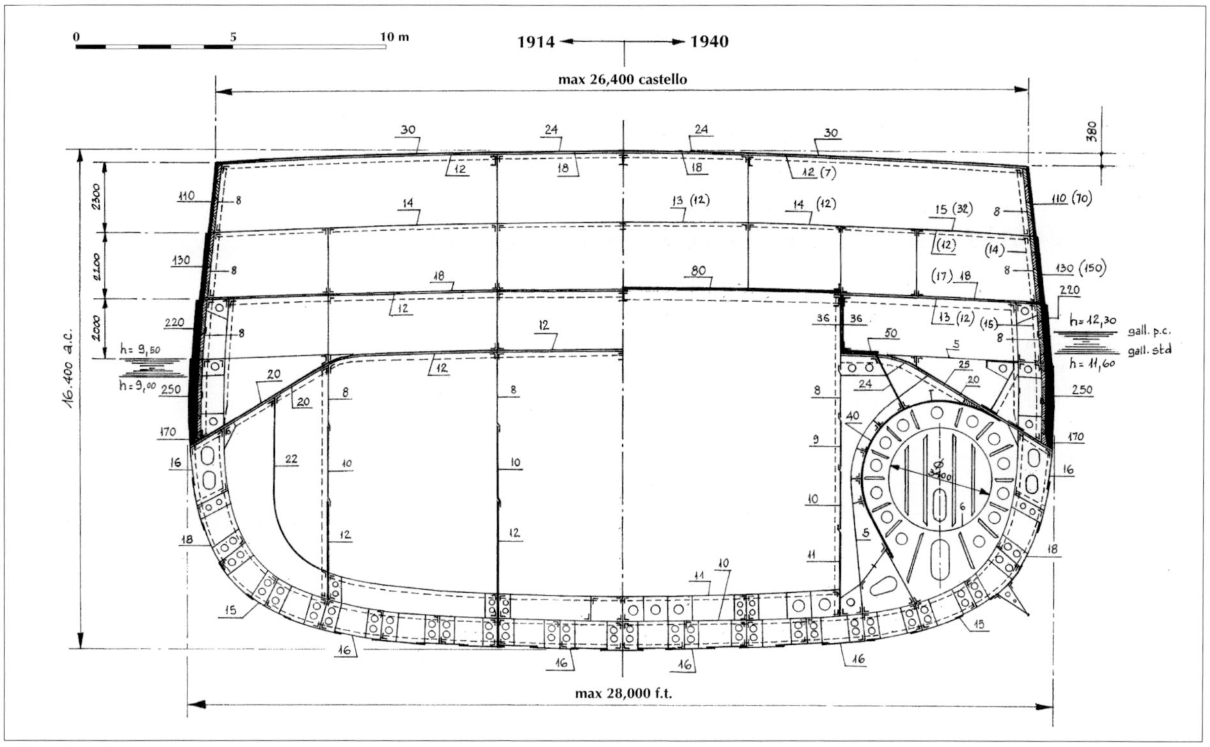

Left: Midship section comparing the armour scheme and scantling thicknesses of the 'Cavour' and 'Duilio' classes as built (to the left of the centreline) and as reconstructed (to the right). (Drawing by R Maggi)

( ) Figures for the 'Duilio' class
_ Figures for the 'Cavour' class

Below: Photo of the diesel dynamo controls of the battleship *Andrea Doria*. (F Petronio collection)

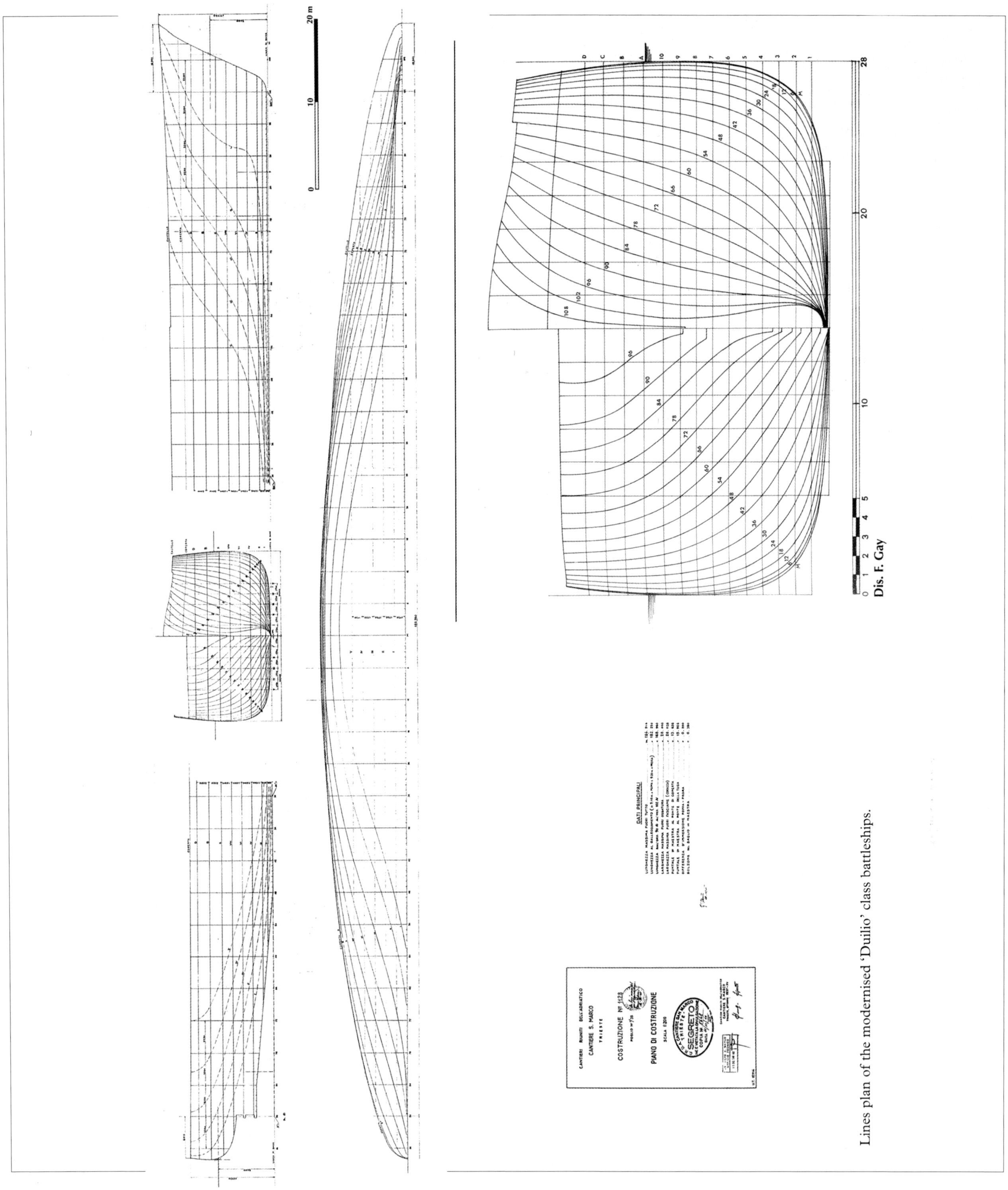

Lines plan of the modernised 'Duilio' class battleships.

Above: Partial view of the unarmoured command bridge of the *Andrea Doria* after modernisation.

Left: Detail of the machinery telegraphs in the original version of the unarmoured command bridge of the battleship *Andrea Doria*.

Left: A partial view of the armoured conning tower on the *Andrea Doria*.

Below: One of the machinery control stations on the *Andrea Doria* following the modernisation.

A photo of the *Andrea Doria* at Pola in October 1940. (F Petronio collection)

External bow and stern views of the modernised 'Duilio' class. (Drawing by R Maggi)

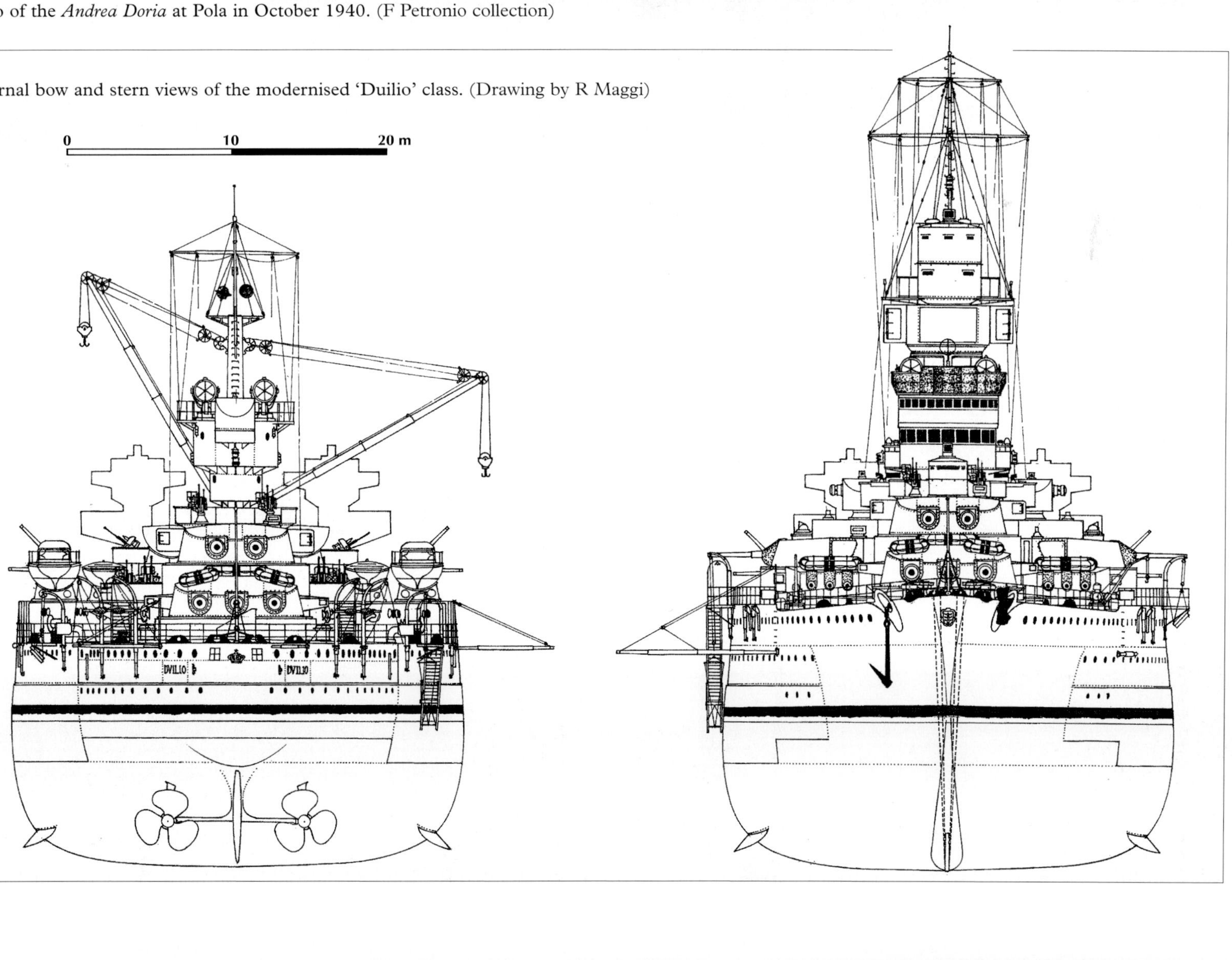

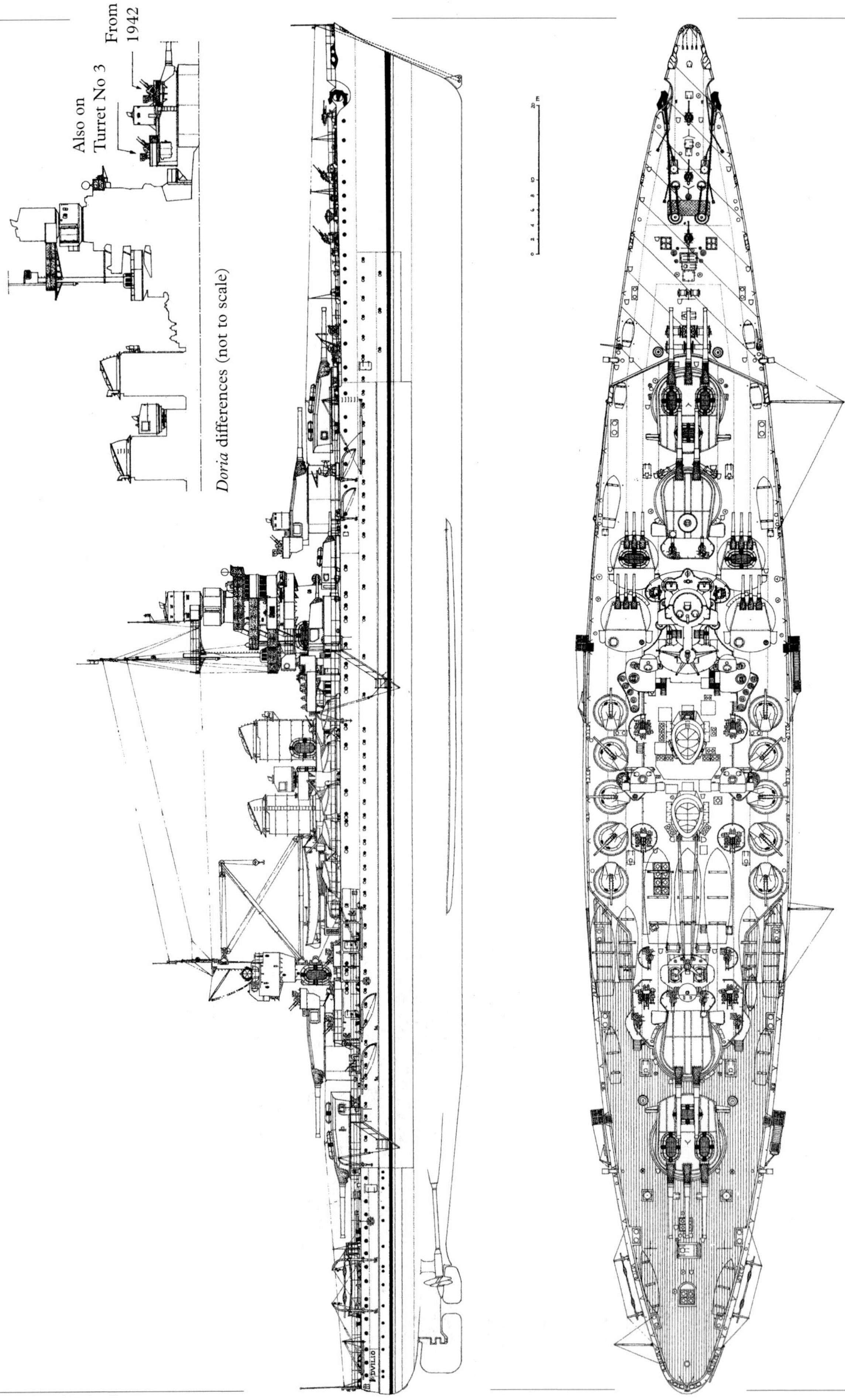

Modernised 'Duilio' class battleships. External views.
(Drawing by R Maggi)

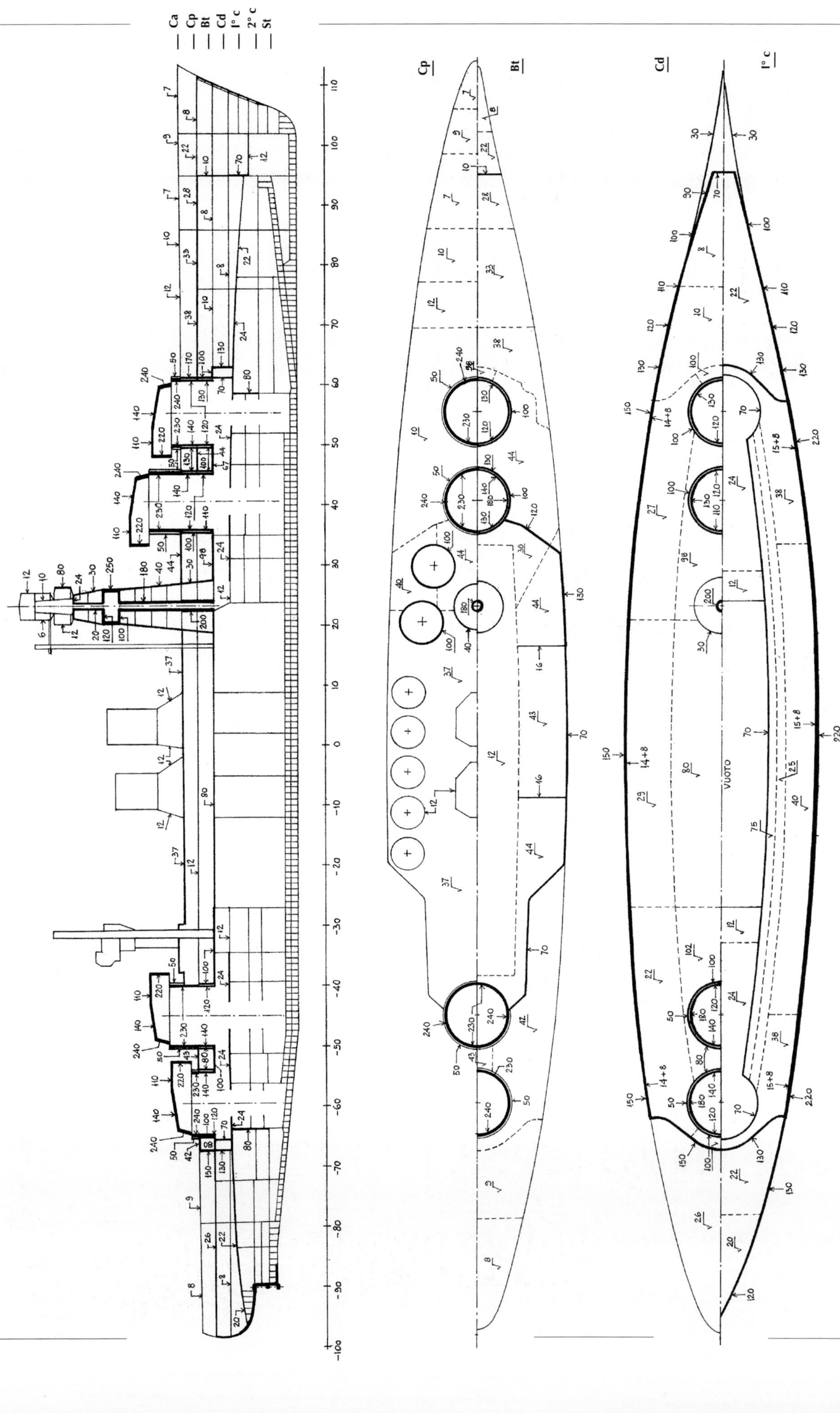

Armour scheme of the modernised 'Duilio' class.
(Drawing by R Maggi)

Note: measurements in millimetres

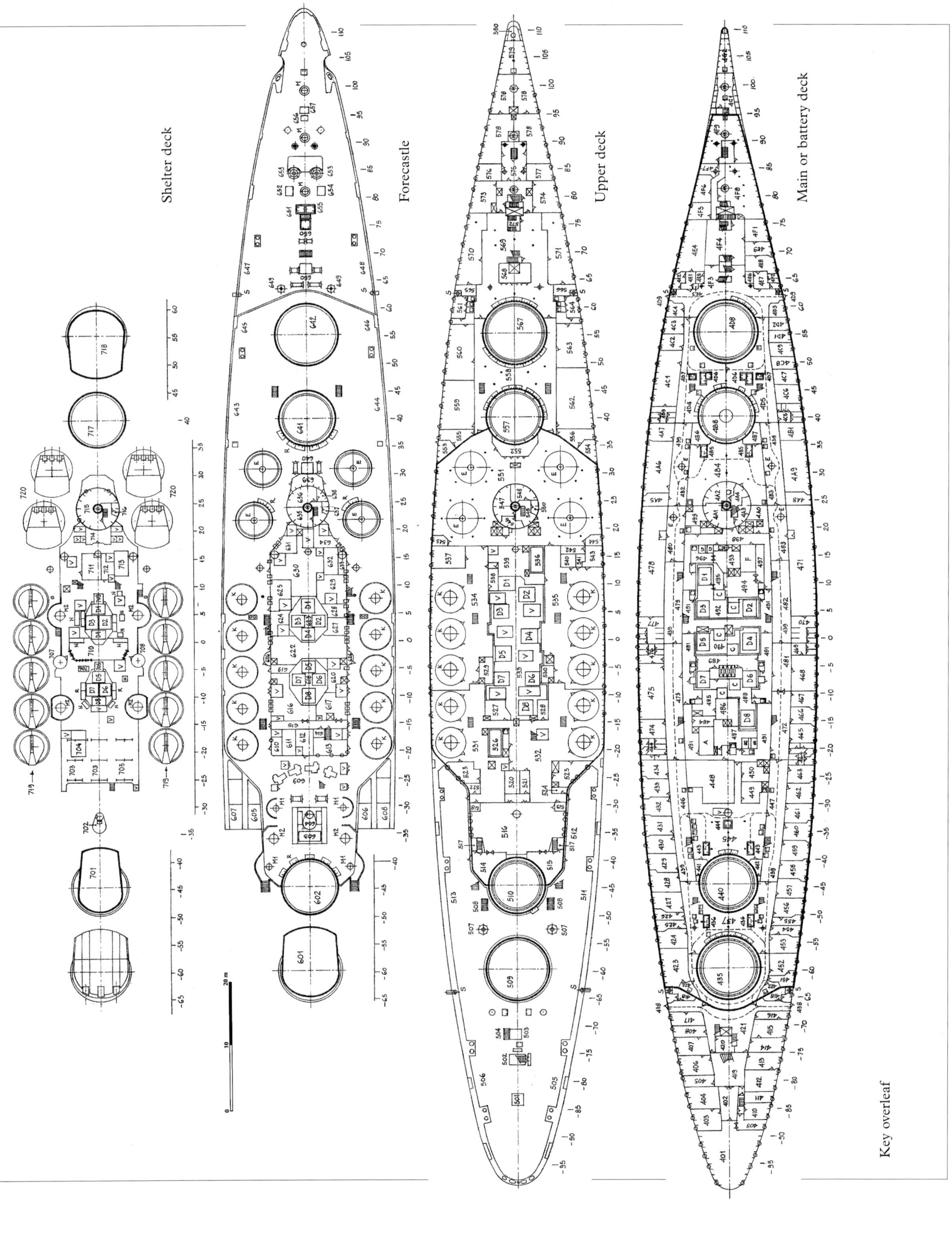

Plan of upper decks of the modernised 'Duilio'. (Drawing by R Maggi)

Transverse sections of the modernised 'Duilio' class.
(Drawing by R Maggi)

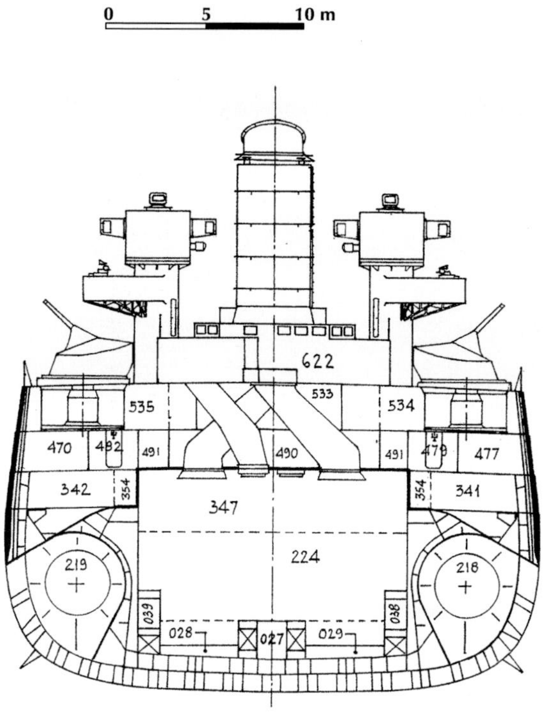

Frame Ø (midship) looking aft

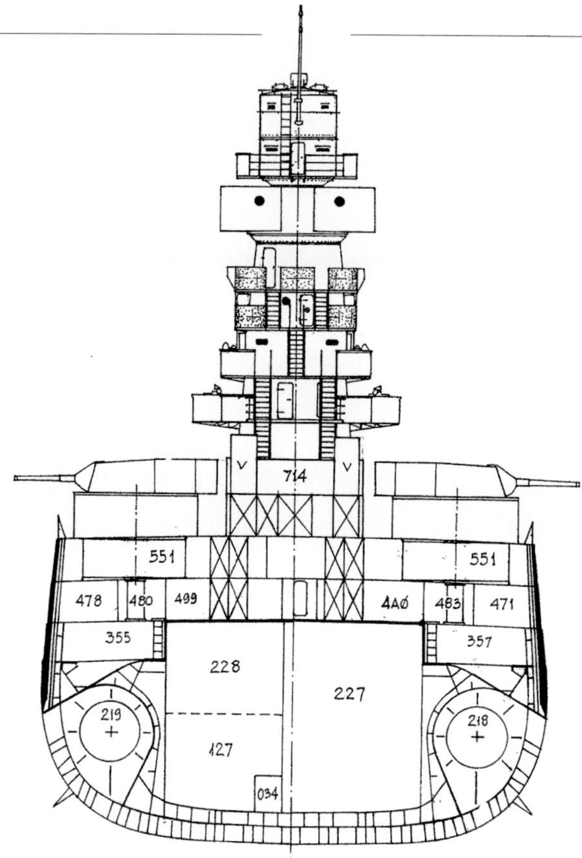

Frame 20 looking aft

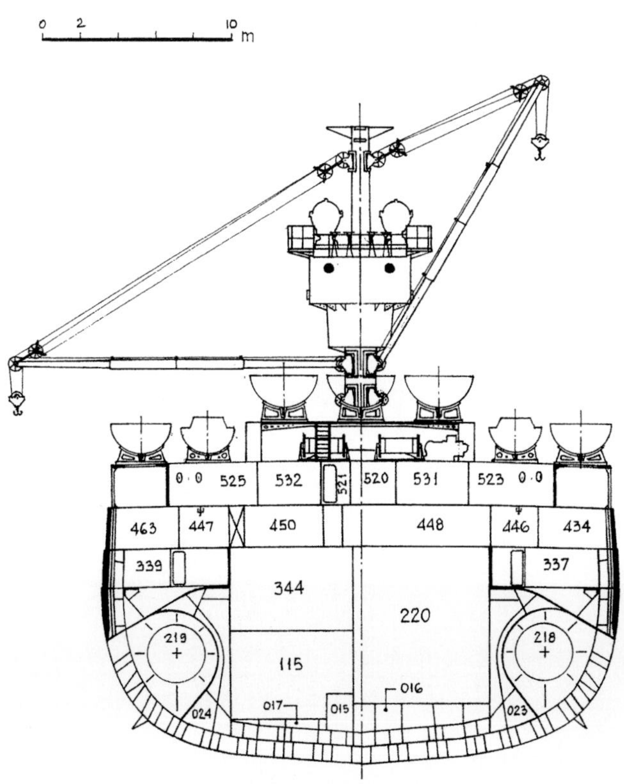

Frame 24 looking aft

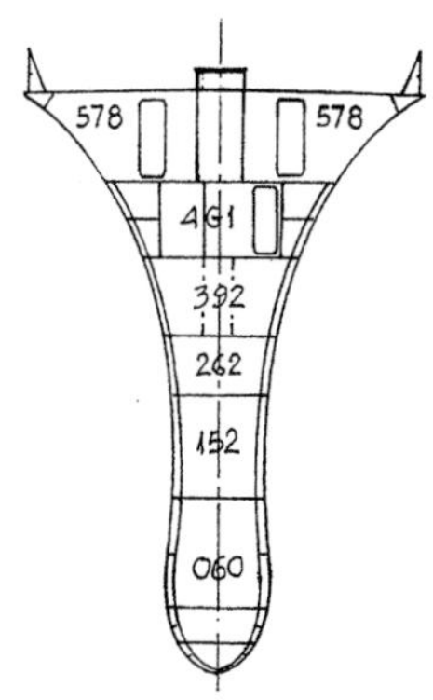

Frame 96 looking aft

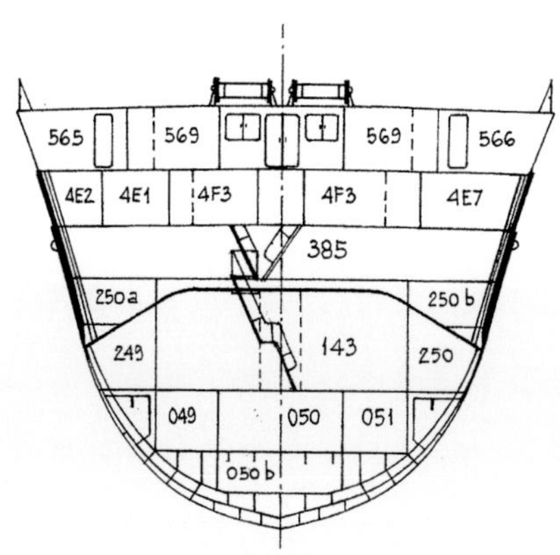

Frame 64 looking forward

Key overleaf

Key to drawings on pages 84 and 130-131.

HOLD
002 No 4 320mm turret baseplate pivot
003 No 4 320mm turret lower shell room
010 No 3 320mm turret baseplate pivot
011 No 3 320mm turret lower shell room
012 MG ammunition magazine
015 Aft passage
016 Aft engine room (port shaft)
017 Aft auxiliary machinery room
023 Port cofferdams
024 Starboard cofferdams
027 Middle passage
028 No 5 boiler bedplate
029 No 4 boiler bedplate
034 Fore passage
038 Port oil tanks
039 Starboard oil tanks
042 135mm & 90mm lower shell magazine
043 No 2 320mm turret shell room
044 No 2 320mm turret shell handling room
045 No 1 320mm turret shell room
046 No 1 320mm turret shell handling room
049 Assistant's store room (port)
050 Fore pump room
050b Bilge
051 Assistant's store room (starboard)
056 Diesel oil compartment
057 Log room
059 Trim control tanks
060 Trim water tank

PLATFORM DECK
101 Second afterpeak
102 Electric cables store
103 Sewage tanks & pumps room
104 No 4 320mm turret shell handling room
105 No 4 320mm turret upper shell room
106 No 3 320mm turret shell handling room
109 No 3 320mm turret middle shell room
110 MG ammunition magazine
115 Aft auxiliary machinery room
127 Fore auxiliary machinery room
134 135mm & 90mm middle shell magazine
135 No 2 320mm turret shell room
138 No 2 320mm turret shell handling room
139 No 1 320mm turret shell room
140 No 1 320mm turret shell handling room
143 Assistant's store room
146 Main pantry
150 Chain locker
151 Block & tackle store
152 Trim tank

LOWER DECK
201 Main steering gear compartment
202 Steering gear machinery compartment
203 Rudder handling room
208 Aft diesel generator room
211 No 4 320mm turret charge handling room
214 No 4 320mm turret shell room
215 No 3 320mm turret charge handling room
216 No 3 320mm turret shell room
217 Aft medium/small calibre shell magazine
218 Port shock-absorbing cylinders
219 Starboard shock-absorbing cylinders
220 Aft engine room
223 Nos 6 &7 boiler rooms
224 Nos 4 & 5 boiler rooms
225 Nos 2 & 3 boiler rooms
227 Fore engine room
228 Fore turbo-generator room
235 Gyro-compass room
236 Armoured W/T receiving station
238 Middle medium/small calibre shell magazine
239 Fore medium/small calibre shell magazine
242 Main 135mm & 90mm shell magazine
248 Fore diesel generator room
249 Port electrical engineering store
250 Starboard electrical engineering store
250a Port diesel generator muffler
250b Starboard diesel generator muffler
253 Pantry access lobby
259 Wine casks store
260 b Bed linen store
262 Clothing store
263 New stem cofferdams

MIDDLE DECK
301 Ensigns' showers
302 Ensigns' washbasins
303 Ensigns' quarters
303 b Officers' baggage room
305 Ensigns' wardroom
306 Lobby
309 Non-commissioned officers' showers
310 Crew space No 1
311 Officers' baggage room
313 No 4 320mm turret shell hoist and motors
318 Frequency converters room
325 No 3 320mm turret shell hoist
329 Electric power station
332 Various machinery room
337 Crew co-op shop store
339 WOs' pantry & wine store
341 Port sea water cofferdams
342 Starboard sea water cofferdams
343 Aft engine room
344 Aft turbo-generator room
345 No 8 boiler room
347 Nos 4 & 5 boiler rooms
349 No 1 boiler room
350 Fore turbo-generator room
351 Fore engine room
354 Sea water tanks
355 Signal & lifesaver store
357 Underwater & anti-gas apparatus store
369 Communication & order broadcasting room
370 Main fire control station
371 Refrigeration machinery compartment
372 No 2 320mm turret shell hoist
373 Main air-cooling machinery room
374 No 1 320mm turret shell hoist and motors
385 Crew space No 2 with fore warping windlass motors
386 Crew space No 3
387 Crew space No 4 with capstan motors
391 Prison
392 Clothing store room
393 Boatswain store

MAIN DECK
401 Meeting room
402 Admiral's lobby
403 Admiral's stateroom
404 Admiral's cabin
405 Admiral's bathroom
406 Commanding Officer's stateroom
407 Commanding Officer's cabin
408 Commanding Officer's bathroom
409 Admiral's closet
410 Admiral's secretariat
411 Chief of staff's bathroom
412 Chief of staff's cabin
413 Chief of staff's stateroom
414 Executive officer's stateroom
415 Executive officer's cabin
416 Executive officer's bathroom
417 Flag officer's cabin
418 Officers' WC
419 Officers' lobby
420 Command secretariat
421 Crew space No 5
422 Anti-gas safety access
423 Officers' library
424 1st gunnery officer's cabin
425 1st gunnery officer's bathroom
426 1st paymaster's cabin
427 1st paymaster's bathroom
428 2nd gunnery officer's cabin
429 VII-VIII departments chief officer's cabin
430 Port AA fire control officer's cabin
431 Hull control officer's cabin
432 4th gunnery officer's cabin
433 Powerplant control officer's cabin

434 Port medium calibre fire control officer's cabin
435 No 4 320mm turret shell transfer room
436 Ammunition loading hatches to magazine No 4
437 Crew space No 6
438 Aft ammunition loading scuttle
439 Ammunition transfer rails
440 No 3 320mm turret shell hoist and motors
441 IX deptartment secretariat
442 Modifications secretariat
443 Ammunition loading hatches to magazine No 3
444 Ammunition loading hatches to medium & small calibre magazines
445 Crew space No 7
446 Port officers' rear corridor
447 Starboard officers' rear corridor
448 Mechanical workshop
449 Electrical workshop
450 Gunnery workshop
451 C.D. commissioned officer's bathroom
452 C.D. commissioned officer's cabin
453 Engineering service chief officer's cabin
454 Engineering service chief officer's bathroom
455 1st medical officer's bathroom
456 1st medical officer's cabin
457 Navigating officer's cabin
458 E.C. officer's cabin
459 3rd gunnery officer's cabin
460 Starboard medium calibre fire control officer's cabin
461 Store administration officer's cabin
462 Starboard AA fire control officer's cabin
463 Personnel officer's cabin
464 Officers' showers & WC
465 Weapon service chief officer's cabin
466 2nd medical officer's cabin
467 2nd paymaster's cabin
468 Stewards & cooks quarters
469 Stewards & cooks WC
470 WOs' quarters
471 Port WOs' quarters
472 Port officers' forward aisle
473 Starboard officers' forward aisle
474 WOs' quarters
475 Engineer POs' quarters
476 Engineer POs' showers & WC
477 WOs' showers & WC
478 Starboard WOs' quarters
479 Port WOs' rear aisle
480 Port WOs' middle aisle
481 Lobby
482 Starboard WOs' rear aisle
483 Starboard WOs' middle aisle
484 Service personnel washbasins
485 Service personnel showers
486 Crew showers
487 Crew showers & washbasins
488 Nos 1-2-3 boiler covers
489 Midship athwartship aisle
490 Nos 4-5 boiler covers
491 Access to engine rooms & boilers
492 Nos 6-7-8 boiler covers
493 Permanganate showers
494 Hot rinse showers
495 Locker room
496 Washbasins
497 Washbasins
498 Bridge platforms access lobby
499 Engineering accountant store
4A0 VII-VIII departments secretariat
4A1 Powerplant control room
4A2 Ship control technical secretariat
4A3 Engine control technical secretariat
4A4 Lobby
4A5 Port WOs' closets
4A6 Port WOs' mess
4A7 Gunnery WOs' quarters
4A8 Starboard WOs' closets
4A9 Starboard WOs' mess
4B1 Engineering & fire control WOs' quarters
4B2 Port WO's forward aisle
4B3 Starboard WO's forward aisle
4B4 Crew space No 8
4B5 Ammunition loading hatches to magazine No 2
4B6 II department secretariat
4B7 Weapon secretariat
4B8 No 2 320mm turret shell hoist
4B9 POs' showers & WC
4C1 POs' quarters
4C2 1st shipwright WO & 1st medical aid WO cabin
4C3 1st adjutant WO cabin
4C4 1st W/T WO cabin
4C5 Loading control WOs' showers & WC
4C6 Quartermaster service WOs' cabin
4C7 1st engineering WO cabin
4C8 1st signal service WO cabin
4C9 1st boatswain WO cabin
4D1 1st electrical service WO cabin
4D2 1st gunnery WO cabin
4D3 1st hull control service WO cabin
4D4 Crew berthing area No 9
4D5 Crew berthing area No 10
4D6 Ammunition loading hatches to magazine No 1
4D7 Ammunition loading hatches to medium & small calibre magazines
4D8 No 1 320mm turret shell transfer room
4D9 Fore ammunition loading scuttle
4E1 Crew sick-bay lobby
4E2 Sick-bay bathroom & WC
4E3 Linen store
4E4 Crew sick-bay
4E5 Pharmacy
4E6 Infected linen closet
4E7 Disinfection room
4E8 Isolation hospital
4E9 Officers' surgery
4F1 WO, PO & crew surgery
4F2 Isolation bathroom & WC
4F3 Lobby
4F4 Crew berthing area No 11
4F5 Dental surgery
4F6 Ironing room
4F7 Taylor's workshop
4F8 Laundry
4F9 Crew washbasins
4G1 Shipwright store
4G2 Boatswain store
A Aft engine room vent
B Aft turbo-generator vent
C Boiler rooms vents
Dx Boiler No 'x' funnel funnel uptake
E Medium calibre mount baseplates
F Fore engine room vent
G Fore turbo-generator vent
H Armoured communication pipe
S Diesel generator exhaust
M 37mm MG storage cylinders
V Fan

UPPER DECK
501 Admiral's quarters ventilation skylight
502 Admiral's quarters hatch
503 Officers' quarters ventilation skylight
504 Officers' quarters hatch
505 8m oar launch stowage
506 9m gig stowage
507 Aft warping windlass
508 Crew spaces hatch
509 No 4 320mm turret – loading room
510 No 3 320mm turret – transfer room
511 8m oared launch stowage
512 5m whaler stowage
513 8m oared launch stowage
514 Port officers' wardroom lobby
515 Starboard officers' wardroom lobby
516 Officers' wardroom
517 Filters room
518 Wardroom closet
519 Anti-gas safety access
520 Officers' closet
521 Dish washing room
522 Paymaster's office
523 Paymaster secretariat
524 Officers' pantry store
525 Personnel secretariat
526 Aft engine room cover
527 III & IV departments secretariat
528 Technical secretariat
529 Crew secretariat
530 Telephone switchboard
531 Crew berthing area No 12
532 Crew berthing area No 13
533 Funnel uptakes

534 Crew berthing area No 14
535 —
536 Fore engine room cover
537 Crew barber shop
538 Post office
539 Crew showers
540 X department secretariat
541 Photographic workshop
542 Photo dark room
543 WO & PO barber shop
544 Port battle-stations WC
545 Starboard battle-stations WC
546 Acoustical transmitting station
547 Frequency converters room
548 Weapon usage secretariat
549 Bridge access
550 Bridge WC
551 Crew space No 16
552 Battle-stations rations distribution room
553 Port oil loading room
554 Starboard oil loading room
555 Port POs' showers
556 Starboard POs' closet
557 No 2 320mm turret – shell hoist & motors
558 Crew space No 17
559 Port POs' mess
560 Port aft POs' quarters
561 Port POs' WC
562 Starboard POs' mess
563 Starboard aft POs' quarters
564 Starboard POs' WC
565 Port POs' WC
566 Starboard POs' WC
567 No 1 320mm turret – transfer room
568 Canteen
569 Crew berthing area No 18
570 Port fore POs' quarters
571 Starboard fore POs' quarters
572 Crew berthing area hatch
573 Port crew washbasins
574 Starboard crew washbasins
575 Crew access
576 Crew urinals
577 Crew washbasins
578 Crew WC
579 Canvas store
580 Paint store
Dx Boiler No 'x' funnel uptake
E Medium calibre mount – loading room
H Armoured communication pipe
K 90mm AA mount basement
S Diesel generator exhaust
M 37mm MG storage cylinders
V Fan

FORECASTLE
601 No 4 320mm turret – gunhouse
602 No 3 320mm turret – loading room
603 Officers' wardroom ventilation skylight
604 Electrical engineer stand-by room
605 10m motorboat stowage
606 10m motorboat stowage
607 12.25m motor launch stowage
608 12.25m motor launch stowage
609 Derrick winches
610 Security guard room
611 Aft engine room skylight
612 Shipwright workshop
613 Accountants' mess
614 Closet
615 Galley corridor
616 WO's & POs' galley
617 Officers' galley
618 Aft funnel smoke ducts
619 Vegetable handling room
620 Senior officers' galley
622 Crew galley
623 Fore funnel smoke ducts
624 Cafeteria
625 Mess-tin washing room
626 Closet
627 Mess-tin washing room
628 Smelting furnace
629 Forge
630 Bakery
631 Engine & boiler engineers' watch room
632 Fore engine room skylight
633 Sick-bay galley
634 Accumulator recharge room
635 Admiral's stateroom
636 Commanding Officer's stateroom
637 Admiral's bridge WC
638 Commanding Officer's bridge WC
639 Venereal disease prevention treatment room
640 Crew space ventilation skylight
641 No 2 320mm turret – transfer room
642 No 1 320mm turret – loading room
643 7m motorboat stowage
644 7m motorboat stowage
645 3.5m raft stowage
646 3.5m raft stowage
647 3.8m dinghy stowage
648 3.8m dinghy stowage
649 Fore warping windlass
650 Staircase ventilation skylight
651 Wine loading hatch
652 Ironing room ventilation skylight
653 Capstans
654 Laundry ventilation skylight
655 Diesel oil loading hatch
656 Jail ventilation skylight
657 Signal store skylight
Dx Boiler No 'x' funnel uptake
R Ammunition lockers
K 90mm AA mount
M Single 37mm MG
M1 Twin 20mm MG
M2 Twin 37mm MG
S Diesel generator exhaust
E Medium calibre turrets – operation room

SHELTER DECK
701 No 3 320mm turret – gunhouse
702 Electrical switchboard room – lighting section
703 Three 13m motor launch stowages
704 Aft engine room skylight
705 Fresh water tank
706 Auxiliary boilers oil tank
707 Port gunnery & fire-control stations
708 Starboard gunnery & fire-control stations
709 Washing water tank
710 Crew galley over-roof
711 Crew library
712 Staff archive
713 Fore engine room skylight
714 Potable water refrigerators
715 Secondary W/T station
716 Bridge WC
717 No 2 320mm turret – loading room
718 No 1 320mm turret – gunhouse
719 90mm AA mounts
720 135mm turrets
721 No 2 320mm turret – gunhouse
Dx Boiler No 'x' funnel uptake
N Ventilation pipe
H Armoured communication pipe
M2 Double 37mm. MG
V Fan

PLATFORMS
801 Lower chart room
802 Bridge staircase
803 Open-air gasoline tanks
804 Lookout station
805 Director basement
806 Lower radio-signalling platforms
807 Night fire director platform
808 3m director
809 Signal & flag platform
810 Signal & flag locker
811 Armoured bridge
812 Navigation bridge
813 Upper radio-signalling platform
814 Armoured admiral's bridge
815 Admiral's navigation bridge
816 Searchlight storage room
817 7.5m main director
818 Crow's nest
819 Surface lookout station
820 1st fire control station
821 Electrical switchboards – low voltage & AC sections
822 Electrical switchboards – main power & artillery sections
823 Searchlight storage room
824 Searchlight container cylinders
825 Rangefinder basement
826 Searchlight platform
827 3m director
B Magnetic compass
B1 Detecting compass
B2 Gyrocompass repeater
B3 Standard compass
K Ventilation pipes
G Ecogoniometer (sonar)
P 120cm searchlights
T Searchlight control devices
A Night fire control devices
L A.A. fire aiming devices

Simplified sections
A Admiral & senior officers' quarters
AP High-pressure turbines
B Officers' quarters
BP Low-pressure turbines
C Steering & rudder machinery
D Storerooms & closets
E Heavy gun turret machinery & services
F Magazines
G Machinery (various)
H Boiler rooms
J Fire control stations
K Funnel uptakes
KN Oil boilers
KC Mixed oil-coal boilers
L Service rooms & departments
M Engine rooms
N Command & control stations
P Crew berthing area
R WO & PO quarters
S Tanks (oil, water)

Above: Gunnery trials with the after 320mm guns of the *Andrea Doria* in the roadstead at Pola in October 1940.

Right: Detail of the bridge tower and the SDT located on the forward twin 320/44 turret on the *Andrea Doria* in late 1942. (E Leproni collection)

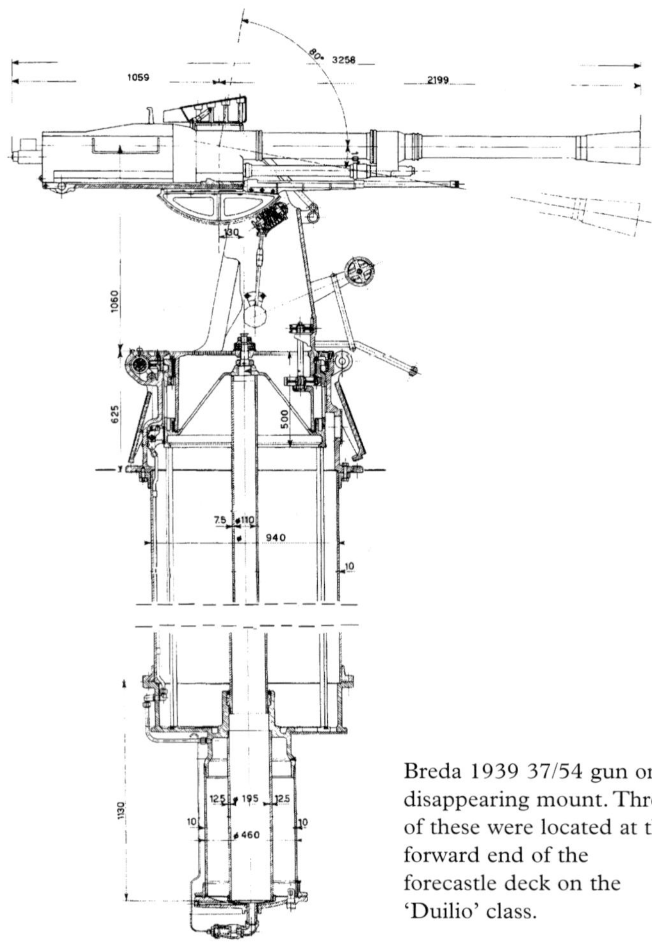

Breda 1939 37/54 gun on a disappearing mount. Three of these were located at the forward end of the forecastle deck on the 'Duilio' class.

The battleship *Andrea Doria* turning to starboard at speed in late 1942.

searchlights. All of the main fire control centres were located at the base of the bridge tower, beneath the armoured deck; the smaller types were in the 320mm and 135mm superfiring turrets.

Although in 1943 plans had been drawn up for the two 'Duilios' – and for the *Cesare* as well – to embark a type EC3 ter 'Gufo' radar on the bridge tower, no radar equipment was fitted to these ships before the end of the war. It was not until 1947 that the *Duilio*, flagship of the chief of naval forces, was fitted with two 'LWG' type air search radars. These were British mobile radars, characterised by a large antenna consisting of dipoles which formed two pyramids that were joined at their apexes; they were

Partial view of the machinery control room of the modernised battleship *Andrea Doria*.

'DUILIO' CLASS BATTLESHIPS

Principal technical characteristics after reconstruction[1]

		Duilio	*Andrea Doria*
Displacement (tons):	standard	26,176	26,140
	at normal load	27,726	29,455
	at full load	29,032	29,100

Dimensions (metres):	overall length	186.9
	length between perpendiculars	168.9
	breadth overall	28.03
	maximum draught full load	10.5

Powerplant: 8 Yarrow type water tube boilers
2 Belluzzo type geared turbines on 2 shafts; 2 three-bladed propellers, 4.8-metre diameter
Maximum total designed power: 75,000 shp; during trials 86,400 shp

Speed (knots): 26 maximum at normal load (trials 27)

Range (miles/knots): 4000/18; 1825/25 with 2548 tons oil and 471 tons reserve water for boilers

Protection (mm):	maximum vertical at waterline	250
	maximum total horizontal	150
	main gun turrets	280
	main gun barbettes	290
	medium calibre turrets	120
	maximum conning tower	260
	underwater:	Pugliese system 'absorbing cylinders'

Armament (mm):
10–320/44 guns (in 2 triple and 2 twin turrets)
12–135/45 guns (in 4 triple turrets)
10–90/50 guns (in single turrets)
15–37/54 rapid-fire guns (in 6 twin and 3 single mounts)
12–20/65 guns (in 6 twin mounts)
Later modifications:
19–37/54 guns (in 8 twin and 3 single mounts) [1942]
16–20/65 guns (in 8 twin mounts) [1942]

Complement[2] 1520 men (of whom 70 officers) and 1450 petty officers and ratings

Notes
[1] In the absence of significant differences between the two ships, median values are shown.
[2] Staff of any higher commands (Squadron, Division) are not included.

Shown purely by way of example are the median values of *deadweight* and *net tonnage* (volume of internal spaces) expressed in tonnes of space (1 tonne = 2.83m3) and are valid for both ships: 13,407 and 5058. These values were used to determine agreements for ports (outside of naval bases), towage and canal transits (Suez, etc).

MODERNISED 'DUILIO' CLASS BATTLESHIPS

Duilio
Reconstruction/modernisation: Cantieri del Tirreno, Genoa
Start of work: 1 April 1937
Completion of work and return to the Regia Marina: 26 October 1940
From 1953 laid up at La Spezia
Stricken: 15 September 1956
Broken up: La Spezia, 1958–1960

Andrea Doria
Reconstruction/modernisation: Cantieri Riuniti dell'Adriatico c/o 'San Marco' shipyard, Trieste
Start of work: 8 April 1937
Completion of work and return to the Regia Marina: 26 October 1940
From 1953 gunnery school ship at Taranto
Stricken: 1 November 1956
Broken up: La Spezia, 1961–1963

Detail of the two starboard 135/45 turrets on the battleship *Andrea Doria* in a photo probably from 1940.

installed, along with the associated towed trailer that acted as a base for the antenna, one port and one starboard at the far end of the platform located abaft the tower. On completion of the major work carried out in Taranto between 1947 and 1950, in addition to taking advantage of major improvements in radio communications equipment, the *Andrea Doria* was equipped with a 'Centrale

The *Andrea Doria* at Pola in October 1940 'swinging the compass' – calibrating of the ship's magnetic compasses.

The battleship *Duilio* entering La Spezia in May 1941. (Courtesy De Gaetano family)

The *Andrea Doria* at anchor in an anti-torpedo net enclosure in Taranto's Mar Grande in 1943.

Impiego Armi' (CAI, or Weapons Employment Centre) located abaft the bridge tower, and also finally embarked radar sets. There were three of these: one air search 'NSA 1' type (a modified 'LWG') placed on the mainmast top; another of the same type located on the aft 'mushroom', replacing the backup SDT and one sea search type 'NSM 1' with rotating antenna located on the masthead.

One last modification made to the *Andrea Doria* – the sole remaining battleship in Italian Navy service – stemmed from her final role as a gunnery training ship for cadets of the Crew School at Taranto. This involved the removal of some of the remaining 37/54 guns and placing on board a number of Oerlikon 20/70, Breda 20/65 and Isotta Fraschini 20/70 single mounts.

Chapter 9.1

FROM THE INITIATION OF HOSTILITIES TO THE BEGINNING OF THE WAR AGAINST GREECE (NOVEMBER 1940)

Italy's entry into the war, Regia Marina operational orientation

In late May 1940, with Belgium and Holland overrun by the Germans and the French front in the Ardennes broken through, Italy's entry into the war became a practical proposition. On 29 May Mussolini told the military chiefs that any date after 5 June was acceptable and confirmed directives that had been issued on 31 March that assigned the navy, unlike the two other armed forces, the mission of acting offensively within and outside the Mediterranean. This led to a worried reaction by the Undersecretary of State and Navy Chief of Staff, Admiral Domenico Cavagnari, expressed on 14 April, which managed to institute a more prudent policy. This was summarised in the 30 May meeting of the Chief of the General Staff, Marshal Pietro Badoglio, with the service chiefs of staff, as: defensive posture in the east and west and control of the Sicilian Channel. This concept inspired Direttiva Navale (Di Na = Naval Directive) 0 dated 29 May 1940 that foreshadowed an active defence, consisting, among other things, of:

- hindering the transfer of forces between the two basins of the Mediterranean;
- taking advantage of every occasion in which the Italian Navy had partially superior or equal forces;
- engaging the bulk of enemy forces as soon as possible, on condition that those forces had not been reinforced and that the encounter could take place not far from Italian bases;
- to defend shipping to Libya and Albania;
- and acting with stealth, light units and aircraft near enemy bases and against his lines of communication.

In effect, from a qualitative standpoint, compared with British and French forces in the Mediterranean, Italy's entry into the war

Taranto, afternoon of 7 July 1940. On board the *Giulio Cesare*, preparations to transfer the ship's battle ensign from its ceremonial casquet near the Captain's quarters where it was normally kept, to the signal station on the tripod mast, ready to be hoisted to the peak.

on 10 June 1940 found the Regia Marina in a situation of great inferiority in capital ships (battleships and aircraft carriers), but almost equal with respect to cruisers and superior only in surface and underwater torpedo craft:

Ship category	RM	RN Eastern Med	RN Western Med	MN Western Med	MN Eastern Med	Total RN + MN
Battleships (fast)	2(2)	4	1	4(2)	1	10(2)
Aircraft carriers		1				1
Heavy cruisers	7			4	3	7
Light cruisers	12	8	1	6	1	16
Destroyers/ Torpedo boats	118	22	9	31	3	65
Submarines	107	12		40	6	58
MAS	61					

RM = Regia Marina; RN = Royal Navy; MN = Marine Nationale

In addition, the two enemy navies could easily increase or replace their forces from other areas – as happened in late June with the establishment of Force H at Gibraltar to neutralise and replace the French fleet in the western Mediterranean – while the Italian fleet could only count on new construction. However, thanks to this new construction, the relative numbers would soon change to Italy's advantage because of France's departure from the scene and the entry into squadron service of four new Italian battleships. The British Mediterranean Fleet was concentrated at Alexandria, as Malta had been evacuated because of fear of air attack. The French forces, aside from a few ships in the eastern Mediterranean, were located in the western basin between the North African and metropolitan bases. British plans were aimed at ensuring control of their sea lanes in the eastern Mediterranean, including the Aegean, to prevent the Italians from resupplying those possessions, while offensive action was not envisioned in the central Mediterranean and against shipping between Italy, Libya and Albania, because of both the threat by the Regia Aeronautica, whose actual danger was yet to be measured, and the Regia Marina, especially its large submarine component. French plans were more aggressive, calling for bombardment of the Ligurian and Sicilian coasts, attacks against shipping to Libya in collaboration with the Mediterranean Fleet, and even landings on Pantelleria and the island of Elba. At the outset of hostilities, the two Allied navies abstained from taking any drastic action, but did, however, carry out intense activity with unchallenged incursions in the Aegean, coastal bombardments on the Libya-Egypt front and against Vado and Genoa on 14 June by a division of French heavy cruisers.

Supermarina, the newly constituted Italian naval operational command, was guided by criteria of prudence, which led to several sorties by light fleet units, but none made any contact with the enemy. The only offensive action was taken by the underwater arm, with some success and initially with light losses. However, the *Conte di Cavour* and the *Giulio Cesare*, which on 10 June had been put on a wartime footing, remained inactive at Taranto; their last sortie for an exercise with the VIII Destroyer Squadriglia had taken place on 6 June. It was in these early weeks of the war that the bow section of the upper deck of both ships, like that of the cruisers, was covered with a coat of white lime to make recognition from the air easier; this measure rapidly proved ineffective because of the limited resistance of the coating to weathering.

Operations TGM and MA5 and the battle of Punta Stilo (6–15 July 1940)

In early July 1940 it was decided to send a fast convoy with

The battleship *Conte di Cavour* steaming at sustained speed in the central Mediterranean on 8 July 1940.

Admiral Inigo Campioni, C-in-C of Italian naval forces at Punta Stilo, photographed on the bridge of the battleship *Giulio Cesare*.

troops, vehicles and other equipment to Benghazi for an offensive against Egypt. There had been earlier, largely isolated, passages of merchant ships and fast warships, but now for protection of the first major convoy Badoglio requested that the navy employ the entire fleet and that the air force commit large numbers of reconnaissance and bomber aircraft. The operation was designated TGM and the convoy consisted of five fast merchant ships. The bulk of the convoy was to sail from Naples at 18:00 on 6 July, with arrival at Benghazi scheduled for the afternoon of 8 July, and was to be escorted by six torpedo boats (IV Squadriglia plus two), by the 2nd Division and the X Destroyer Squadriglia. Long-range escort consisted of: to the east, the *Pola* (flagship of the commander-in-chief of II Squadron, Admiral Riccardo Paladini), the 1st and 3rd Divisions; to the west were the 7th Division, and the 5th, 4th and 8th Divisions were in a support role. The long-range escorts and the support group would disengage from convoy protection at 11:00 on 8 July, as long as there was no enemy presence in the central Mediterranean, otherwise they were to continue on until 13:00; command at sea was assumed by Admiral Inigo Campioni, commander-in-chief of I Squadron aboard the *Cesare*. The cited units and associated destroyer formations put to sea on the afternoon of 7 July. Between the 6th and the 11th, Supermarina arranged for two submarine barrier lines: four boats to the west and seven to the east. Aircraft from the air force and maritime reconnaissance would ensure surveillance of the routes that the ships were to cross and in addition bomber and fighter units were kept ready for incursions against Malta and Alexandria and to support the fleet at sea.

At the same time as Operation TGM, the British planned the transit of two convoys from Malta to Alexandria, beginning on 7 July – one fast convoy, MF1 of three ships, and one slow, MS1 of four ships – to transport civilian evacuees and equipment. From Alexandria the Mediterranean Fleet was to furnish cover split into three groups: Force A with the 7th Cruiser Division (light cruiser *Orion*, Vice-Admiral John Tovey, with *Neptune*, *Sydney*, *Liverpool*, *Gloucester*) and one destroyer; Force B with the battleship *Warspite*, flagship of the commander-in-chief of the Mediterranean Fleet, Admiral Andrew B Cunningham, and five destroyers; Force C with the 1st Battleship Division (*Royal Sovereign*, *Malaya*), the aircraft carrier *Eagle* and eleven destroyers. These groups were to set sail from Alexandria at 24:00 on 7 July, proceeding until they met 120 miles east of Cape Passero, then to continue towards the Italian coast. The Royal Air Force (RAF) was to carry out reconnaissance from 8 to 13 July in the central-eastern Mediterranean. Finally, on the morning of 8 July, leaving from Gibraltar on a separate mission (an air attack against Cagliari) was Force H (battlecruiser *Hood*, Vice-Admiral James Somerville, with the battleships *Valiant* and *Resolution*, the carrier *Ark Royal*, three light cruisers and ten destroyers).

In Rome reports had been received on the evening of 5 July of the movements of Force H from Gibraltar (this was the sortie for a second attack against the French squadron at Mers el Kebir, a few days after the French armistice with Germany) and, on the night of the 6th, of an imminent operation by the Mediterranean Fleet from Alexandria. The next day additional decoding pointed to its presence at sea and thus the possibility of action against the convoy or the Italian coast. The Italian naval and air commands were informed to prepare for reconnaissance and bombing. In the opposing camp, shortly after 08:00 on the 8th, Cunningham received a message that about three hours earlier the submarine *Phoenix* had attacked two Italian battleships that were proceeding south about 180 miles east of Malta (the attack was not observed); this led to the supposition that the Italian fleet had put to sea to protect a major convoy to Libya. Cunningham, therefore, continued on his way west and ordered Malta to carry out a reconnaissance to find and follow the Italian forces. On the morning of 8 July Campioni and Cunningham were therefore, aware of their respective presences at sea.

The Italian convoy, after a well-considered detour to the south, resumed its course for Benghazi. That same morning the Mediterranean Fleet was discovered and attacked without hesitation by the submarine *Beilul* and, later, several times by Italian aircraft but with negligible results; only the *Gloucester* suffered damage from a 250kg bomb on the bridge and because of damage the destroyer *Imperial* had to return, as did the *Beilul*, which was subjected to a lively anti-submarine attack. Shortly after 15:00 on the 8th Campioni received a report from maritime reconnaissance from Tobruk about the presence of three battleships and eight destroyers southeast of Crete headed west. The distance and the insufficient speed of the British ships would not have allowed them to reach the Italian convoy and therefore Campioni decided to cease providing protection but, fearing that at dawn on the 9th the enemy could appear off Benghazi and bombard the ships while they were unloading, he decided to proceed towards that location in order to engage them an hour before dusk. At 16:00 he ordered the *Cesare* and *Pola* groups to rendezvous and at 18:00 ordered that, if contact was not made within an hour, the fleet should resume its course to return to base. However, at 18:45, Supermarina, informed of his intentions, ordered him not to engage, considering the great distance from the metropolitan coast and the unfavourable visibility conditions in which he would find himself, with the waning light to his back, and to allow the air force to intervene pre-emptively in order to damage the enemy and allow the fleet to face it in relatively advantageous conditions. As a result, Campioni set a return course. Meanwhile, on the evening of the 8th, the convoy had reached Benghazi, while the 2nd Division and the X Destroyer Squadriglia continued on to Tripoli.

Cunningham, in turn, informed by aerial reconnaissance of the presence of the Italian fleet northeast of Cyrenaica, decided to break off his original mission covering the two convoys heading to Alexandria and to sail northwest in order to place himself between Alexandria and Taranto under cover of darkness. These movements went unnoticed by Supermarina, which, also on the basis of inexact information from the Kriegsmarine cryptographic service in Berlin, convinced itself that the Mediterranean Fleet was headed towards the eastern coast of Sicily to conduct an air-sea incursion on the afternoon of the 9th. So, on the evening of the 8th it ordered Campioni to head for the southeastern coast of Calabria, to assemble all of the forces at 14:00 on the 9th and to lie in wait, having an open return course to Taranto. It also ordered a picket line of five submarines south of the Gulf of Squillace and air reconnaissance along the probable enemy approach routes and requested Superaereo (the air force operational command) to plan bombing and observation flights around the naval bases of Taranto, Messina and Augusta. Supermarina's intentions were to have the Italian fleet attract the Mediterranean Fleet force towards the submarine picket line and to subject it to pre-emptive air attacks before engaging it, and with the Mediterranean Fleet already having been hit and in separate groups, on the afternoon of 9 July, taking advantage of Italian numerical superiority and greater speed as well as being close to their bases.

At 06:00 on the 9th, having been authorised by Supermarina, Campioni sent three destroyer squadriglie to Messina to refuel

Conti di Cavour conducting main armament firing exercises in the late 1930s.

and to join I Squadron by 14:00; in addition, he ordered the XIV Squadriglia that had remained in Taranto to reach him within the same hour. Paladini decided against refuelling his own destroyers at Augusta, considering that they would not have made it in time to reach the assembly point, but ordered the 7th Division and the XIII Squadriglia to try to join him after having refuelled. In addition, between 10:30 and 12:30, another three destroyers (*Dardo*, *Strale* and *Antonio da Noli*) had to be sent back to Taranto because of machinery problems. At 09:00, as per Supermarina's instructions, Campioni advised the admirals subordinate to him of his plan of action: once the fleet had gathered east-southeast of Cape Spartivento (Calabria), the fleet would deploy in four parallel columns at five-mile intervals; the inner lines would be formed by the 5th Division and by the heavy cruisers, the outer lines by light cruisers ready to deploy in the direction the enemy was coming from. The columns were to steam at 18 knots on an east-southeast/west-northwest heading then doubling back, keeping between the coast of Calabria and the deployed submarine barrier. In Campioni's plan, this arrangement would have allowed the battleship group to be in the centre, including the heavy cruisers, to compensate for the numerical, firepower and protective inferiority of his battleships, and to have a light group leading; the tail-end group would be able to reach the leading group thanks to its high speed. All of this arrangement was based, however, on the mistaken assumption that the British fleet was further to the south headed towards Sicily, while in reality it was much further north, headed towards the coast of Calabria.

The movements of the Mediterranean Fleet remained unknown for the rest of the morning of the 9th, with increasing apprehension within the Italian headquarters. In effect, because of the mistaken assessments, maritime reconnaissance had searched the waters to the east of the island and the approach routes to Puglia, with the result that the swathe between these two sectors, where the enemy was in fact located, was not searched. Conversely, on the same morning aircraft from the *Eagle* were able to spot and track the Italian ships at sea for long distances, so that an aerial torpedo attack was made possible. At 11:25 the 5th Division, having reached Punta Stilo, reversed course to join the *Pola* group that was 60 miles further south. Because of this manoeuvre, the *Eagle*'s torpedo aircraft did not find the two battleships that they had intended to attack, but at 13:25 discovered the heavy cruisers.

The attack was unsuccessful, but delayed the *Pola* group's attempt to get to the head of the 5th Division. At that hour the Italian forces were assuming the deployment desired by Campioni, with the exception of the 7th Division, which was still far off. However, more importantly, at 13:30 a seaplane on an anti-submarine patrol sent a message that it had spotted two battleships and eight destroyers 80 miles northeast of the Italian fleet. Although the position reported was 30 miles to the north of the actual position – as soon determined by embarked reconnaissance aircraft from 8th and 4th Divisions – this was the first news regarding the Mediterranean Fleet force that Campioni received on the 9th. At 14:00, therefore, he reversed course and manoeuvred to adjust his deployment, putting the *Pola* group in the vanguard ahead of the 5th Division, increasing speed to 25 knots (the maximum sustainable by the 'Cavour' class steaming in formation) and requested Marina Messina, Marina Taranto and Supermarina, in accordance with the cumbersome procedures of the time, to have bombers from the air force join the action. Because of the course reversal, 7th Division still lagged behind and would not be able to take part in the now impending encounter.

Meanwhile, at 13:10, instructions had arrived from Supermarina concerning the criteria to be followed in any encounter:

- not to distance themselves too far from aeronaval bases to allow pre-emptive or contemporaneous air attacks;
- to engage, if possible, the enemy battleships separately, being aware of the different speeds;

ITALIAN FLEET (senior commander at sea and commander-in-chief of I Squadron, Admiral Inigo Campioni aboard *Cesare*)

Starboard column	**Centre column**	**Port column**
8th *Division*; light cruisers *Abruzzi*, *Garibaldi*;	3rd Division: *Bolzano*, *Trento*	7th Division(*)*Eugenio*, *Attendolo*, *Montecuccoli*
4th Division; light cruisers *da Barbiano*, *da Giussano*;	1st Division: *Gorizia*, *Fiume*, *Zara*	
IX Destroyer Squadriglia: *Alfieri*, *Oriani*, *Carducci*, *Gioberti*;	*Pola* (flagship C-in-C II Squadron)	
XIV Destroyer Squadriglia: *Vivaldi*, *Pancaldo*.	XI Destroyer Squadriglia: *Artigliere*, *Camicia Nera*, *Aviere*, *Geniere*;	
	XII Destroyer Squadriglia: *Lanciere*, *Carabiniere*, *Corzziere*, *Ascari*;	
	5th Division: battleships *Cesare*, *Cavour*;	
	VII Destroyer Squadron: *Freccia*, *Saetta*.	(*) Manoeuvring to join 5th Division

MEDITERRANEAN FLEET (Commander-in-Chief Admiral Andrew Cunningham aboard *Warspite*)

Force A (vanguard)	**Force B and C (main force)**	***Eagle* Group** (about to separate)
7th Division: light cruisers *Orion*, *Neptune Sydney*, *Liverpool*	Battleship *Warspite*	Carrier *Eagle* (*)
	14th Destroyer Flotilla: *Nubian*, *Mohawk*, *Hereward*, *Decoy*;	Light cruiser *Gloucester* (**)
	1st Battleship Division: *Royal Sovereign*, *Malaya*;	Destroyers *Vampire* (*), *Voyager* (*)
	10th Destroyer Flotilla: *Stuart*, *Dainty*, *Defender*, *Juno*, *Janus*;	
	2nd Destroyer Flotilla: *Hyperion*, *Hero*, *Hostile*, *Hasty*, *Ilex*	(*) Detached from Force C (**) Detached from Force A

- delaying surface contact in order to allow the air force to do damage to the enemy;
- to withdraw the battleships at sunset;
- to engage the torpedo craft at night.

These counsels of caution proved irrelevant, as Campioni intended to steer north immediately in order to get to the north of the Mediterranean Fleet as quickly as possible and to engage it in battle as he had an open line of retreat to Taranto, at the price, however, of finding himself with a somewhat disorganised deployment at the moment of contact. He also had to forego the light cruisers *Armado Diaz* and *Luigi Cadorna* of the 4th Division, which had been authorised to return to Taranto and Messina because of problems with their evaporation gear.

While the Italian fleet sailed north, the *Pola* group – which had reversed course so as not to fall back behind 5th Division and was now disposed with *Pola* trailing and *Bolzano* leading – was able to take position ahead of the battleships, made easier by their reduction in speed from 25 to 20 knots. The cruisers of the 8th and 4th Divisions could not reach the head of the formation, but were able to assume a position to starboard of the battleships, on the side from which the enemy would approach, which was satisfactory enough to carry out their scouting duties. Cunningham, informed by the RAF of the Italian fleet's movements, continued on to the northwest until 14:00, when, having ascertained that he had put himself between the Italians and Taranto, he headed west in order to hasten contact. At 14:52 *Neptune* and, at 15:00 *Orion* spotted several Italian destroyers off their bows and, between 15:05 and 15:08, the 4th and 8th Divisions and the IX Destroyer Squadriglia spotted Force A to the east. With gunfire contact imminent (15:10) the opposing forces had assumed the deployments shown in the table opposite.

The *Conte di Cavour*, which is astern of the *Cesare* in a line ahead formation, with her 320/44 guns at maximum elevation against the British battleships.

At 15:10 and at 15:26, respectively, the 8th and 4th Divisions, which had increased speed to 30 knots, began exchanging fire with the Force A cruisers at a range of 20,000 metres, under conditions of excellent visibility and with a fresh wind from the northwest. The enemy cruisers directed fire on their counterpart Italian cruisers and on the IX Squadriglia's destroyers, which did not return fire due to insufficient range of their 120mm guns. The encounter between the two light forces stretched on until 15:31 while heading north, with no rounds finding their mark; only one shell, which exploded near the *Neptune*, damaged its catapult and

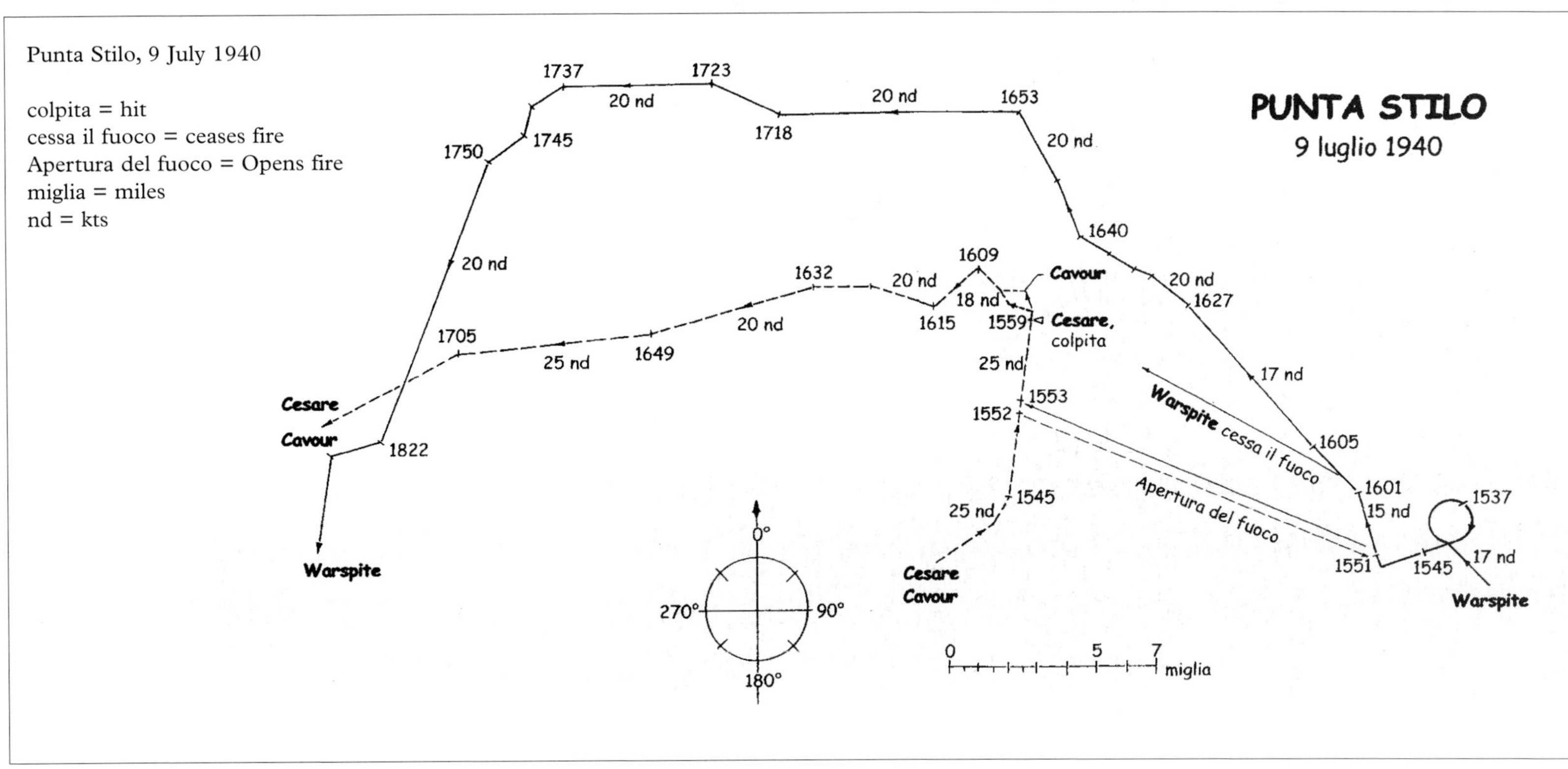

Punta Stilo, 9 July 1940, 15:53 hours. The battleship *Giulio Cesare* opens fire with her main armament against HMS *Warspite* at a distance of 26,000 metres.

seaplane with splinters, and the plane was dumped overboard to avoid a fire. The firing ceased when *Warspite* joined action at 24,000 metres with its 15in (381mm) guns in support of Force A, while the *Pola* group and the 5th Division hurried to join the action. At 15:23, in fact, after the six heavy cruisers had struggled into position ahead of the battleships, Campioni turned 60 degrees to starboard to close the range and increased speed to 25 knots. In this phase, which preceded the encounter between the battleships, the 8th Division and the IX Squadriglia in a brilliant manoeuvre freed the field of fire for the major ships, passing between the tail end of the *Pola* group and the head of the 5th Division, while the 4th passed astern of the battleships, but ended up trailing behind the main force and, in effect, the two units took no further part in the encounter. On the British side, after the Italian light cruisers had disengaged, *Warspite*, followed by Force A, executed a wide turn to join the slower *Malaya* – the *Royal Sovereign*, which could make no more than 18 knots, was now out of the picture – and the destroyers took positions to starboard to clear the field of fire.

At 15:53 *Cesare* and shortly thereafter *Cavour* opened fire on *Warspite* at a measured distance of 26,000 metres, close to the maximum range of their 320mm guns. The *Cavour* believed that her fire had been directed against another battleship at a range of 30,000 metres – greater, that is, than the range of the 320mm guns – but the British side confirmed that both Italian battleships had directed their fire on the nearer *Warspite*. At the same time, Campioni ordered the *Pola* group to close the distance, deploying the cruisers on a line of bearing of 040 degrees, but the enemy

The *Conte di Cavour*, shortly after, opening fire against the same target.

Cesare, in the foreground, and *Conte di Cavour* in the first minutes of firing at the Battle of Punta Stilo on 9 July 1940.

At 15:59, a 381mm (15in) salvo from *Warspite* brackets the *Giulio Cesare*. In this famous photo, taken by an cameraman from the LUCE Institute on board a destroyer, two 'long' rounds can be seen; a third round, however, has hit the Italian battleship amidships.

battleships remained beyond the range of the Italian 203mm guns, so that only the *Trento* managed to fire three salvos at 26,000 metres. After this, from 15:55 until 16:12, the ships of the *Pola* group began to fire on the closer Forcer A at an initial range of 25,000 metres. This kept them busy from 15:59 until 16:15 at distances between 21,000 and 18,000 metres, at the limit of the range of the 152mm guns, but managing, nevertheless, to distract them from the *Warspite*. During this phase the British fire was well executed: *Neptune* (or according to some sources the *Orion*) hit the *Bolzano* (the leading ship of the *Pola* group) three times in rapid succession.

Meanwhile, the most important development of the day had occurred. The fire of the Italian battleships had proven to be moderately accurate, even with rounds that straddled the target but that were somewhat dispersed; only a few rounds fell dangerously close to the *Warspite*'s bow and fragments from a couple of 'overs' damaged the destroyers *Decoy* and *Hereward*. Fire from *Warspite* was repeatedly well aimed with salvos that were well grouped and at 15:59 a 15in shell hit *Cesare* on the after funnel, penetrating it and exploding on the port side of the shelter deck. A violent fire ensued on the upper decks and superstructure and the smoke that was generated was sucked in by the fans in boiler spaces 4, 5, 6 and 7, which had to be evacuated and the boilers banked (for details see Appendix 4). Speed fell to 18 knots and as a result the *Cesare* fell astern of the *Cavour*.

In view of the new situation, Camponi decided to break off the action. He could not in fact wait to ascertain the extent of damage suffered and the time needed to restore his flagship to its proper state, nor did he feel inclined to leave the *Cavour* and the *Pola* group engaged with the large enemy force, but it would have been impossible to skirt the British fleet to the north and set a course for Taranto if the fleet was confined to the maximum speed that the *Cesare* could make. Therefore, at 16:05 he decided to disengage, turning to 270 degrees, laying a smokescreen and throwing the destroyers into a torpedo attack. The new course was soon altered to 230 degrees, and the *Cesare* resumed the division lead. For about ten minutes the battleships and the heavy cruisers continued to fire as they withdrew, while the destroyers of the five squadriglie went on the attack, covering themselves with smokescreens while disengaging. This continued until 16:45, without, however, being pressed to the limit, with torpedoes launched at ranges between 12,500 and 11,250 metres, which caused the enemy little concern. On the other hand, laying the smokescreens proved very effective and made the Italian disengagement much easier.

British reaction was likewise not very effective: the destroyers of the 10th Flotilla, which were slightly to the northeast of *Warspite*, counterattacked, supported by fire from Force A, from *Warspite* and from *Malaya*, but no Italian ships were damaged, except, very slightly, the destroyer *Alfieri*. An aerial torpedo attack made by nine Swordfish aircraft from the *Eagle* between 16:10 and 16:45 against *Bolzano* and *Trento*, which had been mistaken for battleships, produced no results. Cunningham did not feel like pushing through the smokescreen but preferred to go around it to windward from the north. By 17:00, when his destroyers had completed the manoeuvre, the Italian fleet was out of sight. At 17:35, having determined that it would no longer be possible to intercept the Italian fleet, he headed south and then southeast. Finally, at 21:15, after a report at 19:05 from the *Warspite's* reconnaissance aircraft placed the Italian fleet near Cape Spartivento on a course of 230 degrees at 18 knots, Cunningham turned to make for a point south of Malta where he would meet with the major ships while waiting for his destroyers to refuel.

Meanwhile, at 16:45, the *Cesare* had lit six of its eight boilers and was able to make 25 knots. Campioni, however, did not take advantage of the conditions to resume contact with the Mediterranean Fleet and head to Taranto, which risked being caught against the coast of Calabria, nor to engage the destroyers in night-time attacks due to the shortage of torpedoes and fuel. With respect to the squadriglie that had already been sent to their bases to refuel, these would join the fleet around 20:00 near Cape dell'Armi, too late and too distant to attempt any further attacks without precise information on the enemy's position and course. In view of the fact that the enemy was not in direct pursuit, Campioni gave up the idea of changing course to engage in combat while withdrawing at the speed dictated by the *Cesare*. This was discovered by British reconnaissance, which indicated to Cunningham that the Italian fleet was distancing itself in some disorder. Campioni continued on towards Cape dell'Armi to reach the bases in eastern Sicily and in the Lower Tyrrhenian; the *Cesare*, the 3rd Division, the *Cadorna* escorted by *Freccia* and *Saetta*, and the 7th Division made for Messina and the straits, while the *Pola*, the 1st, 8th and 4th Divisions and the *Cavour* headed for Augusta.

From that point on, operations were confined to air activity. The missed opportunity to spot MF1 in the early morning had prevented the Regia Aeronautica from acting before the meeting of the two fleets. Intervention by units of the II Air Squadron and by the IV Territorial Air Zone in Puglia, although on alert, did not begin until after Campioni's request to Supermarina at 14:00, which was then relayed to Superaereo that did not receive it until 14:50. Seventeen sorties were made with attacks by small formations at high altitudes (from three to twelve bombers) between 16:45 and 21:10 on 9 July. A total of 126 aircraft were involved, which dropped 514 bombs (almost all of which were 250 and

100kg) without hitting any ships, even though the British noted the danger of the bombings. The most regrettable fact, however, was that because of the vague nature of the information on the position and course of the Mediterranean Fleet, the scattering of the Italian fleet and the air force's inability to recognise Italian ships from high altitude, about half of the attacks were directed – without registering any hits – against the Italian ships that were heading in groups to the Sicilian bases.

From the night of 9/10 July and throughout the day the British destroyers and the *Royal Sovereign* refuelled at Malta. During those same hours fast convoy MF1 left Malta bound for Alexandria, escorted by four destroyers, then *Gloucester*, and a few hours later slow convoy MS1 left with a screen of three destroyers. With the bulk of the Mediterranean Fleet, Cunningham resumed his return at 09:00 on the 11th, maintaining a covering position west of convoy MS1, but intending first to strike another blow by an aerial torpedo attack at dusk on the 10th against Augusta, where reconnaissance from Malta had reported the presence of ships. At 21:00 on the 9th, the *Cesare* and the 3rd Division had entered Messina, while the 7th Division continued on to Palermo through the straits and the main force headed to Augusta. Earlier, on 7 July, thanks to partial deciphering of a coded enemy message, Supermarina picked up hints of an air raid against Augusta. Additionally, on the 10th, Regia Marina cryptographers in Rome had deciphered a radio message from Cunningham at 09:24 on pending movements that clearly pointed to a night attack against the Ionian bases. Based on the decryption from the 7th, on the night of the 9th Supermarina had alerted the naval bases and had ordered Paladini to leave Augusta, which he had just reached, and to move to Naples with the *Pola*, the *Cavour* and the 1st Division, which he did on the night of the 10th after a hasty refuelling. On the morning of 10 July it was the turn of the IX and XI Destroyer Squadriglie, while the 8th and 4th Divisions followed in the late afternoon to Taranto. The 7th Division, which had already entered the Tyrrhenian, was redirected to Naples because of fear stemming from the presence of Force H in the western Mediterranean. The *Cesare*, along with 3rd Division, remained in Messina to offload wounded and dead and to clean up the ship.

As assumed by Supermarina, on the afternoon of the 10th the

The effects of the fire on the *Cesare* resulting from the enemy shell hit. The flames were quickly put out, but the smoke caused the temporary shutting down of several boilers, with a notable loss in the Italian battleship's speed and the consequent breaking of contact with the British naval forces.

Ships lost and damaged during operations TGM and MA5 (6–15 July 1940)[1]

	Italian naval forces			Mediterranean Fleet and Force H		
Type of attack	Ships lost	Ships damaged by direct hits	Ships damaged by near misses	Ships lost	Ships damaged by direct hits	Ships damaged by near misses
Torpedo (submarine)				*Escort*(1)		
Torpedo (aircraft)	*Pancaldo*[2](1)					
Bomb					*Gloucester*(1)	*Warspite*(2) *Malaya*(1)
Main gun (381/20)		*Cesare*(1)				*Decoy*(1) *Hereward*(1)
Medium-calibre gun (152)		*Bolzano*(3) *Alfieri*(1)	*Bolzano*(3)			*Neptune*(1)

1 Added to these losses are four Regia Aeronautica aircraft and damage to the submarine *Beilul*.
2 Sunk at Augusta but subsequently raised.
() Following the ship names, in parentheses, are the number of rounds that hit or that were near misses.

Mediterranean Fleet had taken up its planned position in the western Ionian Sea for a launch from *Eagle* at 18:50 of nine Fairey Swordfish aircraft, all of which were armed with torpedoes. Three of these planes spotted and attacked the destroyer *Leone Pancaldo*, which had been delayed in its turn at refuelling, in the roadstead at Augusta. The ship, hit by a torpedo, sank rapidly while the attackers headed for Malta. On 11 July the Mediterranean Fleet resumed its return to base, without having been disturbed by the Italian air force because of its poor reconnaissance, if one excludes a fruitless operation on the morning of the 10th against Malta, targeting the aircraft that were refuelling. From Alexandria, the battleship *Ramillies*, the 3rd Cruiser Division and four destroyers set sail to reinforce the escort of convoy MS1. During this phase, which ended between 13 and 15 July with the return of the Mediterranean Fleet to Alexandria and the convoys split into three groups, British forces were subjected to a total of thirty-one high-altitude bombing raids by 235 Regia Aeronautica aircraft that dropped 914 bombs of varying sizes, without any of them making a direct hit on any target. Both *Warspite* and *Malaya* suffered superficial damage caused by near misses.

Meanwhile, in the western Mediterranean, Force H, which had set sail from Gibraltar for a diversionary action against the airbases at Cagliari, was spotted on the morning of the 9th by Italian reconnaissance south of Mallorca and subjected to aggressive high-altitude bombardment by aircraft based in Sardinia, but with no material effect. Nevertheless, this was enough to induce Somerville to abandon the mission, judging it not worth the risk of damage to the *Ark Royal*. At 22:15 on 9 July he reversed course to return and, on the eve of the 11th, the submarine *Guglielmo Marconi*, which was part of a group of four boats stationed in the Alboran Sea to track the movements of Force H, while surfaced spotted and attacked a section of destroyers, sinking HMS *Escort*.

From the standpoint of losses, the dual operating cycle that culminated in the battle of Punta Stilo can be summarised by the table above.

In conclusion, both fleets had accomplished their respective missions, allowing their own convoys to reach their destinations unharmed. But the course and development of operations lent themselves, even then, to many assessments, some of which are worth mentioning.

On the Italian side, it was the first wartime test of air-naval cooperation and employment at sea of the air arm. Results were disappointing and, from certain aspects, worrying. Maritime reconnaissance worked well enough on 8 July to enable Campioni to have the convoy reach Benghazi safely, but it failed on the morning of the 9th, not all of which was his fault, and on 10 July when it did not find the Mediterranean Fleet south of Malta. The most critical aspects, however, had to do with doctrine and execution of the air attacks at sea; of a total of about 2000 bombs dropped by about 500 aircraft, only one hit the target. Despite the exaggerated estimates at the time, faith in high-altitude bombing was badly shaken and with this the reliance that the navy placed on weakening enemy forces before engaging them; this disappointment was even more accentuated by errors in recognising Italian ships. Communication arrangements between the two services were also inadequate; in the absence of direct radio contact between naval ships at sea and aircraft, communications were effected only by being routed through the respective headquarters on shore, with the result that they were often too slow, imprecise and of little use, added to which were insufficient training and the lack of experience of the air observers; air observation by the shipboard aircraft proved to be better. All in all, cooperation between the two arms was lacking and not very susceptible to improvement in the short run, except for target identification. Campioni raised the question of an aircraft carrier, the only thing that could ensure timely air support at sea, and asked that priority be given to building one ahead of the oceanic cruisers that had been authorised by the last peacetime budget.

In operational terms Campioni showed a more offensive spirit than did Supermarina, conscious of the advantage represented by superior speed. Tactically, the Italian fleet manoeuvred well enough, taking into account the large number of ships and the fact that it was the first time the two squadrons were operating under a unified command; but the *Pola* group, which was to have supported the 5th Division against the enemy battleships (in truth only the *Warspite*) was late in taking up its planned formation, remained at the extreme range of its 203mm guns, and when it finally engaged Force A found itself with the flagship behind it. Furthermore, the light cruiser divisions remained on the margins of the encounter, briefly engaging their enemy counterparts and only partially attending to their scouting tasks.

With respect to gunnery, the 5th Division engaged the enemy at almost the extreme limit of its 320mm guns, according to the prevailing doctrine that sought to take advantage of the greater average range of the Italian guns to give a favourable turn to the course of the battle by scoring an early hit, in view of the fact that it was only at steep angles of fall that the 320mm rounds could penetrate the horizontal protection of the enemy battleships. These were, in truth, remote possibilities because of the lack of precision of the guns at those ranges and confirmed that the 'Cavour' class were not capable, in terms of either armament or protection, of facing the British battleships by themselves. The *Cesare* fired seventy-four 320mm rounds, of which forty-four were armour-piercing and thirty-seven semi-armour-piercing, all against the *Warspite*, but to no result. On the other hand, guns and ammunition functioned satisfactorily, but the 100/47 anti-aircraft guns were barely effective, due partly to the 'primitive' fire direction system; the fire of the 37/54 guns seemed to be more effective.

The powerplants caused no problems on the larger ships, but there were many breakdowns on the less modern lighter ships, attributed to equipment problems, fatigue and the poor competence of the machinery personnel. Above all, the limited range of Italian destroyers under wartime conditions came to light; all complained of high consumption, especially of water, and a full four squadriglie were unavailable during the decisive phase of the operation as they had to return to their bases for resupply. Campioni concluded that it was necessary to maintain slower speeds while on prolonged wartime operations, as had been the case during TGM.

But the fact that marked the course of the battle and which was not noticed for a long time in the post-war period, was the surprise appearance of the Mediterranean Fleet between the Italian fleet and Taranto, a circumstance in the first instance blamed on the Italian decoding service – which nevertheless achieved some good results – and the German service in Berlin, which on 9 July were mistaken in assessing the enemy routes and objectives and sent the reconnaissance aircraft on a false trail. On the 13th, the day of his return to Alexandria, Cunningham wrote to the First Sea Lord, Admiral Dudley Pound, that for him the Italian codes were an open book, thanks to the capture of the codebooks from a sinking submarine (the *Uebi Scebeleli*, on 29 June). It was, perhaps, an exaggeration, but it is certain that the intelligence system that assisted him, including air reconnaissance, gave him an awareness of Italian movements, much more consistent and precise than that which Campioni was able to enjoy. It should also be stressed that from the afternoon of the 9th until the morning of the 11th the Mediterranean Fleet was the almost unchallenged master of the Ionian Sea, inasmuch as the threat represented by a handful of torpedo bombers was enough to drive almost all of the Italian fleet into the Tyrrhenian.

As he again wrote to Pound, Cunningham himself was not pleased with the results. Thanks to its greater speed the Italian fleet had escaped him: his battleships were too slow, with the partial exception of the *Warspite*; the light units were insufficient in number, especially with respect to heavy cruisers, of which he was entirely devoid; and because of the modest air component and the imperfect state of personnel training, the *Eagle* appeared to him to be ill-suited as a fleet carrier. He therefore requested that a battleship be assigned him that would be able to fight in the line alongside *Warspite*, as well as a modern carrier, a couple of heavy cruisers, an AA cruiser and a couple of sloops. He was quite impressed by the grouping of the Italian bombers, despite the fact that there was an extremely low percentage of bombs that hit the target (estimated at 1 per cent). Nevertheless, even if that were to be doubled, it would have represented a more than acceptable risk for future operations in the central Mediterranean.

Movements of the *Cavour* and *Cesare* after the battle of Punta Stilo

On the afternoon of 10 July, the *Cavour* reached Naples with the bulk of the squadron, after having cleared the 320/44 guns of several rounds that had failed to fire, firing them out to sea.

The *Giulio Cesare*, with power restored to all of her boilers on 13 July 1940 steaming from Messina to La Spezia.

Detail of the port side amidships of the *Giulio Cesare* while moored at Messina on 9 July 1940. Note the gash at the base of the after funnel made by the British 381mm shell and the blackening of the structures from the smoke following the fire. (A Fraccaroli collection)

Campioni, arriving by land from Messina along with his staff, raised his flag on the morning of 13 July. In the afternoon the ship set sail for Taranto escorted by destroyers of the VII Squadriglia, the *Corazziere* and *Carabiniere*. In the Strait of Messina the *Cadorna* and *Vivaldi* joined, while the two 'Soldati' class destroyers entered Reggio Calabria. In the late afternoon of the 14th the battleship moored at the buoy in Mare Grande.

On the evening of 12 July at Messina *Cesare* and *Bolzano* set sail for La Spezia, escorted by the destroyers *Aviere*, *Geniere*, *Malocello*, *Pigafetta* and *Zeno* and, during the daylight hours, by aircraft in an anti-submarine role. They crossed the Tyrrhenian at speed and during the late evening of the 13th the group reached La Spezia. There the next day the *Cesare* began repair work. The repairs were completed on 31 July and the time was also used to replace the 13.2mm machine guns with the same number of 20mm guns. On the morning of 1 August, the battleship transferred to Genoa for graving, but in leaving the base at La Spezia she had to stop her machinery and bank her boilers because mud had blocked the sea intakes for the condensers. This was a danger that plagued the manoeuvres of large ships until the end of the war at La Spezia due to the insufficient depth of water there. The ship resumed passage to Genoa in the afternoon, and was again in drydock for repairs there from 2 to 7 August. Having re-entered La Spezia on the 8th, that same evening she weighed anchor to join the rest of the 5th Division in Taranto, escorted as far as Messina by the XIII Destroyer Squadriglia (*Alpino*, *Bersagliere* and *Fuciliere*) and from there by the destroyers *da Recco* and *Usodimare*.

Small splinter holes on the *Giulio Cesare*'s superstructure. The damage sustained during the Punta Stilo engagement was repaired within a few days by work carried out at La Spezia.

Strengthening the Italian battle squadron and its lack of effect on the conduct of the naval war

In July 1940 the entry into squadron service of the two 'Littorio' class battleships, followed by that of the *Duilio*, coincided with the fall of France. These two factors did much to improve the relative strength compared with the British squadrons at Alexandria and Gibraltar, each of which was numerically inferior to the Italian naval opposition. This scenario prompted Mussolini to issue new directives on 11 July that, insofar as the naval war was concerned, expressly anticipated the imminent full operational status of the two new battleships and pointed out that the Regia Marina's main mission was to conduct energetic operations against the two separate groups of the British fleet. The naval hierarchy considered these plans to be excessive and on that same day were able

Inscription on the barbette of No 3 turret of the battleship *Giulio Cesare* celebrating the ship's participation in the battle of Punta Stilo.

to get them rescinded and replaced by others that were more sensible. Soon after, Supermarina issued a new edition of the Di Na [Naval Directive] 0 that confirmed the provisions of the earlier directive, but also planned to support the operations of the Italian army in North Africa. But each time that these plans faced concrete realities, the navy ended up assuming quite a different attitude.

The first problems surfaced in July 1940 when Badoglio requested that the army's flank be protected during the planned advance into Egypt in case of a sortie by the Mediterranean Fleet, and with the request by the German navy's high command (the Seekriegsleitung, Skl) for information concerning operational possibilities in the Mediterranean with a view to cooperation between the two navies. In the first case Cavagnari and Campioni excluded engaging the enemy in the eastern Mediterranean because of its distance from the major Italian bases, because the new battleships and the *Duilio* were insufficiently worked up, and because of the delay in making final adjustment to the main guns of the *Vittorio Veneto*. In the second case, the navy held that because of the characteristics of the Mediterranean theatre and the distance of sensitive enemy targets, there was no possibility of offensive action by the Italian fleet with the likelihood of even partial success; instead, its role should consist of the defence of the sea lanes to Libya and in tying up large portions of the Royal Navy, thus easing pressure on German shipping in the Atlantic trying to evade the surface blockade. In turn, the Italian Navy would have gained an advantage from German operations and collaboration between the two fleets would consist of these indirect effects. The Skl was disappointed. In its judgement, the fall of France opened suitable opportunities for action in the eastern Mediterranean, in order to expel the British from Egypt and from the Levant; this was, in truth, an optimistic assessment but which in part corresponded to Badoglio's initial thoughts. Here we should only note that the significant strengthening of the fleet, rather than fostering a greater offensive spirit ended up embedding the concept of the 'fleet in being' more deeply in Supermarina. This was a line of thinking that would not change for the rest of the war, regardless of its progress.

Entry into squadron service of the *Duilio*, re-entry of the *Cavour* and the air-naval exercises of 10 August 1940

At the outbreak of the war the *Duilio* was undergoing training at Pola, making brief sorties into the Upper Adriatic. The ship left Pola in a combat-ready status for Taranto at 05:00 on 14 July with an escort consisting of the destroyers of the XV Squadriglia (*Confienza, Solferino, San Martino, Palestro*) as far as the Ancona parallel. From Ancona to Taranto escort was assumed by the XIV (*Partenope, Polluce, Pleiadi*), along with two maritime reconnaissance aircraft. At Taranto, which she reached shortly after 08:00 on the 15th, the *Duilio* moored at the buoy in Mar Grande, joining the 5th Division. Until almost the end of July she was engaged in protective sweeping exercises and in naval and AA gunnery practice, either at anchor or in the gulf.

On 10 August *Cesare*'s return to Taranto provided an opportunity to hold an air-naval exercise, exactly in the waters of Punta Stilo, with the entire division: in addition to the *Cesare* and the XVI Destroyer Squadriglia, this comprised the *Conte di Cavour*, Rear Admiral Bruno Brivonesi's flagship, the *Duilio*, the VII

Squadriglia (*Freccia*, *Dardo* and *Strale*) and the VIII Destroyer Squadriglia (*Folgore*, *Baleno* and *Lampo*) from Taranto, as well as units of the Regia Aeronautica, of the I Squadron and of the seaplane command from Taranto. The meeting of the two groups occurred at 06:00 on 10 August. Fleet evolutions and zig-zag exercises were followed by various concentration and dispersion and defensive manoeuvres against air attacks. In the early afternoon *Cavour* and *Duilio* fired their 320mm guns at charges III and I and all of the ships, including the destroyers, fired with their medium-calibre guns. *Cavour* and *Cesare* returned to Taranto at 14:30 while *Duilio*, which needed more training, continued gunnery exercises until after 15:00, then returned to Taranto.

One aspect of these exercises deserves particular mention – experiments in aerial recognition, after the application of white lime on the bows had proved so ineffective at Punta Stilo. These trials were carried out under decidedly favourable conditions of aerial visibility and were among the last held before the definitive adoption of the diagonal white and red stripes on ships' decks. The assessments in this respect expressed by Brivonesi to Campioni can be summarised as follows:

- The white and red stripes painted on the forward deck were clearly visible even at an altitude of 3000 metres and at a horizontal distance of 5000 metres; those on the *Cavour* and *Duilio* were more visible as they were on a larger surface area; the diagonal white stripes on the after deck were quite visible, except for those at the extreme stern, which could be confused with the ship's wake; visible, but of little use, were the red circles painted on the main gun turret roofs;
- The red smoke trails emitted from the mast, which had been tested the previous May, were judged to meet the requirement; those emitted by the *Cesare* were spotted at a horizontal distance of 10,000 metres, but those by the *Cavour* were not so visible;
- The red smoke for submarines was not spotted, except for some from 1500 metres altitude [Authors' note: submarines did not participate in this exercise];
- Searchlight signals were effective; Brivonesi, however, specified that the periods in which the searchlights were shut off should be very short.

Ultimately, the 5th Division commander judged the system of diagonal white and red stripes to be adequate, but that they could be improved upon and should be added to the stern sections for the benefit of aircraft approaching from that direction. He also brought attention to the ease of recognising several characteristic features of the ships such as the 90/50 turrets of the *Duilio*, visible even from high altitude, and of the advantage of retaining smoke and searchlights in practical recognition tests.

On 12 August at Taranto, Campioni transferred his flag from the *Cavour* to the *Cesare* and on 29 August the 6th Division was established, at that moment consisting only of *Duilio* and the VIII Destroyer Squadriglia while awaiting squadron entry of the *Andrea Doria*. On 21 August *Duilio*, *Cesare* and the destroyer *Pessagno* carried out another gunnery and manoeuvring exercise in formation in the Gulf of Taranto.

Action against Operation 'Hats' (31 August–2 September 1940) and breakdown of the *Giulio Cesare*'s condensers

After the battle of Punta Stilo and in view of the imminent Italian offensive in Egypt, the British admiralty planned to reinforce the Mediterranean Fleet with more modern radar-equipped ships,

A photo taken during the attempted action against the British Operation 'Hats' in which four of the five Italian battleships (*Littorio*, *Vittorio Veneto*, *Cavour*, *Cesare* and *Duilio*) took part. (G Tomaselli collection)

without having them transit around the Cape of Good Hope, and to resupply Malta at the same time. Designated 'Hats' and set in motion in late August, this complex operation had a number of aims: the transfer from Gibraltar to Alexandria of the battleship *Valiant*, the carrier *Illustrious* and the AA cruisers *Calcutta* and *Coventry*; resupplying Malta with a convoy from Alexandria; carrying out air and naval bombardments of Italian bases in Sardinia and in the Aegean; and to escort a convoy from Nauplia to Port Said (Operation MB3). Thus converging towards the central Mediterranean were: Force B from Gibraltar (battle-cruiser *Renown*, carrier *Ark Royal*, light cruiser *Sheffield* and sixteen destroyers), constituting the main element of Force H; Force F, consisting of the Mediterranean Fleet reinforcing units, and from Alexandria the Mediterranean Fleet (battleships *Warspite* and *Malaya*, carrier *Eagle*, heavy cruiser *Kent*, light cruisers *Gloucester*, *Liverpool*, *Orion*, *Sydney* and thirteen destroyers) and convoy MF2 consisting of three merchant ships with four escorting destroyers.

On 30 August Supermarina became aware of both movements and made arrangements with Superaereo to act against them: in the west with aircraft and submarine ambushes, in the east with surface and air forces. The naval forces (FN) put to sea at first light on the 31st, heading towards the central Ionian as joint squadrons. Their composition consisted of the battleships *Littorio* (Admiral Campioni, C-in-C) and *Vittorio Veneto* of the 9th Division; *Cavour* and *Cesare* of the 5th Division and *Duilio* of the 6th, the six light cruisers of the 7th and 8th divisions and twenty-two destroyers in six squadriglie (I Squadron) in addition to the *Pola* (Admiral A Iachino), plus another five heavy cruisers (1st and 3rd Divisions) and twelve destroyers in three squadriglie (II Squadron).

These forces were superior to those of the Mediterranean Fleet, even considering that the two 'Littorio' class ships and the *Duilio* were not fully worked up, and the absence of the *Cesare* in the initial phase of the operation. *Cesare* got under way without problem at 05:35, but some ten minutes later, after clearing the port, the ship had to stop because of blockage of the condensers. She dropped anchor shortly before 06:00, near San Vito and, at 07:00, having cooled the water, the main and auxiliary condensers could be opened. It was then discovered that the tubes and the condenser structures themselves were clogged with algae and other vegetation from the bottom. With the assistance of divers from the naval yard the intakes were cleaned out, as well as the condenser tubes and the fire pump circuits. At 09:25, with machinery stopped and manoeuvred by tugs, the ship was towed to a new anchorage position. The cleaning operations were completed, and the ship was ready to move by 11:45, but she did not set sail until the night of 30 August and, escorted by the torpedo boats *Pleiadi* and *Partenope*, was able to join the FN the next morning.

Meanwhile, in the Ionian, there was no encounter between the fleets, even though Italian air reconnaissance had worked fairly well. The departure of the FN was delayed until it had some knowledge of enemy movements and then it was restricted by Supermarina orders to proceed at a speed of only 20 knots and to avoid night-time engagements, and to reverse course and head to the centre of the Gulf of Taranto by dusk if contact was not made with the enemy force. Such constraints were not conducive to interception, except in the unlikely event that the British were heading towards the Italian coast. At 14:30 on the 31st Supermarina called for the fleet's return, ordering a reversal of course for 16:00 hours. This interrupted the advance of II Squadron, which preceded I Squadron, when it seemed possible to intercept the enemy forces around 18:30. On the morning of 1 September, from the Gulf of Taranto, the FN, which had now been joined by the *Cesare*, resumed searching for the enemy on the earlier course heading (155°) with the restriction of not being able to go beyond the Malta–Zante line. In addition, on 1 September the wind, which had freshened since the previous evening, had turned into a violent storm from the north-west and, shortly after 13:00, the FN were ordered to return at speeds that were gradually reduced to 10 knots, as the destroyers could not hold their formation, nor could they use their guns, in the prevailing conditions.

During the return passage the *Abruzzi* was missed by two torpedoes fired by the submarine *Parthian* that passed under her hull, and the *Littorio*, *Duilio* and *Cavour* opened fire several times with their port AA and medium-calibre batteries against Sunderland flying boats that stood off at a great distance. Towards evening Italian aircraft arrived in the skies over the FN, which reached their departure bases on the night of 1/2 September and were kept ready to move until the afternoon of the 3rd. Meanwhile the air attacks made in the western and central-eastern Mediterranean had led to meagre results and to the loss of several aircraft. Only the merchant ship *Cornwall* was damaged, which, through great effort, managed to reach Malta, and the Polish destroyer *Garland* was also lightly damaged.

Sortie by the Naval Forces on 7–9 September 1940

As soon as Operation 'Hats' was concluded, Force H left Gibraltar on 6 September, pretending to make a sortie into the Mediterranean, in order to mask its move to Freetown in the Atlantic to participate in the attack against the French forces at Dakar. On the night of the 6th Supermarina received news of the sortie to the east and arranged to counter it with submarine ambushes and intervention by the FN, whose departure it ordered, so that at 16:00 on the 8th it would be 50 miles south of Cagliari. In the event of lack of contact with the enemy, they were to return to the Lower Tyrrhenian to the east of the Cape Carbonara–Marettimo Island line, thence to reach the 80 east meridian at 07:00. The two squadrons left Taranto on the afternoon of the 7th with a composition of five battleships and a like number of heavy cruisers, equal to the force that challenged Operation 'Hats'. At Brindisi and at Taranto the cruisers of the 7th and 8th Divisions with their respective destroyer squadriglias and the MAS based in Sicily were kept ready to deploy to face any Mediterranean Fleet sortie into the Ionian.

On the night of the 7/8th the FN passed through the Strait of Messina and at 16:00 reached the waters south of Sardinia. From there, lacking any news of the enemy, they withdrew to the Lower

The battleship *Giulio Cesare* at the buoy in Taranto's Mar Grande in late summer 1940. (Courtesy A Amici)

Tyrrhenian. But at 24:00 on the 8th, Supermarina ordered the return of I Squadron to Naples, of the *Pola* and of the 1st Division to Palermo and of the 3rd Division to Messina, where they arrived on the morning of the 9th. There they resupplied, keeping themselves ready to move. In the absence of any further news concerning the enemy, the FN left Naples and Palermo on the afternoon of the 10th to return to their bases.

The sortie ended in a lack of action, as on the night of the 7th Force H had changed course and headed for the Atlantic – a diversion that was missed by the Italians – which turned it into an exercise that merely highlighted the difficulty of handling a formation of five dissimilar battleships at more than 24 knots. In the event of combat, Campioni suggested taking advantage of the greater speed of the 9th Division (28 knots) to manoeuvre independently, with the smaller battleships working together at a speed of 25 knots that, on their own, they could make more easily.

Opposition to British Operation MB5 (29 September–1 October 1940) and the failed Operation CV

At the end of September, the British organised an operation to reinforce Malta with about 1200 men and supplies from Alexandria by fast transport in the light cruisers *Gloucester* and *Liverpool*. Covering them, and with the aim if possible of engaging the Italian fleet, the Mediterranean Fleet also left with the fastest battleships, *Warspite* and *Valiant*, the carrier *Illustrious*, the light cruisers *Orion* and *Sydney* and the heavy cruiser *York* and eleven destroyers. At the same time another convoy, AN4, escorted by the AA cruiser *Calcutta* and four destroyers, left Port Said for Piraeus, where it would arrive on 1 October. The operation was designated MB5 and the Mediterranean Fleet departed from Alexandria on the night prior to 29 September. The next morning it was spotted and reported several times between Crete and the African coast by Italian reconnaissance aircraft, which however overestimated the number of battleships at four. In the afternoon of the 29th Supermarina ordered the FN, consisting of both squadrons, to sortie, with orders to steer on a course of 160 degrees at a speed of 18 knots to 25 miles north of the intermediate point of the Malta–Cerigo axis, and at 22:10 alerted the submarines in the eastern Mediterranean. I Squadron consisted of the same five battleships from the previous sortie in addition to four light cruisers and fourteen destroyers; II Squadron comprised all seven heavy Italian cruisers and eight destroyers.

The FN left their bases after 18:00 on the evening of 29 September and the next morning Supermarina ordered that, at 08:00, once the designated point had been reached, they should cruise between the 37th and then the 38th and later the 39th parallel. At 14:00 it again ordered that the FN set a course to the southwest and to cruise as far as the 37th parallel. Finally, at 17:20, as there was no clear idea as to the situation of the enemy battleships and with the warning of a storm from the southeast that would have put the destroyers in difficulty, Supermarina ordered the FN to return, which occurred on the night before 1 October. It was not until the afternoon that air reconnaissance was able to provide a more precise picture of the enemy, which, however, was returning to Alexandria and no longer within interception range. The Mediterranean Fleet, in fact, had steamed towards Malta until 23:00 on the 30th, suffering several attacks on the 29th by Italian bombers and torpedo bombers without result. At 12:30 on the 30th British reconnaissance had spotted the Italian fleet, underestimating its size (two battleships rather than five) and while *Gloucester* and *Liverpool* were concluding their mission, Cunningham was waiting for them in the central Mediterranean. But when at 12:45 he became aware of the presence of four or five battleships at a distance of 116 miles, he gave up the idea of launching an attack with the few torpedo bombers still available on the *Illustrious*, doubting its outcome, and at 23:00 he reversed course. In this phase, *Orion* and *Sydney* carried out a diversion in the Aegean, shelling Italian positions at Stampalia, to no effect, on the night of 2/3 October. The destroyers *Havock* and *Hasty*, coming from Piraeus after having escorted convoy AN4, on the morning of 2 October surprised the submarine *Berillo* on the surface and sank it. The attacks made by the Regia Aeronautica on 1 October were ineffective and on the afternoon of the 3rd the Mediterranean Fleet completed its return to Alexandria.

The attempt to head off Operation MB5 repeated what had happened with Operation 'Hats'. Supermarina's orders to the FN were such that they prevented, right from the outset, any contact with the enemy, while air attacks and submarine ambushes proved to be ineffective as well as risky. The Mediterranean Fleet easily carried out its resupply and associated missions, but Cunningham was no better served by his reconnaissance assets than Supermarina and the FN, so he was surprised by the presence at sea of five Italian battleships. That he did not attempt to engage them led to some criticism from London, where a greater degree of aggressiveness was expected once the *Valiant* and *Illustrious* had joined as reinforcements.

Having returned to their bases, on 6 October the FN were supposed to have undertaken Operation CV, consisting of 'urgent' transport of supplies from Taranto to Leros with two fast merchant ships that had long been ready. Both squadrons were to

Detail of the battleship *Duilio* in October 1940. Note the absence of blast bags (known as 'pants' to the Italians) protecting the guns of No 1 main (320/44) turret.

take part: II Squadron preceding the convoy as far at the Aegean, while I Squadron was to provide long-distance cover. The XII Destroyer Squadriglia was responsible for close escort, but shortly after 12:00 on 6 October, when 1s and 3rd Divisions had already put to sea from Taranto and Messina and I Squadron was preparing to sail, Supermarina cancelled the operation after erroneous sightings of heavy British forces in the western Mediterranean. The operation was not attempted again.

'Exigency G' and the failed landing at Corfù (October–November 1940)

The attack on Greece, designated 'Exigency G' and scheduled for late October 1940, called for, alongside an advance in Epirus, the occupation by sea of the Ionian island of Corfù facing Albania and northern Epirus. The operation had been planned for months as a surprise landing, to be made upon declaration of war, and was to have seen the use of the 'Bari' infantry division and the participation by almost the entire FN, which was given the mission of direct support and long-distance cover to the convoys. Once the island had been occupied, the Regia Marina was to be responsible for maintaining and defending the new line of communication.

Leading up to the 28 October deadline, on the 24th Supermarina had taken steps to issue the general operation order, followed by specific instructions for the commanders-in-chief of the I and II Squadrons of the Special Naval Forces (FNS), which had been expressly constituted on 25 October for amphibious operations. The original plan was to put the landing forces ashore at dawn on the 28th at four points on the island, transported by two convoys from Taranto, one convoy and a group of auxiliary merchant ships from Brindisi escorted by ships of the FNS. The 4th Division's light cruisers would reconnoitre and provide any support needed in the waters north of Corfù and the 7th Division's light cruisers from Brindisi were to engage in surveillance operations southwest of the island. Two 'Spica' type torpedo boat squadriglie would sweep any minefields in the essential channels around the Ionian islands and daily air reconnaissance over western Greece as far as Corinth was to be assured. The main portion of the two battle squadrons, including the two 'Cavours' and the *Duilio*, was to be kept ready to move in three hours, to intervene in the event that the British fleet appeared. Submarine ambushes were arranged in the central-eastern Mediterranean, as was strategic reconnaissance over Alexandria and Malta. But at the beginning of hostilities against Greece the operation was postponed several times because of bad weather that would have made it difficult for the many FNS merchant ships. In reality, the military top brass were rather lukewarm, considering that there was little advantage in seizing from the sea an island that was just off territory that could be rapidly occupied by a land advance and, in the final analysis, wary of the increasing difficulties that the 'Bari' division would face on the ground while assaulting Greek territory.

In November, because of the continuing stalemate on the Greek front, Mussolini ordered planning to resume for a landing at Preveza, as an alternative or in conjunction with that against Corfù, to take the enemy by surprise from the rear. This time, with the battle squadron reduced by half because of the Taranto episode – which will be discussed later – it was Cavagnari who opposed the plan: a first time on 27 November, as he could not guarantee the safety of the transports, as mastery of the Upper Ionian against the powerful British fleet had been lost, and again on 2 December because it was impossible for the navy, even assuming that the landings were successful, to protect the shipping that would have been subjected to the inevitable attacks by British forces that were just a short distance from the Otranto Channel. These problems and the deterioration of the situation on the Greek front induced Mussolini to order, on 28 November and 3 December, that plans be updated. Seen in retrospect, if Cavagnari's opposition to a landing at Corfù – an operation, moreover, that was within the capabilities of the Italian armed forces – is indicative of a defensive mentality, it does not appear to be unreasonable. If in actuality an Italian advance in Epirus had taken place, the occupation of Corfù from the sea would not have been of any great benefit because the island would have fallen on its own or would have not had any influence on the course of operations. If the ground campaign had gone differently, as it did later, possession of the island would have become a burden because of the dispersion of energy and resources to hold it, or worse yet, it would have required a humiliating evacuation.

Detail of the 320/44 guns of the forward battery of the battleship *Conte di Cavour* in a 1940 photo.

Chapter 9.2

FROM THE 'NIGHT OF TARANTO' TO THE BOMBARDMENT OF GENOA (NOVEMBER 1940–FEBRUARY 1941)

British Operation MB8 (6–14 November 1940) and the 'Night of Taranto' (11–12 November 1940)

Ever since the 1935–1936 Mediterranean crisis, in the event of war the Royal Navy had planned of an attack on the Taranto naval base with carrier-based torpedo aircraft, designed to damage or put the Italian fleet out of action. The idea gained impetus in autumn 1940 as, since Operation 'Hats', the Mediterranean Fleet included the modern carrier *Illustrious* in addition to the older *Eagle*, deploying squadrons of Fairey Mk I Swordfish biplanes, which were slow but very effective as torpedo bombers. For some time, the crews had been trained to drop their torpedoes in shallow waters, such as those in Taranto's Mar Grande, in order to reduce the initial running depth and avoid the torpedo burying itself in the mud. In addition, the Mark XII torpedoes had been fitted with Duplex percussion and magnetic fuses, adjusted for a depth that would allow them to pass under the torpedo nets and explode, if they did not hit the hull, by magnetic impulse under the hull with devastating effect. This technical preparation was accompanied by accurate air reconnaissance of Taranto, which kept track of the presence and anchorages of the Italian ships as well as the base's active and passive defences, up to the day of the attack.

The genesis of the operation, designated 'Judgment', was somewhat troubled. Originally scheduled for 21 October 1940, the anniversary of the battle of Trafalgar, it had to be delayed, first because of a fire aboard the *Illustrious*, which destroyed two Swordfish and damaged another three, and then because of a sortie by the Mediterranean Fleet to the western coast of Greece. The date was then fixed for a day between 11 and 19 November, during a favourable period of moonlight. However, there were yet other mishaps. The action had envisaged the use of both carriers with an attack force of thirty aircraft, but *Eagle* was not fully oper-

Some of the Italian battleships moored in Taranto's Mar Grande in a British air reconnaissance photo taken a few days before the torpedo aircraft attack on 11 November 1940. From the left they are: *Conte di Cavour* (which was hit), *Andrea Doria* and *Vittorio Veneto*. (IWM photo)

Taranto, 11/12 November 1940

Plan of moorings in Mar Grande. For *Littorio*, *Cavour* and *Duilio*: A, position in which the ships were hit; B, position where they were later run aground. Note the considerable extension of the enclosure protected by obstacles and torpedo nets where the battleships were anchored. (From *STORIA militare* No 26, November 1995)

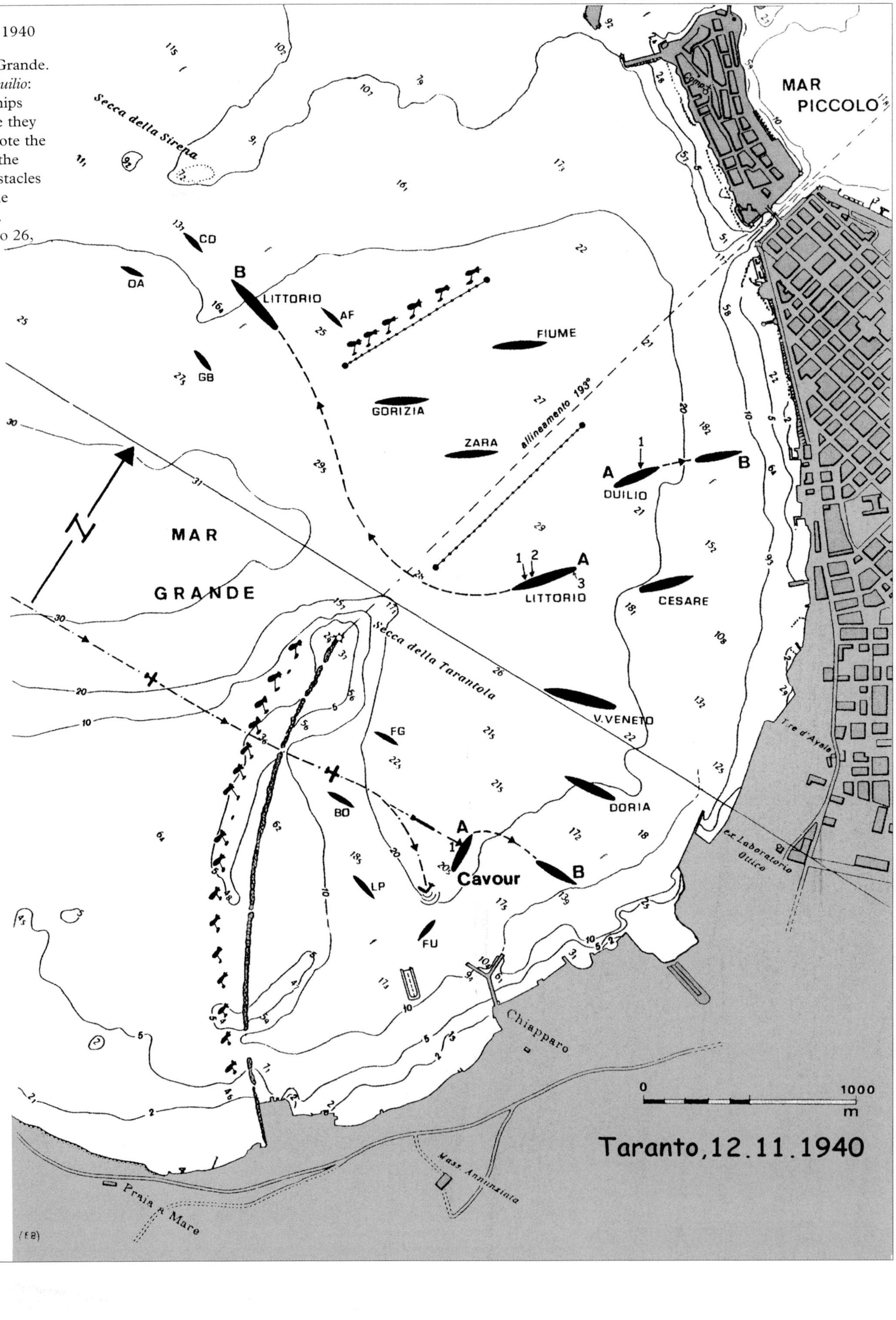

ational because of near-miss bomb damage sustained in the Aegean and it was decided to do without her participation. Five of her Swordfish and eight crews were transferred to *Illustrious*, but the operational aircraft fell to twenty-four; another three were lost in accidents in the initial phase of the operation and the total fell to twenty-one. 'Judgment' was finally inserted as part of an impressive operation, designated MB8, which involved the entire Mediterranean from Alexandria to Gibraltar, including a total of ten movements and operations that were combined and connected. These saw the employment of a British force totalling five battleships, two carriers, two monitors, ten cruisers and thirty destroyers; taking place between 6 and 14 November 1940, all phases, except for one, met with success and encountered little or only ineffective response by Italian forces.

For the sake of brevity, we shall dwell only on 'Judgment' itself. On the afternoon of 6 November the Mediterranean Fleet, with *Warspite, Valiant, Malaya, Ramillies* and *Illustrious*, with the light cruisers *Ajax, Sydney, Gloucester* and the heavy cruiser *York* along with thirteen destroyers, left Alexandria for the central Mediterranean and on the morning of the 9th the *Ramillies* and three destroyers were detached to reinforce the escort assigned to convoy MW3 from Alexandria to Malta. The Mediterranean Fleet's departure and movements did not escape Italian observation, along with the Force H departure from Gibraltar, and Supermarina and Superaereo instituted a series of measures to find and engage them. Submarine ambushes were set up south-east of Malta and light units were sent on scouting missions, some of which could not be carried out because of poor sea conditions. On the morning of the 8th the Italian naval forces were kept ready to move within three hours but did not put to sea because, in Supermarina's judgment, enemy positions and movements had not been determined with sufficient accuracy, and when they were, it was too late to take action. In conclusion, engaging Force H to the west and the Mediterranean Fleet to the east was carried out on 9 and 10 November by the air force and by submarines, but with no results and with the loss of several aircraft. At 18:00 on the 10th the *Illustrious*, along with *Gloucester, Glasgow, York* and *Berwick* and four destroyers, detached from Force A and headed north-northeast, constituting the strike element of the Mediterranean Fleet, to conduct the aerial torpedo strike against Taranto, while Force A remained further to the south as a covering force.

The latest moves by the Mediterranean Fleet escaped Italian observation, but not those that had preceded them. At 17:00 on the 10th, air reconnaissance had spotted them 20-30 miles south-west of Malta heading east, but Supermarina decided not to order the FN to sea, as it was on three-hour readiness. Had it put to sea in the evening, it could have been in the Lower Ionian on the morning of the 11th with a fair chance of intercepting the enemy. Instead it limited itself to making arrangements for night-time reconnaissance and ambushes by destroyers, torpedo boats and MAS in the Sicilian Channel, none of which resulted in any contact. On the morning of the 11th other movements of enemy vessels to the east were detected, especially of convoy ME3 (from Malta to Egypt) on the same heading. These latest reports, and the fact that on the afternoon of the 11th nothing was spotted, led Supermarina to assume that the Mediterranean Fleet was returning to Alexandria. Accordingly, it waited for the enemy to move off to the east, then to have the freedom to carry out a scheduled naval bombardment mission at Suda (see below). Furthermore, Supermarina did not follow up on the request by the Comando Superiore Traffico dell'Albania [Albania Convoy High Command] to carry out security patrols in the Otranto Channel given the presence at sea on the night of 11/12th of a total of four convoys. Offensive action against the enemy was entrusted to the air force, but it did not materialise because of poor weather conditions.

While the British were preparing to attack Taranto, almost all of the Italian fleet was concentrated in that base, distributed around the following anchorages:

- Mar Grande, Tarantola cove: 9th Division (*Littorio* and *Vittorio Veneto*); 5th Division (*Giulio Cesare* and *Conte di Cavour*); 6th Division (*Duilio* and *Andrea Doria*); VIII Destroyer Squadriglia (*Folgore, Fulmine, Baleno, Lampo*).
- Mar Grande, south of the merchant port: 1st Division (*Zara, Gorizia, Fiume*); IX Destroyer Squadriglia (*Alfieri, Gioberti, Carducci, Oriani*).
- Mar Piccolo, at the buoys: 3rd Division (*Trieste* and *Bolzano*); XIII Destroyer Squadriglia (*Granatiere, Fuciliere, Bersagliere, Alpino*).
- Mar Piccolo, torpedo boat quay and Porta Ponente: *Pola* and *Trento*; 8th Division (*Duca degli Abruzzi* and *Giuseppe Garibaldi*); aircraft support ship *Giuseppe Miraglia*; salvage ship *Teseo*; minelayer *Vieste*; VII Destroyer Squadriglia (*Freccia, Strale, Dardo, Saetta*); X Destroyer Squadriglia (*Maestrale, Libeccio, Grecale, Scirocco*); XI Destroyer Squadriglia (*Camicia Nera, Geniere, Lanciere*); XII Destroyer Squadiglia (*Carabiniere, Corazziere, Ascari*); XVI Destroyer Squadriglia (*da Recco, Usodimare, Pessagno*); XIV Torpedo Boat Squadriglia (*Partenope, Polluce, Pleiade, Pallade*).
- Mar Piccolo, submarine quay and other moorings: thirteen submarines of the 3rd, 4th, 8th and 10th groups, as well as subsidiary and auxiliary vessels.

Such a high concentration of forces was due to the developing strategic situation and to the fact that Taranto was considered to be the best protected naval base. Active defence consisted of 21 anti-aircraft batteries with 101 guns, 68 heavy machine gun installations with a total of 84 guns, 109 light machine guns in fixed and moveable positions, all of which were fully operational even though some of the weapons were antiquated; the warning network had 13 sound locators and 22 high-powered search-lights. These defences were augmented by the massive AA armament on such a large number of ships. Passive defence consisted of aerial obstructions, but with only 27 tethered balloons at an altitude of 200 metres, as 60 had been torn away by the wind in the previous days and had not yet been replaced due also to insufficient local production of hydrogen. In Mar Grande, 4200 metres of torpedo nets were in place, with an average depth of 10 metres, which was insufficient to stop the run of torpedoes that could be set for a greater depth; the nets were arranged so as to form two large enclosures, one of which included all of the Tarantola cove, east of the breakwater of the same name, and another was a smaller enclosure west of it. Actually, for the protection of ships moored in Mar Grande a total of 12,800 metres of nets had been planned, of which 2900 still lay in warehouses waiting to be laid while the rest were still being manufactured. But, even when that was completed, there were no plans for individual nets around the anchorages of the capital ships, but only of simple subdivision of the water's surface with anti-torpedo nets and other devices. This was partly because of the shortage of materials (nets, buoys, floats, cables) and vessels (lighters, tugs, etc) to position them, but also because letting ships swing around a single forward mooring buoy allowed them to manoeuvre more freely when arriving and departing, so very large areas would need to be enclosed; the average depth of the nets would also remain unchanged. Finally, there was a complete lack of smoke generating equipment to obscure the area.

Between 20:35 and 20:40 on 11 November, from a point 170 miles southeast of Taranto, twelve Swordfish of the first wave took off from *Illustrious*. Drawn from 813, 815 and 824 Naval Air Squadrons, six were torpedo aircraft, four carried bombs and two carried flares. They reached their objective at 23:00 with good weather and light conditions: calm sky, breeze from the northeast, high moon, excellent visibility. The two flare-droppers flew along the eastern shore of Mar Grande illuminating the targets from the rear, and then bombed the oil tanks. To create a diversion, the four bombers attacked the ships anchored in Mar Piccolo and a semi-armour-piercing 250-pound bomb hit the *Libeccio* without exploding. The torpedo bombers split into two sections of three planes each and attacked the battleships at very low level: the first section from the southwest flying over the Tarantola breakwater, the second from the northwest, flying over Punta Rondinella. The first section launched against the *Cavour*, which at 23:15 was hit by a torpedo that exploded under the hull below No 2 main gun turret; the other two Swordfish missed their targets and their torpedoes exploded on the bottom not too far from the *Andrea Doria*. At 23:15 the second section launched against the *Littorio* and hit the ship with two torpedoes, one starboard near the two forward main gun turrets and one aft to port.

The British attack did not come completely without warning, as it had been preceded by three alarms during the course of the evening but, notwithstanding the very violent anti-aircraft fire, only the plane that torpedoed the *Cavour* was shot down by fire from *Cavour* and *Fulmine*; the plane's crew survived and was captured.

Between 21:28 and 21:34 the nine Swordfish of 813, 819 and 824 NAS, comprising the second wave, took off, of which six were torpedo planes, one a bomber and two carrying flares. During take-off two planes collided slightly; one of them, hastily repaired, took off half an hour later. As a result, the initial attack was made by only seven aircraft coming from the northwest, which arrived on target shortly before 24:00. The two carrying flares made the same approach as did the earlier flare-droppers and also bombed the oil tanks. The torpedo planes again flew over Punta Rondinella and attacked the *Littorio*, *Duilio* and *Vittorio Veneto*; one aircraft was quickly shot down, probably by the *Gorizia*, but at 23:59 one torpedo each hit the *Littorio* on the starboard bow and the *Duilio* from starboard under the hull at the forward main gun turrets; another torpedo buried itself in the mud under the hull of the *Littorio* without exploding; the *Vittorio Veneto* was missed (the torpedo hit the bottom and exploded) and the attacking aircraft was damaged. The final aircraft to arrive was the bomber that had been delayed, which attacked the ships in Mar Piccolo, hitting the *Trento* with a 250-pound semi-armour-piercing bomb that did not detonate. The raid lasted until almost 01:00 on 12 November and by 02:50 all of the Swordfish,

The battleship *Conte di Cavour* on the morning of 12 November 1940, resting on the bottom in the shallows after having been seriously damaged by a torpedo the previous evening.

Detail taken on 12 November of the midships section of the *Conte di Cavour* sunk in Mar Grande.

less the two that had been shot down, returned to the carrier, which at 07:30 joined the rest of the Mediterranean Fleet.

The British were immediately aware of the success of the operation and Cunningham thought about renewing the attack with fifteen aircraft on the night of 12/13th, but he did not take action only because of the forecast poor weather conditions. To crown this success, in the early hours of the 12th in the Otranto Channel, Force X intercepted and destroyed the 'Locatelli' convoy of four merchant ships sailing from Valona to Brindisi. In the afternoon Force X joined the Mediterranean Fleet, which returned to Alexandria on the 14th having been attacked in vain by the Regia Aeronautica during its passage.

This was the picture on the morning of 12 November in Taranto's Mar Grande: the *Littorio*, hit by three torpedoes, had been beached near the Sirena bank to prevent her from sinking; the *Duilio*, hit by one torpedo, had been grounded by the bow facing the city; the *Cavour*, also hit by one torpedo, sank in the shallows where she was towed when it was clear she would not remain afloat. In Mar Piccolo, *Trento* and *Libeccio* had each been hit by unexploded bombs and suffered minor damage; two seaplanes had been destroyed at the seaplane base and negligible damage had been suffered by the naval dockyard and the oil tanks. Human loss was quite low: thirty-two killed aboard the *Littorio*, sixteen on the *Cavour*, one on the *Duilio*, in addition to several victims among the civilian population. Wounded aboard the ships that had been hit amounted to 150.

At the cost of only two Swordfish, the Royal Navy had temporarily reduced the Italian battle squadron by half and destroyed an entire convoy. The attack had been planned and executed with skill and determination; however, the main cause of the British success is to be found in the shortcomings of the base's defences, especially its passive defences – poor organisation, especially the inability of the sound locators to pick up the approaching aircraft at low level, and the failure to use the searchlights. Furthermore, this was not the first successful aerial torpedo attack against ships in harbour: in July at Tobruk three destroyers had been sunk and a fourth in Augusta (the *Pancaldo*, later recovered); in addition, at Mers el Kebir the French battleship *Dunkerque* had been torpedoed, the details of which were known to Supermarina through the Italian armistice commission with France. Not least, Supermarina prevented the Italian fleet from making any sorties throughout the course of MB8, even though there was adequate information on the Mediterranean Fleet, leaving it undisturbed to carry out its movements in the central Mediterranean. All of this appears even more serious, because the failure of the air force and of the submarines to even slightly hinder enemy initiatives could not have been overlooked, as the experience of the previous months had clearly demonstrated.

From a technical standpoint, the rapid spread of flooding in all of the torpedoed ships came as a nasty surprise. From the early examination of the *Littorio* and *Duilio* it was possible to ascertain that the phenomenon was due not to any structural deficiencies but rather to the poor watertight performance of the doorways, by the ventilation ducts and imperfect fitting out, as well as the ineffective damage control arrangements (layout of the electrical systems and of the distribution, location and output of the high-capacity drainage pumps), inadequate training and equipment (portable pumps, respirator masks, ineffectiveness of gas masks) and because of the vulnerability of the electrical systems in general. From this standpoint, the bitter experience of Taranto was providential. In the months that followed it was in fact possible to remedy the generality of shortcomings in the battleships through extensive revision of all aspects that had been found wanting, generally improving resistance to damage, with positive effects when faced with later underwater threats. The exception was the electrical systems, which remained one of the major vulnerabilities on Italian ships, capital ships included, not only in combat but also in heavy weather.

The failed bombardments of Suda and Zakynthos

An immediate consequence of the attack against Taranto was cancelling the naval bombardments of Suda and Zakynthos,

The central area of the wreck of the *Cavour* seen from a different angle.

Taranto, afternoon of 12 November 1940. Beyond the after upper main gun turret of the *Cavour*, the battleship *Andrea Doria* can be seen, preparing to leave Taranto for Naples along with the *Vittorio Veneto* and *Giulio Cesare* and their escorts.

planned on 10 November, while British Operation MB8 was in full swing. The targets of the first bombardment were the ships anchored and the military installations at Suda and Chania in Crete. The operation was to have begun on the 12th with the return of the Mediterranean Fleet to Alexandria. On 11 November Admiral Campioni had issued a general operational order and that same day the scheduled air reconnaissance over the objective and over vast areas of the eastern Mediterranean took place. Participating in the action were to have been the *Pola*, the 1st Division, the IX, XII and XV destroyer squadriglias, which were tasked with bombarding Suda, with long-range cooperation by 9th Division and 8th Division. The operation was to take place once air reconnaissance had determined that the Mediterranean Fleet, which at that moment was present in the central Mediterranean, was found to the east of the 25° east meridian while returning to Alexandria.

The objective of the second attack was to have been Zakynthos and Cape Katakolo (the northeastern Peloponnese at the mouth of the Zakynthos channel) with the targets being the ships at anchor, the oil depots in the Bay of Kieri and the railway line north of Cape Katakolo. The *Pola* and the 3rd Division were to make the attack, supported by *Duilio* and 7th Division. This operation also was to have taken place after air reconnaissance had verified the absence of major British forces in the central Mediterranean. The two groups were to have weighed anchor after dusk on Day X and be at their objectives during the early hours of Day X + 1, with protective sweeping in waters that might be mined. Return was envisaged as the evening of that same day.

Transfer of the Naval Forces from Taranto to Naples and the changed relative force posture in the Mediterranean

The day following the attack on Taranto Supermarina decided to move the battleships that were still operational from that base and most of the cruisers for the time needed to improve defences and to concentrate the local technical and logistical resources on repairing the three ships that had been put out of action. Naples was chosen as the new base, because it was less spread out than La Spezia and La Maddalena and was considered to be more easily defended. On the afternoon of the 12th the battleships *Vittorio Veneto*, Admiral Campioni's new flagship, *Doria* and *Cesare*, the cruiser *Pola*, which was Iachino's flagship, and the 1st Division cruisers, *Gorizia* and *Fiume*, with their respective destroyer squadriglias, left Taranto for Naples, arriving on the afternoon of the 13th. At the same time, the cruisers of the 3rd Division transferred to Messina. The *Zara* left Taranto on the 12th for La Spezia, where she arrived on the 14th, followed on the 16th by the *Andrea Doria* to proceed to that location for training. The 8th Division remained in Taranto.

With three battleships out of action and the transfer to Naples of the bulk of the residual forces, the strategic picture in the Mediterranean had changed. The deterioration of its strength relative to the Mediterranean Fleet – which in mid-November numbered five battleships (*Warspite*, *Valiant*, *Barham*, *Malaya* and *Ramillies*) and two aircraft carriers (*Illustrious* and *Eagle*) – in Supermarina's judgement effectively deprived the Italian Navy of the ability to operate in the central Mediterranean. The only area of action that remained was the western basin, where Force H at the time comprised only the battlecruiser *Renown* and the carrier *Ark Royal*. The new situation allowed the British to redistribute their major ships, transferring some from Alexandria to other theatres. Thus, at the end of November and early December 1940, *Malaya* and *Ramillies*, the heavy cruiser *Berwick* and three light cruisers left the Mediterranean for the Home Fleet, and Force H was free to cover convoys as well as to hunt down German surface raiders attacking merchant shipping in the Atlantic. Thus, even the minimal strategic effect of the Italian 'fleet in being' tying down significant heavy British forces in the Mediterranean was lost.

British Operation 'White' and the sortie of Italian naval forces of 16–18 November 1940

On the night of 14/15 November Force H, commanded by Vice Admiral James Somerville, left Gibraltar with the *Renown*, the *Ark Royal*, the light cruisers *Sheffield*, *Despatch* and *Newcastle* (this last direct from England with 200 men and equipment from the RAF), and eight fighter aircraft to support a flight to Malta by several Hurricanes from the small and antiquated carrier *Argus* in order to reinforce the island's defences against the Italian air force

Detail of the forward main gun turrets of the *Cavour* on 12 November 1940.

The battleship *Duilio* at Taranto: operations to raise the fore part of the ship from the bottom where it had been beached to avoid sinking after it had been hit by a torpedo on 11 November.

(Operation 'White'). At the time an air attack from *Ark Royal* was also planned against the airfield at Alghero.

The departure of Force H from Gibraltar was quickly reported by observers on the spot and Supermarina ordered a sortie by the two naval squadrons, which put to sea from Naples and Messina on the morning of the 16th composed as follows:

- I Squadron: *Vittorio Veneto* (Admiral Campioni, C-in-C), *Cesare*, XIII Destroyer Squadriglia with four ships;
- II Squadron: *Pola* (Admiral Iachino); 1st Division (*Fiume* and *Gorizia*), IX Destroyer Squadriglia with three ships, 3rd Division, from Messina (*Trento*, *Bolzano*, *Trieste*), XII Destroyer Squadriglia (from Palermo) with four ships.

Lacking precise information on the position and course of the enemy, the bulk of the two Squadrons headed towards the Lower Tyrrhenian, where in the afternoon it joined with the 3rd Division and its accompanying escort. Then Campioni headed to the southwest of Sardinia at a speed of 18 knots, reduced to 14 knots on the night of 16/17th to allow the destroyers to cope better with the big sea that was whipped up by a southwest wind. Not until 10:15 on the 17th did air reconnaissance report the enemy's presence, without however giving any indication of course or speed. Following that vague information Campioni steered south (towards Bone), in order to intercept in the early afternoon hours, in the event that the British had continued on to the east. Later information from Supermarina did not clarify anything and the aircraft catapulted from *Pola*, *Gorizia* and *Trieste* only determined that the enemy was not in western Algerian waters. In doubt, Supermarina decided to order a return to base, which occurred between the morning and afternoon of 18 November.

For his part, Somerville did not fare any better with his own air reconnaissance. On the afternoon of the 16th Malta-based reconnaissance informed him that it had spotted a large Italian force south of Naples, which prompted him to launch the Hurricanes from as far west as possible. At first light on the 17th, southwest of Sardinia and 400 miles from Malta, the *Argus* launched two waves of six Hurricanes and a Skua each; eight Hurricanes and one Skua were lost due to course errors and erroneous estimates of the effect of the wind. Late in the afternoon of the 17th, following the spotting of the German heavy cruiser *Admiral Scheer* near the Azores, Somerville cancelled the air raid against Alghero to return quickly to Gibraltar, refuel the *Renown* and *Ark Royal* and head for the Atlantic. Force H made its return to Gibraltar in the early hours of 19 November, while *Newcastle* reached Malta with no problem.

Operation 'White' was only a partial success for the British, due both to bad weather and mistaken assessments, but also because the presence at sea of the Italian naval forces deterred Somerville from allowing *Argus* any closer to Malta before launching her aircraft. On the Italian side the sortie was worthwhile as it raised morale a little following Taranto, but there was no immediate awareness of its effect on the enemy operation. The sea state (long waves from the southwest) also troubled Campioni. All of the ships, including the battleships, suffered heavy rolling, judged to be enough to affect the use of the guns on a southerly course. Upon returning, the admiral requested and was granted authorisation to carry out gunnery exercises in the rough seas against the La Botte reef, but the results, however, are unknown.

Action against British Operation 'Collar' and the battle of Cape Teulada/Spartivento (16–28 November 1940)

The need to resupply Greece and Malta induced the British to send a fast merchant convoy through the Mediterranean direct from Britain (MT) with two ships for Malta and one for Alexandria and, simultaneously a convoy of four merchant ships from Alexandria to Malta (MW4), as well as a convoy of five from Malta to Alexandria (ME4). At the time it was also decided to reinforce Force H with a battleship transferred from the Mediterranean Fleet, which now enjoyed a substantial operational and numerical advantage after the halving of Italian battleship strength and the withdrawal of the surviving ships from Taranto. The overall operation was designated MB9 and the western part, specifically, as 'Collar', with the forces arrayed as follows:

- From the west: Force B (*Renown*, Admiral Somerville); *Ark Royal*, light cruisers *Sheffield* and *Despatch*, nine destroyers); Force F (light cruisers *Manchester* and *Southampton* with about 1400 men on board, one destroyer, four corvettes and the MT convoy with three merchant ships bound for Alexandria).
- From the east: Force A (*Warspite*, Admiral Cunningham C-in-C, *Valiant*, *Illustrious*, nine destroyers); Force C (*Malaya, Ramillies, Eagle*, light cruisers *Orion, Sydney, Ajax*, heavy cruiser *Berwick*, eight destroyers); Force E (light cruisers *Glasgow, Gloucester*, heavy cruiser *York*); Force D (light cruisers *Calcutta, Coventry*, four destroyers and convoy MW4 from Alexandria with four merchant ships); after leaving Malta for Gibraltar on the afternoon of the 26th Force D included *Ramillies, Berwick* and *Newcastle* (which had remained at Malta after Operation 'White'), the *Coventry* and five destroyers.
- From the west Force B and Force F were to escort convoy MT as far as Sardinia to join Force D coming from the east around midday on the 27th; once they had joined, they were to continue in the Sicilian Channel until the night of the 27th, after which Force F, the *Coventry* and five destroyers were to proceed to the eastern Mediterranean, where Force A was to await it, while Force B was to return to Gibraltar with the remainder of Force D.

The operation began in the east on the morning of 23 November with the departure from Alexandria of Forces C and D which, crossing the Aegean, reached Malta on the morning of the 26th, following an incursion over Tripoli by eight planes from the *Eagle*; on the afternoon of the 26th Force C minus *Ramillies* and *Berwick*, was to assume cover for convoy ME4 from Malta to Alexandria and Port Said. On the night of 24/25th, Force A also set sail from Alexandria, which in the afternoon joined with Force E, already at sea for exercises. Force A entered the Aegean by the Strait of Casos and on the night of 25/ 26th the *Illustrious* was detached for an air attack against Portolago on the island of Leros, while the main element put in at Suda to replenish the destroyers. From there it departed on the evening of the 26th to reach a position about 160 miles east of Malta on the 27th, where it was to remain cruising while awaiting the ships from Gibraltar to escort them to Alexandria. Finally, also on the 25th, convoy MW4 left Alexandria for Malta, covered by Force E. To the west Force B put to sea from Gibraltar on the morning of 25 November to support Force E, which had entered the Mediterranean the night before. Transit of the Sicilian Channel by the convoy and the ships bound for Alexandria was to be accomplished on the night of 27/ 28th, while from the east the *Ramillies*, the *Berwick* and *Newcastle* were to rejoin Force H at noon on the 27th south of Sardinia to proceed together to Gibraltar.

The first reports of the two enemy operations reached Rome on the morning of 25 November; in the west from observers around Gibraltar and in the east from a civilian airliner that spotted large enemy forces, including a carrier and a battleship 150 miles southeast of Malta. Lacking more precise information and given the presence of the carrier, Supermarina thought that the enemy might attack Italian bases. It thus alerted the coastal defences and ordered the departure of the 10th Torpedo Boat Flotilla from Trapani (*Vega, Sagittario, Alcione* – which soon had to return because of machinery breakdown – and *Sirio*), to keep a watch on the waters of Cape Bon, an ambush by nine MAS in the Sicilian Channel, a deployment of four submarines south of Sardinia and three others near Malta, as well as readying I and II Squadrons at Naples and Messina. As it was not possible, given the position (and presumably unfavourable force ratio), to engage the Mediterranean Fleet in the east, but only Force H in the west, at mid-morning on the 26th Supermarina issued operational orders to the two squadrons, directing that they should be in position south of Sardinia on the morning of the 27th, but that they should engage only if the situation was favourable. I Squadron and the 1st Division left Naples around 12:00 on the 26th and at 17:40 met in the southeastern Tyrrhenian with the 3rd Division coming from Messina. The *Andrea Doria*, since 23 November attached to the 5th Division but still in training at La Spezia, did not take part in this sortie. Thus, the Italian naval forces which headed to the waters south of Sardinia consisted of the following:

- I Squadron: *Vittorio Veneto* (Admiral Campioni, C-in-C), *Giulio Cesare*; XIII Destroyer Squadriglia (*Granatiere, Fuciliere, Bersagliere, Alpino*); VII Destroyer Squadriglia (*Freccia, Saetta, Dardo*).
- II Squadron: *Pola* (Admiral Iachino); 1st Division (*Fiume* and *Gorizia*); IX Destroyer Squadriglia (*Oriani, Carducci, Gioberti*);

3rd Division (*Trento, Bolzano, Trieste*); XII Destroyer Squadriglia (*Lanciere, Carabiniere, Corazziere, Ascari*).

Finally, Superaereo kept numerous fighter and bomber groups based on Sardinia ready to join the action.

On the night of 26/27th first contact was made. At 00:33 the torpedo boat *Sirio*, on patrol in the Sicilian Channel, near Cape Bon spotted ships of Force D proceeding to the northwest and at 00:55, after an unsuccessful and unobserved torpedo attack, signalled the discovery, which was quickly received by Supermarina and by the *Vittorio Veneto*. At first light on the 27th Campioni ordered reconnaissance by embarked aircraft. The message from the *Sirio* was also intercepted by the British, who then knew that they had been spotted. In mid-morning both of the commanders at sea received reports from their respective reconnaissance elements, uncertain as to the enemy's composition and course. Campioni, who had reached the 8th meridian southwest of Sardinia, received a report from an aircraft from the *Bolzano*, and learned that the force consisted of only one battleship and thus considered the possibility of engaging it. But, at 11:00, he ordered his ships on a heading of 70 degrees, thus on a course that distanced itself with respect to the enemy's probable course, and not until 11:28 did he set a course of 135 degrees, orienting the deployment towards the probable enemy heading.

At the same time reconnaissance aircraft from *Ark Royal* had spotted the Italian naval forces, while Force B and D were about to meet west of the island of Galite. The overlap of their messages led Somerville to believe that he was facing a force that was much larger than it actually was. In the late morning, having sighted Force D, he ordered convoy MT to sail at maximum speed to the east-southeast escorted by several ships of Forces B and F and from Force D, which had also arrived while he, with *Renown*, *Ramillies* and five modern cruisers, including the *Manchester* and *Southampton* with troops aboard, headed to the northeast, ordering *Ark Royal* to manoeuvre behind the battleships and to ready its torpedo bombers. He intended to catch and deal with the Italian forces, trusting that the torpedo aircraft would hit and slow down the Italian battleships to 20 knots (the maximum speed of the *Ramillies*) or less.

The Italian force had only just assumed the deployment ordered by Campioni on a heading of 135 degrees when more precise information was reported by an air force reconnaissance plane. Having learned by this report that he now faced two battleships and a carrier as well as the presence of a convoy, he judged that he was in an unfavourable position relative to the British force, especially because of the presence of the carrier and decided not to engage, keeping strictly to Supermarina's instructions. At 12:07 he ordered all of his groups to steer east and ordered II Squadron not to engage, to increase speed to 30 knots and to join the battleships, which were some 24,000 metres distant. At the moment that Campioni was ordering the withdrawal, the British cruisers, followed by the *Renown*, which because of machinery problems could not make 28 knots, spotted the Italians and Somerville learned their exact makeup from air reconnaissance. The five British cruisers closed the distance advancing on a line of bearing towards the direction in which the Italian ships had been spotted and at 12:20 opened fire at the limit of the range of their 152mm (6in) guns. At 12:24 *Renown* joined in at 23,800 metres; at 12:26 *Ramillies*, which was not able to make 21 knots, fired her only two salvos to verify range, which were significantly short, after which the battleship remained on the margins of the encounter. The Italian cruisers responded, between 12:20 and 12:22, at an average range of 21,500 metres for the 3rd Division and 22,000 metres for the 1st Division, while they steered east and increased speed, in accordance with Campioni's orders. In this phase British fire, including that of the *Renown*, was directed against the closer 3rd Division.

The situation worried Iachino, who ordered 3rd Division to retire to the north at maximum speed with their sterns to the enemy, while he with his 1st Division steamed to the northeast to join the battleships and to keep the enemy in the area of maximum range. At around 12:45 the distancing of the 3rd Division, which was cloaking itself in a smokescreen and firing with only its after turrets, caused the British to concentrate their fire on the 1st Division, which was unable to open the distance because *Fiume*'s boiler problems meant she could not make more than 28 knots, and so ended up bearing the brunt of the battle. A little earlier, at 12:27, in order to hasten the meeting with his cruisers, Campioni had ordered his squadron to make two successive course changes so as to make a large circle and lose way, but he refrained from heading directly towards the enemy to support them, even though he knew they were engaged with a capital ship. Between 12:38 and 12:50, while making this manoeuvre, the *Vittorio Veneto* and the *Cesare* ware attacked, in two successive waves, by five and seven Swordfish torpedo planes that, by inserting themselves between their targets and the escorting destroyers, flew at a height of 700–800 metres under violent anti-aircraft fire to drop their torpedoes; the torpedoes were avoided by rapid manoeuvring: two of the torpedoes passed 150 metres ahead and 90 metres aft of the *Cesare*.

The action between the cruisers continued, in a more or less intense fashion, on a northeast heading until 13:15 at ranges between 22,500 and 17,000 metres, with the Italian ships firing as they withdrew and the British firing forward. British fire was judged to be neither well-directed nor effective, but with well grouped salvos; Italian fire was more on target, but with salvos that were more dispersed. Fire from the *Renown*, first against 3rd Division and then against the 1st, scored no hits but worried Iachino, who did not have the support of the battleships. Using her superior speed to get within range, *Vittorio Veneto* joined the action at 13:00. While also retiring, she fired seven salvos or a total of nineteen rounds against the *Manchester* from her after 381mm (15in) turret in the space of ten minutes, at ranges between 28,500 and 32,500 metres. The fifth and seventh salvos were on target, but the cruiser was hit only by fragments. The *Cesare* did not get within useful range (28,600 metres).

Shortly after, at 13:12, Somerville broke off the action, disengaging towards the southeast, and three minutes later the 1st Division also ceased firing when range had increased to 23,000 metres. The reasons the British admiral disengaged can be summarised as: deteriorating visibility due to smoke and smokescreens; the difficulty of pursuing the faster Italian ships, which had not been slowed down by torpedo bomber attacks; lack of confidence in renewed carrier attacks because of the poor state of pilot training; the increasing risk of air and submarine attacks as the Sardinian coast loomed closer; and the need to accord priority to the security of the convoy that was sailing towards the Sicilian Channel.

In the encounter's initial phase, the *Berwick* was hit by two 203mm (8in) shells fired by the *Pola* or the *Fiume*: the first (12:22) pierced the 'Y' turret barbette, putting it out of action and killing seven men and wounding nine; the second (12:35) penetrated and exploded in the officers' quarters with no serious damage. *Berwick*, with one turret out of action, nevertheless remained in formation. The armoured belt of the *Southampton* was also hit by a 203mm shell without penetrating it or exploding. More critical was the situation in which the destroyer *Lanciere* found itself, having fallen back to the starboard of the 3rd Division. At 12:35 she had been hit by a 152mm (6in) shell from the *Southampton*, which exploded in the aft engine room, and shortly after by two more shells that did not explode. The *Lanciere* continued to steam on only her forward engine at a speed of 23 knots, but around 14:00, with the action ended, the destroyer had to stop because of a total lack of water in the boilers. A quarter of an hour later she was able to restart the boilers using sea water and began to slowly make headway. At 14:40, on Iachino's orders, the entire 3rd Division and the XII Destroyer Squadriglia came to her assistance. *Lanciere* was taken in tow by the *Ascari* and brought in to Cagliari.

The gunnery phase had been reciprocally carried out under excellent visibility conditions, except for problems caused by gun-smoke and by smokescreens, with a calm sea and a force 2 wind from the east-northeast. The volume of fire from the Italian ships against British ships and aircraft is summarised in the following table.

Ship/calibre	381	203	152	100	90	37	20	13.2
Veneto	19		3[2]		214	921	2409	nd
Cesare				nd		nd	nd	nd
Pola		110		113		108		500
Gorizia		123		60		432		600
Fiume		210		42		420		60
Trieste		96		2		140		nd
Bolzano[1]		27		-		44		17
Trento		92		-		160		150
Total	19	658	3 (**)	217	214	1304	2409	1327

[1] *Bolzano* fired only a few salvos, as its fire control was thrown off by smoke generated by the *Trento*.
[2] In an anti-aircraft role.
nd = data not known

Considering surface fire alone, only two 203mm rounds hit the target, a percentage of just 0.3. On the other hand, the performance of the equipment was excellent; there were only a few breakdowns, which were quickly remedied. The *Cesare* was the only major ship not to take part in any firing, as she never got within practical range. With respect to British fire, although complete data has not been found, the number of rounds fired was more than the Italian figure: if the *Renown* fired eighty-six 381mm rounds and *Ramillies* only a few more, of the light cruisers *Manchester* alone fired 912 rounds, more than all of the Italian ships combined, and the three rounds that hit the *Lanciere* amounted to a very modest percentage.

Once contact was broken, Somerville ordered a second aerial torpedo attack against the Italian battleships, but at 15:30 the Swordfish came across the cruisers of the 1st Division en route and attacked them with no result. At 13:35 the British admiral was informed that an Italian cruiser – in reality the destroyer *Lanciere* – had been immobilised; he did not attempt to close and destroy it, for more or less the same reasons that had prompted him to refrain from pursuit. He limited himself to launching an attack by Blackburn Skua dive-bombers that, at 15:35, instead encountered and attacked the 3rd Division, which had set out to assist the *Lanciere*. No ships were hit or damaged. In the afternoon the Regia Aeronautica joined the action with three high-altitude attacks against Force H: the first against the *Renown*, and the others against *Ark Royal*. In this instance as well, no ships were hit or damaged.

The British operation concluded as programmed. To the west, Forces B, D and F joined with convoy MT and accompanied it until dusk; then, Force B and D put about and returned to Gibraltar on the 29th. On the night prior to the 28th the convoy and the other British ships wandered into the Italian defensive arrangements in the Sicilian Channel which had been set up by Supermarina on the afternoon of the 27th and which consisted of the 10th Torpedo Boat Flotilla, twelve MAS, of which two had to return because of breakdowns, and two submarines. The Italian opposition was ineffective and all British movements ended without loss.

The Italian squadrons returned while split into three groups along independent courses: the I Squadron reached Naples shortly after 13:00 on the 28th; the 3rd Division, after having escorted the *Lanciere* to Cagliari, met on the morning of the 28th with the 1st Division near Ponza and together returned to Naples that afternoon.

The 'changing of the guard' at the top of the navy and of the fleet (7 December 1940)

The battle of Cape Teulada (or Cape Spartivento as it was known to the British) of itself was a secondary event in the context of Operation MB9, but its consequences were of major importance. In the British camp, Somerville's conduct did not seem beyond criticism to the Admiralty, the successful outcome of Operation 'Collar' notwithstanding. Having returned to Gibraltar, he was subject to a court martial, where his breaking off contact and the failed second torpedo plane attack against the Italian battleships were questioned. As to the first point, he made the arguments that have already been outlined; as to the second point, he noted that the decision to attack the cruisers was within the discretion of the flight commander. Both of the arguments convinced the court and the Admiralty.

The consequences on the Italian side were quite different. The sortie by the fleet was intended to demonstrate that after Taranto the Regia Marina's fighting spirit had not diminished, but with the unstated reservation of not taking risks and not engaging to the limit. Taken as a whole, once again naval and air action proved to be ineffective; but it was the fleet's action that caused the greatest disappointment to the head of the government. Supermarina did not want to risk its only two operational battleships and Campioni held to that criteria in a restrictive fashion, as seen by his hesitancy in heading for the enemy when he thought that the British had only the *Renown* facing him, and the lack of support to the cruisers, even though they were engaged by a battlecruiser. The result was an unpleasant image of an engagement carried out exclusively while withdrawing, battleships included. The fact that in the days that followed Cavagnari defended such a line of conduct, and that he supported it even for future action, irritated Mussolini. In truth, his disappointment with the naval leadership had been increasing since the summer because of their reluctance to employ the fleet more incisively to the point of passivity and abdication in the face of an enemy who operated all across the Mediterranean almost unchallenged. The episode of Taranto, the disappointment of Cape Teulada and Cavagnari's obstinacy finally induced Mussolini to a 'change of the guard' at the top levels of the navy, along with other changes in the highest military echelons stemming from the negative progress of the conflict. On 7 December, admirals Domenico Cavagnari and Odoardo Somigli were replaced in their posts as Chief of Staff (and Undersecretary of State) and Deputy Chief of Staff of the Navy, respectively, by Vice Admirals Arturo Riccardi and Inigo Campioni, who was replaced by Admiral Angelo Iachino as C-in-C of the naval forces, which had been reorganised as a single squadron. But, as soon would become clear, little or nothing was to change in the conduct of operations at sea.

The bombing of Naples of 14–15 December 1940 and transfer of the battleships to La Maddalena

The main reason why the bulk of the fleet was moved from Taranto to Naples was to safeguard it against further aerial torpedo attacks, as bombing by high-altitude aircraft had so far proved to be ineffective. But, in November 1940, the British War Cabinet had prepared a plan to employ bombers that were laying over while transferring to Egypt, and later 148 Squadron RAF, which had been expressly constituted to operate from Malta against ports in southern Italy. Thus, in late autumn 1940, Vickers Wellington medium bombers attacked Naples four times, although with negligible results, except for a raid on the night of 14/15 December 1940, when they struck a devastating blow.

The *Vittorio Veneto*, Admiral Iachino's flagship, and the *Cesare* were moored at the Luigi Rizzo quay, as well as the heavy cruisers *Pola*, *Zara* and *Gorizia* moored at the Italo Balbo pier with eleven destroyers of the VII, IX and X squadriglias. There were, in addition, two large passenger liners, *Giulio Cesare* and *Lombardia*, and the hospital ship *Arno*. The attack was made by nine Wellingtons in two waves, the first targeting the warships and port installations, and the second the airport and railway junctions. With visibility good enough not to need flares, both groups came from

The *Giulio Cesare* riding at anchor in the La Maddalena archipelago (between Sardinia and Corsica) in December 1940. (Courtesy Presidenza Nazionale ANMI, Rome)

seaward at altitudes estimated between 1000 and 2000 metres and made several runs over the targets. The damage to ground installations was of little account. The damage done to the ships by 250-pound semi-armour-piercing bombs was more serious. The worst damage was suffered by the *Pola*, which, hit by two bombs, was in danger of sinking. Minor damage was sustained by two merchant ships. Overall, the anti-aircraft defences were confused and ineffective and the ships spotted the attacking aircraft only three times. The ships did not lay smoke, while on the ground the smoke generators were not operating. The bombing laid bare the inadequacy of anti-aircraft defences at Naples and Supermarina decided to move the major ships until these defences were improved. On the afternoon of the 15th the two battleships and the two cruisers with their respective destroyer squadriglias departed Naples for La Maddalena (in the north of Sardinia), where they arrived on the morning of the 16th.

The move of the two battleships from Naples was the strategic outcome of the raid. This fell on the eve of the complex British operation MC2 – centred upon the dispatch of a convoy from Alexandria to Malta and of another from Malta to Alexandria and of the transfer of the battleship *Malaya* with three destroyers from Alexandria to Gibraltar (16–24 December 1940) – and forestalled any possible interference by the Italian fleet.

At the time the Italian military situation had deteriorated on all fronts. Since the end of November in the Balkans, the Greeks, having rebuffed the Italian invasion, had gone on the offensive and struck deep into Albania, putting the entire Italian deployment in danger. In North Africa, the British counteroffensive under General Archibald Wavell had been in full swing since 9 December, which threw the Italians out of Egypt and which would soon lead to the defeat of the 10th Army and the loss of Cyrenaica. These setbacks and the inability to challenge the naval power exercised by the British in the Mediterranean marked not only a serious crisis for Italy, but a threat to Germany and the European balance that had been created by its victories on the Continent. This led to Hitler's insistence that Mussolini allow German assistance in the Mediterranean, in North Africa and in the Balkans, which would act to stabilise the southern fronts. Its first manifestation was the transfer to Sicily, in the second half of December 1940, of the X Fliegerkorps, consisting of air units specialised in maritime warfare. This did not signal a change in Hitler's strategy – as had been advocated by the Skl for months to strike Britain in the area it considered to be weak, the Mediterranean and Middle East – but it constituted a new and important reality in the war in that theatre.

The bombings of Naples in December 1940 and January 1941 and Operation 'Excess' (10-12 January 1941)

On 20 December 1940 the *Vittorio Veneto*, the *Cesare* and the 1st Division, along with the VII, IX and XIV destroyer squadriglias, had returned from La Maddalena to Naples, as the anti-aircraft defences had been strengthened and chlorohydrin systems to generate artificial fog installed. Two days later *Zara* and *Gorizia* left Naples for Taranto; this second basing of the battleships in Naples would not last for very long.

For early January 1941 the British had planned a new complex operation throughout the entire Mediterranean in order to strengthen their position in Malta, in Greece and in the Levant, which would involve all of the naval forces present in the theatre, from the Mediterranean Fleet to Force H (7–13 January 1941). The main operation, designated MC4, consisted in sending supplies from Gibraltar to Malta and Piraeus by means of the 'Excess' convoy, made up of five merchant ships. The associated operations involved sending supplies from Alexandria to Malta and two convoys from Malta to Alexandria. To cap off Operation MC4, a second operation, MC6, was to be conducted against Italian coastal targets and Libyan convoys by part of the Mediterranean Fleet, including the carrier *Illustrious*. Escort for the 'Excess' convoy from Gibraltar to the Sicilian Channel was assigned to Force H and, in the final leg to Malta, also to a part of the Mediterranean Fleet with Admiral Cunningham's flagship, *Warspite*, along with the *Valiant* and the *Illustrious*. Three submarines were placed in ambush positions north of the convoy route in the Sicilian Channel, while the RAF was to conduct anti-submarine reconnaissance of Italian ports.

It is not clear if the air attack against Naples on the night of 29/30 December 1940 was connected to this cycle of operations. It developed in two waves, targeting the ground installations and the port area where the *Vittorio Veneto* and the *Cesare* were moored. This time air observation worked well, because their approach was spotted and reported by the watch stations at Marsala and a timely alarm led to a decent laying of an artificial fog screen which covered a large portion of the port area. No ships were hit or damaged and damage on shore was minimal. All of the ships in port took part in the anti-aircraft defence with barrage fire from their machine guns. The fog generation proved to be effective, especially the fog created by the army's smoke generators. Iachino had requested, in fact, that both the fixed as well as the mobile positions be strengthened, so as to reduce reliance on the ships' own smoke-making apparatus, which was less effective and which at times produced large flames that revealed their positions.

On 8 January 1941, during the initial phase of Operation MC4, RAF reconnaissance had determined the presence of three battleships in Naples. That led to the decision to make a pre-emptive attack against the base to damage them. This assessment was fairly precise, but the ships were the *Vittorio Veneto*, the *Cesare* and the cruiser *Pola*, which was undergoing work. The raid was conducted by Wellingtons of 148 Squadron from Malta on the evening of 8 January. Once again they were favoured by good visibility, but this time the Italian warning system in the Strait of Messina also functioned satisfactorily and the bombers did not arrive unexpectedly. It was thus possible for the ships and army chemical sections ashore to lay an artificial fog screen over the Luigi Rizzo quay in time. The air incursion took place shortly before 20:00 and was greeted by anti-aircraft fire from the Dicat [Difesa Contraera Territoriale, Territorial Air Defence] and that from the ships. The Wellingtons again came from seaward in several waves and made multiple low-level runs over the targets in port. Once again, the targets were in large measure hidden by the artificial fog: the *Vittorio Veneto* completely and the *Cesare* for only about a quarter of its length forward, a fact that made it the primary target. No bombs hit the ships, but at 19:59 some exploded in the water a short distance from the starboard side of *Cesare*, causing slight damage to the hull with flooding limited to the Pugliese protection system. Two bombs exploded on the Luigi Rizzo quay close to the battleship near the aft main gun turrets, hurling a large number of fragments that caused losses among the personnel; another landed on the *Vittorio Veneto* with no effect. There was no other appreciable damage ashore or to the ships that were in port.

The material effects of the January 1941 bombing were, therefore, of minor relevance, but for Iachino Naples did not offer adequate security to function as a base for the main nucleus of the fleet. In addition, the repair work on the *Cesare* required a drydock, and Naples did not have any large enough. Also, as the *Doria* had not yet completed her training programme, the *Vittorio Veneto* was left as the only operational battleship of the entire fleet and Supermarina did not feel like risking her in a base that was

The battleship *Giulio Cesare* being manoeuvred to its mooring at Naples in late 1940. (D Zambon collection)

not yet secure. Because of this, on the afternoon of the 9th, both battleships weighed anchor for La Spezia, arriving there on the afternoon of the 10th. That same day the admiral's staff of 5th Division were transferred from the *Cesare* to the *Doria*, in light of the ship's move to Genoa for work in drydock. The *Cesare*, escorted by the destroyers *Libeccio* and *Grecale*, arrived on the 12th, but could not be put into drydock until the 16th because of a strong and persistent north wind that was strong enough to part one of the ship's mooring cables in port, forcing her to spend the entire night of the 14/15th held into the wind with the assistance of a tug. She entered drydock on the 16th and remained there, camouflaged with tarpaulins (the white and red stripes forward were quite visible in the moonlight) until 30 January, when she returned to La Spezia for the final adjustments.

With this latest raid the British were thus able to relegate the three remaining operational or nearly operational Italian battleships to the margins of the theatre of war and to prevent any possible interference by them against Operation MC4, whose opposition was left to light forces and the air force, which for the first time saw the intervention of the X Fliegerkorps. On 10 January, in an encounter in the waters off Pantelleria, the torpedo boat *Vega* was lost but the same day German aircraft seriously damaged the *Illustrious* in the Sicilian Channel and on the 11th, the *Gloucester* and *Southampton*, the latter of which was later scuttled, to which was added the irreparable damage caused by an Italian mine to the destroyer *Gallant*.

On the night of the 10/11th, having learned of the damage to the *Illustrious*, Supermarina ordered Iachino's flagship, the *Vittorio Veneto*, and the *Doria*, which was still undergoing training, to sortie from La Spezia in an attempt to intercept the British in the Sicilian channel, that is, at a distance of more than a day's steaming. The two battleships set out around 04:00 on the 11th, escorted by a section of the XIII Destroyer Squadriglia consisting of *Granatiere* and *Alpino*, by the X Squadriglia (*Maestrale, Libeccio, Grecale, Scirocco*) and by a section of VII Squadriglia, *Freccia* and *Saetta*, proceeding south at a speed of 20 knots. This group was to be joined in the waters off Augusta at 08:00 on the 12th by the 3rd Division's cruisers from Messina and by those of the 1st and 7th from Taranto. But by the evening of the 10th the *Illustrious* had reached Malta and Supermarina, having received the news, at 14:00 on the 11th ordered Iachino to return. The squadron, which had just passed the Scoglio d'Africa (a small skerry in the Tuscan archipelago), reversed course and returned to La Spezia on the morning of the 12th while executing several manoeuvring and gunnery exercises.

For the first time since the beginning of the war the British had paid a high price for carrying out their operations in the Mediterranean, thanks primarily to the X Fliegerkorps and, so as not to run any additional risks, cancelled Operation MC6. The use of Italian light forces proved once again to be ineffective, partly because of the tactic of scattering the torpedo boats in small and disconnected formations, which then found themselves facing greatly superior enemy forces without even being able to surprise them. With respect to the battle squadron, even allowing for the delay to the mission – the battleships put to sea when the *Illustrious* had already been in Malta for some time – and the decision to not employ only the cruisers from Taranto and Messina (an attempt that would have been too late in any case), it was obvious that basing the battleships at La Spezia excluded, from the outset, any possible role for them in the central Mediterranean.

The bombardment of Genoa and opposition to Operation 'Grog' (8–11 February 1941)

After the incursions against Taranto and Naples the British persisted in their aeronaval offensive in order to strike the Italian Navy both materially and psychologically. In the second half of January 1941, according to information they possessed, there were two battleships and a heavy cruiser at Genoa, of which one battleship in drydock was to return to La Spezia on 31 January. The situation gave Somerville the idea of bombarding the city, which was lightly defended, to cause damage to the major ships present there and to industrial sites, as well as making an aerial torpedo attack against the dam of the Tirso hydroelectric station in Sardinia. The operations went badly: the first was broken off because of poor weather conditions, and the second because of a failed attack with the downing of one plane, and Force H returned to Gibraltar on 4 February. its movements, however, had not escaped Italian observation and the bulk of the naval squadron was held ready to move to La Spezia.

Two days later the British once again attempted the operation against Genoa, prompted by the news of an imminent meeting between Mussolini and Spain's Franco. In their calculations an attack in internal Italian waters would persuade the Spanish Caudillo to adopt a more cautious attitude to neutrality and, in particular, to not grant air and naval bases in the Balearics. For this second operation, designated 'Grog' and which also called for an air attack against the refineries at Livorno, Force H took to sea initially split into three groups: I (*Renown*, with Admiral Somerville, *Malaya*, *Ark Royal* and *Sheffield*), and III (four destroyers) left Gibraltar on the afternoon of 6 February, headed for the Atlantic, simulating a convoy escort; group II (six destroyers) entered directly into the Mediterranean, simulating an anti-submarine exercise. With the onset of darkness, groups I and III entered the Mediterranean and on the night of 6/7th met with II east of Gibraltar. After which, Force H headed to the Balearics and, having sailed between Ibiza and Mallorca, proceeded to the northeast, keeping to the north of the archipelago and then following a route below Provence, thus finding itself on the morning of the 9th in the Gulf of Genoa. Two destroyers were left to cruise close to the Balearics and to send radio signals to confuse enemy observation. Supermarina was already aware of the departure as early as the morning of the 7th thanks to observers posted around Gibraltar and for the morning of the 8th instituted along with Superaereo a reconnaissance effort west of Sardinia. While awaiting the outcome, the battleships were made ready at La Spezia and shifted the 3rd Division to Genoa, a move that had already been scheduled in view of the planned meeting between Mussolini and Franco at Bordighera on 11 February. Aerial reconnaissance provided no appreciable intelligence, other than of the alleged spotting of destroyers 100 miles south of Minorca, which led to the presumption that Force H was at sea, but left uncertain what its purpose might be – launching aircraft to Malta, escorting a convoy through the Sicilian Channel, air attack against targets in southern Sardinia, landing Gaullist troops on Corsica, air raids against Genoa and La Spezia, coastal bombardment in the Gulf of Genoa were all possibilities.

Supermarina arranged for departure of the three battleships from La Spezia on the evening of the 8th and their meeting, at dawn on the 9th, slightly to the north of Asinara with the 3rd Division, which had already left Messina at 07:00 on the 8th; from there the squadron was to have sailed as far as the 6th east meridian to await news of the enemy, having the option of either heading north or south of the Strait of Bonifacio (in this second case, however, the possibility of a timely encounter in the morning would have been problematic); in the absence of any sightings the naval squadron was to return to La Spezia on the morning of the 10th. The battleship group weighed anchor with some delay because of problems with *Cesare*'s condensers due to the intake of mud while manoeuvring to exit from the Duca degli Abruzzi basin and on the night of the 8th the Italian forces at sea were as follows:

- Battleship group (from La Spezia): *Vittorio Veneto*, Admiral Iachino C-in-C; 5th Division: *Cesare*, *Doria*; X Destroyer Squadriglia: *Maestrale, Libeccio, Scirocco, Grecale*; XIII Destroyer Squadriglia: *Granatiere, Fuciliere, Alpino*.
- Cruisers (from Messina): 3rd Division: *Trieste, Trento, Bolzano*; XII Destroyer Squadriglia: *Corazziere, Carabiniere, Camicia Nera*.

In addition, the submarines *Diaspro*, *Corallo* and *Santorre di Santarosa* were arrayed as scouts south of Sardinia.

While the battle squadron (SN) was gathering near Asinara and air reconnaissance resumed searching the waters to the west of Sardinia, Force H had penetrated, unobserved, into the Gulf of Genoa. At 06:00 on the 9th the *Ark Royal*, escorted by three destroyers, took station about 70 miles from Livorno to launch an air attack against the local refineries and, at 07:50, the rest of the force, which had arrived off Portofino, to the east of Genoa, prepared to shell the city, proceeding from east to west at a speed of 18 knots. Firing began at 08:14 at a range of 19,000 metres with quite good visibility. The action continued until 08:45 with the assistance of aerial observation and a total of 273 15in rounds, 782 6in and 400 4.7in were fired, half of which landed in the water and many of which did not explode. There was a certain amount of damage: the port installations did not suffer much; the old school ship *Garaventa* and one steamship, which was later recovered, 14 lighters, one floating stage and a motor sailer were sunk; a ship in drydock was damaged and 32 of 55 steamships present were slightly damaged. None of the naval vessels under repair, the *Duilio* and the destroyer *Bersagliere*, suffered any damage. In the industrial area the Ansaldo works suffered only property damage, while damage to the Società Italiana Acciaierie Cornigliano works was somewhat more serious as it involved

The battleship *Giulio Cesare* alongside at Naples in December 1940 while an artificial fog (smokescreen) exercise is under way; the *Vittorio Veneto* can be seen in the background.

several plants. The city, including the cathedral of San Lorenzo, suffered 250 buildings damaged or destroyed and 2500 people were left homeless. The human cost was 144 killed and 242 wounded. The coastal defences, totalling two 381mm guns on barges, two 190mm (idem) and eight 152mm, reacted with slow, sporadic and ineffective fire because of the difficulty of seeing the targets from the ground and because of shortcomings in the organisation of the gunnery; the *Duilio* also joined the action, opening fire with light armament against an enemy reconnaissance plane. Once the bombardment was over, the British ships headed south to join the *Ark Royal* at 09:00, which was returning from the east, after having carried out with little result a raid against the ANIC refineries in Livorno and, by mistake, against targets at Pisa, with the loss of one Swordfish. Four other aircraft dropped mines in the access channels into La Spezia, which however were quickly discovered. At 11:35 Force H continued to proceed south, then to steer to the southeast and to more or less double back on the course it had previously taken along the coast of Provence and north of the Balearics.

The British ships had made it to the Ligurian coast unobserved, where no arrangements had been made to patrol the sea despite the fact that the local commands had been alerted. They were spotted from shore and by port security only shortly before the bombardment began; moreover, the ships were mistakenly identified as Italian. But neither these sightings, nor later reports, were passed on by radio by local stations and commands, contrary to what was prescribed and, to top it all off, Supermarina was unaware of this development. It did not become aware of it until 09:00 and at 09:50 Iachino received the message and order to head to the north. Until that moment the Italian squadron had headed southwest, a course deemed to be ideal for launching the shipboard Ro 43 scout planes and because it was thought, based on the alarm regarding the Tirso dam the previous night, that the enemy was in that direction. Therefore, when at 09:50 Iachino steered north, with the cruisers 10,000 metres ahead of the battleships, the battle squadron ended up 30 miles to the south of what had been planned. Despite the time that had been lost, there was still a chance of intercepting the enemy, except that once it had steamed away from Genoa, nothing was known of its positions or its course. In addition, air reconnaissance had to be reoriented to the area of sea between Provence and Corsica, which for several reasons was lacking. Among these was the breakdown of the *Vittorio Veneto*'s catapult, which prevented launching the two Ro 43 scout planes for the rest of the morning of the 9th. The sparse information that reached Iachino in those hours was vague, contradictory and did not provide any reliable indication regarding the withdrawal route of Force H. For the entire morning the battle squadron steamed north, but at 12:44, in the absence of any reliable information as to the enemy's position and movements, Iachino set a 330° heading, assuming that the British were withdrawing along the coast of Provence and launched a Ro 43 from *Trieste* to scout in that direction. If the squadron had proceeded for another half hour in that direction it would have intercepted Force H with a favourable force ratio and in an area of the sea where Axis air assets could have easily joined in the action.

It was in this confused situation that the decisive turn of the day took place. Around 13:00 messages reached Iachino from Supermarina regarding sightings that put the British carrier, at 10:45, still in the Gulf of Genoa with a course to the south and three other ships west-southwest of Cape Corso heading to the northeast. This last sighting was of French convoy CN4 bound from Toulon to Bone, but passing through the Tyrrhenian Sea east of Corsica and Sardinia; this was mistaken for Force H, even though because of armistice regulations its movement should have been well known to the Italian commands. The misunderstanding led Iachino to conclude that the two enemy groups were about to join together west of Cape Corso with the intention of escaping to the south along the western coast of Corsica. This interpretation was given credence by the fact that the Ro 43 from *Trieste* had not seen anything in the waters of Provence and that (mistaken) radio direction intercepts of the enemy had confirmed this assessment. Accordingly, at 13:07 Iachino steered north-northeast at a speed of 30 knots for the cruisers and 24 knots for the battleships, certain of intercepting the enemy; at 13:21 all ships were ordered to prepare for action and at 15:24 and 15:38 the *Trieste*, 15,000 metres ahead of the battleship group, spotted the suspect ships. However, as the squadron made ready for battle, Supermarina provided new, belated reports of sightings and of an air attack against Force H between 12:00 and 13:00 in the waters south of Provence, which now convinced Iachino to search to the west. Until that time, therefore, he had steamed in a direction that diverged from that of Force H and when, at 15:50 he set a course for 270 degrees with the cruisers leading at 30 knots followed by the battleships at 24, it was now too late because the British ships were now showing their sterns. At dusk the Iachino abandoned the search and during the night, by Supermarina's orders, he remained to cruise in the Ligurian Sea. On the morning of the 10th Supermarina ordered the 3rd Division to return to Messina and the battleship group to Naples, in anticipation of the access routes to La Spezia being cleared of mines dropped by British aircraft. Late in the morning of the 11th the three battleships reached Naples and in the late afternoon they weighed anchor again for La Spezia, arriving there on the afternoon of the 12th. The air force, including the X Fliegerkorps units, had not achieved any better results, despite the total of 194 reconnaissance, bomber and fighter aircraft that had been committed (two were shot down). On the afternoon of the 11th, moreover, Force H had returned to Gibraltar with the loss of only one aircraft.

Operation 'Grog' had ended with a blow to Italian arms and a resounding loss of prestige for Italy on the eve of the summit between Mussolini and Franco. Force H had audaciously penetrated Italian waters, had conducted the bombardment of a major city like Genoa with good results, in addition to air attacks against Livorno and La Spezia, and had withdrawn undamaged, escaping the hunt by Italian naval and air forces. An attempt was made to lay the blame, in part, on weather conditions for the failure to discover the British in confined waters, but in truth they had been favoured by an incredible combination of negligence, imprudence, disfunctions, misunderstandings, delays, mistaken information and assessments at all levels, of which we have mentioned only a few. It showed up the inadequacy of coordination between the navy and the air force, but equally demonstrated disconnects and frictions in the communications system and the lack of preparation to conduct an air war over the sea. The mistaken identification of the French convoy, of itself, was perhaps the least serious of the errors (it was, moreover, crossed by Force H during its initial withdrawal to the south), if one considers that around 13:45 aircraft bombed two Italian MAS boats (MTBs), mistaking them, first, for a battleship and an aircraft carrier, and then for two cruisers (!!), or that the two Fiat BR 20 bombers reported their attack at 13:00 against the *Ark Royal* only after they had returned to their base (Iachino received the news two and a half hours later), or that in three sightings Force H was mistaken for the Italian battle squadron, because the observers did not think that they would find the enemy in that area of the sea, based on information they had been given prior to take-off. In effect, probably the fundamental error made by the Italian commands was not seriously considering the possibility that the enemy might retire along the quickest exit route from the Ligurian Sea.

Superaereo bitterly chastised its subordinate commands for the complete failure of air operations and Supermarina sent similar notes to its subordinates, Iachino excepted. Confronted by Mussolini, Supermarina defended the action (and its own) including the mistaken assessment of the enemy early on the morning of the 9th; it cautiously challenged the fact that it had not used the cruisers as a scouting force, pushing them as far as and beyond the line of horizon (20,000–30,000 metres). Iachino alleged that their number was insufficient and that he could never imagine such a total failure of air reconnaissance. However, later operations ('Halberd', Second Sirte) revealed that, although he understood the shortcomings of air reconnaissance even in the pre-tactical phase, he always had a tendency not to use his cruisers as long-range scouts, preferring to hold them close to the bulk of the force. This is also confirmed by his written directives and doctrine for the use of the fleet.

Chapter 9.3

THE ITALIAN BATTLESHIPS IN DEFENCE OF CONVOYS TO LIBYA (WINTER 1941–1942)

The lack of employment of the smaller battleships during 1941 and the Libyan convoy crisis

After the failed action against Operation 'Grog' the modernised battleships were no longer employed in operations until late November 1941. Their participation was only envisaged for the planned, but never implemented, Operation 'Orione' at the end of October 1941, an offensive operation in the waters west of the 25th meridian east between Cyrenaica and Crete, for which almost all of the Italian fleet was to have taken part. It was intended to engage the Mediterranean Fleet, in the event that it sortied to protect British convoys to Tobruk, which had remained cut off after the reconquest of Cyrenaica by the Italo-German Armoured Army (ACIT) or, alternatively, to force the British to cancel the operation. The decision to forego their employment had its origins in technical factors and reasons of economy of force. From the first perspective, their maximum speed was a few knots below that of the 'Littorio' class and the clearly demonstrated difficulty of operating in formation with those ships eroded their contribution, considering that one of the major advantages of the Italian battleships over the British was their superior speed. From the second, shortages of fuel began to make themselves felt from the summer of 1941– which was to afflict the Regia Marina for the rest of the war – and the availability of fleet destroyers declined, due more to wear and lack of training than to losses, brought about by the increasingly intense requirements of convoy defence.

The outlook changed when it became necessary to intervene in force to deal with the serious emergency situation that arose towards the end of 1941 in defence of convoys with Libya, a period that coincided with *Vittorio Veneto* being out of service for about three months after being torpedoed at Cape dell'Armi (14 December 1941). The crisis affected the operational capability of the ACIT and facilitated the British 8th Army's offensive (Operation 'Crusader') which began on 18 November and led to the loss of Cyrenaica again in December. The greatest threat to the Axis convoys came from light units, Force K, from submarines and from several torpedo aircraft squadrons, all operating from Malta. The main (but unknown) cause of Italian difficulties in supplying North Africa resided in the effectiveness reached by 'Ultra' code-breaking during that period, but there was also a marked gap in preparation for night combat, exacerbated by the lack of radar equipment. The situation reached such a dramatic point that between December 1941 and early January 1942 Supermarina went so far as to propose to Comando Supremo [the Supreme High Command] the suspension of convoys with Libya.

That same autumn, in order to ease the difficult situation in the Mediterranean, the Kriegsmarine sent several U-boat flotillas and, later, torpedo boats. The Luftwaffe sent another air formation, the II Fliegerkorps, with the specific mission of neutralising Malta and which, along with X Fliegerkorps and Fliegerführer Afrika, constituted the II Luftflotte. With the arrival of these new units the Deutsche Marinekommando Italien (German Naval Command in Italy) was formed, assigned to Vice Admiral Eberhard Weichold, and the Oberbefehlshaber Süd (OBS) or High Command South under Field Marshal Albert Kesselring, to which all the German forces in the Mediterranean were nominally subordinate, although in reality it was able to exercise full authority over only II Luftflotte. Participation by German submarines quickly produced significant results: on 14 November *U 81* sank the carrier *Ark Royal* and on the 25th *U 331* sank the battleship *Barham*. Within a short time the strategic picture would further improve because of serious damage in Alexandria to the Mediterranean Fleet's two remaining battleships, the *Queen Elizabeth* and the *Valiant*, by Italian Decima MAS frogmen, by elimination of Force K, which ran into a minefield between 18 and 19 December and, most of all, because of the neutralisation of Malta thanks to the II Fliegerkorps offensive in the early months of 1942.

Night-time gunnery exercises by the *Giulio Cesare* on 24 September 1941

From the late spring of 1941 the ships of the battle squadron (*Squadra Navale*, SN) were engaged in day and night gunnery exercises, the latter of which were designed to verify the effectiveness of the new procedures and instrumentation, in an attempt to deal with one of the Regia Marina's most worrisome technical and operational disadvantages. Documentation survives relating to these exercises for the nights prior to 22 June and 24 September in the Gulf of Taranto.

The *Littorio*, the *Duilio* and the XIV Destroyer Squadriglia participated in the first exercise, in order to test the effectiveness of illuminating fire and of night-time gunnery. The *Duilio* played the role of target ship and the C-in-C of the SN, Admiral Iachino, embarked on the *Littorio*, was able to verify that the new procedures for night firing met the requirement, but that the ammunition was still inadequate: in particular, the old 120/40 guns for illuminating fire of the 'Littorio' class were completely inadequate, while the 90mm guns had only a short range. He deemed it necessary to replace the 120mm of the 'Littorios' and to adopt a long-range 90mm illuminating round (9000–10,000 metres); with respect to the negative impact of the searchlights on firing, he proposed an adequate distribution of Zeiss-Septar binoculars for all of the surface ships and to equip the APG and the night-firing apparatus with optical instruments of the same characteristics, although he remained dubious about the possibility of observing the fall of the salvos in order to adjust fire.

Only the *Cesare* took part in the exercise on the night (with no moonlight) of 23/24 September. The main purpose was to test the new simplified night instrumentation for the main and medium guns through the use of new installations placed on the sides of the command bridge. A series of 320mm salvos with three turrets were fired at charge III and a series of 120mm at charge III with two starboard turrets at distances between 4000 and 6200 metres. Each series was preceded and accompanied by illuminating fire from the starboard forward 100/47 mounting and the starboard midships 120mm turret. Illuminating fire was ineffective, mainly because of the short range and restricted coverage of the illuminated area. The night-firing instruments, however, worked very well and the location of the instrument stations on the sides of the command bridge offered the advantage of immediate contact between the three fire direction centres and the commanding officer, but also led to numerous problems among which were the flash and blast caused by the rounds as they were fired. In order to attenuate the flash effect of the main gun rounds, the only remedy was for the crew to close their eyes upon the fire director's order to fire, but anyone did not do so in a timely manner lost their night vision for about two minutes. With respect to accuracy, overall, the gunnery proved to be fair.

The mission of the 5th, 8th and 7th Divisions protecting convoys with Libya (29 November–1 December 1941)

In late November 1941, in support of Operation 'Crusader' and as a reinforcement to Force K, Force B was sent from Alexandria to Malta. Commanded by Rear Admiral H B Rawlings, it consisted of the light cruisers *Ajax* and *Neptune* and the destroyers *Kimberly* and *Kingston.* During those same days, following the destruction of the 'Maritza' convoy by Force K, Supermarina made arrangements for the movement of numerous transports based on the concept of several small convoys sailing to Libya from a number of ports and along different routes that were distant from each other, in the hope that at least some of them would get through. However, Supermarina gave these many movements indirect protection by major ships by sending an impressive naval force into the central Ionian. Accordingly, putting to sea from Taranto were the *Duilio* (5th Division under Admiral Guido Porzio Giovanola, senior commander at sea) with four destroyers and the 7th Division (light cruisers *Duca d'Aosta, Montecuccoli* and *Attendolo*) with three destroyers, and from Messina the light cruiser *Giuseppe Garibaldi* (8th Division) with two destroyers. Agreements were also reached with Superaereo for reconnaissance over the Sicilian Channel, around Malta and over the area of sea where the Italian groups were to operate on 29 and 30 November. A line of three submarines was set up east and southeast of the island to watch for any sortie by Force K.

The battleship *Andrea Doria* seen from the *Giulio Cesare* in the central Mediterranean during Operation M 42 (16–19 December 1941).

The *Andrea Doria* in her first camouflage scheme, dating from the preceding October, taken from another Italian battleship in December 1941.

Unfortunately, beginning on 28 November, a large part of the radio messages relating to the planning were quickly decoded by the British and confirmed by air reconnaissance. At 05:00 on the 30th, therefore, setting out from Valletta were Force K (light cruisers *Aurora*, *Penelope* and *Lively*) and Force B, headed first to the south and then to the east so as to intersect the course between Taranto and Benghazi, staying out of range of the Stukas based on Crete as much as possible. Two submarines were posted in the central Ionian and a third in the southern Ionian. That same day the 14th Destroyer Flotilla with four destroyers and the 15th Cruiser Division (*Naiad*, *Euryalus*, with two destroyers) departed Alexandria to reconnoitre the waters north of Marmarica.

The passage of the Italian naval groups southward was slowed down for all of 29 and 30 November by bad weather and in the meantime, at 17:25 on the 29th, 25 miles east-southeast of Point Alice, the *Montecuccoli* was the target of torpedoes fired from the submarine *P 31*, which were avoided by manoeuvring, but which revealed that the Italian movements had been discovered. On the morning of the 30th the 'Duilio' group and the 7th Division were spotted a number of times by British reconnaissance and, in turn, Supermarina and the embarked commands received confirmation from air reconnaissance of the sighting by the submarine *Tricheo* of the British light forces south-southeast of Malta following a course to the east.

Because of the potential threat posed by the British forces Supermarina ordered the 'Duilio' group to steam 20 miles away from the 7th Division and for the division to manoeuvre as a consequence. Around 15:00 the 'Duilio' and 'Garibaldi' groups met and the cruiser took up station aft of the battleship. But just at that moment a dramatic event occurred that would determine the outcome of the operation. Supermarina was putting the final touches to the earlier dispositions, ordering that once the 'Duilio-Garibaldi' group had joined the 7th Division, it was to proceed south until 22:00 to cover one of the convoys and then to reverse course and head for Taranto, when the *Garibaldi* first reported that her steering gear had broken down and, shortly thereafter, that she had to stop engines as all of the boilers had shut down because of the lack of water to supply them, due to unknown causes. The *Duilio* moved closer to the cruiser while waiting to determine the extent of the breakdown and to decide what to do, including the possibility of towing the cruiser, for which preparations were begun aboard the battleship. At 16:10 the *Garibaldi* was able to relight two of her boilers and to restart the starboard engine, first moving at 6 knots and then at 15 knots, but half an hour later reported that the cause of the breakdown was still not clear, that the evaporation gear could not be relied on and that it would be prudent to return to base under escort. Shortly after 17:00 Supermarina issued orders to the three forces at sea that were already heading north to return to Taranto. The rest of the cruise offered no surprises and ended on the morning of 1 December. Other boilers on the *Garibaldi* were gradually lit again, but without any guarantee they would function reliably because of abnormal consumption of the water supply. The return of the three Italian groups left the field open for Forces B and K. We cannot dwell on the epilogue here. It suffices to recall that of the five merchantmen only one reached Libya, three were sunk and one returned with minor damage; a destroyer was also lost with no offsetting loss on the British side. Some supplies transported by naval ships were, however, able to reach the Libyan ports unharmed.

On 13 December Admiral Iachino, commenting on the way the mission of the three groups had unfolded, observed to what extent it had been conditioned, mainly with respect to the destroyers, by bad weather, but also by the excessive worry of keeping radio silence, which caused many errors. Finally, he noted the incidence of seasickness among the battleship crews because of their too little sea-time.

Italian technological inferiority in the fields of reconnaissance and communications, which at the time was only partially recognised, meant that the sortie by the strong naval force did not prove to be of any help to the mission. The reason can primarily be found in the great (and justified) apprehension of the risk of engaging in night encounters, which conditioned movements in the daylight hours as well. Supermarina had actually planned to continue the operation until 19:00 and later, even until 22:00 of the 30th, but when the incident with the *Garibaldi* occurred, in tune with the view of the senior commander at sea, it deemed the priority to be the safety of the cruiser compared to the fate of several convoys. Supermarina did not feel that it should have the 7th Division go to their assistance, as it might find itself alone in facing a night-time action against the British forces.

Operation M 41 and its cancellation (13–14 December 1941)

The urgent need to get supplies to Libya, the ineffectiveness of earlier convoy measures and a desire to counteract the sense of impotence that was making itself felt almost everywhere prompted Supermarina in early December to organise a complex operation, designated M 41. It consisted of sending three separate convoys from Taranto, Argostoli (Cephalonia) and Navarino (western Peloponnese) between 12 and 13 December, but this was then scaled back to two because two modern merchant ships were torpedoed by a submarine in the Gulf of Taranto. The protection for this operation comprised almost all Italian naval forces capable of putting to sea, including the 9th Division (*Littorio* and *Vittorio Veneto*), sailing directly from Naples, and the two 'Duilio' class ships. Arrangements were also made for scouting and offensive submarine screens and measures for air and naval cooperation and cover.

The British learned of M 41 through 'Ultra' intercepts and put Operation ME9 into motion to oppose it with light forces and submarines from Malta and Alexandria. Once under way, however, ME9 was cancelled after the British learned that the Italian operation itself had been cancelled. The cruisers from Alexandria, which in the meantime had put to sea, were recalled and on the 14th, by now close to its base, the *Galatea* was sunk by *U 577*. In fact, it so happened that on the afternoon of the 13th Italian reconnaissance had spotted the cruisers that had left Alexandria headed towards the central Mediterranean. Having mistaken them for battleships, Supermarina concluded that the Mediterranean Fleet was at sea with three battleships – it was not yet aware of the loss of the HMS *Barham* – and at 20:00 decided to suspend M 41 and to have the convoys and the naval forces at sea return home. In its judgement, although the total Italian forces (assuming the combination of the two 'Duilios' with the 'Littorios') would be superior to the British, this advantage would be cancelled out by the over-arching need to protect the convoys, and by the lack of enough escort ships and of air cover; above all, it feared the prospect of a night encounter. Instead, the 9th Division made its way to Taranto, with a view to a repeat of the operation. During this passage, on the morning of 14 December, just to the south of the Strait of Messina, the submarine HMS *Urge* managed to hit the *Vittorio Veneto* with a torpedo. Although damage was not very serious, the ship took on 3000 tons of water, but was able to reach Taranto at high speed. However, the ship was not available for later operations of the same type.

Operation M 41 failed at its inception with the loss of the two modern motorships, with damage to two steamships due to collision and damage to the *Vittorio Veneto*, only in part offset by the sinking of the *Galatea*. The torpedoing of the battleship made a strong impression on Supermarina, which had already reached the point of proposing that all convoys to Libya be suspended in order to husband the naval forces for the defence of the homeland; supplies were to be ferried only by destroyers, submarines and aircraft. But two days later, in the very midst of Operation M 42, it further requested that the destroyers be withdrawn from the Libyan route so that they could be returned to fleet duties, which would have simply meant abandoning the Italo-German ground forces and Libya to their fate.

Operation M 42 and the First Battle of Sirte (16–19 December 1941)

Mussolini and the chief of the general staff, General Ugo Cavallero, obviously overruled Supermarina and on 15 December at Taranto Admiral Riccardi made a rousing speech to the crews. The operation was again attempted in a simpler form: two convoys were organised, which were to depart from Taranto together at 14:00 on 16 December and which would separate at 18:00 on 17 December north of the Gulf of Sirte, one to head to Tripoli and one to Benghazi, where they were to arrive at first light on 18 December. The first convoy consisted of three merchant ships with a direct escort of six 'Navigatori' class destroyers; the second convoy consisted of a single merchant ship with one destroyer and one torpedo boat.

Close escort was assigned to a naval group consisting of the *Duilio* and the 7th Division (light cruisers *Aosta, Attendolo* and *Montecuccoli*) with the XI Destroyer Squadriglia (*Aviere, Ascari, Camicia Nera*), which was to have departed Taranto at 15:00 on the 16th. Long-range cover was assigned to a support group consisting of the *Littorio* (Admiral Iachino, commander of the battle squadron), the *Doria* and the *Cesare*, by the 3rd Division (heavy cruisers *Gorizia* and *Trento*), by the XIII Destroyer Squadriglia (*Granatiere, Fuciliere, Bersagliere, Alpino*), by the XII (*Corazziere, Carabiniere* plus *Usodimare*) and by the X (*Maestrale, Oriani, Gioberti*) leaving Taranto at 20:00 on the 16th. The 'Littorio' group was to assume cover of the convoy to the east. The 'Duilio' group was to maintain visual contact with the convoy, thus divided: the battleship to the east and the 7th Division to the west. On the evening of the 18th the 'Duilio' group was to reverse course to return to Taranto, as would also the 'Littorio' group. Supermarina set up a submarine screen and adequate air cover.

Contemporaneously, the British had arranged to send the supply ship *Breconshire* from Alexandria to Malta, escorted by the 15th Cruiser Division (*Naiad*, Vice Admiral Philip Vian, and *Euryalus*), by the light cruiser *Carlisle* and by the 14th Destroyer Flotilla, while Force K (*Aurora, Penelope* and the 4th Destroyer Flotilla) would leave from Malta to join with Admiral Vian's force and, on the afternoon of the 17th, Force B (light cruiser *Neptune* and destroyer *Kandahar*) to search for the Italian convoy. Admiral Cunningham decided against using his two remaining battleships because of the shortage of escort destroyers. Vian left Alexandria in the late evening of the 15th (the *Carlisle* and two destroyers returned soon after because of breakdowns) and at 08:30 on the 17th joined up with Force K north of Cyrenaica, continuing on to Malta.

Intelligence provided by 'Ultra' regarding M 42 was accurate and timely, especially in the initial phase. However, Vian had to dedicate himself to protecting the *Breconshire* until the evening of the 17th and not until the next night could he search for and attack the Italian naval forces. The Italian codebreaking service also functioned well and by 24:00 on the 16th Iachino knew that he had been spotted. From the morning of the 17th Vian's formation was observed many times by German and Italian aircraft, including by the two scout planes from *Littorio*, which, however, consistently mistook the *Breconshire* for a battleship. This fact had more than a little effect on Iachino's decisions, who adjusted his plan so that he could close with and engage the enemy with three battleships, rather than do so only with the faster *Littorio* and the 3rd Division, assuming he could fall back upon the two smaller battleships if he found himself facing superior forces. However, as dusk was approaching, Iachino felt that he could not intercept the enemy before dark and had the convoy and the 'Duilio' group

The *Andrea Doria* seen bow-on during Operation M 42 which led to the brief encounter known as the first battle of Sirte on 17 December 1941.

change course to avoid the possibility of being attacked at night, while the support group, with the 3rd Division leading, would still continue on a southerly heading. But, simultaneously, shortly before 17:30, there was a succession of sightings of the British forces oblique and to port of the *Littorio*, split into two groups and subjected to one of the many air attacks of the day. Iachino, still convinced that he faced at least one battleship, quickly steered in that direction until he got within range and then, at 32,000 metres, turned to the south so as to bring all of his guns to bear, choosing not to reduce the range any further.

Vian, who likewise had spotted the Italian forces, all of which, however, were out of range, had the *Breconshire* and two destroyers head south at the supply ship's maximum speed of 16 knots and to execute a diversionary manoeuvre to the north with the rest of the force, laying smokescreens. At 17:53, the engagement began in the faint light of dusk, which favoured the British ships as they had darkness behind them. The *Littorio* opened fire at an initial distance of 32,000 metres, followed by the *Doria* and the 3rd Division, which was further ahead to the south and closer to the enemy. Soon after the destroyers of the XIII and X squadriglias fended off an attack by enemy destroyers. Despite the enormous distance and the imperfect visibility due to the impending darkness, fire from the *Littorio* appeared to the British to be accurate, but no rounds hit the target. Only the destroyer *Jervis* was hit by fragments by a 203mm round from *Gorizia*, suffering one casualty. The short-lived gunnery action by the Italian ships is summarised in the following table:

Ship	Time opened fire/ Range (metres)	Time ceased fire/ rounds fired
Littorio	17:53/32,000	18:02/27
Doria[1]	17:53/32,000	17:59/13
Cesare[1]	-/30,000	-/-
Gorizia	17:55/22,400	18:04/58
Trento	17:57/22,400	18:02/34

[1] Maximum range of the 320/44 guns on the 'Duilio' class was 29,400 metres.
[2] Maximum range of the 320/44 guns on the *Cesare* was 28,600 metres and the distance shown here is that measured by rangefinder.

In the brief contact with the enemy the *Cesare* did not join in with her main armament because of abnormal vibration at high speed, which made target observation and rangefinding for its 320mm guns difficult. She engaged only in harassing fire with her medium-calibre guns against destroyers towards the smokescreens laid by the enemy ships. With the onset of darkness, Iachino broke off the action, turning away and ordering the destroyers to rejoin the main body. At 18:26 he headed north, the direction in which the convoy and the 'Duilio' group had already been heading for half an hour. Until 22:00 the convoy and the naval squadron continued on that course, which took them into less threatening waters, but also led them further from their destination and brought them closer to Malta. At that hour, Iachino made the convoy and the 'Duilio' group steer to the southwest, while the support group again assumed cover to the east. At 12:30 on the 18th at the entrance to the Gulf of Sirte, the two convoys split up with their respective direct escorts and both reached their destinations on the morning of the 19th. This second part of the mission was marked by several incidents (a collision between two destroyers and one between a merchant ship and a destroyer), which, nevertheless, had no effect on the successful outcome. Around 15:00 on the 18th the force set a course for Taranto, where it arrived on the 19th. Only the 7th Division continued to escort the convoy to Tripoli and returned the following day, after having avoided torpedoes fired by the submarines *Unbeaten* and *P 31* on the morning of the 19th.

The main worry for Admiral Vian was ensuring that the *Breconshire*, which had slipped to the south of the Italian forces, got to its destination. He assigned Force K to escort it, reinforced on the morning of the 18th by Force B, which in the preceding hours had searched in vain for the Italian convoy. The *Breconshire* finally arrived at Malta on the 18th. That night, Vian had already set course to return to Alexandria after a fruitless attempt to intercept the second convoy off Benghazi. As soon as it had resupplied at Malta, Force K put to sea again that same evening to search for the Italian convoy in the waters off Tripoli, but on the night of 18/19th ran into a field of 'T' mines laid by Italian

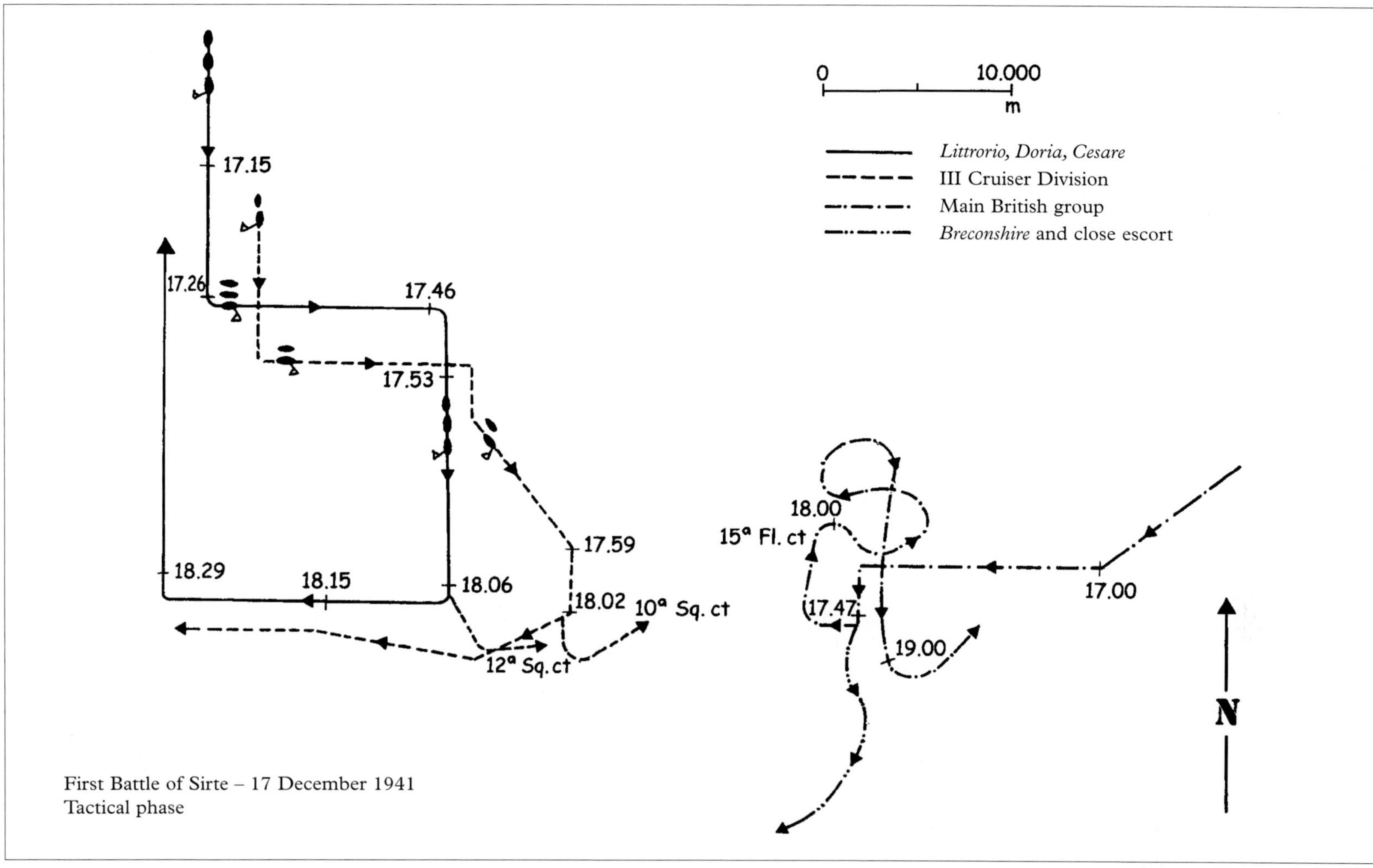

First Battle of Sirte – 17 December 1941
Tactical phase

ships the previous June. The light cruiser *Neptune* and the destroyer *Kandahar* were sunk, and the light cruiser *Aurora* was badly damaged and *Penelope* slightly damaged. For some months the surviving ships of that force continued to operate from Malta, but without their earlier offensive vigour.

Operation M 43 (3–6 January 1942)

The success of M 42 encouraged the Italian high commands to repeat the action in early January 1942. However, the Regia Marina hierarchy remained in two minds about this type of operation. Iachino thought it was wasteful and too risky to commit the whole of the fleet and, in particular, the only large battleship still operational, especially as the conflict was assuming a predominantly maritime character with the entry of the United States and Japan into the war, a fact that, in his opinion, should make preserving the fleet the guiding principle of the Italian naval war. These statements of position came at a time when there was still no full awareness of the serious losses suffered by the British in the Mediterranean and in the Pacific during the last part of 1941, but reflected the priorities of the highest echelons of the Italian Navy. The new operation, designated M 43, was to consist of sending three fast convoys departing on 3 January and with a single destination, Tripoli (Benghazi had fallen in December). It was made up as follows: Convoy No 1, from Messina, formed with three merchant ships and escorted by four destroyers; Convoy No 2, from Taranto, formed of two merchant ships escorted by four torpedo boats of which two were fitted with sonar gear; Convoy No 3, from Brindisi, consisting of one merchant ship escorted by a destroyer and a torpedo boat. The convoys were to meet at sea and to proceed to Tripoli, where they were scheduled to arrive late in the afternoon of the 5th.

Close-in protection was assigned to a group made up of the *Duilio*, the 8th (*Duca degli Abruzzi* and *Garibaldi*) and 7th Divisions (*Aosta* and *Attendolo*), with the X Destroyer Squadriglia (*Maestrale, Scirocco, Oriani, Gioberti*) as well as the destroyers *Saetta* and *Malocello*. Long-range cover was assigned to a group formed by the *Littorio* (C-in-C of the naval squadron, Admiral Iachino onboard), by the *Doria* and by the *Cesare*, by the 3rd Division (heavy cruisers *Gorizia* and *Trento*) and by the destroyers *Carabiniere, Alpino, Antonio Pigafetta, da Noli, Ascari, Aviere, Geniere* and *Camicia Nera*. The 'Littorio' group was to furnish long-range cover to the east, that is, against any threats by the Mediterranean Fleet from Alexandria, while the 'Duilio' group would be mixed in with the convoys, according to a plan devised by Admiral Bergamini. In fact, compared with M 42, the escort was to sail in immediate contact with the merchant ships, almost as if to form a single formation. This ensured there would always be a decisive superiority in case of attack by Force K, but also acknowledged the counterbalancing high risk of being torpedoed, by either submarines or aircraft, and the limits imposed by slow speed and difficulty of manoeuvre. Supermarina also deployed nine submarines east and south of Malta and Crete, while air force, naval aviation and Luftwaffe assets would be involved in reconnaissance and air escort.

The operation began on 3 January with the departure of the three convoys, of the 'Duilio' group, which joined Convoy No 2 soon thereafter, and finally of the 'Littorio' group. Soon after departure, at 21:44, the *Doria* suffered a machinery breakdown because of overheating of the starboard turbine's central reduction gear bearing. As a result, the battleship had to reduce speed to 6 knots but, as she was not able to continue steaming safely, Iachino ordered the ship to return to Taranto, escorted part of the way by *Ascari* and *Carabiniere*, which would later rejoin the main body. The support group thus continued its mission with only two battleships. The next day the convoys met and at 17:20 the 'Duilio' group merged with the convoy, while the support group provided cover to the east. In the late afternoon of the 4th, while on the way to meet with the convoy, Bergamini tested the maximum power output of the *Duilio*, achieving a less than satisfactory result: the ship did not exceed the revolutions for 24 knots (200 instead of 225), even with a displacement of 29,400 tons compared with the 27,500 tons during trials, which was the basis for the revolutions table.

M 43 continued on without any problems. At 18:45 on 4 January Iachino ordered the support group to return to Taranto, once the lack of threat from surface forces from Alexandria had been determined, as well as to escape any attacks at night, which were deemed probable following the repeated sightings of British reconnaissance aircraft. The 'Littorio' group reached its bases at Taranto and Messina on the afternoon of the following day. On the night prior to the 5th the 'Duilio' group left, in turn, the convoy while it was a short distance from Tripoli and returned to Taranto on the night of 5/6th. The convoy, which on the last leg of the voyage was protected only by its direct escort, had meanwhile reached Tripoli unscathed at noon on 5 January. In fact, despite the numerous sightings by aircraft there was no reaction by the British because after the losses suffered by running into the minefield near Tripoli Force K was out of the fighting and the aircraft based in Malta had not been able to find the Italian ships.

The operation was crowned with complete success, but upon his return Admiral Bergamini drew attention to the grave state of wear of the destroyers, characterised by a long succession of engine breakdowns, and concluded that a 'period of consolidation' was needed for the fleet. He also pointed out that ships camouflaged with dark colours were less visible at night and under varying light conditions, and because it was much more important to be less visible at night than during the day, he suggested that it would be appropriate for ships earmarked for these convoys to adopt dark camouflage schemes. This was also the last proper wartime operation in which the *Cesare* took part. This least modern of the smaller rebuilt battleships would in fact remain inactive at Taranto for the rest of 1942: that is, until transferred to Pola while waiting to undergo a major upgrade.

Operation T 18 and the loss of the motorship *Victoria* (22–25 January 1942)

Towards the end of January 1942, after the British advance in Cyrenaica had been halted at Agedabia and Rommel prepared for a counteroffensive, Supermarina made plans to send two fast convoys of five merchant ships to Tripoli, among which was the modern passenger ship *Victoria*, which was making its thirty-sixth wartime mission, along the Levant route passing about 90 miles east of Malta. Despite the fact that Supermarina thought at the time that an operational battleship of the 'Queen Elizabeth' class was still present at Alexandria, it relied on the speed of the convoys and did not contemplate providing a naval covering force, but only direct escort by a single battleship, the *Duilio*. The convoys were formed as follows: No 1, from Messina, with four merchant ships; No 2, from Taranto with the *Victoria*. The escort was split as follows: the 'Duilio' group, consisting of the battleship flying the flag of the II Squadron commander, Admiral Bergamini, with the XV Destroyer Squadriglia (*Pigafetta*, *Oriani*,

The *Andrea Doria*, foreground and the *Giulio Cesare* during Operation M 42. Note that on the *Cesare* the paint scheme is incomplete as application of the camouflage had to be suspended to allow the ship to put to sea at short notice on 16 December to replace the battleship *Vittorio Veneto*, which had been damaged by a torpedo two days earlier.

The battleship *Giulio Cesare* in January 1942 with its first experimental 'Claudus' camouflage scheme.

Scirocco, Ascari); the 7th Division (light cruisers *Aosta, Attendolo* and *Montecuccoli*) with the XIII Destroyer Squadriglia (*Alpino, Bersagliere, Carabiniere, Fucliere*); the 'Vivaldi' group, consisting of the XIV (*Vivaldi, Malocello, da Noli*) and the XI Destroyer Squadriglia (*Aviere, Camicia Nera, Geniere*); the torpedo boats *Orsa* and *Castore*, both equipped with sonar gear. Supermarina also deployed the usual submarine screen north of Cyrenaica, east of Lampedusa and off Malta, while the Regia Aeronautica and II Fliegerkorps were to ensure air cover during the daylight hours, as well as reconnaissance and anti-submarine patrols.

The two convoys were to steer courses 190 miles to the east of Malta – that is, outside of the presumed range of torpedo aircraft based there – and were to join together with the naval groups in the lower Ionian on the 23rd. North of Sirte the 'Duilio' group, first, and the 7th Division later, were to separate from the convoy to assume a waiting position in the middle of the Ionian to protect from any incursions from Alexandria and, then, to return to Taranto. Finally, the 'Vivaldi' group was to escort the combined convoy as far as Tripoli and then return to Palermo. Convoy No 1, which formed up in the Strait of Messina, and the 'Vivaldi' group left those waters at 08:00 on 22 February. That same day, at 11:00, the 7th Division left Taranto, followed at 17:00 by the 'Duilio' group and by convoy No 2, into which *Duilio* was integrated, as the *Victoria* had a maximum speed of 23 knots, almost equal to the battleship's sustained speed at that time (24.5 knots); the two ships were to sail in formation at a speed of 19 knots until they met up with Convoy No 1 and the other two groups.

The Italian movements were soon discovered by 'Ultra' beginning on 22 January itself and transmitted to the British naval commands in the Mediterranean, making the work of the submarines and reconnaissance aircraft based in Malta easier. The remaining operational ships of Force K were also thrown into the mix on the night of 23/24 January, but action was deferred because of the substantial superiority of the Italian forces at sea. Opposition, therefore, fell upon only three submarines and air assets. It was one of those submarines, HMS *Torbay*, that on the afternoon of the 22nd spotted the 7th Division

The single Breda 1939 37/54 guns on 'disappearing' mounts on the forecastle of the battleship *Andrea Doria*.

20 miles east-northeast of Cape Colonne heading south and sent a report of the sighting, which was however quickly intercepted by the Italians.

At 18:00 the 7th Division joined with the 'Vivaldi' group and Convoy No 1, while further to the north the 'Duilio-Victoria' group changed course to the east to deceive observation by a presumed submarine, a deviation that brought with it a significant delay in the planned meeting of the two convoys. During the night of 22/23rd the second group, discovered and shadowed by British flare-dropping aircraft, engaged in evasive manoeuvres that increased the delay with respect to joining with the 7th Division and Convoy No 1, so that on the morning of the 23rd Convoy No 1 was ordered to temporarily reverse course while the 7th Division zig-zagged nearby. At dawn on the 23rd both groups of ships were met by an air escort of Junkers Ju 88 aircraft from II Fliegerkorps and by several Regia Aeronautica Cant Z 506 floatplanes, although their presence did not deter British reconnaissance from establishing contact and maintaining it from a distance. Foreseeing air attacks at dusk, at 15:00 Bergamini directly requested II Fliegerkorps provide an increased fighter escort, which was provided by the addition of three more Ju 88s before any attacks occurred. In the early afternoon the two groups met in the Lower Ionian. Accordingly, a new sailing formation was assumed with an east-southeast heading at a speed of 14.3 knots: the merchant ships formed up as a single convoy in two columns with the *Victoria* at the head of the port column with the close-in escort of the 'Vivaldi' group; the 'Duilio' group took up station aft to starboard and 7th Division oblique to port.

At 17:25, as dusk approached, a squadron of three RAF Bristol Beaufort torpedo bombers from Cyrenaica came in from the direction of the sun that was low on the horizon and attacked the *Victoria*, hitting her at 17:30 with a torpedo on the starboard quarter. The attack went almost unobserved, so much so that an evasive manoeuvre was barely attempted and it was thought that the torpedo was from a submarine. The motorship, with its No 3 and 4 holds flooded, was down by the stern and immobilised, but still with a fairly good chance of staying afloat. The air escort, which had grown to twelve Ju 88s, had not been able to prevent the action and only one enemy plane was shot down. Bergamini detached the *Camicia Nera*, the *Aviere* and the *Ascari* to try to tow the *Victoria* and, if that was not possible, to see to picking up the shipwrecked survivors and proceed to Tripoli, while the rest of the group was to continue along the scheduled course. In truth, Bergamini was very impressed by British reconnaissance and the idea was briefly considered of reversing the convoy's route at dusk, but he dismissed the idea because he concluded that it would not be easy to escape British observation even in the hours of darkness.

Between 18:42 and 18:48, in the fading light, while the three destroyers detached to assist her had given up on towing the *Victoria* because of her size and parlous condition and were picking up survivors – including those who improvidently had abandoned ship well ahead of time – a renewed attack by five Fairey Albacore aircraft of the Fleet Air Arm from Cyrenaica sealed her fate with a second torpedo hit, even though one plane was downed by the *Aviere*. The *Victoria* sank at 19:10, taking with her 354 of the 1400 men who had been on board.

Meanwhile, at 17:15 on the 23rd, forty-five minutes early because of the persistent air threat, the 'Duilio' group, followed at 10:00 the next day by the 7th Division, separated from the convoy in order to cruise in an area north of the 36th parallel and east of the 19th meridian to protect against any incursion by

Detail of the after main 320mm turrets on the battleship *Duilio*.

A famous photo taken on 23 January 1942 from the forecastle of the battleship *Duilio*, with the modern motorship *Victoria* loaded with troops in the background.

surface vessels from Alexandria. The convoy escorted by the 'Vivaldi' group continued steaming during the night while being subjected to alarms and air attacks carried out by seven Vickers Wellingtons that had taken off from Malta and led by an eighth plane equipped with radar. At 07:30 on the 24th, the torpedo boats *Calliope* and *Perseo* from Tripoli met to reinforce the convoy, just before the last attack made at 09:00 on the 24th by the submarine *Urge*, whose torpedoes barely missed the motorship *Monviso*. Operation T 18 ended with no further losses and the convoy's arrival in Tripoli between 14:00 and 16:00 on the 24th, and the separate return of the naval groups the next day.

It was in this phase that the *Duilio* suffered an annoying breakdown of the evaporation system. At 14:40 on 24 January the group had begun its return passage, but at 18:00 there was an infiltration of salt water in the main condenser of the battleship's starboard engine through the cooling unit. For a time the ship proceeded on its port engine alone, but at 18:25, considering the hour, the area and the lack of any sighting, Bergamini decided to stop both engines for seventeen minutes, take the main starboard condenser off-line, disconnect the starboard low-pressure turbine, find the infiltration and resume steaming with both engines at a speed of 20 knots rather than proceeding on only one engine across an area that presented the most danger from enemy submarines in the entrance to the Gulf of Taranto. The 'Duilio' group returned to that base at first light on the 25th with no further problems, while the 7th Division and the 'Vivaldi' group returned in the early afternoon, respectively, to Taranto and Palermo.

T 18 can be considered only a partial success because of the painful loss of the modern *Victoria*. Bergamini – who, like everyone else, was ignorant of the existence and capabilities of 'Ultra' – ascribed (and overrated) the timely discovery of the Italian ships to highly effective British air and submarine reconnaissance, and to their ability to maintain contact and coordination with air attacks, which were mainly made by twin-engine Bristol Beauforts that had much greater range and were faster than the old Swordfish biplanes and which were better able to evade the German Junkers Ju 88s. He could not know that, despite everything, of the thirty RAF and Fleet Air Arm aircraft that were committed to offensive action, half of them were unable to find the Italian ships. Bergamini did not fail to point out positive aspects: for the first time direct radio contact, which worked reasonably well, had been established with the escorting German aircraft, and the direct request for air support made by the commander at sea to the shore commands and to II Fliegerkorps materialised in an effective manner. With respect to employment of the ships, the *Attendolo* had to deal with a breakdown of her evaporator system, which reduced the operational boilers from six to three, as well as the steering machinery, which forced her to operate the rudder manually. Minor breakdowns were experienced by several destroyers due in part to the turbulent sea state during the last phase of the operation. If the problems connected to wear and tear in the smaller ships are excluded, these were minor faults that could be quickly repaired while the ship was afloat, but during the course of a mission they could have serious consequences. Lastly, the *Duilio*'s anti-aircraft APG system was not able to find the targets easily and precious time was lost before opening fire, even when the attacking aircraft were perfectly visible to the naked eye. Bergamini prompted Supermarina to bear that in mind with regard to similar systems installed on the new battleship *Roma*, which was fitting out in Trieste.

Opposition to British Operation MF5 (14–16 February 1942)

On 21 January 1942 the Italo-German forces resumed the initiative in Libya and with a brilliant counteroffensive retook Benghazi and almost all of Cyrenaica, getting almost as far as Tobruk and thus changing the strategic situation in the central-eastern Mediterranean in their favour. Meanwhile, the air offensive that until then had been carried out against Malta by II Fliegerkorps had significantly reduced its effectiveness as an air and naval base and threatened its ability to hold out. The urgent need to resupply Malta induced Admiral Cunningham to organise a convoy of fast ships for the middle of February from Alexandria, designated MW9 and split into two sections (MW9A and MW9B); at the same time a convoy of empty ships was to set sail from Malta to Alexandria, designated MW10. The entire operation was designated MF5 with the composition of the convoys and naval forces as follows: MW9A with two merchant ships, protected by the *Carlisle* and four 'Hunt' class escort destroyers; MW9B with one merchant ship escorted by four 'Hunts', both convoys departing from Alexandria on the 12th; ME10 of ten steamships escorted by Force K (*Penelope* and six destroyers) which was to leave Malta on the night of 12/13 February.

Cover for convoy MW9 was assigned to Force B, consisting of the 15th Cruiser Division (light cruisers *Naiad, Dido, Euryalus*) and by the 14th and 2nd destroyer flotillas. Force B was to leave Alexandria on the night of 12/13 February and join with convoy MW9A on the morning of the 13th. The two sections would then sail west in order to meet at dusk on the 14th off of Tobruk, which leads one to believe that this was their destination; after this they were to steer to the northwest. In the Lower Ionian, north of Benghazi, MW9 was to cross with ME10 and there Force K and Force B would exchange convoys; the first would escort MW9 to Malta and the second ME10 to Alexandria. Between 9 and 12 February scouting and offensive deployments of three submarines from Malta were set up in the Gulf of Taranto and one south of Messina; as a result, HMS *Una* sank the tanker *Lucania*, while HMS *Tempest* was sunk by the torpedo boat *Circe*. RAF units from Malta were to furnish minimum air cover and make harassing attacks against airfields in Sicily. Operation MF5 was a failure, as between 13 and 15 February two merchant ships from MW9 were lost to German air attacks and a third ship, which was damaged, was forced to return. ME10 fared better and, despite repeated Axis air attacks, managed to reach the Egyptian ports with only modest damage.

Informed of the sightings and the early attacks against the

Detail of the forecastle and port forward superstructure of the battleship *Duilio* in early 1942.

enemy convoy from Alexandria, in the afternoon of 13 February Supermarina immediately assumed that its destination was Malta and alerted Admiral Iachino for possible action, warning, however, that because of a shortage of fuel a sortie could not be made to no purpose and that, therefore, opposition would be entrusted to air and submarine forces only. However, although there were already ten submarines at sea north of Cyrenaica, even though they were able to make several contacts, they achieved no results. While the convoy from the east was making its way to Malta with a presumed arrival time of the afternoon of the 15th, and having confirmed the departure of the other convoy from Malta, the Axis high command examined the possibility of action by the Italian surface forces. The fuel problem having been overcome by then, the question hinged on the availability of adequate and continuous air cover for the forces at sea and on the continuation of air attacks against Malta. Italian reluctance was overcome by the German guarantee of offensive action against the island and air cover for the ships at sea, and by Superaereo of interdiction flights by aircraft based in Sicily. The German bombers and Italian torpedo bombers were to repeat their attacks in order to damage and slow down the enemy, which would then be finished off by the Italian naval forces. On the afternoon of the 14th the following units were assigned for the action: *Duilio* (Admiral Carlo Bergamini, senior commander at sea) with the X Destroyer Squadriglia (*Maestrale, Scirocco, Usodimare*) and the 7th Division (light cruisers *Aosta* and *Montecuccoli*) with the XIII Destroyer Squadriglia (*Alpino, Carabiniere, Fucliere, Bersagliere*) from Taranto; 3rd Division (heavy cruisers *Gorizia, Trento*) with the XI Destroyer Squadriglia (*Aviere, Geniere, Camicia Nera, Ascari*) from Messina. The battleship and the 7th Division would set sail at 19:00 and the 3rd Division at 24:00 on the 14th. German liaison parties were embarked on the three division flagships to provide radio contact with the German aircraft and there was a cryptographic unit aboard the *Duilio* as well. The two cruiser divisions were to meet at 08:00 on the 15th 70 miles east of Malta, followed at a distance of 10 miles by the *Duilio* in a supporting role, so as to put themselves between the convoy and its destination. In addition, five ships from the German 3rd Torpedo Boat Squadron would be posted in an ambush position east of Malta.

The *Duilio* passed through the defensive barrages at 19:15 on the 14th, but at 19:55 was ordered by Iachino to return as the absence of battleships escorting the enemy convoy had been confirmed. Thus ended the battleship's participation in the mission, and as a result the mission was left to the two cruiser divisions and command of the combined cruiser forces at sea devolved on Admiral de Courten on the *Aosta*. In the hours that followed, because of a mistaken appreciation of the situation by Supermarina, there was no interception and at 18:30 on the 15th, after having cruised south of the Malta parallel, de Courten was ordered to return. During the night the Italian ships suffered an attack by Albacore torpedo aircraft with the assistance of flare-droppers, but without results. At first light on the 16th the Italian and German air escort reappeared over the Italian ships which by now were heading back to base. During this phase, on the approach route to the Strait, the destroyer *Carabiniere* was torpedoed in rough seas by the submarine *P 36* and had its bow blown off, suffering twenty-one killed and forty wounded, but managed to make it to Messina under tow at 18:30 on the 17th.

Operation K 7 (21–24 February 1942)

After the almost complete reconquest of Cyrenaica, Supermarina organised resupply operations escorted by significant portions of the naval forces, in order to make up the losses and consumption by the Italo-German desert forces during that prolonged operational cycle. The result was Operation K 7, which in late February 1942 saw the gathering from various ports of six modern merchant ships divided into two fast convoys for Tripoli on routes passing east of Malta. These were Convoy No 1, from Messina: three merchant ships with the destroyers *Vivaldi, Malocello, Zeno, Premuda Strale* and torpedo boat *Pallade*; Convoy No 2 from Corfù: three merchant ships with the destroyers *Pigafetta, Usodimare, Pessagno, Maestrale, Scirocco* and the torpedo boat *Circe* equipped with sonar gear. Defending the convoys was a cover force consisting of the *Duilio* (Admiral Carlo Bergamini, senior commander at sea) with the XI Destroyer Squadriglia (*Aviere, Generie, Ascari, Camicia Nera*) from Taranto, and the 3rd Division (heavy cruisers *Gorizia*, with Admiral Angelo Parona, *Trento*, and the light cruiser *Giovanni delle Bande Nere*) with destroyers *Alpino*, *da Noli* and *Oriani* from Messina. In addition, an air escort from II Fliegerkorps based in Sicily was deployed. Convoys No 2 and No 1 departed on 21 February with their close escorts. That same day the 'Duilio' group left Taranto at 16:00 and the 3rd Division left Messina at 18:30. Convoy No 1 and the 3rd Division met at 23:15 that same day and continued on to Tripoli on a course passing about 190 miles from Malta. On the morning of 22 February, they met up with and joined Convoy No 2 and the 'Duilio' group; whereupon the 3rd Division took station ahead of the convoys and the 'Duilio' group took up station astern and then continuing on a southerly heading.

Weather conditions were not good with cloud cover and an increasingly rough sea whipped by a southeast wind from the afternoon of the 22nd; however, the roughness tended to decrease as the ships headed south. The operation and its progress did not escape British intelligence, and air and submarine forces from Malta were prepared to meet the Italians. With respect to underwater forces, a submarine barrier was established along the Italian route with four boats that were already at sea and an additional four submarines left Malta but did not reach their assigned ambush positions in time. Air attacks were made from 14:00 to 16:00, but were all driven off by German fighters and three British aircraft were shot down. Meanwhile, at dusk on the 22nd, the 3rd Division merged with Convoy No 1, while No 2 followed 8 miles behind and the 'Duilio' group reversed course to return to Taranto. The northerly move by the *Duilio* and the XI Destroyer Squadriglia was, however, bedevilled by a violent gale, which reached its maximum intensity on the night and morning of the 23rd with a strong southeasterly wind and atrocious visibility, forcing speed to be reduced to 14 and then to 12 knots.

During the night and the next morning Bergamini struggled to

The battleship *Cesare* at sea in January 1942. This sketch, the work of the late Elio Andò, was part of a group of lithographs done by him in the early 1970s.

keep the group together, especially in case an emergency required a return to a southerly course, but the *Duilio* suffered enough through the force of the sea alone (see Appendix 4); at the same time the destroyers suffered damage, especially to their electrical systems because of the amount of water leaking in the upper decks and superstructures. Towards evening, as they drew closer to the Gulf of Taranto, the gale lost its intensity and Bergamini was able to increase speed to 18 knots. In the early hours of the 24th the group entered Taranto's Mar Grande along the secure channels, where because of the wind the *Duilio* had to anchor in the roadstead, before she could moor the following morning inside the net enclosure. Further to the south the mission had gone well. At 10:30 on the 23rd the 3rd Division reversed course and returned to Messina at 12:00 on the 24th, while the *Bande Nere*, which during the passage north had to head east to reduce the effects of the southeasterly gale, lagged behind until the morning of the 25th. The convoys with their close escorts continued on separately to Tripoli, where they arrived on the afternoon of the 24th escorted during their final leg by two torpedo boats from the base and by Italian aircraft. In that context on the morning of 23 February the *Circe* spotted and sank, along with the destroyer *Usodimare*, submarine *P 38* approximately 30 miles east of Tripoli.

Apart from the breakdowns suffered by the ships due to the gales, Operation K 7 ended perfectly. Bergamini was satisfied by the work of the German aircraft on 22 February, which was a crucial day for the mission. Air cover was lacking on the 23rd, but that was due to the terrible weather conditions, while further to the south the Italian air force was present in the skies over the 3rd Division and the convoys.

Chapter 9.4

INACTIVITY OF THE SMALLER BATTLESHIPS FROM SPRING OF 1942 TO 8 SEPTEMBER 1943

Operation K 7 was the last escort mission on which Italian battleships were employed. The neutralisation of Malta by II Fliegerkorps and the weakening of the Mediterranean Fleet in late 1941 – even though its size continued to be overestimated – no longer made them necessary. Supermarina never felt that the risks were worth it and in operations always sought to expose them as little as possible, but the massive use of major vessels in defence of Libyan convoys that winter had been essential to guarantee resupply during a period of maximum crisis. The priority for Italian naval forces (FN) once again became the mission of challenging British attempts to resupply Malta. Although the smaller battleships had not taken part in the second battle of Sirte (23 March 1942), the experience prompted Supermarina to reposition them with a view to possible offensive use. In fact, in early April it decided that to have a better chance of intercepting convoys from Alexandria to Malta, it would make more sense to sortie from Augusta and Messina rather than from Taranto. The use of the more forward Sicilian bases would allow the FN to respond with less warning time (eighteen instead of twenty-three hours) in case of late sightings of enemy movements.

The transfer of the 'Duilios' from Taranto to Messina and their return (April–May 1942)

In spring 1942 the two aforementioned bases presented no particular security problems against enemy air attacks. But the impossibility of transferring the two 'Littorio' class, the shortage of destroyers and of fuel as well as of anti-submarine vessels equipped with sonar made it impossible for Supermarina to spread the naval forces over the three Ionian bases. It thus opted for Messina only, which provided an acceptable compromise. With respect to composition, the tactical group could have been formed by one, or at most two 'Duilio' class ships, by the 3rd Division and by a squadriglia of 'Soldati' class destroyers, plus possibly three or four 'Navigatori' class destroyers. It would have been difficult to move other major ships to this port because of congestion due to the intense merchant shipping in transit. In addition, Supermarina felt that a group such as that could not deal adequately with an enemy force, meaning that it would be necessary to commit other ships based at Taranto, even if it was only cruisers. All of this, however, would require intensive air

Detail of the *Andrea Doria* at the beginning of 1942. For a colour view of this camouflage scheme see page 245.

The battleship *Andrea Doria* on passage between Taranto and Messina on 15 May 1942. The ship had worn the new standard two-tone grey camouflage scheme since the previous month. In the background are the destroyers *Mitragliere* and *Corazziere*.

reconnaissance in the waters south of Crete to ensure timely employment. Based on these assumptions, on 5 April 1942 it decided to immediately transfer the *Duilio* to Messina and, when her working-up was completed, the *Andrea Doria* as well, where they would be based along with the 3rd Division and a squadriglia of modern destroyers.

The move of the *Duilio*, the flagship of the II Squadron commander, Admiral Bergamini, and of the cruiser *Attendolo*, escorted by the destroyers *Pigafetta*, *Zeno* and *Malocello*, took place between the afternoon of 7 April and the morning of the 8th. During the night the group was sighted and trailed, without consequence, by British flare-dropping aircraft, from which it defended itself by laying smoke. The *Doria* followed her twin a month later, as she had been engaged in trials and exercises, including the sortie on 23 April, when, escorted by three destroyers, the ship carried out daytime anti-ship and anti-aircraft gunnery exercises with all guns as well as carrying out machinery trials, during which she easily reached a speed of 26 knots. The move to Messina along with the 7th Division (*Eugenio di Savoia* and *Duca d'Aosta*) with the escorting destroyers *Oriani, Mitragliere, Geniere, Legionario, Alpino* and *Carabiniere* was made between 15 and 16 May and was marked at dawn on the 16th by the presumed sighting of a submarine, to which *Geniere* gave chase. The stay of the two battleships at Messina was brief. By 25 May, without having once put to sea, they returned to Taranto escorted by the destroyers *Alpino, Legionario, Mitragliere, Geniere, Bersagliere* and *Corazziere* and took up their usual anchorages in Mar Grande. This transit was the last wartime mission prior to 8 September 1943.

Indeed, the transfer of the two 'Duilios' was part of a larger plan of deployment of the FN that had developed in April 1942. This assumed that, as a result of the strategic situation caused by Japan's entry into the war, it was unlikely that the Mediterranean Fleet would be reinforced and that, as a result, the main enemy threat would come from Gibraltar. Because of this, Supermarina contemplated bringing part of the fleet along with the two 'Littorio' class battleships to Naples and moving the light forces to Messina and Augusta supported by one or two of the 'Duilios', which were deemed to be capable of dealing with enemy moves from the east. These forces would also be in an ideal position to act to the west with the 9th Division from Naples and to participate in the planned execution of operations C 2 (the occupation of Corsica) and C 3 (the invasion of Malta). But it made its implementation subject to maintaining pressure on Malta from the air, which would hinder any large-scale attacks against Naples, Messina and Augusta, and to the availability of an adequate number of destroyers and of a minimum amount of fuel in the three bases. The deployment had thus been temporarily achieved with respect to the 'Duilios'.

Planned participation of the Naval Forces in the invasion of Malta (Operation C 3)

In the spring of 1942 the military situation in the Mediterranean took a turn that was decidedly favourable to the Axis, thanks in large measure to the neutralisation of Malta, which was close to exhaustion, leading the Italo-German commands to plan its invasion (Operation C 3, or 'Herkules' for the Germans). Two scenarios were considered: a short-term plan, to be achieved by a raid with limited forces by the end of spring at the culmination of the island's neutralisation; and the summer plan, to be achieved by a large-scale operation. In the event, nothing at all was done, either because of the scepticism of Hitler and, more to the point, by the Wehrmacht high command (Oberkommando der Wehrmacht, OKW), or because Rommel's triumph at Tobruk in June seemed to open the door to the Nile without having to first eliminate the island.

In the case of the large-scale operation, intervention by almost the entire naval force was envisioned, including the two 'Littorios' and the two 'Duilios' in the event of opposition by enemy naval forces in the Malta area or diversionary actions (such as landings on Corsica) or of convoys that attempted to resupply the island. Supporting the landings by naval bombardment was assigned solely to the 'Duilio' class. All of the submarine forces were to be deployed on reconnaissance and interdiction duties in the western and eastern Mediterranean basins and the Aegean forces were to oppose any enemy initiatives in that sector. The landing operations were to be made by the Forza Navale Speciale (FNS, or Special Naval Force). For C 3, it was estimated that a total of 70,000 tons of fuel oil would be needed, 40,000 for the FNS and 30,000 for the FN. For this latter requirement an extraordinary supply from the Kriegsmarine was assumed and a request to that effect was sent in June by the Comando Supremo to the OKW. The Seekriegsleitung (Skl) in principle was not opposed to Operation Herkules, but it believed that Romania would have to supply the extraordinary demand for fuel. These fields had never achieved the planned output and never kept up with current demands; at most, the Skl was prepared to grant 10,000 tons for use by the light forces. In reality, the Italian request came at a time when the Skl was getting ready to employ its own major ships against the Arctic convoys (Operation Rösselsprung), which it did not intend to sacrifice. Finally, on 25 June, OKW gave a negative response, which meant that in the event of an invasion of Malta the Regia Marina would have to make other arrangements for the exceptional supply of fuel. The attitude of the Skl seems to be questionable: the Italian request undoubtedly required a substantial sacrifice, but the German standpoint ran counter to one of the most important agreements reached by the Axis navies at Garmisch in January 1942, namely, that in the event of contemporaneous operations they would consult in order to establish the priority based on the availability of fuel, but no such consultations took place.

New deployments of the Naval Forces (August–November 1942)

With the fall of Tobruk on 20 June 1942 and with the British Eighth Army severely battered, Operation C 3 was set aside in favour of the advance of the Italo-German armies in Egypt. The advance, however, came to a halt in July at El Alamein, where the front stabilised until the end of October. Under these conditions the British undertook two major initiatives to resupply Malta: in June with convoys from Gibraltar (Operation 'Harpoon') and from Alexandria (Operation 'Vigorous'), and in August with the massive Operation 'Pedestal' from Gibraltar. These were opposed by the Axis air and naval forces, giving rise to the battles of mid-June (Operation 'Vigorous') and mid-August (Operation 'Pedestal'), neither of which involved the small battleships. It was only while planning for action against Operation 'Harpoon', on the afternoon of 12 June, that the *Duilio* was readied for sea along with the main body of the FN, when it appeared that 'Harpoon' was the more important enemy convoy. But on the morning of the 13th air reconnaissance reported the movements of a larger convoy from the east, so Supermarina came up with a new operational plan that no longer involved the *Duilio*, as the two 'Littorios' ensured a sufficient advantage. For Operation 'Pedestal', Supermarina did not consider the use of any battleships because of the shortage of

The battleship *Andrea Doria* entering Taranto's Mar Piccolo at some time in 1942. (Courtesy F Mesturini)

fuel and of destroyers, relying only on participation, with respect to large ships, of the two cruiser divisions at the western entrance of the Sicilian Channel, where it assumed that enemy battleships would not venture.

In the months that followed, although opportunities for the use of the small battleships became increasingly improbable, especially after the entry into squadron service on 22 August 1942 of the *Roma*, the third ship of the 'Littorio' class, they continued to remain in the naval force's relocation plans. These mostly originated in pressure from Comando Supremo and from the Germans in anticipation of new attempts to resupply Malta from Gibraltar or Alexandria, of landings in French North Africa, or in support of Operation C 4 (occupation of Tunisia), the latter of which became increasingly probable in late summer that year.

From mid-August to mid-November 1942 Supermarina examined no fewer than six options for relocating the naval forces, some of which had several versions, almost all of which tended to shift the centre of gravity in the central-western Mediterranean, leaving enough forces in the central-eastern sector to be able to protect traffic to Libya or to oppose resupply operations to Malta from the east. The two 'Duilio' class ships and to a lesser degree the *Cesare* found a place in these schemes, either to reinforce the Tyrrhenian forces, centred on the three 'Littorios' in Naples, or the forces in the east (Navarino, Suda or Leros). It did not, however, envisage their participation in actions against enemy landings in North Africa east of the 7th meridian, which was the only intervention considered to be practical by the FN. None of these moves were put into effect before November 1942, nominally because of a shortage of fuel and of escort destroyers. In the final analysis, they were inspired by the theory of the 'fleet in being' – as Supermarina was again to enunciate on 24 September 1942 to the Comando Supremo – in that moving the major portion of the FN to the west was intended to exert a deterrent effect that would force the enemy to assemble a force so large that it would be incompatible with the limited resources at Gibraltar.

Between late October and early November 1942, the entire strategic picture in the Mediterranean changed with the British Eighth Army's offensive at El Alamein and the Anglo-American landings in Morocco and Algeria (Operation 'Torch'). The Axis reacted by occupying the rest of continental France, of Corsica (Operation C 2) and of Tunisia (Operation C 4), which became the last stronghold in North Africa, and acting against enemy naval forces and convoys with submarines and air assets. There was no intervention by the Italian surface forces, partly because the Allies did not risk landing in Tunisia, the only sector in which the Italian fleet could in theory intervene. The fuel situation improved in November due to a large supply provided by the Kriegsmarine, but only three days after the Allied landings in French North Africa, and following German pressure, the 9th Division was transferred from Taranto to Naples, too late to take action against any landings in Tunisia or to exert any dissuasive influence. The three smaller battleships remained in Taranto. But by 18 November Supermarina had reconsidered the relocation of the FN with an apparently more aggressive view, considering, among other things, moving the 9th Division from Naples to La Spezia, with the declared intent of bringing it 45 miles closer to Algeria, and the entire 5th Division from Taranto to La Maddalena, in anticipation of acting against Allied shipping in Algerian waters.

In reality, the new dispositions once again reflected a reliance on the concept of the fleet in being, which was now oriented towards defence of the homeland, according to which the location of the FN in the Tyrrhenian basin, where there were powerful Axis air assets, would have probably of itself been sufficient to inhibit the enemy from undertaking any dangerous initiatives. This plan was in part realised with the move, on 6–7 December, of the three 'Littorio' class from Naples to La Spezia shortly after the very heavy 4 December bombing; within the navy this was clearly seen as the abandonment of any action with the nucleus of the fleet in the last operational theatre that remained for it. The three smaller battleships of the 5th Division, however, did not move from Taranto.

The 5th Division exercise of 17 September 1942

Despite the shortage of fuel, in September and October 1942 the naval forces present in Taranto carried out several exercises at sea, in particular for working-up the very new *Roma*, which had entered service with the 9th Division on 22 August. One exercise also involved the 5th Division, whose two main ships had not left their moorings for almost three months. It took place in the afternoon and evening of 17 September 1942 in the waters of the gulf, with the *Duilio*, flagship of Admiral Bergamini, C-in-C of II Squadron, the *Doria* and the destroyers *Aviere, Bersagliere, Legionario* and *Euro* taking part. Weather conditions were a calm sea, light wind and good visibility during the daylight hours (20,000 metres) and at night (from 4000 to 10,000 metres). To save fuel the two battleships lit only four of their eight boilers. The *Doria* was the first to leave from her net enclosure in Mar Grande in order to conduct some progressive trials, then anchoring near the island of San Paolo. Then the destroyers put to sea, followed finally by the *Duilio*. Shortly after 14:00 the formation, except for the *Euro*, which had turned back because of engine problems, passed the barrages and was joined by the fighter and anti-submarine aircraft as well as by the target-towing plane for the anti-aircraft gunnery practice. The exercises included formation evolutions and use of smokescreens, firing with medium-calibre and anti-aircraft guns against a towed target sleeve, anti-ship gunnery with the main armament (at charge III) and with the medium guns (at charge I), and with the 90/50 guns. In the late afternoon the ships returned to their moorings; only the *Duilio*, after having anchored near the island of San Paolo, in the evening again went through the barrages for a night exercise with the main and medium guns, returning at 22:30.

The results of these exercises provide the final measure, albeit partial, of the degree of effectiveness of the 'Duilio' class prior to the summer of 1943. During the daytime firing of the main guns the equipment functioned well with no lost rounds on the *Duilio* and only one on the *Doria*. Gunnery (speed and accuracy) was judged to be excellent for the *Doria* and good for the *Duilio* in the series conducted by the main SDT, but inadequate for the series

Detail of the bridge tower of the battleship *Andrea Doria* in 1942.

conducted using the APG of the 2nd DT [Fire Director]. This was due to mechanical lapses in the transmission of data from these APG, which had already been experienced on previous occasions, which led to considerable errors and significant variation from salvo to salvo. The navy's technical departments and the manufacturing company (San Giorgio) had already investigated the problem without being able to resolve it. Doubting that it could be resolved, Bergamini concluded that fire control should not be passed from the 1st DT to the 2nd DT and that, if necessary, each turret should assume independent fire direction. He went so far as to propose that the SDT from No 2 turret be removed, thus saving 50 tons of weight in the forward section, where the need was greatest. During daylight firing of the medium guns the equipment also functioned well, with only two failed rounds on the *Duilio* and four on the *Doria*, all due to causes that could be remedied. Fire direction was assessed to be good; it was excellent, in particular, for the starboard battery on the *Doria* and for the port side battery on the *Duilio*. During anti-aircraft fire against a towed target sleeve the equipment performed well. Fire direction on the *Duilio*, for the first time with a stabilised SDT, was quite satisfactory; on the *Doria*, lacking stabilisation, the firing was rapid and accurate, but several rounds burst in mid-trajectory due to poor functioning of the automatic fuses, which were activated by the shell elevators of the 90/50 guns. Gunnery with the medium- and small-calibre time-fused rounds against torpedo aircraft silhouettes were carried out while turning, with good results for the 135/45 guns but less so for the 90/50s, especially on the *Doria*, with salvos landing short in the sea because of aiming errors due to smoke obscuring the APG. Night gunnery with the main and medium guns on the *Duilio* was judged to be quite satisfactory.

The same could not be said for the smoke apparatus: production of smoke from the funnels was rapid and abundant, but the four smoke generators on the stern of the *Duilio* produced very little and the two on the *Doria* did not work at all because of ignition problems. Things were better on the destroyers, but in general, the output of the stern smoke generators was meagre and Bergamini proposed supplementing them with chlorohydrin generators, which were widely used ashore.

With respect to the powerplants, the two ships lit four boilers instead of six (of a total of eight), never developing a speed of more than 18 knots during the exercise. Despite the fact that they had been idle for all of 115 days and that the crews were for the most part new and not well trained, everything went well. Admiral Bergamini complained that using only four boilers did not allow the engines to be run as they would be in action and asked if it would not be better to activate six, considering that fuel consumption would not be very different as at a speed of 18 knots the four boilers had to work harder than would be the case with six.

Radiotelegraphic and telephony systems did not experience any problems except for interruptions of alternating current for a few minutes' duration caused by the violent concussion when 320mm and 135mm salvos were fired simultaneously. Bergamini pressed for installing small backup generators on board for those systems, given the importance of the short-wave equipment for squadron voice communications.

All things considered, the performance of the 'Duilio' class was fairly good, but the exercises made it obvious that these ships could not be considered fully operational. Supermarina shared Bergamini's doubts about the effectiveness of the shipboard systems because of the prolonged period of inactivity, but did not see any possibility of remedying them as long as there continued to be a shortage of fuel (priority was accorded to the 'Littorios'). It did not, however, share the concern about activating only four boilers as, in its opinion, even with only four he would have been able to apportion the evaporation equipment as if for a wartime mission.

Placing the *Cesare* in reserve at Pola and the 'Duilios' in reduced readiness at Taranto (January 1943)

In December 1942 the shortage of destroyers – mainly engaged in convoy defence – and the scarcity of fuel led Supermarina to conclude that by this phase of the war the simultaneous employment of all of the capital ships was not possible; nor was there any hope of a change in the situation in the short term, while enemy air superiority made the surface forces increasingly vulnerable. It came to the realisation, therefore, that they could no longer keep all of the battleships and cruisers ready for action. As a result it was decided to bring forward the transfer of the *Cesare* to the Upper Adriatic, to make the ship available for a period of major upgrade work; she would be replaced by the *Cavour*, which was scheduled to be ready by May 1943. The *Duilio* and *Doria* would be retained in service but with reduced manning so that they could be ready for employment within forty-five days of returning the crews to full strength. It hoped that by that process it would be able to recover enough officers and specialised personnel to address their acute shortage in smaller ships.

The remaining large ships would in any case have formed an adequate nucleus of forces. These comprised the three 'Littorios' and eight cruisers, which number did not include the *Cadorna* at Pola but which did count the *Bolzano* and *Attendolo* that were badly damaged.

Thus, after nearly a year of inactivity at Taranto, the *Cesare* was sent for refit to the CRDA yards at Trieste. In view of the transfer, in December 1942, day and night exercises with all guns were intensified, conducted at the anchorages in Mar Grande, except for a move under tow near the island of San Paolo, where AA gunnery against a towed target sleeve and against torpedo plane silhouettes was practised. On 29 December, fuel and other supplies were taken aboard and that night the battleship weighed anchor for Trieste escorted by the destroyers *Premuda* and *Lubiana* and by the torpedo boat *Castelfidardo*. As soon as the ship had left the secure channels in the Gulf of Taranto, the *Cesare* had to manoeuvre to avoid an alleged submarine attack and as she continued steaming received a message from Supermarina that changed its destination to Pola, where the ship arrived at 06:50 on 31 December, anchoring in the roadstead.

There *Cesare* was placed in reserve and on 1 January 1943 began to disembark its main and secondary gun ammunition. The following day, the wake of a MAS boat running at high speed sent an ammunition lighter crashing against the hull; the collision tore a hole in the lighter, which capsized, dropping 132 320mm rounds to the bottom. These rounds were salvaged in the days that followed with the assistance of divers and on 11 January offloading of the ammunition was completed. Later the 20/65 and some of the 37/54 guns were disembarked, to be used for other purposes. Meanwhile, on 5 January the battleship had moved to a stern anchorage at the submarine barracks quay, which remained her habitual mooring station until the armistice.

During all of that time the *Cesare* never left Pola, engaging in only modest training activity.

Even after the *Cadorna* left in mid-June 1943 the battleship did not take on a training role for cadets of the school of the CREMM (Corpo Reali Equipaggi Militari Marittimi, or Royal Naval Crew Corps) at Pola and Venice, a possibility that had previously been examined. On the other hand, alertness against attack by submarines was constant and intense. Unfortunately, documentation could not be found relating to the nature of the work that the *Cesare* was supposed to have undergone at Trieste, where she was to have taken the place of the *Cavour* in the San Marco yard as soon as the latter entered service with the personnel from her sister-ship. However, from a Supermarina memorandum dated 14 January 1943 it appears that at the time an upgrade programme (the installation, on a light trellis mast abaft of the 1st SDT, of an E.C.3/ter 'Gufo' radar set) had already been shelved. With respect to the *Duilio* and the *Doria*, they were placed in reduced readiness at Taranto on 5 and 7 January 1943 respectively.

The threat of invasion of the national territory and return to service of the 'Duilio' class (March–June 1943)

From January 1943 the significant flow of men and equipment through the Strait of Gibraltar reinforced the impression amongst the Axis political and military hierarchies of imminent enemy landings at one or more points of the southern front, the clear Allied air and naval superiority allowing them many potential options. In mid-March there was more evidence that the Allies were about to undertake a major operation in the western Mediterranean, even before the campaign in Tunisia was concluded. In particular, the Comando Supremo considered an imminent landing in Sardinia was more likely than one in Sicily, as long as there were still Axis forces in Tunisia, and even more effective if the Allies wished to deal Italy a decisive blow. Comando Supremo accordingly asked the chiefs of staff of the three services to study the appropriate defensive measures to meet such an eventuality. Supermarina agreed that it expected a major Allied operation, even though it considered the ultimate objective to be Sicily, in order to ensure free movement in the Mediterranean and provide a focal point for future operations. The March 1943 defensive plans, and the later discussions with the Germans, contained no mention of the two 'Duilios', for which, apart from their technical limitations, there was no fuel.

In the early days of May the aggravation of the crisis in Tunisia, the major concentration of landing craft in Algeria and on Malta and the numerous naval forces at Gibraltar, and the intensification of air bombardment of air and naval bases all reinforced the belief that a major enemy operation in the Mediterranean was imminent. On 10 May, with the end of fighting on the last strip of Axis territory in Africa, Comando Supremo turned its attention decisively to the major islands, issuing rather desperate directives to employ every means to oppose from the outset any attempt at invasion. This included the fleet, as Comando Supremo found it inconceivable that it should not put to sea in the event of an attack against Sicily or Sardinia. On 26 May, therefore, it put together the directives for the defence of national territory based on three possible enemy landings: in Sicily (Case 'Si'), in Sardinia (Case 'Sa'), in Sicily and Sardinia simultaneously (Case 'S.S.'). In its opinion, although the fall of Sicily would have inexorably split the Mediterranean into two basins, with serious repercussions for the Greek theatre, the threat against Sardinia continued to be the more feared – its defence was more problematic because of its distance from the mainland and because its occupation would lead inevitably to the loss of Corsica.

These considerations and the fact that the navy and air force would suffer more defending Sicily compared to defending Sardinia induced Comando Supremo to assign primary defence responsibilities for Sardinia to the navy and to the army for Sicily. Supermarina agreed with this arrangement, proclaiming that it was ready to intervene with the Forze Navi da Battaglia (FNB, or Naval Battle Force) – a designation assumed by the main naval forces on 5 April 1943, now under the command of Admiral Bergamini – in Sicily as well as Sardinia, so long as it enjoyed adequate naval and air escort. In addition, two days later, in another meeting with Comando Supremo, faced with the problems of scraping together air cover of the required size, Admiral Riccardi declared that the FNB would sortie to face the British fleet for the sake of the navy's honour, independently of any escort that could be promised. At the end of May Supermarina issued directive Di Na 12 for Case 'Si' to its subordinate commands, which posed no restrictions for the employment of submarines, motor torpedo boats and MAS. However, employment of the FNB was made subject to numerous conditions – on verification of an enemy landing on the Tyrrhenian shore of the island, on the size of the enemy forces at sea, on the possibility of attacking enemy convoys, on the extent of air cover and, significantly, on a politico-strategic assessment of further developments of the war.

On 5 June 1943, following a heavy bombing of La Spezia, the *Vittorio Veneto* and the *Roma* were rendered unfit for combat for a few months and this development seemed to cancel out any possibility of employing the FNB, which was now reduced to only the *Littorio*. The next day, faced with this situation, Comando Supremo asked Supermarina what its orders were for the FNB, in view of the temporary unavailability of the two 'Littorios'; it was also asked to examine the possibility of reactivating the *Duilio* and *Doria* at Taranto by transferring the crews of the *Vittorio Veneto* and *Roma* and, if that were possible, to assess the most suitable location to base them. Supermarina gave assurances that the *Vittorio Veneto* would return to the squadron in late June and the *Roma* in late July and, above all, that even though it had been impaired, the FNB would join action in any of the cases envisioned. Readying the 'Duilios' would have taken forty-five days and thus it would not have been worth the effort to bring them back on line with the crews of the damaged 'Littorio' class; better to use those of the *Gorizia* and the *Trieste*, the first of which had been seriously damaged and the second of which had been sunk in the bombing of La Maddalena on 10 April. With respect to employment, Supermarina excluded the possibility that the 'Duilios' could join the larger ships because of their slower speed and assigned them to act as a small 'fleet in being' in Taranto and thus an independent nucleus in the Ionian. Although not suitable to challenge enemy battleships because of their patent inferiority, they would have at least forced the Allies to use battleships for any offensive in the area, in this view, making it more difficult to carry out more than one major landing operation at a time.

The Allied landings in Sicily and the lack of employment of the Naval Battle Force (July 1943)

The attack against the major islands did not come as early as expected, but was prefaced from 10 June by the air bombardment of the island stronghold of Pantelleria, which had political and morale repercussions that outweighed the military effects. It was particularly galling to Comando Supremo, which expressed dissatisfaction with the fatalism being shown by the navy under these new circumstances, despite the repeated assurances that the fleet would be used to defend the homeland. That same day the order was given to make ready the two 'Duilios' by beginning training that was to have brought them back to full wartime readiness in forty-five days. On 10 July 1943 the Allies landed on the southeastern coast of Sicily (Operation 'Husky'). At that time, the FNB at La Spezia comprised only the *Littorio* and *Vittorio Veneto* (which was not yet fully operational), five light cruisers and nine destroyers. It would have had to face, with insufficient air cover, an enormously superior naval force almost two days' sailing away and in waters dominated by enemy air power. The Allies would have had enough time to concentrate almost all of their available six battleships, two carriers and fifteen cruisers, in addition to many smaller vessels, assuming that the Italian fleet were able to make it to the waters south of Sicily without being destroyed or severely mauled from the air during its approach. In Taranto, which was closer, in addition to the 5th Division, there was a heterogenous group consisting of the light cruisers *Cadorna* (of very modest combat value) and the excellent but small *Pompeo Magno*, which would be joined, following a brilliant success against British MTBs in the Strait of Messina, by her sister, *Scipione Africano*, and by two barely capable destroyers *Nicoloso da Recco* and the French war prize *FR 23*. Action by this naval force was not even considered, partly because the two battleships had not completed their training, but mainly because of their absolute inferiority compared to the enemy forces and the lack of air cover. For those reasons, on 10 July Admiral Riccardi requested and was granted by the Comando Supremo and Mussolini to not engage the FNB; opposition at sea was left to submarines and fast coastal vessels.

Once they were fitted out, the two 'Duilios' were engaged in intense training activity, especially in daytime and night gunnery with all weapons, almost always, however, from their moorings or with brief moves from Mar Grande. From 16 to 29 June the *Duilio* was put into the Ferrati drydock for graving, followed by the *Doria* from 1 to 11 July, and It was not until 21 August that the 5th Division carried out a formation exercise at sea along with the light cruiser group (*Cadorna, Scipione, Pompeo*) and the only two destroyers that were still operational, the *da Recco* and *FR 23*. Other sorties out to sea were made on 26 July and on the night of 26/27th by the *Duilio* and on the afternoon and evening of the 27th by the *Doria*, both along with the *da Recco*.

At the end of July the FNB was irremediably divided in two groups, by now fated to act separately. The main group, at La Spezia and Genoa, consisted of the *Italia* (formerly the *Littorio*), the *Vittorio Veneto* and the *Roma*, whose return to the squadron was imminent, by five light cruisers (two 'Abruzzi' and

The battleship *Conte di Cavour* being repaired and modernised at Trieste in autumn 1942. Part of the superstructure of the ship is being rebuilt, involving a significant commitment of resources and manpower.

three 'Aosta' class) and eight destroyers. The smaller group, recently constituted at Taranto, consisted of the two 'Duilios', by the ageing *Cadorna* and by the two 'Scipione' class, with a like number of destroyers. On 15 August the I Torpedo Boat Squadriglia (five 'Spica' class ships) was also attached to the 5th Division but, because of the inferiority of the 'Duilios' compared with any enemy battleship and the lack of air and naval escort, the Taranto group could only be used for close-in defence of the gulf or for a few sorties by the cruisers against enemy shipping or to lay mines.

The employment possibilities of the Taranto group following the loss of Sicily (August–September 1943)

Only a few days after the landings in Sicily it was clear to the Italo-German commands that it would no longer be possible to throw the Allies back into the sea and, indeed, as their advance proceeded the situation in the Tyrrhenian and the Ionian would likewise become even worse. Any intervention by the FNB being ruled out, Supermarina assigned the mission of opposing enemy forces exclusively to submarines and small fast surface attack craft, alongside similar German assets, but overall did not achieve any noteworthy results. Comando Supremo was not satisfied with such a showing and on 24 July questioned Supermarina as to what measures it intended to adopt for convoy protection, for the defence of coastal centres and to oppose enemy activity in the Tyrrhenian and Ionian in the event of the occupation of Sicily, which by now was taken for granted. In its 3 August reply Supermarina did not hold out any possibility of employing surface ships of any importance because of insufficient air cover and reconnaissance, limiting action only to submarines. Faced with this continuing denial and the growing and unchallenged Allied naval activity along the coasts of Sicily and Calabria, Comando Supremo was more than a little dissatisfied, considering it unacceptable that enemy activity continued uninterrupted by any naval opposition. Although Supermarina reiterated the reasons that dictated the inactivity by the main naval forces, it felt compelled by this pressure – more than the intention of keeping the Germans at bay – to adopt a more proactive approach. This is the genesis of the two missions of the 7th Division on 4–6 August and of the 8th Cruiser Division on 6–7 August to bombard the port of Palermo (although both actions were broken off), and of the light units of the Taranto group on 4 and 6 August for laying mine barriers along the Ionian coast of Calabria. This latter action was cut short by the suspected sighting of an enemy light cruiser, a disengagement that was strongly criticised for its lack of offensive spirit by the new Minister and Chief of Staff of the Navy, Admiral Raffaele de Courten. Apart from that, and of a planned operation using only cruisers against an enemy convoy in transit from Gibraltar on the night of 18 August (which was soon abandoned), the options for employment of the FNB were by now reduced to opposing any enemy landings on other parts of Italian national territory.

With the fall of Sicily, there was a meeting on 21 August at Comando Supremo of high-ranking Italian and German officers

Detail of the battleship *Giulio Cesare* showing, in the foreground, the centre port side 120/50 twin turret; a Breda 20/65 twin mount had been located on its roof since 1941.

to propose measures to counter any possible enemy landings in Sardinia, Corsica and southern Italy (Salerno and Gaeta). Admiral de Courten assured the meeting of the unconditional employment of the fleet, but reiterated the need for air cover by at least thirty aircraft constantly in the skies over the ships, corresponding to a total availability of not fewer than 150 aircraft, obtaining assurances from General Renato Sandalli, the new Minister and Chief of Staff of the Air Force, and from Kesselring. In conformity with these promises, Supermarina issued Di Na 15 ('Directive for naval actions to oppose enemy landings in southern Italy') for action by the FNB and 'stealth' forces (small fast surface craft and submarines) in the event of an enemy landing on the Tyrrhenian coast and in the Gulf or Taranto. The directive also took into account the possibility of facing large enemy forces, if that were necessary to reach the enemy convoys or the landing areas; in particular, the two 'Duilios' would seek to reach the landing areas at high speed, following coastal routes behind the minefields and act as mobile gun batteries in shallow waters, while in the event of relatively small landings on the Ionian coast of Calabria, the use of only light forces was envisaged.

Chapter 9.5

FROM THE ARMISTICE TO THE SCRAPPING OF THE 'DUILIOS'

From 25 July to 8 September

The events of 25 July, with the dismissal and arrest of Mussolini and the appointment of Marshal Pietro Badoglio as head of government, also affected the navy. In the new ministerial structure, Admiral Raffaele de Courten, who from 15 March 1943 had held the post of Assistant Deputy Chief of Staff, assumed that of Minister and Chief of Staff (CSM); Admiral Luigi Sansonetti kept his post as Deputy Chief of Staff.

Badoglio and the Chief of the General Staff, General Vittorio Ambrosio, conducted negotiations in utmost secrecy that led to the signing of an armistice with the Allies at Cassibile on 3 September 1943. However, they were not aware when it would come into force (or so they led others to believe) as the Allies, who did not trust them, had reserved the right to make it public only a few hours before the planned landing at Salerno. Based purely on conjecture, Rome formed the opinion that the armistice would not be announced before the 12th. The naval clauses prescribed that all naval and merchant vessels that were able to move were to transfer to ports controlled by the Allies and an attachment, 'Memorandum Dick' – named after its author, the Chief of Staff to the Commander-in-Chief of Allied Naval Forces in the Mediterranean, Admiral Andrew Cunningham – set forth the procedures to be followed relative to transfer and disarming, which also specified that the movement of the ships was to begin at the time the armistice was proclaimed. The drama that followed would dreadfully involve all of Italy but will be addressed here only as they relate to the Taranto group, the FNB and the *Giulio Cesare* in Pola.

De Courten knew of the signing of the armistice on 3 September itself, but it was not until the night of the 6th that he became aware of 'Memorandum Dick'. On the morning of the 7th he wrote two memoranda, which he did not hand personally to Ambrosio until noon on the 8th: in one he protested that the navy had been kept in the dark about such an important question that affected him directly, but in the other he set forth the possibility of sending the three 'Vittorio Veneto' class with Italian crews to fight the Japanese in the Pacific, observing that the three major ships had been spared from bombings. This latter proposal, apart from the cynical and naive idea of 'helping' the Anglo-Americans in the Far East, lays bare de Courten's thoughts concerning the use of the fleet. In his eyes the armistice would again put it in play as a political factor, rendering a service to Italy much greater than it would have been able to achieve by its sacrifice, either in a last desperate battle or in scuttling, which he never seriously considered. He did not see the fleet as a means of barter for more favourable peace terms, but rather as removal of a potential threat to the Allies that would have left them free to use many more assets in the war in the Far East and, in addition, to benefit from a significant nucleus of modern battleships in Italian hands. Ambrosio reassured him, stating that 'Memorandum Dick' was out of date, as a request had already been made to the Allies to allow all of the ships to move to La Maddalena and that there were good reasons why this should be granted. It was not true and, indeed, negotiations on that point had already failed.

The 8 September at Taranto and the 'transfer' of the 5th Division to Malta

Before his meeting with Ambrosio, de Courten had called a meeting in Rome on 7 September with the commanders of the naval forces and departments, during which he mentioned nothing of the armistice and 'Memorandum Dick', but only set forth verbally the contents of a memorandum No 1 to the Comando Supremo, nominally regarding measures of public safety, but in which arrangements were made to act, if necessary, against the Germans. He spoke of the unpredictability of the political and military situation and of the risk of a German coup in an attempt to restore Fascism; to deal with such an emergency, the warships were to be kept ready, upon receipt of a proper order, to move to Sardinia, Corsica, Elba, Sebenico [Šibenik] and Spalato [Split], while merchant ships were to make for ports south of Livorno and Ancona. These instructions conflicted with the terms of the armistice and in general de Courten was rather cryptic; he sought to make it understood, without explicitly stating so, that an armistice was being prepared. He did not deliver memorandum No 1 – even though the army staff had issued it to its subordinate commands – except to Rear Admiral Bruno Brivonesi, C-in-C of the Sardinia Maritime Department, because the bulk of the fleet was to have concentrated there. He did not trust the C-in-C of the FNB, Lieutenant Admiral Carlo Bergamini, who was most involved in the movement of the fleet, and in fact in one or two discussions that he had on the margins with him that same day, he added nothing more except for the possibility of scuttling the ships as an extreme measure. The conference was also attended by Vice Admiral Bruto Brivonesi (the brother of Bruno), C-in-C of the Military Maritime Department of the Ionian and Lower Adriatic, and Admiral

Arrival at Malta of Italian ships from Taranto on the morning of 10 September 1943. The escort destroyer HMS *Hursley*, top left, was tasked with leading the ships through the safe channels to the island; astern are, in order, the battleships *Duilio* and *Doria* and the cruisers *Cadorna* and *Pompeo Magno*. (NH 111451 photo)

Alberto da Zara, commander of the 5th Division, who did not grasp, as neither did all of the others in attendance, the ultimate sense of the Minister's words, which were intended to imply the imminence of the armistice, as Sansonetti, who was aware of the situation, declared after the war. According to him, only the admirals stationed in Rome, who had heard rumours, understood the subtext, as well as possibly Bruto Brivonesi, who learned from other sources.

While the conference was taking place, there had already been warnings for hours of an amphibious operation on the coast of Campania (Operation 'Avalanche') and, thus, of the imminent announcement of the armistice. Bruto Brivonesi and da Zara left Rome for Taranto early on the morning of the 8th. As soon as he boarded the *Duilio*, shortly after dusk, da Zara learned of the armistice. The situation in Rome had, in fact, taken a dramatic turn, when later in the afternoon of the 8th an ultimatum had come from the Commander-in-Chief of the Allied forces, General Dwight Eisenhower, which ordered that the commitment to collaborate in view of the landings be put into action, scheduled for the early hours of the 9th on the Salerno plain, while Radio Algiers and other transmitters were reporting the news of Italy's unconditional surrender. After a hectic Council of

The battleship *Duilio*, which flies the ensign of Admiral Da Zara, riding at anchor off Valletta on 10 September 1943. (IWM)

the Crown, which met at 18:00, Marshal Badoglio announced the armistice over the radio beginning at 19:45.

Compared to La Spezia, the situation at Taranto was less urgent, as it lacked any direct and (apparently) significant German threat. This, however, resulted in laying mines in Mar Grande at night by two German MTBs and a motorised barge that were authorised to leave the base in order (according to them) to reach Greece. On the night of 10 September 1943 these mines would sink the fast minelayer HMS *Abdiel* with a significant loss of the troops she was carrying. This episode did nothing to improve post-armistice relations with the Royal Navy.

On the night of the 8/9th in the headquarters of the Taranto Military Maritime Department there was an initial meeting between Bruto Brivonesi, Vice Admiral Giuseppe Fioravanzo, his subordinate and Military Maritime Commander of Taranto, da Zara and Rear Admiral Giovanni Galati, who since 15 August had been the commander of the cruiser group. In vain, attempts were made to establish telephone contact with Rome and in the uncertainty, around midnight of the 8th, Bruto Brivonesi issued orders aimed at preventing the handing over of the ships to anyone and, if that were not possible, to prepare to scuttle them, informing Supermarina. The situation at Taranto changed on the morning of the 9th when communications were re-established with Rome. At 06:31 Supermarina reported that the Germans were marching on the capital, that it would no longer be able to communicate and to follow the clauses of the armistice faithfully; at 07:00 it ordered the light cruiser *Scipione Africano* to raise steam and proceed to Pescara, where she was to take on a high-ranking person (the King) and where she was to meet with the corvette *Baionetta* from Pola and *Scimitarra* from Venice. At 07:15 it transmitted the executive order of memorandum No 1 of Comando Supremo and at 09:20 transmitted the order directly to da Zara to set sail for Malta with all of the ships able to move, to take aboard the British commission, giving assurances that the ships would not be turned over and that the flag would not be lowered, and providing instructions on daytime recognition signals (black pennant, black circles on the decks, weapons at maximum depression) and for night ('gamma alfa' semaphore signals, dimmed navigation lights). Finally, at 11:50 a message by de Courten began to be broadcast to all Italian sailors.

The 09:20 message reached da Zara (10:05) while a meeting was being held on the *Duilio* of officers in command positions to prepare the ships for scuttling, which, as he wrote, 'for one who had lived in a cult of supreme sacrifice, represented the logical and instinctive act for which one had prepared with calm awareness'. In Taranto the news of the armistice had been greeted by the personnel ashore and on the ships with varied, but not general, displays of joy, which were short-lived. For the officers, however, with few exceptions, it was painful because of the defeat and a sense of anguish, and almost all of the officers expressed themselves in favour of scuttling. Da Zara interrupted the meeting and went ashore again with Galati to confer with Brivonesi and Fioravanzo. The discussion was contentious: da Zara and Galati declared themselves for scuttling, Brivonesi and Fioravanzo for the observance of the orders from Rome; Fioravanzo went so far as to declare that he was ready to replace da Zara as commander of the ships if he did not feel like leading them to Malta. Finally, even da Zara agreed to obey the orders of the King and the government, while Galati remained a lone voice. Having returned to the *Duilio*, da Zara resumed the conference to bring the commanders up to date, but faced with doubts and complaints found himself forced to ask each one of them for a written declaration of loyalty in executing their orders. Everyone consented, with the exception of Galati, who remained immovable, and of Captain Alberto Banfi, captain of the *Pompeo Magno* who, however, declared himself willing to follow da Zara. Galati was sent ashore along with his Chief of Staff and flag adjutant, and was replaced as commander of the cruiser group by Captain Paolo Mengarini, captain of the *Luigi Cadorna*. Da Zara set the time of departure from Taranto at 17:00 in order to give the commanding officers enough time to explain the new state of affairs to the crews. Preparations for scuttling were cancelled and resupply of the ships was begun; at 15:48 he notified Supermarina that he would put to sea in accordance with the orders he had received. That evening Brivonesi placed Galati under arrest in the fortress following altercations with other officers, whom he accused of traitorous conduct because of their meek acceptance of the surrender order.

Da Zara had fixed the departure time for 17:00 but, when he learned of the imminent arrival of British landing forces at Taranto (Operation 'Slapstick'), he hastened preparations and, from 16:18, the 5th Division (*Duilio* and *Andrea Doria*) and the cruiser group (*Cadorna*, *Pompeo* and the destroyer *Nicoloso da Recco*) weighed anchor, following the western safe channel (along the Calabrian coast), while on the eastern route (along the coast of Puglia) Force Z was approaching with the battleship *Howe* and the landing forces. Remaining in Taranto were the destroyer *Granatiere* undergoing major work and the *FR 23* (ex-French *Tigre*), *FR 31* (ex-*Trombe*) nominally being worked on, and several torpedo boats. The FNB group followed the coastal route until evening, then headed for Malta. It was in turn followed at a distance by the battleship *King George V* and by destroyers detached from Force Z. Around dusk the Italian ships were attacked by German aircraft, to which they responded, with no damage done to either side, despite the fact that two bombs had fallen close to the *Duilio*. The voyage continued undisturbed and on the morning of the 10th the Italian ships were joined in several phases by escort vessels and British fighters and anti-submarine aircraft and by the *King George V*. The Italian ships were led through the safe channels approaching Malta, where around 19:00 on the 10th they anchored along a line parallel to the northeastern coast between St Paul's Bay and slightly to the north of Grand Harbour.

The Taranto group was the first to reach Malta. During the passage da Zara had learned from radio intercepted messages from Supermarina of the fate of the *Roma*, which had been sunk by German aircraft off Sardinia, but not of Bergamini's death, who was thought to be aboard the *Italia* (formerly the *Littorio*) as the survivors of the La Spezia FNB group did not arrive until the morning of the 11th. The fact was not reported to him by Admiral Romeo Oliva, commander of the 7th Division, who succeeded Bergamini. In turn, da Zara became the most senior Italian admiral at Malta and, as such, had the first contacts with Cunningham and the naval authorities. In an initial climate of tension and distrust he became aware of the text of the armistice, of the details relating to disarming the ships (removal of the firing mechanisms except for the anti-aircraft guns, of fuses and scuttling charges, deactivation of telecommunications equipment, taking aboard security parties that were later removed, etc), of the need to transfer at least some of the ships to another location, and he began early cooperation with the former enemy. All of this, while not actually constituting a handover, left little doubt as to the significance of the surrender of the Italian ships, a condition that was soon confirmed and made all the more difficult by the so-called 'long armistice' signed by Badoglio at Malta on 29 September.

8 September aboard the *Giulio Cesare*

The base at Pola, where the *Giulio Cesare* had been since 31 December 1942, was the headquarters of the Military Maritime Command and Port, both commanded by Admiral Gustavo Strazzeri. The base hosted numerous schools of the Corpo Reale Equipaggi Militari Marittimi (CREMM, or Royal Naval Crew Corps) and submarine and MAS training schools, a section of reserve cadets from the Naval Academy and the navy section of the Guardia di Finanza [Revenue Service]. For shore defence of the base Strazzeri was subordinate to the XXIII Army Corps, which was headquartered in Trieste, and all told there were no fewer than 18,000 men, excluding embarked personnel. On the night of 8 September in addition to the *Cesare*, which organisationally was subordinate to the 5th Division, were the torpedo boat *Sagittario*, the corvettes *Urania* and *Baionetta*, the gunboats *Aurora* and *Cattaro* (undergoing work), three tankers, local service vessels as well as the ships assigned to the submarine school (submarines *Serpente*, under repair, *Goffredo Mameli* and *Vettor Pisani*, torpedo boat *Insidioso*, a support ship and smaller vessels) and two MAS from the MAS school; the midget submarine *CB 7* was also undergoing work, while another four of the same type were fitting out in the Scoglio Ulivi yard. Finally, aircraft of the 184th Naval Air Squadriglia were deployed at

Minister of the Navy, Admiral Raffaele de Courten, in khaki service uniform, on the quarterdeck of the battleship *Duilio* in 1944.

various airstrips. Scoglio Ulivi was also the base of the German 29th U-Bootflotille with *U 407* and *U 453* (undergoing work) and motor torpedo boats *S 30* and *S 33*; excluding the crews, there were no more than 160 Germans. There were no German forces in Istria, but Tito's partisan bands had grown in strength, which began to worry the local population and the Italian military commands. On the night of the 8th the *Insidioso* departed Trieste and at midnight the school ships *Amerigo Vespucci, Cristoforo Colombo* and *Palinuro* also sailed.

As early as August 1943, with the deterioration of Italian-German relations, the commander of the *Cesare*, Captain Vittore Carminati, joined the ranks of those who favoured scuttling the ships. It is not clear if he first consulted Strazzeri or da Zara, his immediate superior, but he went to La Spezia to propose the idea to the C-in-C of the FNB from whom, however, he was instructed only to secretly prepare the ship for departure from Pola. Upon his return he had all available fuel oil, water and main gun ammunition taken aboard, with the excuse of making space in the shore installations for new supplies.

On the evening of 8 September Carminati accelerated the preparations and called the officers and crew together, notifying them of the new situation. On the morning of the 9th Strazzeri delivered to Carminati a 09:00 telegram from da Zara that ordered the *Cesare* to set sail for Malta and to join the rest of the division, to receive the British watch party aboard, and gave instructions for navigation procedures and arrangements, giving assurances that the ship would not be turned over nor was the flag to be lowered. That same morning the Pola Naval Command ordered Carminati to make for Brindisi (the destination was modified in the early afternoon to Cattaro), where the ship was to complete its refuelling and receive further instructions. Carminati made all of this known only to his deputy and, in addition, due to a series of errors, only those two officers received the news of the proclamation distributed by de Courten relating to execution of the armistice clauses. At the same time police and security forces ashore all around Scoglio Ulivi were strengthened against the Germans, while the *Baionetta* left Pola to head for Pescara at maximum speed.

On the German side, in execution of Operation 'Achse', designed to neutralise the Italian armed forces, at 06:00 on the 9th the submarines at Pola received orders to suppress any Italian resistance and to prevent any attempts by Italian ships to escape, but when *U-407*, the only one of the two boats that was operational, tried to pass through the barrages and take up a position in front of the port, it was forced to return under the threat of Italian weapons directed against the small German base and its ships. Full Italian control of the base allowed the departure of all of the major ships and of the tanker *Verbano*. At 16:00 on the 9th, based on an erroneous report that German forces were approaching, the *Cesare* stopped embarking ammunition and left the base with only some of its boilers working, escorted for a short time by the *Sagittario* and the *Urania*. In an atmosphere of uncertainty and tension, generated in part by the fact that the personnel were not aware of the messages from da Zara and de Courten, but had been able to hear one from Cunningham that indicated the ports that the Italian ships should head for, it was enough to give weight to the idea that the ships would be handed over to the former enemy.

That same evening, after several meetings and the evasive answers given by Carminati to the requests for explanations, a group of officers, mostly from the Naval Engineers, and a large group of NCOs, led by Naval Engineer Major Giancarlo Fornasari and by Naval Engineer Captain Giacomino Spotti, put together a plan to oppose surrendering the ship. The plan called for seizing and confining the commander and deputy commander, disconnecting the controls of the bridge to the orders room, immobilising other officers of the executive branch and diverting the ship to Ortona, where the crew would be taken off and the ship scuttled; then the authors of the coup would turn themselves over to Italian authorities. The takeover, in which some seamen also took part, was put into action as planned at 02:15 on the 10th, while the *Cesare* was steaming near Lissa. There was hardly any reaction or protest; there were no incidents, nor was it necessary to transfer the rudder controls from the bridge to the orders room. The commander was stopped on the bridge and brought to the chart house; conning the ship was assumed by Captain Giacomo Borgogno who, after having steamed at maximum speed on the original course, at 03:45 on the 10th headed for Ortona. Around 04:00 Carminati had a talk with Fornasari and Spotti, bringing them up to date on da Zara's message, pointing out the risk of German or British air attacks once the ship reached Ortona and, most importantly, gave his word that he would head for Cattaro where, in the event the British were there, he would disembark the crew and scuttle the ship in more than 100 metres of water, rather than hand it over. Having received these assurances and after conferring with each other, the coup plotters again placed themselves under Carminati's command, who at 04:15 resumed his post and steered once more for Cattaro at reduced speed. At 09:19 on the 10th the commander finally addressed the assembled crew and the episode was over – not, however, without some difficulty in persuading some of the NCOs.

Around noon on the 10th the *Cesare* was joined by the seaplane carrier *Giuseppe Miraglia*, coming from Venice and also bound for Cattaro; the two ships travelled in convoy and command of the improvised group was assumed by Captain Gaetano Correale, captain of the *Miraglia*, as senior ranking officer. Followed throughout the morning by German reconnaissance aircraft, at 13:48 the two ships were attacked by ten German bombers that focused their sights on the battleship, which replied with AA fire. There were no consequences, even though two bombs were near misses. In the afternoon both ships received orders from Supermarina to no longer head for Cattaro (nor for Brindisi, where the King and his retinue had just arrived) but rather for Taranto. The change of destination led to a serious range problem for the battleship, as fuel consumption relative to the amount of fuel oil believed to be on board indicated that the ship would run out of fuel off Otranto. However, as always happened on the major ships, the fuel that had been saved during its period of activity (and inactivity) and appropriate shifting among the various tanks in order to drain the tanks to the last drop enabled the ship to reach Taranto at 16:05 on 11 September under its own power – and, importantly, without having to be towed by any other ship, either Italian or British, as has often been reported. On the last leg of the voyage, at 18:30 on the 10th, the *Cesare* suffered a slight problem with the rudder, which was quickly remedied and, at 13:35 on the 11th, while already in the western safe channel to Taranto, the ship stopped to pick up a man who had fallen overboard.

At Taranto the *Cesare* anchored near Cape San Vito, where on the afternoon of the 11th and the night following the ship was refuelled and supplied with water by lighters in view of her planned move to Malta. Rear Admiral Sesto Sestini, former captain of the ship, boarded, in order to check on what had happened, along with a British picket, which removed the breechblocks of the main and medium guns. Also, some of the NCOs who had taken part in the attempted coup were taken off the ship, preferring to remain in Italy rather than go to Malta with the ship. At 14:10 on the 12th the *Cesare* set sail for the British island along with the *Miraglia*, escorted in an anti-submarine capacity by a Cant Z 506. At 07:25 on the 13th, off of Cape Passero the two ships were met by the battleship *Warspite*, *Cesare*'s opponent at Punta Stilo, and by smaller British ships that led them as far as Malta. There they anchored at 12:24 off St Paul's Bay, then in the evening of the 14th moving on, the *Miraglia* to Marsa Muscetto [Marsamxett in Maltese] and the *Cesare* to Marsa Scirocco [Marsaxlokk in Maltese], where she joined the *Duilio* and *Andrea Doria*.

The coup involving some officers, NCOs and seamen of the *Cesare* was one of the relatively few episodes of reaction to the armistice within the navy, either at sea or ashore. The commission of inquiry that met in September 1944 to address the matter recognised that the mutiny could be attributed to a praiseworthy and understandable sentiment, to an unwarlike atmosphere resulting from the prolonged period at a base far from the fighting, as well as to the mistakes and shortcomings in communication and the closed nature of the commander, who did not even inform his own officers of what he knew about the armistice

The battleship *Duilio* with uniform paint scheme in two shades of grey typical of the period of co-belligerency with the Allies. (A Starace collection)

clauses; also considered were fears of leaving the homeland for an uncertain and obscure future. In view of these factors the commission did not refer the matter to a military court and proposed only mild disciplinary measures, in part so as not to advertise episodes of dissatisfaction regarding what should have been complete obedience within the navy to the orders of its leaders and of the King. In 1946 the navy's disciplinary council adopted minimal sanctions against the protagonists in that rebellion. During the post-war period a similar line was taken in the official historiography, which passed over the event almost without mention. Although complete documentation was available, it did not consider in depth that these and other acts of disobedience and reaction did not undermine the honour of the navy, but only demonstrated that there were men who were not resigned to defeat and the overturning of alliances, or were not inclined to mechanically place the ships in the hands of their former enemies.

Internment of the 5th Division at Malta (September 1943–June 1944)

The continuing arrival of Italian ships at Malta made the harbours and facilities on the island overburdened and unsafe to receive them, so from 14 September they were redistributed. Initially, the two 'Vittorio Veneto' class, four cruisers and four destroyers were transferred to Alexandria, while that same day the three smaller battleships were concentrated at Marsa Scirocco, at the extreme southeastern side of the island. The exodus from Malta was intensified as a result of an agreement between Cunningham and de Courten on 23 September 1943 that, even before the signing of the long armistice, set the parameters for the Italian Navy's cooperation with the Allied navies as outlined in the Québec accord dated 15 August 1943 concerning the support that Italy would give to the Allied cause. However, the battleships were excluded, as the accord required their disarming, and later rearming only if that seemed desirable by the Allies. Thus, on 16 October the two 'Vittorio Venetos' were moved to the Great Bitter Lakes in the middle of the Suez Canal, where they sadly remained interned until 1947; a similar fate befell the three smaller battleships, which remained interned at Malta at reduced manning. Some days earlier, at St Paul's Bay, the surplus crew from the *Duilio* and the *Doria* – the *Cesare* was already at reduced manning – were transferred to the light cruisers *Duca degli Abruzzi, Giuseppe Garibaldi* and *Pompeo Magno* and sent back to Taranto between 4 and 5 October, escorted by the destroyers *Legionario* and *Alfredo Oriani* and by the torpedo boats *Libra* and *Calliope*.

The three small battleships remained confined at Marsa Scirocco until June 1944, swinging at their anchors there until February, as the British had continued to put off laying buoys and moorings. Throughout that period, connections with Italy for exchange of personnel and for leave, resupply and various other services were made by Italian vessels, while relations with the island were limited strictly to service needs. Onboard activity and training were limited, as was the maintenance of machinery, equipment and facilities, which could only be carried out with whatever tools were already on board; nevertheless, it was enough to preserve the ships in fairly good condition. Despite the confinement, morale and discipline remained high; the major worries related to the fate of family members who remained in the area of Italy occupied by the Germans and under Allied bombardment. There was also concern about the post-war period and the prospects for those who would not be able to find a place in a downsized navy and, for many officers who were progressively taking positions against the King, in whose name they had made the sacrifice of obedience to the armistice clauses, the political status of the country.

The salient events of those months were few. On 30 December 1943 Admiral Arturo Catalano Gonzaga di Cirella replaced da Zara as commander of the 5th Division; the change was made by way of the *Legionario*. On 25 and 26 February 1944 a violent southeast wind hit the bay and severely tested the moorings of the ships, in particular the *Cesare*, which began to drift to leeward, dragging her anchor up to 50 metres away from the bow of the *Duilio*. The British would not authorise a move into the open sea to find shelter in Valletta Bay and the *Cesare* was only able to maintain a safe distance by manoeuvring with her engines for about thirty hours with the help of two tugs that were authorised to give assistance. It was only after this episode that the British put in moorings for the greater safety of the ships in Marsa Scirocco, but not, as had been likewise requested, nets for submarine defence. There was great apprehension generated in March 1944 when the President of the United States, Franklin Delano Roosevelt, announced the unexpected handing over of part of the Italian fleet to the Soviet Union, which had been agreed at the Teheran Conference (28 November–1 December 1943). Catalano Gonzaga declared that he was in favour of scuttling his ships if they were part of the deal, finding support from de Courten, who assured him of the maximum involvement of the government to prevent such an eventuality. He succeeded, temporarily, in his intention and Moscow's claims were satisfied by the Allies with the loan of British and American ships.

In this situation, on 3 May 1944 Catalano Gonzaga sent a detailed report to the Navy Staff, laying out the operational readiness status of the three battleships and a plan for the works that would be necessary to return them to fully operational status, in the optimistic hope that they would be rearmed. It is worth summarising the essential points of that document.

Artillery. The main and medium guns were deactivated, while the anti-aircraft guns and machine guns, except for the 37/54 disappearing mounts on the 'Duilio' class, were still operational. However, the anti-aircraft gunners periodically tested the turrets of the larger-calibre guns. Overall, the artillery components only needed limited work, most of which related to the rangefinders on the revolving director on the top of *Doria*'s bridge tower and improvements to the anti-aircraft fire direction stations. This work could be performed without any interference in the four months of training and exercises needed to bring everything back up to satisfactory working condition.

Powerplant. Engines, boilers and auxiliary machinery were in good condition overall. However, the inspection of the turbines was overdue, as were the regular tests of the evaporation systems. The rest of the powerplant needed only to be checked and have periodic maintenance carried out to eliminate minor problems that could not be dealt with by onboard personnel. Only the *Cesare* had some degree of wear to her evaporation system and auxiliary condensers for potable water production and for supply of some other onboard services.

Hull. The outer plating, the decks, the bulkheads and hull machinery were in good repair. All of the ships had leaks in the inaccessible areas between the old and the new bows and, to a lesser degree, in other parts of the hull. the Maintenance of the normally closed watertight compartments was poor (especially on the *Cesare*) because of the shortage of anti-rust paint. The state of the watertight doors was also unsatisfactory because of the deterioration of the gaskets, which had thinned and hardened; in present circumstances the normal replacement as they deteriorated was impossible, and it was now an urgent requirement. In addition, those on the *Cesare* also suffered from an inherent weakness in their locking mechanisms. The refrigeration systems in the ammunition and food spaces, although needing maintenance, were in good condition; their condition, however, would deteriorate as the summer approached if there were a prolonged stay at Marsa Scirocco. The general condition of the steering gear was good; only the steam engine of the *Duilio*'s rudder had too much play. Pipework, exhausts and sea intakes were likewise in good condition except, here and there, for excessive incrustations, but they too were in need of extensive maintenance. Finally, the ships required graving to remove marine growth and fouling due to the prolonged immobility. All or most of the work needed could be performed only with personnel and equipment in shipyards or naval dockyards.

Safety measures. Safety equipment on all of the ships was in a precarious state, especially with respect to the fire extinguishing apparatus, due to the lack of replacement parts; the *Cesare* also suffered from insufficient personnel training.

Electrical system. The state of conservation and maintenance of the electrical system could be considered fairly good, but would inevitably deteriorate because of the lack of replacement parts and of repair equipment. The main concerns were the diesel generators, which were well past their maximum working hours limit; the four on the *Cesare*, one of which was not operational, were capable of generating 60 per cent of normal power. All told, the electrical system needed repair and overhaul, which could be accomplished only in a shipyard or dockyard.

Personnel. Except for the *Cesare*, which had seen a long period of laying in reduced readiness prior to internment at Malta, the level of crew training could be considered fair.

All things considered, after eight months of internment the two 'Duilios' were in a fair state of readiness; less so for the *Cesare*. But – as Catalano Gonzaga had noted – that did not mean that merely bringing the crew up to strength and allowing a brief period of training would be sufficient for them to resume some form of wartime activity. This was not entirely attributable to the internment, as the three ships had not undergone scheduled work since December 1942 because of the priority assigned to smaller vessels for all resources in the shipyards and naval dockyards.

The battleship *Giulio Cesare* lying decommissioned in July 1947, with some vestiges of its last wartime camouflage scheme still visible on its superstructure. A few months earlier the clause of the peace treaty ceding the ship to the Soviet Union had been made public. (A Fraccaroli photo)

Left: The battleship *Andrea Doria* leaving Taranto's Mar Piccolo, probably in 1948.

Below: Detail of the bridge tower of the battleship *Andrea Doria* in 1949. Note the British LWS type radar located on the main top.

The battleship *Duilio* proceeding in rough seas during a training cruise in the Upper Tyrrhenian on 7 June 1951.

The battleship *Andrea Doria* passing Taranto's swing bridge, headed for Mar Piccolo, some time before the end of the 1940s.

Above: The original mobile mounting of the British type LWS air search radar.

From the 5th Division's return to Italy to the peace treaty (June 1944–February 1947)

From November 1943 de Courten had tried to negotiate with British naval authorities for the return to Italy of at least some of the interned battleships – in particular, the damaged *Italia*, in order to make repairs, and the two 'Duilios', to assign them to training duties. On 18 May 1944 the new Commander-in-Chief of Allied Naval Forces in the Mediterranean, Admiral John Cunningham, gave his consent to repatriate the three smaller battleships, and resolved the humiliating question of deactivating the main and medium-calibre guns by the compromise of offloading their ammunition at Augusta to depots under Italian control. But it was not until 5 June that Catalano Gonzaga was authorised to transfer them to Augusta, although he was obliged to move them separately and at different times because of the shortage of escort vessels and so as not to overcrowd that base. The *Doria* was the first to leave Marsa Scirocco, setting out on the morning of 8 June 1944 escorted by the torpedo boats *Aliseo* and *Libra* to reach Augusta that same afternoon. There, from 9 to 12 June, the main and medium-calibre ammunition was disembarked. Later, in late morning of the 14th, the ship moved to Siracusa (Syracuse), anchoring near the remains of the hospital ship *California*. This anchorage was considered unsatisfactory by

Right: The *Duilio* being overflown by an Italian air force P-38 Lightning during an exercise in the early 1950s. On the right is the characteristic antenna of one of the two LWS type radars with which the ship was equipped. (G Apostolo archives)

The battleship *Andrea Doria* anchored in the roadstead at Augusta (Sicily) in April 1952.

Catalano Gonzaga (who expected a prolonged stay in that roadstead) because of its proximity to the wreck and because the poor holding ground did not give the anchors enough security, especially during the bad weather season. As soon as the ship was at anchor, he therefore requested that a proper mooring be provided, in order to allow the ship to manoeuvre on its engines in case of emergency or to slip its moorings quickly and to put to sea for safety reasons.

On the morning of 17 June, the *Cesare* left, escorted by the destroyer *Artigliere* and the torpedo boat *Fortunale*. They reached Augusta that afternoon, and from 19 to 24 June offloaded the main gun and medium gun ammunition.

Duilio finally left Marsa Scirocco on the morning of 27 June, escorted by the torpedo boats *Aliseo* and *Sirio*. The ship reached Augusta that afternoon, where she offloaded her ammunition between 27 June and 4 July.

The transfer of the three ships took place at a speed of 21 knots, the maximum sustainable with a reduced complement of engine room personnel, and experienced no machinery problems. The voyage was used to carry out anti-aircraft gunnery exercises, which gave satisfactory results, with the partial excep-

The battleship *Duilio* at La Spezia in 1953 shortly before being decommissioned.

The battleship *Andrea Doria* in one of the large graving docks in the Taranto naval yard in 1954.

The battleship *Duilio* manoeuvring in the port of Bari on 13 September 1948. (A Fraccaroli collection)

The battleship *Andrea Doria* – moored at Naples between the cruisers *Duca degli Abruzzi*, right, and *Montecuccoli* – during a ceremony held on 20 March 1950 for awarding the Gold Medal for Valour to the Navy Flag.

tion of the *Cesare*, because of the failure to return to battery of two 100/47 installations and jamming of one of the 37/54 guns. For all of the ships, disembarking the ammunition was under the auspices of the British authorities and executed without urgency or regularity because of the shortage and inadequacy of the equipment that was provided (lighters and barges of various sizes) and because of priorities accorded to other base services. Storage of the ammunition was also under British supervision, with few vehicles available and with civilian workers who were reluctant to handle the ammunition; only the storage sites (the hangar of the seaplane station and the Brucoli powder magazine) were ideally suited to receive the ammunition. As a result, the ballistic caps of many of the main gun shells were broken or bent and the copper driving bands were also damaged; armourers had to be sent from Taranto to make the repairs and the need to assign them to Augusta to recondition and reorganise that base was recognised. Finally, on 30 June 1944 the British authorities at Augusta handed over the firing mechanisms of the main and

The *Andrea Doria* in a graving dock at Taranto in 1954.

Detail of the fore-foot of the *Andrea Doria* during graving in 1954.

medium guns for the *Duilio* and the *Doria*, as well as those for the *Cesare*, which at the time was still at Taranto.

On 1 August 1944, with the 5th Division's return to Italy, the Inspectorate of Naval Forces was established, which replaced the Naval Forces Training Directorate, that had been instituted on 24 October 1943 for cooperation with the Allies. The new inspectorate was meant to mark a step towards establishment of a true and independent naval command, which the status of co-belligerence, however, did not yet allow.

Between June 1944 and December 1946, the *Cesare*, moored in

The *Duilio*, now lying decommissioned at the Scali Quay at La Spezia in 1954.

The hull of the battleship *Duilio* being scrapped at La Spezia in late summer 1958. (E. Bagnasco photo)

Another view of the hull of the battleship *Duilio* undergoing demolition at La Spezia in late summer of 1958. (E. Bagnasco photo)

The *Andrea Doria* entering Genoa on 21 July 1951. (A Fraccaroli collection)

Taranto's Mar Piccolo at reduced readiness, remained inactive, except to function for some periods as the headquarters of the above-mentioned inspectorate and headquarters of the CREMM schools. On 20 January 1946 she was placed in 'available' status and on 10 January 1947 back in reduced readiness, directly subordinate to the commander of the Taranto naval dockyard, while awaiting the fate reserved for her by the peace treaty.

The *Doria*, at reduced readiness, remained between Augusta and Siracusa until March 1945, acting as a school ship for cadets from the Naval Academy and from the CREMM. On

The *Andrea Doria*, flagship of the commander-in-chief of the Italian naval forces, moored at Naples in 1953. (US Navy photo)

Midship detail of the *Andrea Doria* in April 1960 leaving Taranto under tow for La Spezia where she will be broken up. (A Starace collection)

The *Andrea Doria* being towed through the Taranto swing bridge en route to the breaker's yard in April 1960. (A Starace collection)

20 February 1945 she left Siracusa for Taranto, but had to return to Augusta because of bad weather. The voyage was resumed on 13 March, reaching Taranto on the 14th. The ship returned once again to Siracusa on 29 March, remaining there until 12 December 1946 at reduced readiness and with school functions. She returned to Taranto on 13 December, disembarking the school personnel, and was placed in dockyard hands until autumn 1949, remaining in reserve.

The *Duilio* was the only one of the small battleships to engage in appreciable training activity with various sorties for exercises in the Gulf of Taranto and a brief move to Siracusa in March 1945, being the only one of the three that was still active after the *Doria* was decommissioned in December 1946.

28 April 1960, another view of the *Andrea Doria* being towed through the Taranto channel towards Mar Grande for transfer to La Spezia for breaking up. (USMM)

The peace treaty and the fate of the *Giulio Cesare* and of the 'Duilios'

On 10 February 1947 Italy signed the peace treaty imposed by the victors in Paris. It involved great territorial, material and moral sacrifices that did not spare the navy, and was greeted very negatively in naval circles, as it destroyed all the hopes that had been generated by the navy's cooperation with the Allied cause. The greatest bitterness came from the treatment of the Italian fleet as if it were war booty to be divided up among the victors. There were warning signs of this attitude going back to March 1944, but the government and navy had always hoped that – apart from compensation to the powers whose ships had been taken and not returned – Italy would be allowed to keep a nucleus of ships sufficient for its essential defence needs and that the same would be the case for new construction. Instead, not only was the navy left with ships completely inadequate for probable requirements in number and quality, but limitations for the future were even more punishing. With respect to battleships, the *Vittorio Veneto* was assigned to Great Britain, the *Italia* to the United States and the *Cesare* to the Soviet Union, while the two 'Duilios' were left to Italy. Once these last two ships were decommissioned, Italy could no longer possess any battleships nor guns with a range greater than 30,000 metres. While the peace treaty was being drawn up, Rome, which took no part in the negotiations, tried unsuccessfully with memoranda and declarations to soften the provisions that the twenty-one victorious powers were specifying with respect to the navy. In particular, the navy sought to keep the two 'Vittorio Venetos' as school ships, citing, in addition to Italian sacrifices and contributions to co-belligerency with the Allies, the symbolic value of these ships, the negative impact of their transfer on public opinion and on the navy, and the superior space and modern character of their equipment compared with that of smaller ships.

The failure of all attempts – which continued even after the treaty had been signed – induced de Courten to resign as Chief of Staff on 31 December 1946, after having given up his portfolio as Minister earlier on 14 July. That act signified the failure of the political calculation that had inspired his actions from the eve of the armistice, which were intended to save the navy from defeat and to maintain the core of the fleet by changing alliances, by active cooperation with the victors, and finally, by distancing itself

The *Andrea Doria* and other ships awaiting breaking at La Spezia in 1961.

from the monarchy as made clear by tacit acceptance, in June 1944, of the new formula for swearing in new ministers that ignored the figure of the King; de Courten, however, used the act of swearing allegiance to the King to force officers and crews to obey the clauses of the armistice.

The peace treaty was ratified, not without opposition, by the constituent assembly on 2 August 1947 and came into force on 16 December 1947, three months after the ratification was delivered to Paris (16 September 1947). During this interlude, Rome began negotiations with each of the four major powers, aimed at avoiding the humiliating act of handing over the ships in exchange for their scrapping. This aim was almost completely achieved with Washington and London but only partially with Paris. On 5 October 1947 the United States renounced its entire share of ships, including the *Italia*, with the obligation to demolish the major combat ships (the term 'demolish' was understood to mean the minimum destruction necessary to negate the ship's military potential). A similar agreement was reached with Britain, which, in turn, gave up the *Vittorio Veneto* and two submarines, in exchange for their demolition or sinking by 15 June 1948, but also of 20,000 tons of steel products. Both powers left minor combat vessels (motor torpedo boats, MAS) to Italy, prior to declassification, as well as auxiliary vessels. However, within the navy the disappointment and bitterness engendered by physically handing over ships to the remaining victorious powers (France, the Soviet Union, Greece and Yugoslavia) was great and palpable – so much so that the new Chief of Staff, Admiral Franco Maugeri, despite earlier doubts about his sympathies for the Allied cause, applied himself between February and September 1947 to preventing any moves towards scuttling the ships.

As previously mentioned, the peace treaty allowed Italy to keep the two modernised 'Duilio' class ships in service 'extra quota', but without the possibility of replacing them once they had reached the age limit for decommissioning – that is, forty years after their entry into service. These ships were, however, by now essentially outdated, and with operating and maintenance costs that were rather high for the tight Italian naval budgets in the difficult post-war years.

The new Italian Navy was born out of the institutional changes following the 2 June 1946 popular referendum that instituted the Italian Republic. Its hierarchy decided that the battleships would be assigned exclusively to training roles and, from spring of 1947, as headquarters (C-in-C of the Naval Forces and/or C-in-C of the naval divisions). In addition, because of their high operating costs, it was de facto established that only one of the two would remain fully manned and equipped, alternating periods of work, reduced readiness, reserve or decommissioned status.

In very brief summary, the *Duilio* remained fully active until November 1950, then passed into reserve at Taranto from where, in 1953, she was transferred to La Spezia and shortly after decommissioned. Following a long period of work at Taranto completed in late 1949, the *Andrea Doria* returned to service, replacing her sister as a headquarters ship, a function that continued until mid-1953 when, moored at Taranto and with a skeleton crew, the ship became a gunnery school. The *Duilio* was decommissioned on 15 September 1956, being scrapped at La Spezia between 1958 and 1960. Disarmed in August 1956, the *Andrea Doria* was decommissioned on 1 November; in April 1960, saluted by a sad ceremony for its last transit through Taranto's ship canal, the ship was towed to La Spezia where its demolition was completed in 1962.

Ceding the *Giulio Cesare* to the Soviet Union and its subsequent loss

One of the onerous military clauses of the peace treaty required the handing over to the Soviet Union of forty-five ships totalling 51,464 tons, equal to about a third of the overall available displacement, including the battleship *Giulio Cesare*, the light cruiser *Duca d'Aosta*, three destroyers, three torpedo boats, two submarines and thirty-five small and auxiliary ships. The delivery of these ships was seen by Italian sailors, as well as by the greater part of the population, not only as unfair and humiliating, but also as a renewed and unequivocal sign of defeat, which co-belligerency had managed to erase from the memory of many. The resulting resentment was particularly apparent and there were more than a few voices – especially from the right – calling for the scuttling of those ships. Every ship destroyed by sabotage – as expressly sanctioned by Article 57 of the treaty – would have to be replaced by a corresponding ship chosen from the few remaining in service under the Italian flag, so it was only the discipline of the officers and crews that avoided the real danger of the virtual dissolution of the Italian Navy. Therefore, the deliveries were made reluctantly but without any incidents, except for a few plans for sabotage against the *Cesare* and the *Cristoforo Colombo*, ships bound for the Soviet Union, which the security forces discovered before they could be brought to fruition. These were planned by far-right political youth organisations to be carried out respectively at Augusta and Taranto shortly before handing over the two ships.

When in early 1947 it was confirmed that the *Cesare* was to be ceded to the Soviet Navy, the ship was moored at Taranto, inactive for almost three years, almost devoid of crew and in a very reduced state of readiness. The treaty stipulated that the ships were to be handed over in operational condition – that is, ready for service in every respect and complete in equipment and supplies – no more than three months after 15 September 1947. It was absolutely impossible to meet these conditions with ships that for the most part had been decommissioned for a long period and therefore needed immediate reconditioning. The state of Italian shipyards and the finance of the newly constituted Italian Republic certainly did not allow it, without even considering the general Italian reluctance to fully cooperate in these tasks.

With respect to deliveries to the USSR, in June 1948 none of the ships earmarked had begun to be reconditioned and it was foreseeable that there would thus be long delays in their delivery. In order to speed things up, in July 1948 Moscow agreed that the ships assigned to it could be delivered in the 'condition in which they are currently', with any technical work limited to that necessary for their safe transfer to their ports of destination as had previously been agreed upon with France. Therefore, in late summer of 1948 a series of checks took place on the *Cesare* to verify and restore the proper functioning of the powerplant, the safety systems and all of the equipment necessary for the ship's safe operation. Obviously, this activity was conducted with costs kept to the minimum, limiting any work to the absolutely indispensable. To give an idea of the standard, it is enough to note that even repainting was limited to the exterior hull, excluding much of the superstructure, where traces of the wartime camouflage were still visible. The operational efficiency of the powerplant, of the steering controls and of the major safety systems were checked during a sortie for trials with a reduced crew that was carried out in

Taranto, November 1948. The battleship *Giulio Cesare* returning to Mar Piccolo after a brief sortie to test the machinery on the eve of handover to the Soviet Union, as specified by the 1947 peace treaty.

late autumn of 1948, while checking and stowing the normal complement of shipboard equipment, including ammunition.

Without giving any notice to news agencies, on 9 December 1948 the *Cesare* left Taranto for Augusta, where soon some fifty personnel would arrive from the Soviet Union to serve as the future Russian crews of the former Italian ships that were in the process of transfer (*Cesare, Artigliere, Fuciliere, Marea, Nichelio,* etc). Anchored at the Sicilian base, on 15 December the battleship was officially stricken from the list of Italian warships, assuming the designation of *Z 11* that had been established for the delivery voyage. Along with the other ships involved, the passage from Italy to the destination ports was to be under the flag of the Italian merchant marine, with the ships manned by former military personnel organised for the occasion in a cooperative venture or recruited from among local seamen. The destination established for the former *Cesare* and the former submarines *Marea* and *Nichelio* was the port of Valona in Albania, rather than the Soviet port of Odessa on the Black Sea as for all of the other Italian ships, as the conventions in force for transit through the Turkish Strait did not allow for the passage of large warships and submarines of 'powers that did not border the Black Sea'.

Detail of the battleship *Z 11*, formerly *Giulio Cesare*, at the time of handover to the USSR at Valona, Albania, in February 1949.

Delivery of the ships to Valona

Having embarked all of the stores (including 1100 complete 320mm rounds in addition to the normal issue of 120mm, 100mm, 37mm and 20mm rounds), the *Z 11* departed Augusta on 2 February under the command of Captain Enrico Dodero, reaching Valona the next day, after proceeding at 13–16 knots while encountering very rough weather in the Ionian that caused some damage to the deck fittings. While at anchor at Valona, the Italian civilian crew was replaced – although in a somewhat haphazard manner and earlier than agreed – by the Soviet crew, and left the ship to return to Italy. The documents delivering the *Z 11* to the USSR were finally signed on 6 February 1949 and on the same date the ship assumed, although still provisionally, the name *Novorossiysk*, in honour of the city of that name on the Black Sea that during the war had valiantly resisted a prolonged German siege. The battleship left Valona on 20 February, along with the submarines *TS-3*, formerly *Z 13 Marea*, and *TS-4*, formerly *Z 14 Nichelio*, and a Soviet auxiliary vessel, arriving in Sevastopol in the Crimea on the 26th.

From the outset, the Soviet naval authorities complained about how the ship had been delivered in a somewhat debatable condition. They noted numerous shortcomings, including the presence of only one working gyrocompass, of many systems that were not functioning (the emergency diesel generators, various pumps, electrical systems, etc), blockage of many of the auxiliary piping systems, rust emerging everywhere, and many

Starboard elevation of the battleship *Novorossiysk* (formerly *Giulio Cesare*) in 1952.

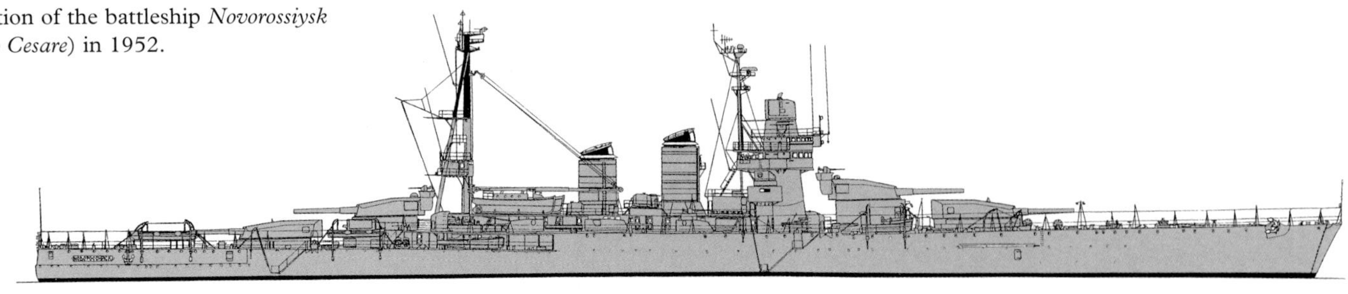

other items. Surprisingly, except for the poor state of maintenance of many of the anti-aircraft guns, there were few complaints about the operational effectiveness of the other guns, although in reality there were problems that could have been found. On the other hand, as reported by Italian personnel, the Russian who was responsible for checking the status during the 'delivery acceptance' of the ship was mainly interested in verifying that all equipment was present, followed by a concern for the presence of any type of sabotage, on more than one occasion inspecting the interior spaces, but without finding anything suspicious. The deficiencies noted were essentially attributable to the superficial maintenance carried out by the increasingly reduced crews during the long period of the ship's inactivity, and to cost-cutting during the ship's final reconditioning, tasks that were in any case carried out unwillingly by disaffected Italian sailors.

The official ceremony for entry of the battleship *Novorossiysk* into the Black Sea Fleet was held at Sevastopol on 5 March 1949, after which the ship underwent a minimum general cleaning up, including an overall painting in the fairly dark grey that was characteristic of Soviet ships. Communist propaganda took advantage of the situation to highlight the acquisition as 'war booty' of the former Italian battleship as yet another triumph of the politico-military plans of the Soviet regime. Despite the fact that the ship was no longer modern and of a type that was largely outdated, it was nevertheless the largest ship in service with the VMF [the Black Sea Fleet] during those years, which was to see rapid development in line with the new Soviet expansionist policy following a long period in which the navy had represented the 'Cinderella' of the Soviet armed forces.

Flagship of the Black Sea Fleet

Assigned primarily to the preparation and training of crews for the new battleships that still figured in the development plans for the Soviet Navy's surface forces during those years, the *Novorossiysk* also had to undertake the duties of flagship of the Black Sea Fleet. However, the ship's general condition and the need to carry out urgent modification and upgrade work (for example, insulation of the crew spaces, which were poorly suited to the local climate; fitting radar and telecommunications gear; restructuring the galleys, etc) determined the ship's employment from the outset. From 1949 the *Novorossiysk* was subjected to frequent periods of work, but it was in 1953, after a series of machinery breakdowns, that the ship was given a major modernisation that dealt primarily with the powerplant and armament. In particular, the boilers were completely overhauled and the original turbine reduction gearing replaced by similar Karkov-type systems of Soviet manufacture for a total of 93,000 horsepower, that is, with a significant increase in power that should have pushed maximum operational speed to more than 27 knots. The emergency diesel generators were also replaced along with many other auxiliary systems, representing a significant overall economic investment. With respect to armament, the major change was removal of all of the Breda 37/54 and 20/65 guns, which were replaced by more modern Soviet 37/67 guns for a total of twelve twin water-cooled systems and six single air-cooled systems; in addition, a new fire control system for the main armament was installed. At the same time several improvements were made to the bridge tower arrangements and new radar and telecommunications systems were fitted. Between 1949 and 1955 the ship underwent eight rounds of work, major and minor. Finally, in spring 1955, it appeared that *Novorossiysk* had reached a sufficient level of readiness, even though it was almost forty-four years since she had first been launched and her crew – now consisting of 1542 men of whom 68 were officers and 243 were NCOs – seemed to have achieved an acceptable degree of familiarity with handling the old battleship.

The Soviet battleship *Novorossiysk*, formerly *Giulio Cesare*, riding at anchor in the Black Sea in late 1949.

The explosion

In the late afternoon of 28 October 1955, while returning from an exercise, the *Novorossiysk* – still flagship of the Black Sea fleet – moored between two of the large buoys in the northern part of Sevastopol's deep bay. This was mooring point No 3, positioned about 300 metres from land over a bottom covered by a significant layer of mud and by 17–18 metres of water, while the ship, at that time, drew about 10. Other buoys were positioned around it, to which other ships were moored, mainly cruisers. The mooring to the shackle of the large bow buoy consisted of a length of chain that was 'unshackled' from the battleship's starboard anchor and that of the stern buoy by a strong steel cable that was 'doubled'. The port anchor, which had been dropped during the mooring operation, was still in the water along with a length of its chain; according to procedure, all of this was to have been recovered the following day with the assistance of a lighter from the base. Both of the buoys were firmly attached to the bottom chain moorings terminating in the traditional 'crow's foot' on whose ends three 'one-armed anchors' (anchors with a single fluke) were arranged 120 degrees from each other. A little later, in the evening, the captain of the battleship and his deputy went ashore on leave, replaced on board by the Number Three. After dinner, 240 men of the crew had gone on liberty or leave, but at the same time 200 cadets from the naval academy in training and some civilian technicians had come aboard, bringing the total number of personnel aboard the battleship to 1530.

That was the situation when, at 01:31 on 29 October, below decks on the starboard side of the hull in the bow area, there was a violent explosion whose intensity was so great that it registered on instruments in the nearby Simferopol seismographic station. The explosion – later assessed as corresponding to 1000–1200kg of TNT – had probably occurred beneath the hull, slightly to starboard of the keel line, impacting a large area of the plating, bending it inwards and making an opening of more than 340 square metres about 22 metres in length. The shock wave had propagated mostly vertically inside the ship, breaking through all of the decks that it met until it 'vented' to the air and opened a gaping external slit 14 by 4 metres in the forecastle deck slightly forward of the muzzles of the 320mm guns of the forward triple turret. The area affected by direct destruction was slightly forward of the ammunition magazine for that main gun turret and was occupied by crew quarters, auxiliary machinery and various storerooms. It was later estimated that 50 to 100 sailors among those present at the time lost their lives immediately. The area consisted of the old bow portion of the battleship's hull, to which the new structures had been grafted and in part superimposed during the course of modernisation in the 1930s. The explosion's energy had displaced much of the forward structure towards the bow, but had also partly compromised the watertight integrity of the magazine's forward bulkhead. It was later calculated that in the first three minutes after the explosion the large hole torn in the hull allowed in so much water that it caused the ship to settle by three to four degrees at the bow and to begin to list to starboard. The ship was initially thrown into complete darkness, but soon after, when the forward diesel generators were brought on line, electricity was restored.

At 01:40, after the first minutes of inevitable confusion, the Commander-in-Chief of the Black Sea Fleet, Vice Admiral Alexandrovi Parkhomenko, was informed of the incident and reached the ship at 02:00. Despite using all the pumps that were still in working order, the list to starboard was worsening, while immersion of the bow continued to increase rapidly. It was estimated that 1200 tons of water had been taken aboard and Parkhomenko was quickly informed, which seemed to calm him down. In reality, as was later recalculated, the water amounted to 3500 tons, or more than 15 per cent of the ship's normal displacement.

Around 02:00 the *Novorossiysk* let go her moorings, passing her cable to some of the tugs that had quickly arrived; but, despite the absolutely calm conditions, some difficulties were encountered that slowed down the manoeuvre. The intention was to tow the ship, which was rapidly losing its buoyancy, to a nearby shallows on which it could safely beach. By 02:20 the forward portion of the forecastle deck was at sea level and, as a result, the fore-foot at the base of the stem post was already burying itself in the viscous mud of the seabed. Several hundred sailors not involved in the rescue operation had gathered on deck, where they were not much use because of the serious damage to the spaces forward of the deck opening, but they were somewhat more effective in the area immediately abaft, where the watertight compartments that were still holding were being shored up and sealed off. At the same time, attempts were being rapidly made to get up some steam so that at least a limited amount of power could be generated for propulsion. The powerplant, in fact, did not appear to have suffered damage as a result of the explosion and leaks in the machinery spaces were minimal.

Parkhomenko had assumed de facto control over attempts to save the ship and around 03:00 decided firmly against a proposal to evacuate the roughly 800 sailors on deck who were not contributing to the operation. The rescue vessels, which by now surrounded the ship, could have been used for this purpose, but in his judgement this would have led to useless panic and, besides, at this point he was still confident that the battleship would not sink. The commander-in-chief was an experienced seaman and felt that the ship, even though damaged, would be able to rest partially on the bottom; he dismissed the possibility that it could turn turtle given the modest depth of the water (about 7 metres) beneath the keel, while the maximum breadth of the hull was all of 28 metres. However, his assessment did not take due account of a layer of very soft mud, which in some places was more than 15 metres deep. Meanwhile, the lower part of the stem was digging ever more deeply into the viscous bottom silt, greatly hindering the work of the tugs that were trying to move the ship. Dragging by the tugs and the hull's resistance because of large amounts of water in the partially flooded spaces, led to a noticeable heeling of the ship, now on its port side, and the redistribution of liquid aimed at reducing the list was too slow and inadequate. On the forecastle deck, the water was by now lapping against the barbette of No 1 main gun turret, and began to flood from above into the bow spaces through the large hole that the explosion had opened just forward of that turret. In that situation, at 3:30, the ship's list had reached 12 degrees. Fifteen minutes later, when the bow was buried several metres into the bottom mud and the efforts of the tugs were almost useless, once again Parkhomenko was asked in vain to order the evacuation of the men on deck. In the meantime, around 04:00, the *Novorossiyk's* list to port reached 17 degrees despite the fact that attempts to right the ship were ongoing.

The sinking

At 04:14, two hours and fifteen minutes after the explosion, with about 7000 tons of water in the hull and a list of more than 20 degrees to port, the ship began to settle rapidly on that side; this rather sudden rotation did not slow until the masts and the upper superstructures began to settle into the mud. The rotating movement continued slowly for about eighteen hours – that is, until around 22:00 on 29 October, with a port side list of 172 degrees – when it ceased and the entire bottom of the hull disappeared beneath the surface.

As the list increased, a large number of the personnel on deck had slid off or had thrown themselves into the water. Many had been picked up by the numerous rescue vessels, while others had been caught in the ship's superstructures as it turned over. Little hope of survival was left to those who were in the interior spaces of the hull; some were able to take advantage of air pockets for a while, but the difficulties encountered in rescuing them allowed only a few of them to be rescued. Total losses amounted to 609 dead and 48 seriously wounded, not only from the crew of the *Novorossiysk*, but also among the rescue teams from other ships.

It was the greatest peacetime disaster in the history of the Russian Navy and, as is always the case, was followed by a serious inquest to determine causes and responsibilities. However, as we shall see, it also led to several absurd, if not ridiculous, conspiracy theories of political fantasy. The *Novorossiysk* was stricken from the list of Soviet ships on 4 February 1956 and the following summer the challenging work of recovery was begun. The wreck was floated with its keel uppermost and with a series of flotation cylinders lashed to both sides on 4 May 1957. Then the combination of ship and cylinders was towed to a small base with a suitable bottom, where the ship was righted and broken up.

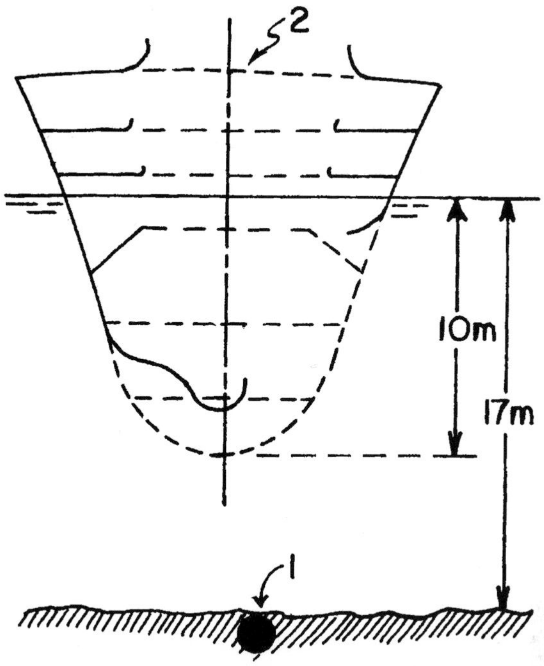

Transverse section of the *Novorossiysk* at the point of the mine explosion.
1. Probable position of the mine, not buried very deep in the mud of the seabed.
2. Structural damage from the double bottom to the forecastle deck.

The 'Malyshev Commission'

The authorities in Moscow reacted immediately to the *Novorossiysk* disaster and within a few days of the sinking a government commission was formed to shed as much light as possible on the event. Consisting of qualified naval technicians, it was headed by an Engineering Corps General, Vyacheslav Aleksandrovi Malyshev, Vice-president in Charge of the Council of Ministers, after which in 1950–1953 he had been Minister of Shipyard Industries. Admiral Sergei Gorshkov, recently appointed as Vice Commandant of the Soviet Navy, was designated to assist him. Moving quickly to Sevastopol, the commission proceeded to examine the hundreds of witnesses while frogmen and divers inspected the battleship's hull, assessing the damage insofar as possible, and sounding the bottom in the area all around mooring position No 3. The work proceeded expeditiously and by 17 November 1955, little more than two weeks after the tragic event, Malyshev was able to present a preliminary report to the Party Central Committee.

The conclusions of the document, which was quickly accepted and approved, indicated that first of all the grave damage to the *Novorossiysk* was not attributable to any malicious or accidental explosion (ammunition, fuel or flammable materials) internal to the ship, but rather to an external underwater explosion (on the seabed and without contact with the bottom of the hull) by a charge equivalent to 1000–1200kg of TNT. In other words, almost certainly, it was by a large German ground mine laid before 9 May 1944 – the date the Germans evacuated Sevastopol – and which surprisingly remained active and undiscovered (perhaps because it was buried in the mud), even though eleven years had passed since it had been laid and the fact that between 1944 and 1953 many mine-clearing operations had been carried out at various times. According to the commission's experts, the mine was probably a German RMH bottom type, suitable for laying by surface vessels and consisting of a robust wooden box (and thus non-magnetic) containing an 'enhanced' TNT charge equivalent to the charge indicated previously. The sensing element was a magnetic induction type, powered by special batteries that were estimated to have a maximum life of nine years. Between the sensor and the activation mechanism for the charge there was a so-called 'trigger clock' that constituted an effective magnetic mine-clearing countermeasure, by which the mine exploded only after a predetermined and variable number of activations or with a delay of several hours.

It was one of the most powerful mines among those discovered in the Bay of Sevastopol during clearing operations carried out at the time of and after the *Novorossiysk* incident, which led to the discovery of another nineteen large German magnetic mines, of which three were within 50 metres of mooring No 3. It is not known if any of these later mines found in 1955–1956 (and even later) were still active. It is likely, therefore, that activation of the mine that exploded at Sevastopol on 19 October 1955 represented an exceptional circumstance, both because its battery was still active and because of the abnormal functioning of the trigger mechanism. During the post-war period mooring No 3 had in fact been used 134 times by large ships (and thus with a large magnetic field), among which was the *Novorossiysk* herself on ten previous occasions. Among the many hypotheses put forward, one of the most likely was that there had been a mechanical blockage of the activation mechanism, which had occurred when the mine was laid or caused by the accidental bumping of the mine against an anchor or a chain, which would have rendered it temporarily 'deaf' to magnetic impulses, and then reactivated by a later contact with a chain during the battleship's final mooring manoeuvres. The Soviet frogmen carried out detailed soundings of the bottom around the presumed point of explosion and found a crater, even though it was not very pronounced, right under the estimated position of the ship's hull at 01:31 on 29 October. Finally, a series of tests with underwater charges confirmed that the impact on the *Novorssiysk*'s hull (plates bent inwards, structural damage, etc) was consistent with the explosion of a ground mine with a large 'enhanced' TNT charge.

Dutifully, the commission's report made reference to its assessments of other hypotheses for the possible origin of the explosion that led to the loss of the ship: a) torpedo fired by a submarine; b) attack by frogmen; c) sabotage. However, none of these hypotheses, in the light of the relevant technical discoveries, was judged to be credible.

Having dealt with the issue relating to the nature of the explosion, the Malyshev commission's report then addressed the issue of a more sensitive nature: an examination of the events and of the behaviour that led to the capsize and sinking of the *Novorossiysk* with the aforementioned heavy loss of human life. The conclusions led to serious disciplinary measures for several high-ranking officers, up to Vice Admiral Parkhomenko, who was held to be chiefly responsible for such substantial casualties and removed from his post in December 1955. At almost the same time the Commander-in-Chief of the Soviet Navy, Admiral of the Fleet Nikolai Kuznetsov, was forced to leave his post, as he was falsely charged with being part of the measures connected with the Sevastopol tragedy and was accused of responsibility in connection with the technical and organisational shortcomings that had come to light. However, in the opinion of almost every scholar of Russian military history, his replacement was driven by other considerations and had much larger ramifications, which went back to his strategic choices concerning development of the fleet. These differed substantially from the views of the powerful Minister of Defence, Marshal Zhukov, and most of all from the ideas of the First Secretary of the Communist Party Central Committee of the USSR, Nikita Khrushchev.

The early news issued by the Kremlin relating to the loss of the battleship was that it was 'an explosion caused by several accidental fires', a version that almost immediately proved to be false, but which remained the official line until almost the end of the 1980s. This was despite the fact that, even during the Cold War, it had become known unofficially that the cause of the explosion was a German mine, which in the West was accepted without much surprise by many authoritative specialised publications. In 1991, the year of the dissolution of the Soviet Union, a volume appeared in Russia in which the first doubts were expressed regarding the entire '*Novorossiysk* event': the 'mine theory' was challenged, while at the same time an attack by frogmen – and Italian veterans of the Decima MAS, no less – was presented as a more realistic possibility! Since that time, there has been a repetitious cycle of fanciful publications, with a flood of theories, each less likely than its predecessor, all however coming from the same Italian sources, none of which provide any direct witnesses or documentary evidence to back them up.

Forward section of the overturned wreck of the *Novorossiysk* shortly after its salvage at Sevastopol in May 1957. Note the large hole in the hull caused by the powerful underwater explosion that caused the ship to sink. (A Starace collection)

Chapter 10

RAISING, SECOND MODERNISATION AND LOSS OF THE *CONTE DI CAVOUR* (1940–1945)

Shortly after the *Conte di Cavour* was sunk at Taranto, Supermarina decided to raise the ship. The general plan was completed in early December by the Comitato Progetti Navi (CPN, or Ship Plans Committee), with the cooperation of the Direzione Generale delle Costruzioni Navali e Meccaniche (Maricost, or General Office for Naval and Mechanical Construction). Following his 'exoneration' in 1939 (under the racial laws he had been debarred because of Jewish ancestry), Naval Engineer General Umberto Pugliese had been recalled to service and was able to lend his valuable assistance. The project

Pumping water from the interior spaces of the *Cavour* that had been rendered watertight. (Courtesy G Chesi)

to raise the ship and its execution were entrusted to the CPN. The plan was based on the gradual pumping out of the watertight compartments, approaching them from the decks and isolating the spaces directly affected by the gash in the hull, as it was impossible to seal off the opening because of its inaccessible position and its large jagged shape. The ship was to be raised gradually through a series of phases, reversing those that had led to its grounding and, thus, to be brought to float in a condition of trim and stability corresponding to three contiguous flooded compartments, a condition this class of ship was designed to survive. It was necessary to make the hull, the forecastle and upper deck watertight by sealing the many existing openings and building up

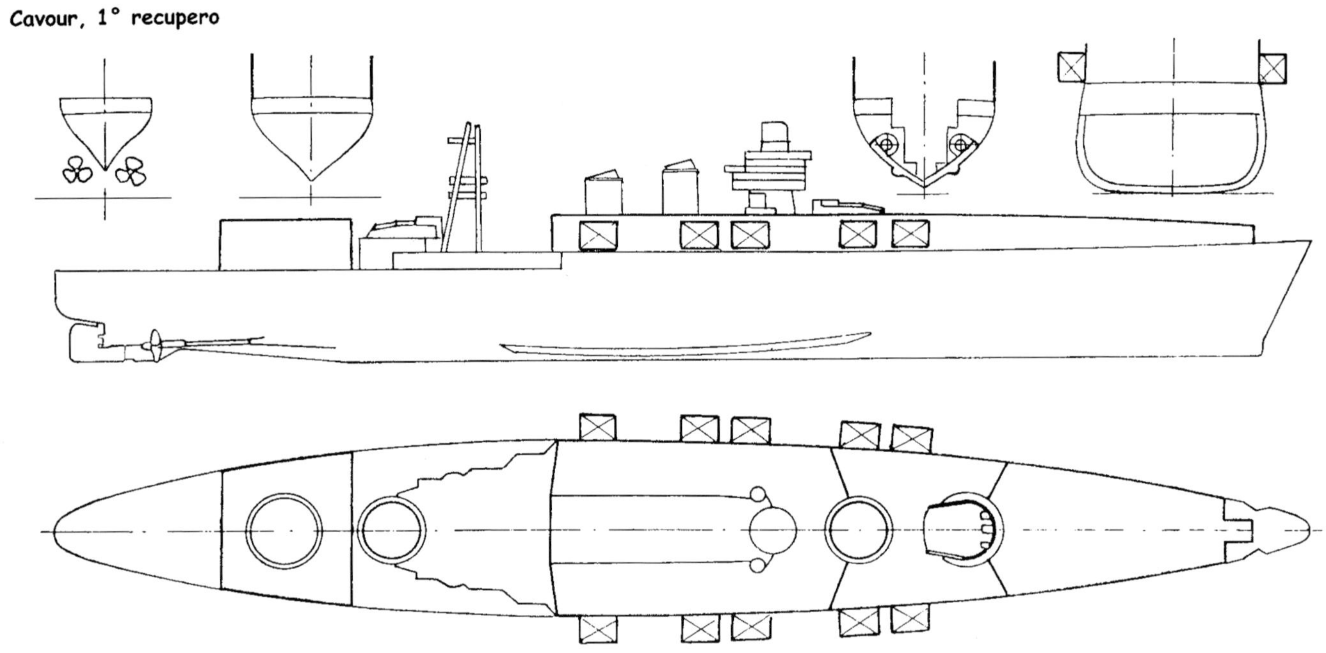

Construction of the cofferdams and positions of the lifting cylinders for the raising of the *Conte di Cavour* at Taranto in 1941. (Courtesy *Rivista Marittima*)

Building the cofferdam around the fore portion of the hull of the *Cavour*. (Courtesy G Chesi)

a cofferdam of solid plates fixed to the deck-edge from the bow to midship and closed thwartship abaft the second funnel, in order to provide sufficient freeboard; once this was done, it would be possible to proceed directly to emptying the spaces beneath the upper and forecastle decks. Air-tight caissons were to be applied to the external sides of the sealed area in order to provide lift and to stabilise the ship during the critical phase of raising. For the stern, it was proposed to apply the lifting cylinders so that the aft spaces would be drained as the ship was raised, as well as a concrete saddle under the stern in order to ensure stability during the operation. Provisions were to be made at the outset to remove equipment, material, and most of all, the guns and their

The advanced state of work during recovery of the *Conte di Cavour* at Taranto on 1 April 1941: the guns have been removed, the general lightening of the ship has been completed, and the large cofferdam forward is under construction. (Courtesy G Chesi)

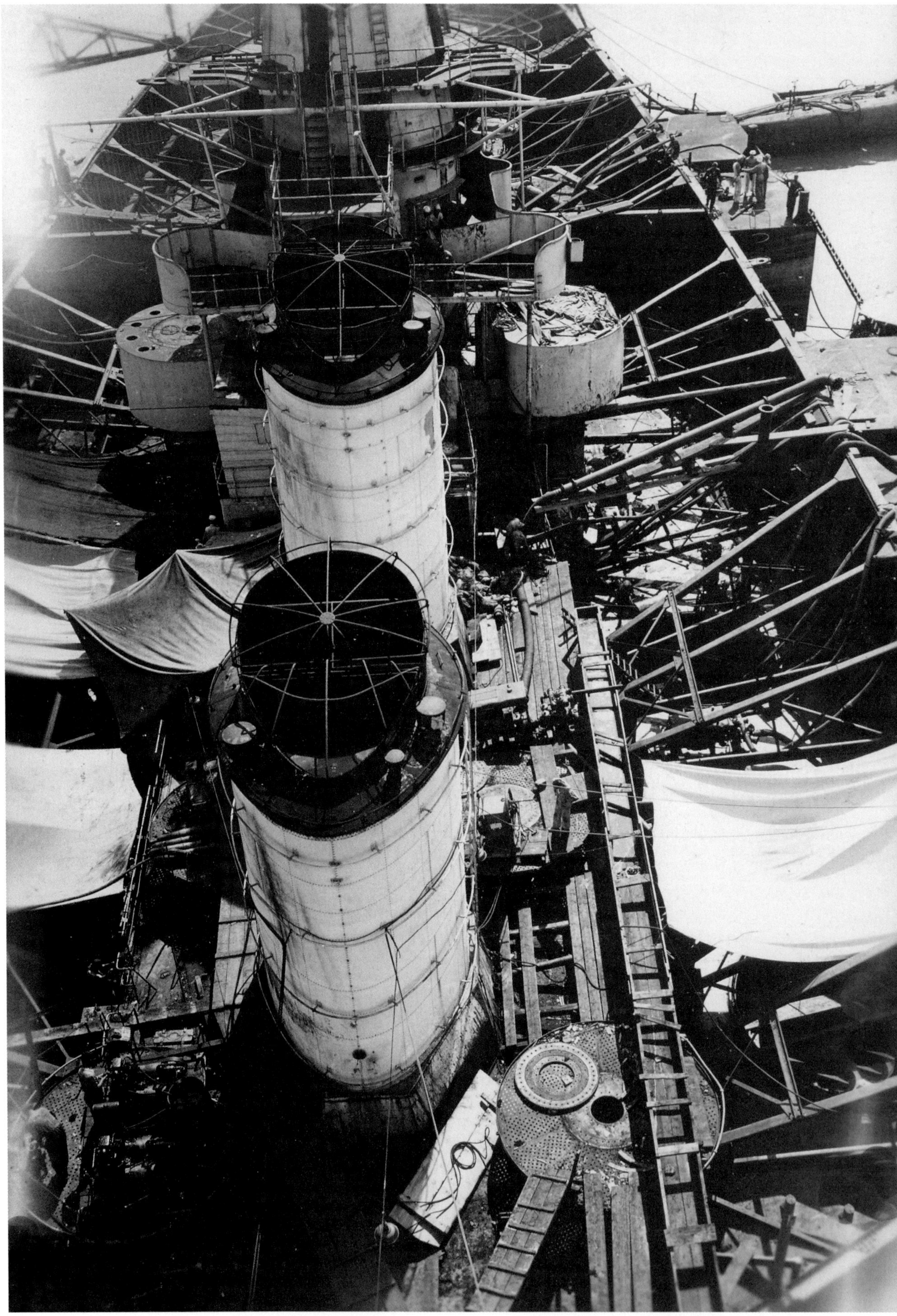

Advanced stage in the construction of the *Cavour's* forward cofferdam on 26 June 1941. (Courtesy G Chesi)

Partial view of the work in progress on the *Cavour* in late June 1941. (Courtesy G Chesi)

mountings so that they could be reconditioned and repaired, as well as to lighten the ship. The commission for the recovery was given to the specialised firm of Tripcovich s.a of Trieste in order to not siphon off men and equipment from the Taranto naval dockyard, which was already heavily committed to the tasks of a major naval base, including the recovery of the *Littorio* and the *Duilio*. CRDA of Trieste was assigned to build the lifting cylinders and the cofferdam.

Raising and reconditioning operations until transfer to Trieste (December 1940 – December 1941)

Throughout December 1940 work on the ship languished while awaiting the equipment and materials needed and because of the inability of the naval dockyard to provide support for the removal of guns and equipment from the ship. Operations could not begin until January 1941 with removal of the smaller guns and fire direction equipment, followed by removing the fire control stations, armour and guns of the main and secondary mountings. In early March the first elements of the large cofferdam were installed; it was completed on 1 April. Then the work of pumping out the water began and arrangements were made to place the two large lifting cylinders aft. During this phase the initial plan was revised to add the building a second cofferdam abaft around the No 4 main gun turret, with work assigned to be done by the Taranto naval dockyard, which completed the work in late May.

The operations to empty and seal off the fore section continued throughout April using high-capacity steam and electric pumps – whose power was supplied, respectively, by the submarine tender *Teseo*, by the tug *Ciclope* and by the submarine *Antonio Sciesa* – and, as the ship continued to dry out, with motor pumps. In early May the aft cofferdam was closed, after which, with some difficulty, all of the compartments above the first lower deck were drained; having been lightened by some 15,000 tons at this point, the ship began slowly to lift from the bottom. By early June the ship was floating freely and was in good vertical trim, with a displacement of about 45,000 tons and an average immersion of almost 15 metres, more than 23,000 tons of water having been discharged.

Raising continued with great caution because of the risks associated with large amounts of water still present in the hull. On

Taranto, 9 July 1941. The *Conte di Cavour* has been refloated. Note, on the hull the series of 'tidemarks' left by the ship's increasing immersion. (Courtesy G Chesi)

20 June the forecastle broke the surface, while aft work continued on dismantling and removing the roof armour and guns from turret No 4, which by now was dry inside the cofferdam. On 27 June part of the aft hull sides were above sea level while draining the aft spaces continued. Finally, on 2 July the upper deck emerged and the cofferdams, which had served their purpose, now began to be dismantled.

Meanwhile the problem of placing the ship in drydock for the initial reconditioning work had been solved. For technical and availability reasons placing the ship in one of the stone drydocks of the navy yard had been discounted, so it was decided to do the work in *GO 12*, then the largest floating drydock in Italy. However, this had a capacity of only 22,000 tons and a maximum depth of slightly more than 17 metres, so, on the one hand,

Above: The aft portion of the now floating *Cavour*. In the background, above the balancing cylinders, two 'Littorio' class battleships can be seen at anchor. (Courtesy G Chesi)

Left: The salvaged hull of the *Conte di Cavour* being towed through the ship canal towards Mar Piccolo in July 1941. (Courtesy G Chesi)

Left: Midship detail of the *Cavour* transiting the canal towards Mar Piccolo where the ship will soon be put in drydock. (Courtesy G Chesi)

Below: The *Conte di Cavour* entering floating drydock *GO 12*, which is positioned over the trench that had been previously dredged in the bottom of Mar Piccolo to allow the overturned hull of the battleship *Leonardo da Vinci* to be righted. (Courtesy G Chesi)

Left: Drydock *GO 12*, with the *Cavour* now high and dry, while being towed in September 1941 near the dockyard workshops that were heavily involved in reconditioning the main machinery. (Courtesy G Chesi)

Below: Another image of the move towards the dockyard being made by the *GO 12* with the *Cavour* in September 1941. (Courtesy G. Chesi)

modifications were required to increase its depth and capacity, while measures were taken to lighten the ship as much as possible, as it seemed preferable to move it into Mar Piccolo through the navigable canal rather than attempting to bring the floating dock into Mar Grande. Both operations turned out exceptionally well as, among other things, it had been possible to drain all of the ship's undamaged spaces; it was only necessary to place three large cylinders (which had been used to raise the ship) on the aft deck, filling them with many tons of seawater, in order to correct the trim by the head.

On the morning of 12 July, the *Cavour* was moved to Mar Piccolo, manoeuvred by six tugs, and the same afternoon was put into *GO 12*, which had already been flooded down and placed over the large trench that had been dredged after the First World War for righting the *Leonardo da Vinci*. The recovery operations were concluded on 16 July when the ship was completely dried out. It was then possible to fully ascertain the extent of damage for the first time and, thus, to proceed with clearing the debris, removing the remaining salvage equipment and cleaning the interior spaces. This was followed by thoroughly reconditioning the hull and as far as possible getting the ship in a state to allow a move to Trieste under its own power where the remaining repairs and planned upgrading could be carried out. The work was to be done mainly by the local Maricost and CRDA personnel.

The damage was greater than expected. The keel was rebuilt for a length of more than 25 metres; the outer plating, the double and triple hull structures, the ammunition space deckheads as well as the central pivot of No 2 main gun turret, the longitudinal and transversal bulkheads in the area of the opening and adjacent areas were all rebuilt. The deformed areas on the bottom between forward frames 26 and 47 were straightened, but the smaller deformations abaft forward frame 26 to aft frame 11, made by the ship accidentally scraping on the bottom of Mar Grande on 14 April 1939, noted previously, were not repaired. Other work related to reconditioning or rebuilding the bilge keels that had been torn off or damaged by the impact with the bottom and during the salvage operations, reinforcing the stern post, checking all of the rivets of the outer plates and inspecting all of the watertight bulkheads. On a positive note, except for the electrical system, the powerplant, including the auxiliary systems, the donkey boilers, the shafts and propellers, was essentially undamaged. The rudders, as well as the steering gear and associated machinery, the high-capacity pumps and various other components, including the outboard intakes and vents, scuppers, galleys, etc were examined and reconditioned; the shafts and propellers, which were slightly bent or damaged, were removed and reconditioned, and the electrical system was repaired to the extent necessary to enable the ship to make the move to Trieste. The hull bottom was completely cleaned and painted with a coat of rust-proofing and another coat of anti-fouling. At the same time, significant changes to the armament

Above and left: Taranto, December 1941. Two views of the *Cavour* ready to transfer to Trieste under her own power (note the temporary camouflage colours applied for the passage) to complete refitting and modernisation work. (A Molinari collection)

External views of the battleship *Conte di Cavour* based on the plans for the second moderrnisation

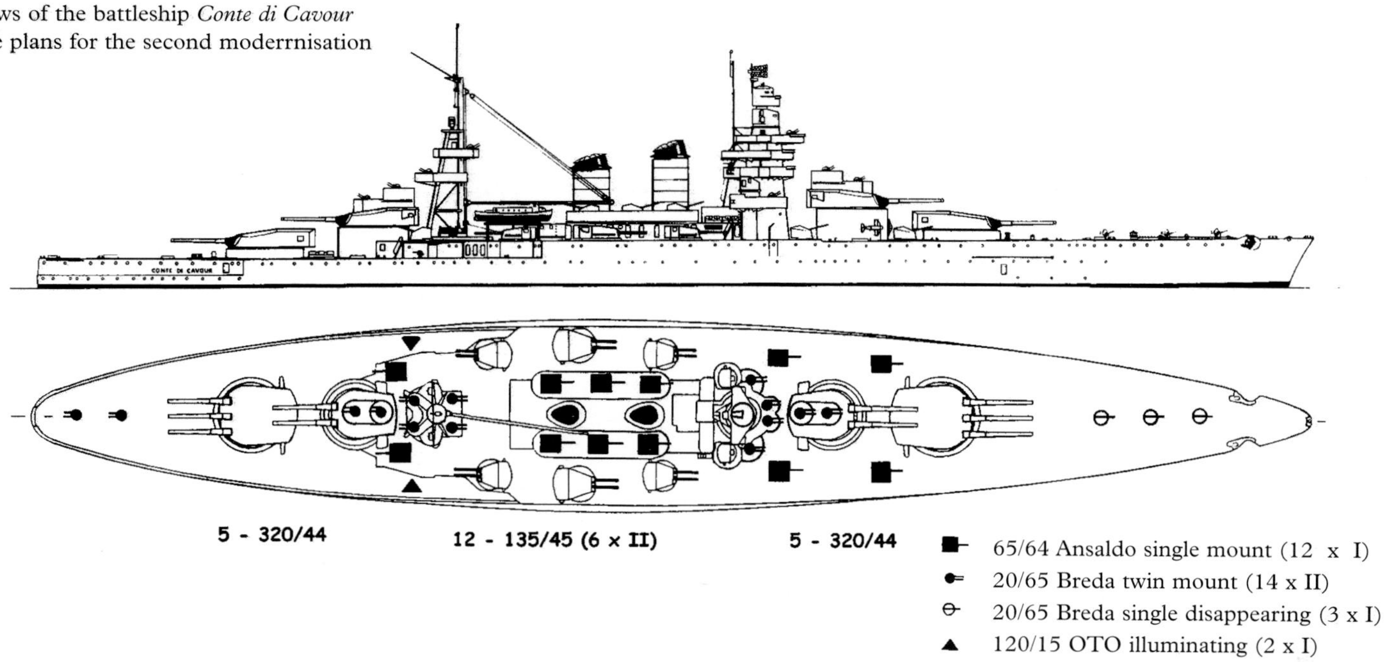

were considered that would have changed the original configuration by completely replacing the anti-torpedo-boat and anti-aircraft weapons, the main fire control centre and other systems associated with the guns.

The initial schedule of March 1941 called for all the work to be completed by 31 January 1942, but things went differently. Raising and drydocking the ship was only delayed by one month, attributable mainly to logistical problems, due in part to the priority given to repairing the *Vittorio Veneto* (which had been torpedoed at Gaudo on 28 March 1941), and to technical problems associated with the preparation and construction of the cofferdams. But the repair work done while the ship was in drydock encountered significant delays because of a shortage of manpower caused by the overriding requirement for the repair and construction of naval and merchant vessels during the second half of the year. The *Cavour* left floating drydock *GO 12*, after the dock had again been moved over the *da Vinci* trench, and in the following days was prepared and resupplied for the passage to Trieste under its own power, completely stripped of its guns, except for sixteen 37/54 and four 20/65 guns for anti-aircraft defence. Painted in an experimental 'Claudus' camouflage scheme (see Appendix 1), the ship departed Taranto on the morning of 22 December 1941 escorted by the destroyers *Sebenico* and *Freccia*, and reached the San Marco shipyard at Trieste on the afternoon of the 23rd, having maintained an average speed of about 20 knots, with the hull and powerplant standing up well during the voyage.

Preparations for readiness at Trieste until 8 September 1943

In early 1942 Italian industry experienced the first serious production hitches and delays due to the lack of qualified workers, which became acute in some shipyards (OTO in Livorno and the Cantieri Riuniti of Ancona), to the lack of raw materials, and the limitation on electricity consumption decreed by the Ministry of Corporations to the point that it reduced the working week by one or two days in shipyards where electrical welding was used extensively. These factors led to establishing priorities in the construction and fitting out of new warships that favoured anti-submarine and escort vessels. The *Conte di Cavour*, which had just arrived in Trieste, escaped those restrictions for the moment, partly because it did not require much new material (which moreover had already been assigned through March 1942), and because the capabilities of the San Marco yard of the CRDA enabled the work to be done without interfering with the simultaneous fitting out of the *Roma*, the construction of four new 'Aliseo' class torpedo boats and repair of the battleship *Vittorio Veneto* in Taranto following its torpedoing on 14 December 1941. The only impact was on the *Impero*, which at

The battleships *Conte di Cavour*, left, and *Roma*, respectively under repair and fitting out at Trieste in 1942.

The *Conte di Cavour* moored at the fitting out quay at the CRDA San Marco shipyard in Trieste in early 1942.

In a photo presumably from the early months of 1943, detail of the forward 320/44 turrets of the *Cavour* while fitting out at Trieste. The installation of the ten main guns had been completed the preceding October, along with several improvements to the mountings and systems for fire control. (A Molinari collection)

Left: The construction of two long platforms, abreast the funnels of the *Conte di Cavour*, designed to mount six new model 65/64 anti-aircraft guns, three per side. (A Starace collection)

the time was in Venice and whose transfer to Trieste was not deemed appropriate in order to avoid having three battleships in a restricted area of water being used for fitting out and because the workforce was already busy with the aforementioned work.

In mid-January 1942 the time needed to ready the *Cavour* was dictated by its armament, whose completion was forecast for August 1942. All of the other scheduled work was to have been completed within the same time frame (January–July). The situation envisaged at the time can be summarised as follows: armament, installation of new motors in the main gun turrets and other equipment by San Giorgio, mounting of the main guns (with tests and trials between late August and early September 1942), preparation of the 135/54 guns by OTO (almost completed at La Spezia) and producing the 65/64 AA guns (under way at Ansaldo in Genoa), reinstallation of the firing systems with modifications; for the electrical system, replacement of the aft diesel generator group, completing the main cable and distribution systems and the rest of the light and power systems, replacing or reconditioning various electrical motors; for fitting out, modification of the ventilation system, installing new refrigerators, clean-up of accommodation spaces, galleys and other spaces; for the powerplant, replacement of some auxiliary machinery with more modern types, replacement or modification of some turbine components and of the evaporation system tubing; for the hull and steering gear, overhaul and improvement of watertight compartmentation and installation of a new auxiliary rudder.

In the following months the work did not make the hoped-for headway because of the priority given to new vessels that were needed more urgently: torpedo boats, 'Gabbiano' class corvettes, motor torpedo boats, motorised barges, merchant ships, and the repair at Taranto of the *Littorio*, which had been torpedoed during the battle of mid-June. At the end of July 1942 the first doubts as to the wisdom of completing work on the *Cavour* began to surface officially within the navy's technical departments. On 22 July officials at Maricost presented the situation to the Navy Staff (Maristat), observing that, without even including the weapons, 300,000 work days [man-days] would be needed to ready the ship. On 9 August Maristat reiterated that work on the battleship was to continue and invited Maricost to evaluate withdrawal of personnel from the *Cavour* in order to assign them to priority tasks and to avoid completion being put off indefinitely. The Inspectorate for Construction, Fitting Out and Testing New Ships (Marinalles) organised the work so as to not interfere with more urgent construction and the workforce available was used to make operational the essential parts of the ship (hull, armament and powerplant) before doing other work.

Around the end of August 1942, the 320/44 guns were

Left: Ansaldo-Terni 1939 65/64 anti-aircraft guns in single shielded mounts. These were modern guns with a high rate of fire (one round every three seconds), but they were only produced in limited numbers.

The forward twin 320/44 superfiring turret of the *Cavour* photographed at Trieste in late spring 1944 showing the new arrangements for the twin 20mm guns on its roof. (A Starace collection)

installed and the roofs of the main gun turrets were once again closed, while the machinery and other components of the gun mountings would soon be ready as well; the first trials were scheduled for early November and the official tests between December and January. The medium-calibre turrets, which had already been mounted, were ready to receive the new 135/54 guns and by December installation of the new main fire control centre (the same type used on the 'Capitani Romani' class cruisers) and firing network were to be completed. Progress on the electrical system was running further behind schedule: the forward diesel generator group and the aft turbo-generator and the replacement cables were not yet ready, whereas the electric motors being repaired ashore were completed. That same month modification work to host the new SDT and radiotelegraph station was completed on the bridge tower. Up to the end of November 1942, work continued at a moderate pace, considering the continuous modifications and improvements being made to the structures and systems. At that date all of the main

The original 120mm twin turrets of the *Cavour*, modified to mount two OTO Mod 1938 135/45 guns, shown being installed at Trieste in the early months of 1943. (A Starace collection)

Trieste, spring 1943. The crew of the battleship *Conte di Cavour* drawn up on the quay in front of their ship on which can be seen a pair of the newly installed 135/45 guns.

gun mountings were functional, except for the shell carousels, and the medium-calibre installations were in more or less the same state. Final tests for both types were now scheduled for mid-March 1943. On the other hand, the anti-aircraft armament, which now included four 90/50 guns, had not yet been installed. The 90mm guns were being tested by Ansaldo at Genoa and the 65/64 guns were awaiting assembly, while arrangement of the associated mountings was still under study; the 90/50 guns were intended as one-for-one replacements of 65mm guns, probably the four that were located abreast of No 2 320mm turret. All of the fire control instrumentation, a large part of which was new (main SDT, revolving rangefinder turret, medium-calibre SDT, cables, night APG for the main guns, anti-aircraft fire control centres), was to be embarked by March 1943, except for the two independent main gun fire control positions, which were already in place on turrets Nos 2 and 3, along with the old but reconditioned rangefinders.

The powerplant was to be ready for trials at the ship's moorings in March, but not so the electrical system because of delays in laying the cables for the various outlets, which would not be ready before May 1943, although the generators, new or reconditioned, would be ready by February. With respect to the communications systems, it was intended to install an ultra-short wave IMCA radio system, which would have been of an experimental nature with a view to its possible employment on the carrier *Aquila* for naval air use. Work on the hull, which included improvements to the watertight compartmentalisation, repositioning some of the deck plating that had been dismantled to remove the old bow, and replacement of the armoured belt where it had been removed, was to have been completed in February 1943. Fitting of the safety and floatation systems (large and small pumping network, fire suppression systems, ventilation arrangements, etc) were behind schedule, as well as personnel services (accommodation, galleys, washing facilities, sick-bays, laundries). Finally, there were major changes being made to the bridge tower (admiral's, command and searchlight bridges) and the aft tripod (signals bridges). At the time, work on the *Cavour* saw some 1500 personnel on board and 500 ashore but, according to Marinalles, even with those numbers and at that pace the ship would not be ready before the end of June 1943.

On 17 January Supermarina decided, as a general principle, that for new construction priority was to be given to destroyers, torpedo boats and corvettes and, specifically, that workers assigned to the *Cavour* should be considered as reserves for the six 'Ariete' class torpedo boats awarded to the San Marco shipyard. In February the main and medium gun turrets were tested 'dry' [without firing]; live-fire tests were scheduled for March. The platforms for the 65/64 and 90/50 guns were also prepared and the main fire control centre was installed, while the medium-calibre SDTs were to be installed as work continued on modifications to the bridge tower and associated platforms. Progress was also being made on the electrical systems: all of the turbo-generator groups were practically complete and the forward diesel generators were ready; the power and lighting systems were 55 per cent and 50 per cent complete. Moored testing of the powerplant remained scheduled for March. Unfortunately, no documentation has been found on the progress of work from the end of February to June 1943 when, with the invasion of Italian national territory imminent, work was suspended, along with all work on all of the other major ships.

At that time the following remained to be done: modifications to the superstructures, embarkation of the anti-aircraft armament, completion of the gunnery networks and of the electrical and safety systems. In addition to the officers and crew on the manning list, 200 workers remained on board to perform maintenance and to complete work on the safety and anti-aircraft armaments systems, while it was estimated that another six months of work with 1000 workers would be needed to complete all work on the ship. As a result of the suspension of work, on 25 July 1943 the ship was moved to the head of the fitting out pier so as to leave the quay free for readying other vessels. The Navy Staff estimated that refitting work on the *Cavour* could not be finished before the end of winter 1943, but at the time of the armistice, it was far from complete. Because of continuous changes to the reconditioning and upgrading programme, all of the forecast schedules had been rendered invalid, not through serious obstacles, but because of the incremental effect of small delays due to prioritising other building requirements.

The fundamental error was wanting to save and modernise a ship of modest combat value, a fact that was evident in the early months of the war. Most of all, from early 1942 the shortage of fuel oil and of escort destroyers had practically halted the activities of the other three surviving small battleships. No one, however, put forth the case in time to give up the project and limit it to raising the wreck and salvaging its materials. That being said, it must be added that the attempted overhaul did not interfere very much with programmes for new construction and ship repairs, either naval or mercantile, at least insofar as it related to the CRDA workload. The only ship to be sacrificed was the much more important *Impero*, which was also fitting out; but she could not have been completed in a reasonable time frame, even if work on the *Cavour* had been suspended. The subject of the workforce retained in Trieste on pretence of completing work on the *Cavour* is another story. There, at the insistence of the most capable Italian shipyard complex, the navy agreed not to scatter its specialised and well-qualified personnel to other yards that were in need.

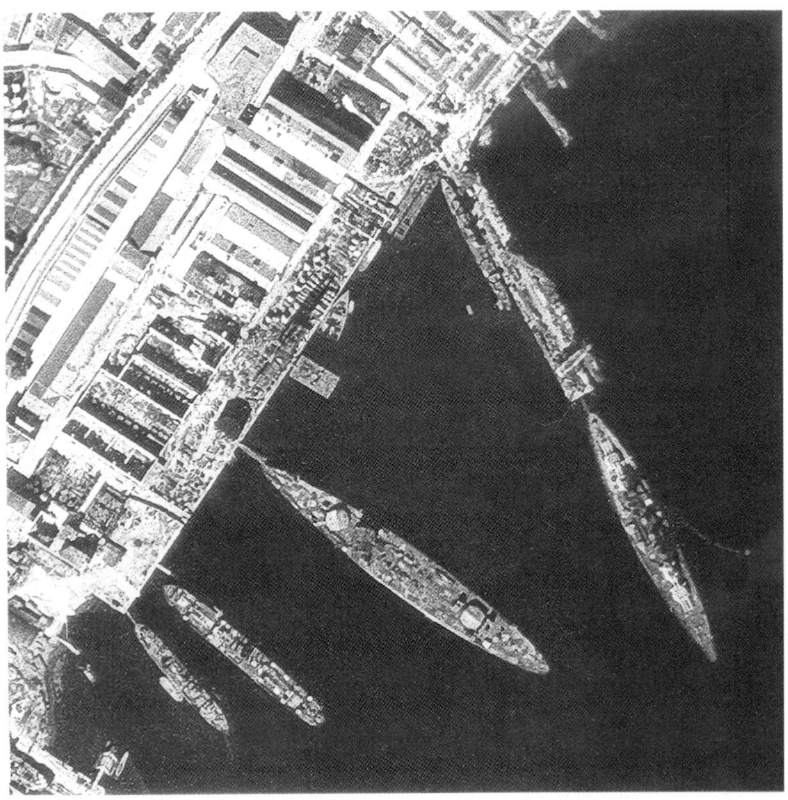

Aerial photo of the San Marco yard at Trieste taken on 8 July 1944. From the left can be seen two merchant ships, the uncompleted battleship *Impero* moored bow-on to the fitting out quay, and the *Conte di Cavour*.

From 8 September 1942 to breaking up in 1952–1953

At the time of the armistice, in Trieste there were under construction or fitting out two battleships, two cruisers, two destroyers, six torpedo boats and a corvette, without counting the merchant shipping. Operational naval forces were very meagre: on the afternoon of 8 September 1943 setting sail for Pola were the school ships *Amerigo Vespucci*, *Cristoforo Colombo* and *Palinuro*, the old torpedo boat *Insidioso* and *MAS 516*; remaining were only the corvette *Berenice* nearing the end of its fitting out, the minelayer *Fasana*, the auxiliary cruiser *Ramb III (D 6)* and two small local use ships. Bound for Venice at the same time were the large motorships *Saturnia* and *Vulcania*, on which the cadets from the normal and reserve naval academy courses were embarked, later to head south. Trieste was also the location of the headquarters of XXIII Army Corps and was, therefore, the transit point for German army units to the Balkans. Using this as a pretext, in preparation for Operation 'Achse' (the neutralisation of Italy in case of defection), during those days various German units had bivouacked on quay VI in the port, with Italian authorisation.

On 8 September, in the hours following the announcement of the armistice, Captain Giuseppe Lazzani, ranking officer of the local Marinalles and the officer in charge of the *Cavour*, increased security measures at the naval shore installations and in the areas adjacent to the shipyards (San Marco and the adjacent Trieste naval dockyard). At 05:00 the German troops present in the Duca d'Aosta port easily took control of the area, of the merchant ships that were moored there, and of a 76mm battery that was in place to defend the seaward barrages. From there on the morning of 9 September they sank the *Berenice*, which was attempting to

The battleship *Conte di Cavour* in Trieste following suspension of work in June 1943, here in a photo probably taken in late 1944.

Detail of forward turrets and the new bridge tower of the *Cavour*, now in a state of abandonment in late 1944.

The capsized wreck of the *Conte di Cavour* – sunk at Trieste by air bombardment in February 1945 – in a 1946 photo.

leave the port to reach Pola and, from Opicina, where a battalion of the German 71st Infantry Division was billeted, they drove off the torpedo boats *Audace* and *Insidioso*, which had just arrived to escort the *Duilio* and *Giulio Cesare* to the base at Pola. The same morning, the commander of Marina Trieste, Captain Lorenzo Stallo, having determined that it was not possible for any ships to leave, had many of the naval personnel who were ashore assemble on the *Cavour*, joining the crew. Then, based on orders received by telephone from Pola and confirmed by Venice, he proceeded to render inoperable for about three months machinery and engines of naval vessels about to enter service (torpedo boat *Gladio* and corvette *Egeria*). Nothing was done for the *Cavour* and the *Impero*, the first of which needed at least six months, and the second eighteen, to reach completion. During the 10th, when units of the German 71st Division had entered the city and were occupying the army corps and territorial defence headquarters, which had been abandoned or cleared, Stallo and Lazzani saw to the destruction of secret files, what was left in the safes, of small arms in the naval shore installations, destruction of the *Cavour*'s combat ensign and of the weapons on board all of the ships, as well as dispersing the personnel. On the 11th all of the ships were captured by the Germans, but the two officers, even though authorised to leave Trieste, stayed behind for some time, locating and helping navy personnel.

Very little information has been found regarding what happened to the *Cavour* during the months of German occupation. Having discarded the possibility of using the ship as a floating battery, it was stripped of materials that could be used for other purposes. It did not become part of the Kriegsmarine and was left in a state of almost complete abandon. The ship survived until February 1945 without any apparent damage from the numerous Allied air raids conducted against Trieste beginning in April 1944 – but not from those made on 17 and 20 February 1945, carried out by the US 15th Air Force, based at fields on the Foggia plain. Due to damage suffered most probably in the second of these attacks, the *Cavour* sank on the night of 23/24th or, less likely, on the night of 24/25th. Based on an examination made in 1950 in preparation for raising the wreck, a single leak of modest size was found near the aperture for the rudder-post, caused by a bomb that had exploded nearby. Other bombs hit the port side of the *Cavour*, causing widespread destruction to the topside and above the armoured deck between forward frames 15 and 55 with extensive stripping of the hull side and upper deck plating. In the absence of any preventive action the flooding spread through piping and open watertight doors and the ship went down by the stern until it hit the bottom.

The reaction to contact with the seabed caused the water within the hull to shift and the ship to turn over. The ship rested on the bottom at an average depth of 12 metres, with a 15-degree heel to starboard; the superstructures, the funnels, masts and main gun turrets all buried themselves almost completely in the

The hull of the *Cavour*, raised from the bottom in March 1952, was soon after towed, while still upturned, to the area of Punta Sottile in the Bay of Muggia (Trieste) where it would be scrapped. (M Cigona photo)

Situation of the wreck of the *Conte di Cavour* in 1945–1946 (R Maggi drawing)

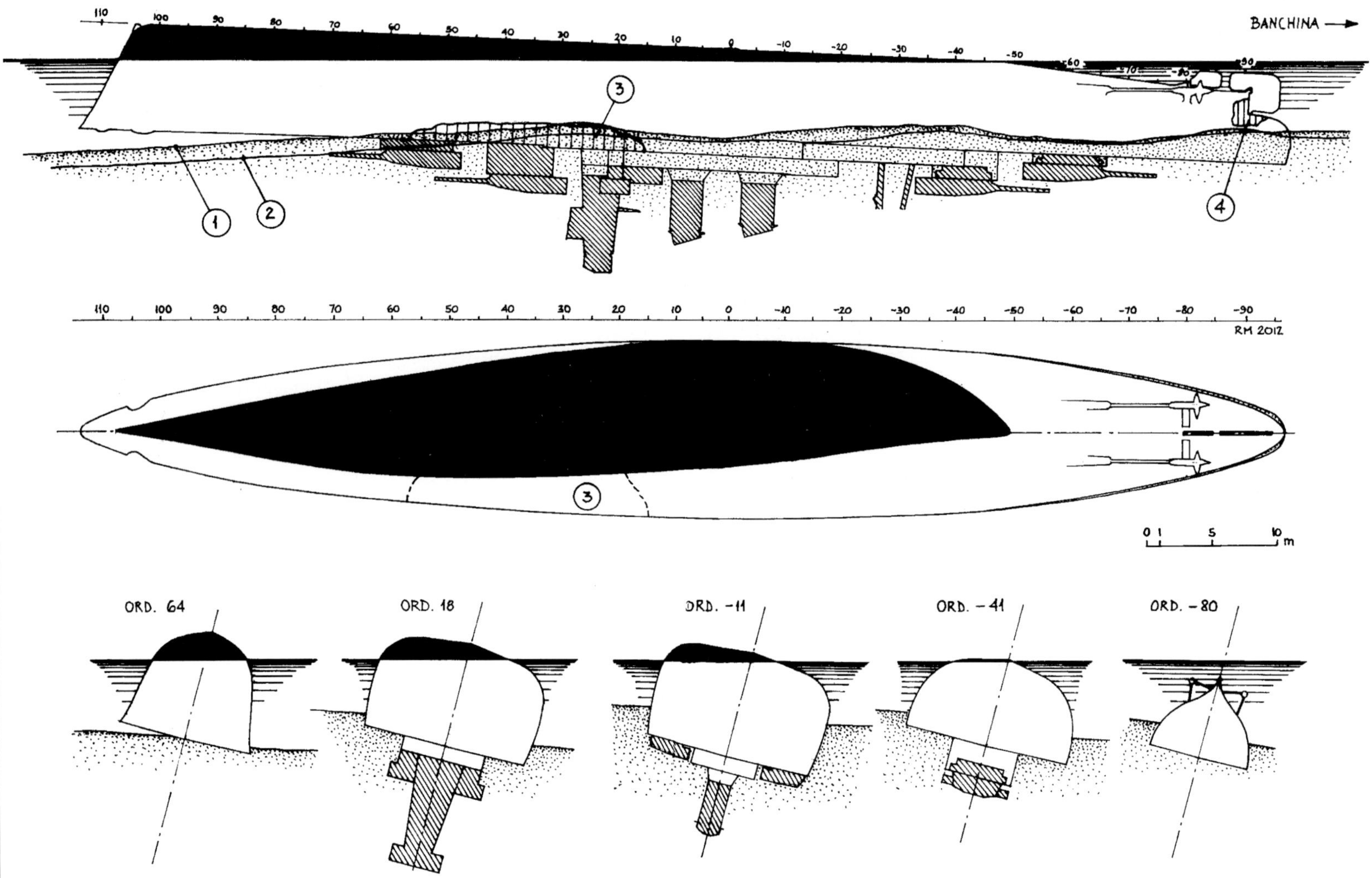

■ Portions above water
□ Visible submerged portions
Portions sunk in mud
Portions destroyed, removed or loosened prior to salvage

1. Profile of seabed, left side
2. Profile of seabed, right side
3. Area damaged on port side
4. Hole in external plating near the main rudder

Note
Port and starboard refer to the ship afloat looking forward. The transverse sections are represented looking aft.

mud; the sturdier features retained their original shape, but the less robust were broken and twisted. Only part of the hull bottom showed above the surface. The wreck lay there for a long time, until on 8 December 1950, at the time of the Allied military administration in Trieste, work began to raise the ship and clear the waters in front of the shipyards. The operation, which was awarded to the Officine Armando Vasi of La Spezia, was completed on 29 March 1952 and the wreck, still upside-down but floating, was towed to the Punta Sottile beach on the bank opposite the Bay of Muggia, where it was broken up.

Chapter 11

COMPARISONS AND CONCLUSIONS

Compared with the 'Littorio' class – which belonged to a generation of battleships that were relatively similar to each other, as some of their main characteristics derived from international agreements – it is more difficult to make comparisons between the rebuilt 'Conte di Cavour' and 'Duilio' classes and other ships of equivalent category, as no battleships from any other country had undergone such radical transformation. In truth, many battleships from that era had undergone extensive modernisation during the 1920s and 1930s, such as three of the five 'Queen Elizabeth' class and the battlecruiser *Renown* and all of the Japanese dreadnoughts that the 1922 Treaty of Washington had left to that country. None of those, however, had seen substantial modification of their main gun armament, as they already had effective guns that were also of large calibre (from 356 to 406mm); finally, they were all ships whose original size and characteristics were superior to the Italian ships and as such do not allow for a useful comparison. The case was somewhat different for the new French 'Dunkerque' class, against which the 'Cavours' were a direct response to the first of that class and which served as a design benchmark. With this as a premise and considering that it was impractical to compare the four Italian ships with the Japanese battleships, below is an illustrative comparison with the 'Dunkerque', for reasons already mentioned, and with the *Warspite* – with her sisters *Valiant* and *Queen Elizabeth* – which was the main adversary of the two 'Cavours' among the modernised British battleships in the early months of the conflict in the Mediterranean.

Thus, the 'Cavour' and 'Duilio' classes were undoubtedly inferior in armament and protection to the *Warspite* and superior to it with respect to speed. They might seem almost equal to the 'Dunkerque' with respect to armament, but inferior in speed and protection. The limited electrical power installed on the *Warspite* should be noted, a characteristic of all British battleships, where hydraulics were preferred for many of the systems.

A comparative study by the Regia Marina Staff in 1937

It is more interesting to assess the level of knowledge that the Regia Marina hierarchy had of the combat power of the 'Cavour' class at the end of the 1930s, that is to say, at the time of their re-entry into service. When their reconstruction was decided upon between 1932 and 1933, only France figured in the group of great naval powers as a possible enemy; but when in 1937 rebuilding was complete, the politico-military picture had changed and Britain was now among those. Therefore, in a manual for combat

THE REBUILT ITALIAN BATTLESHIPS COMPARED

Principal characteristics on entry in service (approximate values)	'Conte di Cavour' class, 1937 (variations for 'Duilo' class, 1940)	*Dunkerque*, 1937 (*Strasbourg*, 1938)	*Warspite*, 1937
Displacement full load	29,050 t (29,200 t)	35,500 t (36,380 t)	37,000 t
Maximum power output	95,000 shp (85,000 shp)	114,000 shp (115,000 shp)	81,000 shp
Maximum speed (knots)	28 (26.5) at full load	30 at normal load	23.5
Range (miles at knots)	6300 at 12 knots (4400 at 12 knots)	7850 at 15 knots	7580 at 12 knots
Main gun (mm)	10–320/44	8–330/52	8–381/42
– Anti-torpedo	12–120/50 (12–135mm)	16–130/45	8–152/45
– Anti-aircraft	8–100/47 (10–90/50)	8–102/45	
	8–37/54 (15–37/54)	10–37/50	32–40/40
	12–13.2 (16–20/65)	32–13.2	16–12.7
Protection (mm)			
– Vertical (max)	250	225 (283 inclined)	330
– Horizontal (max)	30 + 80	115/125 + 40	146/159 total
– Underwater	Reduced Pugliese system	Multiple longitudinal bulkheads	Outer blisters
– Main gun turrets (max)	280	330 (360)	330
– Main gun barbettes (max)	50 + 240	310 (340)	254
– Conning tower (max)	260 (250)	270	76
Installed electrical power (Kw)	2600 (3000)	4800	2400

The *Andrea Doria*, ready to return to service after modernisation, in October 1940. (F Petronio collection)

at the time the Navy Staff looked at the question of selection of combat ranges of the 'Cavours' compared with the French battleships ('Dunkerque', 'Courbet' and 'Bretagne' classes) and British ('Queen Elizabeth', 'Royal Sovereign', 'Nelson', 'Renown' classes and *Hood*) then in service, based on experimental data and as a function of the characteristics of armament, vertical and horizontal protection and of the range and angle of impact. The data had been calculated based on the information available at the time and on the basis of tests with modern armour; the protective capability of armour prior to 1918 was assumed to be equal to the modern plates with a thickness reduced by one-tenth. The quality and characteristics of the steel of the plates and of the projectiles was assumed to be equivalent. The picture that emerged, and of which a brief account will be given, appeared to be quite worrying for the Italian Navy hierarchy.

The vertical protection on the 'Cavours' was capable of being pierced by the British 381/42 (where 'piercing' was understood to be the complete penetration of the armour by an intact armour-piercing round and exploding inside the ship) up to 18,000 metres, while the horizontal armour could be penetrated from 16,500 metres on up, as long as there were no 'immune areas', whatever the range. With respect to the 406/45 guns of the 'Nelson' class, vertical protection could be penetrated up to about 22,500 metres and horizontal from 18,000 metres on up, with no immune areas. With the parties reversed, the vertical protection of the 'Queen Elizabeth' and 'Royal Sovereign' classes appeared to be able to be penetrated by the 320/44 guns of the 'Cavour' up to 16,000 metres and horizontal protection from 20,500 metres on up; these values, referred to the 'Renown' class and the *Hood*, rose, respectively, to almost 22,000 metres and up to about 18,000 metres for vertical protection, as well as from 20,000 metres and from 20,500 metres and up for horizontal; the horizontal protection of the 'Nelson' was practically impenetrable and vertical only at less than 11,500 metres.

As to the French battleships, the vertical protection of the 'Cavours' appeared to be capable of being penetrated by the 330/52 guns of the 'Dunkerque' class up to 26,000 metres – this gun was obviously credited with a penetration capability greater than that of the British 381/41 (correctly) and greater than that of the 406/45 (incorrectly) – and horizontal from 22,500 metres on up; the 340/45 guns of the 'Bretagne' class would have prevailed over the vertical protection of the 'Cavours' up to almost 14,000 metres and horizontal from 20,500 metres and up; the 305/45 guns of the 'Courbet' class, respectively, up to about 12,500 metres and from 25,000 metres and upwards. With the parties reversed, the 320/44 of the 'Cavours' would have been able to penetrate the vertical protection of the 'Bretagne' up to almost 20,000 metres and horizontal from 21,500 and up, as well as the vertical protection of the 'Courbet' to almost 20,500 metres and horizontal from 23,000 metres and up; there were no data on the effectiveness of the 320/44 against the 'Dunkerque', probably because the characteristics of the armour were not known.

Based on these calculations, against the gun/armour combination the 'Cavours' could successfully challenge only the oldest French battleships, compared with which they had better zones of immunity, but they were unable to face off against any British battleship, with the partial exception only of the 'Renown' class. Compared with the 'Dunkerque' class they likewise appeared to be at a decided disadvantage. However, the 'Cavours' were even more disadvantaged if their most favourable ranges for opening fire are taken into account – as reported in the same document, these were 22,000 metres under conditions of good visibility and 24,000 metres under conditions of excellent visibility. In other words, the 320/44 guns were effective against the vital parts of most enemy ships only at great distances, when, as was already known, the accuracy of fire could not be relied upon.

The high-ranking officers of the Italian Navy downplayed these unfavourable comparisons based on two considerations, namely: that in the French and British ships the areas protected by maximum-thickness armour were generally less in surface area than on the 'Cavour' types, and that the protection outside the areas of maximum protection was of lesser thicknesses than those of the two Italian battleship classes. That led to the conclusion that the disadvantages of the 'Cavour' could be nullified or very much reduced. In truth, it was all meant to demonstrate the greater surface of maximum thickness of the 'Cavours' compared with the French and British battleships; in addition, at the time the doubts about the actual usefulness of protection outside of the armoured redoubt were already well known and widely disseminated.

It is easy to observe how the performance of the 320/44 was much inferior to that of the 381/50 of the 'Littorio', for which similar comparisons were made. But, the difference in penetration was significantly reduced regarding the horizontal armour because of the very flat trajectory of the main guns of the larger Italian battleships.

Ultimately, the Regia Marina Staff, even before the conflict, had clear and accurate knowledge of the marked ballistic inferiority and protection of the rebuilt battleships even compared with older rival ships.

Concluding considerations

Conclusions as to the value of these ships can be drawn from the preceding chapters, except for a few clarifications. From the structural point of view the partial reconstruction of the hull with its lengthening improved the hull's performance but, especially on the 'Cavours', the outer plating was plagued by persistent leaks where the new structure met the old hull in areas that it was impossible to drain, with the resultant weighing down of the bow with several dozen tons of water. Later remedies – which seem to have been confined to *Cavour* herself – limited the problem. These problems were also manifest in the 'Duilios', but to a lesser degree.

Much has been said about the main armament. The 320/44 were far less capable than either the British 381/42 or the French 330/52 guns. But the most serious shortcoming, and the one that most worried the Regia Marina commands and technical offices, was the significant salvo dispersion, which between 1937 and 1940 could only be minimised. However, the 330/52 of the 'Dunkerque' class turned out to be an even greater source of concern in the Marine Nationale, as the excellent capabilities of these guns were offset by serious shortcomings in the functioning of the quadruple turrets and a very alarming salvo dispersion in extent and irregularity (from 200 to 1000 metres); when added to other design and construction deficiencies, such as mediocre seakeeping qualities or the sensitivity of the steering, it considerably reduced their fighting potential. The secondary, anti-aircraft and anti-torpedo armament, of the 'Cavours' proved to be barely adequate, even though it was equal to the most modern Italian, French and German battleships, not to mention the failure to develop a dual-purpose anti-aircraft and anti-torpedo gun. Added to that, the 100/47 guns were fewer in number than those embarked on many cruisers, both light and heavy. Compared with the 'Cavours', armed with the mediocre 120/50 and 100/47 guns, the 'Duilios' received the excellent 135/45 guns and the 90/50 AA guns that had been adopted for the 'Littorio' class. The biggest problems, however, stemmed from the inadequacy of the mountings, especially with respect to the 90/50 stabilisation system which was soon deactivated, and the organisation of the AA and night-time fire direction; remedial steps were eventually taken in light of wartime experience, but not until 1941 and then with some difficulty, but it never came close to progress being made by other navies. This was, however, a shortcoming common to all Italian vessels.

The battleship *Giulio Cesare* on a wartime operation in January 1942.

No comment is necessary with respect to the armour other than its inadequacy; the layout and thickness of the horizontal armour was similar to that of most of the modernised battleships and to some of the latest generation. In any case, during their wartime activity the 'Cavours' and the 'Duilios' did not suffer direct bomb damage and only one hit by artillery rounds, namely the 15in shell that struck the *Giulio Cesare* at Punta Stilo. The episode was not critical, as the shell exploded outside of the hull, after having gone through a funnel; however, the cap, projected downward by the explosion, penetrated the forecastle deck, protected by 30mm of armour, and the upper deck before coming to a halt against the internal facing of the side armour, which suffered no appreciable damage.

Underwater protection was also barely adequate. In order not to compromise speed, it consisted of a modification of the Pugliese protective system inside the original hulls and not of an external application of blisters, as on the 'Littorios'. Because of this limitation there was already an awareness at the time that the system would not absorb all of the energy of a torpedo explosion, especially at the extreme end of the redoubt as a result of the narrowing of the hull. As a consequence, the survival of the ships against such threats would have depended in large measure on the structural strength and compartmentalisation of the hull, and the effectiveness of the damage-control systems, which even

The battleship *Duilio* at a mooring in one of the battleship net enclosures in Taranto's Mar Grande in 1942.

before the experience of Taranto had proved rather lacking. There is no direct proof of the effectiveness of the underwater protection, as the torpedoes fitted with magnetic fuses that hit the *Cavour* and the *Duilio* during the 'night of Taranto' exploded under the hull, therefore in an area that lacked any protection apart from the triple bottom; this was true of all other battleships of every era, with only the partial exception of the Japanese 'Yamato' class super-battleships.

This damage could be compared to that suffered by the British battleship *Valiant* from a 230kg high-explosive warhead (compared to the 176kg of the torpedoes used at Taranto) that was placed under the hull during the incursion made by the Decima Flottiglia MAS at Alexandria on the night of 18/19 December 1941. In all three cases, in fact, the charges exploded under the hull as well as reacting with the seabed, which accentuated the effect, in the area of the fore main gun turrets (on the *Valiant* exactly under A turret, on the two Italian battleships between turrets 1 and 2). Thus, the relative underwater protective systems were not affected. It seems, however, more difficult to extend the comparison to the attack against the *Queen Elizabeth* at the same time, as the charge was placed by another pair of Italian frogmen on the bottom of the hull, but beneath the boiler spaces and further spread out than during the other attack, so the target was likely to ship a greater amount of water. As a result of the explosion, the *Valiant* suffered a breach and some deformation of the bottom over a total area of 9.15 x 18.30 metres, between frames 29 and 52, with the keel bent to a maximum distortion of 20cm, but without breaking. The damaged ship settled 1.6 metres down by the head with a 4-degree list to port, but did not touch bottom; the hull structure was destroyed or seriously damaged around A turret, whose trunk was distorted, preventing use of the guns; flooding extended to all of the spaces as far as the lower deck. There was, however, no appreciable flooding in other parts of the hull thanks to the fact that the bulkheads remained watertight and to the effectiveness of the damage-control arrangements, so that the adjacent B turret remained operational. In addition, the ship would have been able to move under its own power if necessary. Repairs, which were carried out in two phases, were completed in mid-July 1942 in the United States, some seven months later. Comparing the damage to that suffered by the two Italian battleships at Taranto, the *Valiant* demonstrated a much greater degree of structural strength, better fitting out and greater effectiveness of its safety arrangements, at least compared with the 'Cavour' and 'Duilio' classes at the end of 1940.

The powerplant proved to be the most successful aspect of the modernisation, especially on the 'Cavours'. Apart from the criticism that power was transmitted through only two shafts, it reflected an operational reliability equal to or exceeding expectations, working consistently and with no major problems. On the 'Cavours' maximum power and speed greatly exceeded contract specifications: in the pre-tactical phase of the battle of Punta Stilo both reached a speed of 27 knots with no difficulty at a displacement close to full load and, before the war, a speed of 28 knots, also at full load; under conditions of extra power, they could make 29 knots. The range of the 'Cavour' class was superior to that of the 'Littorios' and more than sufficient for any operations in the Mediterranean. The performance of the 'Duilio' class powerplants was somewhat lower in terms of speed and range, but equally reliable, so that even after a prolonged period of inactivity and insufficient maintenance, they suffered fewer problems than had been feared. Only the 'Cavours' experienced persistent corrosion problems with the propeller shafts and the white metal seals of the stern tubes and brackets, which required repeated periods of major maintenance. In substance, compared with most of the British battleships – excluding the 'King George V' class and the battlecruisers – the 'Cavour' and the 'Duilio' classes had a marked speed advantage that enabled them to operate with the larger and fast 'Littorios' and with lighter vessels, and disengage if necessary when faced with superior but slower enemy forces, as happened at Punta Stilo. By contrast, the larger and slower British battleships, such as the 'Royal Sovereign' class and the *Malaya* and *Barham*, soon proved to be unsuitable for first-line operations and in time were assigned to secondary roles or theatres, such as convoy escort in distant waters; and the operational speeds of the three 'Warspite' type modernisations and of the 'Nelsons' were only slightly greater.

The seakeeping qualities of the 'Cavours' and 'Duilios' did not prove to be as satisfactory. Quite apart from leaks in the area where the old and the new bow sections were joined, the ships were rather wet forward because of the excessive weight that reduced the freeboard and increased the moment of inertia, and the hull tended to trim by the bow. In heavy seas they were unable to sustain high speeds and use of the armament, both main as well as secondary, was hampered or compromised. During the war, ineffective efforts were made to lighten them. These were, however, problems common to many other battleships with fine hull lines and insufficient freeboard, such as the 'Dunkerque' and the German 'Gneisenau' designs, which were also unable to use their foremost or both of their forward turrets in even moderately bad weather.

Overall, the rebuilt 'Cavour' and the 'Duilio' classes were ships whose armament, protection, speed and range were balanced. They represented the best technical solution achievable given the original characteristics of these ships; in addition, the 'Duilios' were more successful thanks to technical solutions derived from the design and experience of the 'Littorio' class, as well as from more modern armament and equipment. But none of this altered their modest combat value and the judgment expressed in this book cannot be stressed enough: namely, that while it might have been reasonable in 1932–1933 to proceed with rebuilding the first two ships when faced by only the *Dunkerque*, it was a mistake, especially from the financial standpoint, to replicate the experience with the 'Duilios' in 1937, when the inferiority of these ships to almost every type of potentially enemy battleship was perfectly well known.

The battleship *Conte di Cavour* seen from her twin *Giulio Cesare* in the late 1930s.

The ships' mottos

***Conte di Cavour*:**
A NESSUNO SECONDO (SECOND TO NONE)
[In addition, from 1937: an inscription on the front of the 1st DT:
MOLTI NEMICI MOLTO ONORE! (MANY ENEMIES MUCH HONOUR!)

***Andrea Doria*:**
ALTIUS TENDAM (ALWAYS HIGHER)

***Giulio Cesare*:**
AD QUAMVIS VIM PREFERENDAM (TO WITHSTAND ANY BLOW);
From 1920: CAESAR ADEST (CAESAR IS HERE)
[in addition, from 1937: an inscription on the front of the 1st DT: GUAI AGLI INERMI (WOE TO THE HELPLESS]

***Duilio*:**
NOMEN NUMEN (THE NAME SIGNIFIES POWER)

***Leonardo da Vinci*:**
NON SI VOLTA CHI A STELLA E' FISO (HE WHO IS FIXED ON A GOAL DOES NOT GIVE UP)
[after being raised: OGNI TORTO SI DIRIZZA (EVERY INJUSTICE IS RIGHTED)]

La Spezia, 20 July 1941: Admiral Bruto Brivonesi, centre, presiding over the change of commanders of the battleship *Giulio Cesare*. (G Vaccaro collection)

Appendix 1

'CONTE DI CAVOUR' AND 'DUILIO' CLASS COLOUR SCHEMES (1940–1956) – A SUMMARY

At the time Italy declared war in June 1940 the Regia Marina ships operating in the Mediterranean carried the traditional uniform paint scheme of vertical surfaces in *grigio cenerino chiaro* (light ash grey) with decks in *grigio piombo* (lead grey) when not covered, as on large ships, totally or partially in teakwood planking which retained its natural colour. As described in Chapter 3, this type of paint scheme had been resumed in the early 1930s and saw no major changes until July 1940, when an 'anti-camouflage' measure was introduced to allow recognition of Italian ships by Regia Aeronautica aircraft. For this purpose, on the occasion of the action at Punta Stilo on 9 July 1940, the stern deck area of major Italian ships was painted with water-soluble white lime, but the measure proved to be wholly inadequate. Therefore, in the days following that encounter, the staff issued an order to paint the extreme forward portion of the upper decks of Italian ships with oil-based paints in alternating bands of *rosso mattone* (brick red) and *bianco opaco* (opaque white). These diagonal bands were to have an inclination of –45 degrees to port and +135 degrees to starboard, but at times this orientation was slightly different, and it also happened that on some of the major ships even the extreme stern of the upper deck was temporarily painted in this banded scheme. The provision remained in force for the duration of the war, although photographic evidence shows its progressive removal from some of the larger ships beginning in early 1943.

From early 1941 the first experiments began with 'camouflage' paint schemes on Italian naval ships by applying special multi-colour patterns that, in reality, were intended to deceive an attacker about the ship's size, speed and course, rather than to 'hide' the vessel – widely understood to be a very difficult if not impossible task on the open sea. As shown in the series of colour profiles that appear below, the modernised battleships were also involved in three experiments: the first was the *Duilio* in May 1941 with a design called the 'fishbone' pattern, followed later that year by *Doria*, *Cesare* and *Cavour* (only temporarily, after being raised at Taranto) with complex schemes designed by noted marine artist Rodolfo Claudus that, like the earlier patterns, did not yield the desired results.

Finally, in December 1941 the Regia Marina staff issued general principles for wartime paint schemes for ships, where the 'camouflage' component consisted of only two colours (with few exceptions) called 'base', or more appropriately, standard

The forecastle of the battleship *Andrea Doria* in autumn 1940: detail of the alternating white and red diagonal stripes applied from July 1940 for identification of Italian ships by aircraft.

Cavour in 1916, in light grey with white false bow wave.

(Colour rendering by Maurizio Brescia from line drawings drafted by Roberto Maggi.)

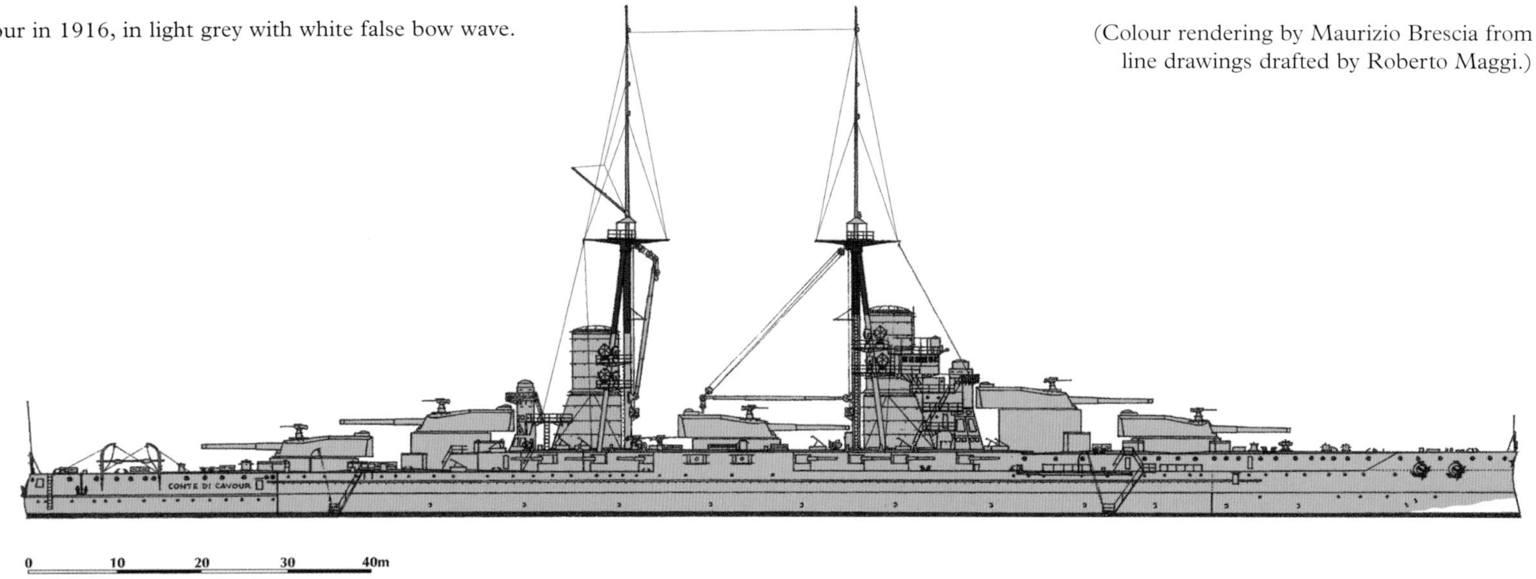

Duilio in the early 1920s in the dark grey overall scheme adopted by Regia Marina's ships after the First World War and maintained until 1929.

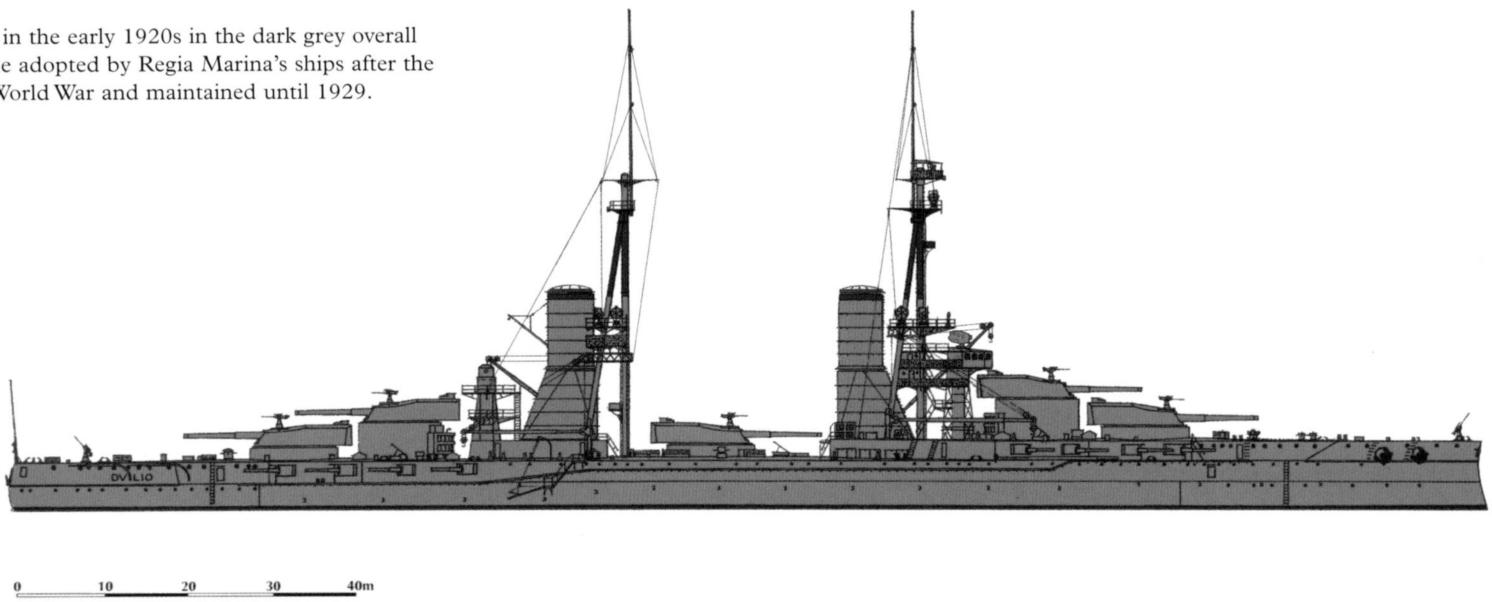

Dulio in the light grey overall scheme in use since 1929–1930, before reconstruction in the first half of the 1930s; notice the catapult on the port side of the forecastle deck.

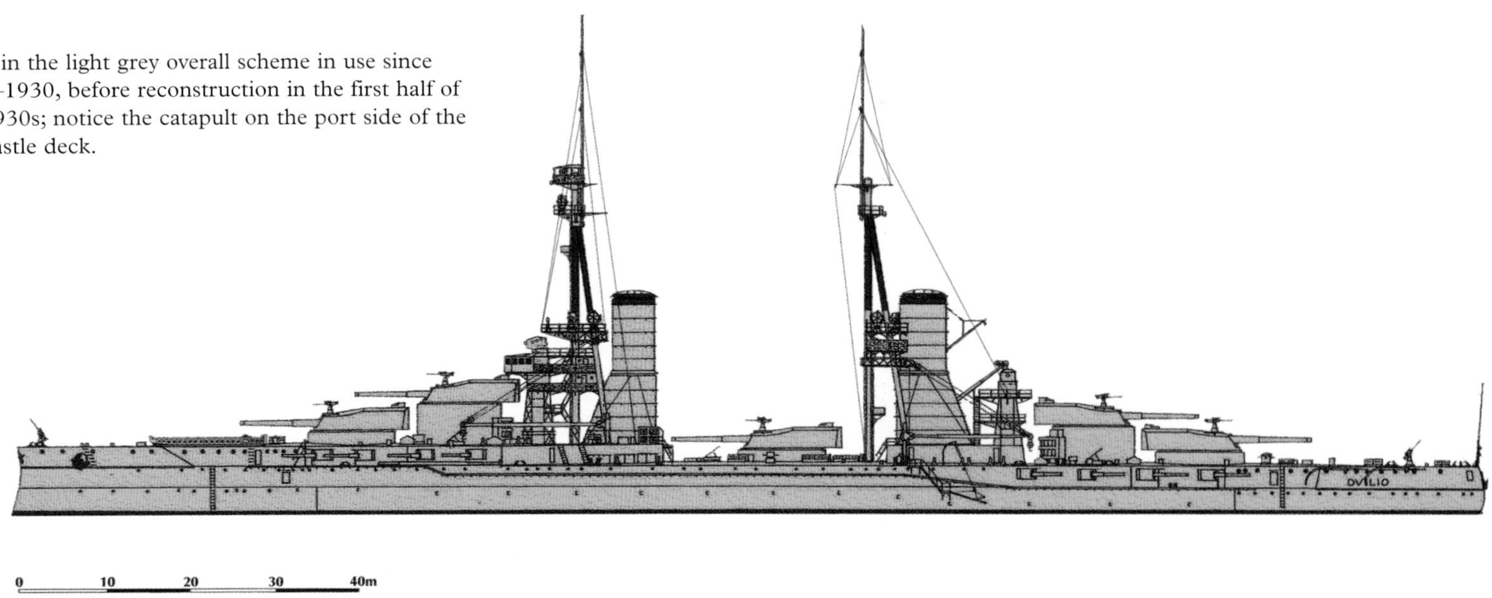

Cavour as rebuilt, in light grey overall scheme.

(Colour rendering by Maurizio Brescia from line drawings drafted by Roberto Maggi.)

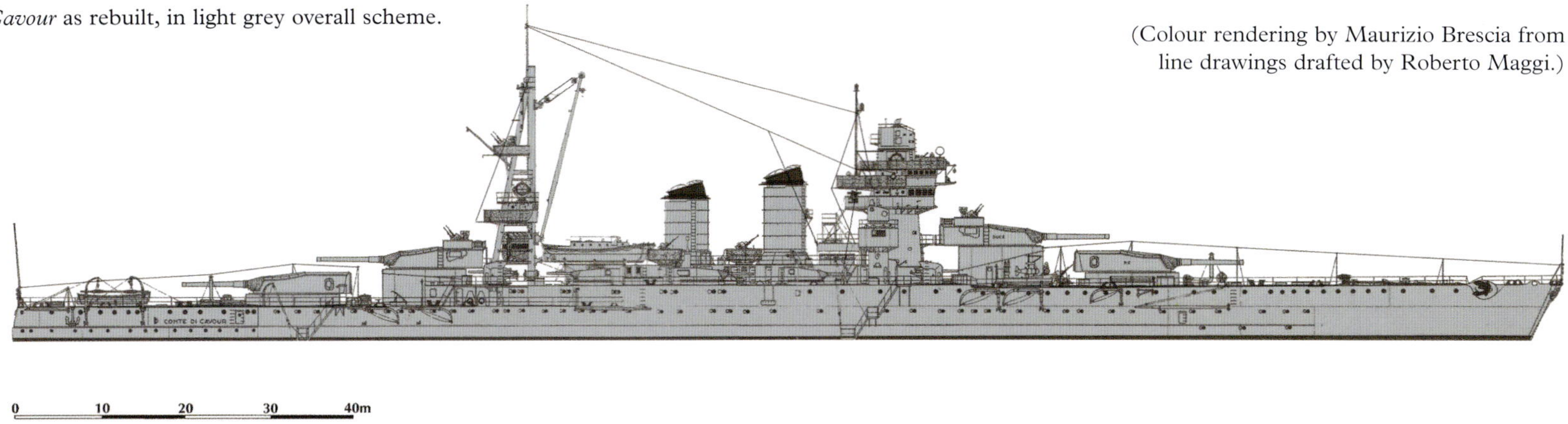

Duilio as rebuilt, in light grey overall scheme.

Cavour in December 1941 in a 'Claudus' dazzle camouflage (same on both sides). This scheme was adopted for the voyage from Taranto to Trieste, where the ship was to have been rebuilt.

Notice that, in order to save weight when the ship was refloated, the main calibre guns, the 120/50 and the 100/47 guns have been landed; also, masts have been reduced in height. Colours are white, black and light grey.

Cesare in December 1941 wearing a 'Claudus' dazzle camouflage (same on both sides).

Colours are black, light grey and light blue, but it is quite similar to *Cavour*'s 'Claudus' scheme (see drawing 6).

(Colour rendering by Maurizio Brescia from line drawings drafted by Roberto Maggi.)

Cesare June 1942, in a dazzle scheme with the standard light and dark grey colours.

In summer 1943 *Cesare*'s camouflage was modified in the forward part of the hull on both sides; the ship's port bow was painted light blue.

Doria in October 1941 in a 'Claudus' dazzle camouflage (same on both sides). Colours are white, black, light grey and light blue.

(Colour rendering by Maurizio Brescia from line drawings drafted by Roberto Maggi.)

Doria in May 1942, in a dazzle scheme with the standard light and dark grey with additional areas in light blue fore and aft.

Duilio in May 1941 in a 'fishbone' pattern with greenish triangles superimposed over dark grey hull and superstructure.

Duilio in mid-1942 in a dazzle scheme with the standard light and dark grey with additional areas in light blue fore and aft. Notice areas in white in the lower bow and right aft to simulate high speed.

(Drawings by Maurizio Brescia.)

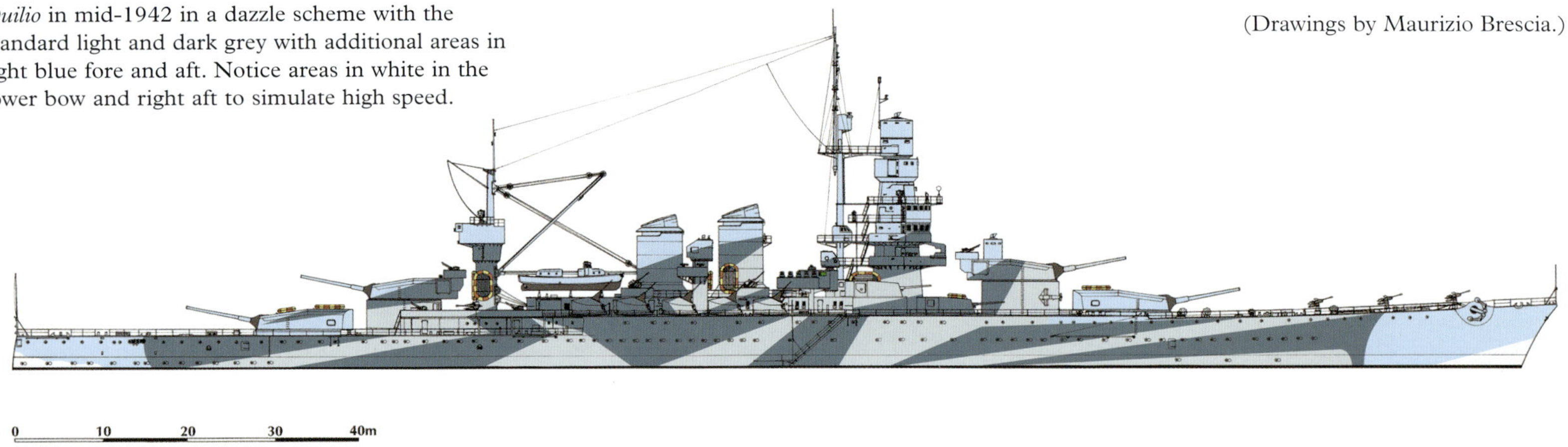

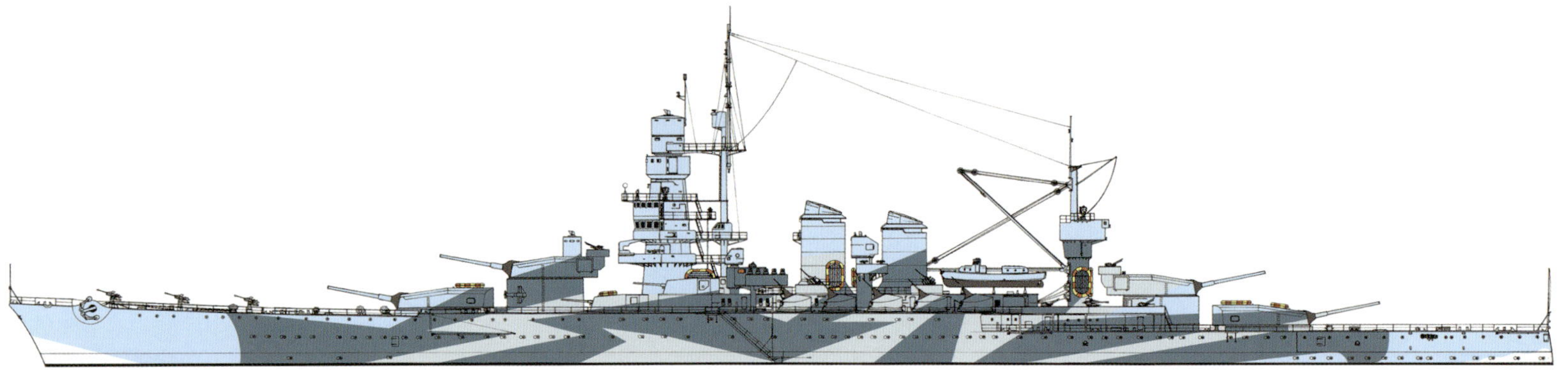

Duilio in 1946 in an 'Allied' scheme, with dark grey hull and light grey superstructure.

In 1950, *Duilio* and sister-ship *Doria* reverted to the pre-war light overall scheme, still in use today in the Italian Navy.

(Colour rendering by Maurizio Brescia from line drawing drafted by Roberto Maggi.)

Gulf of Naples, Naval Review of 5 May 1938. Sailors of the battleship *Giulio Cesare* with the heavy cruiser *Pola* in the background.

The damaged battleship *Duilio* at Taranto in November 1940.

Battleship *Giulio Cesare* being completed at Genoa in 1913.

Battleship *Duilio* fitting out at Genoa in 1914. (Courtesy Ansaldo Archives)

Battleship *Conte di Cavour* at the Naval Review in the Gulf of Naples, 5 May 1938.

Gulf of Naples, Naval Review of 5 May 1938. The cruiser *Zara* photographed from the battleship *Conte di Cavour*.

A 320/44 armour-piercing shell preserved in the Venice Naval Museum. (Photo M Cicogna)

A preserved splinter from the 381mm (15in) shell of the battleship HMS *Warspite* which struck the *Giulio Cesare* at Punta Stilo on 9 July 1940.

Gulf of Taranto, summer 1941. Gunnery exercise with *Duilio*'s main armament.

Taranto naval base, October 1941. The battleship *Andrea Doria* wears her first deceptive scheme designed by marine painter Rudolfo Claudus.

colours: light ash grey and dark grey (or steel grey, similar to that used for the upper decks), both in an opaque finish, while the 'camouflage' was achieved by applying special patterns (splotches, broken lines, etc) and/or by the use of opaque *bianco sporco* (dirty white) applied to the extreme bow and stern portions of the hull. During 1942 the *Doria*, *Duilio* and *Cesare* were successively repainted in colours that, with minor variations over time, the first two kept until 1944 and *Cesare*, which was decommissioned during the period of co-belligerence, until 1948 when the ship was ceded to the Soviet Union as required by the peace treaty. In 1944 *Andrea Doria* and *Duilio* were given a unique livery consisting of the uniform painting of the vertical hull surfaces in dark grey and those of the superstructures in light grey. Probably in order to use up reserve stocks of paint that were stored in relative abundance, this colour scheme was retained by the two 'modernised' ships that survived the war until 1951, when they returned to a uniform livery in light ash grey that they kept until their decommissioning five years later.

The *Andrea Doria* in 1942 in her second dazzle scheme.

Appendix 2

GUNNERY PERFORMANCE

MAIN GUN AND MEDIUM-CALIBRE GUN PERFORMANCE DATA OF THE 'CONTE DI CAVOUR' AND 'DUILIO' CLASSES

Perforation capabilities of the 320/44, 120/50 and 135/45 guns

(from Direttive e norme per l'impiego della Squadra navale, Impiego delle artiglierie, settembre 1942)

Thickness of KC type armour capable of being penetrated by 320/44 guns at charge I, with armour-piercing round (with semi-armour-piercing, figures in parentheses) by distance and angle of impact

	Vertical armour in mm					**Horizontal armour in mm**
Distance (m)	90°	80°	70°	60°	50°	
24,000	221 (150)	216 (150)	202 (150)	179 (148)	150 (124)	108 (99)
22,000	238 (150	232 (150)	218 (150)	194 (150)	162 (135)	91 (82)
20,000	256 (152)	249 (150)	235 (150)	209 (150)	174 (140)	75 (68)
18,000	276 (162)	270 (152)	254 (150)	225 (150)	189 (142)	61 (55)

These are values on average lower than 'gunnery test ranges', usually used to compare equivalent weapons, of which however no trace has been found.

Thickness of OD [nickel-chromium-steel] type armour capable of being penetrated by 135/45 guns at charge I, with semi-armour-piercing round by distance and angle of impact.

	Vertical armour in mm					**Horizontal armour in mm**
Distance (m)	90°	80°	70°	60°	50°	
17,000	no data	no data	no data	no data	no data	48
16,000	38	37	30	30	30	36
13,000	49	48	45	40	33	25
11,000	53	52	49	43	36	17

Thickness of OD type armour capable of being penetrated by 120/50 guns at charge I, with semi-armour-piercing round by distance and angle of impact.

	Vertical armour in mm					**Horizontal armour in mm**
Distance (m)	90°	80°	70°	60°	50°	
15,000	38	37	35	31	–	43
13,000	45	44	37	30	32	
12,000	45	48	48	42	42	23
10,000	58	56	53	47	47	16

Salvo from the battleship *Giulio Cesare*'s forward 320/44 battery in 1942.

Main armament gunnery exercise by the battleship *Duilio* during the period of co-belligerence with the Allies.

SUMMARY OF PRINCIPAL RESULTS RELATING TO GUNNERY EXERCISES IN TRAINING YEARS 1939/1940 AND 1940/1941

Regia Marina Navy Staff, 25 November 1941 (extract)

	Ansaldo guns – 1939/1940					
Calibre	320/44			381/50		
Charge	I	II	III	I	II	III
Range	23,600	17,100	13,600	22,500	17,400	15,000
Effective salvos (%)	44.0	35.5	48.5	35.0	27.0	26.0
Rounds on target (%)	9.0	2.6	10.5	3.7	9.5	8.5
Average rate (seconds)	48.0	51.1	46.0	59.0	47.0	42.0
Irregular rounds (%)	4.5	2.6	4.2	1.2	0.0	3.0
Lost rounds (%)	12.0	6.0	17.5	28.0	28.4	9.6
Longitudinal dispersion (m)	620	347	168	416	360	127
Longitudinal spread (m)	769	610	257	364	315	130

	OTO guns – 1939/1940					
Calibre	320/44			381/50		
Charge	I	II	III	I	II	III
Range	18,200	16,400	13,400	21,000	17,000	15,600
Effective salvos (%)	40.0	27.5	35.0	25.0	24.0	55.0
Rounds on target (%)	2.5	12.5	9.6	7.0	10.7	16.0
Average rate (seconds)	43.5	50.7	45.5	63.0	37.5	48.5
Irregular rounds (%)	0.0	3.5	5.7	1.5	0.0	1.6
Lost rounds (%)	22.0	5.7	17.2	26.7	29.0	18.1
Longitudinal dispersion (m)	no data	400	143	290	185	185
Longitudinal spread (m)	no data	547	200	267	344	202

	Ansaldo guns – 1940/1941					
Calibre	320/44			381/50		
Charge	I	II	III	I	II	III
Range	–	18,100	14,000	–	18,800	15,500
Useful salvos (%)	–	22.5	53.5	–	48.0	26.0
Rounds on target (%)	–	6.0	10.9	–	6.2	8.5
Average rate (seconds)	–	48.7	41.0	–	30.6	42.0
Irregular rounds (%)	–	0.8	3.8	–	6.5	3.0
Lost rounds (%)	–	10.2	6.9	–	11.6	9.6
Longitudinal dispersion (m)	–	276	140	–	309	123
Longitudinal spread (m)	–	315	193	–	360	153

	OTO guns – 1940/1941					
Calibre	320/44			381/50		
Charge	I	II	III	I	II	III
Range	–	15,100	–	–	20,000	15,800
Useful salvos (%)	–	48.5	–	–	65.0	32.0
Rounds on target (%)	–	14.7	–	–	7.3	6.7
Average rate (seconds)	–	54.7	–	–	29.7	34.1
Irregular rounds (%)	–	5.2	–	–	3.6	1.3
Lost rounds (%)	–	8.4	–	–	8.9	4.9
Longitudinal dispersion (m)	–	145	–	–	422	139
Longitudinal spread (m)	–	216	–	–	500	190

Note: In these tables 'spread' relates to the opening salvo, while 'dispersion' covers the following salvoes.

Aiming exercises on board the battleship *Giulio Cesare* moored at Taranto in late summer 1942. (Courtesy V De Gaetano family)

Appendix 3

MOVEMENTS AND LOCATIONS OF THE 'CONTE DI CAVOUR' AND 'DUILIO' CLASS BATTLESHIPS DURING THE WAR

The tables of movements and changes of bases that follow are derived from the 'Statini dell'attività bellica delle navi' (Summary of statistics of combat activity of ships), held at the AUSSM [Archivio Ufficio Storico Stato Maggiore Marina – Italian Navy Staff Historical Office Archives], drafted after the war for administrative purposes. There are some inaccuracies, but we have opted to use the format and data, making corrections and additions only in cases of significant discrepancies. For a better understanding, it should be borne in mind that generally:

- departure and arrival times refer to the commencement of unmooring and mooring
- for the hours under way, for purposes of graphic simplicity, hours and minutes are separated by a comma;
- the references to attacks on bases and ports are included only when the ship is known to have been damaged or to have engaged in anti-aircraft activity;
- the times of air attacks refer to the beginning and end of such attacks, or to the beginning and end of anti-aircraft fire.

CONTE DI CAVOUR

Date	Time	Location	Hours, minutes under way	Miles covered	Notes
10 October 1940 6 July 1940		Taranto			Ship ready; operationally ready in port.
7 July 1940 10 July 1940	13.50 00.50	from Taranto to Augusta	59,10	1135 approx	Sortie by combined squadrons (Naval Forces, FN) in the central Ionian to cover and escort two convoys bound for Libya (Operation TCM). Battle of Punta Stilo (9 July 1940); at 15.59 the *Cesare* is hit by a 381mm shell from battleship *Warspite*, which causes some appreciable damage and leads the FN to disengage.
10 July 1940	01.30 16.13	from Augusta to Naples	14,43	236 approx	Move because of threat of attack by torpedo aircraft.
13 July 1940 14 July 1940	20.29 18.36	from Naples to Taranto	22,07	473	Transfer.
9 August 1940 10 August 1940	23.40 14.55	from Taranto to Taranto	15,15	297	Air-naval and gunnery exercises in the northern Ionian with *Duilio* and *Cesare*, the latter ship returning from La Spezia.
31 August 1940 2 September 1940	23.40 14.55	from Taranto to Taranto	46,28	734	Sortie by the FN into the central Ionian to oppose British Operation 'Hats'. No contact with enemy naval forces.
7 September 1940 9 September 1940	15.50 12.07	from Taranto to Naples	44,17	839	Sortie by the FN to south of Sardinia to oppose a presumed sortie by Force H from Gibraltar. No contact with the enemy.
10 September 1940 11 September 1940	17.20 18.20	from Naples to Taranto	25,00	461	Transfer.
21 September 1940	12.36 17.21	from Taranto to Taranto	4.45	97	5th Division gunnery exercises in the Gulf of Taranto.
29 September 1940 1 October 1940	18.39 03.05	from Taranto to Taranto	32,26	587	Sortie by the FN into the central Ionian to oppose British Operation MB5. No contact with enemy naval forces.
11 November 1940	23.05	Taranto			Torpedo aircraft attack on the base at Taranto (Operation 'Judgement'). At 23.14 the *Cavour* is hit by a torpedo sustaining major damage. At 04.20 on the 12th, with the aid of tugs, an attempt is made to beach the ship in shallow water, but it sinks at 08.00 on the 12th.
13 November 1940 21 December 1941		Taranto			Work to raise the ship from the bottom, refurbishing hull and powerplant.

Taranto, December 1941: the battleship *Conte di Cavour* about to sail for Trieste under her own power to complete a refit after being raised following the serious damage suffered in November 1940.

The battleship *Giulio Cesare*, foreground, and *Conte di Cavour* moored at the buoys in Taranto's Mar Grande in summer 1940.

22 December 1941 23 December 1941	10.00 17.16	from Taranto to Trieste	31,16	600	Move under own power to San Marco (CRDA) shipyard to complete refitting and modification.
23 December 1941 8 September 1943		Trieste			Undergoing work at San Marco yard (CRDA). Work proceeds slowly and In June 1941 is definitively suspended.
8 September 1943 10 September 1943		Trieste			Upon proclamation of the armistice (8 September 1943) the ship was not ready to move and on the evening of the 10th is abandoned without being sabotaged. Captured by German forces, it is not placed in Kriegsmarine service and was stripped of much of its equipment and material.
17 February 1945 20 February 1945	14.50 16.46 11.46 12.50	Trieste			Bombing of the Trieste port and dockyards, during one or both of which the ship, in an abandoned state, suffers multiple damage with no action taken to limit flooding.
24 February 1945		Trieste			Following damage caused by the bombings, the ship sinks, capsizing at the head of the fitting out quay of the San Marco (CRDA) shipyard.
8 December 1950		Trieste			Start of operations to raise the wreck from the bottom.
29.March 1952		Trieste			End of salvage work and towing the upturned wreck to the Punta Sottile beach (Muggia) for demolition.

GIULIO CESARE

Date	Time	Location	Hours, minutes under way	Miles covered	Notes
10 June 1940 6 July 1940		Taranto			Ship ready; operationally ready in port.
7 July 1940 9 July 1940	13.50 00.50	from Taranto to Messina	56,57	1135	Sortie by combined squadrons (Naval Forces, FN) in the central Ionian to cover and escort two convoys bound for Libya (Operation TCM). Battle of Punta Stilo (9 July 1940); at 15.59 the *Cesare* is hit by a 381mm shell from battleship *Warspite*, which causes some appreciable damage and leads the FN to disengage.
12 July 1940 13 July 1940	20.30 22.47	from Messina to La Spezia	26,17	540	Transfer.
15 July 1940 31 July 1940		La Spezia			Work in naval dockyard.
1 August 1940	13.35 18.15	from La Spezia to Genoa	4,20	72	Transfer.
2 August 1940 7 August 1940	Genoa				In graving dock.

Continued overleaf

7 August 1940	15.30 19.45	from Genoa to La Spezia	4,15	72	Transfer.
8 August 1940 10 August 1940	21.37 15.00	from La Spezia to Taranto	4,15	820	Transfer and air-naval and gunnery exercise in the northern Ionian with *Cavour* and *Duilio*.
21 August 1940	14.22 20.15	from Taranto to Taranto	5,53	90	Gunnery exercises in the Gulf of Taranto.
31 August 1940 1 September 1940 2 September 1940	05.35 05.55 03.26 07.42	from Taranto to Taranto from Taranto to Taranto	0,25 28,16	350	Sortie by the FN into the central Ionian to oppose British Operation 'Hats'. The ship had to stop in Mar Grande because of condenser blockage. It later joins the FN. No contact with enemy naval forces.
7 September 1940 9 September 1940	15.47 12.00	from Taranto to Naples	44,13	864	Sortie by the FN to south of Sardinia to oppose a presumed sortie by Force H from Gibraltar. No contact with the enemy.
10 September 1940 11 September 1940	16.15 18.01	from Naples to Taranto	25,46	468	Transfer.
21 September 1940	12.34 17.55	from Taranto to Taranto	5,21	103	5th Division gunnery exercises in the Gulf of Taranto.
29 September 1940 1 October 1940	18.40 03.26	from Taranto to Taranto	32,46	582	Sortie by the FN into the central Ionian to oppose British Operation MB5. No contact with enemy naval forces.
30 October 1940		Taranto			Moored at buoy. Firing against probable reconnaissance aircraft.
11 November 1940 12 November 1940	23.05 00.20	Taranto			Torpedo aircraft attack on the base at Taranto (Operation 'Judgement'). The ship participates in anti-aircraft defence.
12 November 1940 13 November 1940	14.48 16.30	from Taranto to Naples	25.42	466	Transfer of the FN.
16 November 1940 18 November 1940	11.00 12.13	from Naples to Naples	49,13	910	Sortie by the FN to oppose British Operation 'White' in the western Mediterranean. No contact with the enemy, but the presence at sea of the FN leads to partial failure of the enemy operation.
26 November 1940 28 November 1940	12.05	from Naples to Naples	51,55	880	Sortie by the FN to oppose British Operation 'Collar'. Battle of Cape Teulada (27 November 1940). The *Cesare* does not get within useful range to engage enemy naval forces. From 12.37 to 13.47 she is attacked by torpedo aircraft to no effect.
2 December 1940	20.55 21.50	Naples			Air attack. Ship participates in anti-aircraft defence.
14 December 1940	20.55 22.31	Naples			Air attack. The ship participates in anti-aircraft defence.
15 December 1940 16 December 1940	17.26 09.40	from Naples to La Maddalena	16,14	265	Transfer.
17 December 1940	10.04 11.55	from La Maddalena to La Maddalena	 1,51	 7	 At anchor. Change of mooring.
19 December 1940 20 December 1940	22.33 13.28	from La Maddalena to Naples	 15,05	 263	 Transfer.
22 December 1940 23 December 1940	20.23 15.18	from Naples to Naples	18,55	306	Exercises.
28 December 1940	14.15	Naples			Firing against enemy reconnaissance aircraft.
29 December 1940 30 December 1940	20.36 01.25	Naples			Air attack. Ship participates in anti-aircraft defence.
6 January 1941	…	Naples			Fire against enemy reconnaissance aircraft.
6 January 1941 7 January 1941	18.05 17.00	from Naples to Naples	22,55	371	Various exercises.
8 January 1941	19.35 23.00	Naples			Air attack. The *Cesare* is slightly damaged by bombs exploding nearby. Participates in anti-aircraft defence.
9 January 1941 10 January 1941	16.53 14.05	from Naples to La Spezia	21,12	400	Transfer.
12 January 1941	09.29 15.08	from La Spezia to Genoa	5,39	70	Transfer.

15 January 1941 29 January 1941		Genoa			Undergoing work.
30 January 1941	09.55 15.02	from Genoa to La Spezia	5,07	67	Transfer.
8 February 1941 11 February 1941	19.09 10.28	from La Spezia to Naples	63,19	1125 approx	Sortie by the Naval Squadron [SN] to opposed British Operation 'Grog' (bombing of Genoa). No contact with the enemy.
11 February 1941 12 February 1941	18.41 15.24	from Naples to La Spezia	20,43	352 approx	Transfer.
24 February 1941	10.06 20.20	from La Spezia to La Spezia	10,14	172	Gunnery exercises in the Gulf of Genoa.
27 February 1941	13.05 20.04	from La Spezia to La Spezia	6,59	95	Gunnery exercises in the Gulf of Genoa.
1 March 1941	14.00 17.00	from La Spezia to La Spezia	3,00	227	Night gunnery exercises in the Gulf of Genoa
2 March 1941	21.30 05.10	from La Spezia to La Spezia	7,00		Night gunnery exercises in the Gulf of Genoa
20 March 1941 21 March 1940	05.05 00.10	from La Spezia to La Spezia	19,05	144	Daytime gunnery exercises in the Gulf of Genoa.
4 April 1941 5 April 1941	15.41 11.14	from La Spezia to Naples	19,33	365	Transfer.
30 April 1941 1 May 1941	13.20 04.31	from Naples to Naples	15,11	255	Gunnery exercises.
2 May 1941 24 June 1941		Naples			Ship inactive in port.
25 June 1941 26 June 1941	12.33 07.30	from Naples to Naples	18,57	320	Day and night gunnery exercises.
11 July 1941 12 July 1941	17.36 14.10	from Naples to La Spezia	20,34	382	Transfer.
13 July 1941 26 August 1941		La Spezia			Ship inactive in port.
27 August 1941 29 August 1941	19.32 18.02	from La Spezia to Taranto	46,30	907	Transfer.
8 September 1941	11.20 19.40	from Taranto to Taranto	8,20	146	Gunnery exercises in the Gulf of Taranto.
24 September 1941	11.21 20.00	from Taranto to Taranto	8,39	290	Daytime gunnery exercises.
25 September 1941	20.57 04.28	from Taranto to Taranto	7,31		5th Division night gunnery exercises in the Gulf of Taranto
26 September 1941 15 December 1941		Taranto			Ship riding at anchor.
16 December 1941 19 December 1941	18.58 18.00	from Taranto to Taranto	71,02	1450	Participation in Operation M 42 (convoy escort to Libya). First Battle of Sirte (17 December 1941). From 17.53 to 18.07 on 17 December engages enemy light vessels with no outcome.
3 January 1942 5 January 1942	19.15 17.30	from Taranto to Taranto	46.15	900	Participation by the SN in Operation M 43 (convoy escort to Libya).
6 January 1942 10 April 1942		Taranto			Ship inactive at anchor.
11 April 1942 4 May 1942		Taranto			In drydock undergoing work.
5 May 1942 29 December 1942		Taranto			Ship inactive in port.
30 December 1942 31 December 1942	01.00	from Taranto to Pola	29,10	592	Transfer.

Continued overleaf

1 January 1943 22 May 1943		Pola			Ship inactive in port.
23 May 1943		Pola			Air alarm. Ship participates in anti-aircraft defence.
24 May 1943		Pola			Air alarm. Ship participates in anti-aircraft defence.
25 May 1943 28 June 1943		Pola			Ship inactive in port.
29 June 1943		Pola			Air alarm. Ship participates in ant-aircraft defence.
30 June 1943 18 July 1943		Pola			Ship inactive in port.
19 July 1943		Pola			Air alarm. Ship participates in anti-aircraft defence.
20 July 1943 8 September 1943		Pola			Ship inactive in port.
9 September 1943 11 September 1943	16.30 16.05	From Pola to Taranto	47,35	640	Following proclamation of the armistice (8 September 1943) the ship leaves Pola. On the night of 9/10 September uprising by a group of officers to prevent handing the ship over to their former enemies but is quelled after a few hours. At 13.48 on 10 September ship opens fire against German aircraft, which make an unsuccessful attack.
12 September 1943 13 September 1943	14.10 12.24	from Taranto to Malta	22,14	330	Transfer. At anchor outside St Paul's Bay.
14 September 1943	16.50 19.35	from Malta to Malta	...	8	Change of mooring; anchored at Marsa Scirocco.
8 October 1943	06.50 14.30	from Malta to Malta	7,40	...	The *Cesare* passes the booms and runs her engines in the roadstead.
9 October 1943 16 June 1944		Malta			Ship at anchor at Marsa Scirocco.
17 June 1944	07.30 14.40	from Malta to Augusta	7,10	113	Transfer.
27 June 1944 28 June 1944	16.10 08.40	from Augusta to Taranto	16,30	285	Transfer.
29 June 1944 8 May 1945		Taranto			Ship inactive in port.

DUILIO

Date	Time	Location	Hours, minutes under way	Miles covered	Notes
10 June 1940 10 July 1940	Pola				Ship inactive in port.
11 July 1940	11.30 17.35	from Pola to Pola	6,05	62	Gunnery exercises.
14 July 1940 15 July 1940	05.03 08.07	from Pola to Taranto	27,04	520	Transfer.
18 July 1940	15.17 19.08	from Taranto to Taranto	3,51	60	Gunnery exercises in the Gulf of Taranto.
20 July 1940	09.15 09.44 16.47 18,05	from Taranto to Taranto from Taranto to Taranto	0,29 1,18	5	Change of mooring for gunnery exercises in Mar Grande. Return to usual mooring.
22 July 1940	12.45 15.40	from Taranto Taranto	2,55	48	Gunnery exercises in the Gulf of Taranto
25 July 1940	14.18 18.22	from Taranto Taranto	4,04	65	Gunnery exercises in the Gulf of Taranto.
9 August 1940 10 August 1940	23.45 16.41	from Taranto to Taranto	16,56	343	Air-naval and gunnery exercises in the central Ionian with *Cavour* and *Cesare*, the latter ship returning from La Spezia.
21 August 1940	14.34 20.13	from Taranto to Taranto	5,39	92	Gunnery exercises in the Gulf of Taranto.

The battleship *Duilio* in transit from Pola to Taranto on 14 July 1940. The ship has just concluded its preliminary training phase at the base following completion of the modernisation. (F Bargoni collection)

The *Duilio* at the buoy in Taranto's Mar Grande in summer 1940. (Courtesy A Amici)

29 August 1940	13.30 20.00	from Taranto	6,30	93	Gunnery exercises in the Gulf ofTaranto.
31 August 1940 2 September 1940	05.05 03.17	from Taranto to Taranto			Sortie by the Naval forces (FN) to the central Ionian to oppose British Operation 'Hats'. No contact with the enemy.
7 September 1940 9 September 1940	15.42 10.50	from Taranto to Naples	43,08	566	Sortie by the FN to south of Sardinia to oppose a presumed sortie by Force H from Gibraltar. No contact with the enemy.
10 September 1940 11 September 1940	16.52 17.40	from Naples to Taranto	24,48	431	Transfer.
13 September 1940	13.06 17.32	from Taranto to Taranto	4,26	73	Gunnery exercises in the Gulf of Taranto.
25 September 1940	13.38 16.51	from Taranto to Taranto	3,13	90	Daytime gunnery exercises in the Gulf of Taranto.
	20.18 23.12	from Taranto to Taranto	2,54		Night gunnery exercises in the Gulf of Taranto.
29 September 1940 1 October 1940	18.30 03.00	from Taranto to Taranto	32,30	563	Sortie by the FN in the central Ionian to oppose British Operation MB5. No contact with enemy naval forces.
16 October 1940	12.34 17.09	from Taranto to Taranto	4,35	78	Gunnery exercises in the Gulf of Taranto.
24 October 1940	13.50 21.59	from Taranto Taranto	8,09	108	Gunnery exercises in the Gulf of Taranto.
6 November 1940	05.30	Taranto			Air alarm. Participates in anti-aircraft defence.
11 November 1940	22.53	Taranto			Torpedo aircraft attack on the base at Taranto (Operation 'Judgement'). At 23.59 on 12 November the *Duilio* is hit by a torpedo that causes serious damage. As a precaution the ship is beached in shallow water. Participates in anti-aircraft defence.
12 November 1940	12.49	Taranto			Air alarm. Brief anti-aircraft firing.
12 November 1940	19.37 19.42	Taranto			Air alarm. Anti-aircraft firing.
13 November 1940	19.53 19.57				
13 November 1940	20.08	Taranto			Air alarm. Anti-aircraft firing.
15 November 1940	03.44 04.47	Taranto			Double air alarm. Anti-aircraft firing.
16 November 1940	19.40 20.06	Taranto			Air alarm. Anti-aircraft firing in two phases.
19 November 1940	19.40 20.35	Taranto			Double air alarm. Anti-aircraft firing.

Continued overleaf

22 November 1940	19.43 20.57	Taranto			Air alarm. Anti-aircraft firing.
28 November 1940	20.05 20.50	Taranto			Air alarm. Anti-aircraft firing.
23 December 1940	13.10 13.13	Taranto			Air alarm. Anti-aircraft firing.
30 December 1940	20.07 21.47	Taranto			Air alarm. Anti-aircraft firing.
25 January 1941	12.23 16.37	from Taranto to Taranto	4,14	35	Test of provisional watertight repairs to hull.
26 January 1941 28 January 1941	15.55 17.32	from Taranto to Genoa	49,37	768	Transfer.
3 February 1941		Genoa			Put into graving dock at Le Grazie.
9 February 1941		Genoa			British Operation 'Grog' (bombardment of Genoa). Participates in anti-aircraft fire against planes flying over the port.
3 May 1941	10.17 19.05	from Genoa to La Spezia	8,48	110	Leaves drydock and during transfer carries out gunnery exercises.
10 May 1941	10.30 16.15	from La Spezia to La Spezia	5,45	70	Gunnery exercises in the Gulf of Genoa.
14 May 1941	11.12 15.57	from La Spezia to La Spezia	4,45	59	Gunnery exercises in the Gulf of Genoa.
14 May 1941 16 May 1941	11.12 09.47	from La Spezia to Taranto	39,48	733	Transfer.
16 June 1941	12.20 19.49	from Taranto to Taranto	7,29	215	Daytime gunnery exercises in the Gulf of Taranto.
17 June 1941	20.30 02.06	from Taranto to Taranto	5,35		Night gunnery exercises in the Gulf of Taranto.
22 June 1941 23 June 1941	19.53 02.10	from Taranto to Taranto	6,17	82	Night gunnery exercises in the Gulf of Taranto with the battleship *Littorio*.
15 July 1941	14.30 15.30	Taranto			Air alarm, anti-aircraft firing.
1 August 1941	07.50 08.02	Taranto			Fire against enemy reconnaissance plane.
11 August 1941	10.02 21.10	from Taranto to Taranto	11,08	163	Gunnery exercises in the Gulf of Taranto.
20 August 1941	10.42 17.42	from Taranto to Taranto	7,00	181	Daytime gunnery exercises in the Gulf of Taranto.
21 August 1941	20.16 03.20	from Taranto to Taranto	4,04		Night gunnery exercises in the Gulf of Taranto.
24 September 1941 25 September 1941	19.00 04.06	from Taranto to Taranto	9,06	90	5th Division night gunnery exercises in the Gulf of Taranto.
26 September 1941 28 November 1941		Taranto			Ship riding at anchor.
29 November 1941 1 December 1941	17.44 11.11	from Taranto to Taranto	41.27	673	Indirect escort for convoy to Cyrenaica. Firing against enemy aircraft at 09.46 on 30 November.
13 December 1941 14 December 1941	18.27 02.50	from Taranto to Taranto	8,23	83	Participates in Operation M 41 (escort convoys for Libya); cancelled.
16 December 1941	00.03 02.03	Taranto			Air alarm; anti-aircraft firing.
16 December 1941 19 December 1941	13.44 17.44	from Taranto to Taranto	76,00	1,182	Participates in Operation M 42; direct escort for convoys to Libya; First Battle of Sirte (17 December 1941), in which *Duilio* does not participate.
3 January 1942 6 January 1942	16.02 05.06	from Taranto to Taranto	61,04	1,065	Participates in Operation M 43; direct escort of convoy to Libya.

22 January 1942 25 January 1942	16.24 16.10	from Taranto to Taranto	61,46	1,160	Participates in Operation T 18; direct escort of convoys to Libya. Fires against enemy aircraft on afternoon of the 23rd.
14 February 1942	18.37 22.50	from Taranto to Taranto	4,13	54	Sortie with light forces to oppose British Operation MF5 (convoy to Malta). Mission broken off; no contact.
21 February 1942 24 February 1942	15.14 02.02	from Taranto to Taranto	58.48	935	Participates in Operation K 7 (escort for convoys to Libya). Fires against enemy bomber on afternoon of the 22nd.
10 March 1942 24 March 1942		Taranto			In graving dock.
7 April 1942 8 April 1942	16.57 09.29	from Taranto to Messina	16,32	304	Transfer.
9 April 1942 24 May 1942		Messina			Ship inactive in port.
25 May 1942	05.08 20.00	from Messina to Taranto	14,52	292	Transfer.
26 May 1942 16 September 1942		Taranto			Ship riding at anchor.
17 September 1942	13.03 22.19	from Taranto to Taranto	9,16	107	Day and night gunnery exercises with *Doria* in the Gulf of Taranto.
18 September 1942 12 February 1943		Taranto			Ship at anchor.
13 February 1943	13.45 13.53	Taranto			Air alarm. Firing against enemy aircraft.
13 February 1943	15.42 16.30	Taranto			Air alarm. Firing against enemy aircraft.
14 February 1943 3 May 1943		Taranto			Ship inactive in port.
4 May 1943		Taranto			Air raid. Several bombs fall close to the ship without causing any damage. Participates in anti-aircraft fire.
17 May 1943		Taranto			Air alarm. Firing against enemy aircraft.
18 May 1943 16 June 1943		Taranto			Ship inactive in port.
16 June 1943 29 June 1943		Taranto			Ship in drydock for graving.
29 June 1943 14 July 1943		Taranto			Ship inactive in port.
15 July 1943		Taranto			Air alarm. Participates in anti-aircraft defence.
26 July 1943 27 July 1943	14.36 01.57	from Taranto to Taranto	11,21	96	Gunnery exercises in the Gulf of Taranto.
27 July 1943	18.16	Taranto			Air alarm. Firing against enemy aircraft.
28 July 1943	18.08 18.24	Taranto			Air alarm. Firing against enemy reconnaissance aircraft.
7 August 1943	14.09 20.15	from Taranto to Taranto			Gunnery exercises in the Gulf of Taranto.
18 August 1943	09.35 10.06	at Taranto	0,31	120	At the buoy for calibration of radio direction gear and magnetic compasses.
19 August 1943	14.20 00.45	from Taranto to Taranto	10,25		Gunnery exercises in the Gulf of Taranto.
21 August 1943 22 August 1943	13.05 00.03	from Taranto to Taranto	10,58	132	Gunnery exercises in the Gulf of Taranto.
26 August 1943	03.31 05.31	Taranto			Air alarm. Anti-aircraft fire.
28 August 1943	12.52 13.55	Taranto			Air attack. Participates in anti-aircraft defence.

Continued overleaf

29 August 1943	02.34 03.38	Taranto			Air attack. Participates in anti-aircraft defence.
5 September 1943	17.00	Taranto			Firing against enemy reconnaissance Plane.
9 September 1943 10 September 1943	16.18 18.55	from Taranto to anchorage In Malta	26,37	530	Following proclamation of the armistice (8 September 1943) the 5th Division leaves Taranto to transfer to Malta. German air attack at 18.55 on the 9th; unsuccessful, against which *Duilio* responds.
14 September 1943	16.10 18.20	from Malta to Malta	2,10	8	Transfer to anchorage at Marsa Scirocco.
8 October 1943	...	from Malta to Malta	...	...	Change of mooring at Marsa Scirocco.
9 October 1943 26 June 1944		Malta			Ship inactive at anchor at Marsa Scirocco.
27 June 1944	06.05 14.14	from Malta to Augusta	8,09	106	Transfer.
5 July 1944 6 July 1944	19.17 12.52	from Augusta to Taranto	17,35	296	Transfer.
7 July 1944 17 September 1944		Taranto			Ship inactive in port.
18 September 1944	06.00 14.55	From Taranto to Taranto	6,55	92	Gunnery exercises in the Gulf of Taranto.
12 October 1944	08.50 15.13	from Taranto to Taranto	6,23	98	Gunnery exercises in the Gulf of Taranto.
18 November 1944	08.03 12.37	from Taranto to Taranto	4,34	72	Gunnery exercises in the Gulf of Taranto.
19 November 1944 31 December 1944		Taranto			Ship inactive at anchorage.
27 January 1945	08.18	from Taranto	5,47	86	Gunnery exercises in the Gulf of Taranto
28 January 1945 13 March 1945		Taranto			Ship inactive at anchorage.
14 March 1945 15 March 1945	08.05 08.00	from Taranto to Siracusa	23,55	365	Transfer.
28 March 1945 29 March 1945	18.05 17.48	from Siracusa to Taranto	23,44	317	Transfer.
30 March 1945 8 May 1945		Taranto			Ship inactive in port

ANDREA DORIA

Date	Time	Location	Hours, minutes under way	Miles covered	Notes
10 June 1940 3 September 1940		Trieste			Fitting out at San Marco yard (CRDA)
4 October 1940	09.00 14.30	from Trieste to Pola	5,30	117	Transfer.
7 October 1940	07.00 13.00	from Pola to Venice	6,00	91	Transfer to be put in Principe di Piemonte drydock.
20 October 1940	07.15 13.10	from Venice to Pola	5,55	80	Transfer.
25 October 1940 26 October 1940	08.00 18.15	from Pola to Taranto	34,15	839	Transfer.
30 October 1940	...	Taranto			Air alarm. Participates in anti- aircraft fire.
1 November 1940	...	Taranto			Fire against enemy reconnaissance aircraft.
5 November 1940	12.07 19.45	from Taranto to Taranto	7,38	98	Gunnery exercises in the Gulf of Taranto.
11 November 1940	11.57 18.40	from Taranto Taranto	6,43	115	Gunnery exercises in the Gulf of Taranto.

Andrea Doria and *Vittorio Veneto* in the Tyrrhenian Sea on 11 January 1941.

The *Andrea Doria* photographed from another battleship during Operation M 42 in December 1941.

11 November 1940 12 November 1940	23.10 00.20	Taranto			British torpedo aircraft attack on the base at Taranto (Operation 'Judgement'). Participates in anti-aircraft defence.
12 November 1940 13 November 1940	15.02 17.34	from Taranto to Naples	26,32	420	Transfer of the Naval Forces.
15 November 1940 16 November 1940	18.08 14.02	from Naples to La Spezia	19,54	370	Transfer.
25 November 1940	11.05 18.31	from La Spezia to La Spezia	7,26	120	Gunnery exercises in the Gulf of Genoa.
5 December 1940	11.15 21.41	from La Spezia to La Spezia	10,26	173	Gunnery exercises in the Gulf of Genoa.
19 December 1940	11.35 20.53	from La Spezia to La Spezia	9,18	140	Gunnery exercises in the Gulf of Genoa.
29 December 1940	09.30 17.11	from La Spezia to La Spezia	7,41	119	Gunnery exercises in the Gulf of Genoa.
11 January 1941 12 January 1941	22.00 09.18	from La Spezia to La Spezia	11,18	500	Sortie by the Naval Squadron [SN] to find the carrier *Illustrious*, damaged in the Sicilian Channel. Operation cancelled. Tactical and gunnery exercises during return voyage.
13 January 1941	07.00 23.40	from La Spezia to La Spezia	16,40	96	Gunnery exercises in the Gulf of Genoa.
8 February 1941 11 February 1941	10.20 11.47 18.57 11.54	from La Spezia to La Spezia from La Spezia to Naples	1,14 65,47	1,354	Sortie by the SN to oppose British Operation 'Grog' (bombardment of Genoa). No contact with the enemy.
11 February 1941 12 February 1941	18.00 20.08	from Naples to La Spezia	26,08	326	Transfer.
24 February 1941	10.20 23.30	from La Spezia to La Spezia	13,10	160	Gunnery exercises in the Gulf of Genoa.
1 March 1941 2 March 1941	10.00 08.00	from La Spezia to La Spezia	22,00	170	Trials and gunnery exercises in the Gulf of Genoa.
20 March 1941 21 March 1941	07.00 03.00	from La Spezia to La Spezia	20,00	135	Gunnery exercises in the Gulf of Genoa.
4 April 1941 5 April 1941	16.00 11.40	from La Spezia to Naples	19,40	364	Transfer.
30 April 1941 1 May 1941	13.00 06.00	from Naples to Naples	17,00	256	Gunnery exercises.
2 May 1945 24 June 1941		Naples			Ship inactive in port
25 June 1941 26 June 1941	13.00 08.00	from Naples to Naples	19,00	321	Exercises.

Continued overleaf

9 July 1941 10 July 1941	23.06 02.07	Naples			Air raid. Participates in anti-aircraft defence.
10 July 1941 11 July 1941	23.08 02.22	Naples			Air raid. Participates in anti-aircraft defence.
11 July 1941 12 July 1941	17.30 16.00	from Naples to La Spezia	22,30	364	Transfer.
4 August 1941 6 August 1941	06.30 03.00	from La Spezia to Taranto	44,30	849	Transfer.
11 August 1941	10.05 21.17	from Taranto to Taranto	11,14	163	Gunnery exercises in the Gulf of Taranto.
20 August 1941 21 August 1941	11.00 02.00	from Taranto to Taranto	15,00	178	Gunnery exercises in the Gulf of Taranto.
25 August 1941 26 August 1941	10.00 01.23	from Taranto to Taranto	15,23	65	Gunnery exercises in the Gulf of Taranto.
24 September 1941 25 September 1941	12.40 03.50	from Taranto to Taranto	15,10	203	5th Division day and night gunnery exercises in the Gulf of Taranto.
13 December 1941 14 December 1941	18.40 01.30	from Taranto to Taranto	6,50	103	Participates in Operation M 41 (escort of convoys to Libya), suspended.
16 December 1941 19 December 1941	18.40 18.25	from Taranto to Taranto	71,45	1,519	Participates in Operation M 42 (escort of convoys to Libya). First Battle of Sirte (17 December 1941). From 17.53 to 17.59 on the 17th engages light enemy units with no outcome.
3 January 1942 4 January 1942	19.10 04.40	from Taranto to Taranto	9,30	70	Participates in Operation M 43 (escort of convoy to Libya). Mission cancelled because of engine breakdown.
20 February 1942	09.06 09.26	from Taranto to Taranto	0,20		Change of mooring.
21 February 1942 8 April 1942		Taranto			In drydock for work.
12 April 1942	07.00 11.00	from Taranto to Taranto	4,00	...	Change of mooring and machinery tests.
23 April 1942	12.40 18.12	from Taranto to Taranto	5,32	105	Machinery trials and gunnery exercises in the Gulf of Taranto.
15 May 1942 16 May 1942	13.10 08.08	from Taranto to Messina	18,58	364	Transfer and gunnery exercises.
25 May 1942	04.40 20.20	from Messina to Taranto	15,40	296	Transfer.
26 May 1942 17 September 1942		Taranto			Ship inactive in port.
17 September 1942	13.00 19.10	from Taranto to Taranto	6,10	101	Daytime gunnery exercises with *Duilio* in the Gulf of Taranto.
18 September 1942 17 February 1943		Taranto			Ship inactive in port.
18 February 1943	13.53 17.06	from Taranto to Taranto	3,13	15	Change of mooring.
1 April 1943	07.36 13.10	from Taranto to Taranto	5.34	...	Change of mooring.
1 April 1943	...	Taranto			Fire against enemy reconnaissance plane.
1 April 1943 3 June 1943		Taranto			Ship inactive at anchor.
4 June 1943	01.30 06.30	Taranto			Alarm against presumed enemy submarine. Explosive charges dropped from ship and patrol craft.
17 June 1943		Taranto			Fire against enemy reconnaissance plane.
22 June 1943	12.40 13.10	Taranto			Fire against enemy reconnaissance plane.

1 July 1943	06.15 10.10	from Taranto to Taranto	3,50		Change of mooring.
1 July 1943 11 July 1943		Taranto			In drydock for graving.
19 July 1943	08.16 08.50	from Taranto to Taranto	0,34		Move to train engine room personnel.
22 July 1943	05.30 06.55	from Taranto to Taranto	1,25	7	Move to train engine room personnel.
	11.44 12.55	from Taranto to Taranto	1,41		Move to train engine room personnel.
27 July 1943	14.31 19.00	from Taranto to Taranto	4,29	38	Gunnery exercises in the Gulf of Taranto.
27 July 1943 28 July 1943	21.03 01.13	from Taranto to Taranto	4,10	38	Night gunnery exercises in the Gulf of Taranto.
7 August 1943	16.48 21.20	from Taranto to Taranto	4,32	35	Gunnery exercises in the Gulf of Taranto.
21 August 1943	13.25 20.40	from Taranto to Taranto	7,15	119	Gunnery exercises in the Gulf of Taranto.
26 August 1943	03.31 05.30	Taranto			Air attack. Participates in anti-aircraft defence.
28 August 1943	12.52 13.56	Taranto			Air attack. Participates in anti-aircraft defence.
5 September 1943	17.00 17.14	Taranto			Fire against enemy reconnaissance aircraft.
9 September 1943 10 September 1943	16.25 19.10	from Taranto to anchorage at Malta	26,36	435	Following proclamation of the armistice (8 September 1943), the 5th Division leaves Taranto to transfer to Malta.
8 October 1943	07.17 16.55	from Malta to Malta	9,38	22	Transfer to anchorage at Marsa Scirocco.
9 October 1943 7 June 1944		Malta			Ship inactive at anchor in Marsa Scirocco.
8 June 1944	07.06 14.12	from Malta to Augusta	7,06	122	Transfer.
14 June 1944	10.48 17.04	from Augusta to Siracusa	1,16	21	Transfer.
15 June 1944 9 October 1944		Siracusa			Ship inactive in port.
10 October 1944	12.00 15.07	from Siracusa to Augusta	3,07	46	Transfer and exercises.
13 October 1944	12.33 14.17	from Augusta to Siracusa	1,44	35	Transfer and exercises.
14 October 1944 19 February 1945		Siracusa			Ship inactive in port.
20 February 1945 21 February 1945	16.57 12.55	from Siracusa to Augusta	19,58	364	Transfer to Taranto but returned to Augusta because of bad weather.
25 February 1945	13.25 15.05	from Augusta to Siracusa	1,40	20	Transfer.
13 March 1945 14 March 1945	16.28 20.00	from Siracusa to Taranto	27,32	410	Transfer.
21 March 1945	08.00 14.35	from Taranto to Taranto	6,35	99	Various exercises in the Gulf of Taranto.
29 March 1945 30 March 1945	14.00 07.00	from Taranto to Siracusa	17,00	264	Transfer.
31 April 1945 8 April 1945		Siracusa			Ship inactive in port.

Appendix 4

DAMAGE SUSTAINED BY MODERNISED 'CONTE DI CAVOUR' AND 'DUILIO' CLASS SHIPS

The description of the damage sustained before and during the war is drawn from reports and messages from headquarters and technical offices, for the most part written in the days and weeks following the events or while repair was in progress. Some of the graphics have been taken from period drawings or from reconstructions based on the text of the aforementioned documents.

Conte di Cavour

Contact with bottom in Mar Grande at Taranto, 14 April 1939

At 11:20 on 14 April the *Conte di Cavour*, while leaving Taranto's Mar Grande through the San Paolo passage, scraped the seabed at a speed of 6 knots. A lengthy drag and hull vibrations were experienced and the commander, Captain Lorenzo Gasparri, had the engines stopped and steered to port to quickly free the channel. Early examination revealed no problems with the steering gear or powerplant, but shortly afterwards oil leaks were noticed in cell No 55 of the triple bottom and it was discovered that it was under pressure because it was exposed to the sea, that the chain holding the repair mat (which was placed transversally beneath the hull) had parted and that the body of the mechanical log would not retract. The ship was anchored near the breakwater, while contamination of water in cell 49 of the port side triple bottom was also reported. The ship was ordered to return and at 14:50 was again at its mooring in Mar Grande, where divers resumed inspection of the hull, which continued into the following days.

The contact with the bottom had distorted an area of almost 40 metres of the bottom plating on the port side, between frames 40 forward and 2 aft about 3 metres from the keel, about 40cm wide and with a maximum warping of 10cm. In that stretch some of the rivets had sheared or loosened, and damage had been done to some of the floors and sea intakes for flooding the No 2 ammunition magazines and the bilge pump of the forward engine. Oil storage tank 55 and water tank 47 were open to the sea and there were minor leaks in the adjacent spaces and in the forward engine room. There were also minor leaks in water tank 49, in laundry space 45 and in dry cells 53 and 59 and in several lateral double hull spaces. Large areas of paint were stripped away, but the propellers and rudder were in perfect order.

The extent of the damage did not affect the ship's combat worthiness. Because of that a complete repair, which required placing the ship in drydock, was postponed and interim repairs were made with the ship afloat by using plugs and pouring concrete, and where possible, with electrical welding, and drying out the flooded spaces. The *Cavour* was later put into the Taranto naval dockyard's General Ferrati drydock in June 1939, but for other urgent work. In a later period in drydock (10 December 1939–4 January 1940) no leaks were found in the plates, while in the double bottom, which had been made watertight by using cement, some of the watertight flooring was found to have minor leaks that were eliminated by adding more cement.

Torpedo aircraft attack against Taranto, night of 11/12 November 1940

During the course of the first torpedo attack the *Conte di Cavour* was hit at 23:15 on 11 November by an 18in (450mm) Mark XII torpedo, with an explosive charge of 176kg of TNT and a duplex fuse (that is, triggered either by contact or by magnetic influence). The torpedo, dropped at low height and coming from the ship's port side, passed beneath the hull and exploded just abaft No 2 main gun turret, where the bottom of the ship is almost horizontal, which meant that the explosive energy was absorbed by the ship's structure to a very high degree, in addition to the shock wave of the explosion rebounding off of the seabed itself. The explosion did not, therefore, affect the Pugliese underwater protective system, which protected only the flanks of the ship's vitals and which thus was not able to absorb any of the explosion's blast energy.

The explosion caused extensive structural damage, opening a gash about 12 metres long in the keel and 8 metres in the frame floors between forward frames 24 and 36. Normal lighting was lost immediately in the ship's forward and midship areas, but the backup lighting system quickly came on line; within three minutes the ammunition stowage spaces of the fore main and medium gun turrets were flooded, as were the lower portions of the main gun turret installations, the high-capacity pump room, the bilges beneath the fore diesel generator room, refrigerated spaces Nos 1, 2 and 3, and there were leaks between forward frames 35 and 59 through the vents in the air spaces between the longitudinal bulkhead and the curved bulkhead that internally bordered on the Pugliese absorbing cylinder; in addition, the concussion broke the port anchor stopper and the second bower fell to the bottom. The attempt to engage the forward high-capacity pump immediately failed because it could not be started nor could the discharge valve be activated properly. Despite closing the watertight doors, the flow of water from the pump room below the forward electrical station prevented starting up one of the two diesel generators; the space itself had to be evacuated and the distribution panel deactivated. Thus, the *Cavour* was quickly without its main means of pumping to cope with the flooding in the area that had been damaged. However, from examinations made in the spaces below the lower deck within the twenty minutes following the explosion, there were no leaks forward of the bulkhead corresponding to forward frame 68, while under the orders room and the fire control centre there were small leaks making their way through pipes, cable conduits and air vents, as well as leaks along the electrical circuits for the forward main gun turrets and the forward turbo generator, and backup of water in the toilets.

The immediate actions taken involved checking the closure of all of the vertical and horizontal doors and hatches in the ship's fore and midship sections, plugging the water infiltration in the bathrooms and reactivation of the normal lighting system by using jury-rigged circuits. The ship's captain, Captain Ernesto Ciurlo, also ordered that preparations to start the main engines, which were already under way at the time of the air attack, should be speeded up. At 20:30 and in the minutes that followed he transmitted in clear to the C-in-C of I Squadron aboard the *Littorio*, Admiral Inigo Campioni, three messages containing an urgent request for tugs and pumping equipment and a summary description of the flooding. He also sent an officer to the *Littorio* to confirm receipt of the messages he had sent. As the captain declared in a subsequent report, his intention was, in the event that the ship began to settle rapidly, to bring the ship to rest on the nearby 12-metre bottom. At 23:40 and 23:45, the tugs *Tenace* and a 'Lipari' type came alongside the *Cavour*, to which were passed, respectively, a towing cable fore and aft. Around 24:00 Admiral Bruto Brivonesi, commander of the 5th Division, came on board on his own initiative (although he was simultaneously ordered to do so by Campioni), and assumed direction of the salvage operations.

Up to this point the narrative has followed the reconstruction of events made by Captain Ciurlo in the ship's log and in a later report by him. What follows is the reconstruction, as uneven as it may be, and observations by Admiral Brivonesi, relating to the subsequent controversy concerning the causes of the ship's sinking.

As soon as he came on board and was informed by Ciurlo of the state of affairs, he agreed the plan to move the ship to the shallows. The unmooring operations had proceeded slowly because of the lack of electrical power or because of damage to the capstans, but were completed at 03:00 on the 12th and the ship was ready to move by its own power and the assistance of the two tugs, remaining attached to only the bow mooring buoy, ready to be released. At that moment, however, Lieutenant Giulio Cipollini, the *Cesare*'s fire direction officer, boarded the ship bringing Campioni's order to not beach the ship, without, however, specifying any reasons. In the hours that followed, other instructions in the same vein were issued by Campioni through two high-ranking officers. Brivonesi followed them and ordered that the final mooring not be released and that salvage operations be carried out using external pumps provided by the tugs that were already alongside and by other vessels that were on their way, in particular the salvage ship *Teseo*. Ciurlo and other *Cavour* officers made repeated attempts to beach her in the light of the increased flooding and the diminishing effectiveness of the external pumps, but in vain. The operation, in fact, was not going well. The *Tenace*, which had released its towing cable and which had come alongside the port side of the forecastle in order to get its pumps into action, did not have the appropriate hoses and the small tug *Boeo* was sent to the dockyard to pick them up, but seems to not have returned. At 01:00 the draught at the bow was about 14 metres (about 3.5 metres more than normal) and kept on sinking by about 30cm each hour. At 01:40 the tug *Vigoroso* arrived and came alongside the *Tenace*, in the space of a few minutes laying a 150mm hose, but despite repeated attempts, it was not able to draw any water from the lower deck until 04:00.

Meanwhile, at 02:30, the tanker *Volturno* had come alongside

Taranto, 11-12 November 1940. Successive phases of immersion of the battleship *Conte di Cavour* from the time of the torpedo ('siluro') hitting the ship until being run aground and sinking. (Erminio Bagnasco drawing)

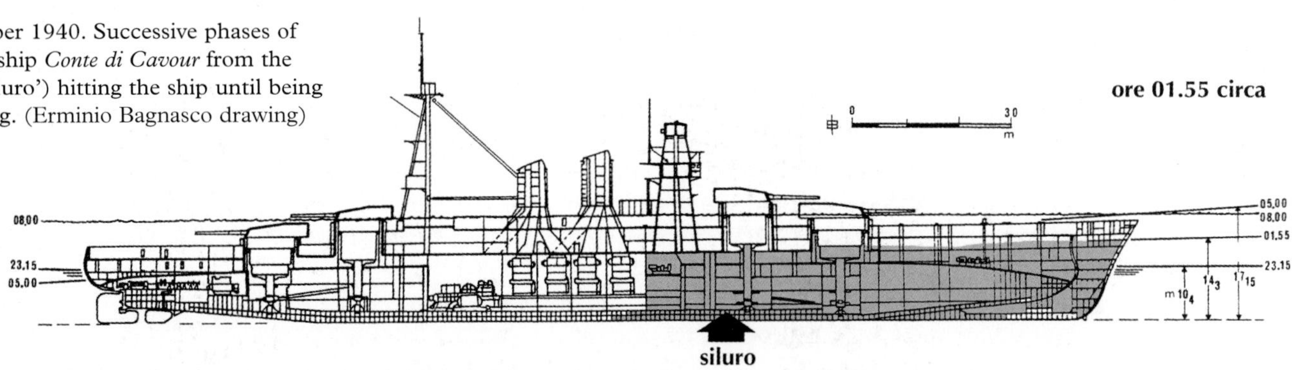

Progression of immersion of the bow of the *Cavour* (*) until running aground (12 November 1940)

Time	01.00	01.55	03.00	03.53	04.15	04.45	05.00
Immersion (metres) (**)	14.00	14.30	15.80	15.30	15.80	16.30	17.15

(*) From the log of the *Cavour* and report by Admiral Brivonesi dated 7 December 1940.
(**) At the moment of being torpedoed (23.15) the immersion of *Cavour* at the bow was 10.42 metres.

The battleship *Conte di Cavour* resting on the bottom of Mar Grande at Taranto on the morning of 12 November 1940.

aft on the port side of the *Vigoroso* and had laid a 120mm hose, which it had lowered to the first lower deck, where the water had reached a height of 35cm; the hose, however, only worked between 03:00 and 03:30 because of various problems that occurred. At that time immersion had reached 14.80 metres, progressing at a rate of 50cm in less than an hour. Meanwhile, at 02:50, the tanker *Frigido* came alongside on the starboard side towards the bow, whose 120mm hose was lowered through the skylight into the prison spaces below the first lower deck, where overflowing water could be heard; this was the only external equipment that worked regularly and continuously from 03:15. At 04:15, on the battleship's starboard side, astern of the *Frigido*, the *Teseo*, along with some tugs, had come alongside, and whose 120mm hose was placed forward of No 1 main gun turret on the first lower deck, but its pumps did not begin to work until the battleship's run to the shallows, and with little result.

Shortly after 04:00 the fate of the *Cavour* seemed sealed; immersion at the bow had reached 15.80 metres and was progressing rapidly, despite shifting fuel oil from the fore compartments to aft compartments and flooding one of the aft balancing cells as ordered by Brivonesi. At 04:20, when water was lapping the forecastle deck (at 04:45 immersion reached 16 metres, and at the stem the forecastle had dipped below sea level), Brivonesi ordered the mooring at the buoy to be released and the tug *Porto Pisano*, which had already attached a cable, to tow the ship towards the shallows, without the aid of the battleship's engines, whose assistance Captain Ciurlo had requested. During the tow, which was already delayed because of the significant level of immersion at the bow, the situation continued to get worse and around 05:00 the *Cavour*, which was down by the bow as far as the capstans (17.15 metres immersion), hit bottom. Until that time, the ship had remained in perfect transverse trim, but ten minutes after it had run aground lost stability and heeled progressively to starboard, despite the flooding of five of the port balancing cells that had been quickly ordered, until at 06:00 it reached 25 degrees and, later, 45–50 degrees, appearing to be about to capsize. During this phase the admiral had the boilers shut down (05:30) and the crew evacuated by the nearby tugs and tankers. At the conclusion of the operation (06:15) all of those ships pulled away from the sinking battleship. After 08:00, as the flooding extended aft, the ship began to right itself when the stern hit the seabed. The ship rested, almost

Detail of the damage caused to the hull of the *Conte di Cavour* by the British torpedo that hit the ship on the evening of 11 November 1940.

completely submerged, settling on a level bottom that was rather muddy and covered with algae, with only its superstructures above water.

The sinking of the *Cavour* led to a train of controversy between Admiral Brivonesi and Captain Ciurlo because of their differing views on how best to save the ship. The admiral wanted to keep it afloat, avoiding beaching it for fear of the ship's reaction with the bottom and putting faith in external pumping systems; the captain, having ascertained the uselessness of the ship's pumping equipment, intended to beach it quickly to avoid its complete sinking. These divergences came fully to light after their initial reports reached Supermarina; the controversy was sharpened in early December 1940 when the Chief of Staff of the Navy, Admiral Domenico Cavagnari, interrogated Ciurlo and the declarations he made, set down in a memorandum, were submitted to Brivonesi for rebuttal, which he then presented to Campioni. It should be stated at the outset that on the night of 11 November, as soon as he became aware of the torpedoing of the *Cavour*, the C-in-C of I Squadron entrusted the management of the salvage operation to Brivonesi and left him free to act as he felt best, 'keeping in mind that beaching the ship by the bow could present the danger that the ship might overturn'. This directive was repeated to Brivonesi several times throughout the night, but (according to Brivonesi) without any explanation being given, which led him to assume that it stemmed from a fear that beaching would cause damage to the keel structures, which were probably weakened by the explosion [in effect, broken]. Therefore, he held to that guidance, even though he had initially agreed with Ciurlo's opinion, and in the rebuttal submitted to Campioni he had recognised that at 01:00 on the 12th the fate of the ship was already sealed without the aid of effective external assistance, but for which he still had hope.

The difference also had to do with the beaching manoeuvre. Brivonesi, afraid of causing further damage to the hull structures, rejected Ciurlo's proposal to speed up the beaching with the ship's engines and, in fact, ordered the tug on the bow to proceed at minimum speed. Then, when the ship's stem had touched bottom, and when the ship lost stability and heeled to starboard, he rejected Ciurlo's proposal to have the other tug on the stern pull to port and to have that side of the hull rest on the bottom, fearing that it could cause the ship to overturn. Instead, he ordered five of the port balancing cells to be flooded, but filling these took much longer than Ciurlo's proposed manoeuvre. Seen with hindsight and ignoring other insignificant differences in the reconstruction of events and assessment of the situation, it appears obvious that Captain Ciurlo had immediately correctly judged the state of affairs and had identified the immediate grounding of the ship as the only measure capable of saving her, as was done for the *Littorio* and the *Duilio*. At first Brivonesi was of the same mind, but once he had received directives from Campioni, he held strictly to them, ignoring the fact that the C-in-C was not in a position to follow the evolving situation in a close and continuous manner, and forgetting that he himself had been given the freedom to make decisions. It was mainly that situation that led to the fate of the *Cavour* being different from that of the other two torpedoed battleships.

Giulio Cesare

Contact with bottom in Mar Grande at Taranto, 14 April 1939

At 10:26 on 14 April the *Giulio Cesare*, while leaving Taranto's Mar Grande through the San Paolo passage, scraped the bottom at a speed of 6 knots. The commander, Captain Angelo Varoli Piazza, felt four shocks in rapid succession and ordered the engines to be stopped. After headway had carried the ship past the defensive barrages, he had the engines restarted in order to free the channel. At 10:38 he again stopped engines to recover the chains of the collision mats that had parted. The initial impression was that the *Cesare* had scraped against some obstacle associated with the barrages, as the depths shown on the charts were all greater than 12 metres. At 10:45 the captain resumed the operation and carried out the scheduled exercise at a sustained speed. At the same time the hull and spaces assumed to be affected were checked, without any damage being found. It was not until 16:28 on the 14th, while the ship was resuming its mooring in Mar Grande, having re-entered through the San Vito passage, that it was noticed that the forepeak was completely flooded. By evening the ship was down slightly by the bow (10.60 metres draught at the bow and 10.10 metres immersion at the stern) with a displacement of 28,424 tons; checks carried out that same evening and the following day using divers, discovered the damage described below.

On the port side, from the fore-foot bulb to forward frame 32 there were slight but numerous distortions, damage and separation of the outer plates (decreasing aft of forward frame 2) as well as distortion of frames and floors, especially between forward frames 6 and 10 with a maximum warp of 12cm. Damage was minor on the port side, running from the bulb to forward frame 34. The forepeak was completely flooded, as was the bilge below the provisions room in the area between the old and the new bow between forward frames 76 and 66 and the dry cells between forward frames 1 and 7; there were slight leaks between forward frames 66 and 60, as also in dry cell 24 and in the well of the log meter. Large areas of paintwork were completely or partially scraped off, but the propellers and rudder were in perfect order. The damage to the *Cesare* was slightly greater than that suffered by the *Cavour* – the bulbous fore-foot, in particular, was quite damaged – but did not compromise operational effectiveness. Because of that its complete repair, which required placing the ship in drydock, was postponed and interim repairs were made with the ship afloat by using plugs and pouring concrete, and where possible, with electrical welding, and drying out the flooded spaces. No specific documentation has been found concerning any later, more complete, repairs, but it does not appear that the distortions to the bottom of the hull were completely eliminated.

Battle of Punta Stilo, 9 July 1940
Damage due to enemy fire

At 15:59 the *Giulio Cesare* was hit by a 381mm (15in) round from the battleship *Warspite* at a very high plunging angle given the range of 24,000 metres. The round struck the aft funnel on the starboard side at the height of the second handrail and exploded, exiting from the base of the funnel itself. The head of the shell, which took a downward path, penetrated the forecastle between forward frames 0 and 1 at 5.5 metres from the port bulwark, through the casemate, causing the charges in the stand-by lockers of No 4 120/50 turret to catch fire, penetrated the upper deck and the bulkhead at forward frame 4, penetrated into the 'mixed petty officer quarters' (petty officers of different departments) on the first lower deck and came to rest against the inner face of the port side armour (120mm) between forward frames 4 and 5, after having broken through the backing plating and wooden cushion. On the forecastle deck the blaze generated by the burning of the stand-by charges vented up through the entry hole made by the head of the shell, set fire to the individual life-preservers lashed to the guardrails and the heat caused the ammunition stored in the lockers of No 4 37/54 gun mounting to explode. The fires caused by the combustion of the No 4 medium gun turret charge lockers were fed by the embers, mats and wooden material, spreading throughout the port side casemate and then spread further to the starboard side. Flames and gases made their way to Nos 2 and 4 medium gun turrets, through the casing ejection ports and elevator openings. The fires did not cause excessive concern to the staff captain and the head of damage control as they involved areas that were not vital and which were quickly limited. As we shall see later, the C-in-C of the Naval Forces, Admiral Campioni, was of a different opinion.

In greater detail, the damage suffered by the ship can be summarised as follows:

Estimated path of the 381mm shell and of its cap which hit the *Giulio Cesare* at Punta Stilo.

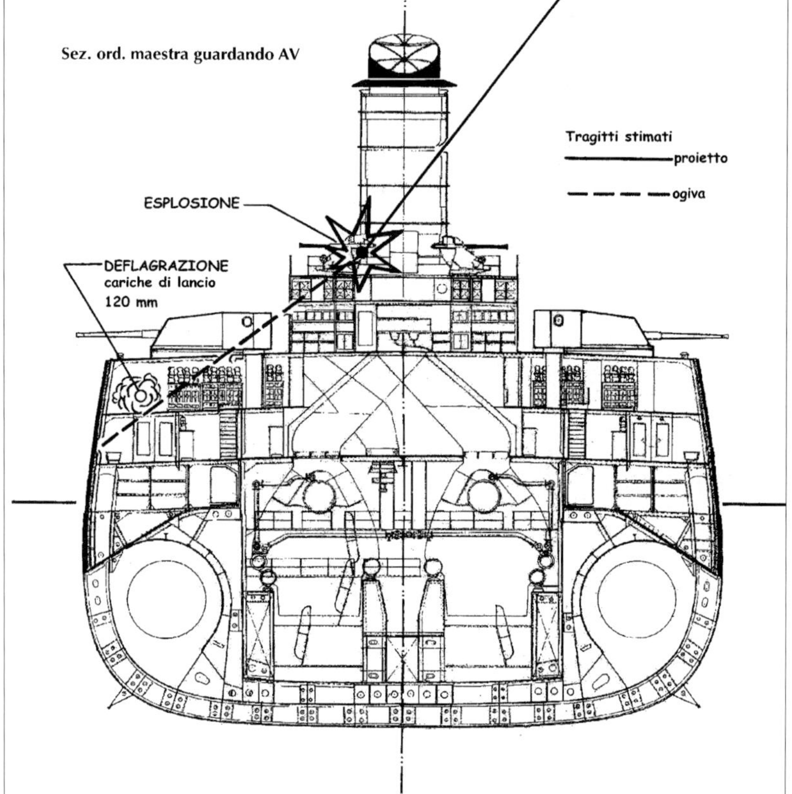

Hull and superstructure

The starboard side of the aft funnel showed an entrance hole made by the projectile and, on the port side, a large gash 5 metres by 3.5 metres on the funnel casing due to the explosion as well as demolishing the steam pipes (vent pipes for boiler steam), damage to various smoke vents for boilers 5, 7 and 8, destruction of the fog laying apparatus with escape of hot oil, which splashed into spaces below the base of the funnel, producing oil vapour and a fire in the donkey boiler space. The fore funnel was marked only by splinter holes. The forecastle was torn open on the port side between forward frames 0 to 2 with about a metre of the beam ripped away at forward frame 1 and heavy damage to other structures in that area of the deck, including the space below it. On the same side of the forecastle the officers', petty officers' and crew galleys were partly demolished as well as the firefighting pipes and systems near the aft funnel. There were also holes and damage to the upper deck between frames 0 and 4 with damage to and destruction of access hatchways and stairways to the forecastle. On the first lower deck there were large holes in the bulkhead at forward frame 4 and twisting of forward frame 5. Various spaces and systems (ventilation ducts, bathrooms, etc) in the officer and petty officer accommodations were damaged or destroyed.

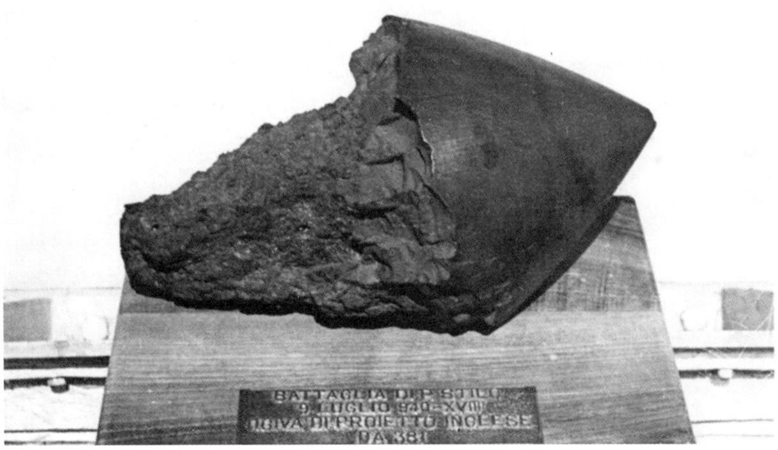

Fragment of the cap of the 381mm (15in) shell fired by HMS *Warspite* at Punta Stilo that hit the battleship *Giulio Cesare*.

Armament

The trunnion of the port side aiming device of No 2 medium gun turret was perforated and the rangefinder optics were damaged. The water used to put out the fires caused damage to the electrical circuits of various networks and the charge locker was destroyed by the explosion of the charges it contained. The turret, however, was quickly made serviceable. No 4 medium gun turret had its guns only slightly damaged by splinters, but the armour was pierced in several places on the roof and sides and many plates were bent. The turret trunk was also damaged in several places by splinters and traverse was jammed, rendering the turret non-operational, as was also the rangefinder. The portion of the inclinometer that protruded from the tower was broken off and various electrical circuits were damaged because of the water

Entrance hole of the shell in the after funnel of *Giulio Cesare*.

Area of the forecastle deck of the *Giulio Cesare* damaged by fire that followed the explosion of the British shell at Punta Stilo.

pumped into the casemate to put out the fires. The fire direction centre was not damaged. No 6 medium gun turret suffered only slight damage to its electrical circuits because of the water, but the turret was able to be made operational. Both of the 37/54 guns of station 4 were put out of action by the explosion of the charge lockers and by the fire, and their mountings were twisted. One 37/54 gun of station 3 (starboard side) was out of action because of damage to the breechblock caused by the heat of the fire.

Powerplant

The damage that had the greatest effect on the ship's operational status, even though temporary, was to the main machinery. Because of the fire that spread on the upper decks, boiler rooms 4-5 and 6-7 were filled with smoke sucked in by the ducts and turbo-ventilators, accompanied by light burning material and a few splinters; the duty personnel donned their masks, but were unable to hold their stations with the resultant shutdown of the four boilers. There were two casualties. The same thing happened in the aft engine room but there, once the crew had put on their masks, they were able to remain at their posts.

The almost simultaneous shutdown of the four boilers mentioned led to a significant drop in pressure of the port side aft engine that continued to be fed only by boiler 8, as well as a slight lowering of pressure in the starboard engine. The Chief Engineering Officer at first ordered the speed of the forward engine to be decreased in order to maintain pressure and, then, once the cause of the shutdown of the four boilers had been determined, ordered the maximum number of revolutions possible based on the pressure furnished by the four boilers that were still working, corresponding to a speed of 20 knots. At 16:45, with fresh personnel equipped with masks, boilers 4 and 5 were reactivated, allowing a speed of 25 knots. This could not be done for boilers 6 and 7 because of the persisting dense smoke that hampered visibility. It does not appear that they were brought on line subsequently, as the ship was able to maintain a sufficient speed of 23–24 knots. In addition, the crew were able to put out the fires in the port side casemate and on the lower deck, to deal with a flood of hot oil in the boiler smokeboxes that was caused by a break in the oil delivery line for the aft funnel smoke generators, and to deal with the flooding on the port side lower deck caused by the water used in extinguishing the fires above and because of the discharge of water from a broken firemain.

Electrical and telephone systems

In general, there was no breakdown worthy of note in the generation and distribution of electrical power before and after the 381mm hit, except for the area directly affected. There the major damage – caused by the use of salt water to put out the fires and by the effects of the explosion – affected the light and power circuits of No 4 medium gun turret, the power circuits in the crew and petty officer galleys, which were not in use, the lighting circuits of the lines and lamps above the forecastle, which were also out of service and, most of all, the lighting circuits in the port side casemate, in the donkey boiler space and in the port side petty officers mess. Also damaged were the storage batteries of the port side medium gun turrets and of the 37/54 gun that had been hit. There were also breakdowns of the telephone networks in the area affected by the 381mm round.

Personnel

Losses were high. According to initial estimates by the medical service on board there were forty-eight killed and sixty-eight wounded, of which fifteen lightly wounded remained on board, while the seriously wounded were taken off the ship at Messina. According to other sources the dead increased to sixty-six and wounded to forty-nine. Most of the losses were attributed to burns, followed by fragmentation wounds and asphyxiation.

Damage due to concussion of outgoing salvos

Minor damage was registered because of the effect of the ship's gunnery itself, especially after steering to disengage, when the

Cesare fired with her main guns while withdrawing. The biggest problem was caused by the overload of the fuse circuit that fed the aft fire control centre, which was quickly eliminated by using the backup circuit. The same salvo caused minor problems to the rudder machinery. There were short circuits in the extreme stern accommodations. At 18:09, some time after firing had ceased, the electrical fuse on the manual rudder gear was tripped, caused by a sharp change in course, a problem that was eliminated in about a minute. Also as a result of the concussion, some plates of the medium gun SDT were warped, as were some support arms for the rangefinders and other fire direction instruments and there was damage in several places in the ventilation ducts of the turbo-generator spaces, as there were also problems with the elevation, loading and aiming mechanisms of the aft 13.2mm machine guns because of the aft main gun turrets firing astern. It is likely that similar damage due to the effects of firing the guns was experienced by the *Conte di Cavour*.

As Campioni wrote in his report, the damage to the *Cesare* was 'magnified' by the fires. In reality, they were more spectacular than they were serious: only one medium gun turret and several 37/54 and 13.2mm guns were put out of action and the ship's combat worthiness was in danger only to the extent that smoke from the fires had been sucked into some of the boiler rooms. However, the flames had spread rather easily and Campioni laid out a series of measures to remedy the situation, which in part were applicable to all other major Italian ships, such as reduction or different stowage arrangements for individual lifesavers (to be made fireproof) and hammocks, the latter having proven to be dangerous sources of spreading fire; elimination or reduction of ammunition stored in the ready-use lockers and adoption of watertight ready-use lockers for the machine guns; draining the smoke-generating feed tubes located in the funnels during combat, keeping only the stern smoke generators ready for use; increasing the fire suppression pipe system on the superstructures and installing overhead flooding sprinklers in the anti-torpedo and anti-aircraft ammunition lockers; installing fireproof doors on the first lower deck. The smoke that filled the boiler rooms from the fires sucked in by the fans had shown the shortcomings of the systems that provided air to the boiler rooms. Campioni proposed that spaces in which personnel were on duty be made completely independent of air ducts. In the meantime, the availability of gas masks, respirators and fire extinguishers was to be increased, as had for some time already been requested in vain.

Transferred to Genoa for repairs, work on the *Cesare* was completed in less than a week. It is not known if and when the above-mentioned technical measures were adopted on this and other ships, as no documentation in this regard has been found.

Bombing of Naples, evening of 8 January 1941

At 19:59 several 250-pound (113.5kg) armour-piercing or semi-armour-piercing bombs exploded in the water to starboard of the *Giulio Cesare* at varying distances, one of which, however, was only 4 metres away. Another two bombs of the same type exploded on the southern end of Luigi Razza quay near the two aft main gun turrets a few dozen metres from where the ship was moored, scattering a great number of splinters that caused the

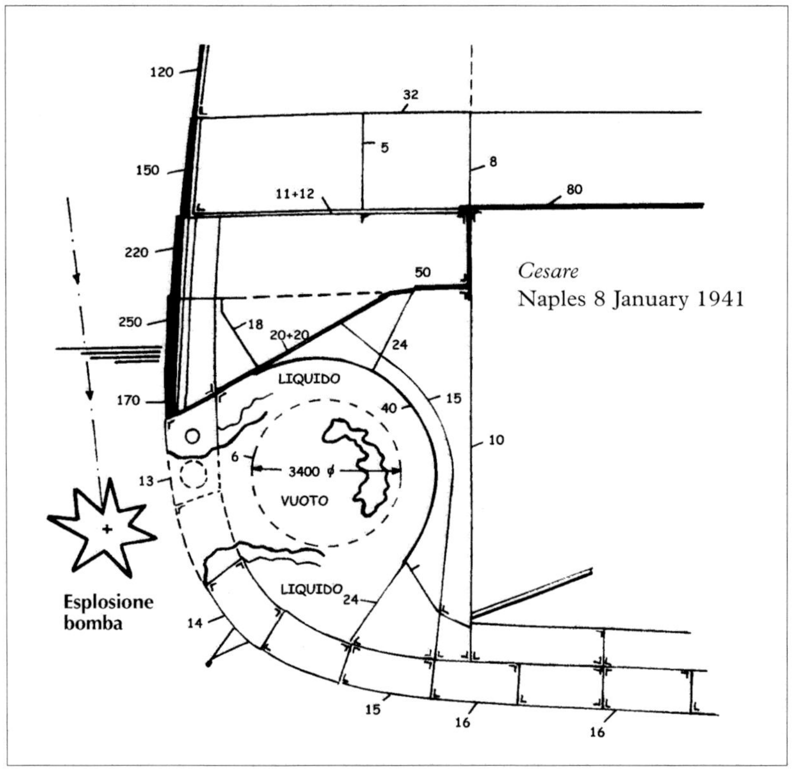

Cesare
Naples 8 January 1941

deaths of a cadet midshipman and four sailors, as well as wounding other personnel. The bomb that exploded in the water 4 metres from the hull made a hole with inward-facing edges 2.40 metres long by 1.40 metres wide astride forward frame 10 about 8 metres below the waterline. Fore and aft of the opening there was twisted metal and rivets missing from the plates up to the lower edge of the armoured belt (about 3.5 metres below the waterline) and, finally, severing the attachment points of the bilge keels for a length of about 5 metres. Despite the size of the opening, the underwater protection system absorbed the explosion well, distributing the force of the blast laterally but not downwards. Only one dry cell of the double bottom (cell 023) was flooded and, by means of the automatic balancing system, the corresponding cell on the opposite side (cell 024) was also flooded. In all, the battleship took on 200 tons of water with an increase of immersion at the bow of 8cm and at the stern of 3cm. Initially, the ship listed 1 degree to starboard, but soon after, the automatic balancing system returned it to an even keel.

The *Cesare* was first transferred to La Spezia to disembark ammunition and fuel and then to Genoa for repair. There, from 15 to 19 January 1941, the ship was put into the largest drydock in the area of Le Grazie, where the work was done. On 30 January the ship returned to La Spezia for final preparations and re-embarking stores.

Duilio

Torpedo aircraft attack against Taranto, night of 11/12 November 1940

During the second wave of the attack, at 12:59 on the 11th the *Duilio* was hit by a torpedo of the same type as the one that struck the *Conte di Cavour*. The torpedo was dropped at low level, on the starboard side at a distance estimated at 400 metres and an angle of impact of about 80 degrees; it passed below the hull and exploded under the keel roughly under No 2 main gun turret, where the bottom of the ship was almost horizontal and where the force of the explosion absorbed by the ship's structure was greatest, exacerbated by the proximity to the bottom, which reflected the shock wave. As previously mentioned for the *Cavour*, the explosion in this case did not affect the Pugliese underwater protection system.

The explosion caused considerable damage and, in particular:

- A gash in the outer plating astride the keel between forward frames 32½ and 49 starboard and forward frames 37 and 49 port side, with an opening at the keel of 14.50 metres starboard and 11 metres port side and for the floors of 8.50 metres starboard and 4.50 port side;
- Breaking and partial ripping away of the keel in the area affected by the explosion;
- Damage to the plating of the double and triple bottom above the opening and minor damage to the lower deck;
- Destruction of the No 2 main gun turret magazine and shell room and damage to the turret central pivot, charge and projectile carousels, displacement of the turret trunk and damage to several adjacent structural elements;
- Destruction of the No 1 main gun turret shell room; the turret installation itself did not, however, suffer any appreciable damage, the turret being able to traverse freely;
- Damage to various fire direction systems due to the concussion.

The ammunition stowage spaces of Nos 1 and 2 main gun turrets were quickly filled with toxic gases through the vents between the flooded areas and the first lower deck spaces. Fortunately, the two transverse watertight bulkheads that enclosed them at forward frames 31 and 59 were intact, even though this did not stop the spread of flooding due to leaks in other compartments fore and aft of the stowage spaces themselves. Loss of human life was limited to one dead, as the explosion took place in an area of the ship where only a few of the crew were present, but the gas generated poisoned 150 men and prevented a full damage assessment, partly because of the unsuitability of the gas masks for that type of smoke and the shortage of the more effective individual respirators. The immediate responses involved activating the ventilators and fans to disperse the fumes, shoring up the bulkheads surrounding the forward magazine and shell rooms, closing off all of the horizontal and vertical hatches above the armoured deck, closing the open scuppers and blocking all other openings as well as starting the high-capacity drainage pumps at the bow to contain the flooding in the adjacent diesel generator space. Unfortunately, this last measure proved to be useless, because of

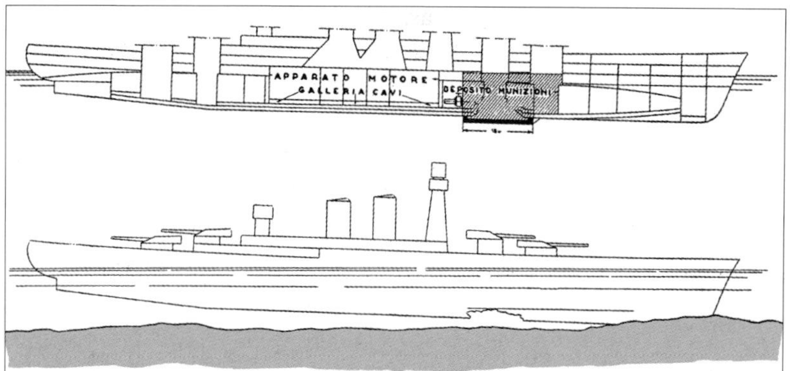

Flooding experienced by the battleship *Duilio* following torpedo damage on 11 November 1940 and position of the hull with its bow resting on the bottom to prevent the ship from sinking.

The battleship *Duilio*, badly damaged by a torpedo on the evening of 11 November 1940, photographed a few days later with her bow still resting on the shallow bottom of Taranto's Mar Grande where she was quickly moved to in order to avoid her sinking.

damage to the outlet pipe as well and because the flooding produced an electricity cut after just fifteen minutes. To assist the *Duilio* the naval dockyard sent a tug equipped with a pump and the *Po*, a tanker, which, at least initially, was not much help. Despite the measures taken, heavy flooding continued to spread in many spaces not directly affected by the explosion (armoured RT station, fore compass space, electrical control centre, cypher office, orders room, fire control centre, air cooling and refrigerator systems, medium gun magazines, forward diesel generator) through access doors to the ammunition spaces, the cable tunnel, the ventilation and electrical cable ducts and the riveting of the armoured decks. The powerplant, however, remained completely operational.

At first, despite the spread of the flooding, the ship's situation did not appear alarming. But, as time passed, the increasing bow-down attitude made it advisable to run her aground in shallow water in order to prevent further spread of the flooding. At 00:30 on the 12th an order came from the *Littorio* to light the boilers and to make ready to get under way, and at 01:30 it was decided to beach *Duilio* by the bow. At 02:55, with her own engines and with the assistance of two tugs, the ship was rotated 180 degrees and made to run aground on a 12-metre deep mud bottom. Once the bow had come to rest on the bottom the situation stabilised and there was no further concern. The ship had taken on a total of 5800 tons of water, with an immersion at the bow of 3 metres, corresponding to a trim by the bow of 1 degree 25 minutes. Transverse trim was unchanged, and the forecastle was completely submerged. With respect to the spread of flooding on the *Duilio*, it was a repeat of what has been said about the *Cavour*.

Of the three battleships torpedoed at Taranto, the *Duilio* fared best of all. Theoretically, it would have been possible to carry out a more rapid recovery compared with the other two, but the rupture of the keel below the two forward main gun turrets argued against immediately drydocking the ship at Taranto for fear of compromising the hull's alignment; it was preferred to first apply an external metal caisson attached to the undamaged parts of the hull in order to seal it. Once the caisson was in place, the *Duilio* was to be moved elsewhere for a complete repair, since the large Ferrati drydock in Taranto was scheduled to host the *Littorio*. In the days following the torpedoing, measures were taken to protect the ship, placing a double layer of anti-torpedo nets, except to the north because of its proximity to the shore, and arranging for protection by generating artificial fog by a torpedo boat moored nearby. Admiral Carlo Bergamini, appointed as head of Marinalles (the inspectorate for construction, fitting out and testing new ships) assumed command of the salvage and repair operations and the work was contracted, in addition to the local naval dockyard, mainly to the Cantieri Riuniti del Tirreno as well as, for specific items, to CRDA and Ansaldo.

As for the *Littorio*, Bergamini established the following priorities for carrying out the repair work:

- Work indispensable to ready the ship for a wartime mission, except for No 2 turret;
- Work necessary, but that could be completed with the ship ready;
- Work to be delayed, as not essential to the ship's combat effectiveness, unless it interfered with indispensable work.

By mid-December all of the spaces not directly open to the sea had been drained. It was thus possible to pump out 1900 tons of water and the greater buoyancy achieved was enough to raise the bow from the bottom and to float the ship. Thus, with increasing difficulty, as progress was made closer to the damaged areas, another 1400 tons of water were discharged and by Christmas all of the damaged machinery could be removed for repair or replacement. At the same time a caisson of mild steel was built in the Tosi shipyards in Taranto as well as a 120-ton cellular structure that was shaped to conform to the bottom part of the hull affected by the explosion. The structure, launched on 23 December, was towed to the battleship's bow, where it was slung from two sheers and slipped under the ship's bow in the desired position by emptying the tanks and raising the sheers; it was then attached to the intact exterior bottom plating with nuts and bolts (at the time, underwater electrical welding was unknown); the watertight seal between the caisson and the hull was achieved by 'gargami' (fothering mats covered by large cables sealed with raw wool cloth) and by wooden wedges sealed with the same type of covering. It was a very challenging operation from the nautical point of view and executed in thirty-five hours of demanding work by divers.

In January, with the hull made watertight, work was begun to pump out the spaces directly affected by the opening, where 2500 tons of water were still present, as well as removal of wrecked and damaged equipment, repair of the transverse bulkheads at the ends of the affected area between the triple bottom and the lower deck and hooking up the lowest part of the hull to the condenser circulation pumps. Because of its very poor condition, it proved impossible to render the triple bottom completely watertight and thus to form an internal watertight area. In the end, a contoured fairing was made between the forward edge of the plug and the hull, thus reducing the resistance to movement and stresses on the caisson itself.

On 25 January 1941 the ship was ready for a trial to see if the provisional repairs to the hull were watertight, which provided positive results that afternoon, as the ship reached a speed of 20 knots without experiencing any problems. On 26 January the *Duilio* began her transfer to Genoa for a complete repair, arriving on the 28th having steaming at an average speed of 16 knots. On 3 February the battleship was put into drydock No 3 of Le Grazie, which could hold the ship with the additional caisson under the hull, and was prepared for active and passive anti-aircraft defence. The ship remained there until 3 May, when she moved to La Spezia to re-enter squadron service. While in drydock, the caisson was removed, the hull was restored, and main gun turrets Nos 1 and 2 were repaired, as were the ammunition stowage spaces and other damaged areas and equipment. No other details regarding the work have been found, which involved the Cantieri del Tirreno, Ansaldo and San Giorgio, or of subsequent tests and trials. All of the work was done to the complete satisfaction of Bergamini, as it was completed more than a month earlier than expected.

Operation K 7 (21–24 February 1942). Damage from heavy seas

On the morning of 23 February 1942 while returning from Operation K 7, the *Duilio* ran into very heavy weather in the Ionian caused by a southeastern storm with winds up to force ten and the ship was significantly battered by the sea in its after areas. As the squadron commander, Admiral Carlo Bergamini related, the battleship handled far worse than expected because of a series of breakdowns and problems, almost all due to leaking water which reduced its operational efficiency, as shown here following:

- Major leaks in the spaces between the turret trunk and the starboard 90/50 turret platforms with the resulting flooding of the battery below. The water reached the upper level of the coamings of all of the hatches, which had already been raised, and the use of the portable pumps was not enough to lower the level. As a result, the deck hatches and the vertical shell elevator shafts could not be opened, making it impossible to resupply ammunition on the starboard side throughout the course of the storm. There was also other damage to the electrical systems.
- Major leaks in boiler spaces 6, 7 and 8 through aspiration by the turbo-ventilators of boilers 6 and 8; the water caused varied damage and deterioration of conditions and put the fans out of action causing much discomfort to the personnel there.
- Leaks in the crew bathroom spaces and in the chain locker through the deck anchor pipes.
- Major leaks through the turret trunk and the turntable of No 4 main gun turret, which was most exposed to the force of the sea because of the southerly wind, with flooding of the turret's pivot which could not be emptied by the normal pump system, with damage to the turret's electrical system so that ammunition could be loaded only by hand and the normal turret traverse and gun elevation were impeded. The entire turret complex was temporarily out of action.
- Small leaks through: the ventilation ducts because of the poor closure of the intakes on the open decks, with flooding of the spaces and accommodations below and damage to electrical equipment, which was not always waterproof; the watertight side access hatches (loading hatches) because of poor gaskets and excessive play in the locking systems of the hatches; the openings in the deck for the 90/50 turret electrical cables with flooding of accommodations and spaces below; the watertight doors of the upper deck casemate and its flooding; the seam of the side plating where it met the armour with flooding of the accommodations and other spaces.
- Other problems: loss of the centre starboard gangway and of various nearby stanchions; partial opening of several armoured plugs in the spaces beneath the forecastle; entry of seawater into the fuel oil tanks in the double bottoms and oil in the water tanks, respectively, through the gas vents on the forecastle and the plugs on the sounding rods; prolonged submersion of the stern smoke generators; leaks through the stuffing gland of the propeller shafts; because of pitching and rolling, contamination of the oil in the service tanks by bottom sediment with consequent cleaning through a filter system every four hours; tearing away and breakage of various pieces of equipment and other problems of a minor nature.

A difficult moment during the voyage of the battleship *Duilio* in the Ionian Sea on the morning of 22 February 1942 in a very rough sea with a southeast wind from astern.

In the light of this experience, Bergamini formulated a long list of proposals to eliminate or improve the quality of seals for the ventilation duct intakes, gas vents, electrical cable runs and of other openings on the deck, closing by leather aprons of the spaces between main, medium and anti-aircraft turret trunks and turrets, improvements to the closure system of various hatches on the decks and hull and, not least, removal of the 90/50 stabilisation systems. He also added proposals to improve crew mobility on the decks and superstructures during bad weather.

The problems were repaired, initially, with the ship afloat and later in drydock in Taranto. Similar repairs were carried out on the *Andrea Doria* and *Giulio Cesare*. But, in general, Bergamini was not satisfied with the ship's behaviour in rough seas; if the mission had been prolonged, even under better weather conditions, it would not have been possible to remedy the major problems with the equipment on board; in particular, No 4 main gun turret and the entire starboard 90/53 battery would have been useless and there would also have been problems with moving the rudder by electrical power. He had previously expressed doubts about the seaworthiness of these battleships to the Navy Staff, proposing a reduction of displacement by 1000 tons to limit immersion and the moment of inertia, to disembark the ineffective stabilisation systems of the 90/50 guns and to carry out a series of improvements to the steering gear. Ultimately, in his opinion, the *Duilio* (and the two similar ships) showed themselves unable to maintain speeds greater than 14 knots, nor to fight, in a very rough sea. The widespread weakness and vulnerability of the electrical systems of Italian ships was later confirmed, which were extremely sensitive to the effects of water (and of fire), due in part to the lack of proper insulation of equipment and circuits.

SOURCES AND BIBLIOGRAPHY

What follows is not a comprehensive list of documentation and publications relating to the subject, but includes only the sources actually used by the authors in writing this book.

Primary Sources

Archivio dell'Ufficio Storico della Marina Militare, Roma: *Raccolta di Base*: - b.260, f.5: *1912.Varie;* - b.1718, f.3*: Comitato progetti navi. Promemoria circa rimodernamento delle corazzate;* - b. 1727, f.1*: Commissione Suprema di Difesa (Sezione XII – Febbraio 1936); f. Situazione politico-navale dell'Italia nel Mediterraneo;* f. P.N. *[Programmi navali];* - b. 2312, f. *Crociera 1a e 2a Squadra Navale Spagna e Portogallo;* - b. 2364, f. *Uscita dal Mar Grande del Cavour e Cesare per il passo di San Paolo* [...]; f. *Strisciamento Cavour-Cesare;* - b. 2373, f. *Ufficio di Stato Maggiore della R. Marina. Occupazione Albania Aprile 1939 – XVII; - b. 2516, f. La nostra politica marittima (Febbraio 1929);* - b. 2631, f.2*: Lavori di rimodernamento Navi Cesare – Cavour – Duilio. 1934; - b. 2675, f. 9, s.f. Progetto di corazzate da 26.500 t;* f. *Promemoria dell'Ispettore di Marinalles* [...]. *Approntamento e prove di naviglio di nuova costruzione; - b. 2684, f. Sanzioni; -b. 2688, f. Promemoria dell'Ispettore di Marinalles* [...]. *Approntamento e prove di naviglio di nuova costruzione;* f. [...]. *Progetti operativi 1937;* - b. 2695, f. *Comitato esame progetti navi;* - b. 2703, f. b/2: [...] *Anno 1938 – Bilancio e pratiche relative;* f. *Programma navale (Anno 1938*); - b. 2709, f. *1938:Visita in Italia di S.E. Hitler;* - b.2713, f. *Restituzione della visita da parte della flotta italiana alla flotta inglese;* f. *Visita di navi italiane a porti jugoslavi;* - b. 2714, f. *Visita di S.E. il Capo del Governo a Genova;* - b. 2727, f. *Commissione Suprema di Difesa (Programma navale 1937);* - b. 2729, f. *Rimodernamento delle RR.NN. Duilio e Doria;* - b. 3183, f. 2; - b. 3268, f. *Italia. Programmi navali;* f. 2/3. ***de Courten Memorial Archive***: *b. 1, ff. 14 e 25*; ***Base attack file***: - b. 1, f. 959: *Attacco aereo Napoli 15-12-1940*; -b. 1, f. 962 ter: *Attacco aereo su Napoli l'8-1-1941*; - b. 2 f. 958: *Attacco aereo su Taranto 11–12. Nov.1940*; f.964: *Attacco Aereo-Navale Genoa 9.2.1941.* ***Naval Command Complex file (1940–1946)***: -b. 1: *Comando in Capo FF.NN.BB. (Navi V. VENETO – LITTORIO – ROMA – ITALIA)*; - b. 6: *Comando 1a Squadra Navale (Navi Cesare – Littorio – Veneto)*; - b. 12: *Comando 5a Divisione Navale*, ff. 1, 5, 7 e 8; - b. 13: Comando 5a Divisione Navale, f. 9; - b. 17. ***Admirals Committee file*** [...]: - reg. *Verbali delle adunanze. Anni 1932-33-34-35-36-37-38-39-1940*, ***Special Inquest Commission file (C.I.S.) – Navi***: - b. *1 Corazzate Roma e Cavour [e Cesare].* ***Maristat file I.A.M (Ispettorato Artiglierie e Munizionamento)***: - b.37, f. 576: *Verbale della 27a sessione del Comitato superiore tecnico per le armi e munizioni (14–15 e 22 novembre 1938).* ***Maristat file. I.S.G.N. [Ispettorato Servizio Genio Navale].*** :*Lavori alle unita di superficie*: - b. A 6, f. 1: *Andrea Doria*; - b. C 27, f. 6: *Conte di Cavour*; - b. D 29, f.11: *Duilio*; - b. G 43, f. 2: *Giulio Cesare.* ***Maristat file – Reparto Naviglio e Addestramento***: - b. 34, ff. 333 e 341; - b. 35, ff. 342 e 343; - b. 36, ff. 353 e 354, ss.ff. 1 e 2; -b. 55 ff. 533, 534, 535; - 56, ff. 536, 537; - b. 57, f. 538; - b. 58, ff. 539, 540; - b. 61, f. 561; - b. 62, ff. 5631/1, 563/2, 563/3. ***Naval ship file***: - b. C 10, f. *R.N. Cavour*; -b. C 11, f. *Corazzata 'Giulio Cesare'*; -b. C11 bis: *R.N. G. Cesare*; - b. D 7, f. *Andrea Doria*; -. D 12, f. *Duilio.* ***Maristat publications file (2a Serie)***: - b. 76: *Lavori di riparazione dell'apparato motore della R.N. 'Giulio Cesare', parte 1 [...]*,1934; *Lavori di riparazione dell'apparato motore della R.N. 'Giulio Cesare' – Capitolato d'oneri speciale, parti ll – lll – Vl: [...]*,1934. ***Registry file***: - b. *Regia Nave Conte di Cavour [ammodernata]*; -b. *Regia Nave Duilio. Prima della trasformazione*; - b. *R.N. Duilio [ammodernata]*; -b. *Andrea Doria [ammodernata].* ***Historical Office Secretariat, class A***, b. 58, ff. 578 e 587. ***Historical Office Secretariat, no classification***: - b. 34, f. 149: *Monografia dell'US n. 309: L'opera di preparazione della Marina italiana nel campo delle artiglierie, munizionamento e chimica degli esplosivi.* ***Statistics of wartime ship activity***: - b. 1; *Navi da battaglia*; - b. 2–6: *Incrociatori*; - b. 7–16: *Cacciatorpediniere.* ***Supermarina file. Comando Supremo***: - b. A, f. 5, ss.ff. 1 e 10; -b. C, f. 3, s.f. 3; - b. D, f. 10, s.f. 1. ***Supermarina file. Confirmation and assessment of damage inflicted on the enemy***: - b. 6: *Apprezzamenti e promemoria sull'attivita operativa del nemico.* ***Supermarina file. Promemoria di Supermarina***: - b. *1940*; -b. *1941/l*; - b. *1941/ll*: - b. *1942*; - b. *1943.* ***Supermarina file. Promemoria Sansonetti***: bb. 1, 2. ***Supermarina files. Scontri navali e operazioni di guerra***: - b. 3: *Battaglia di Punta Stilo 6–9 luglio 1940*, f. A 4: - b. 8: *Operazione 'Hats' (31 agosto – 2 settembre 1940)*; - b. 10: *Uscita forze Navali da Gibilterra – 9 settembre 1940*; - b. 46: *Operazione 'M 41' 13–14.12.1941. Operazione 'M 42' 16–19.12.1941*; -b. 47: Operazione 'M 43': 3–6/1/1942; - b. 48: *Operazione 'T 18' 22–25/1/1942*; - b. 49: [...] *Uscita 7a Divisione Aosta e 3a Divisione Gorizia* [...] *Uscita della Forza B e K di Alessandria e Malta per scorta navi mercantili* [...].***Supermarina file. Situazioni delle forze navali italiane e dei reparti aerei per la R. Marina*** [c.d. *Situazioni Gialle*, n.d.a.]: - b. *Dicembre 1941*; - b. *Giugno 1942*; - b. *Settembre 1943.* ***Supermarina file. Squadra Navale***: - b. 2, f.8: *Raccolta di pubblicazioni contenenti direttive e norme per l'impiego della Squadra*, s.f. 6: *Norme per il combattimento diurno*; s.f. 11: *Impiego dell'apparato motore*; s.f. 18; *Impiego delle artiglierie*; -b. 3, f. 13: *Direttive impartite alle unità nel 1943*: - b. 4, f.15, s.f. 4: *Operazione C.V. (non eseguita)*; f. 16: *Impiego della squadra per impegnare le forze navali nemiche nella zona della Spezia [sic] nei giorni 11-12 gennaio 1941*; -b. 10, f.86: *Lavori e approntamento delle unità nel 1941*

Central State Archive: Ministero della Marina file, Gabinetto (1934–1950): b – 178

F. Bargoni Archive, Rome: - *Relazione del Direttore generale delle Costruzioni navali a S.E. il Ministro della Marina:* - vol. *Anno X – Esercizio 1914–1915; - vol. Anni Xl e Xll – Esercizi 1915–16 e 1916–17;* - vol. *Anni Xll, XlV e XV – Esercizi 1917–18, 1918–19 e 1919–20*

Civico Museo del Mare Library, Trieste: - *Lavori di riparazione dell'apparato motore della R.N. Nave 'Conte di Cavour', parte l: Capitolato d'oneri speciale, 1943*; - Officine Armando Vasi – *La Spezia, Progetto ricupero della nave 'Conte di Cavour' – Relazione dicembre 1950*

Printed Sources and Press Items

Atti Parlamentari, Senato del Regno: - Legislatura XXVI, 1a Sessione 1921–1922, Discussioni, tornate del 28 e 29 marzo 1922; - *Legislatura XXVI, 1a Sessione 1921–1923, Discussioni*, tornata del 16 febbraio 1923

'll bilancio di previsione del Ministero della Marina per l'esercizio finanziario dal 1o luglio 1934 al 30 giugno 1935', *Rivista Marittima*, suppl. al n. di giugno 1934. Idem per 'l'esercizio finanziario dal 1o luglio 1937–XV al 30 giugno 1938–XVI', *Rivista Marittima*, suppl. al n. di luglio–agosto 1937. Idem per 'l'esercizio finanziario dal lo luglio 1938-XVl al 30 giugno 1939-XVll', *Rivista Marittima*, suppl. al n. di giugno 1938

Naval Staff Histories, *Second World War, Selected Operations (Mediterranean, 1940)*, London, Admiralty, Historical Section, 1970

Naval Staff Histories, *The Royal Navy and the Mediterranean, vol. 1: September 1939 – October 1940* & vol. ll: November 1940 – December 1941, Frank Cass, London & Portland, 2002

Simpson, M. A. (editor), *The Cunningham Papers, vol. l: The Mediterranean Fleet, 1939–1942*, Aldershot & Brookfield, The Navy Record Society, 1999

Simpson, M. A. *The Somerville Papers*, Aldershot & Brookfield, The Navy Record Society, 1995

Secondary Sources – Books

Bagnasco, E , *In guerra sul mare. Navi e marinai italiani nel secondo conflitto mondiale*, Parma, Albertelli, 2005

Bagnasco, E, *Le armi delle navi italiane nella seconda guerra mondiale*, Parma, Albertelli, 1978

Bagnasco, E, de Toro, A, *Le navi da battaglia classe 'Littorio' 1937–1948*, Parma, Albertelli, 2010

Bargoni, F, Gay, F, Andò, E, *Corazzate classe 'Conte di Cavour'*, Rome, Edizioni dell'Ateneo, 1972

Bargoni, F, Gary, F, Andò, E, Corazzate classe 'Caio Duilio', Rome, Edizioni dell'Ateneo, 1972

Bernardi, G, *Il disarmo navale fra le due guerre mondiali (1919–1939)*, Rome, USMM, 1979

Catalano Gonzaga di Cirella, A, *Per l'onore dei Savoia*, Milan, Mursia, 1996

Da Zara, A, *Pelle d'Ammiraglio*, Milan, Mondadori, 1949

De Toro, A, Cicogna M, *Navi d'Italia a Trieste 1918–1945*, Trieste, Lega Nazionale, 2018

Gill, G H, *Royal Australian Navy 1939–1942* (Series 'Australia in the War of 1939–1945'), Canberra, Australian War Memorial, 1957

Giorgerini, G, Nani, A, *Le navi di linea italiane 1861–1969*, Rome, USMM, 1973

Halpern, P G, *La Grande Guerra nel Mediterraneo 1914–1918*, 2 vols, Gorizia, Libreria Editrice Goriziana, 2009–2010

Iachino, A, *Le due Sirti. Guerra ai convogli in Mediterraneo*, s.l., Mondadori, 1953

Jordan, J, Dumas, R, *French Battleships 1922–1956*, Barnsley, Seaforth Publishing, 2009

Mattesini, F, *La battaglia di Punta Stilo*, Roma, USMM, nd [about 1999]

—, *La battaglia di Capo Teulada (27–28 novembre 1940)*, Rome, USMM, 2000

Meier-Doernberg, W, *Oelversorgung der Kriegsmarine 1935 bis 1945*, Freiburg, Rombach, 1973

Pack, S W C, *The Battle of Sirte*, Shepperton, Ian Allan, 1975

Raven, A, Roberts, J, *British Battleships of World War Two*, London, Arms and Armour, 1976

Santarini, M, *La condotta del tiro navale da bordo nella Regia Marina 1900–1945*, Rome, USMM, nd [about 2018]

Santoni, A, *Il vero traditore. Il ruolo documentato di Ultra nella guerra del Mediterraneo*, Milan, Mursia, 1981

Schofield, B B, *La notte di Taranto (11novembre 1940)*, Milan, Mursia, 1974

Smith, P C, Walker, E, *The Battles of the Malta Striking Forces*, Shepperton, Ian Allan, 1974

'La Marina italiana nella Seconda Guerra Mondiale' Series, Rome, Ufficio Storico della Marina Militare - vol. IV: Fioravanzo, G, *Le azioni navali in Mediterraneo dal 10 giugno 1940 al 31 marzo 1941, 1976*; vol. Vll: Cocchia, A, *La difesa del traffico con l'Africa Settentrionale dal 1o ottobre 1941 al 30 settembre 1942*, 1976; vol. XV: *Fioravanzo, G, La Marina dall'8 settembre alla fine del conflitto*, 1971; vol. XXl: *Fioravanzo, G, L'organizzazione della Marina durante il conflitto*, 3 volumes, 1972

Secondary Sources – Papers and Articles

Bagnasco, E, 'Grandi navi ai lavori negli Anni Trenta' in *Rivista Marittima*, May 1992

Bagnasco, E, 'La tragedia e le favole (perdita dell'ex Giulio Cesare – parti 1a e 2a)' in *STORIA Militare* Nos 298 & 299 (June and August 2018)

Bagnasco, E, 'Perdita e recupero della RN *Conte di Cavour*' in *STORIA Militare*, November 1995

Bagnasco, E, Brescia, M, 'll camouflage delle navi italiane 1940–1945' (*STORIA Militare* Briefing n 33, September–October 2017)

Colliva, G, 'La Marina fa la spesa' in *Rivista Marittima*, November 2002

Colliva, G, 'Guerra di spie. Il colpo grosso della Marina italiana nel primo conflitto mondiale' in *Bollettino d'Archivio dell'USMM*, September/December 2010

De Toro, A, 'Dalle *Littorio* alle *Impero*' in *Bollettino d'Archivio dell'USMM*, March 2012

Cuniberti, V, 'An ideal battleship for the British Fleet', in Jane, F T (editor), *All the World's Fighting Ships 1903*, London & New York, Naval Syndicate, 1903

Halpern, P G, 'French and Italian Naval Policy in the Mediterranean 1898–1945', in Hattendorf, J B (editor), *Naval*

Strategy and Policy in the Mediterranean, London & Portland, Frank Cass, 2000

Mattesini, F, La Marina del 'Regno del Sud' in Bollettino d'Archivio dell'USMM', June, September, December 1994

Mattesini, F, 'L'armistizio dell'8 settembre e il dramma delle Forze Navali da Battaglia' in *Bollettino dell'A.I.D.M.E.N.*, June 2006

Mattesini, F, 'La Marina italiana nel contrasto dell'operazione britannica M.F. 5. 13–15 febbraio 1942' in *Bollettino d'Archivio dell'USMM*, March/June 2010

Poddighe, G M, 'R. Marina Italiana. Artiglierie e tiro navale, 2019' in www.Academia.edu

Rizza, C, 'Il caso *Da Vinci*' (parti 1a e 2a), in *STORIA Militare* n. 283 e 284 (April and May 2017)

Roseti, C, 'La condotta del salvataggio della *Duilio*' in *Rivista Marittima*, October 1955

Somma, A, 'Il ricupero della nave da battaglia *Conte di Cavour*, Taranto 1940–1941' in *Rivista Marittima*, April 1957

Turrini, A, 'Le corazzate classe "Cavour" con motori diesel' in *Rivista Marittima*, January 2010

ACKNOWLEDGEMENTS

This work was able to be completed by the assistance of all of those who offered their contributions during the lengthy period of searching for and evaluating documents, drawings and photographs and through observations, suggestions and advice prior to and during its writing. The authors wish to express their sincere gratitude to Stefano Bagnasco, Maurizio Brescia, Mario Cicogna, Giorgio Giorgerini, Roberto Maggi, Ermanno Martino, Francesco Mattesini, Fulvio Petronio, Mario Piovano, Franco Prosperini, Claudio Rizza, Nicola Siracusano, Aldo Starace, Stelio Zoratto as well as our late friends Elio Andò, Franco Bargoni, Arrigo Barilli, Gino Chesi, Giuliano Colliva, Mauro De Pinto, Armando De Stefano, Aldo Fraccaroli, Franco Gay, Renato Mancini, Augusto Nani, Franco Papili, Achille Rastelli and Francesco Roncallo.

The authors also wish to give heartfelt thanks to the Museo Storico Navale di Venezia, to the Archivio di Stato and to the Civico Museo del Mare di Trieste, whose courteous cooperation proved to be very important. Particular thanks are owed to the Historical Office of the Italian Navy in Rome, both for access to the relative archives as well as for the competent and patient assistance by its personnel throughout the research process, which lasted for so many years, without which it would have been impossible to publish this book as it is here.

And finally, a heartfelt thanks to our friend Ralph Riccio who, after the challenging translation of *The Littorio Class* and of other earlier works of ours, assumed the burden of this new volume as well.

E.B. – A,d.T.

The *Andrea Doria* steaming towards Malta on 10 September 1943. Note on the port quarter a minor variation of the camouflage scheme, an eloquent example of the frequent small changes and amendments made in painting the ship's exterior. (IWM photo)

INDEX

Page numbers in **bold** refer to illustrations and those in *italic* refer to tables.